"This edition of *Crime and Criminal Justice in America* is even better than the last, and the last edition was fantastic. Pollock describes complex concepts so clearly and concisely that students grasp them on the first reading. Her examples are up to date, relevant, and instructive. Many texts talk about race and gender in general terms, but Pollock brings these crucial issues to life in a way that motivates students to reflect upon the basic fairness of our system of justice. My students love this text. Yours will, too."

—**Richard R. Bennett**,
Professor of Justice, American University

CRIME AND CRIMINAL JUSTICE IN AMERICA

Crime and Criminal Justice in America, Third Edition, addresses the major controversial issues in U.S. policing, courts, and the correctional system. This book features unique graphical displays and contemporary data and research, developed by Joycelyn Pollock, criminologist, and University Distinguished Professor of Criminal Justice, Texas State University. The text's question-and-answer model promotes a critical thinking process for students new to criminal justice, encouraging student engagement and the application of learned skills through end-of-chapter exercises. Timely, comprehensive, and visually stimulating, *Crime and Criminal Justice in America,* Third Edition, is the go-to text for introductory criminal justice students and educators.

Joycelyn Pollock started her career in criminal justice as a probation and parole officer in the state of Washington. She earned a Bachelor of Arts in Sociology at Whitman College in Walla Walla, Washington, and was nominated to Phi Beta Kappa. She earned a Master's and Ph.D. in Criminal Justice at the State University of New York at Albany. She also obtained a J.D. at the University of Houston, and passed the Texas Bar in 1991.

Her other books include *Ethical Dilemmas and Decisions in Criminal Justice,* Ninth Edition (2016), *Criminal Law,* Eleventh Edition (2016), *Case Studies in Criminal Justice Ethics* (with Michael Braswell and Larry Miller, 2006), *Prisons and Prison Life* (2004), Second Edition (2012), *Women's Crimes, Criminology, and Corrections* (2014), and many others.

She served as Chair of the Department of Criminal Justice at Texas State University (1993–1996) and graduate director (2002–2006).

In 2006 she received the Outstanding Texas State Woman Faculty Award and also the Bruce Smith Award from the Academy of Criminal Justice Sciences for "outstanding contributions to criminal justice." In 2008 she received the Distinguished Alumni Award from The University of Albany, School of Criminal Justice.

She was formerly a member of the Crime and Justice Research Alliance (CJRA), a shared project of the American Society of Criminology and Academy of Criminal Justice Sciences. CJRA is a clearinghouse and source for objective criminal justice research. It refers policy members to authoritative experts to inform public debate on criminal justice issues.

CRIME AND CRIMINAL JUSTICE IN AMERICA

Third Edition

Joycelyn Pollock

Routledge
Taylor & Francis Group

NEW YORK AND LONDON

Third edition published 2017
by Routledge
711 Third Avenue, New York, NY 10017

and by Routledge
2 Park Square, Milton Park, Abingdon, Oxon, OX14 4RN

Routledge is an imprint of the Taylor & Francis Group, an informa business

First edition published by Anderson Press 2008
Second edition published by Anderson Press 2011

Library of Congress Cataloging-in-Publication Data
Names: Pollock, Joycelyn M., 1956– author.
Title: Crime and criminal justice in America / Joycelyn Pollock.
Other titles: Crime and justice in America
Description: Third edition. | New York, NY : Routledge, 2017. | Earlier
    editions published as: Crime and justice in America : an introduction to
    criminal justice.
Identifiers: LCCN 2016035212 | ISBN 9781138697478 (hardback) | ISBN 1138697478
    (hardback) | ISBN 9780323290692 (pbk.) | ISBN 0323290698 (pbk.)
Subjects: LCSH: Criminal justice, Administration of—United States.
Classification: LCC HV9950 .P65 2017 | DDC 364.973—dc23
LC record available at https://lccn.loc.gov/2016035212

ISBN: 978-1-138-69747-8 (hbk)
ISBN: 978-0-323-29069-2 (pbk)
ISBN: 978-1-315-26970-2 (ebk)

Typeset in Arno Pro
by Apex CoVantage, LLC

Test questions and a wealth of additional instructor support materials, prepared by Andrea Joseph, Department of Criminal Justice, New Mexico State University, are available on a password-protected website at www.routledge.com/cw/pollock to faculty and administrative staff who have been approved to request Review Copies by Routledge.

To Eric and Greg, as always . . .

Contents

Preface   xv

Acknowledgments   xix

Section 1 The Criminal Justice System and Social Control   1

    1 Criminal Justice as Social Control   3

        What Is the Criminal Justice "System"? Is It a System?   4

        What Is Social Control? How Does The "Social Contract"

        Justify State Power?   11

        What Is the Historical Foundation of Our Legal System?   13

        How Big Is the Criminal Justice System Compared to 50 Years Ago?   14

        What Are Some Current Issues in Criminal Justice Today?   16

        How Do Ideologies Affect Objective Analysis of

        Criminal Justice Issues?   21

        Focus On Data: Are Illegal Immigrants More Likely to Be Criminal?   23

        Summary   28

        Critical Thinking Exercises   29

    2 Crime in Society   31

        What Is Crime?   31

        What Is the Role of Legislators, Victims, Police, and Prosecutors

        in Defining Crime?   32

        What Sources Do We Use to Find Out About the Patterns of Crime?   35

        What Crimes Are People Most Frequently Arrested For?   44

        What Do We Know About Homicide?   46

        What Has Been the Pattern of Crime Over the Years?

        Has It Declined?   49

        Does the Public Have an Accurate Perception about the

        Prevalence of Crime?   50

        How Do the Crime Rates of the United States Compare

        to Other Countries?   51

        Focus On Data: Is There a Ferguson Effect? Is There a Current

        Crime Wave?   53

        Summary   62

        Critical Thinking Exercises   63

3 Why Has Crime Declined?   67

What Are the Explanations for the Decline of Crime?   67
What Are Some Methodological Issues in the Question: Why
Do People Commit Crime?   69
Who Commits Crime?   71
Focus On Data: Are Blacks More Criminal Than Whites?   78
What Are the Major Criminological Theories of Crime?   84
What Do Biological Theories of Crime Say About Who
Commits Crime and Why?   85
What Do Psychological Theories of Crime Say About
Who Commits Crime and Why?   90
What Do Sociological Theories of Crime Say About Who
Commits Crime and Why?   92
What Are Some Other Theories of Crime?   96
Summary   102
Critical Thinking Exercises   103

Section 2 Law Enforcement as Social Control   109

4 Police in America   111

What Is the Function of Policing?   112
What Are the Major Issues Facing Policing Today?   113
Focus On Data: Are Police Officers Under Attack?   116
How Many Police Officers Are There and Who Are They?   118
What Is the Difference Between Federal, State, and
Local Law Enforcement?   124
How Did Modern Policing Evolve?   129
What Is Community Policing?   134
Summary   139
Critical Thinking Exercises   141

5 Police Operations   143

How Are Police Officers Selected and Trained?   143
What Is the Difference Between Proactive and Reactive Policing?   147
How Has Technology Affected Policing?   150
Is Police Officer Stress a Problem and, If So, What Is the
Role of Organizational Justice?   152
What Is the Police Subculture?   153
What Are Some Types of Police Misconduct?   155
Do Police Officers Discriminate Against Minorities?   159
What Is the Law and Policy Concerning Police Use of Force?   168

Focus On Data: Do Police Officers Abuse Their Power to
Use Lethal Force?   171
What Were the Recommendations of the 21st Century
President's Task Force on Policing?   175
Summary   177
Critical Thinking Exercises   178

6 Policing and the Legal Process   185

What Is the Source of Our Rights Against Police Power?   185
When Can Police "Seize" a Person in Any Way?   187
When Can Police Search Without a Warrant?   194
Do Police Need a Warrant to Obtain a Blood Sample?
Breathalyzer Test? Saliva? Urine? Hair? DNA?   201
Do Police Need a Warrant to Obtain a Handwriting Sample?
Clothing? Line-Ups or Photo Arrays?   203
What Are Our Rights During Interrogation?   204
What Is the Exclusionary Rule?   207
Focus On Data: Do Gun Control Laws Reduce Gun-Related Violence?   209
Summary   214
Critical Thinking Exercises   215

Section 3 The Law as Social Control   219

7 Law and Society   221

What Is the Purpose of Law? What is the Purpose of Criminal Law?   222
What Is the Origin of Our Legal System?   225
What Are Some Differences Between Civil and Criminal Law?   228
What Are Some Constitutional Challenges to Creating Laws?   228
What Are the Elements of a Crime?   238
What Are Some Defenses to Criminal Culpability?   242
What Are Some Recent Issues in Criminal Law?   252
Focus On Data: Is Medical Marijuana Crime or Cure?   253
Summary   255
Critical Thinking Exercises   256

8 Criminal Prosecution   259

What Are the Different Levels of Courts?   259
What Are Specialized Courts?   263
Focus On Data: Are Specialized Courts Effective?   264
How Do Prosecutors Decide Whether and What to Charge?   267
What Are the Duties of a Defense Attorney?   268
What is the Role of a Judge? How Are They Selected?   272

What is the Jurisdiction of Federal Courts?   274
How Does Due Process Protect Individuals Against
Error in the Criminal Justice Process?   278
What Are the Steps of a Trial?   287
Summary   293
Critical Thinking Exercises   294

9   Criminal Sentencing   297

What Happens in a Sentencing Hearing?   298
What Are the Goals of Sentencing?   299
What Are the Types of Sentences That Might Be Given
to Criminal Offenders?   299
What Are Three-Strikes Sentencing Laws?   300
What Is the Most Common Sentence?   302
What Is the Criticism Regarding Fines and Fees?   303
What Recent Events Have Occurred with Federal
Drug Sentencing?   306
What Is Restorative Justice?   313
What Are the Legal Arguments Against the Death Penalty?   317
Focus On Data: Is There Racial Disparity in Sentencing?   322
Summary   327
Critical Thinking Exercises   329

Section 4   Corrections as Social Control   333

10 Community Corrections and Correctional Classification   335

What Are the Goals of Corrections? What Was the
"Rehabilitative Era"?   336
How Do Theories of Crime Relate to What We Do to Criminals?   340
What Is Probation and How Is It Different from Parole? How
Is It Different from Pre-Trial Diversion?   342
What Is the History of Probation?   343
What Are Some Typical Conditions for a Probationer?   344
What Is the Profile of Offenders Under Correctional Supervision?   348
Do Women On Probation Have Different Backgrounds and
Needs Than Men; If So, What Are They?   351
How Many Drug Offenders Are Under Correctional Supervision?
What Are Their Issues?   353
What Are Some Current Issues of Probation Supervision?   354
What Is Revocation? How Many Probationers Fail?   356
What Is Classification? What Is Third-Generation Classification?   359
Focus On Data: Does R/N/R Classification Accurately
Predict Recidivism?   361

Summary   365
Critical Thinking Exercises   367

11 Confinement: Jails and Prisons   373

How Many People Are Incarcerated in Jails and Prisons
in the United States?   373
What Rights Do Prisoners Have?   380
What Is Prison Like Today Compared to Previous Eras?   383
Who Are the Prisoners in State and Federal Prisons?   389
What Are the Elements of the Prisoner Subculture?   391
Is Sexual Assault in Prison a Problem?   394
What Are the Issues Concerning the Mentally Ill in Jails and Prisons? 396
Why Are Some Prisons and Jails Privately Run? Are Private
Prisons Less Expensive?   399
What Are the Differences and Similarities of Jails and Prisons?   401
Focus On Data: Did the Increase in Incarceration Reduce
the Crime Rate Between 1995 and 2010?   405
Summary   409
Critical Thinking Exercises   411

12 Re-Entry and Recidivism   417

What Is the History of Parole?   417
Who Is on Parole?   419
What Are the Problems of Re-Entry?   424
What Are Collateral Consequences of a Criminal Conviction?   427
What Is the Second Chance Act?   430
What Is the Process for Parole Revocation?   431
How Many Offenders Recidivate and Who Is Most Likely
to Recidivate?   433
Focus On Data: What Is The "Justice Reinvestment Initiative" and
"Justice Realignment"? Have These Approaches Increased Crime?   438
Summary   442
Critical Thinking Exercises   444

13 Juvenile Justice and Corrections   449

How Is the Juvenile Justice System Different from the Adult System?   449
What Have Been the Trends in Juvenile Crime?   454
What Is the Profile of the Juvenile Offender?   458
Focus On Data: Are Girls Becoming More Violent?   465
What Rights Do Juvenile Offenders Have?   469
Can Juveniles End Up in Adult Courts? How?   470
What Are People Referring to by the Terms "Zero Tolerance"
and "School-To-Prison Pipeline"?   472

How Many Juveniles Are On Probation?   475
How Many Youths Are Sent to Secure Detention Facilities?   478
Are Juveniles as Recidivistic as Adults?   481
Summary   483
Critical Thinking Exercises   484

Section 5 Concluding Our Critical Thinking Approach to Criminal Justice   489
      14 A Critical Thinking Approach to Criminal Justice   491
How Are the Major Issues in Studying Crime Today?   492
What Are the Major Issues in Policing Today?   495
What Are the Major Issues in Courts Today?   498
What Are the Major Issues in Corrections Today?   500
What Is the Role of Criminal Justice Actors in the War On Terror?   501
Focus On Data: Last Thoughts   511
Critical Thinking Exercises   513

Glossary/Index   515

Preface

This is a major, new revision of a text I earlier published with Anderson/Elsevier in 2012. I have taken a fairly radical approach to the revision after carefully considering reviewers' comments and my own experience in teaching criminal justice classes, and therefore have retitled the book *Crime and Criminal Justice in America*. This text was originally developed in response to a perceived need for a shorter, less expensive, introductory book for instructors who desire an alternative to the comprehensive textbooks that are currently available. I have continued to provide the "bare bones" of theory, law, and organizational descriptions without burying the student in extraneous detail.

There are three major changes to this edition. The first is that I have rewritten the book to emphasize and model a critical thinking approach to introducing our system of criminal justice to undergraduate students. While it is true this phrase is over-used in academia today, the importance of encouraging students to understand policies, practices, and hot-button issues using *evidence* is no less important despite its rhetorical prevalence. To adopt this approach in a way that would be fully useful to fellow instructors and their students required that I fully rewrite chapters to address the key questions facing the criminal justice community and American citizens today, while also providing the most relevant information in clear, accessible form. At the same time, it remained important that I continue to introduce students to the basic information about each important element of our criminal justice system.

The second major change is that the publisher and I have made a concerted effort to present data in a visually accessible manner, employing a graphic designer to create over 30 of the more than 160 exhibits in the book as a whole, including more than 50 very current photographs. There is no doubt that "infographics" are the way information is processed today, especially by younger people, and this text attempts to provide the same type of easily absorbed visual data that one can find on FiveThirtyEight.com, the *New York Times* infographics, or other sources.

The third major change is an explicit treatment of the major controversial issues of our day in the United States—e.g., gun control, whether law enforcement officers abuse their power to use lethal force, whether immigrants are more criminal, and many others—in the new "Focus on Data" sections in each chapter of the text. This may make the book less palatable to some instructors, but I hope it does not, since the goal is to practice the same critical thinking approach that is used and advocated throughout the book. Reviewers asked for more current discussions and factually based treatment of relevant, topical issues. I have provided that while at the same time keeping the "nuts and bolts" of what is necessary in an introductory criminal justice text.

This third edition retains the same chapters and basic organization of the first edition although the juvenile justice chapter has been moved to follow the corrections chapters. I have continued to include women and minorities in each chapter, rather than relegating these groups to isolated chapters. I have also updated all statistics where new data were available. I have eliminated the "Focus on Crime" and "Breaking News" boxes thanks to discussions with instructors teaching from the book who suggested that such discussions were better presented within the text so that students would read them. In the "margin notes" I have also added many more Internet links to useful information and debates on practices and policies, links that should remain durable and updated over time. Important concepts are in **bold** font and explained, in context, within the text and are again fully defined in the Glossary/Index at the back of the book. Each chapter concludes with a helpful summary, and suggested Critical Thinking Exercises for instructors to use, inside or outside of class.

For those instructors who have used the prior edition, more detail on revisions to each chapter are as follows:

Chapter 1—kept basic introductory chapter that briefly describes the system of criminal justice and philosophical foundation for it (social contract); added discussion of President Johnson's Commission on Law Enforcement and Administration of Justice and *The Challenge of Crime in a Free Society* to set in context current issues in criminal justice; reduced discussion of systems theory; added discussion of current issues; added focus on data on illegal immigrants and crime.

Chapter 2—kept discussion of crime as constructed reality and sources of crime data; updated all statistics and provided more visually accessible graphs and pie charts, e.g., one of arrests displayed as most frequent to least frequent; added focused section on homicide; provided longitudinal data on trends to show crime decline; added focus on data on Ferguson effect.

Chapter 3—reworked theory material to more directly focus on whether or not theory helps explain crime decline; moved crime correlates from Chapter 2 to Chapter 3 in this edition to begin discussion of theory; shortened theory sections considerably, especially biological theory section from last edition; added focus on data on whether Blacks are more criminal.

Chapter 4—begin chapter on policing with current issues section rather than history; add focus on data on whether police killings are increasing (which unfortunately became more topical because of the Dallas and Baton Rouge attacks); updated statistics on policing; kept description of federal, state, and local policing; shortened history discussion and moved community policing to follow discussion of policing history.

Chapter 5—kept discussion of selection, training, and subculture (shortened), but added new section on technology and policing, including cybercrimes; kept discussion of proactive and reactive policing; added discussion of organizational justice in discussion of stress; shortened discussion of police misconduct; added discussion on allegation of discrimination against minorities and focus on data section on whether police are more likely to kill Blacks after discussion of legal principles in the use of force and research findings.

Chapter 6—reworked this chapter to set up questions about police legal powers at each stage of the interaction with individuals; added discussion of New York City's rise and fall of the use of stop-and-frisks; added box on types of searches; expanded discussion of electronic searches; added focus on data about whether gun control reduces crime.

Chapter 7—added comments to show how legal analysis is critical thinking; kept common law versus statutory law discussion, incorporation, and differences between civil law and criminal law but added a box summarizing differences in selected crimes/torts; provided a greater emphasis on the Bill of Rights as source of determining state's power to create law; kept major challenges discussion, e.g. vagueness; updated relevant cases; added focus on data section on medical marijuana; kept elements of a crime section (*actus reus* and *mens rea*); added new section on criminal defenses (this was not in previous editions and is part of the field test for criminal justice so now this gap has been addressed).

Chapter 8—kept description of courts; added expanded discussion of specialized courts in focus on data section; kept discussions of defense attorneys, prosecutors, and judges but updated with new material, e.g., new studies on the lack of legal assistance for indigents.

Chapter 9—reworked old material between Chapter 8 and Chapter 9 to limit Chapter 9 to sentencing; expanded and updated information on three strikes; added section on the "poverty penalty" (the burden of fines, fees, court costs on poor defendants); consolidated discussion of restorative justice by moving material from two chapters in last edition to here; added focus on data section on whether there is racial discrimination in sentencing.

Chapter 10—kept all of probation material but updated numbers; consolidated classification discussion from two chapters in the last edition to only in this chapter; added focus on data for expanded treatment of effectiveness of R/N/R classification approach.

Chapter 11—shortened history and subculture sections of old chapter and updated all numbers regarding incarceration; expanded discussion of differences between jail and prison; updated PREA numbers; updated private prison information; added focus on data section on whether imprisonment reduced crime.

Chapter 12—kept history of parole (somewhat shortened); added discussion of Second Chance Act, Realignment, and Justice Reinvestment; updated recidivism material; added focus on data on whether Justice Reinvestment has been effective.

Chapter 13—new placement for this juvenile chapter; kept most material but reworked it for better clarity; added focus on juvenile rights; added focus on data on whether girls are becoming more violent; added more discussion of zero tolerance and school resource officers.

Chapter 14—added new opening to place chapter in context of critical thinking approach; added current issues sections for crime, police, courts, and corrections; reduced discussion of events after 9/11; added new material on surveillance; added new discussion of sources of data (e.g., Bureau of Justice Statistics) and provided hyperlinks to suggested sources.

INSTRUCTOR SUPPORT MATERIAL

Test questions and a wealth of additional instructor support materials, prepared by Andrea Joseph, Department of Criminal Justice, New Mexico State University, are available on a password-protected website at www.routledge.com/cw/pollock to faculty and administrative staff who have been approved to request Review Copies by Routledge.

Acknowledgments

I would like to thank Mickey Braswell for the opportunity to create the first edition of this text. I am extremely grateful for the friendship and support that have come my way from Mickey and Susan Braswell and everyone at Anderson over the years. For this edition, Steve Rutter has been a tireless editor and his vision, ideas, and cheerleading have been instrumental to the book's completion. Emily Barrett has been a talented graphics creator and Sarah Calabi has helped in obtaining permissions and great photos that will enhance the readers' experience. I want to thank the anonymous reviewers who provided their opinions about the second edition and the first drafts of this edition.

Dana Botello	California State University, Sacramento
Clairissa Breen	Cazenovia College
Mary Eckert	Texas State University
Abigail Ellis	University of North Florida
Kathryn Elvey	Northern Kentucky University
Michelle Foster	Kent State University
Kimberly Hall	Florida State College
John Hepburn	Arizona State University
Patrick Ibe	Albany State University (Georgia)
Veronyka J James	Virginia Union University
Stephanie Jirard	Shippensburg University
Andrea Joseph	New Mexico State University
Sara Kitchen	Chestnut Hill College
Jospeter Mbuba	Indiana University
Kerry Muehlenbeck	Mesa Community College
Akwasi Owusu-Bempah	Indiana University (Bloomington)
Marlene Ramsey	Albany State University (Georgia)
Martin Schwartz	George Washington University
Mahendra Singh	Grambling State College
Gary A. Sokolow	College of the Redwoods

Floyd Stokes	College of the Redwoods
Jennifer Sumner	California State University, Dominguez Hills
Kevin Wozniak	University of Massachusetts Boston

I also want to thank the folks at Taylor and Francis for their assistance in the production of this book.

I encourage any instructor using this book to contact me with criticisms or suggestions for improvement. I welcome your contribution: jp12@txstate.edu.

Section 1

THE CRIMINAL JUSTICE SYSTEM AND SOCIAL CONTROL

CRIMINAL JUSTICE AS SOCIAL CONTROL

Criminal justice refers to the system of social control that encompasses police, courts, and corrections. The academic field of study includes aspects of the sociology of law, along with sociology, psychology, management science, and other fields. In this textbook, we will present what we know about crime, the theories that have been developed to explain why people commit crime (Chapter 3), law enforcement (Chapters 4–6), courts (Chapters 7–9), corrections (Chapters 11–13), and juvenile justice (Chapter 13). The final chapter (Chapter 14) will recap what we know and don't know, and how to address emerging issues. Throughout the book, our approach will be to address our inquiry using a critical thinking approach. Critical thinking is an approach to problem solving that utilizes the following steps:

(a) identify and clearly formulate relevant questions or issues
(b) gather and assess relevant information, noting the source of the information to identify any bias or vested interest

Chapter Preview

- What Is the Criminal Justice "System"? Is It a System?
- What Is Social Control? How Does the "Social Contract" Justify State Power?
- What Is the Historical Foundation of Our Legal System?
- How Big Is the Criminal Justice System Compared to 50 Years Ago?
- What Are Some Current Issues in Criminal Justice Today?
- How Do Ideologies Affect Objective Analysis of Criminal Justice Issues?
- Focus on Data: Are Illegal Immigrants More Likely to Be Criminal?
- Summary
- Critical Thinking Exercises

(c) utilize data to develop well-reasoned conclusions and solutions and test them

(d) at all times be aware of assumptions that may bias your perception of data and lead to selective perception, tunnel vision, or cognitive distortion

(e) be aware of the implications and practical consequences of findings.[1]

The intent of this book is to provide information, but also develop the skills necessary for critical thinking and analysis. New issues in criminal justice continue to emerge. New research findings shape our understanding of old problems. A textbook that describes the facts is helpful, but providing the research skills and sources to help you find out the facts is, arguably, even more important, because the facts of criminal justice are dynamic.

Unlike most introductory textbooks, we outline the chapters through a series of questions and then the text provides information relevant to the questions posed. In each chapter we also have a "Focus on Data" section which deals very specifically with a current and, sometimes, controversial issue: we present the question, apply the available evidence, and provide a summary answer to the question, noting any weaknesses or gaps in the data available that may call into question what we think we know. These questions are sometimes complicated with conflicting findings; there may be no easy answer. That is the challenge of social science—to address difficult issues and attempt to find the truth while resisting preconceptions, assumptions, and bias.

WHAT IS THE CRIMINAL JUSTICE "SYSTEM"? IS IT A SYSTEM?

Police, courts, and corrections comprise the elements of what we think of as the criminal justice system. Police take center stage up to arrest; their role is to investigate crimes, arrest the suspect, and gather evidence. Courts are obviously involved in the process of adjudication, which determines guilt or innocence and sets the amount of punishment for the guilty. The sub-system of corrections takes over after sentencing. Exhibit 1.1 is an illustration of these elements as a flowchart.

We tend to think of these sub-systems as distinct; however, these simple categories don't accurately describe the realities of criminal justice. In reality, police work with probation and parole officers to investigate offenders who may already be on probation or parole. Pretrial adjudication programs often use probation officers to supervise clients who haven't been found guilty along with those who have been convicted. Probationers who violate the conditions of their probation may go back to court for re-sentencing. It is even possible for someone on parole (after a prison term) to get a probation sentence. However,

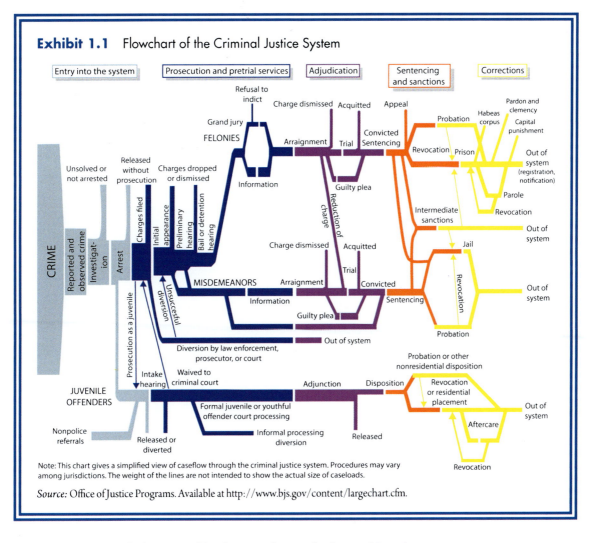

Exhibit 1.1   Flowchart of the Criminal Justice System

Note: This chart gives a simplified view of caseflow through the criminal justice system. Procedures may vary among jurisdictions. The weight of the lines are not intended to show the actual size of caseloads.

Source: Office of Justice Programs. Available at http://www.bjs.gov/content/largechart.cfm.

the use of these three "sub-systems" has become the standard way of describing the criminal justice system and this textbook arranges the chapters in a way that is consistent with this standard flowchart.

In Exhibit 1.2, more description is provided for each of the steps. We speak in very general terms when we describe the steps of the system, with the caution that it may not accurately describe your own jurisdiction. We will discuss this process in more detail in Chapter 8.

In general, law enforcement exists at state and local levels to enforce the law, although, just because a law is broken does not necessarily mean there will be an arrest or prosecution. Typically, a state law enforcement agency (e.g., highway patrol) enforces the state's highway laws, but the agency might also be called in to help investigate local crime. There is usually a county-level law enforcement

Exhibit 1.2 The Criminal Justice Process

Arrest Police need probable cause for an arrest. There does not need to be an arrest warrant in order for an arrest to take place, but there must be probable cause that the suspect has committed a crime.

Booking is basically an administrative entry into jail. The suspect's fingerprints are taken, officers take his or her property, issue jail clothing and, sometimes, the suspect undergoes some form of health screening before being placed in the jail population.

First appearance is usually within the first 24 hours of arrest (and it must take place within a "reasonable" period after arrest). In this short hearing before a magistrate, the charges are read and the magistrate determines if there is sufficient probable cause for the arrest. The magistrate may also begin the process of determining if the suspect is indigent, in which case an attorney will be appointed.

Preliminary hearing is basically to determine whether there is sufficient evidence to go forward with a trial. Often, the preliminary hearing is waived. In some states, the grand jury system completely takes the place of the preliminary hearing.

Grand Jury is a group of people appointed by the administrative judge of a jurisdiction. This group hears the evidence presented by a prosecutor to determine if there is probable cause to go forward to trial. If they agree that there is, they issue an indictment. Not all states use the grand jury system and, instead, the prosecutor issues an "information" as the charging document instead of an indictment. It should not be confused with the **petit jury**, the jury that decides guilt or innocence at trial.

Arraignment is where the offender may plead guilt or innocence and, if indigent, has an attorney appointed if one has not been appointed yet.

Pretrial diversion may occur at any time before trial and after charges have been filed. Typically, the suspect must admit guilt and agree to conditions that range from work and restitution programs to community service.

Plea bargaining is an agreement between the defendant, represented by his or her attorney, and the prosecutor to plead guilty in exchange for a recommended sentence. It may take place at any time up to a determination of guilt or innocence in a trial, but, typically, takes place soon after arraignment.

Pretrial hearings are when judges decide procedural issues relevant to the trial, such as the admission of evidence or change of venue.

Trials may be "**bench trials**," which means that they are held only in front of a judge with no jury. If the defendant requests a jury trial, **voir dire** takes place before the jury is seated, which basically involves ensuring that jury members will be unbiased in their judgment.

Sentencing hearing is a separate proceeding, although appointed attorneys are required to continue to represent the offender through the sentencing hearing (and first appeal). There may be some time between the trial and the sentencing hearing in order for a presentence report to be written. While some states allow juries to sentence, others release the jury and have the judge do the sentencing.

Jail/prison/probation or a combination of them are the basic sentencing options in felony cases. Some states have strictly limited which crimes are eligible for a probation sentence; in other states, potentially any felon can be sentenced to probation. **Split sentences**, where an offender serves a short period of time in jail or prison and is then released on probation, are possible. While, generally, only felons go to state prisons and misdemeanants go to jails, some states have created "state jails" that house lower-level felony offenders.

Parole comes *after* a prison sentence, while probation is *instead* of a prison sentence (in most cases). They are very similar in that both involve supervised release into the community.

agency (county sheriff and deputies) and a municipal law enforcement agency within the city limits. Most of us are familiar with the municipal police officer (whether it is a police department for a city of millions or a small town of only several thousand), but there are also other types of law enforcement officers depending on the state, such as constables, park or airport police departments, port authority police, transit police, and university police departments. These specialized police forces must be created by the state legislature. Law enforcement will be discussed more fully in Chapters 4–6.

There are also various layers of courts that prosecute the laws. City ordinances and code violations are typically heard in municipal courts, while misdemeanors and felonies are heard in county and state courts. Every state has a court structure that allows for appeals, and the highest appellate court in the state is often called the *state supreme court*, not to be confused with the United States Supreme Court, the highest court in the country. Issues relevant to the courts and criminal prosecution will be explored more fully in Chapters 7–9.

Each state also has a corrections system. Jails are generally county-level agencies while prisons are state-level agencies. Probation (generally used in lieu of a prison or jail sentence) is usually county-level with state oversight, and parole (generally coming after a prison sentence) is usually a state agency. There is no consistency across 50 states in the management and organization of corrections. We will explore these differences more closely in Chapters 10–12.

The juvenile justice system has a different history, mission, and language from the system for adult defendants and offenders. For this reason, it is helpful to discuss the juvenile justice system separately and we do so in Chapter 13.

You can find the US Code at https://www.law.cornell.edu/uscode/text.

For more information, go to www.dhs.gov/

For more information, go to http://www.justice.gov/archive/ll/highlights.htm

The federal criminal justice system parallels the state systems. Federal laws are passed by Congress and can be found in the **United States Code**. Despite the limitations on federal power created by the Constitution, we have a large number of federal laws that are investigated and enforced by federal law enforcement agencies. We are most familiar with the Federal Bureau of Investigation (FBI), but other federal agencies such as Immigration and Customs Enforcement (ICE), post office inspectors, and treasury agents, also investigate and enforce federal criminal laws. Federal prosecutors prosecute federal crimes and, if convicted, the offender enters the federal correctional system.

As you may know, the **Department of Homeland Security** was created after the terrorist attacks of September 11, 2001, by the **USA Patriot Act**. One of the purposes of creating this department was to create better communication among the many federal law enforcement agencies that are involved with protecting the country from terrorist acts. It is important to note that federal laws have made a distinction between domestic crimes and terrorism when allocating powers of investigation and prosecution to federal agencies. Typically, federal agencies, such as the FBI and Central Intelligence Agency (CIA), have greater powers when investigating foreign suspects of terrorism than federal, state, county, or municipal law enforcement agencies investigating "regular" crimes by U.S. residents. Of course, there are often blurry lines between domestic crimes, such as bank robbery or smuggling drugs, and international terrorism. The power of government agents and the privacy rights and civil liberties of individuals are different when national security interests are at stake. Such topics go beyond the scope of this text; however, we will discuss the role of local law enforcement in the fight against terrorism in Chapter 14.

Is the Criminal Justice System a System?

The concept that law enforcement, courts, and corrections form a system can be traced back directly to President Johnson's Commission on Law Enforcement and Administration of Justice and their report, *The Challenge of Crime in a Free Society*,[2] issued in 1967. President Johnson, in response to widespread fear of crime and social unrest in the 1960s, called for legislation to create an Office of Law Enforcement Assistance (LEAA) which supported law enforcement training, education, and hardware. He also established the Commission on Law Enforcement and Administration of Justice, which studied every aspect of law enforcement, court administration, and corrections. Its report became a blueprint for the study and prevention of crime, and included 202 recommendations. In the development of the report, task forces on juvenile delinquency, policing, courts, corrections, organized crime, and drugs were created. This was the first ever effort to describe the process of crime, investigation, prosecution, and corrections as a system. It was the first nationally coordinated attempt to create or gather together statistics to understand what was happening across the country, including the first crime victimization survey, and the first attempt to gather correctional population figures.[3] National crime reports did exist to some degree and had been collected since the 1930s, first by the International Association of the Chiefs of Police, then by the Federal Bureau of Investigation. The Uniform Crime Reports (UCR) in the 1960s, however, did not include all jurisdictions since participation was voluntary.

Exhibit 1.3   A police officer escorts a protestor to a squad car surrounded by dozens of anti-Vietnam War demonstrators outside the 1968 Democratic National Convention, Chicago. President Johnson created the Commission on Crime and the Administration of Justice to address public concern about crime and disorder.

Source: Getty

The President's Commission resulted in major changes in the criminal justice system; not the least of which was considering the vast patchwork of law enforcement, prosecutorial, and correctional agencies across 50 states and the federal government, a system which implies the various parts work together for a single goal. States can be quite different in their laws and/or the organization of their court and corrections system. Mere possession of marijuana, for instance, is a crime in most states and under federal law, but by 2016, four states had legalized possession in some way. States may have different definitions of other crimes, including, for instance, the dollar amount that moves a theft from a misdemeanor to a felony, the age of legal culpability, and the distinction between simple assault and aggravated assault. There are differences in terminology and even in the order of the steps illustrated in Exhibit 1.2. For instance, jurisdictions may combine the first appearance and arraignment. Many jurisdictions will have either the grand jury hearing or the preliminary hearing, but not both. For that reason, it is difficult to write about the "criminal justice system" because there are actually 51 systems (including the federal criminal justice system); and, additionally, the U.S. territories of Puerto Rico and American Samoa should be considered. Courts are called by different names; some states have grand jury systems while others do not; some states have parole while others do not. Certain elements are present in all systems, however, so we can utilize one book to describe (generally) the nation's system of justice as long as you are aware that your own state may do things a bit differently.

Almost all discussions of our crime control agencies utilize a **systems approach**, meaning that the various elements of police, courts, and corrections are viewed as working together as an integrated whole toward a single goal, which is crime control and prevention. In general, this is true, although the various sub-systems sometimes have contradictory objectives. In fact, some might say that the court system works "against" the police by letting offenders out on bail after police officers arrest them; or, the corrections system works "against" the court system by reducing a prison sentence through good time.

In other ways, the concept of a system does seem to describe what we know to be happening: parole agencies receive pressure to adjust their release numbers when prisons are overcrowded; prosecutors work with police to adjust charges and/or sentence recommendations to help police persuade informants to testify, and police work with parole agents to closely monitor high-risk parolees. Despite the sometimes contradictory objectives of the sub-systems, a systems approach is helpful to understand how these various elements of social control work together, and how sometimes the worldview held by the professionals employed within the various substems conflict.

WHAT IS SOCIAL CONTROL? HOW DOES THE "SOCIAL CONTRACT" JUSTIFY STATE POWER?

Where does the state's power to control people come from? We rarely stop to think about the right of police officers to arrest or the authority of judges to sentence someone to prison, but what is the legal, philosophical, and moral justification for such power? The underlying function of the criminal justice system is social control. Every society needs to control the actions of citizens when they threaten the social order.

Social control is either implicit or explicit. **Socialization** is implicit social control. Our institutions of family, church, and school socialize us to adopt the norms of society. We act the way we do and even think the way we do partially because of the socializing influences of these institutions. Social control can be informal—when your friends, neighbors, peers, and/or family disapprove of your actions, you feel pressure to conform. In contrast, we can think of the criminal justice system as exercising explicit and formal social control. We know that, in addition to social disapproval or informal sanctions, we face the risk of formal punishment for resisting the formal rules of society known as laws, ordinances, regulations, and other terms.

Philosophers, political scientists, and sociologists have asked the question why anyone would voluntarily subject themselves to onerous rules imposed by society. One of the most well-known answers to this question is the **social contract**. This concept comes out of the work of Thomas Hobbes (1588–1679), John Locke (1632–1704), and Jean-Jacques Rousseau (1712–1778).[4] According to Hobbes, before civilization, man lived in a "war of all against all" and life was not very pleasant. A more peaceful existence for everyone could only come about if every person agreed to give up the liberty to aggress against others in return for society's protection against aggressors. Rousseau's "social contract" is the idea that citizens agree to abide by the law in return for the law's protection. Of course, it is not really the case that we all consciously agree to such a contract. Our agreement is implicit when we choose to accept the benefits of living within a society. Part of the idea of the social contract is that if we break the law, we have agreed to the consequences; specifically, arrest, prosecution, and punishment.

The establishment of written laws marks the advance of what we consider civilized society. Hammurabi's reign (1975–1750 BCE) is noted for many things, but one of the greatest is his celebrated code of laws. It is not the earliest code of laws, but one of the most complete. It is also noteworthy in that this ruler made public the entire body of laws, arranged in orderly groups, so that the citizenry would know what was required of them. The code was carved upon a black stone monument, eight feet high, and clearly intended to be in public view. Hammurabi's 282 laws, arguably some of the oldest laws in existence, include many laws that would seem familiar to us today as well as many laws that would not. For instance, this law punished false reporting:

> If any one bring an accusation of any crime before the elders, and does not prove what he has charged, he shall, if it be a capital offense charged, be put to death.

The laws revealed discriminations such as those based on the status of the victim:

> If any one steal cattle or sheep, or an ass, or a pig or a goat, if it belong to a god or to the court, the thief shall pay 30-fold therefore; if they belonged to a freed man of the king he shall pay 10-fold; if the thief has nothing with which to pay he shall be put to death.

There were also laws that supported the oppression of women and slaves:

> If he put out the eye of a man's slave, or break the bone of a man's slave, he shall pay one-half of its value.
>
> If the "finger is pointed" at a man's wife about another man, but she is not caught sleeping with the other man, she shall jump into the river for her husband.

The importance of these ancient laws is not necessarily their content, but that they impose order and control for individual members of society, even if the specific laws of any society (or time) may vary. Public laws educate and protect. They educate the citizenry by giving notice that certain acts will be punished, assuming that rational people will choose not to engage in such behavior. They protect because rulers are put on notice that citizens cannot be punished *unless* they break such laws. History is replete with tyrants who oppress their citizenry; however, the presence of law provides some restrictions on their actions. The phrase "a nation of laws, not men" refers to the idea that in a society governed by law, no one person is above the law; and laws, once created, supposedly apply to everyone.

Gradually, rudimentary court systems were created to administer the laws. Historically, citizens had a much bigger role in assessing guilt and punishment. For instance, in ancient Greece it was common to have several hundred people on a jury to decide a case. Prosecutors did not exist and any person could bring a charge against any other person. Only much later, public police agencies and public prosecutors were created to enforce laws. Modern policing began less than 300 years ago.

Because law is so much a fabric of our social reality, we forget what it would be like without it. Apocolyptic movies are one exercise in imagining a society without law. Inevitably, the perception of screenwriters is that relationships between people break down to resemble Hobbe's "war of all against all" where the strong prey upon the weak. In this view of humanity, the socal contract keeps us all in check and law protects us as well as controls us. While law school primarily teaches the "is" of law today, the academic field of sociology of law examines the "why" of how laws are created, the use of law as a tool of social control as well as social reform, and the interactions between law and morality, among other issues. Our discussion in this textbook will focus almost exclusively on the system of law and the agencies of social control in the United States and it should be noted that other nations may have quite different criminal justice systems.

WHAT IS THE HISTORICAL FOUNDATION OF OUR LEGAL SYSTEM?

Our legal system in the United States comes from English **common law**, except for the state of Louisiana, which, because of its history as a French possession, has evolved from the continental civil law (or code) system. The continental code system predominates in Europe and in areas colonized by France and Spain, and is based originally on the Napoleonic code. Common law, in contrast, developed from hundreds of years of magistrates' decisions in England. Over time, these decisions were expected to follow past decisions (a concept known as *stare decisis* or "let the decision stand"). At some point, some decisions were written down to be used as guidance when similar cases were brought by different people and/or in different courts. The English common law refers to the compilation of all those decisions. In the 1700s, William Blackstone, a famous English jurist, undertook the mammoth effort of organizing and identifying the principles of law that derived from these decisions. Blackstone's *Law Commentaries* collected the common laws together in a single source for the first time.

After the American Revolution and early state creation, England's common laws gave way to **penal codes**, developed by the legislatures of the emerging states. The American Constitution set forth the basic structure of the federal court powers, and also limited the federal government's power to create law. The federal government's powers are specifically enumerated in the Constitution in Article 1 and are limited to certain mandates, such as to protect the borders of the country and to regulate interstate commerce, although in recent decades the scope of federal crimes have expanded exponentially. The power of the federal government to regulate interstate commerce has been used as a basis for federal laws on drug possession and sales, weapons charges, various frauds, and other crimes.

The Constitution gave state legislatures broad powers to create new crimes. This is called **police power** and is specifically delegated to the states by the 10th Amendment of the Constitution. States' police power allows states to pass a myriad of laws related to the health and welfare of the citizenry as long as such laws do not conflict with federal constitutional rights.

Exhibit 1.4   10th Amendment of the U.S Constitution

The powers not delegated to the United States by the Constitution, nor prohibited by it to the states, are reserved to the states respectively, or to the people.

U.S. Constitution, Amendment X

Source: http://constitutioncenter.org/constitution/full-text

States can also delegate this authority to local political bodies, such as counties and cities. City ordinances (i.e., no skating on the sidewalk) are created by city councils or the local political entity, and are usually punishable by fines. City code violations (i.e., keeping livestock within city limits) are also created by local political bodies and punished by fines. The power these local political entities possess comes to them from the state and can be restricted and modified by state legislatures.

The Texas Penal Code, for instance, can be found at http://www.statutes.legis. state.tx.us/?link=PE; California's criminal laws can be found at http://www. leginfo.ca.gov/cgi-bin/calawquery? codesection=pen. You can probably find your own state's code by simply using a web-based search engine.

You can see some of these laws that supposedly still exist at http://www. dumblaws.com/

Now all states have their own penal codes that lay out the laws for that state, and we have many more laws than what existed under the common law.

You may have seen an Internet item that lists obscure and ridiculous old laws that supposedly still exist, such as no kissing in public or no shooting buffalos from a moving train, although it is doubtful because states' penal codes are periodically reviewed by legislators aided by the state bar association.

HOW BIG IS THE CRIMINAL JUSTICE SYSTEM COMPARED TO 50 YEARS AGO?

As noted earlier, about 50 years ago, President Lyndon Johnson addressed Congress on the need for a national response to the problem of crime. The first challenge was the absence of knowledge about crime and criminal justice agencies. In 1965, there was not even the most basic information about the criminal justice system. No operational data on the police, courts, and other justice agencies existed. There was no central repository for data on the number of police, the number of people in prison, or how much the criminal justice system cost taxpayers. There were no criminal justice or criminology departments on college and university campuses and few law enforcement departments; the field of study simply did not exist.

President Johnson's attention to the criminal justice system was in response to widespread fear of crime and disorder. Public protests over the Vietnam War and civil rights created a pervasive sense that the country was descending in violent chaos. Crime was a major concern, but citizens were also upset by the television coverage of law enforcement officers using clubs against peaceful protestors. For the first time, race relations and urban strife entered everyone's living room through the medium of television; everyone watched peaceful civil rights protesters being assaulted with tear gas, clubs, high-pressure waterhoses, and dogs. This exposure created pressure not only to pursue civil rights goals, but also to reform the system of social control and address a perceived crime problem.

In response, President Johnson created the Commission on Crime and the Administration of Justice, mentioned earlier in this chapter. The effects of the President's Commission were substantial. In response to recommendations, police departments became more racially and ethnically diversified. Police officers sought college degrees and were supported with federal funds by LEAA, resulting in more departments of police science in colleges and universities which then evolved to departments of criminal justice. The Office of Justice Programs in the Department of Justice eventually included the National Institute of Justice (NIJ), the Bureau of Justice Statistics (BJS), the Bureau of Justice Administration (BJA), and the Office of Juvenile Justice and Delinquency Prevenion (OJJDP). These have become the major federal funding sources for criminal justice research and program implementation and evaluation. The Bureau of Justice Statistics is our main source for national statistics on victimization, correctional populations, and other criminal justice data.

Go to the Bureau of Justice website to explore the different types of data you can access: www.bjs.gov/

Our criminal justice system has grown into a leviathan costing $265 billion each year when including federal, state, and local costs. The cost of corrections alone is $80 billion and states spend increasing amounts of their budget on prisons. Since the mid-1980s, the share of states' general funds that go to prisons doubled in 15 states and increased by at least half in 31 states. In the aggregate, state-level prison costs have grown from 4.7 percent of general fund spending in fiscal 1986 to 7.0 percent in fiscal 2012.[5] With many states now struggling to support public education and fund projects to maintain and upgrade the state infrastructure (roads, bridges, public works), serious consideration of alternatives to ever-increasing criminal justice costs are being considered.

WHAT ARE SOME CURRENT ISSUES IN CRIMINAL JUSTICE TODAY?

Similar to 50 years ago, there is currently a great deal of interest in criminal justice issues. At least one writer suggested that 2015 was the "the year of criminal justice reform."[6] It seems that we are at a watershed moment in history, similar to 1965 when President Johnson created his Crime Commission. Similar to the Commission's report in 1965, the issues and concerns that have been identified recently can be seen as challenges to overcome in the quest to have a more effective and just criminal justice system. In the paragraphs to follow, we will briefly examine current challenges in all areas of the criminal justice system.

Crimes

One issue today is the perceived inappropriate expansion of federal criminal laws, especially when such laws eliminate the requirement of criminal intent. Some point out that no one even knows how many federal crimes there are because they are not presented in any organized way and are interspersed in federal regulations as well as the federal code. "**Overcriminalization**" refers to the idea there are too many "crimes." The Sensenbrenner-Scott Over-Criminalization Task Force Safe, Accountable, Fair, Effective (SAFE) Justice Reinvestment Act[7] of 2015 (H.B. 2944), for instance, is a comprehensive criminal justice reform bill (for the federal system) that is best known for the provisions to reduce mandatory minimum sentences for low-level drug offenders; however, other sections of the bill addressed the "overcriminalization" of violations of federal regulations.

Another area of overcriminalization targeted by critics is the juvenile justice system. Public attitude seems to be shifting against "**zero tolerance**" in school discipline and the use of the criminal justice system (through arrest and municipal tickets) to respond to school fights and other misbehavior that have historically been dealt with by school officials. The so-called "school-to-prison pipeline"[8] describes the correlation between school suspension or expulsion and future involvement in the court system. Teenagers have always consumed alcohol, smoked cigarettes, and skipped school, but now these activities are acts that result in a formal criminal justice system response. Many people question whether a formal criminal justice response is the most effective intervention to youthful misbehavior.

We have witnessed a historic decline in most crime categories since the late 1990s. The homicide rate of 4.7 per 100,000 in 2011 was about half of what it was in 1991 (9.8 per 100,000) and the rate in 2014 was even lower at 4.5. In fact, the homicide rate is even lower than what it was in 1962 (4.6 per 100,000). Other crime categories have mirrored this decline of crime.[9] Obviously our understanding of major crime trends hinges on accurate reporting, just as it did 50 years ago. Computers have provided a boon to the researcher unimaginable to researchers in 1965, but gaps in what information we collect or our inability to compare particular data over time frustrates our efforts to understand what is happening. Questions have arisen over the accuracy of crime reports,[10] the ability to utilize the national victimization survey for longitudinal comparisons of crime victimization statistics,[11] and the lack of current national data on crime reports or arrests because the FBI's data is only available months or years later.

To see the FBI's crime data, go to https://www.fbi.gov/about-us/cjis/ucr/crime-in-the-u.s

One of the major challenges in criminology today is to understand what caused the dramatic decline of crime over the last twenty years. Was the crime decline caused by our expansive use of imprisonment as punishment or simply a function of the aging of the "baby-boom" population? Did more police on the street reduce crime? Numerous researchers have attempted to isolate the most important causal factors.[12] Most recently, the Brennan Center for Justice has published *What Caused the Crime Decline*? Also, the National Academy of Sciences has created a Roundtable on Crime comprised of major criminological and statistical experts who have been exploring factors in the crime decline. Their multi-year effort will culminate in a final report as well.[13]

Since the President's Commission did its work in 1965–67, the growth of the academic fields of criminology and criminal justice has been exponential, with a steadily increasing number of academic programs across the country, dozens of journals, and thousands of researchers devoted to the study of crime. One challenge is to avoid conducting and disseminating research in a way that is not biased toward any political/social ideology. Unlike some other areas of academic inquiry, it seems everyone thinks they know what causes a person to commit crime or what correctional programs should work to reduce **recidivism**, but these issues require carefully constructing questions and answering them with the best and most accurate facts available.

Policing

Recently, law enforcement officers have been the subject of intense public scrutiny, not seen since the early 1990s. The perception then, as now, is that police officers are not held accountable when using inappropriate force against minority groups. Widespread protests in 2014 led to President Obama's 21st Century Panel on Policing. This panel, comprised of both academics and practitioners, issued its report in early March 2015 with recommendations for major changes in training, accountability, and the culture of policing. In 2016, "**Black Lives Matter**" protests ignited again after the deaths of two Black men in Louisiana and Minnesota. Perceived injustice has been cited as a motivation for

Exhibit 1.5   President Obama meets with members of the Task Force on 21st Century Policing, which ultimately called for for major changes in training, accountability, and the culture of policing.

Source: https://www.whitehouse.gov/blog/2015/03/02/what-21st-century-policing-means

You can view the Cato Institute's website at www.policemisconduct.net/

individuals who ambushed and killed police officers, first in New York City in December 2014 and, then, in Dallas and Baton Rouge in the summer of 2016.

Across the country, formal and informal groups have targeted police for scrutiny. Some groups, such as the Cato Institute, publish websites that collect and display news stories of police misconduct. Others, such as the American Civil Liberties Union (ACLU), have utilized open records requests to acquire disciplinary records from major cities. Legislative efforts exist now in several states to roll back privacy protections that exempt police officers' personnel records from open records requests. Apps have been created to encourage people to upload cellphone videos of police misconduct and there are loosely formed groups in some cities that promote various forms of "cop watches" based on the premise that there is widespread abuse of power.

This heightened scrutiny has come about because of a perception that police officers across the nation engage in misconduct, especially in the use of illegal force. While some isolated events have received a great deal of media attention, whether there is a widespread problem or whether the prevalence of misconduct has increased are questions that must be answered with objective data. Efforts are now underway to begin the collection of accurate data on the number of police shootings that result in death and injury. We need to know how many individuals are killed by police, but also what the elements are in the fatal exchanges. What patterns exist in the use of force across cities? What are the correlates of the officer involved or the targets of the shootings? Is it true that race is a factor after "controlling for" (meaning holding constant) all other variables?

Recently, the "Ferguson Effect" has been in the news referring to the observed work slowdown of police officers (measured by dramatic reductions in arrests) in places such as Ferguson and Baltimore where police feel unfairly judged and some have linked it to increases in violent crime.[14] We will explore these questions in subsequent chapters.

Courts

Increasingly prevalent in the news in the last decade or so have been stories of the wrongfully convicted. Innocence Projects now exist around the country where volunteer lawyers and students investigate cases and, in a growing number of cases, are successful in exonerating their clients. The National Registry of Exonerations notes that 1,570 people have been released from prison because their conviction has been found to be the result of inaccurate eyewitness testimony, false confession, and/or misconduct on the part of system actors. Some prosecutors' offices have also established **conviction integrity units**. These prosecutors either work with Innocence Projects or identify cases on their own to investigate as potential wrongful convictions. Prosecutors have come under scrutiny themselves for unethical and illegal actions with a few being criminally charged for their actions in sending innocent people to prison.

The first question is what is the prevalence of wrongful convictions, and what are the elements that lead to them. Thus far, we have only estimates that range drastically depending on whether they come from prosecutors or defendants. Several preliminary studies, which will be discussed in a later chapter, find some causal factors that suggest how to reduce the number of wrongful convictions.

One area identified in the research on wrongful convictions is the use (or misuse) of **forensic science**. Forensic science refers to science used in the

For more information, see www.law.umich.edu/special/exoneration/Pages/about.aspx

administration of law. Forensic scientists analyze physical evidence, including ballistic testing, blood spatter analysis and other fields. The National Academies of Science published a scathing report in 2009 criticizing most forensic fields except for DNA because of a lack of scientific method in developing and measuring the reliability of the testing. Even the FBI's vaunted crime lab has come under fire for shoddy work and/or misleading testimony. The questions in this area include which forensic techniques are supported by science, which are not, and how they are being used in the courts.

A major challenge in the area of courts is the problem of providing adequate representation to the indigent. In 2012, Attorney General Eric Holder announced that significant new resources would be directed to indigent aid. A number of private and public advocacy groups (Sixth Amendment Center, Brennan Center, The Constitution Project, the Gideon at 50 Project, the American Bar Association) have brought attention to the fact that indigent legal aid is so overburdened that representation likely falls below constitutional requirements.[15] Some evidence indicates that some jurisdictions do not provide indigent defense as early in the process as they are constitutionally required or have policies and procedures that serve to deny the poor their legal rights. An important question is whether the indigent receive adequate legal representation and whether having a public defender results in "less justice." We need to know much more than we do about what is happening in the courts and prosecutors' offices of this country before addressing these questions.

Corrections

In 2015, President Obama was the first sitting president to visit a federal prison. Virtually every major policy and legal group in the United States has criticized this nation's "mass imprisonment." We incarcerate approximately 700 per 100,000 residents, compared to other Western country's rate of less than 200. The United States incarcerates six times as many people as Canada, between six to nine times as many as most western European countries, and as much as ten times as many people as northern European countries.[16] People think this is because we have more crime in this country; data indicate this is true only for violent crime and our property **crime rates** are similar to other countries.

Recently, there have been legislative efforts to address the problem. The Colson Commission was formed by Congress to evaluate the problem of over-imprisonment at the federal level. Legislation introduced in 2015 mandated eliminating five- and ten-year mandatory minimums based on the weight of the drug involved if the person was not a leader of a drug ring, and promoted diversion, drug courts, and probation instead of prison for non-violent low-level offenders. Although it has not emerged from the Justice Committee for a vote, it is possible that it will in the next legislative session. At the state level, Justice Re-investment grants from the Office of Justice Programs have been awarded to help states reduce the numbers sent to prison and re-invest the savings into community resources. The question is whether these interventions are successful in reducing prison populations with no unacceptable risk to the public. We need to understand what is happening across the country and what elements have allowed some states to reduce their prison population. More fundamentally, we ask the question—did the increase of imprisonment reduce crime in any significant way?

HOW DO IDEOLOGIES AFFECT OBJECTIVE ANALYSIS OF CRIMINAL JUSTICE ISSUES?

The paragraphs above raise questions in every part of the criminal justice system. We have a challenge in that, for many of these questions, we do not have good data. Another problem is that ideology sometimes slants our understanding of the problem.

Ideologies

An **ideology** is a body of doctrines or beliefs that guides an individual or group. It is a way of organizing knowledge, in that we interpret things we see and hear with reference to our existing belief systems. In fact, we may even reject information that doesn't fit our existing ideology and only accept information that does. In 1968, Herbert Packer described two models of law enforcement that are extremely helpful in understanding the issues and the decision making that occur in reference to the entire criminal justice system, not just law enforcement. What he termed models could also be called ideologies. Packer called his two models crime control and due process.

In the **crime control ideology**, the basic belief is that controlling crime and punishing the criminal are more important than anything else, best expressed by a Supreme Court justice who argued that the criminal should not be set free because "the constable blundered." Some of the beliefs that are consistent with Herbert Packer's crime control ideology follow:

- Reducing crime is the most important function of law enforcement.
- The failure of law enforcement means the breakdown of order.
- The criminal process guarantees social freedom.
- Efficiency is a top priority.

- The emphasis is on speed and finality.
- There is a presumption of guilt once the suspect is in the system.

The **due process ideology** supports controlling crime, but in this ideology crime control is not the most important goal. The most important mission of the criminal justice system is the enforcement of law in a fair and just manner, as characterized by the comment: "It is better to let ten guilty men go free than punish one innocent." Beliefs that are consistent with this ideology include:

- There is a possibility of error in the system.
- Prevention of mistakes is more important than efficiency.
- Protection of the process is as important as protection of innocents.
- The coercive power of the state is always subject to abuse.
- Every due process protection is there for a reason and should be strictly adhered to.

These basic ideologies are very pervasive in our thinking and opinions regarding criminal justice issues. You can see evidence of them in television dramas, in politicians' statements, in television and radio talk show hosts' conversations, and in "letters to the editor" in the local newspaper.

If one's ideology is purely "crime control," then some consistent beliefs would include that criminals are the "enemy" and any means necessary is acceptable to control them. On the other hand, if one has a dominant ideology of due process, then consistent beliefs might include the idea that criminals have the same rights as "good people" and the protections put in place to protect civil rights are more important than any individual case. Probably no one holds purely crime control or purely due process belief systems, but the inclination to lean one way or the other often influences how we receive information. One's ideology also influences perceptions of acceptable crime control and security strategies.

There are substantial differences in how Americans view any debate based on ideology. In a 2011 poll, of those who identified as liberal, 85 percent believed the criminal justice system should invest more money in rehabilitation and job programs for offenders, but only 49 percent of conservatives agreed; only 13 percent of liberals believed that more money should be spent on police, prisons, and courts compared to 47 percent of conservatives.[17]

More concerning is the fact that research foundations and "think-tanks" are labeled conservative (e.g., The Heritage Foundation, Manhattan Institute) or liberal (The Sentencing Institute, The Brennan Center). If such sources of information can be identified by their ideology, should we be concerned about the objectivity of the reports generated? It is unfortunate that few sources of information regarding criminal justice issues are perceived as ideologically neutral (e.g. the Bureau of Justice Statistics, the FBI's Uniform Crime Reports). Recently, there has been a convergence of conservative and liberal groups in championing reform in criminal justice; specifically, in reducing mandatory minimum sentences and the extremely high rates of incarceration, addressing collateral consquences of imprisonment (e.g., lifetime bans on voting), over-criminalization, and other issues. More generally, however, in criminal justice, ideology shapes the debate and influences proposed solutions.

We have many questions that require careful collection of facts and analysis. While our knowledge today, as compared to 1965, is incredibly more detailed and comprehensive; there are still large gaps in what we know about crime and how the criminal justice system works. It is important to continually improve our collection and analysis of data to understand crime and crime prevention. In each chapter, we will offer a focused investigation of a specific topic. In this first chapter, we take a very current controversial issue—whether illegal immigrants are disproportionally responsible for crime—and offer available data and evidence to attempt to answer the question objectively using the critical thinking approach we will use throughout the text.

FOCUS ON DATA: ARE ILLEGAL IMMIGRANTS MORE LIKELY TO BE CRIMINAL?

The presidential nomination process for the 2016 election led to a renewed argument about whether there is a link between immigration and crime; more specifically, are illegal immigrants more likely to be criminal than native-born? This is a question that can be researched and has been. It is a good example of an issue rife with ideological bias that requires an objective collection and careful analysis of data; however, it also offers a host of methodological challenges that may make any clear answer impossible. First, we must identify any preconceptions or bias. Groups and individuals who are in favor of a hardline approach to immigrants who are in this country without legal authorization may be more tempted to see a link while those who are advocates for immigrant groups would be disinclined to accept evidence that the millions who are in this country without legal authorization are more likely than native-born to be criminal. Some of these interest groups publish findings that must be evaluated keeping these potential biases in mind; likewise, academics are not immune from bias based on personal views and so careful weighing of various findings are important. One way to more objectively analyze facts is to "triangulate" data if possible. That means collect data from more than one source to note consistencies or inconsistencies.

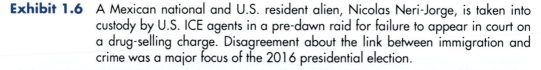

Exhibit 1.6   A Mexican national and U.S. resident alien, Nicolas Neri-Jorge, is taken into custody by U.S. ICE agents in a pre-dawn raid for failure to appear in court on a drug-selling charge. Disagreement about the link between immigration and crime was a major focus of the 2016 presidential election.

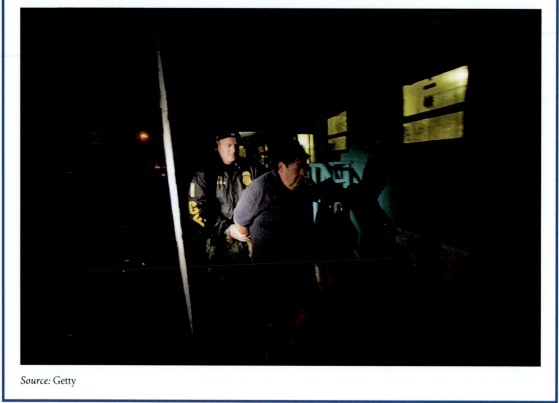

Source: Getty

Are immigrants more likely to commit crimes than native-born? Generally, such allegations are directed toward Latinos and immigrants coming across our southern border from Mexico and Central and South America, thus the question itself lacks specificity. Even though most people think of those countries when one says immigrant or, especially, illegal immigrant, there are thousands of people in the United States from Canada, Great Britain, Europe, and other countries without legal authorization as well. Does the question presuppose a particular geographic source of the immigrant or not? Many reports don't bother to specify.

Some reports have indicated that criminal aliens are responsible for a disproportional amount of crime, are more likely to recidivate, and are the target of a disproportional number of homicide warrants.[18] In the summer of 2015, the killing of Kate Steinle in San Francisco by a man who had been deported five times ignited the issue even further. He had been recently released from the San Francisco jail because that city approved **sanctuary city** rules which prohibited local law enforcement from holding illegal immigrants for Immigration and Customs Enforcement (ICE) agents unless there were formal detainers or warrants issued. As a result, Congress has threatened to withhold federal monies to cities with sanctuary laws in place. While some argue immigrants are more likely to commit crime; others argue they are actually *less* likely to be involved in crime than other groups. Neither side presents a definitive answer because we don't have complete information.

An individual who comes across the border without legal authorization or stays longer than his or her visa is considered to have committed a *civil* (not a *criminal*) violation. Only when they ignore an order of deportation or return after being deported have they committed a federal crime and become an illegal immigrant. Federal laws have been passed so that someone who is a legal immigrant may lose that status after committing any crime. This poses a methodological difficulty because there is an overlap in the definitions used—one cannot examine the link between being an illegal immigrant and criminality when the commission of a crime may be the essential element in the definition of being an illegal versus legal immigrant.

Whether these individuals are more likely than others to commit other types of crimes (such as drug crimes, burglary, or robbery) is the question that we will address here. It should also be noted that identifying a correlation does not provide the "cause" of the correlation. Even if there is a correlation between illegal immigration and crime, it may not be because "criminals" and "rapists" are coming across the border; the correlation may exist because illegal immigrants can't find legal employment and so resort to illegal sources of income.

Studies have consistently found that first-generation immigrants have lower crime rates than their children and subsequent generations. Other studies show that even within the demographic group of young males, immigrants have lower **incarceration rates** that native-born.[19] A recent study, using a national survey of adolescents, found that immigrant teens are 50 percent less likely than native-born to be involved in drug use or selling.[20] In fact, there has been a long series of studies over the decades that show immigrants are *less* likely to be involved in crime than native-born.[21] These findings do not address the question of whether illegal immigrants are more likely to be criminal since the numbers represent, for the most part, legal immigrants, not those who are in this country illegally.

Researchers, including Ramiro Martinez,[22] have found no differences over time in homicide or other crimes between geographic areas with high concentrations of Latino immigrants and those with lower numbers of immigrants. This approach is problematic, however, in that illegal immigrants are not differentiated from legal immigrants, although in the aggregate these communities are more likely to have large numbers of both legal and illegal immigrants. Another potential problem with this methodology is that it is possible that neighborhoods with high numbers of illegal immigrants may be less likely to report victimization to police agencies, thereby suppressing official crime numbers.

Some studies use prison or jail population numbers to show that the percentage of foreign-born in prisons and/or jails is higher than their representation in the community.[23] Using prison or jail as a proxy for criminality is a methodologically weak approach, however. Incarcerated populations are not representative of those who commit crime and the number of criminal illegal immigrants may be low in that many would probably be deported rather than sent to prison. It may also be the case that they may be more likely than native-born to remain in jails because they could not make bail or obtain any form of pre-trial release. The point is that prison or jail populations are influenced by a range of factors not controlled for by such studies, making incarcerated populations a poor measure to compare criminality between native-borns and immigrant groups.

Hickman and Suttorp attempted to address the question by looking at recidivism. They compared "deportable" aliens to legal immigrants released from the Los Angeles county jail.[24] They found while 65 percent of the non-deportable immigrants had no re-arrests, 57 percent of the deportable immigrants had no re-arrests. When these researchers controlled for a variety of independent variables that might affect recidivism, including type of crime, age of defendant, and other factors, they found no significant differences in the **recidivism** rate after one year between the two groups. These findings arguably show that illegal immigrants are not more recidivistic than legal immigrants; at least they are not any more likely to be re-arrested. Weaknesses of the study are that deportable aliens may not have re-entered the criminal justice system because of deportation. Also, it doesn't tell us anything about whether illegal immigrants are more likely to be arrested than legal immigrants for a first crime, only that they are not more likely to be re-arrested for a second crime after controlling for other variables that might affect recidivism.

Another recent study carefully examined the federal government's Secure Communities program which enlists local law enforcement to help identify and deport illegal immigrants. Under this program, local law enforcement agencies send fingerprints of recent arrestees to the federal government who check to see if the person is deportable because of immigration violations. If so, federal agents take the individual into federal custody for deportation hearings. The researchers found that the removal of illegal immigrants did not reduce crime in those communities as compared to other communities without the program in any significant way.[25] Another study of the Secure Communities program analyzed nearly 3,000 counties over nine years. Findings indicated no significant crime declines in those counties that utilized Secure Communities to deport immigrant offenders.[26]

The best methodology to answering the question would be to use self-reported crimes of each of the three groups (native-born, legal immigrants, and illegal immigrants) to see if any group reported higher participation rates than the other two groups. Because that type of study is unlikely, the next best approach would be to use arrest numbers, even with the caution that arrest figures are not strictly a measure of crime, but, rather a measure of official response to suspected crime. Using arrest numbers, one would want to construct a **rate** of crime commission for illegal immigrants and compare it to the rate of crime for legal immigrants, and the rate of crime for native-borns; that is, out of every 100 illegal immigrants, how many have committed crimes, out of every 100 native-born, how many have committed crimes, and so on. It is important to note, however, that the illegal immigrant population is more likely to be male and young than either of the other populations, so the other population bases should be similarly age and sex restricted for a true comparison.

One would think these numbers should be relatively easy to obtain, but they are not. According to the FBI, the general arrest rate in 2014 was 3,512 per 100,000. That is, for every 100,000 people in the country, 3,512 were arrested.[27] The FBI's Uniform Crime Report also provides total arrest numbers by age range and race, but not ethnicity. Even if arrest figures by ethnicity (as opposed to race) were available, the arrest numbers would include legal immigrants, illegal immigrants, and native-born. In short, the respective arrest numbers for these three groups is not readily available.

In the absence of the best data, researchers resort to available data (such as jail or prison population numbers). After a careful examination of the available studies, research does not seem to support the proposition that illegal immigrants are more criminal; however, it doesn't disprove it either. We do know that first-generation immigrants (not differentiated as legal or illegal) are less likely to commit crime than their children (who would be native-born if born in this country). Studies also show that removing deportable aliens does not reduce crime. Unfortunately, our ability to answer the question definitively is limited by lack of the best data to answer the question.[28]

SUMMARY

What is the Criminal Justice "System"? Is It a System?

The criminal justice system is comprised of law enforcement, the courts, and corrections. We consider it a system because one can argue these "sub-systems" have a shared goal of crime prevention and justice. However, one could also argue the sub-systems do not comprise a system because of differing and conflicting goals.

What Is Social Control? How Does the "Social Contract" Justify State Power?

Social control is what pressures individuals in society to conform to societal norms of behavior. When the informal institutions of family, church, and school fail and individuals break the formal rules of society (laws, regulations, ordinances), then the criminal justice system takes over as the institution of social control. The "social contract" refers to the idea that we all give up certain liberties (the liberty to act in any way we please) in return for societal protection.

What Is the Historical Foundation of Our Legal System?

Our legal system's foundation is British common law, although over time states have adopted state penal codes that specify all criminal laws. The federal system also has the Uniform Code which specifies federal laws.

How Big Is the Criminal Justice System Compared to 50 Years Ago?

The "system" of criminal justice, including law enforcement and corrections, eclipses most state budget items and, combining federal and state expenditures, exceeds $265 billion.

What Are Some Current Issues in Criminal Justice Today?

Current issues include the legalization of marijuana, overcriminalization, and the "school to prison pipeline." Law enforcement has come under intense scrutiny in their use of force and, especially, use of lethal force. Mandatory minimums and other harsh sentencing practices have also come under recent critical scrutiny. In general, on any given day, the newspaper is full of not just stories of crime, but also of criminal justice policy issues.

How Do Ideologies Affect Objective Analysis of Criminal Justice Issues?

Ideologies can sometimes affect our ability to process information objectively. Two ideologies recognized in criminal justice are the crime control and due process models.

Critical Thinking Exercises

1. Identify at least three criminal justice stories in today's newspaper—can you identify an ideology associated with the story? What questions are presented by the issues presented? What data is presented? Is the data (if any) from a biased source or an unbiased source in your opinion?

2. Set up an ideal way to study whether those in this country illegally are more likely than legal immigrants or native-born to commit crime. What would you want to know? How would you make sure that there wasn't some other factor influencing your results? Why can't we use prison figures to determine the relative likelihood of criminality among different groups?

NOTES

1 Adapted from The Critical Thinking Community, 6/9/2016 from http://www.criticalthinking.org/pages/our-concept-of-critical-thinking/411.

2 The President's Commission on Law Enforcement and Administration of Justice, *The Challenge of Crime in a Free Society*. Washington, DC: Government Printing Office, February 1967, available at www.ncjrs.gov/pdffiles1/nij/42.pdf.

3 T. Feucht and E. Zedlewski, *The 40th Anniversary of the Crime Report*. Washington, DC: Office of Justice Programs, 2007. Available at http://www.nij.gov/journals/257/pages/40th-crime-report.aspx.

4 See T. Hobbes, *Leviathan*. New York: Penguin Classics, 1651/1982. See also J. Rousseau, *The Social Contract*, New York: Penguin Classics, 1762/1968.

5 National Association of State Budget Officers, *State Spending for Corrections: Long-Term Trends and Recent Criminal Justice Policy Reforms*. Washington, DC: NASBO, 2015. Available at: http://www.nasbo.org/sites/default/files/pdf/State%20Spending%20for%20Corrections.pdf

6 T. Lynch, "2015 can be the year of criminal justice reform." The Cato Institute, February 9, 2015. Available at: http://www.cato.org/publications/commentary/2015-can-be-year-criminal-justice-reform.

7 As of December 2016, the HB 2944 had not been brought forward for a vote and was still being considered by the Judiciary Committee.

8 See, for instance, https://www.aclu.org/fact-sheet/what-school-prison-pipeline.

9 J. Fox and M. Zawitz, *Homicide Trends in the United States: 2000 Update*. Washington, DC: Bureau of Justice Statistics, 2003. A. Cooper and E. Smith, *Homicide in the U.S. Known to Law Enforcement*. Washington, DC: Bureau of Justice Statistics, 2013. Available at http://www.bjs.gov/index.cfm?ty=pbdetail&iid=4863. FBI. *Crime in the United States, 2014*. Washington, DC: FBI, 2016, Table 1. Available at: https://www.fbi.gov/about-us/cjis/ucr/crime-in-the-u.s/2014/crime-in-the-u.s.-2014/tables/table-1

10 J. Eterno and E. Silverman, *The Crime Numbers Game: Management by Manipulation*. New York: CRC Press, 2012.

11 S. Ansari and N. He, "Convergence revisited: A multi-definition, multi-method analysis of the UCR and the NCVS crime series (1973–2008)." *Justice Quarterly* 32 (2012): 1–31.

12 F. Zimring, *The Great American Crime Decline*. Boston: Oxford, 2006.

13 O. Roeder, L. Eisen and J. Bowling, *What Caused the Crime Decline?* New York, New York: Brennan Center, 2015. Available at: http://www.brennancenter.org/. See, The Roundtable on Crime Trends website: http://sites.nationalacademies.org/DBASSE/CLAJ/CurrentProjects/DBASSE_081065.

14 H. MacDonald, "The new nationwide crime wave." *Wall Street Journal*, May 29, 2015. Available at http://www.wsj.com/arti cles/the-new-nationwide-crime-wave-1432938425. R. Rosenfeld, *Was there a Ferguson Effect on Crime in St. Louis? Washington,* DC: Sentencing Project, 2015. Available at: http://sentencingproject.org/doc/publications/inc_Ferguson_Effect.pdf

15 N. Mariano, "Justice denied: The high price of justice." TheSouthern.com, April 19, 2015, http://thesouthern.com/news/ local/justice-denied/the-high-price-of-justice-sixth-amendment-guarantee-deteriorating-under/article_2992e476-c4ca-5124- a433–23a025a26bf8.html

16 http://www.washingtonpost.com/blogs/fact-checker/wp/2015/04/30/does-the-united-states-really-have-five-percent-of worlds-population-and-one-quarter-of-the-worlds-prisoners/.

17 Gallup Poll, Table 2.0025.2010, "Attitudes toward profiling of airline passengers to prevent terrorism, 2010." *Sourcebook of Criminal Justice Statistics Online.* Retrieved 9/5/2010 from http://www.albany.edu/sourcebook/pdf/t200252010.pdf.

18 Reported in R. Martinez, "The impact of immigration policy on criminological research." *Criminology and Public Policy* 7 (2008): 53–58.

19 B. Bersani, "An examination of first and second generation immigrant offending trajectories." *Justice Quarterly* 31 (2012): 315–343. C. Kubrin, S. Desmond, "The power of place revisited: Why immigrant communities have lower levels of adolescent violence." *Youth Violence and Juvenile Justice* (October 2015) 13: 345–366, first published on August 24, 2014.

20 C. Salas-Wright, M. Vaughn, S. Schwartz and D. Cordova. "An 'immigrant paradox' for adolescent externalizing behavior? Evi-dence from a national sample." *Social Psychiatry & Psychiatric Epidemiology* 51 (2015). Also available at ResearchGate: https:// www.researchgate.net/publication/281406948_An_immigrant_paradox_for_adolescent_externalizing_behavior_Evi dence_from_a_national_sample.

21 See review of studies: A. Nowrasteh, *Immigration and Crime: What the Research Says.* Cato Institute, July 15, 2015, available at http://www.cato.org/blog/immigration-crime-what-research-says.

22 R. Martinez, "The reality of the secure communities program: Are our communities really becoming safer?" *Criminology and Public Policy* 13 (2014): 339–344.

23 S. Camarota and J. Vaughn, *Immigration and Crime: Assessing a Conflicted Issue.* Center for Immigration Studies, 2009. Available at: http://cis.org/ImmigrantCrime.

24 L. Hickman and M. Suttorp, "Are deportable aliens a unique threat to public safety? Comparing the recidivism of deportable and nondeportable aliens." *Criminology and Public Policy* 7 (2008): 59–82.

25 E. Treyger, A. Chalfin and C. Loeffler, "Immigration enforcement, policing, and crime: Evidence from the secure communities program." *Crime and Public Policy* 13 (2014): 285–322.

26 T. Miles and A. Cox, "Does immigration enforcement reduce crime: Evidence from secure communities." *Journal of Law and Economics* 57 (2014): 937–946.

27 Retrieved from *Crime in the United States, 2014* at: https://www.fbi.gov/about-us/cjis/ucr/crime-in-the-u.s/2015/preli minary-semiannual-uniform-crime-report-januaryjune-2015.

28 See for more critical analysis of the methodology issues: D. Mears, "The immigration crime nexus: Toward an analytic frame-work for assessing and guiding theory, research, and policy." *Sociological Perspectives* 44 (2001): 1–19.

CRIME IN SOCIETY

2

Chapter Preview

- What Is Crime?
- What Is the Role of Legislators, Victims, Police, and Prosecutors in Defining Crimes?
- What Sources Do We Use to Find Out About the Patterns of Crime?
- What Crimes Are People Most Frequently Arrested for?
- What Do We Know About Homicide?
- What Has Been the Pattern of Crime Over the Years? Has It Declined?
- Does The Public Have an Accurate Perception About the Prevalence of Crime?
- How Do the Crime Rates of the United States Compare to Other Countries?
- Focus On Data: Is There a Ferguson Effect? Is There a Current Crime Wave?
- Summary
- Critical Thinking Exercises

WHAT IS CRIME?

What is crime? This seems like an easy question, and it is, in a way. However, the answer is not necessarily murder, robbery, or rape. Those may be examples of crime, but the definition of **crime** is simply "an action that is prohibited by law." For instance, the definition of simple **assault** in one state is as follows:

1) Intentionally, knowingly, or recklessly causes bodily injury to another, including the person's spouse.
2) Intentionally or knowingly threatens another with imminent bodily injury, including the person's spouse.
3) Intentionally or knowingly causes physical contact with another when the person knows or should reasonably believe that the other will regard the contact as offensive or provocative.[1]

So, if you pushed or even hugged someone who you knew would consider it to be provocative or offensive, you have committed simple assault.

This is a Class A misdemeanor unless some other conditions are met; therefore, it is not a very "serious" crime. Most simple assaults are not brought to the attention of the criminal justice system. However, many other, more serious crimes are also never reported. This creates what is known as the **dark figure of crime**, which is crime that does not find its way into official numbers. Crimes such as domestic violence, acquaintance rape, and even theft, are more likely than other crimes to be part of this dark figure of crime.

Because the dark figure of crime is so high, it makes theorizing about who commits crime difficult. We do not know if the offenders who never come to the attention of authorities are similar to those who do. We do not know if these unknown offenders have similar motivations and patterns of criminal offending. Studies that are based only on known offenders may be faulty in that they are not able to present findings on all offenders—only those we know about. It is important to ask relevant questions about crime, e.g. has homicide increased or not; but, it is also important to note the weaknesses of our data sources when trying to understand crime patterns.

WHAT IS THE ROLE OF LEGISLATORS, VICTIMS, POLICE, AND PROSECUTORS IN DEFINING CRIME?

Crime is called a "constructed reality" because it is created by the definitions and perceptions of the legislators, perpetrators, observers, victims, and formal system actors (such as police and prosecutors). Take for instance, the following scenario: Person A shoves Person B. Is it a crime? It might be simple assault if Person A did it intentionally, believing it to be offensive to Person B. Is it prosecutable? It might be, only if Person B reports it to police or perhaps if a police officer happened to be close enough to see it and chose to arrest. Will it be prosecuted? A variety of factors affect the decision to prosecute, including the wishes of the victim, the resources of the prosecutor's office, the nature of the evidence and, some would say, perhaps the race and ethnicity of the offender and/or victim.

Exhibit 2.1   Crime: A "Constructed Reality."

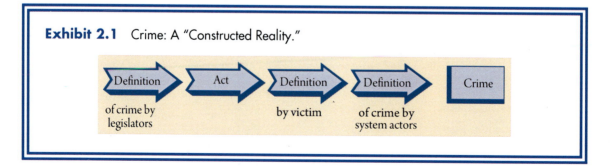

Before we can punish any act as a crime, a law has to be created by legislation. As we learned in the last chapter, most of our laws come from common law; however, state and federal legislators are constantly fine-tuning our criminal codes and adding new laws or changing existing laws. Recent changes in some states have legalized possession of small amounts of marijuana, and the carrying of guns on college campuses. Other changes in some states' laws have criminalized talking on your cellphone while driving, and posting nude pictures of someone on social media sites without their permission. As mentioned in the last chapter, states are free to create new crimes as long as they do not violate individuals' federal constitutional rights. It is not at all unusual to have one state legislature pass a new law that criminalizes behavior that is still legal in other states or vice versa.

Before a crime can be counted by officials, it must be reported by the victim. Why might someone *not* report a crime to authorities? The most common

Exhibit 2.2   According to statistics, in 2014, 431,000 people were injured and 3,179 were killed in car accidents involving distracted drivers, which has prompted many states to pass laws banning texting or cellphone use while driving.

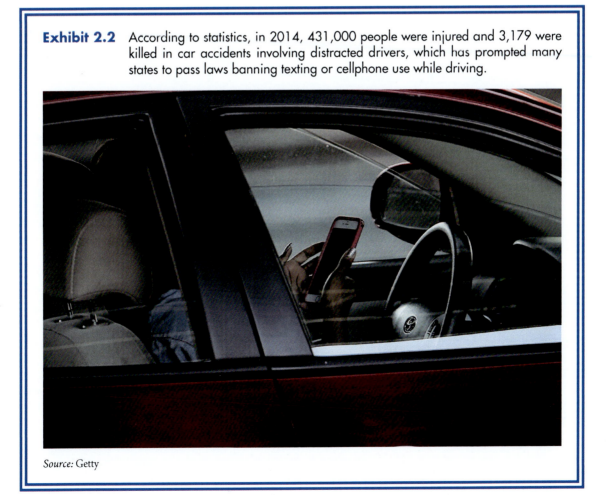

Source: Getty

reason is that they believe police can't do anything about it, but they might also interpret the event as a private matter and not a crime. Domestic violence victims sometimes do not want the involvement of the police, even though they are obviously victims of assault. Rape victims also may not report their own victimization, sometimes because they do not want formal intervention, but sometimes because they do not interpret the event as a crime. Studies have shown that female victims who are raped in "date-rape" scenarios by someone they know in circumstances where the lack of consent may be somewhat ambiguous sometimes do not define what occurred as a crime. If the victim does not perceive the event as a crime, or does not want formal system intervention, then the event is never reported to police and does not appear in our crime statistics.[2] In 2007, only 40 percent of all criminal victimizations were reported to police. Robberies with injury and auto theft were reported by 85 percent of victims, but only a quarter of some other types of crimes were reported to police.[3] In Exhibit 2.3, we display 2013 figures, but also show those for 2004. We see that the percentage of individuals who report their victimization to the police has decreased in many crime categories since 2004, but has increased in some crime categories.

To find the most current statistics regarding victim reporting, go to the website of the Bureau of Justice Statistics. The 2014 report can be found at: http://www.bjs.gov/content/pub/pdf/cv14.pdf.

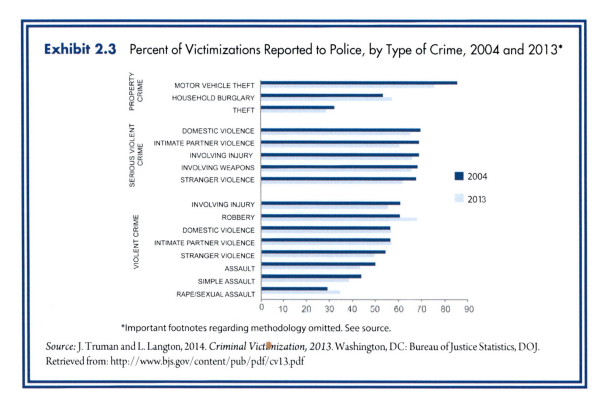

Exhibit 2.3   Percent of Victimizations Reported to Police, by Type of Crime, 2004 and 2013*

*Important footnotes regarding methodology omitted. See source.

Source: J. Truman and L. Langton, 2014. *Criminal Victimization, 2013.* Washington, DC: Bureau of Justice Statistics, DOJ. Retrieved from: http://www.bjs.gov/content/pub/pdf/cv13.pdf

Even if the victim calls police, there may not be an arrest. Police do not arrest in a large percentage of cases where an arrest is legally justified; perhaps in as many as half of all cases. Although arrests are usually made in serious felony cases, or in situations in which victims demand an arrest, even assaults may be dealt with informally rather than by initiating a formal report or arrest.[4] Obviously, arrest statistics represent only the cases in which police officers receive a report and decide to make an arrest. These numbers represent only a small portion of the total number of criminal incidents.

Before we can ask Chapter 3's question "Why do people commit crime?" we need to become familiar with the patterns and characteristics of crime. We use a number of sources that provide crime data. These are not perfect and each has inherent weaknesses, but they are the source of everything we think we know about crime in this country.

WHAT SOURCES DO WE USE TO FIND OUT ABOUT THE PATTERNS OF CRIME?

The two most common sources of crime data are the Uniform Crime Reports (which includes both reports to police and arrests) and the National Crime Victimization Survey. It is important to note that everything that we think we know about crime is derived primarily from these sources; thus, if there is some bias (inaccuracy) in the way these sources present the patterns of crime, then what we think we know is not necessarily accurate. It is important to know when you are looking at crime statistics whether the numbers reflect "reports to police," "arrests," or respondents reporting in a victimization survey. Each reflects slightly different realities of crime.

The Uniform Crime Reports

The most well-known and used source of crime statistics in this country is the **Uniform Crime Reports**. This collection of local crime reports and arrest data began in 1929 and is now produced by the Federal Bureau of Investigation. The numbers come either directly from local law enforcement agencies or from a state agency that collects the data from local agencies and delivers it in a centralized format. About 98 percent of law enforcement agencies submit crime data to the FBI.[5]

You can find the UCR at https://www.fbi.gov/about-us/cjis/ucr/ucr

The Uniform Crime Reports present crime reports in terms of **rates** as well as raw numbers. The rates you will see in the Uniform Crime Reports are the number of crimes divided by the population and then multiplied to display by a standard number. You can compute a rate (per 100,000) using the following mathematical formula. The rate tells you how many crimes took place for each 100,000 people.

$$\textbf{Rate} = (\textbf{Number of Crimes} \div \textbf{Population}) \times \textbf{100,000}$$

The advantage of a rate is that it allows us to compare patterns of crime in very different populations. For instance, with rates, we can compare the same city in two different periods, even if the city's population has dramatically changed. We can also compare two different cities, even if one is very large and the other very small. Knowing, for instance, the raw number of burglaries in New York City; Portland, Oregon; Austin, Texas; and Los Angeles, California, tells us something, but it doesn't tell us the relative risk of victimization in these cities because they do not have similar populations. The only way to compare the crime of two different populations is to compute the rate of each city, then compare the rates. In 2013, the *numbers* of reported burglaries and the *rates* for these cities looked like this:[6]

City	Population	Number of Burglaries	Rate
New York City	8,396,126	16,606	197
Portland	609,136	4,128	678
Austin	859,180	6,550	752
Los Angeles	3,878,725	15,728	405

Who would have thought that there were more burglaries per 100,000 people in Portland, Austin, and Los Angeles than in New York City? Compare other big cities which also show quite different rates for burglary.

City	Population	Number of Burglaries	Rate
Houston	2,180,606	23,733	1088
Chicago	2,720,554	17,775	653

The FBI cautions against anyone using these numbers to compare the crime risk between cities because there are so many variables that go into them, including police departments' recording practices, urban density, victim reporting practices, and so on. If city limits extend out into the suburbs, the crime rate will be lower because crime occurs less often in suburban than in urban areas. Any or all of these factors may help to explain why New York's burglary rates are so much lower than other cities. New York City also may have a low rate of burglaries because of a higher percentage of buildings with security, a lower percentage of occupied dwellings than other metropolitan areas, or a number of other factors that affects the number of burglaries in that geographic area. Even though we want to be cautious when comparing rates across cities, an examination of these rates do tell us that just because New Yorkers report over 16,000 burglaries and citizens of Austin report only about 6,500 does not mean necessarily that an individual has a greater risk of being burgled in New York City.

It is very important to have an accurate population base for rates to mean anything. If the population base is inaccurate, then so too will be the rate. If, for instance, the population base is out of date and the actual population has grown considerably, then the crimes (which inevitably would increase with a larger population) will be divided by an artificially small population indicating that the rate of crime in that locale (the amount of crime per person) is higher than what it actually is. In contrast, if the population used is inaccurate in the other direction and shows a much larger population than what actually exists (perhaps because people have been moving away from that area), and the crime rate is computed using this inaccurately high population, then the crime rate will appear to be lower than it actually is. Usually, the FBI uses the most recent census numbers for the area, but these numbers may be vulnerable to rapid fluctuations in population/migration.

Crime reports are gathered from law enforcement agencies via a standard reporting form so that, for instance, larceny means the same thing in all states whether or not state laws differ in defining the dollar amount that would change larceny from a misdemeanor to a felony. Because these are standard definitions, they may or may not conform to the state's definition for that particular crime.

The UCR provides the total number of reported crimes for the eight **index crimes**: murder and non-negligent manslaughter, forcible rape, robbery, aggravated assault, burglary, larceny-theft, motor vehicle theft, and arson. Violent crimes include the first four crimes and property crimes include the last four crimes. These index crimes are also presented as rates per 100,000. In Exhibit 2.4a and b, we see the UCR rates for violent and property crimes across several decades. Note that all crime categories show dramatic declines in the crimes reported to the police.

Exhibit 2.4a and 2.4b Uniform Crime Reports—Violent Crime and Property Crime, 1986–2014

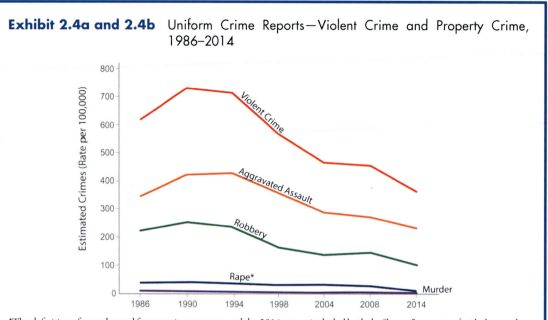

*The definition of rape changed for reporting purposes and the 2014 report included both the "legacy" rape rates (with the word forcible included) as shown here, but also a rate of 36.6 for the new definition: The revised UCR definition of rape is: "penetration, no matter how slight, of the vagina or anus with any body part or object, or oral penetration by a sex organ of another person, without the consent of the victim."

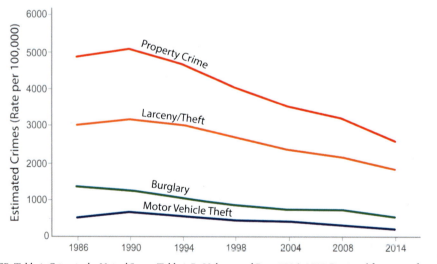

Source: UCR, Table 1, Crime in the United States, Table 1. By Volume and Rate, 1986–2005. Retrieved from www.fbi.gov/ucr/ 05cius/data/table/_.01/html. Crime in the United States, 2008, Table 1. By Volume and Rate, 1989–2008. Retrieved from www. fbi.gov/ucr/cius2008/data/table_01.html. Crime in the United States, 2014. Table 1. By Volume and Rate. Retrieved from https://www.fbi.gov/about-us/cjis/ucr/crime-in-the-u.s/2014/crime-in-the-u.s.-2014/tables/table-1.

One of the most oft-cited criticisms of the UCR is that it represents only reported crimes. If someone does not report a criminal victimization to the police, it does not get counted as a crime. Consequently, there is a "dark" figure of crime that never appears in the UCR. The amount of unreported crime varies by the type of crime. We saw in Exhibit 2.3 that less than half of violent crime victimizations and a little over a third of property crime victimizations are reported to police and, thus, are represented in the UCR. This presents a distinct problem if one uses the UCR as a measure of crime. In fact, it is not a measure of crime, but only a measure of *reported* crime. Another problem is that crimes such as identity theft, cybercrimes, and domestic violence are not easily identified in the traditional UCR because the reporting system is not set up to identify them.

One more potential problem is that some police departments have been exposed as "cooking" their numbers, meaning that they systematically downgrade citizens' reports of crimes in official reports. Scandals in New York City,[7] Chicago, and other cities[8] are troubling reminders that what we think we know about crime is dependent on accurate crime counts. When police departments categorize deaths as "undetermined" despite clear indications of homicide, they are not counted; when they record a robbery as theft instead of robbery, the true nature of the crime is hidden. These troubling incidents potentially make it unwise to utilize the UCR as the only source of understanding crime patterns—at least in specific cities.

The FBI also presents statistics on arrests. Arrest data is presented for 21 crime categories. In addition to the eight index crimes, arrests are also reported for other assaults, forgery, fraud, prostitution, and even curfew violations. The numbers of arrests are by no means a measure of crime, because they capture only the crimes in which a suspect was identified and a decision to arrest was made. Arrest data are presented for 21 crime categories in Exhibit 2.5, arranged in order of frequency. The graph shows that arrests for most crimes decreased. For some crimes, such as prostitution, changes over time are likely due to changes in decisions to arrest; for other crimes, such as homicide, arrest decisions are less likely to change because of discretionary enforcement. We must always remember that fluctuations in arrest rates may be real differences in such behavior, differences in perception and/or enforcement of the behavior, or differences in counting crimes. In this graph, the last several crimes are displayed separately since they show up as almost non-existent when in the same display as more frequent crimes.

Many crimes go unsolved or are not cleared. Crimes are considered cleared when an arrest is made for an offense. The FBI reports on the number of crimes cleared by arrest with a statistic called the **clearance rate**. The clearance rates

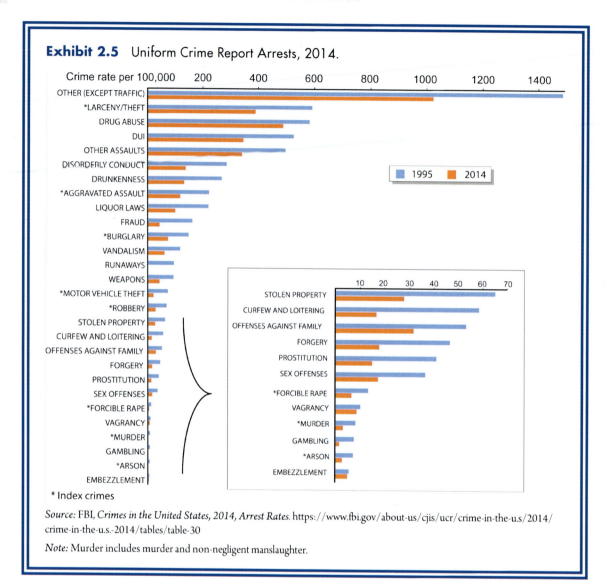

Exhibit 2.5 Uniform Crime Report Arrests, 2014.

*Index crimes

Source: FBI, *Crimes in the United States, 2014, Arrest Rates.* https://www.fbi.gov/about-us/cjis/ucr/crime-in-the-u.s/2014/crime-in-the-u.s.-2014/tables/table-30

Note: Murder includes murder and non-negligent manslaughter.

vary greatly by crime. In 2004, murder and non-negligent homicide had the highest clearance rate (62.6 percent), while burglary had the lowest clearance rate (12.9 percent).[9] In 2009, the clearance rate for murder and non-negligent homicide increased to 66.6 percent, while motor vehicle theft and burglary declined to 12.4 percent and 12.5 percent, respectively.[10] In 2014, the clearance rate for murder and non-negligent manslaughter slipped to 64.5 percent. The clearance rate for motor vehicle theft and burglary was 12.8 percent and 13.6 percent, respectively.[11]

To see clearance rates, go to http://www.fbi.gov/ucr/cius_04/offenses_cleared/index.html

The FBI has also been collecting crime statistics in a different format to address other recognized problems. The National Incident-Based Reporting System (**NIBRS**) gathers much more detailed information about each criminal incident. While the UCR reporting format is hierarchical, meaning that only the most serious crime is counted, NIBRS requires information to be submitted on each crime within a criminal transaction. Instead of reporting crimes via the eight index offenses, NIBRS will display information on Group A offense categories (22 different crimes) and Group B offenses (11 different crimes). More information is obtained about each offense, including information about the victim and offender. For 22 offense categories, the following information is being collected and will be reported in NIBRS reports, also available on the FBI website:

- Victim, offender, and arrestee data
- Location and time of day of incidents
- Weapon data for select offenses
- Drug, alcohol, and gang involvement in offenses
- Attempted versus completed offenses
- Clearances by incidents
- Relationship of victims to offenders.

NIBRS reports are not comparable to the UCR because the way crimes are counted is different. For instance, a robbery, rape, and murder would only be reported as a murder in the UCR, but as three separate crimes under NIBRS. Law enforcement agencies have been slow to adopt the NIBRS reporting procedures, probably because it is much more detailed, requiring more effort to enter the data. There is also the concern that NIBRS will make it appear that there is an increase in crime because it would report each separate criminal incident instead of the hierarchical reporting system of the UCR. In 2012, about 30 percent of the nation's population was represented by crime statistics reported under NIBRS.[12] Currently only fifteen U.S. states have complete NIBRS agency participation, with an additional 18 states that submit both summary UCR and NIBRS data.[13]

Victimization Studies

Another source of crime statistics comes from victimization surveys. The Bureau of Justice Statistics presents findings from the **National Crime Victimization Survey** (NCVS). Begun in 1973 as the National Crime Survey, the U.S. Bureau of the Census has been interviewing household members in a nationally representative sample. In 1992–93, the survey was redesigned and relabeled as the National Crime Victimization Survey. The redesign effort was intended to obtain more information and include less serious crimes. The items in the survey capture more information than what is available through the UCR. For instance, one question asks the respondent whether the crime was reported to the police. This is the source for our information in Exhibit 2.2, about how much crime goes unreported. Findings from the National Crime Victimization Survey can be accessed most easily through the Bureau of Justice Statistics, an agency that also presents other statistics about corrections, police, and specific crimes.

For more information, go to http://bjs.gov/

These two sources of crime data may be compared, but it is important to note their differences. The NCVS excludes homicide, arson, commercial crimes, and crimes against children under age twelve (the UCR includes these crimes). The NCVS also does not include any information on victimless crimes such as drug crimes, gambling, or prostitution. The UCR only collects arrest data on simple assault and sexual assaults other than rape, not reported crimes. Further, the NCVS calculates rates on the basis of 1000 *households,* while the UCR calculates rates based on 100,000 *persons.* Thus, it would be a mistake to treat findings from the two sources as comparable statistically. In general, the UCR gives us a broad picture of crime patterns (as reported to police) in the United States, while the NCVS gives us more information about the characteristics of victimizations in certain selected crime categories and reporting trends by victims.

Because the NCVS is based on a random sample of the population and does not collect reports of all victimizations, it is subject to all the potential problems of sampling and survey weaknesses. If any principles of **random sampling** are violated, then the applicability to the general population is in doubt. The sample size of the NCVS has been decreasing over the years, and some observers have begun to worry that the smaller sample size has begun to affect the representativeness of the sample.[14]

The advantage of having both the UCR (reports to police) and the NCVS (survey respondents' reports of victimization) is that, even if not completely comparable, we can note whether the general crime patterns are similar, thus being more confident in the accuracy of either source. Recall that the UCR shows a dramatic decline in crime reports across the last several decades. We can be more confident that the UCR is accurately representing a crime decline because the NCVS also shows dramatic declines in the number of people reporting victimization (whether or not they reported the victimization to the police). We will explore these patterns more closely when we answer the question about crime patterns below.

Self-Report Studies

Another source of crime data is simply to ask the offender. Self-report studies ask individuals to report the crimes they have committed. Obviously, there are problems inherent in such an approach, such as whether the individual is answering honestly or not. Self-reports are generally only obtained from targeted groups, specifically juveniles (who are still in school) and offenders (who are incarcerated). We do not administer self-report surveys door-to-door to samples of citizens. Self-report studies provide interesting information, but the findings must be considered in light of the characteristics of the sample. For instance, self-report studies of juveniles often use measures of behavior that stretch the definition of "crime" to the breaking point by including minor deviances, such as truancy and other forms of juvenile misbehavior. The definitions of wrongdoing are expanded in such studies because the vast majority of students have not committed any criminal acts. Therefore, in order to get sufficient numbers for statistical analysis, the definition of "offender" is expanded. It should be kept in mind when reading these studies that these "offenders" are not necessarily who we think of as criminals.

Part of the reason that student self-report studies have difficulty obtaining sufficient numbers of offenders for statistical analysis when testing crime theories is that by the time they are administered in junior or senior years, many high-risk juveniles have already dropped out or are not in school the day the study is administered. Therefore, the young people most likely to have committed crimes are likely to be absent from the study, and the reports of criminal activity are likely to under-represent the true nature of juvenile crime.

Like school samples, prisoner samples are relatively easy to obtain, but non-representative. Prisoners do not represent all offenders (only those who are caught and sentenced to prison). They also may not admit or may exaggerate their criminal activities. In addition, these surveys are subject to the potential inaccuracies of all surveys in that respondents may forget or misremember when events occurred. Self-report studies are typically used to understand behavior differences between offenders; for instance, the finding that a small percentage of offenders are responsible for a disproportional number of crimes came from offender self-report studies.

Cohort Studies

One other source of crime data is the **cohort study**, which follows a group of subjects over a long period. For instance, one cohort study followed all males born in Philadelphia in 1948.[15] Another longitudinal study conducted by the Harvard Program on Human Development and Criminal Behavior collected data on a cohort sample.[16] Typically, the follow-up period extends throughout childhood and into adulthood. A large number of factors have been identified as influencing criminality, including family factors, genetic factors, school and neighborhood factors, and peer factors. Proponents of longitudinal research argue that this method of data collection can illuminate how causal factors work at various times in one's life.

WHAT CRIMES ARE PEOPLE MOST FREQUENTLY ARRESTED FOR?

When people think of crime, they probably think of robbery, murder, or violent assault. These crimes fill our newspapers and prime-time television, either as drama or reality television. It is important to note, however, that the most common crimes are fairly mundane. Looking again at Exhibit 2.5, we see that, in reality, the picture of crime is much different than what is reflected in the popular media. Murder, rape, and even robbery arrests are extremely rare. In contrast, the most common arrests are for a wide variety of minor misbehavior ("other"), drug violations (possession and distribution combined), and theft.

Since one of the most frequent types of arrest is for a drug offense, this category bears further scrutiny. In Exhibit 2.6, we see that over 80 percent of all drug arrests are for possession, and the most common drug for those arrests is marijuana. In fact, about 40 percent of all drug violation arrests are for marijuana possession.[17]

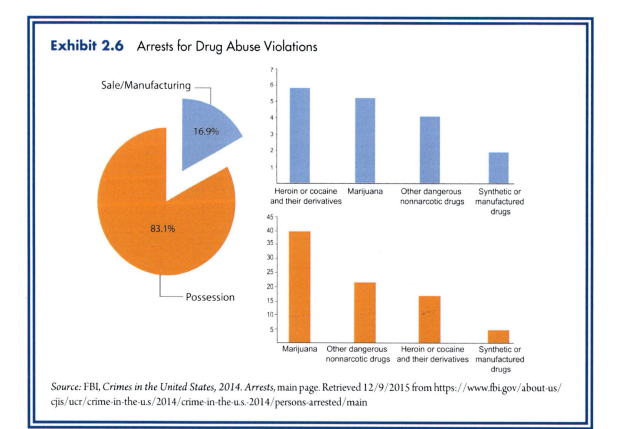

Exhibit 2.6   Arrests for Drug Abuse Violations

Sale/Manufacturing — 16.9%

83.1%

Possession

Source: FBI, *Crimes in the United States, 2014. Arrests,* main page. Retrieved 12/9/2015 from https://www.fbi.gov/about-us/cjis/ucr/crime-in-the-u.s/2014/crime-in-the-u.s.-2014/persons-arrested/main

As we noted before, it is important to remember that arrests are not a true reflection of crimes committed; they only represent who is arrested. Reports to police would provide more information about frequency of crimes, but the UCR only offers information on the eight index crimes. Exhibit 2.7 below presents these reports for 2014. We see that the most frequent crime reports are of larceny/theft, and following far behind are reports of burglaries. Recall, however, that most people report only a fraction of all crimes to police, thus, this picture of crime is also an inaccurate representation of crime.

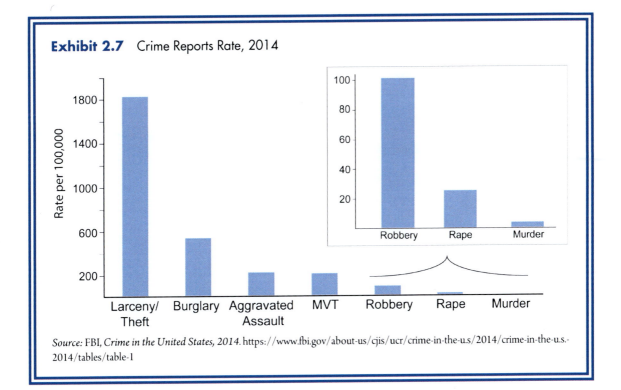

Exhibit 2.7   Crime Reports Rate, 2014

Source: FBI, *Crime in the United States, 2014.* https://www.fbi.gov/about-us/cjis/ucr/crime-in-the-u.s/2014/crime-in-the-u.s.-2014/tables/table-1

Victimization surveys are closer to approximating the true prevalence of crime, but they are not comparable to the crime categories of the UCR or arrest tables. Recall that the most frequent arrests are for drug violations, but that crime category is not represented at all in the victimization reports. In the latest NCVS report, the most frequently reported victimization was theft (at 6.41 reports per 1,000), followed by burglary (at 1.67 reports per 1,000). Thus, these two crimes appear as the most frequent crimes in both reports to the police (UCR) and reports in the NCVS. In contrast, the least frequently reported victimization was serious intimate partner violence (at 0.05 reports per 1,000), which does not have a crime category parallel in the UCR, and rape/sexual assault (at 0.06 reports per 1,000).[18]

To summarize, our crime sources give us fragmented information about the true prevalence of crime. The most frequent arrests in 2014 were for drug offenses, and the most frequent victim-harming crimes seem to be larceny/theft and burglary, as reported to police and in victimization reports. The constant media focus on violent crimes is highly disproportionate to the true prevalence of crime categories.

WHAT DO WE KNOW ABOUT HOMICIDE?

Even though homicide is a very rare occurrence, people are quite rightly more fearful of homicide, rape, aggravated assault, and robbery than property crimes. The rate of homicide has been declining for decades—the murder rate fell by more than half nationally from its peak in 1980, as seen in Exhibit 2.8. It is also true, however, that some cities have experienced increases in some years.

Exhibit 2.8   Homicide Rates Over Time

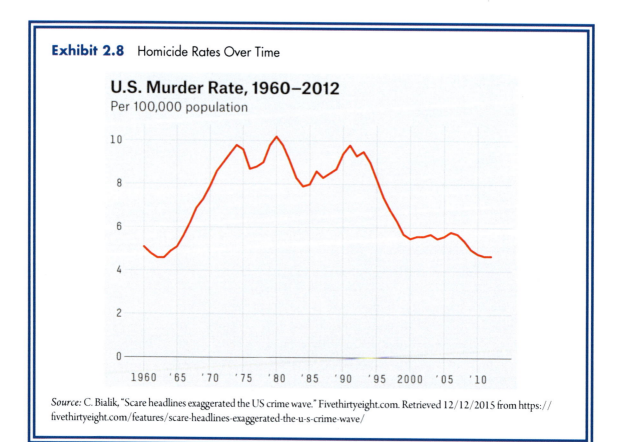

U.S. Murder Rate, 1960–2012
Per 100,000 population

Source: C. Bialik, "Scare headlines exaggerated the US crime wave." Fivethirtyeight.com. Retrieved 12/12/2015 from https://fivethirtyeight.com/features/scare-headlines-exaggerated-the-u-s-crime-wave/

We can obtain more detailed information about homicides from the supplemental homicide reports of the FBI. Exhibit 2.9 shows that the most recent report indicates that homicides are most likely to be single victim and single offender.

You can explore the statistics on homicide by going to a data analysis tool offered by the Office of Juvenile Justice and Delinquency: http://www.ojjdp.gov/ojstatbb/ezashr/asp/off_selection.asp

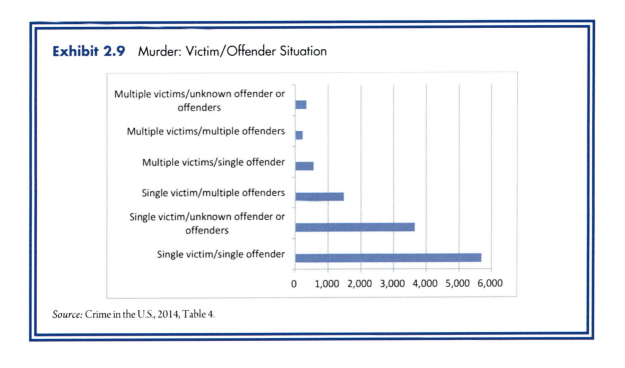

Exhibit 2.9 Murder: Victim/Offender Situation

Source: Crime in the U.S., 2014, Table 4.

Exhibit 2.10 displays information from the FBI's supplemental information on homicides. We see that, in 2012, information was known about the relationship between victim and offender in only slightly more than half of all cases. Of those cases, the most common relationship between victim and offender was acquaintance. The family members most likely to be killed by another family member were wives. Only 12 percent of the victims where the relationship between victim and offender was known were killed by strangers. However, because that information seems to be missing from almost half of all homicides, we must be cautious about assuming anything about the relationship between victim and offender from those cases where we do have the information.

Using 2013 data, it is clear that homicide offenders *and* victims are likely to be male and disproportionately African American (Exhibit 2.11).

Exhibit 2.10   Relationship between Homicide Victims and Offenders

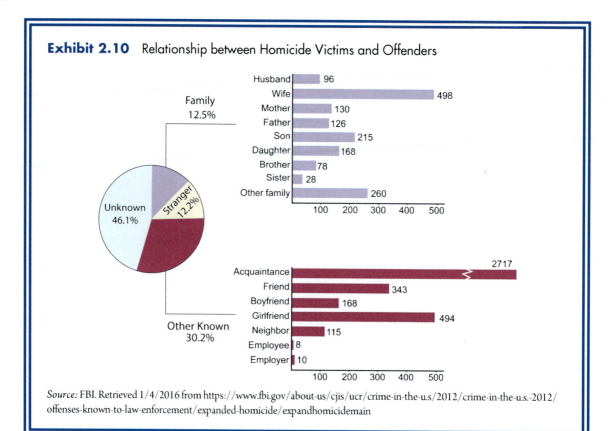

Source: FBI. Retrieved 1/4/2016 from https://www.fbi.gov/about-us/cjis/ucr/crime-in-the-u.s/2012/crime-in-the-u.s.-2012/offenses-known-to-law-enforcement/expanded-homicide/expandhomicidemain

Exhibit 2.11   Homicide Offenders/Victims

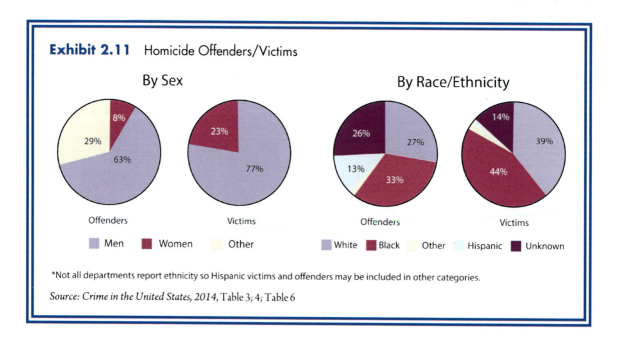

*Not all departments report ethnicity so Hispanic victims and offenders may be included in other categories.

Source: *Crime in the United States, 2014*, Table 3; 4; Table 6

It is important to note that these percentages are of total homicide numbers. Rates (per 100,000) would look much different since African Americans comprise only about 13 percent of the total population; thus, the fact that 44 percent of all murder victims are African American is a truly astounding figure. Data analysis from the time period of the most dramatic decline in homicide illustrated the fact that between the mid-1990s and late 2000s, the most dramatic declines in homicide also took place with African American men (see Exhibit 2.12).[19]

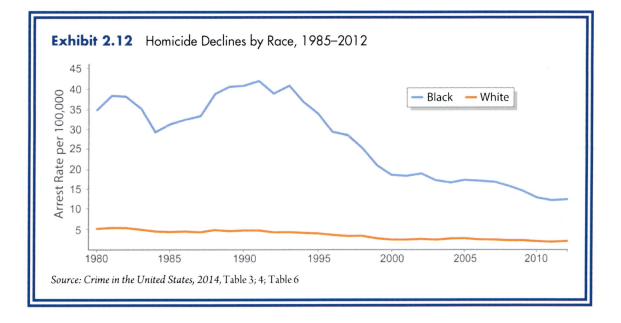

Exhibit 2.12   Homicide Declines by Race, 1985–2012

Source: Crime in the United States, 2014, Table 3; 4; Table 6

It is important to note that when there are changes in the number of homicides, not all racial/ethnic and gender groups are equally at risk. Homicides have increased in some urban areas, but, similar to past patterns, not everyone is equally vulnerable.

WHAT HAS BEEN THE PATTERN OF CRIME OVER THE YEARS? HAS IT DECLINED?

Recall from the above discussion that the UCR has recorded dramatic declines in all crime categories in the last twenty years. This could be due to a true decrease in criminal activity, or it could be due to less people reporting their victimization. The way to know for sure is to compare victimization reports to crime reports. As we discussed in the last chapter, triangulating data utilizes different sources to compare facts. We can be more confident that we have truly experienced a decline in crime because the UCR, the National Crime Victimization Survey, and arrest tables all show a steady overall decline since the early 1990s. Exhibit 2.13 illustrates this consensus. Although there was a bit of an increase in 2012, the decline continued afterwards.

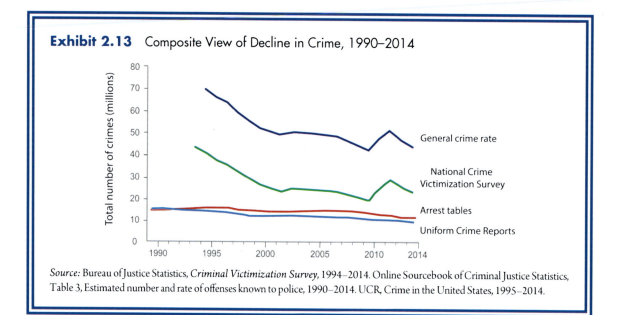

Exhibit 2.13   Composite View of Decline in Crime, 1990–2014

Source: Bureau of Justice Statistics, *Criminal Victimization Survey,* 1994–2014. Online Sourcebook of Criminal Justice Statistics, Table 3, Estimated number and rate of offenses known to police, 1990–2014. UCR, Crime in the United States, 1995–2014.

DOES THE PUBLIC HAVE AN ACCURATE PERCEPTION ABOUT THE PREVALENCE OF CRIME?

There is no doubt that our crime rates are about as low as they have been since the 1970s, but does the public know that? The short answer is no. A Gallup poll indicates that about 70 percent of Americans think there is more crime in the U.S. now than there was a year ago. In fact, in most years, the majority of Americans think crime was higher than the year before, but they have been wrong. The only year the minority of citizens (41 percent) thought crime had declined was in 2001.

It is also interesting to note that women are more likely to think crime has risen. Conservatives (80 percent) are more likely than liberals (57 percent), and those in rural towns are more likely than urban residents to think crime has risen. Exhibit 2.14 shows these differences. In 2015, nearly six in ten Americans (59 percent) said U.S. crime is an "extremely" or "very" serious problem—up slightly from 55 percent in 2014.[20]

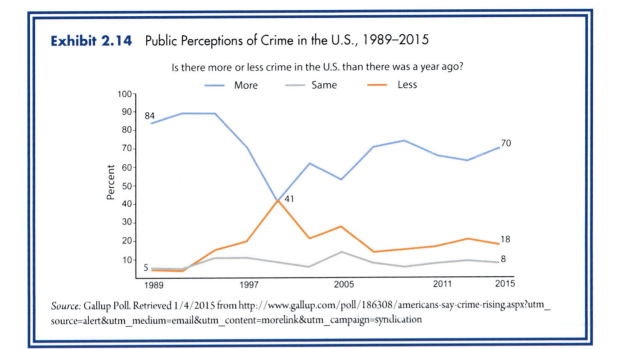

Exhibit 2.14 Public Perceptions of Crime in the U.S., 1989–2015

Is there more or less crime in the U.S. than there was a year ago?

—— More   —— Same   —— Less

Source: Gallup Poll. Retrieved 1/4/2015 from http://www.gallup.com/poll/186308/americans-say-crime-rising.aspx?utm_source=alert&utm_medium=email&utm_content=morelink&utm_campaign=syndication

HOW DO THE CRIME RATES OF THE UNITED STATES COMPARE TO OTHER COUNTRIES?

There is a widespread perception that one of the reasons the United States leads the world in incarceration rates is because there is more crime here than in similar Western countries such as the United Kingdom, France, or Canada. This is true only for homicide. Property crime rates in the United States are roughly comparable to those of other countries. It should be pointed out that comparing crimes cross-culturally is difficult because definitions and reporting practices that affect crime statistics vary. The United Nations Office of Drugs and Crime, however, has collected and makes available crime rates as reported by member nations in order to make some tentative comparisons. In the latest report available, about 138 countries are represented. In Exhibit 2.15 below, certain selected countries and crimes are displayed.

Homicide is perhaps the most consistently reported crime and offers the most reliable comparison. The homicide rate per 100,000 of the United States is about 3.8. That is down from previous years, but still higher than many European countries, Canada, and Australia. On the other hand, the rate of homicide in the U.S. is much lower than Mexico's or other countries in South America and Africa. Mexico's robbery rate is extremely high compared

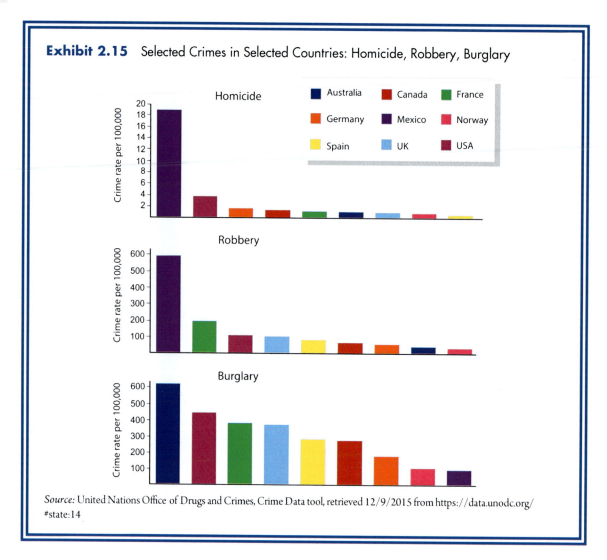

Exhibit 2.15 Selected Crimes in Selected Countries: Homicide, Robbery, Burglary

Source: United Nations Office of Drugs and Crimes, Crime Data tool, retrieved 12/9/2015 from https://data.unodc.org/#state:14

to other countries. France has a higher robbery rate than the U.S. and Australia has a higher burglary rate. While we must be careful with these statistics because it is unknown how accurate or consistent reporting is across all the countries, it does indicate that the crime rate in the U.S. is not wildly disproportionate to other Western, industrialized countries, except for the homicide rate.

To explore for yourself some of these statistics, go to https://data.unodc.org/#state:14

Before we leave this chapter on crime statistics, we will offer a discussion that illustrates how important accurate data and reasonable data interpretation can be when discussing current events. A current controversy playing out in newspapers and other public arenas today is whether there has been a "**Ferguson Effect**" on American policing that has resulted in "**de-policing**" which, in turn, has led to a spike in homicides and violent crimes in major cities. The Focus on Data section below examines this question.

FOCUS ON DATA: IS THERE A FERGUSON EFFECT? IS THERE A CURRENT CRIME WAVE?

In the summer and fall of 2014, the shooting of young Black men by police officers led to a number of violent protests in several American cities, most notably in Ferguson, Missouri and Baltimore, Maryland. Some argued that the public scrutiny and criticism of police led to a change in police behavior, dubbed the "Ferguson Effect," which referred to police officers choosing not to engage with citizens for fear of being labeled racist or violent. This "de-policing," as it was also called, then, arguably, led to a spike in homicide.

Exhibit 2.16 Demonstrators marking the one-year anniversary of the shooting of Michael Brown confront police during a protest in Ferguson, Missouri. Some have argued that criticism of police, both in the media and through protests, has led to the "Ferguson Effect."

Source: Getty

Beginning in 2015, major news outlets began reporting on big-city crime spikes. Eventually the *Washington Post, New York Times*, NPR, CNN, BBC, *USA Today*, Reuters, *Time*, and other major news outlets had "crime spike" stories. In August of 2015, the Major Cities Chiefs Association (MCCA) reported increased homicides as a problem. In contrast, others (*New York Daily News*, Brennan Center, Marshall Project) argued that there was no evidence yet to indicate alarm was warranted. Let's look at the facts.

Heather MacDonald's much publicized article in the *Wall Street Journal* reported that gun violence was up 60 percent in Baltimore with May 2015 as the most violent month the city had seen in fifteen years. A list of cities with percentage increases were offered, including Milwaukee (180 percent by May 17 over the same period the previous year), St. Louis (25 percent), Atlanta (32 percent), Chicago (17 percent), and New York (13 percent). Then she argued that city-wide statistics masked much larger neighborhood increases such as 500 percent in one East Harlem neighborhood. Because the first six months of 2014 continued a twenty-year pattern of decline, her argument was that the increases in the first six months of 2015 were due to a surge of lawlessness because of people's agitation against police departments and media focus on the events. MacDonald noted the "Ferguson Effect" (a term evidently coined by St. Louis police chief Sam Dotson) was the phenomenon of police officers disengaging from discretionary enforcement activity, with a resulting feeling of empowerment by criminals. She pointed to the fact that arrests in St. Louis city and county had dropped a third since the shooting of Michael Brown in August, while homicides surged 47 percent and robberies were up 82 percent through November 2014. Other cities also showed a decline in arrests; for instance, she reported that Baltimore had 56 percent fewer arrests by May 2015 compared to 2014. In New York City, stop-and-frisk policies led to a lawsuit and intense media scrutiny; consequently, stops dropped 95 percent from the 2011 high according to MacDonald. She further argued that aggressive policing has led to urban reclamation and saved thousands of Black lives and warned that continued criticism of police would lead to losing the gains in crime reduction that had been achieved in the last twenty years.[21] There are four arguments to this position:

1) Homicides and other crimes in American cities are increasing.
2) Police officers are not policing in the way they have in previous years, meaning they are less likely to engage in "pro-active" policing such as stop-and-frisks and arrests for minor crimes due to the public and media scrutiny and criticism that has arisen since the summer of 2014.
3) The reduction in pro-active policing, if it exists, caused the increase in homicides and other crime, if the increase exists.

1) Are Homicides and Other Crimes in American Cities Increasing?

Unfortunately, the UCR and the FBIs Supplemental Homicide Report are not as current as we would need to answer this question. It usually takes six months to a year before crime reports are available for public consumption. The latest FBI data (UCR) for 2014 indicate that there was a 2 percent decrease in homicide rates per 100,000 nationwide, however, the pattern was different between cities and suburban and rural areas. In the largest cities (over 1 million), there was a 2.2 percent *increase* in homicides per 100,000, but a 16 percent *decrease* in non-metropolitan counties. Thus, contrary to MacDonald's proposition that the first months of 2015 were an aberration due to changing circumstances after the Michael Brown shooting, homicides had already begun to increase in cities (as opposed to suburban and rural areas) in 2014.

Recent analyses of 2015 homicides for the largest American cities showed that there was probably about a 17 percent increase in homicides in the first six months of 2015 compared to the first six months of 2014—a dramatic increase, but this increase seems to be confined to only some cities.[22] In fact, the pattern is highly skewed: ten cities account for two-thirds of the increase. These cities are characterized by: higher poverty, a falling population, and high unemployment.[23] The National Institute of Justice published an analysis of the increase (using data collected by the *New York Times* and *Washington Post*) and showed that from 2014 to 2015, 127 more people were killed in Baltimore (a 59 percent increase); 61 more people were killed in Milwaukee from the year before (a 73 percent increase); 57 more people killed in Cleveland (a 91 percent increase) and 34 more people killed in Nashville (an 83 percent increase).[24]

Note that, even with over 200 murders in 2015, that number is dramatically lower than the high in 1993 when New York City recorded 1,946 murders.[25] UCR trend data shows that homicide and violent crime has been declining for the last twenty years.

News headlines that refer to large percentage increases in murder rates in specific cities usually neglect to mention that large percentage increases happen more easily with small base numbers. A 50 percent increase in murders sounds ominous, but a 50 percent increase of twelve is six additional homicides. Homicide numbers, because they have been quite small in the last decade, can be influenced by such things as an intra-familial multiple murder, or police recording practices, such as reclassifying cases from undetermined to homicide, or other reporting changes. In fact, several journalists, in articles analyzing crime increases in certain cities such as Chicago, New York, and Los Angeles, have suggested that at least part of the increase might be due to changes in reporting practices after major scandals that exposed police departments as not recording crime reports accurately. For instance, Domanick reported that violent

Exhibit 2.17   Rising Murder Rates in Big Cities, 2014–2015

City	Absolute Increase	% Increase	Cumulative % of Total Increase
Baltimore	127	58.5	15.5
Chicago	61	15.0	22.9
Houston	61	25.2	30.3
Milwaukee	61	72.6	37.8
Cleveland	57	90.5	44.7
Washington DC	57	54.3	51.6
Nashville	34	82.9	55.8
Philadelphia	32	12.9	59.7
Kansas City	29	37.2	63.2
St. Louis	29	18.2	66.7

Source: City police departments, reported in M. Davey and M. Smith. "Murder Rates Rising Sharply in Many Cities." *New York Times* (September 1, 2015), p. A1.

crime in Los Angeles rose more than 20 percent during the first half of 2015, with felony assaults up 26 percent and robberies up 19 percent and suggested that the increase might be due, in part, to a *Los Angeles Times* investigation of the department's crime numbers for the first half of 2014, which discovered the misclassification of 1,200 violent felony assaults as misdemeanors, thus making it appear that serious violent crime was going down when, in fact, it went up by 14 percent.[26] A similar article describing Chicago's crime reporting described how, by categorizing a death as "undetermined," despite clear indices of murder, the number of homicides were artificially reduced.[27] While some amount of misrepresenting the seriousness of crimes probably would not significantly influence percentage increase numbers of burglary because the base numbers are so large, such practices could definitely result in significant increases or decreases in crime categories that involve smaller numbers such as homicide and robbery.

While the MacDonald article presented data from cities that had increased homicides, others have noted that the pattern is not uniform across American cities. An analysis by FiveThirtyEight.com utilized city data, news reports, and other sources to construct a table with 60 cities and homicide numbers for 2015 compared to the same time period in 2014.[28] In 26 cities, homicides were up by 20 percent or more from a year ago, but the number of homicides was down in nineteen other cities.

More generally, crime analysts will warn against year to year comparisons of homicide, or any crime, because year-to-year rates fluctuate. The better way to understand data is by looking at longer periods of time. When we examine murder trends we see that, although there may be year-to-year increases, the general trend has been downward, in this set of tables from a report produced by the Brennan Center.[29]

Exhibit 2.18   Homicide Patterns in Selected Cities: Los Angeles, New York, Chicago

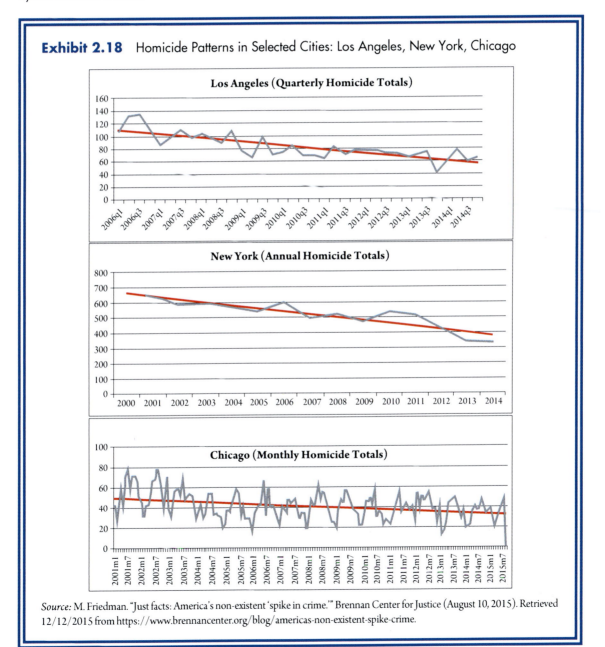

Source: M. Friedman. "Just facts: America's non-existent 'spike in crime.'" Brennan Center for Justice (August 10, 2015). Retrieved 12/12/2015 from https://www.brennancenter.org/blog/americas-non-existent-spike-crime.

Moving from homicide to all violent crime, the UCR reported that nationwide violent crime reports to police were down by 0.2 percent and property crime declined by 4.3 percent in 2014.[30] The latest National Crime Victimization Survey, released in August 2015, reported no significant change in violent crime victimization, and property crime victimization fell from 131.4 per 1,000 to 118.1 per 1,000 in 2014.[31]

In summary, many American cities, but not all, have seen recent increases in homicides. Further, it may be that the increases are occurring in large cities, not in smaller towns and suburban areas. The FBI had reported a small increase in large metropolitan areas in 2014 so this increase began at least as early as 2014. Further, analysts point to trend data to show that year-to-year fluctuations have occurred continuously even throughout the twenty-year decline in homicide and other violent crimes.

2) Are Police Officers Not Policing in the Way They Have in Previous Years? If So, Is This Due to the Public and Media Scrutiny and Criticism That Have Arisen Since the Summer of 2014?

MacDonald reported fairly dramatic declines in arrests in some cities, arguing this was evidence of "de-policing." Interestingly, fewer arrests can be presented as a decline in crime or a decline in policing, depending on one's perspective. While MacDonald reported dramatic declines, criminologists have pointed to other cities that have not shown declines in arrests.[32] Misdemeanor arrests, traffic tickets, and investigative stops are subject to more discretionary decision making by officers than felony arrests, therefore, all three should be considered to determine if "de-policing" is occurring.

New York City has definitely seen a dramatic drop in the number of stop-and-frisks undertaken by New York City police officers, but the decline had begun earlier than the summer and fall of 2014 when the protests in Ferguson, Missouri and Baltimore, Maryland occurred. A report by the John Jay College of Criminal Justice indicated that between 2011 and 2014 the total number of arrests for felonies and misdemeanors, criminal summonses, and stop-and-frisks fell by more than 800,000, or 31 percent. Street stops declined from a high of 685,000 in 2011 to under 46,000 in 2014, a 93 percent decline in only three years. The declines were mostly in poorer and minority neighborhoods where they had grown the fastest over the previous decade. The decline in stops occurred because of a court ruling in 2013 that found such stops unconstitutional as well as a growing public outcry that the stops were unfairly targeting minority and poor residents who had the misfortune to live in certain areas of the city. Despite the multi-year decline in such stops, crime reports continued to decline as well. In 2014, rates of both violent and nonviolent crime in New

Exhibit 2.19   Stop-and-Frisk. The NYPD was sued over its controversial stop-and-frisks, which have since declined substantially.

Source: Getty

York City were lower than the year before, and were almost 90 percent lower than they were in 1980.[33]

Another city that saw arrests and investigative stops decline was Seattle. In May of 2014 it was reported that police enforcement of lower-level crimes, traffic offenses and infractions dropped dramatically, including a 49 percent decline in misdemeanor criminal arrests between 2005 and 2013. While service calls had increased by 9 percent between the first quarter of 2010 and first quarter of 2014, independent officer-initiated activity had dropped by 44 percent, from 15 percent of their time in 2011 to only 8 percent of their time in the same quarter in 2014. Officer checks of suspicious people and suspicious vehicles dropped by 80 percent. Bookings into the jail fell by 51 percent between 2006 and 2013. Between 2007 and 2013, infractions filed in Seattle Municipal Court fell 71 percent, covering unlawful activity such as liquor violations, public urination, and noise problems. Because the Seattle Police Department was investigated by the Department of Justice and entered into a consent decree that required substantial changes in policies and practices to address alleged racism and use of force abuses, the dramatic decline was attributed to "de-policing."[34] Others pointed to alternative explanations such as programs of diversion. Recall, also, that Washington legalized small amounts of marijuana effective December 2012, which must have had a significant effect on the number of police investigative stops and misdemeanor arrests. More importantly, however, there has not yet been a connection shown between decreased police actions and UCR index crimes or victimization reports. Unfortunately, the time lag that occurs in our ability to access this information will prevent any immediate analysis.

We can count arrests, stops, and traffic tickets, and we can document whether or not totals are higher, lower, or the same as the year before, but we can't say for certain why such police actions have declined because we have no way of knowing whether or not the number of underlying acts have changed, other factors have affected the decision (e.g. charging practices of the prosecutor's office or changes in the law), or the officers have changed their policing practices (e.g. less likely to arrest or stop-and-frisk). As noted above, court orders requiring the NYPD to change their stop-and-frisk practices and Washington's legalization of marijuana possession have probably more to do with the observed changes than police officers changing their decision-making practices on patrol in these cities than "de-policing."

Anecdotal evidence has been offered (e.g., quotes from individual officers or police administrators) that police officers felt scrutinized and unfairly criticized after the public protests in 2014 and 2015 and reacted by "de-policing." One small study that surveyed officers in a small police department found that officers reported a decline in motivation to do their job and work with the community because of public criticism, but that they did not change their decisions. Further the decline in motivation evidently was also influenced by administrative and managerial practices of the police department, not simply the "Ferguson Effect."[35]

3) Is the Reduction in Pro-Active Policing (If It Exists), the Cause of the Increase in Homicides and Other Crime (If There Is Significant Increase)?

Proposed explanations for the increase in violent crime, including homicides, in some cities have included (in addition to the Ferguson Effect) a rise in heroin use; increased gang violence; entrenched poverty and hopelessness; release of career criminals from prison (who have served their 25–30-year sentences from the high-crime years of the 1980s); more guns, especially automatic weapons like the AK-47; and, as noted before, simply yearly fluctuations in a two-decade decline. What we do know about these homicides is that they are often gang-related and occur most often in poverty-stricken areas of the city. The only academic study thus far that has addressed this question specifically looked at violent crimes in 81 cities in the year before and the year after the Michael Brown shooting in Ferguson and concluded that the only crime that showed a significant change in direction (from decease to increase) in the second time period was robbery. The study's authors cautioned that even documenting the increase could not "prove" that the increase was due to de-policing because there might be many other factors that affect the increase in robbery.[36] Also, as noted earlier, there have been previous upticks in homicide and violent crime in some cities periodically in the last several decades, even within a general trend of decreasing homicide rates over those years.

A recent study paper from the National Institute of Justice also offered the hypotheses of the growth of heroin markets, an increase in the number of parolees in the community, and a loss of "legitimacy" in Black communities as explanations for the increase in homicide in some American cities.[37] There is no doubt that heroin/opiate deaths have increased, but part of the well-known heroin epidemic is legally obtained opiates through prescriptions so there is no data as yet to prove that illegal heroin markets are fueling the homicide increase. Also, there has been no increase in the number of drug arrests. An increase in the number of parolees contributing to the homicide increase would require a knowledge of whether or not perpetrators were on parole—data we do not have yet for 2015, even for those arrested (and recall that a certain portion of homicides are not ever solved). As for the hypothesis that a legitimacy crisis in the minority community toward the police is causing an increase in homicide, Rosenfeld, in the NIJ analysis referred to above, pointed out that the cities with the largest homicide increases also had higher percentages of Blacks, and public opinion polls show that Blacks have historically low confidence in policing today. He argued that it is a difficult methodolgical problem to determine to what extent a rise is homicides is due to a loss of legitimacy of police and the justice system and suggested ethnographic research.[38] Another possibility is to look at the motivations for killings since part of the loss of legitimacy argument is that people who do not trust the justice system engage in retaliatory behavior. A good question to ask might be: what portion of homicides in these cities are due to retaliation? Also, is the proportion of retaliatory homicides correlated with a decrease in trust in police? We don't have motivation data yet for 2015 (although it will eventually be available in Suppmental Homicide Reports from the FBI).

To conclude, there is no evidence of a trend of increasing homicides at this point. We don't know if the recent increase in some cities will continue nor do we know whether it will spread to more cities. An increase in 2006 spurred similar concern, which proved to be unnecessary since the increase evaporated and the decline in homicides and other violent crimes continued their multi-decade decline after a couple of years.[39] As for "de-policing," there is some quantitative evidence that police discretionary actions (investigative detentions, traffic tickets, and misdemeanor arrests) have declined in some cities, but not the cities that have experienced the most dramatic increase in homicides.

The proposed explanations for the increase in homicides in some American cities offered instead of a "Ferguson Effect" include: growing heroin markets, an increase in parolees returning from prison, and a loss of legitimacy of police and the justice system in the Black community leading to retaliatory and vigilante justice. Absence of current data make any study of these hypotheses difficult.

SUMMARY

What Is Crime? What Is the Role of Legislators, Victims, Police, and Prosecutors in Defining Crimes?

Crime is a "constructed reality" created by legislators who define acts as crimes, acts of the perpetrator, the perceptions of the victim and decision to report to authorities, and decisions by system actors (e.g., the decision to arrest). Only a portion of all crimes find their way into official statistics.

What Sources Do We Use to Find Out About the Patterns of Crime?

The Uniform Crime Reports present data on eight index crimes that are reported to police. They can be accessed from the FBI's website, which also has data on arrests on a larger number of crime categories. Problems with the UCR include the fact that many people do not report crimes to the police and arrests are not necessarily an accurate representation of crimes committed. We also have the National Crime Victimization Survey, which is a random survey of the population to discover the number of people who have been victimized and some characteristics of their victimization. We also use self-report studies and cohort studies in our study of crime.

What Crimes Are People Most Frequently Arrested for?

The largest category of arrests in 2014 was for drug crimes and possession was the most frequent of these arrests. Larceny/theft is the next most frequent arrest category, along with DUI and non-aggravated assault. The crimes the media focuses on (murder, rape, robbery) are extremely rare.

What Do We Know About Homicide?

Homicide, as most crime, has been on the decline since the mid-1990s. It is important to remember that the relative risk of being a homicide offender or a homicide victim is dramatically dependent on population group. Young Black males are much more likely than other population groups to be both homicide victim and offender.

What Has Been the Pattern of Crime Over the Years? Has It Declined?

All measures of crime (UCR, arrests, and victimization reports) show dramatic declines over the last two decades so that today's crime rates—for both violent and property crimes—are about the same as they were in the 1970s.

Does the Public Have an Accurate Perception About the Prevalence of Crime?

The public seems incredibly unaware of the dramatic declines in crime that have taken place in the last decades. A majority of the public thinks that crime is increasing despite all measures showing declines. It is possible that recent upticks in homicides and violent crimes in cities may be a sign that crime rates may be poised to begin an upward trend.

How Do the Crime Rates of the United States Compare to Other Countries?

While the U.S. has higher murder rates than European countries, other crimes do not show any consistent pattern. In general, property crimes in the U.S. are not higher than many other countries.

Critical Thinking Exercises

1. Go to the FBI website for the UCR which is reported in *Crime in the United States*. The 2015 crime statistics have just recently been released at: **https://ucr.fbi.gov/crime-in-the-u.s/2015/crime-in-the-u.s.-2015**. See if homicide and/or violent crime rates are higher than they were in 2014. Write an update to the Focus on Crime section—is there more information available regarding any of the questions raised in the section?
2. Go to the United Nations Office of Drugs and Crime website: **https://data.unodc.org/#state:4**. Look up the crime rates (not raw numbers) for other crimes to see how the United States compares to other countries. Why do you suppose the homicide rates are so much higher here? How would you test your hypothesis?

NOTES

1 Texas Penal Code. Retrieved 4/10/2007 from http://tlo2.tlc.state.tx.us/statutes/docs/PE/content/htm/pe.005.00.000 022.00.htm#22.01.00.

2 See H. Cleveland, M. Koss and J. Lyons, "Rape tactics from the survivor's perspective." *Journal of Interpersonal Violence* 14 (5) (1999): 532–548.

3 *Sourcebook of Criminal Justice Statistics 2010*. Retrieved 9/9/2010 from http://www.albany.edu/sourcebook/pdf/ 13332007.pdf.

4 See C. Mendias and E. Kobe, "Engagement of policing ideals and the relationship to the exercise of discretionary powers." *Criminal Justice and Behavior* 33 (2006): 70–77.

5 N. James, *How Crime in the United States Is Measured*. Washington, DC: Congressional Research Service (CRS), 2008.

6 Federal Bureau of Investigation, *Crime in the United States, 2013*, Table 6, Crime in the United States by State, by City, 2013. Retrieved 9/12/2007 from https://www.fbi.gov/about-us/cjis/ucr/crime-in-the-u.s/2013/crime-in-the-u.s.-2013/ tables/6tabledatadecpdf/table-6.

7 J. Eterno and E. Silverman, "The trouble with Compstat: Pressure on NYPD commanders endangered the integrity of crime stats." *New York Daily News*, February 15, 2010. Retrieved 9/15/2010 from http://www.nydailynews.com/opin ions/2010/02/15/2010-02-15_the_trouble_with_compstat.html; J. Eterno, A. Verma, E. Silverman, "Police manipula- tions of crime reporting: Insiders' revelations." *Justice Quarterly*, 2014. Accessed from: doi.org/10.1080/07418825.2014. 980838.

8 D. Bernstein and N. Isackson, "The truth about Chicago's crime rates, Part I and II." *Chicago Magazine* (May, June, 2014) Retrieved 12/9/2015 from http://www.chicagomag.com/Chicago-Magazine/June-2014/Chicago-crime-statistics/.

9 Federal Bureau of Investigation, *Crime in the United States, 2004*. Retrieved 8/1/2006 from http://www.fbi.gov/ucr/ cius_04/offenses_cleared/index.html.

10 Federal Bureau of Investigation, *Crime in the United States, 2009*. Retrieved 9/15/2010 from http://www.fbi.gov/ucr/ cius2009/offenses/data/table_25.html.

11 Federal Bureau of Investigation, *Crime in the United States, 2014*. Retrieved 12/5/2015 from https://www.fbi.gov/ about-us/cjis/ucr/crime-in-the-u.s/2014/crime-in-the-u.s.-2014/tables/table-25.

12 Bureau of Justice Statistics, NIBRS. Retrieved 12/5/2015 from BJS website, note on methodology on NIBRS. http:// www.bjs.gov/index.cfm?ty=dcdetail&iid=301#_ftnref3.

13 D. Roberts, "Why participating in NIBRS is a good idea." *Police Chief Magazine*, December 2015. Retrieved 12/5/2015 from http://www.policechiefmagazine.org/magazine/index.cfm?fuseaction=display&issue_id=92014&category_ID=4.

14 S. Ansari and N. He, "Convergence revisited: A multi-definition, multi-method analysis of the UCR and the NCVS crime series." *Justice Quarterly*, 32 (2012): 1–31.

15 M. Wolfgang, R. Figlio and T. Sellin, *Delinquency in a Birth Cohort*. Chicago: University of Chicago Press, 1978.

16 M. Tonry, L. Ohlin and D. Farrington, *Human Development and Criminal Behavior: New Ways of Advancing Knowledge*. New York: Springer-Verlag, 1991.

17 Federal Bureau of Investigation, *Crime in the United States, 2014*. Retrieved from https://www.fbi.gov/about-us/cjis/ucr/ crime-in-the-u.s/2014/crime-in-the-u.s.-2014/persons-arrested/main.

18 J. Truman and L. Langton, *Criminal Victimization, 2014*. Table 4. Retrieved from http://www.bjs.gov/content/pub/pdf/ cv14.pdf.

19 See, for instance, J. Cancino and J. Pollock, "Gender, race, and ethnicity: An analysis of homicide rates and trends in San Antonio, 1990–2004." Paper presented at the American Society of Criminology Meeting, Los Angeles, CA (2006, November).

20 Gallup poll. Retrieved from: http://www.gallup.com/poll/186308/americans-say-crime-rising.aspx?utm_source=alert&utm_medium=email&utm_content=morelink&utm_campaign=syndication.

21 H. MacDonald, "The new nationwide crime wave." *The Wall Street Journal*, May 29, 2015. Retrieved 12/12/2015 from http://www.wsj.com/articles/the-new-nationwide-crime-wave-1432938425.

22 R. Rosenfeld, *Documenting and Explaining the 2015 Homicide Rise: Research Directions*. Washington, DC: NIJ, OJP, June 2016, p. 6.

23 J. Gravwert and J. Cullen, *Crime in 2015: A Final Analysis*. Washington, DC: Brennan Center, April 2016.

24 R. Rosenfeld, *Documenting and Explaining the 2015 Homicide Rise: Research Directions*. Washington, DC: NIJ, OJP, June 2016, p. 8.

25 D. Hamill, "Keeping a running score of New York's homicide rate seems a bit ridiculous." *New York Daily News*, June 28, 2015. Retrieved 12/15/2015 from http://www.nydailynews.com/new-york/murder-statistics-don-show-return-bad-old-days-article-1.2273859.

26 J. Domanick, "Why L.A.'s crime rise is no surprise." *Los Angeles Times* (August 27, 2015). Retrieved 12/12/2015 from http://www.latimes.com/opinion/op-ed/la-oe-domanick-los-angeles-rising-crime-20150827-story.html.

27 D. Bernstein and N. Isackson, "The truth about Chicago's crime rates, Part I and II." *Chicago Magazine* (May, June) Retrieved 12/9/2015 from http://www.chicagomag.com/Chicago-Magazine/June-2014/Chicago-crime-statistics/.

28 C. Bialik, "Scare headlines exaggerated the US crime wave." Fivethirtyeight.com. Retrieved 12/12/2015 from https://fivethirtyeight.com/features/scare-headlines-exaggerated-the-u-s-crime-wave/.

29 M. Friedman, "Just facts: America's non-existent 'spike in crime'." Brennan Center for Justice (August 10, 2015). Retrieved 12/12/2015 from https://www.brennancenter.org/blog/americas-non-existent-spike-crime.

30 Federal Bureau of Investigation, *Crime in the United States, 2014*. Tables 12. Retrieved 12/12/2015 from https://www.fbi.gov/about-us/cjis/ucr/crime-in-the-u.s/2014/crime-in-the-u.s.-2014.

31 Bureau of Justice Statistics, *Criminal Victimization, 2014*. Office of Justice Programs. Retrieved 12/12/2015 from http://www.bjs.gov/content/pub/pdf/cv14.pdf.

32 L. Bui, A. Phillip and W. Lowery, "Around St. Louis, bloodshed rises in year since Michael Brown was killed." *Washington Post*, August 11, 2015. Retrieved from http://www.washingtonpost.com/national/around-st-louis-bloodshed-rises-in-year-since-michael-brown-was-killed/2015/08/11/b0ea430c-405c-11e5-bfe3-ff1d8549bfd2_story.html?hpid=z7

33 New York Times Editorial Board, "New York policing, by the numbers." *New York Times*, December 28, 2015, p. A18.

34 S. Miletich, "Report cites plunge in SPD enforcement of low-level crime." *Seattle Times*, May 24, 2014. Retrieved 1/3/2016 from http://www.seattletimes.com/seattle-news/report-cites-plunge-in-spd-enforcement-of-low-level-crime/.

35 Scott E. Wolfe and Justin Nix, "The alleged 'Ferguson Effect' and police willingness to engage in community partnership." *Law and Human Behavior*, 2015; DOI: 10.1037/lhb0000164.

36 D. Pyrooz, S. Decker, S. Wolfe and J. Shjarback, "Was there a Ferguson Effect on crime rates in large US cities?" *Journal of Criminal Justice* 46 (2016): 1–16.

37 R. Rosenfeld, *Documenting and Explaining the 2015 Homicide Rise: Research Directions*. Washington, DC: NIJ, OJP, June 2016.

38 R. Rosenfeld, *Documenting and Explaining the 2015 Homicide Rise: Research Directions*. Washington, DC: NIJ, OJP, June 2016.

39 R. Rosenfeld, *Documenting and Explaining the 2015 Homicide Rise: Research Directions*. Washington, DC: NIJ, OJP, June 2016.

WHY HAS CRIME DECLINED?

3

Now that we have a sense of what crime is and crime patterns over the years, we will turn to whether the theories of crime can help us understand the crime decline or whether we must look for other explanations. Why do people commit crime? In a sense, the entire field of criminology is an exercise in critical thinking because we ask the question, why do people commit crime; and, then, we test various hypotheses to determine if data supports it. In the last chapter, we illustrated how dramatically crime has declined over the last twenty years. Thus, another important question is why has crime declined?

Chapter Preview

- What Are the Explanations for the Decline of Crime?
- What Are Some Methodological Issues in the Question: Why Do People Commit Crime?
- Who Commits Crime?
- Focus on Data: Are Blacks More Criminal Than Whites?
- What Are the Major Criminological Theories of Crime?
- What Do Biological Theories of Crime Say About Who Commits Crime and Why?
- What Do Psychological Theories of Crime Say About Who Commits Crime and Why?
- What Do Sociological Theories of Crime Say About Who Commits Crime and Why?
- What Are Some Other Theories of Crime?
- Summary
- Critical Thinking Exercises

WHAT ARE THE EXPLANATIONS FOR THE DECLINE OF CRIME?

In the last twenty years, we have experienced truly dramatic drops in all crime, including violent and property crimes. Why? Those who favor punitive responses argue that increased incarceration obviously has reduced crime—after all, as the incarceration rate increased, crime declined. Those who favor rehabilitative measures for offenders argue that other factors account for the crime decline. As with our approach throughout the book, we will try to identify any preconceptions or biases such as these that might affect our ability to objectively examine the evidence. An important step is to identify *all* potential factors that might have affected the number of crimes committed. For instance, any of the following factors might be implicated:

- Aging birth cohort of baby boomers
- Stabilization of drug markets
- Higher incarceration rates
- Community policing
- "Zero tolerance" policing
- Home health care and pre- and post-natal health services
- Violence prevention programs in schools
- Reduction of exposure to lead-based paint
- Increased numbers of abortions in the late 1970s and 1980s.[1]

There is no consensus as to whether any of these factors, either alone or in combination, account for the dramatic decline of crime. Analysts have estimated that increased incarceration can explain as much as 58 percent of the property crime drop in the 1990s, but others estimate that it explains none of the drop in violent crime in the 2000s. At least one analysis concluded that increased incarceration did not decrease crime, but, rather, increased crime by about 1 percent. In other words, researchers greatly disagree on the impact of incarceration on the crime rate. When considering many different researchers' findings, however, there are more that concluded increased incarceration has had a real but modest impact on reducing crime in the 1990s, but the continued increase in incarceration rates resulted in diminishing returns in the 2000s.[2]

In a recent comprehensive analysis of incarceration as well as other proposed explanations for the crime drop by the Brennan Center, it was determined that a number of factors affected the crime drop during the 1990s and some, but not all, of these factors continued to affect the declining crime rates of the 2000s. Exhibit 3.1 below shows their findings. The display shows factors that did seem to influence the crime drop, the estimated strength of the influence, and factors that could not be proven as influencing the drop in crime. This statistical analysis was done using reports to police (UCR) as the measure of crime (so consider what weaknesses this might bring to the analysis).

Note that the factors analyzed by these researchers look at societal-level factors, such as increased numbers of police, or the increase in incarceration.

Exhibit 3.1   What Explains the Decline in Crime Rates?

Factors in the Crime Drop	Estimated Influence	Not Proven
1990–99		
Decreased alcohol consumption	5–10%	Right-to-carry laws
Increased incarceration	0–10%	Use of death penalty
Increased numbers of police	0–10%	Decreased crack use
Growth in income	0–7%	Decreased lead in gasoline
Decreased unemployed	0–5%	Legalization of abortion
Aging population	0–5%	
Consumer confidence	(not estimated)	
Inflation	(not estimated)	
2000–13		
Decreased alcohol consumption	5–10%	Aging population
Growth in income	5–10%	Decreased crack use
Introduction of Compstat	5–15%*	Right-to-carry laws
Increased unemployment	0–3%	Decreased lead in gasoline
Increased incarceration	0–1%	Increased police numbers
Inflation	(not estimated)	Legalization of abortion
Consumer confidence	(not estimated)	Use of death penalt

*In cities where it was implemented.

Source: D. Roeder, L. Eisen, J. Bowling. What Caused the Crime Decline? Brennan Center, 2015. Retrieved from https://www.brennancenter.org/publication/what-caused-crime-decline.

A different approach is to ask the question, "Why do people choose to commit crime?" and, arguably, those reasons may also help to explain the drop in crime.

WHAT ARE SOME METHODOLOGICAL ISSUES IN THE QUESTION: WHY DO PEOPLE COMMIT CRIME?

All of the factors in Exhibit 3.1 are considered macro-level factors, that is, broad societal-level elements, such as inflation, increased incarceration or police numbers, and so on. **Macro-level crime theories** predict crime patterns in particular societies or over time. For instance, large social changes (e.g., the number of women in the workforce) might affect crime rates, especially of burglary because of the greater opportunities created when women work leaving houses empty, but say nothing about which individuals are likely to commit crimes. In attempting to explain the crime decline, researchers have tested macrolevel theories to see what changes have taken place in society since the mid-1990s that might have affected people's willingness or ability to commit crime.

Criminology is the study of crime and criminal motivation. It is largely comprised of **micro-level theories** that explain why any particular individual might commit crime. Theories that look at a wide range of biological, psychological, or even sociological causes are considered micro-level theories when they seek to predict the relative likelihood of particular individuals committing crime. A theory that predicts an individual who comes from a broken home, grows up in a disorganized community, does poorly in school, and has peers who are also delinquent is more likely to be criminal is clearly a micro-level theory. Even if correct, it says nothing about whether crime rates are going to go up or down (although, arguably, if one somehow was able to reduce the number of individuals who are "crime-prone" then one might assume there should be a decline of overall crime rates).

Crime theories should be consistent with the facts about crime that we have established thus far or will discuss in the following section:

(a) We have seen dramatic twenty-year crime declines as measured by official reports, arrests, and victimization surveys.
(b) Crime is more likely to be committed by men, by 18–30-year-olds, and, for many crime categories, disproportionally by Blacks.

Almost everyone thinks they know why people commit crimes. Their answers may include family factors (bad parents), individual/personality factors ("bad seed"), peer factors (bad friends), and societal factors (bad economy/neighborhood). Before we begin to explore the theories that have developed, we need to discuss some challenges to developing and testing theories of crime. The first challenge is that "crime" is a broad concept that includes everything from speeding to serial murder. Crime is not synonomous with deviance. Crime is simply behavior that is in violation of a law. **Deviance** can be defined as behavior that is contrary to the norm and that occurs infrequently. Some crimes (such as speeding) are not infrequent and not deviant. Would we expect the explanation to be the same for deviant crimes such as serial murder or any type of homicide and speeding?

It is also complicated to answer the question why people commit crime when the definition of crime changes. For instance, in the past abortion was a crime, and now it is not (at least in the first three months of a pregnancy), but it might be again in the future. Gambling is usually illegal, unless it is buying a state lottery ticket or unless the state has legalized that specific form of gambling. Marijuana possession is illegal in most states, but not all; but always is against federal law. So, how does one construct an explanation for why people commit criminal acts when sometimes those acts are crimes and sometimes they are not crimes at all?

It is important, then, to refine the question, "Why do people commit crime?" to incorporate what specific type of crime you are asking about. Why people break traffic laws is a different question from why someone might commit serial murder, which is a different question from why someone sells drugs. One potential way to categorize crimes might be differentiating crimes that harm others (**victim-harming crimes**) and those crimes where no specific individual is harmed (**victimless crimes**). Most drug laws are victimless crimes, as are gambling, underage drinking, and so on. Some might argue that no crimes are truly victimless because such actions may harm, even if indirectly, family members or friends of the perpetrator, but they are clearly different from such victim-harming crimes as aggravated assault, robbery, larceny/theft, or fraud. Even though crimes such as assault, rape, robbery, burglary, larceny/theft, and fraud are victim-harming crimes, typically we further differentiate personal violent crime from property crimes. There are victims that are harmed in property crimes, however, it is possible that there are differences between those who are willing to physically injure victims from those who are only willing to take property from or defraud victims.

Distinguishing victim-harming and victimless crimes may be important to understand why people commit crime. One can see, for instance, that different explanations might be needed to help explain why someone uses drugs, gambles, or commits DUI from why someone rapes or robs another. It should be noted that some criminologists would argue that the same underlying reason (lack of self-control) explains both victim-harming and victimless crimes.[3]

WHO COMMITS CRIME?

A **correlate** of crime is a factor that is associated statistically with the incidence of crime. A correlate means there is a statistical relationship between two factors. A positive correlation means that as Factor A goes up, Factor B goes up also. A negative correlation is that as Factor A goes up, Factor B goes down. We can think of correlates as predictors. The three strongest predictors of who commits crime seem to be sex (male), age (18–30), and, for some crimes, race (Black).

Sex

We know that men are more likely to be arrested for crime, especially violent crime. There have long been arguments that men and women are equally criminal and it is the criminal justice system that creates the disparity in arrests. The **chivalry theory** proposes the idea that women are less likely to be arrested than men in similar circumstances, and if arrested, are less likely to be tried and convicted. The weight of evidence indicates that it occurred to some extent, for some women, for some crimes, in the past. Although studies often show that women receive, on average, less harsh sentences, it is extremely difficult to control for other variables that also affect sentencing, e.g., criminal history, level of participation, motivation. These factors tend to be different between men and women; so, while women do receive, on average, shorter sentences, it may be because of these other factors, not all of which are taken into account by researchers.[4]

Exhibit 3.2   Men are more likely than women to be arrested, especially for violent crimes. Women who are convicted, like this woman who shot her boyfriend, receive shorter average sentences.

Source: AP

Women's criminality is an issue where preconceptions and biases must be identified. There is a tendency by some to argue that women are, of course, as "evil" as men and, therefore, it must be the system that is affecting the numbers of arrests.

There is a counter-tendency by those who believe that women are inherently less criminal than men to dispute the recent increases in arrest figures. It is important to put bias aside and try to develop a methodology that minimizes any factors that tend to distort the accurate measurement of criminality. Unfortunately, as we have noted before, that is difficult to do because arrest figures are a function of an action by the offender *and* a decision of system actors to arrest or not. Thus, it is not a perfectly accurate measurement of crime. If system actors are less likely to arrest women (as is argued in the chivalry theory) there will be undercounting; if they are more likely to arrest women today than in the past (as is argued below) there will be an inaccurate time comparison of women's criminality.

We are fairly certain that women are much less likely to commit violent crime than men and somewhat less likely to commit most property crimes, although in some crime categories (e.g. embezzlement), they are now just as likely to be arrested as men. Exhibit 3.3 shows men's and women's arrest rates for selected crime categories for 2003 and 2014.

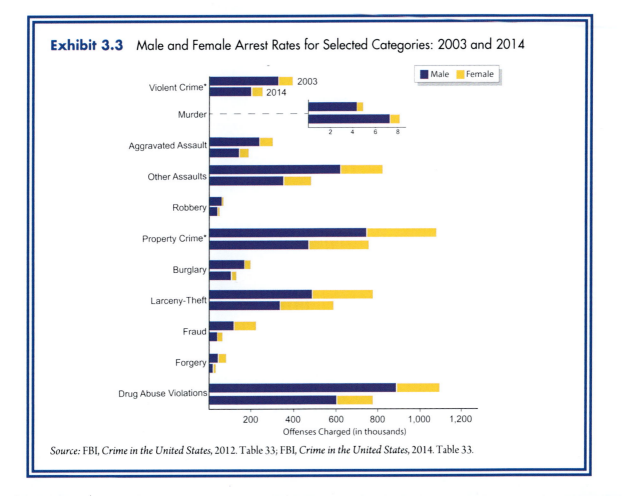

Exhibit 3.3   Male and Female Arrest Rates for Selected Categories: 2003 and 2014

Source: FBI, *Crime in the United States*, 2012. Table 33; FBI, *Crime in the United States*, 2014. Table 33.

Exhibit 3.4 Ten Year Arrest Trends by Sex, Adults Only, 2003–14

Offense charged[1]	Male Total		Female Total	
	2003	2014	2003	2014
Murder and non-negligent manslaughter	7,353	4,368	905	561
Forcible rape	16,578	9,449	210	308
Robbery	63,555	40,077	7,512	6,679
Aggravated assault	239,489	144,654	62,450	42,570
Burglary	170,581	102,293	28,275	24,610
Larceny-theft	486,870	333,813	288,894	253,408
Motor vehicle theft	78,642	26,324	15,531	6,929
Arson	9,153	3,751	1,718	933
Violent crime[2]	326,975	198,548	71,077	50,118
Property crime[2]	745,246	466,181	334,418	285,880
Other assaults	622,089	353,831	199,426	135,174
Forgery and counterfeiting	45,818	17,036	31,184	9,746
Fraud	120,139	39,579	101,513	23,913
Embezzlement	6,301	3,021	6,426	2,762
Stolen property; buying, receiving, possessing	71,587	37,615	16,038	10,658
Vandalism	153,555	77,148	29,910	19,569
Weapons; carrying, possessing, etc.	102,092	62,550	9,001	6,183
Prostitution and commercialized vice	16,382	7,147	32,131	12,511
Sex offenses (except forcible rape and prostitution)	54,794	27,494	5,361	2,290
Drug abuse violations	887,736	601,386	203,212	169,827
Gambling	3,694	1,264	697	322
Offenses against the family and children	68,432	33,927	20,346	12,268
Driving under the influence	780,679	401,904	174,545	130,480
Liquor laws	311,799	93,476	109,377	37,882
Drunkenness	324,213	175,229	54,153	40,028
Disorderly conduct	312,480	139,687	108,318	54,906

(Continued)

Offense charged[1]	Male Total		Female Total	
	2003	2014	2003	2014
Vagrancy	15,521	11,160	4,266	3,154
All other offenses (except traffic)	1,868,452	1,107,783	540,912	375,315
Suspicion	1,447	396	269	148
Curfew and loitering law violations	66,026	21,301	28,679	7,590

[1] Does not include suspicion.
[2] Violent crimes are offenses of murder and non-negligent manslaughter, forcible rape, robbery, and aggravated assault. Property crimes are offenses of burglary, larceny-theft, motor vehicle theft, and arson.

Source: FBI, *Crime in the United States*, 2012. Table 33; FBI, *Crime in the United States*, 2014. Table 33.

Official reports indicate that 73.3 percent of all persons arrested in the nation in 2014 were men. They accounted for 79.8 percent of persons arrested for violent crime and 61.8 percent of persons arrested for property crime.[5] In Exhibit 3.4 we can see that for all crime categories except prostitution, the number of arrests of men exceeded that for women (even though women comprise a bit more than half of the population). For some crimes, the differential was quite extreme (e.g., 4,368 men were arrested for murder and non-negligent manslaughter compared to only 561 women); for others, the difference was negligible (e.g., 3,021 men were arrested for embezzlement compared to 2,762 women).

Arrests of women show an increase in the last ten years in some crimes (robbery, burglary, larceny/theft) while men's arrests for all crimes declined. In Exhibit 3.5 we see that the greatest differential in arrests between men and women occurs in violent crimes. The proportions of men and women arrested are much more similar in property crimes.

What accounts for the decrease in the "**gender differential**" (the disproportional arrest rates between men and women) in embezzlement and other property crimes? Researchers have studied women's increasing numbers of arrests for DUI and found that changes in formal control (e.g., greater willingness to arrest) explains the change better than any change in women's behavior since self-reports and other measures of drinking under the influence have not changed.[6] In other words, women's behavior hasn't changed so much as the

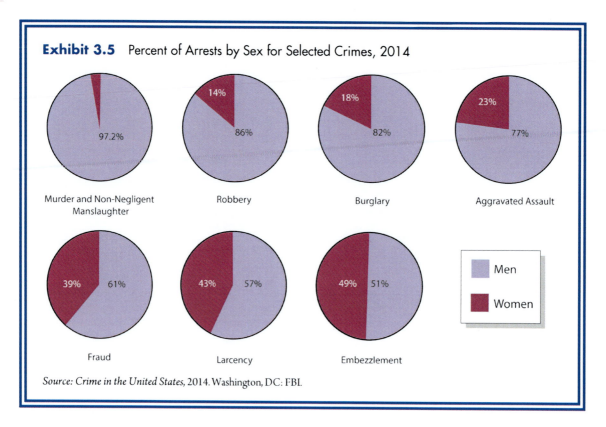

Exhibit 3.5 Percent of Arrests by Sex for Selected Crimes, 2014

Murder and Non-Negligent Manslaughter — 97.2%

Robbery — 14% / 86%

Burglary — 18% / 82%

Aggravated Assault — 23% / 77%

Fraud — 39% / 61%

Larceny — 43% / 57%

Embezzlement — 49% / 51%

Men / Women

Source: Crime in the United States, 2014. Washington, DC: FBI.

willingness to arrest women for behavior they were less likely to be arrested for in the past. Similar research has shown that increased arrests for non-aggravated assaults for both adult and juvenile women also seems to be driven more by changes in system actor decisions to arrest rather than an increase in women's assaultiveness.[7] The way these researchers study this is they look at other measurements of crime (e.g., victim reports). If victim reports don't show an increase over a time period that official arrest numbers increase, then the assumption is that the change is occurring with system actors' decisions to arrest, not the crime patterns.

It is also important to note that most of the change in the ratio between men's and women's violent crime participation is due to the dramatic decline of men's crimes with the relatively modest decline or no change of women's rates rather than any great increase in women's participation in violent crime. Why women's violent crime arrest rates haven't declined as dramatically as men's seems obvious: women's rates have always been low, as shown in Exhibit 3.6. The real question regarding gender and crime is why men's violent crime decreased so dramatically, not why women showed more modest decreases over the same period.[8]

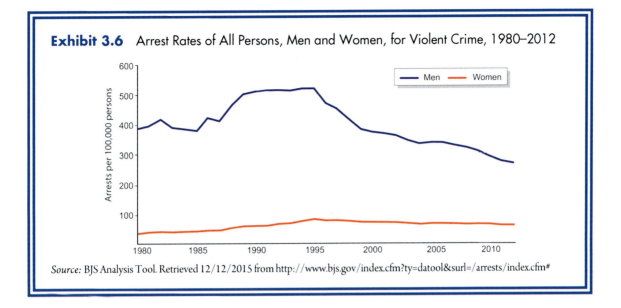

Exhibit 3.6   Arrest Rates of All Persons, Men and Women, for Violent Crime, 1980–2012

Source: BJS Analysis Tool. Retrieved 12/12/2015 from http://www.bjs.gov/index.cfm?ty=datool&surl=/arrests/index.cfm#

Age

Another clear correlate of crime is age. Crime is typically committed by those between the ages of 18 and 25. Exhibit 3.7 illustrates the "crime-prone age years" through arrests, and also shows how arrests decline after age 30.

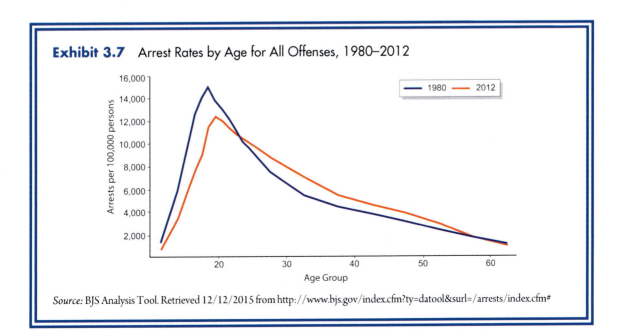

Exhibit 3.7   Arrest Rates by Age for All Offenses, 1980–2012

Source: BJS Analysis Tool. Retrieved 12/12/2015 from http://www.bjs.gov/index.cfm?ty=datool&surl=/arrests/index.cfm#

The fact that crime seems to drop off dramatically after age 30 has been a consistent finding as long as crime statistics have been collected and seems to occur cross-culturally as well.

Race and/or Ethnicity

Race, a third correlate of crime, is controversial and problematic. In the past, FBI arrest statistics did not include information on ethnicity; now ethnicity is identified but in a separate column that overlaps with other columns. In other words, Hispanics are still not separated out from total numbers of Blacks and Whites in arrest totals, although there is now a column showing Hispanics' (both Hispanic White and Hispanic non-White) proportion of arrests.

In 2014, 69.4 percent of all persons arrested were White (including Hispanics), 27.8 percent were Black (including Hispanic), and the remaining 2.8 percent were of other races (including Hispanic). Utilizing the 2014 FBI arrest figures and removing Hispanics' total arrest numbers from Whites, we see that Whites (who account for 62 percent of the population according to the US Census[9]) comprise 55 percent of arrests, Hispanics (who comprise about 17 percent of the population) account for 14 percent of arrests, and Blacks (who are about 13 percent of the population) are responsible for 28 percent of all arrests. This is a very rough computation since by subtracting out the total number of Hispanics from only the White column inaccurately also includes Black/Hispanic or Other/Hispanic which are incorrectly deleted from the total arrests for Whites' numbers. Unfortunately, until the FBI begins to display Hispanics as a discrete and independent group, it is the only way we can isolate the Hispanics as a separate group to see more clearly the relative arrest rates of Whites and Hispanics.

Because the issue of race and crime is so controversial, we explore the topic in more detail in the Focus on Data below.

FOCUS ON DATA: ARE BLACKS MORE CRIMINAL THAN WHITES?

Considering their population percentage of about 13 percent, Blacks are arrested at disproportionate rates for all crimes except for DUI, liquor laws, and drunkenness. Exhibit 3.8 illustrates this disproportional arrest pattern.

Rather than as a percentage of total arrests, another way to view this data is to compare *rates* of arrest between Blacks and Whites. Recall that rates take the population of the group into account, so the way to read Exhibit 3.9 is that these numbers of arrests occur for each 100,000 of Blacks in the population and for each 100,000 of Whites in the population. We see that Blacks are much more

Exhibit 3.8 Percentage of Arrests—Blacks, 2014

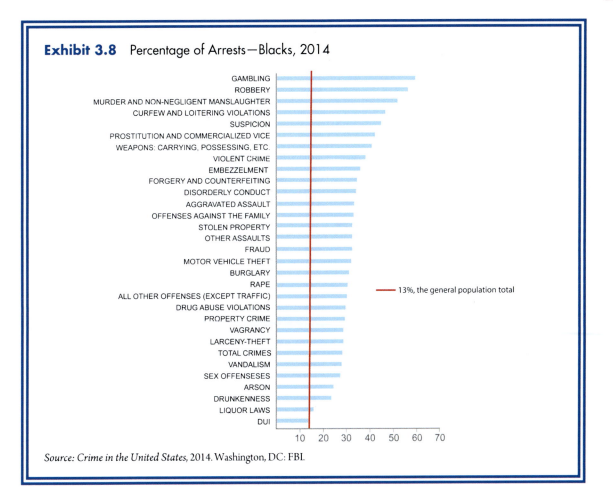

13%, the general population total

Source: *Crime in the United States*, 2014. Washington, DC: FBI.

Exhibit 3.9 Arrest Rates by Race

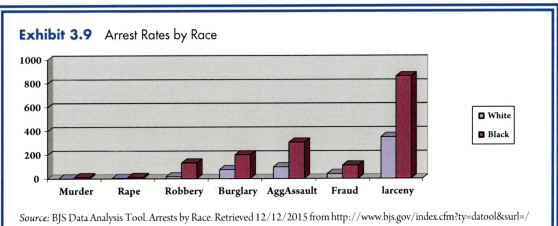

□ White
■ Black

Source: BJS Data Analysis Tool. Arrests by Race. Retrieved 12/12/2015 from http://www.bjs.gov/index.cfm?ty=datool&surl=/arrests/index.cfm#

likely to be arrested taking their population size into account. One important fact Exhibit 3.9 displays is that even though Blacks account for a disproportionate percentage of homicide arrests, these crimes are fairly rare for all racial/ethnic groups when compared to such crimes as larceny.

It is important to remember that these are arrest figures, thus, they are a measure of the choice to arrest or not. There are some who argue, for instance, that police officers are more likely to arrest Blacks than Whites for the same behavior or level of suspicion. Facts to support this proposition are hard to come by since it involves knowing the total number of individuals who would have been in a position to be arrested and then the percentage who were actually arrested and whether this percentage is racially or ethnically disproportional.

We don't have the information of all those who could have been arrested based on their behavior, but we do have self-reports of some types of criminality. According to national surveys, marijuana use is roughly equal among Blacks and Whites. In 2010, 14 percent of Blacks and 12 percent of Whites reported using marijuana in the past year. In the same year, 59 percent of Blacks and 54 percent of Whites reported having never used marijuana. Arrest figures, however, show that in 2010, the arrest rate for Whites was 192 per 100,000 Whites, and the arrest rate for Blacks was 716 per 100,000.[10] Even though some of the difference may be because of differential patterns of use/sales by Blacks and Whites, why arrest rates are so much higher than use rates leads to a hypothesis of differential enforcement.

While differential enforcement is something to be concerned about for lower-level discretionary crimes, it is probably less of a factor in personal violent crime (homicide, robbery, rape) because it is hard to imagine that an arrest would not take place regardless of who the suspect was; however, the possibility of differential enforcement makes any arrest statistics somewhat suspect.

Blacks not only disproportionally commit violent crime; they also are disproportionally victimized by violent crime. Exhibit 3.10 displays findings from the National Crime Survey and shows that although all racial/ethnic groups have experienced substantial declines of victimization, Blacks still experience higher levels than Whites. Hispanics experience victimization levels that are in between the rates of Whites and Blacks.

Even though some evidence indicates probable disparate treatment in arrests (Blacks may be more likely to be arrested than Whites for some crimes), data from victimization studies also shows *victims* identify a disproportionate percentage of their offenders as Black. In one study, Black victims reported about four-fifths of their offenders were also Black.[11] In Exhibit 3.11 below, both White and Black victims report a disproportionate percentage of

To explore drug use figures for young people, go to the Monitoring the Future self-report survey results at http://www.monitoringthefuture.org/pubs/monographs/mtf-overview2015.pdf

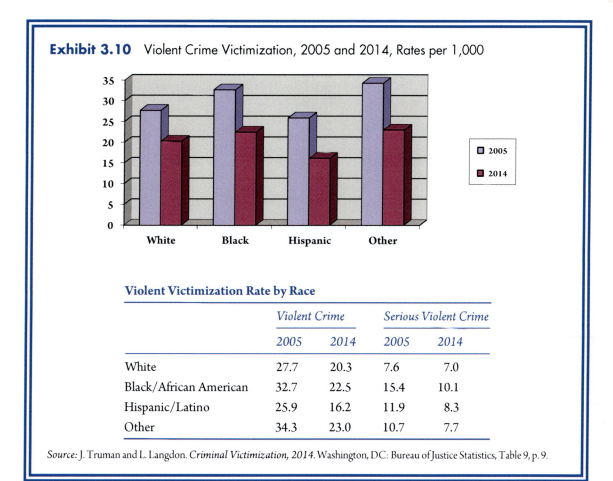

Exhibit 3.10   Violent Crime Victimization, 2005 and 2014, Rates per 1,000

Violent Victimization Rate by Race

	Violent Crime		Serious Violent Crime	
	2005	2014	2005	2014
White	27.7	20.3	7.6	7.0
Black/African American	32.7	22.5	15.4	10.1
Hispanic/Latino	25.9	16.2	11.9	8.3
Other	34.3	23.0	10.7	7.7

Source: J. Truman and L. Langdon. *Criminal Victimization, 2014.* Washington, DC: Bureau of Justice Statistics, Table 9, p. 9.

offenders as Black. About 23.8 percent of victims of violent crime perceived their offender as Black compared to their population percentage of about 13 percent; and almost half (45.4 percent) of robbery victims perceived the offender as Black. Unfortunately, this information from the Bureau of Justice Statistics is from 2008 and it does not appear that similar tables are available for more recent victimization reports. Also remember that victimization reports are not completely comparable to violent crime numbers from the UCR or FBI arrest figures because some crimes (e.g. homicide) are not represented in victim accounts.

Thus, both official reports (arrest data) and victim reports support the conclusion that Blacks are overrepresented in crime, especially violent crime. What could explain the disproportional representation? Other factors may also interact with race. Statistically, if any factor affects crime participation

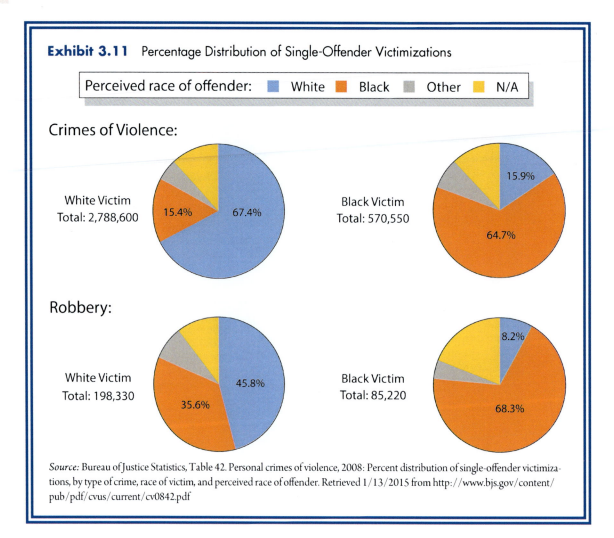

Exhibit 3.11   Percentage Distribution of Single-Offender Victimizations

Perceived race of offender: ■ White   ■ Black   ■ Other   ■ N/A

Crimes of Violence:

White Victim
Total: 2,788,600

15.4%   67.4%

Black Victim
Total: 570,550

15.9%

64.7%

Robbery:

White Victim
Total: 198,330

45.8%

35.6%

Black Victim
Total: 85,220

8.2%

68.3%

Source: Bureau of Justice Statistics, Table 42. Personal crimes of violence, 2008: Percent distribution of single-offender victimizations, by type of crime, race of victim, and perceived race of offender. Retrieved 1/13/2015 from http://www.bjs.gov/content/pub/pdf/cvus/current/cv0842.pdf

and, also, is statistically different based on membership in racial groups, that factor needs to be "**controlled for,**" meaning held constant, if we want to see the true effects of race on criminal involvement. For instance, we know that urban areas have higher crime, even after controlling for the size of the population, and if Blacks are more likely than Whites to live in urban areas, then that factor will account for some of the disproportional representation. In the last report of the National Crime Survey, for instance, the rate of victimization for those in urban areas was 22.2 compared to 18.3 in rural areas for violent crime and 148.8 compared to 103.2 in rural areas for property crime.[12] Thus, it would be more accurate to look at only urban or only suburban Whites' and Blacks' participation in crime in order to control for the variable of urbanity.

Other likely factors to control for include single head-of-household, socio-economic class, and high school graduation rate. These factors have been shown to correlate with criminal offending and also show different patterns by race. The fact that crime is largely intra-racial (Whites offend against Whites and Blacks offend against other Blacks) supports the idea that most crime occurs within neighborhoods. Arguably, the reason that Blacks engage in a disproportional amount of violent crime is because they are more likely to live in neighborhoods where such crimes are likely to occur. This is called the **racial invariance hypothesis** that proposes that crime is stable in a neighborhood regardless of what race/ethnicity predominates.[13]

To compare offending between Whites and Blacks who live in exactly the same circumstances is exceedingly difficult because the fact is, in this country, Blacks are much more likely than Whites to live in distressed, extremely poor disorganized neighborhoods. Peterson and Krivo[14] constructed a data set for 148 predominantly Black and White census tracts in Columbus, Ohio. In Exhibit 3.12 below, their data is presented showing the absence of very highly disadvantaged White neighborhoods and the absence of Black neighborhoods of very low disadvantage.

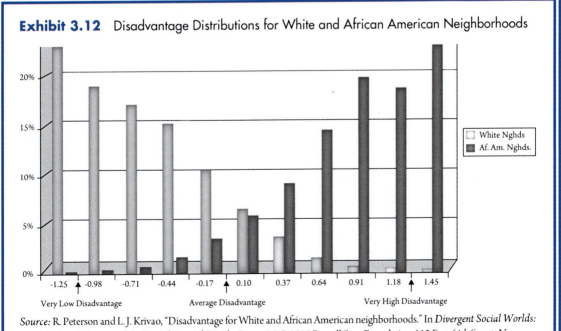

Exhibit 3.12 Disadvantage Distributions for White and African American Neighborhoods

Source: R. Peterson and L. J. Krivao, "Disadvantage for White and African American neighborhoods." In *Divergent Social Worlds: Neighborhood Crime and the Racial-Spatial Divide,* Figure 3.5 © 2010 Russell Sage Foundation, 112 East 64th Street, New York, NY 10065. Reprinted with permission.

These researchers also looked at crime rates within these communities and, not surprisingly, found that crime was higher in disadvantaged neighborhoods. More importantly, the disparity between rates of violent crime between Blacks and Whites was greatly reduced when the type of neighborhood was controlled for, although not entirely eliminated.

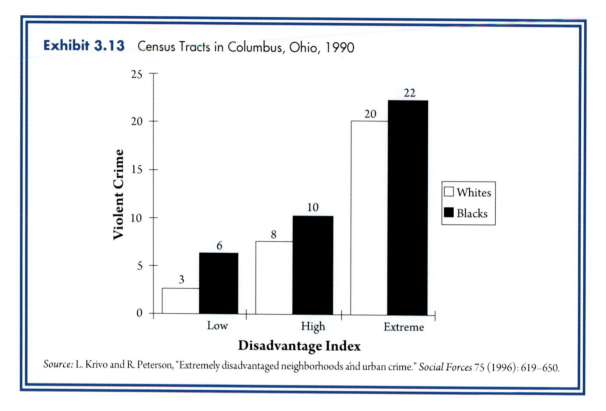

Exhibit 3.13 Census Tracts in Columbus, Ohio, 1990

Source: L. Krivo and R. Peterson, "Extremely disadvantaged neighborhoods and urban crime." *Social Forces* 75 (1996): 619–650.

What the data suggest is that, to a great extent, the disproportional violent crime rates of Blacks can be explained by the type of neighborhood Blacks are likely to live in. Whites who live in similar neighborhoods are almost equally likely to engage in violent crime. The importance of neighborhoods on individuals' decisions to commit crime was one of the earliest identified theories of crime, as we will see later in this chapter. The issue of race and crime clearly shows how important it is to be careful in interpreting crime statistics and explore various hypotheses for why crime patterns occur as they do.

WHAT ARE THE MAJOR CRIMINOLOGICAL THEORIES OF CRIME?

The earliest criminogical theories are usually described as the **classical school** and marked by the contributions of Cesare Beccaria (1738–94) and Jeremy

Bentham (1748–1832).[15] Both theorists, writing in the 1700s, operated under a fundamental assumption that men were rational and operated with free will. Therefore, the elimination of crime could be achieved by the threat of punishment for offenses, which would act as a deterrent to crime. Bentham's "**hedonistic calculus**," for instance, was the idea of carefully weighing punishment to slightly outweigh the potential pleasure or profit that might be obtained, in order to deter. Philosophers during this period did not view women in the same manner as men and viewed their mental abilities to be more akin to children; therefore, their discussions applied specifically to men. The focus of these thinkers was on the legal system; the assumption was that everyone would respond to the legal system in a similar, rational manner.

The field of criminology is generally said to have begun with the "Positivists" in the 1800s. **Positivism** can be described simply as "scientific method" or the search for causes using scientific method. It is typically associated with Cesare Lombroso (1835–1909),[16] who is often referred to as the "grandfather of criminology." Lombroso believed the cause of crime lies in the individual. He developed a typology of criminals, including those he believed were "born criminal" with genetic defects that made them commit criminal acts. Other types included criminals influenced by opportunity, influence, and passion. Later positivists in the early 1900s also looked at individual causes, and both biological and psychological factors were examined. According to positivists, criminals were different from non-criminals and criminologists merely needed to understand those differences. We can say that the field of criminology really began with the positivists because they initiated the search for differences between criminal men and women and law-abiding men and women. Their findings do not hold up over the passage of time and their scientific method was primitive, but their approach is still the basic approach of most criminologists today—that is, to seek out differences that motivate some people to choose crime. Although we will not cover any theories in depth, the sections below briefly introduce you to three different categories of theories in criminology: biological, psychological, and sociological theories.

WHAT DO BIOLOGICAL THEORIES OF CRIME SAY ABOUT WHO COMMITS CRIME AND WHY?

Recall that the three strongest predictors of crime—sex, age, and race—are biological constructs. Of the three, only race shows strongly different patterns cross-culturally. Also, race is mediated by inter-racial mixing so that most people do not represent pure racial **phenotypes**. Further, biologists themselves argue about whether it makes sense to discuss race as a biological construct at all since the genetic difference between the races is minuscule. However, the other two correlates are age and sex and these do show strong cross-cultural patterns. Thus, it would seem that biology should be at least explored as a factor in crime causation. However, research on biological factors has been given little attention in most criminology textbooks. Part of the reason biological approaches in criminology have been so completely rejected is that there are serious policy implications for such theories. It is argued that such theories lead to **eugenics**, which is the idea of improving the human race through controlled procreation, and other forms of control repugnant to our democratic ideals.

Biological factors may be a) inherited genetic traits, or b) biological factors that are not genetic. For instance, a brain tumor that puts pressure on an area of the brain that is instrumental in aggressive impulses and results in irrational violence is obviously a biological cause of crime, but tumors are not thought to be inherited. Chemicals or other environmental toxins, such as lead, can also affect the brain and are non-genetic biological factors that may influence criminal choice. Some researchers are convinced that the reduction in lead-based paint has contributed to some extent to the dramatic decline of violent criminality. There is no question that lead is tremendously detrimental to brain development affecting the pre-frontal lobe and impulse control; and, the percentage of lead in children's blood was alarmingly high as late as the 1970s because of lead-based paints and lead in gasoline. In the United States, blood lead levels in children dropped by 79 percent between 1976 and 1991, the period over which leaded fuel was phased out. The same data showed that blood lead levels, although lower, remained higher among minorities and those with lower socio-economic status.[17] Some research shows a correlation between levels of lead and rates of violent crime, arguing that the greatest spike in crime (early 1990s) corresponded to when cohorts exposed to lead entered their crime-prone age years and, subsequently, the decline of crime occurred when childhood cohorts not exposed to as high levels of lead as past generations grew into the crime-prone age years.[18]

Other researchers have shown that the rise and fall of violent crime was not limited to birth cohorts who were exposed to lead but, rather, all birth cohorts increased their criminality in the 1990s and decreased crime rates could be seen consistently across all birth cohorts in the 2000s.[19] This area of research has become extremely important after it was revealed in the fall and winter of 2015–16 that lead levels in the city water supply in Flint, Michigan, vastly exceeded safe levels because the city did not add a non-corrosive

Exhibit 3.14   Leaded gasoline was widely used until the 1970s. As it was phased out, blood lead levels in children dropped dramatically. Some research shows a correlation between lead levels and crime rates.

Source: AP

agent to the water when it switched from Detroit to the Flint River as a water source. Testing of children has found blood lead levels to be in the range that developmental and behavioral effects might result. To the great misfortune of its residents, Flint may become a natural laboratory in the study of lead and its effects.

More controversial than toxic agents or tumors is the idea that criminality is inherited. Is there a criminal gene? Of course not, but the argument of biological criminologists is that there are some inherited characteristics that predispose individuals to criminal choices.[20] The methodological problem has always been trying to isolate genetic influences from socialization influences. If you are like your mother or father, is it because you have inherited traits from them or because they raised you (nature versus nurture)? Trying to separate these influences is very difficult, even with the use of twin studies which have looked at the **concordance** between the criminality of children and their adoptive parents and biological parents.[21] Statistical and methodological criticisms of twin studies continue to call into question their findings.[22] Opposing arguments strongly refute the methodological criticisms leveled against twin studies, but the two opposing camps agree more than they disagree since both sides accept the importance of both genetics and environment on observable behaviors, including criminal behavior.[23]

Some criminologists estimate that genetics can explain about half of criminality.[24] When a personality trait is believed to be inherited, scientists look for the actual physical components of the trait. These origins lie in the neural structures of the brain, brain chemistry, and hormones. For instance, although such research has been subject to criticism, a fairly impressive body of knowledge has developed on the correlation between testosterone and aggression.[25] If it exists, this biological reality could help to explain the gender differential in violent crime.

Brain chemicals affect personality traits. Monoamine oxidase (MAO) is a chemical found in the brain and low levels have been linked to psychopathy, alcoholism, sensation-seeking, impulsivity, extroversion, schizophrenia, and criminal behavior.[26] Men, on average, have about 20 percent less MAO than women, and this difference exists at all ages. Boys with low MAO levels were found to be more impulsive and sensation-seeking than other boys and were more likely to have drug and alcohol problems.[27] Associations are consistently found between low MAO activity and various correlates of criminal behavior, such as impulsiveness, childhood hyperactivity, learning disabilities, sensation-seeking, substance abuse, and extraversion. MAO activity seems to be correlated with age, sex, and race. Testosterone evidently depresses MAO levels. In fact, testosterone levels are at their highest and MAO levels are at their lowest during the second decade of life (ten to twenty years of age).[28] Thus, these findings provide intriguing possibilities that MAO is perhaps part of the explanation for age and sex differences in crime.

Other research shows interesting connections between serotonin levels and negative emotionality and impulsivity.[29] Serotonin also seems to be linked with norepinephrine levels and, together, they may play a role in conditionability or the ability to learn.[30] Some individuals might be predisposed toward antisocial behaviors because these behaviors are exciting and produce the level of cortical arousal that extraverts seek.[31]

Sex differences exist in cortical arousal levels, and men, in general, are more likely to have low cortical arousal.[32] Hyperactivity and attention deficit disorder (ADD) are more common in boys than girls.[33] These learning issues are also correlated with delinquency. It has been reported that those diagnosed with hyperactivity as children were 25 times more likely to exhibit later delinquency.[34]

Denno[35] reports that chronic delinquency is linked to overactivity, perceptual-motor impairments, impulsivity, emotional lability, attention deficits, minor disturbances of speech, intellectual defects (learning disabilities), clumsiness, neurodevelopmental lag, psychogenic factors, and minor physical anomalies. These features may be the result of genetic transmission, poor living environment, prenatal or birth trauma, or a combination of the above. It is also important to note that critics argue that observed differences in brain chemicals may be due to environmental conditions that also affect the potential for criminality. For instance, studies have found that exposure to abusive, unpredictable, or harsh childhood conditions is associated with changes in the **amygdala** and **prefrontal cortex**, both instrumental in emotional regulation. Severe adversity affects the oxytocin receptor gene which is associated with empathy/callousness so it is possible that the brain molds itself to adapt to the environment.[36] Other researchers have begun to identify how environmental conditions such as violence, emotional abuse, discrimination, and poverty can result in long-term stress creating elevated levels of cortisol that eventually changes brain chemistry, which, in turn, affects the potential to react with aggression to perceived threat.[37] What percent of behavior is "nature" (inherited) versus "nurture" (influenced by the environment) is impossible to determine because the brain itself changes in reaction to the environment.

To summarize: there are sex differences in the relative levels of brain chemicals and hormones associated with delinquency. Furthermore, these chemicals and hormones fluctuate over the life course, and help to explain why younger people are more impulsive and thrill-seeking than older individuals. Biological predispositions don't always result in delinquency and the relationship between these factors is much more complex than what has been sketched here. Critics argue that biological factors can't explain the crime decline of the last two decades because biological factors would be presumed to be fairly stable (the same percentage of the population experience low MAO levels or low cortical arousal). However, we could hypothesize that because situational factors interact with biological factors, something might have changed which affected the relationship between biological factors and criminal behavior. For example, advances in education, earlier intervention in environmental stressors, or other changes, may have taken place and affected particular birth cohorts who did not then grow up to engage in criminality as frequently as prior cohorts. Arrest patterns, however, do not lend strong support to this hypothesis since arrest rates declined across all age groups.

Many criminologists reject biological explanations of criminal choices. This rejection is somewhat understandable given the sordid history of eugenics; however, it is not consistent with the critical approach we are modeling in this text to reject a school of theories without objectively considering the evidence. The field of **epigenetics** is the study of cellular and physiological phenotypic trait differences that result from external or environmental factors that, in effect, switch genes on and off and affect how cells express genes. Great strides are being made in the fields of medicine and nutrition once people accept that the biology is not destiny. Genetic inheritance can only ever explain some portion of health and behavior.

WHAT DO PSYCHOLOGICAL THEORIES OF CRIME SAY ABOUT WHO COMMITS CRIME AND WHY?

Criminologists have largely ignored psychological theories of deviance and crime.[38] This is largely because criminology has emerged as a discipline from the field of sociology, not psychology. To say that psychology is ignored in criminology textbooks is perhaps a misstatement because many of the major theories of criminology could be described as socio-psychological in that they focus on how the individual reacts to his or her environment.

The most obvious contribution of psychological theory to an understanding of criminality is the concept of **sociopathy** or **psychopathy**. The psychopath has been differentiated from the sociopath in the following way: "[the psychopath is] an individual in whom the normal processes of socialization have failed to produce the mechanisms of conscience and habits of law-abidingness that normally constrain antisocial impulses" and the sociopath as "a person whose unsocialized character is due primarily to parental failures rather than to inherent peculiarities of temperament."[39] The *Diagnostic and Statistical Manual* (**DSM-IV**), a type of dictionary for mental health workers to diagnose and categorize all mental health problems, has replaced the terms "psychopathy" and "sociopathy" with the term "**antisocial personality disorder**." Regardless, these definitions describe an individual who is without a conscience and unable to form sincere, affectionate bonds with others. This describes many, but not all, of those who engage in criminal behavior.

Psychological explanations for behavior generally identify agreed-upon personality trait models (i.e., neuroticism, extroversion, openness to experience, agreeableness, conscientiousness), and then identify certain traits as associated with criminal propensity.[40] The traits of sensation-seeking, overactivity, low self-control, emotionality, and callousness, as well as "negative emotionality," which includes aggression, alienation, and anger/irritability as a stress reaction, are associated with persistent criminality.[41] While researchers note that the traits seem to equally predict male and female offending, it is also true that there are fewer female offenders; therefore, there are either fewer young women who possess the predisposing traits, at least to the degree that young men do, or alternatively, there are environmental mediators that operate differently between the sexes so that young men and women with similar personality traits experience life differently and, therefore, take different behavioral paths.

Psychology focuses on the individual and, thus, psychological theories of criminality focus on developmental reasons for criminal choices. A variety of developmental theories propose that delinquent and criminal offenders are "stuck" at lower levels of development and have not reached emotional maturity which includes developing empathy (e.g. caring about others). Delinquents and criminals are immature, either in their response to the world, their interactions with others around them, and/or in their putting self above others.[42]

Learning theory proposes that individuals act and believe the way they do because they have learned to do so. Learning takes place through modeling or reinforcement. **Modeling** stems from the desire to be like others, especially those whom one admires; therefore, children will act as they see their parents or peers act. The other form of learning is through **reinforcement**. That is, one will continue behaviors and beliefs for which one has been rewarded, and eliminate behaviors and beliefs that have been punished or not rewarded. Albert Bandura,[43] for instance, argues that individuals are not necessarily inherently aggressive, but rather learn aggression. He and others also point out that learning is mediated by intelligence and temperament. Personality traits such as impulsivity, aggressiveness, and emotionality affect one's ability to absorb learning.

One of the most enduring explanations of why women commit less crime, by both laypeople and criminologists, is the idea that they learn to be law-abiding and that the social sanctions against deviance for women and girls are much stronger than those boys or men would experience. If true, learning theory is perfectly consistent with the lower crime rates observed for women.

Psychological theories identify individual factors as affecting criminal choice. More sophisticated theories also refer to environmental factors. So, for instance, Andrews and Bonta[44] developed a psychological theory of crime that includes the characteristics of the immediate environment and individual characteristics to explain crime choices. They point to the attitudes, values, beliefs, and rationalizations held by the person with regard to antisocial behavior, social support for antisocial behavior (perceived support from others), a history of having engaged in antisocial behavior, self-management and problem-solving skills, and other stable personality characteristics conducive to antisocial conduct. Then, they relate these to a behavioral explanation of criminality where rewards and costs of crime are mediated by these individual differences. By including environmental factors (e.g. social support) this type of psychological theory overlaps with sociological theories that focus on the environment and situational factors that lead to criminal choices.

Some of the theories above may at least partially help us understand the gender differential in crime and even perhaps the fact that crime is committed disproportionally by the young. No psychological theory of crime by itself would help to explain the crime decline unless psychological factors interacted with environmental changes. Any hypothesis that utilized psychological factors in explanations of crime would first have to establish whether or not there had been changes in the relative levels of such factors in the population; we presume that biological and psychological factors in a population do not change over time, thus any perceived change (such as the decline of crime) would have to be explained by an interaction between the factor and some environmental (societal) change.

WHAT DO SOCIOLOGICAL THEORIES OF CRIME SAY ABOUT WHO COMMITS CRIME AND WHY?

Adolphe Quetelet (1796–1874) and Émile Durkheim (1858–1917) are credited as early sociologists who established the foundations of sociological criminology. Quetelet discovered that crime occurred in reasonably predictable patterns in society, thus supporting the notion that there was something about society that caused crime rather than crime occurring at random or because of individual causes. Émile Durkheim offered the principle that crime was normal and present in all societies. The absence of deviance or crime, in fact, was evidence of cultural stagnation.

Recall the difference between macro and micro theories of crime. Macro theories look at societal factors that affect the amount of crime. We could also call these social structure theories. Micro theories look at how individuals react to their environment by making criminal choices. We could call these social process theories (and they are very similar to some of the psychological theories described earlier). Both approaches reject the idea of the "criminal as different." In these theories, it is assumed that anyone who happens to be exposed to these factors would become criminal.

The so-called **Chicago school** in the 1930s and 1940s truly began the study of societal influences on criminality when sociologists at the University of Chicago observed that crime occurred more often in **mixed zones** of the city. In these zones, residential, commercial, and industrial activity could be observed. The zones were also characterized by low home ownership, property damage, graffiti, and high rates of alcoholism, domestic violence, and mental health problems. Early sociologists discovered that these mixed zones always had higher crime rates, even though different demographic groups moved in and out of them over the decades. Thus, it seemed that there was something about the zone, rather than the people who lived within it, that generated crime.[45]

Observers from the Chicago school noted that **subcultures** emerged in the mixed zone, and these subcultures promoted values and beliefs that were different from the dominant culture and encouraged criminal behavior (such as prostitution, gambling, and other forms of deviance). **Subculture theory** and **cultural deviance theory**, first developed in the 1950s, observed that there are some groups in society who teach antisocial behaviors (instead of socializing its members to follow the norms of the dominant culture). According to this theory, if one lives in these areas of the city, then one will most likely become delinquent because the subculture defines such behavior as acceptable.[46] Cultural deviance theory identifies cultures that clash when individuals migrate to a new culture. Subcultural theories look at subcultures that exist within the dominant culture but have different values and belief systems. Gangs are an example of a subculture, although this stretches the classic definition of a subculture, because members of any gang also participate and are socialized, to some extent, by the dominant culture as well. Women were largely ignored in early subcultural theories even though they obviously lived in the mixed zones alongside the boys and men who were being socialized to criminality.

Another factor observed in the mixed zones was lack of opportunity. The individuals who lived in these neighborhoods had very little hope of economic success. **Strain/opportunity theory**, popularized in the 1960s, argued that lack of opportunity is the cause of crime. Individuals who are blocked from legitimate means of economic success, such as employment, family, or education, will experience strain because of blocked goals and then choose crime as a way to achieve goals according to this theory.[47] A later application of the theory enlarged it to groups, so that those who were blocked from opportunities would form groups (gangs) distinct from those who had legitimate opportunities.[48] Because everyone is socialized to believe that they can and should achieve material success, those who do not have the means feel particular stress. In static cultures, that is, where the poor have no expectations or hope that they will achieve wealth, there is less pressure or inclination to use illegitimate means to get ahead. However, a line of research going back decades has not produced a definitive link between socio-economics and crime on the macro level, and unemployment doesn't have a strong correlation with crime at the micro level.[49] One caution, however, is that much of this research involves examining the effects of employment that involves transitory and low-paying jobs. It is possible that the jobs offenders might be able to obtain are not sufficiently motivating to counteract the lure of criminal opportunities.

More recently, the ideas of the Chicago school have been revived with **social support theory** and **social disorganization theory**. Basically, both point to the community as a prime factor in crime causation, either because of the lack of supportive elements in a neighborhood, or, alternatively the lack of cohesion and elements of "community" of some neighborhoods.[50] These researchers believe that the community is the primary element in social control and can be undercut by oppressive formal control, such as law enforcement.[51]

Social process theories focus on the individual's interaction with the world around him or her and have more in common in this respect with psychological theories. **Differential association theory**, introduced originally by Edwin Sutherland in 1939, is very similar to learning theory.[52] Later, others applied social learning principles to the theory to make it even more similar to learning theory.[53] Researchers have utilized these theories to explain why girls and women are less likely to commit crime—in short, it is because they are socialized to be "nicer" than boys.[54] The increasing participation of women in some crime areas is explained by many as due to changing roles and expectations for women.

Labeling theory assumes that even though almost all of us have engaged in "primary deviance," only certain individuals are labeled as deviant. This results in their accepting and absorbing the deviant role and committing further delinquency because of the label.[55] In constrast, **control theory**, as presented by Travis Hirschi in 1969,[56] presumed that most of us would drift to delinquency, but we don't because of the "bonds" of society that control us—specifically attachment, commitment, involvement, and belief. Delinquency was correlated with the absence of these types of ties. Control theory provides a relatively adequate explanation for the sex differential in crime rates if we can assume that girls have more attachments and other bonds than boys. It is generally found that girls profess stronger ties to friends, family, and school, and they tend to possess more prosocial belief systems than boys. The theory is also consistent with the age correlate because one can assume that "bonds" to society increase as a young man matures and obtains a job, wife, and family. It does not necessarily explain the country's crime decline unless one could identify major changes in schools and other social institutions that created greater attachments that, in turn, led to a decrease in delinquency and subsequent criminality of youth.

While control theory postulates that various bonds to society (attachment, commitment, belief, and involvement) control the individual and prevent delinquency, Hirschi and Gottfredson's[57] **general theory of crime** proposes that individuals are born with and/or are raised to have different levels of self-control and those with low self-control are more likely to commit crime and a host of other dangerous and impulsive behaviors (such as smoking, drinking, using drugs, gambling, having illegitimate children, and engaging in illicit sex). The major cause of a lack of self-control, according to these authors, is ineffective parenting. They argue that the conditions necessary to teach self-control include monitoring behavior, recognizing deviant behavior, and punishing such behavior.[58] Criticisms of the theory argue that self-control does change over the life course and it does respond to different parenting techniques and can be strengthened.[59] A major weakness of the theory is that it does not adequately explain the sex differential in crime unless one was to assume that women generally have more self-control than men.[60] Some research shows, in fact, that moral norms may be more predictive of delinquency/criminality than low self-control.[61]

Agnew's **general strain theory**[62] reformulates strain/opportunity theory, which focused on the level of legitimate opportunities in a neighborhood, into a social process theory that examines how individuals deal with various types of strain, including a lack of opportunity. According to this theory, individuals may experience strain from not getting what they want, losing something that was important, or in other ways being in a situation that is experienced as noxious. The strain generates negative emotions, such as disappointment, fear, depression, and anger, and these negative emotions cause delinquency/crime. Individuals commit delinquent acts in order to relieve the strain of the negative emotions. As the theory was refined over the years, theorists also recognized that different people have different coping abilities and react differently to the strains they experience.

An entirely different direction to explaining crime is offered by Tom Tyler. Hirschi's earlier social control or bond theory in the 1960s asked the question, "Why do people obey the law?" and answered they do so because of their bonds to society like school, attachment to parents, and a belief in their future. Tyler also asks the question, "Why do people obey the law?" but his answer is that they do so when they believe in the legitimacy of the law and the legal institutions of society. Tyler also maintains that individuals are more likely to conform their behavior to the law when they believe in its legitimacy (i.e., people who disobey marijuana laws do so because they believe marijuana should be legal) or they distrust and reject the legal institutions of society.

There is evidence to indicate, for instance, that those who have more distrust of the police are more likely to commit crime. Tyler also notes that legitimacy is tied to **procedural justice**; when people believe that the justice system is fair and just, there is more adherence to the law itself.[63]

WHAT ARE SOME OTHER THEORIES OF CRIME?

The premises of the classical school have been revived with **rational choice theory** and **deterrence theories**.[64] Modern deterrence theory is more complicated, however, than the simplistic approach of the classical school and recognizes the influence of individual factors that mediate how deterrent messages are received, such as low self-control or impulsivity, personal experience, belief systems, and perceptions of punishment.[65] **Routine activities theory** ignores criminal motivation, assuming that a motivated offender exists all the time.[66] According to routine activity theorists, for a crime to happen there must be a motivated offender, suitable targets of criminal victimization, and the absence of guardians of persons or property. Any changes in routine activities lead to changing opportunities for crime. **Environmental criminology** is an area of criminology that explores the factors involved in where crime occurs, but does not focus much on the offender. Theories in environmental criminology test physical and spatial factors in how they encourage or discourage crime (e.g., lighting, door and window placement, presence of "shared space," and so on). The important thing to note about routine activity theory and environmental criminology is that there is little focus on the offender or offender's motivation to choose criminality, although generally these approaches are consistent with deterrence theory.

Integrated theories combine elements of psychological theories and sociological theories, and even accept some elements of biological criminology in a more complicated and comprehensive approach to explaining criminal choices. The methodology typically associated with integrated theories is the cohort study, also called **longitudinal research** because it involves following a sample of individuals for a long period, beginning in childhood and extending into adulthood, looking for factors that correlate with delinquency and adult criminality. For instance, Farrington et al.[67] identified the following as correlates of delinquency and crime:

> We know that the typical high-rate offender is a young male who began his aggressive or larcenous activities at an early age, well before the typical boy gets into serious trouble. We know that he comes from a troubled, discordant, low-income family in which one or both parents

are likely to have criminal records themselves. We know that the boy has had trouble in school—he created problems for his teachers and does not do well in his studies. On leaving school, often by dropping out, he works at regular jobs only intermittently. Most employers regard him as a poor risk. He experiments with a variety of drugs—alcohol, marijuana, speed, heroin—and becomes a frequent user of whatever drug is most readily available, often switching back and forth among different ones.

Thus, individual differences, family influences, school influences, and peer influences were all identified as potential predictors of the onset of, continuation in, and desistance from crime.

Another finding of the longitudinal research studies is that there seem to be two separate groups of delinquents/criminals. The first group begins committing delinquent acts very early and these individuals are chronic and serious criminal offenders; however, the second "late onset" group drifts into delinquency during their teenage years and matures out fairly quickly. Their delinquency seems to be episodic and peer-influenced. The following traits or characteristics seem to be correlated with the group who begin delinquency very early: low intelligence; high impulsiveness; child abuse victimization; harsh and erratic parental discipline; cold and rejecting parents; poor parental supervision; parental disharmony, separation, and divorce; one-parent female-headed households; convicted parents or siblings; alcoholic or drug-using parents or siblings; non-White race membership, low occupational prestige of parents; low educational level of parents; low family income; large family size; poor housing; low educational attainment of the child; attendance at a high delinquency school; delinquent friends; and high-crime area of residence.[68]

Denno utilized biological and sociological factors in an integrated explanation of criminality and delinquency.[69] She identified predisposing factors (that increase the likelihood of criminality), facilitating variables (that, in combination with predisposing factors, increase the likelihood of delinquency), and inhibiting variables (that counteract predisposing factors and decrease the probability of delinquency). At birth, individuals are already affected by such factors as culture, gender, prenatal maternal conditions, pregnancy and delivery complications, socio-economic status, and family stability. By age seven, other factors, such as cerebral dominance, intelligence, and physical and health development, have influenced their predisposition to delinquency; during the pre-teen and teen years, school behavior, achievement, and learning disabilities are affected by intelligence and influence, in turn, the likelihood of delinquency and, eventually, adult crime.

Robert Sampson and John Laub also present an integrated theory of delinquency, suggesting:

- A set of predisposing factors:
  - low family socio-economic status, family size, family disruption, residential mobility, parent's deviance, household crowding, foreign-born, mother's employment;
- Individual characteristics:
  - difficult temperament, persistent tantrums, early conduct disorder;
- And interactions with social control processes as the child develops:
  - family, lack of supervision, erratic/harsh discipline, parental rejection, school, weak attachment, poor academic performance, delinquent influences, sibling delinquent attachment, and peer attachment that leads to delinquency and incarceration.

These factors, in turn, lead to fewer social bonds, weak labor force attachment, and weak marital attachment that influences the continuation of crime and deviance.[70] The other idea proposed by these researchers is that "turning points" in life lead to desistance or continued criminality; for instance, a job or stable marriage might shift a person to law-abiding behavior. Contrarily, the loss of a job or marriage might kick them back into drug use, alcohol use and/or criminal choices. Others argue the causal direction and suggest that there is a cognitive shift in the offender first before a stable job or successful marriage can occur.[71]

Integrated studies are comprehensive in that they include precursors and facilitators of delinquency. In fact, most of the elements identified by all previous theories are incorporated into these integrated theories. While some may say that is the strength of these theories, others argue that it is a weakness because it makes the theory more complicated, and by using every explanation, in effect, there is no explanation that easily explains crime choice. On the other hand, it is probably unrealistic to assume that there is a simple answer to criminal behavior—or any human behavior, for that matter.

One other category of theories basically challenges all theories discussed thus far in that they challenge the very legitimacy of the definition of criminal. Radical, Marxist or **critical criminology** can be distinguished, but, in general, they contest the assumption of criminal as it is defined by official sources of crime. These theories propose that the powerholders of society define criminality and, thus, our official definitions of criminality do not include the activities of the powerful. The argument would be that the typical criminal is minority and poor only because of official definitions of what is defined as criminal. The victim-harming activities of the powerful (e.g., toxic waste dumping, price gouging on life-saving pharmaceuticals, defective products that pose lethal risks to consumers) are never described as crimes. These theories do remind us that, generally, criminology tends to ignore white-collar crimes; however, it is not true that such activities are ignored completely, or are not defined as crimes. It is important to note and ponder whether a trader on Wall Street who sells junk bonds he or she knows to be extremely high risk or even worthless is, in any way, different from someone who shoplifts or engages in credit card fraud since both are willing to profit from victimizing others. Our arrest figures very well may skew our understanding of criminality in that those who have criminal tendencies and are poor will pursue the opportunities open to them (shoplifting, credit card theft, robbery), while those with more opportunities may pursue other criminal activities (embezzlement, fraud, real estate swindles, insider trading and other SEC crimes). These crimes are less likely to be discovered, more likely to be regulatory or punished by fines, and, perhaps, less likely to find their way into our crime statistics. In this sense the only difference between a robber and a real estate swindler or Ponzi schemer (e.g., Bernie Madoff) is the criminal choices open to him or her.

Exhibit 3.15 Criminology tends to ignore white-collar criminals, like Bernard Madoff, whose Ponzi scheme cost his investors an estimated $18 billion.

Source: AP

Courses in criminology cover a multitude of theories that have been created and tested to attempt to answer the question, "Why do people commit crime?" This chapter barely skims the surface of this material, but it provides some general descriptions of the types of theories that have been developed. Any good theory should be able to explain the sex and age differential, as well as why minorities are over-represented in street and violent crimes. Generally, the field of criminology has de-emphasized biological and psychological factors of crime causation and focused solely on sociological causes of crime. More recent theories, such as the general theory of crime and general strain theory, bring the focus back to the individual and, thus, one can argue that the pendulum of scientific/criminological thought has swung from the legal system (classical) to the individual (positivist), to the society and neighborhood (Chicago school), and back to the individual (general strain theory and integrated theories).

New theories continue to be proposed. One new theory proposed by Simons and Burt called **social schematic theory** (SST), proposes that individuals who live in social environments characterized by victimization, poverty, lack of opportunity, and conflict with authority develop a "criminogenic knowledge structure (CKS) that encourages criminality." The specific components of this CKS are: a) hostile views of relationships; b) immediate gratification/discounting the future; and c) disengagement from conventional norms. Expansion of the theory adds that CKS affects routine activities and placing oneself in situations where criminal opportunities are likely to emerge is consistent with CKS.[72] Similar to learning theory and differential organization, this theory proposes that individuals absorb messages from their environment that develop their worldview. It is similar to social disorganization theory in identifying the environment as causal in the development of criminal choice. It is also not inconsistent with some biological theories that propose chronic stress through childhood can affect brain development and the body's reaction to external threats. The CKS of individuals is resistant and helps to explain recidivism presumably. It does not, however, explain white-collar crimes or crimes committed by individuals who are not exposed to criminogenic environments and it presumes that "street crimes" are a true representation of all crimes, a presumption with which critical criminologists would argue.

In Exhibit 3.16, there are very brief descriptions of the theories discussed in this chapter.

Exhibit 3.16   Theories of Crime

Biological Theories

Nongenetic: idiopathic tumors, brain injuries, toxins

Genetic: testosterone, brain chemicals, neural conditionability, other inherited personality traits, such as impulsiveness

Psychological Theories

Personality trait: traits are either conducive to or not conducive to criminal choices

Developmental: individual does not progress to mature social-interpersonal levels

Learning: individual is rewarded for criminal behavior

Sociological Theories

Chicago School: individual lives in the mixed zone of a city where crime occurs

Cultural Deviance: individual is socialized to deviant norms

Strain: individual is blocked from achieving societal goals so resorts to illegitimate means

Social Support: individual lives in area with low social support

Social Disorganization: individual lives in area with indices of social disorganization

Social Process Theories

Differential Association: individual learns to be criminal

Labeling: individual is labeled a deviant and so lives up to the label

Rational Choice (Deterrence): individual weighs options and chooses crime

Routine Activities: crime occurs when there is motivated offender and opportunity

Control (Bonds): individual has few bonds to society

General Theory of Crime: individual has low self-control

General Strain Theory: individual suffers strain, which leads to crime

Procedural Justice: individual is more apt to obey the law when they believe in it

Integrated Theories: different aspects of the theories above explain crime at different periods in the life course

Radical, Critical or Marxist Theories: the power holders in society define crimes which are the actions of the powerless

Source: Author

SUMMARY

What Are the Explanations for the Decline of Crime?

Researchers have studied all of the following as potential factors in the decline of crime: aging birth cohort of baby boomers, stabilization of drug markets, higher incarceration rates, community policing, "zero tolerance" policing, home health care and pre- and post-natal health services, violence prevention programs in schools, reduction of exposure to lead-based paint, and increased numbers of abortions in the late 1970s and 1980s. Although research is continuing, the factors that may be most influential include decreased alcohol consumption, increased use of incarceration, and increased numbers of police.

What Are Some Methodological Issues in the Question: Why Do People Commit Crime?

It is important to distinguish between macro- and micro-level factors when understanding crime. Macro-level theories explain why crime goes up or down in particular time periods or in certain socities (or parts of society). The field of criminology generally is a study of micro factors, or those factors that influence why one individual over another makes criminal choices. In constructing and testing crime theories, it should be remembered that crime and deviance are not synonomous and not all crimes are deviant. Victim-harming crimes may have different motivations and correlational factors than victimless crimes.

Who Commits Crime?

Official reports indicate that 73.3 percent of all persons arrested in the nation in 2014 were men. They accounted for 79.8 percent of persons arrested for violent crime and 61.8 percent of persons arrested for property crime. Further, young people 18–30 account for a disproportional amount of crime. Also, although Blacks represent only about 13–14 percent of the population, their rate of arrest for most crimes, especially violent crimes, exceeds this percentage.

What Are the Major Criminological Theories of Crime?

Criminology is the study of crime and criminal motivation. The classical school and the positivist school form the history of criminology and current theories can be categorized, for the most part, into biological, psychological and sociological theories.

What Do Biological Theories of Crime Say About Who Commits Crime and Why?

Biological theories identify biological factors that may affect criminal choices—either genetic or not. Genetic influences have been identified in neurobiology that affect such things as serotonin, oxytocin, and MAO levels which, in turn, have implications for behavior. There is no criminal gene, but there may be genetic influences that predispose individuals to aggression or a lack of control.

What Do Psychological Theories of Crime Say About Who Commits Crime and Why?

Psychological theories explain crime by looking at personality traits that influence criminal choice or developmental difficulties, e.g., the individual has not progressed to a level of emotional maturity marked by empathy that characterizes normal adult development. Another psychological theory is learning theory and proposes that criminals choose crime because of modeling or rewards.

What Do Sociological Theories of Crime Say About Who Commits Crime and Why?

The beginning of criminology in this country occurred with the Chicago school of the 1930s. Sociological theories identify elements of society (social structure theories) or the interaction of the individual with his or her environment (social process theories) as the reason that people commit crimes.

What Are Some Other Theories of Crime?

Modern deterrence theories and environmental criminology are theoretically consistent with the classical school. Integrated studies are comprehensive in that they include most of the elements identified by all previous theories. Radical, Marxist or critical criminology contest the assumption of criminal as it is defined by official sources of crime. These theories propose that the powerholders of society define criminality and, thus, our official definitions of criminality do not include the activities of the powerful.

Critical Thinking Exercises

1. Find a news story that describes a crime and criminal in detail. What theory of crime best fits the facts of the case? What theories don't fit the facts? What would you want to know (whether or not that information was available in the news reports) in order to see which theory of crime was best able to explain the crime?
2. Ask ten people why they think some people commit crime. Categorize the answers into biological, psychological, and sociological explanations. Did you discover any explanation that does not fit into one of the theories discussed in this chapter? How would you test the theory to determine how well it fits with what we know about crime patterns?

NOTES

1 Steven Levitt's economic analysis indicated that the rising use of abortion by poor women after abortion became legal led to a reduced number of unwanted children who were at the highest risk for becoming delinquents and criminals.

2 D. Roeder, L. Eisen and J. Bowling, *What Caused the Crime Decline?* Brennan Center, 2015. Retrieved from https://www.brennancenter.org/publication/what-caused-crime-decline, p. 22.

3 See M. Gottfredson and T. Hirschi, *The General Theory of Crime.* Stanford, CA: Stanford University Press, 1990.

4 See J. Pollock, *Women's Crimes, Criminology and Corrections.* Long Grove, IL: Waveland, 2014.

5 FBI, *Crime in the United States, 2014.*

6 J. Schwartz and B. Rookey, "The narrowing gender gap in arrests: Assessing competing explanations using self report, traffic fatality, and official data on drug driving, 1980–2004." *Criminology* 46 (2008): 637–671.

7 J. Lauritsen, K. Heimer and J. Lynch, "Trends in the gender gap in violent offending: New evidence from the national crime victimization survey." *Criminology* 47 (2009): 361–401, 378. For a different view, see J. Schwartz, D. Steffensmeier, H. Zhong and J. Ackerman, "Trends in the gender gap in violence: Reevaluating ncvs and other evidence." *Criminology* 47 (2009): 401–427.

8 For a review of research, see J. Pollock, *Women's Crimes, Criminology and Corrections.* Long Grove, IL: Waveland, 2014.

9 Retrieved 7/1/2016 from http://quickfacts.census.gov/qfd/states/00000.html.

10 ACLU, *The War on Marijuana in Black and White.* Washington, DC: ACLU Foundation. June, 2013, p. 17, 21.

11 E. Harrell, *Black Victims of Violent Crime.* Washington, DC: Bureau of Justice Statistics, 2005, p. 5.

12 J. Truman and L. Langton, *Criminal Victimization, 2014.* Washington, DC: Bureau of Justice Statistics, 2015, p. 10.

13 J. Laurence, "Community disadvantage and race-specific Rates of violent crime: An investigation into the 'racial invariance' hypothesis in the United Kingdom." *Deviant Behavior* 36 (2014): 974–995.

14 L. Krivo and R. Peterson, "Extremely disadvantaged neighborhoods and urban crime." *Social Forces* 75 (1996): 619–650.

15 J. Bentham, "The rationale of punishment." In R. Beck and J. Orr (Eds.), *Ethical Choices: A Case Study Approach.* New York: Free Press, 1843/1970, pp. 326–340.

16 C. Lombroso and W. Ferrero, *The Criminal Man.* Montclair, NJ: Patterson Smith, 1895/1972; C. Lombroso and W. Ferrero, *The Female Offender.* New York: Philosophical Library, 1894/1958.

17 J. Pirkle, D. Brody, E. Gunter, R. Kramer, D. Paschal, K. Flegal and T. Matte, "The decline in blood lead levels in the United States. The National Health and Nutrition Examination Surveys." *JAMA* 272 (July 27 1994): 284–291.

18 P.B. Stretesky and M.J. Lynch, "The relationship between lead and crime." *Journal of Health and Social Behavior* 45(June 2004): 214–229.

19 P. Cook and J. Laub, "After the epidemic: Recent trends in youth violence in the United States." *Crime and Justice* 29 (2002): 1–37.

20 O. Jones, "Behavioral genetics and crime, in context." *Law and Contemporary Problems* 69 (2006): 81–100.

21 D. Andrews and J. Bonta, *The Psychology of Criminal Conduct,* 4th edn. Newark, NJ: LexisNexis/Matthew Bender, 2006, pp. 128–129.

22 C. Burt and R. Simons, "Pulling back the curtain on heritability studies: Biosocial criminology in the postgenomic era." *Criminology* 52 (2014): 223–262.

23 J. Barnes, J.P. Wright, B. Boutwell, J. Schwartz, E. Connolly, J. Nedelec and K. Beaver, "Demonstrating the validity of twin research in criminology." *Criminology* 52 (2014): 588–626.

24 D. Dick and A. Agrawal, "The genetics of alcohol and other drug dependence." *Alcohol Research and Health* 31 (2008): 111; J. Barnes, J.P. Wright, B. Boutwell, J. Schwartz, E. Connolly, J. Nedelec and K. Beaver, "Demonstrating the validity of twin research in criminology." *Criminology* 52 (2014): 588–626.

25 E. Maccoby and C. Jacklin, *The Psychology of Sex Differences*. Stanford, CA: Stanford University Press, 1994. See also J. Tedeschi and R. Felson, *Violence, Aggression and Coercive Actions*. Washington, DC: American Psychological Association, 1977; S. Mednick and K. Christiansen (Eds.), *Biosocial Bases of Criminal Behavior*. New York, NY: Gardner Press, 1987; S. Mednick, T. Moffitt and S. Stack (Eds.), *The Causes of Crime*, New York, NY: Cambridge University Press, 1991; A. Walsh, *Intellectual Imbalance, Love Deprivation and Violent Delinquency: A Biosocial Perspective*. Springfield, IL: Charles C. Thomas, 1974.

26 H. Eysenck and G. Gudjonsson, *The Causes and Cures of Criminality*. New York, NY: Plenum, 1991, p. 135. See also A. Walsh, *Intellectual Imbalance, Love Deprivation and Violent Delinquency: A Biosocial Perspective*. Springfield, IL: Charles C. Thomas, 1989, p. 140.

27 A. Walsh, *Intellectual Imbalance, Love Deprivation and Violent Delinquency: A Biosocial Perspective*. Springfield, IL: Charles C. Thomas, 1991, p. 127.

28 A. Walsh, *Biosociology: An Emerging Paradigm*. Westport, CT: Praeger, 1995, pp. 50–54. See also L. Ellis, "Monoamine oxidase and criminality: Identifying an apparent biological marker for antisocial behavior." *Journal of Research in Crime and Delinquency* 28 (1991): 227–251.

29 A. Caspi, T. Moffitt, P. Silva, M. Stouthamer-Loeber, R. Krueger and P. Schmutte, "Are some people crime prone? Replications of the personality-crime relationship across countries, genders, races, and methods." *Criminology* 32 (1994): 163–195.

30 A. Raine, *The Psychopathology of Crime: Criminal Behavior as a Clinical Disorder*. San Diego, CA: Academic Press, 1993, p. 93; J. Portnoy, A. Raine, F. Chen, D. Pardini, R. Loeber and J.R. Jennings, "Heart rate and antisocial behavior: The mediating role of impulsive sensation seeking." *Criminology* 52 (2014): 292–311.

31 H. Eysenck and G. Gudjonsson, *The Causes and Cures of Criminality*. New York, NY: Plenum, 1989, p. 55.

32 P. Wood, B. Pfefferbaum and B. Arneklev, "Risk-taking and self-control: Social psychological correlates of delinquency." *Journal of Criminal Justice* 16 (1993): 111–130.

33 D. Denno, *Biology and Violence: From Birth to Adulthood*. New York, NY: Cambridge University Press, 1990, p. 17; T. Moffitt, "The neuropsychology of juvenile delinquency: A critical review." In M. Tonry and N. Morris (Eds.), *Crime and Justice: A Review of Research*, vol. 12. Chicago, IL: University of Chicago Press, 1990, pp. 99–171.

34 H. Sandhu and H. Satterfield, "Childhood diagnostic and neurophysiological predictors of teenage arrest rates." In S. Mednick, T. Moffitt and S. Stack (Eds.), *The Causes of Crime*. New York, NY: Cambridge University Press, 1987, pp. 146–168.

35 D. Denno, *Biology and Violence: From Birth to Adulthood*. New York, NY: Cambridge University Press, 1990, p. 15.

36 C. Burt and R. Simons, "Pulling back the curtain on heritability studies: Biosocial criminology in the postgenomic era." *Criminology* 52, (2014): 223–262.

37 M. Rocque, C. Posick and S. Felix, "The role of the brain in urban violent offending: Integrating biology with structural theories of 'the streets'." *Criminal Justice Studies*, 2015. DOI: 10.1080/1478601X.2014.1000006.

38 D. Andrews and J. Bonta, *The Psychology of Criminal Conduct*, 4th edn. Newark, NJ: LexisNexis/Matthew Bender, 2006.

39 D. Lykken, *The Antisocial Personalities*. Hillsdale, NJ: Lawrence Erlbaum, 1995, pp. 6–7.

40 J. Miller and D. Lyman, "Structural models of personality and their relation to antisocial behavior: A meta-analytic review." *Criminology* 39 (4) (2001): 765–799.

41 T. Moffit, "Males on the life-course-persistent and adolescent-limited antisocial pathways: Follow-up at age 26 years." *Development and Psychopathology* 14 (2002): 179–207.

42 J. Piaget, *The Moral Judgment of a Child*. New York, NY: Free Press, 1965; L. Kohlberg, *The Philosophy of Moral Judgment*. San Francisco, CA: Harper and Row, 1981.

43 A. Bandura, *Social Learning Theory*. Englewood Cliffs, NJ: Prentice-Hall, 1977.

44 D. Andrews and J. Bonta, *The Psychology of Criminal Conduct*, 2nd edn. New Providence, NJ: Anderson, 2010.

45 C. Shaw and H. McKay, *Juvenile Delinquency and Urban Areas*. Chicago, IL: University of Chicago Press, 1942.

46 See, for instance, C. Shaw and H. McKay, *Juvenile Delinquency and Urban Areas*. Chicago, IL: University of Chicago Press, 1934/1972.

47 R. Merton, "Social structure and anomie." *American Sociological Review* 3 (6) (1938): 672–682.

48 A. Cohen, *Delinquency in Boys: The Culture of the Gang*. New York, NY: Free Press, 1960. See also R. Cloward and L. Ohlin, *Delinquency and Opportunity*. New York, NY: Free Press, 1955.

49 Note this study was conducted in Norway and it may be that the social network system of Norway makes it problematic to generalize to what might be found in the U.S. T. Skardhamar and J. Savolainen, "Changes in criminal offending around the time of job entry: A study of employment and desistance." *Criminology* 52 (2014): 263–291.

50 R. Bursik and H. Grasmick, *Neighborhoods and Crime: The Dimensions of Effective Community Control*. New York, NY: Lexington Books, 1994. See also F. Cullen, "Social support as an organizing concept for criminology." *Justice Quarterly* 11 (4) (1993): 528–559; A. Reiss and M. Tonry, *Communities and Crime*. Chicago, IL: University of Chicago Press, 1989. See also R. Sampson and W. Groves, "Community structure and crime: Testing social disorganization theory." *American Journal of Sociology* 94 (1986): 774–802. See, for instance, R. Sampson, "Local friendship ties and community attachment in mass society: A multi-level systemic model." *American Sociological Review*, 53 (1988): 766–779.

51 M. Carey, "Social learning, social capital, and correctional theories: Seeking an integrated model." In American Correctional Association, *What Works and Why: Effective Approaches to Reentry*. Lanham, MD: American Correctional Association, 2005, p. 9; R. Bursik and H. Grasmick, *Neighborhoods and Crime: The Dimensions of Effective Community Control*. New York, NY: Lexington Books, 1993.

52 E. Sutherland and D. Cressey, *Principles of Criminology*. Philadelphia, PA: Lippincott, 1960/1966.

53 R. Akers, *Deviant Behavior: A Social Learning Approach*. Belmont, CA: Wadsworth, 1966. R. Burgess and R. Akers, "A differential association-reinforcement theory of criminal behavior." *Social Problems* 14 (1973): 128–147.

54 R. Burgess and R. Akers, "A differential association-reinforcement theory of criminal behavior." *Social Problems* 14 (1973): 128–147.

55 See, for instance, E. Lemert, *Social Pathology: A Systematic Approach to the Theory of Sociopathic Behavior*. New York, NY: McGraw-Hill, 1951.

56 T. Hirschi, *Causes of Delinquency*. Berkeley, CA: University of California Press, 1969.

57 M. Gottfredson and T. Hirschi, *A General Theory of Crime*. Stanford, CA: Stanford University Press, 1990.

58 M. Gottfredson and T. Hirschi, *A General Theory of Crime*. Stanford, CA: Stanford University Press, 1990, p. 97.

59 C. Na and R. Paternoster, "Can self-control change substantially over time? Rethinking the relationship between self- and social-control." *Criminology* 50, (2012): 427–462. Also see A. Piquero, W. Jennings and D. Farrington, "On the malleability of self-control: Theoretical and policy implications regarding a general theory of crime." *Justice Quarterly* 27 (2010): 803–834.

60 S. Miller and C. Burack, "A critique of Gottfredson and Hirschi's general theory of crime: Selective (in)attention to gender and power positions." *Women and Criminal Justice* 4 (1993): 115–134.

61 O. Antonaccio and C. Tittle, "Morality, self control and crime." *Criminology* 46 (2008): 479–510.

62 R. Agnew, *Pressured into Crime: An Overview of General Strain Theory*. New York, NY: Oxford University Press, 2007.

63 T. Tyler, *Why People Obey the Law*. Princeton, NJ: Princeton University Press, 2006.

64 D. Cornish and R. Clarke, *The Reasoning Criminal: Rational Choice Perspectives on Offending*. New York, NY: Springer-Verlag, 1986.

65 See, for instance, M. Stafford and M. Warr, "A reconceptualization of general and specific deterrence." *Journal of Research in Crime and Delinquency* 30 (1993): 123–135.

66 L. Cohen and M. Felson, "Social change and crime trends: A routine activities approach." *American Sociological Review* 44 (1979): 588–608.

67 D. Farrington, L. Ohlin and J. Wilson, *Understanding and Controlling Crime: Toward a New Research Strategy*. New York, NY: Springer-Verlag, 1986, p.2.

68 M. Tonry, L. Ohlin and D. Farrington, *Human Development and Criminal Behavior: New Ways of Advancing Knowledge*. New York, NY: Springer-Verlag, 1991, p. 142.

69 D. Denno, *Biology and Violence: From Birth to Adulthood*. New York, NY: Cambridge University Press, 1990.

70 R. Sampson and J. Laub, *Crime in the Making: Pathways and Turning Points through Life*. Cambridge, MA: Harvard University Press, 1993, p. 244.

71 For a review of this argument, see T. Skardhamar and J. Savolainen, "Changes in criminal offending around the time of job entry: A study of employment and desistance." *Criminology* 52 (2014): 263–291.

72 R. Simons, C. Burt, A. Barr, M. Lei and E. Stewart, "Incorporating routine activities, activity spaces, and situational definitions into social schematic theory of crime." *Criminology* 52 (2014): 655–687.

Section 2

LAW ENFORCEMENT AS SOCIAL CONTROL

POLICE IN AMERICA

4

In this chapter we begin our exploration of one of the "sub-systems" of the criminal justice system—law enforcement. Today, law enforcement is under intense scrutiny and weekly, it seems, there are news stories that show police officers seemingly abusing their authority and opinion pieces that allege law enforcement is practiced in a racist manner. On the other side, law enforcement officers and officials and their supporters allege politicians, the media, and some law enforcement leaders are responsible for lowering the morale of all police officers by unfairly sensationalizing a few egregious cases. Many believe that by endorsing the idea that law enforcement officers are abusing the rights of citizens, it makes the job of an officer more difficult and dangerous. Obviously, people have strong opinions in both directions. What we want to do in this text is apply a critical thinking approach to uncover facts, taking care not to allow assumptions or bias affect our understanding of the issues. Before we can explore the current issues of policing today, we need to take several steps back to see where policing has been, and provide

Chapter Preview

- What Is the Function of Policing?
- What Are the Major Issues Facing Policing Today?
- Focus On Data: Are Police Officers Under Attack?
- How Many Police Officers Are There and Who Are They?
- What Is the Difference Between Federal, State, and Local Law Enforcement?
- How Did Modern Policing Evolve?
- What Is Community Policing?
- Summary
- Critical Thinking Exercises

some general facts to understand the issues relevant to policing. In the next three chapters we will cover such topics as: What is the function of policing? How did modern policing evolve? Who are the police officers in this country? Is there a subculture of policing? And, what are the legal parameters of police power?

WHAT IS THE FUNCTION OF POLICING?

What is the function of police? You probably said crime control, but that is not a complete answer. Police officers are dispatched to many different types of calls and crime calls form only a portion of their workload. According to researchers, the majority of police work is divided among patrol, service calls, and paperwork. Further, only 13 percent of their time is taken up with potentially criminal matters, according to these authors.[1]

It is common to identify crime control and **order maintenance** as the two major functions of law enforcement. Crime control includes all the tasks associated with preventing crime and enforcing the law. Patrolling neighborhoods or downtown business districts, responding to dispatched calls, investigating crimes, engaging in sting operations, arresting suspects, testifying in court, and all the other tasks associated with either preventing crime or catching criminals is included in the crime-control function. Order-maintenance tasks, sometimes called "community caretaking," include everything else police do. It is community caretaking when police respond to a car accident and control traffic and see that the victims get medical treatment. Police may be called to perform a "public welfare check" by a worried mother to check on her college-age daughter because she hasn't answered her phone in three days, respond to lost elderly calls, try to mediate neighbor disputes, and counsel recalcitrant teenagers. Increasingly, they are called when a person on a street, in a business, or with family members show signs of mental illness. Police are present when there are medical emergencies, water rescues, traffic problems, public disturbances and organized protests, weather-related and other natural disasters, and civil defense.

Order-maintenance and crime-control functions may overlap and even merge. Police officers may be performing crime control on a domestic disturbance call if someone has been injured, or order maintenance if no criminal charges are warranted. When police are called to a neighbor dispute, this is order maintenance; but if they are unsuccessful in resolving the problem, it may turn into a crime when one neighbor decides to settle the argument with a criminal assault. A mentally ill person may complain to police that their brain is being scanned by an alien, which is obviously not a crime-control issue;

however, if they do not respond in an effective manner to this complaint, the delusional person may commit a crime. When neighbors call police because there is a large group of "suspicious-looking" people in a park late at night, not responding may result in nothing happening, or it may result in a series of vehicle burglaries or other crimes. On the other hand, if the park is open and the "suspicious-looking" people are not committing a crime, there is little the officers can do legally despite the neighbors' unease—they are constantly called upon to resolve issues when there is no clear legal answer.

We consider our police to be the 24-hour one-stop shop for problem solving. Whenever we are in trouble, our first thought is probably to call 911. Police officers, then, have a day that may begin with a person suffering from Alzheimer's who has forgotten where they live or even what their name is, and end with an alligator in someone's backyard pool that has just eaten the family's Chihuahua. Crime calls happen too, but car chases and catching burglars is not the day-to-day routine of most police officers. In fact, one might say that there is no such thing as a day-to-day routine.

WHAT ARE THE MAJOR ISSUES FACING POLICING TODAY?

In 2015 policing came to dominate public discourse and even enter into the presidential campaign platforms. Deaths of Black men while in the custody or at the hands of police officers in Ferguson, Missouri (Michael Brown), Staten Island, New York (Eric Garner), Cleveland, Ohio (Tamir Rice), North Charleston, South Carolina (Walter Scott), Chicago, Illinois (LaQuan McDonald) and Baltimore, Maryland (Freddie Gray) spurred public attention to policing in a way that hadn't been seen since the Rodney King beating in 1991.

The events led to President Obama's creation of a panel of practitioners and experts in 2015 to report on the state of policing. Their report, *Final Report of the President's Task Force on 21st Century Policing*, called for reform in virtually all aspects of policing.[2] Then in the summer of 2016, the shooting deaths of Alton Sterling in Baton Rouge and Philando Castile in a suburb of Minneapolis reignited "Black Lives Matter" protests. In Dallas, a gunman shot and killed five officers and wounded seven others who were on duty at a "Black Lives Matter" public protest. This tragedy has seemed to be a turning point, with community members and law enforcement officials together pledging to work together to find solutions to the problem.

There is no doubt that there is a split between White and minority citizens in this country in how police are perceived. According to a Gallup poll, 59 percent of Whites have a great deal or quite a lot of confidence in the police,

Exhibit 4.1 Eric Garner, a 400-pound man who had asthma, died while being arrested by police in Staten Island.

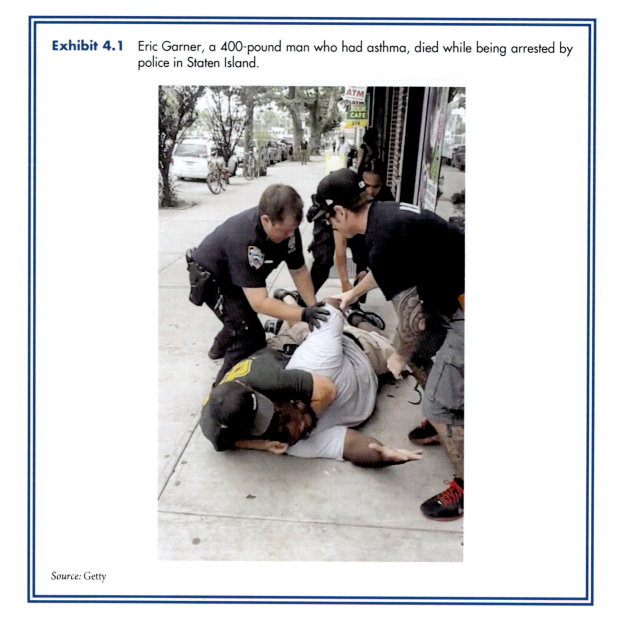

Source: Getty

compared with only 37 percent of Blacks.[3] The Pew Research Center found similar disparities in how Blacks and Whites view law enforcement. Almost half of all Blacks (46 percent) had "little" or "very little" confidence that police treated Whites and Blacks similarly, compared to 20 percent of Whites.[4] After the most recent shootings in the summer of 2016, a *New York Times/*

CBS telephone poll reported that 69 percent of Americans thought that race relations in America were generally bad; in fact, results were about the same as in 1991 after the Rodney King beating. The poll showed a sharp difference in how Blacks and Whites viewed law enforcement as shown in Exhibit 4.2 below.

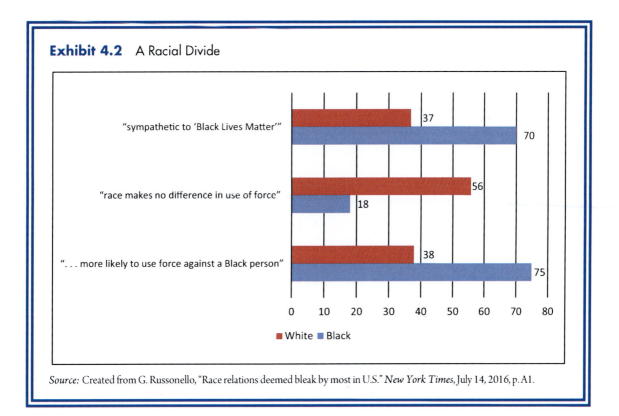

Exhibit 4.2   A Racial Divide

Source: Created from G. Russonello, "Race relations deemed bleak by most in U.S." *New York Times,* July 14, 2016, p. A1.

The antipathy between law enforcement and minority communities is one current issue that must be considered. Another issue, related to the first, is whether police officers abuse their legal authority. Do police officers abuse their stop-and-frisk power and is it used in a discriminatory manner? Police officer use of force, including lethal force, has also been scrutinized. Is there a difference in how quickly officers resort to force when dealing with different race/ethnicity groups? Another current issue is whether police are experiencing heightened danger. This will be the subject of the Focus on Data next.

FOCUS ON DATA: ARE POLICE OFFICERS UNDER ATTACK?

In 2015 and 2016, numerous ambush-style killings of police officers occurred in cities across the United States. The five officers ambushed in Dallas in July 2016 while on duty at a peaceful "Black Lives Matter" protest escalated the concern that policing was under attack. Many argue that the negative media attention related to the police killings of Black men has triggered fatal attacks on police officers. As seen above, this issue threatens to undercut advances in race relations in this nation. Others have argued that policing has never been safer with fewer killings of officers than past decades. Who is right?

An annual report by the nonprofit National Law Enforcement Officers Memorial Fund found that 42 officers were killed by guns in 2015; 49 officers in 2014; 32 officers in 2013; and 50 in 2012. In 2011, 73 officers were killed in gunfire, the most in any year in the past decade. The average since 2004 is 55 police deaths annually. Note that these are deaths by gunfire only; there is about an equal number of additional deaths due to traffic accidents.

These numbers, tragic as they are, are nowhere near the highest numbers of deaths however. In 1973, 156 police officers were killed by gunfire, and the 1970s averaged about 140 officer deaths per year.[5] It is important to note that these are not rates per 1,000, so the 1973 number would have been from a much smaller total number of police officers in the country. The reduction in numbers of police officers killed is probably due to the advent of body armor and better training, now required in most departments.

What worries law enforcement officials, however, is the ambush-style killings where an officer is targeted and killed or injured without warning. Officers Wenjian Liu and Rafael Ramos were assassinated as they were sitting in their patrol car in New York City in December 2014. A man with mental health issues said he did it as a "revenge killing" for Eric Garner and Michael Brown. It has been reported that an average of ten officers per year are killed in ambush style shootings, but there had been five already by March of 2016.[6] Then, in July of 2016, five Dallas police officers—Brent Thompson, Patrick Zamarripa, Michael Krol, Michael Smith, and Lorne Ahrens—were shot and killed. Several others were wounded. The suspect was chased into a parking garage and, after negotiations broke down and officials believed he had explosives that posed a threat, he was killed by a remote-controlled robot that carried explosives.

Exhibit 4.3 shows that the number of officer fatalities goes up and down but has been showing generally a downward direction. Recall from above that about 55 officers on average are killed by gunfire. Exhibit 4.3 shows the total number of fatalities; automobile accidents account for the largest number of officer fatalities.

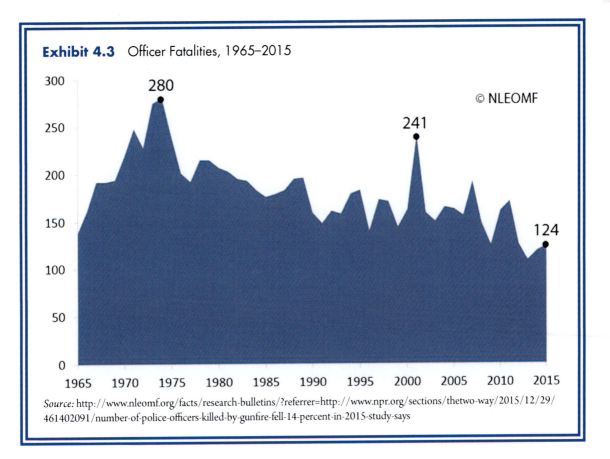

Exhibit 4.3 Officer Fatalities, 1965–2015

© NLEOMF

Source: http://www.nleomf.org/facts/research-bulletins/?referrer=http://www.npr.org/sections/thetwo-way/2015/12/29/461402091/number-of-police-officers-killed-by-gunfire-fell-14-percent-in-2015-study-says

Every officer in the country must experience a sense of dread when these cases arise, knowing that it could happen to them. It is true, as some point out, that, statistically, policing is safer than several other occupations when looking at on-the-job mortality rates; however, there must be some difference in how one experiences the risk of work-related deadly accidents compared to being the victim of an intentional assassination. As Exhibit 4.3 shows, the number of "ambush"-style killings increased dramatically in 2015. There had already been five ambush-style shooting by March of 2016 and the July 2016 killings of five law enforcement officers in Dallas was the single deadliest incident for law enforcement since 9/11. The sniper killings of police officers took place in a city that, by all accounts, had a fairly good relationship between the police force and the minority community. Following that incident, there were several others in the following days involving officers who were shot or shot at by lone assailants in ambush-style situations (e.g., calling 911 and then shooting at the officer who responded).[7]

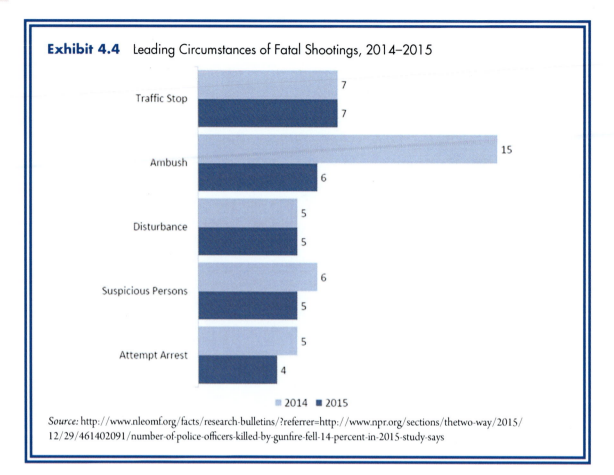

Exhibit 4.4   Leading Circumstances of Fatal Shootings, 2014–2015

Traffic Stop: 7, 7
Ambush: 15, 6
Disturbance: 5, 5
Suspicious Persons: 6, 5
Attempt Arrest: 5, 4

■ 2014 ■ 2015

Source: http://www.nleomf.org/facts/research-bulletins/?referrer=http://www.npr.org/sections/thetwo-way/2015/12/29/461402091/number-of-police-officers-killed-by-gunfire-fell-14-percent-in-2015-study-says

Whether this is a random fluctuation in statistics or the beginning of a troubling trend remains to be seen. Thus, in answer to the question—"Are police under attack or are they more safe now than ever before?"—the answer is yes to both premises. While the number of firearm-related deaths is down dramatically from the 1970s, there has been an apparent increase in 2016 in the number of ambush-style attacks.

HOW MANY POLICE OFFICERS ARE THERE AND WHO ARE THEY?

When we read about police departments in the national news, the focus is almost always on big-city police departments such as Baltimore, New York City, and Chicago. It is important to remember that policing in America includes many very small departments with only a few officers. Most police departments are in suburban or rural areas and may employ 100 or fewer officers. These police departments are usually not the focus of academic research or receive the attention of the mass media, and their issues and concerns do not mirror those of the big-city police departments that are most often in the news.

Information about police departments is available from the Bureau of Justice Statistics. A census done in 2008 reported there 17,876 state and federal police agencies in the United States with about 1.1 million full-time state and local law enforcement personnel and 765,000 sworn personnel with another 44,000 part-time personnel. This translates to about 251 officers for every 100,000 citizens or one officer for every 400 residents.[8] A more recent survey in 2013 reported on 15,388 agencies with 1,045,360 total personnel including 724,690 full-time sworn employees. It appears this survey excluded special jurisdiction agencies.[9]

The BJS census of police agencies in 2013 identified 12,326 local police departments, 3,012 sheriff's agencies,[10] 50 state law enforcement agencies, 1,733 "special jurisdiction" agencies, and 638 other agencies (primarily constables unique to Texas). This figure does not include federal law enforcement agencies. Most police officers work in municipal agencies (52 percent), followed by sheriff's offices (31 percent).[11]

About three-quarters of all law enforcement agencies employ less than 25 people and 48 percent employed fewer than ten officers, but about one-third of all sworn officers work in the few agencies (49) that employ 1,000 or more officers.[12] The largest police department is the New York City Police Department (NYPD) which employed over 36,000 officers in 2008 (34,454 in 2013), nearly three times the next largest department (Chicago) which employed 13,354 in 2008 (12,042 in 2013). Los Angeles (9,727 in 2008, 9,920 in 2013), Philadelphia (6,624 in 2008, 6,515 in 2013), and Houston (5,053 in 2008, 5,295 in 2013) are the next three largest departments.[13] Some departments have increased their numbers while others have experienced a reduction in their numbers between 2008 and 2013. Exhibit 4.5 shows this interesting paradox that most police officers work in large agencies but most agencies are very small.

Historically, most police officers were White males. Today, police departments are beginning to represent the diversity of the population they serve. All police departments require officers to be citizens, and most have age restrictions—that is, applicants must be between 21 and under 35 to 40 to be hired. Some departments now require 60 or 90 college hours. There are written, physical, and psychological tests during the selection process. The average starting salaries of new police officers range from $26,600 to $49,500, with the average

To find numerous reports on police and policing, go to the Bureau of Justice Statistics website at http://bjs.ojp.us doj.gov and look under the heading of "Law Enforcement."

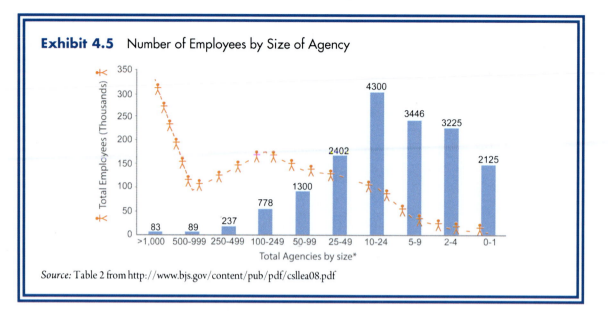

Exhibit 4.5   Number of Employees by Size of Agency

Source: Table 2 from http://www.bjs.gov/content/pub/pdf/csllea08.pdf

salary of $44,400.[14] The median annual wage earned by police officers as of 2011 was $54,230, according to the Bureau of Labor Statistics.[15] Officers with college degrees receive higher salaries in some locations. Seniority and overtime can substantially increase the annual salary of an officer.

The first Black police officer was hired in 1861;[16] however, it wasn't until the mid-1960s that the recruitment and hiring of minority police officers began in earnest. In the most recent survey of local police departments, the BJS reports that about 27 percent of police officers are members of a racial or ethnic minority, up from about 25 percent in 1987. Exhibit 4.6 shows the gradual increase in minority representation in police departments.

From 2007 to 2013, the percentage of Black officers has remained the same at about 12 percent, a slight underrepresentation of their share of the general population (Blacks represent about 13.2 percent of the general population[17]). In general, large cities have higher percentages of minority officers. In 2013, while minorities comprised almost 47 percent of police departments serving cities over 1 million; they comprised only about 16 percent of jurisdictions of less than 2,500.[18] Of course, it is more important to know what the representation of a particular city's police department is and whether the representation of minority officers reflects that city's population. The *New York Times* presents an interactive infographic utilizing 2007 figures from the BJS comparing

Go to the website for this infographic: http://www.nytimes.com/interactive/2014/09/03/us/the-race-gap-in-americas-police-departments.html

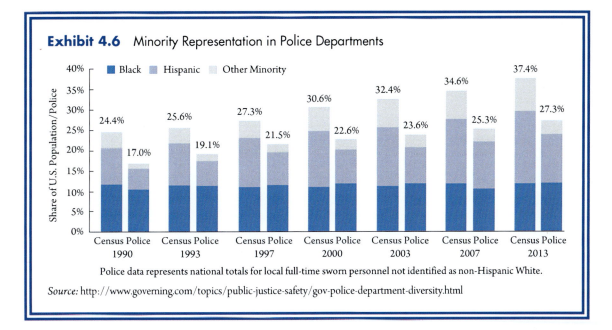

Exhibit 4.6 Minority Representation in Police Departments

Police data represents national totals for local full-time sworn personnel not identified as non-Hispanic White.

Source: http://www.governing.com/topics/public-justice-safety/gov-police-department-diversity.html

the number of Black officers to the percentage of Blacks in the city's population. Some smaller incorporated areas close to large metropolitan areas have especially disparate representation with police forces that are predominately White and populations that are largely minority. For instance, in Greenbelt, Maryland, close to Washington, DC, the population is about 26 percent White, but 79 percent of its police force is White. North Charleston, South Carolina, is about 38 percent White, but 80 percent of its police force was White.[19] Although this data is somewhat outdated, it is still the case that some cities do not have a police force that represents the demographics of the residents served.

Another 11.6 percent of police officers are Hispanic[20] (Hispanics represent about 17.4 percent of the general population). Some cities have large percentages of Hispanic residents, but the police force does not represent them. For instance, Exhibit 4.7 shows the cities that seem to have disproportional representation.

It should be noted that there is little research that proves adequate representation of minority communities improves minority-police relations. A police department that represents the community it serves may be perceived as more accessible and trusted than one that does not, but there is no research that

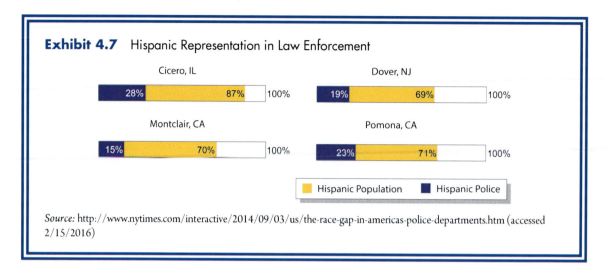

Exhibit 4.7   Hispanic Representation in Law Enforcement

Cicero, IL

28%   87%   100%

Dover, NJ

19%   69%   100%

Montclair, CA

15%   70%   100%

Pomona, CA

23%   71%   100%

☐ Hispanic Population   ■ Hispanic Police

Source: http://www.nytimes.com/interactive/2014/09/03/us/the-race-gap-in-americas-police-departments.htm (accessed 2/15/2016)

shows departments with a better representation of their community are less subject to citizen complaints or use of force lawsuits, or enjoy better relations with the community.

Although women represent about half of the general population, they comprise a small proportion of personnel in law enforcement agencies. The first female police officer was hired in 1910, but her role was restricted to dealing with children and female prisoners. Early policewomen also performed clerical tasks. Policewomen were hired under a separate job category from male police officers, with separate hiring requirements. All that changed in the 1970s, when women were integrated into the patrol ranks.[21]

By 1997, women represented 10.6 percent of all police officers. However, there has been very little increase in the percentage of women in law enforcement since the 1990s. In 2013, women still accounted for only about 12 percent of sworn officers in local police departments. Exhibit 4.8 shows the gradual increase in female officers.

Recently Kringen[22] examined the barriers to hiring and retaining women in a medium-size police department and discovered that certain policies (such as requiring female recruits to cut their hair) were problematic for attracting female applicants and policies such as shift work and mandatory overtime that made childcare difficult were factors that seemed to discourage women from applying or staying in policing. Unlike other professions, generally female officers cannot move to part-time status during the years when pregnancy and childrearing demand flexibility. According to at least one female law enforcement leader, departments that allowed officers to work part-time at some point in their career would probably experience no difficulty in attracting and retaining women.[23]

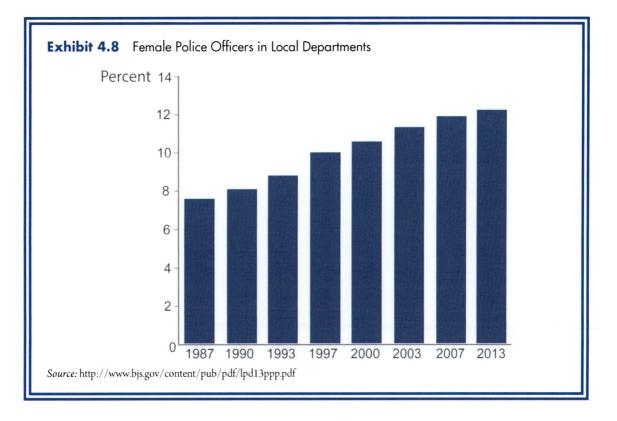

Exhibit 4.8   Female Police Officers in Local Departments

Percent

Source: http://www.bjs.gov/content/pub/pdf/lpd13ppp.pdf

Police departments that serve large cities have larger percentages of female officers (17.6 percent) than small town police departments (6.1 percent).[24] There are also large differences between cities. In an earlier study, Detroit reported 27 percent of their officers were women, compared to Las Vegas with only 9 percent. It was reported that about 15 percent of federal law enforcement personnel were women.[25]

While women represent a small percentage of all police officers, their representation in the command ranks is even smaller. In the most recent survey of police departments, it was reported that less than 10 percent of supervisory personnel in law enforcement agencies were women; and, again, the numbers were higher in big-city police departments serving 250,000 or more residents compared to small town departments. Only about 3 percent of local police chiefs were women.[26] Thus, law enforcement officers are, for the most part, White males with some college education. There are increasing numbers of minority officers, especially in large cities. The percentage of female officers has seemed to plateau at about 11–12 percent.

WHAT IS THE DIFFERENCE BETWEEN FEDERAL, STATE, AND LOCAL LAW ENFORCEMENT?

Law enforcement in the United States is composed of a complex network of overlapping jurisdictions and agencies. There are federal, state, and local police agencies as well as special jurisdictional agencies. Some locales create private police or security forces to protect the citizenry from crime and disorder.

Federal Law Enforcement

Unlike many other countries, the United States has no national police force. Part of the reason for this is the vast area encompassed within the borders of this country, but another reason is that, since the American Revolution, there has been a cultural hostility and suspicion of centralized power. This does not mean, however, that there are no federal law enforcement officers. In fact, there are more than 120,000 federal employees who are considered law enforcement officers.[27] Prior to 2003, the Immigration and Naturalization Service (INS) employed the largest number of federal officers, followed by the Federal Bureau of Prisons, and then the U.S. Customs Service. The Department of Homeland Security (DHS) has absorbed both INS and the U.S. Customs Service, making the DHS the largest federal law enforcement agency today. In 2008, the agencies with the largest number of law enforcement personnel included the U.S. Customs and Border Protection, which employed 36,863; the Federal Bureau of Prisons 16,835; the FBI 12,760; and U.S. Immigration and Customs Enforcement 12,446.[28] Exhibit 4.9 shows these and other federal agencies.

The U.S. Marshals Service, for instance, is responsible for seizing and maintaining property confiscated through civil and criminal forfeiture hearings, providing security for federal courtrooms and judicial officials, transporting federal prisoners, and protecting federal witnesses (some through the Federal Witness Protection Program).

The Department of Homeland Security (DHS), created in 2002, has absorbed a number of other agencies and employs almost half (45.5 percent) of all federal law enforcement personnel. As mentioned previously, the Immigration and Naturalization Service and the U.S. Customs Service are now under DHS. The functions of these two agencies have been reorganized, and now the agency primarily responsible for border protection is called U.S. Customs and Border Protection, and the other agency, called U.S. Immigration and Customs Enforcement, enforces immigration laws within the interior of the country. Other agencies absorbed by the Department of Homeland Security include the U.S. Coast Guard and the U.S. Secret Service. The Transportation Security Administration (TSA) is charged with providing protection at airports.

Exhibit 4.9   Federal Agencies Employing 250+ People with Arrest and Firearm Powers

U.S. Customs and Border Protection	36,863
Federal Bureau of Prisons	16,835
Federal Bureau of Investigation	12,760
U.S. Immigration and Customs Enforcement	12,446
U.S. Secret Service	5,213
Administrative Office of the U.S. Courts*	4,696
Drug Enforcement Administration	4,308
U.S. Marshals Service	3,313
Veterans Health Administration	3,128
Internal Revenue Service, Criminal Investigation	2,636
Bureau of Alcohol, Tobacco, Firearms and Explosives	2,541
U.S. Postal Inspection Service	2,288
U.S. Capitol Police	1,637
National Park Service—Rangers	1,404
Bureau of Diplomatic Security	1,049
Pentagon Force Protection Agency	725
U.S. Forest Service	644
U.S. Fish and Wildlife Service	598
National Park Service—U.S. Park Police	547
National Nuclear Security Administration	363
U.S. Mint Police	316
Amtrak Police	305
Bureau of Indian Affairs	277
Bureau of Land Management	255

* Limited to federal probation officers employed in federal judicial districts that allow officers to carry firearms

Source: B. Reaves, *Federal Law Enforcement Officers, 2008*. Washington, DC: Bureau of Justice Statistics, 2012, p. 2. Accessed 2/1/2016: http://www.bjs.gov/content/pub/pdf/fleo08.pdf

The same Act that created the DHS also changed the Bureau of Alcohol, Tobacco and Firearms (ATF), which is now the Bureau of Alcohol, Tobacco, Firearms and Explosives, and the law enforcement functions of the agency have been transferred to the Justice Department while the revenue functions remain with the Department of the Treasury.[29]

For more information about federal law enforcement, see http://www.bjs.gov/content/pub/pdf/fleo08.pdf

Federal law enforcement agencies enforce federal laws. They share jurisdiction with state and local law enforcement agencies when an action is a violation of both federal and state law. The most common example of this is the sale of controlled substances. While smuggling drugs into the country is a federal crime, sales of controlled substances break both federal and state laws.

State Law Enforcement

State law enforcement agencies are typically called Highway Patrol, Department of Public Safety, or State Patrol, although their mission encompasses more than patrolling the state highways and issuing drivers' licenses. These statewide agencies usually have a state-of-the-art crime lab to assist smaller jurisdictions that have no analysis capabilities. They also provide assistance with investigation and detection to local agencies and carry out their own investigations when the criminal activity is statewide, especially if the criminal activity involves drugs or auto theft rings. The state agency may be the central repository for crime statistics, may have authority over gun registrations and investigations for licenses, and may have supervision over controlled substances registration.

There were 1,733 limited jurisdiction law enforcement agencies employing 56,968 full-time sworn personnel in 2008.[30] Examples include state law enforcement agencies that enforce alcohol and tobacco laws, fish and game agencies that enforce hunting and other laws, agencies that enforce gaming and/or racing laws, and child support enforcement agencies. State universities, state hospitals, state parks, school districts, airports, mass transit, and ports or harbors also may have their own law enforcement agencies. Each state is slightly different in the type and the number of these special jurisdiction agencies.

County Law Enforcement

Sheriffs are elected officials, but sheriff's deputies are hired through civil service selection procedures in a similar manner to municipal law enforcement officers. Usually, county sheriffs also have the responsibility of managing the county jail. In some jurisdictions, sheriff's deputies may be assigned either patrol duties or jail duties, but in other jurisdictions, the position of jailer is a different job from that of deputy. Sheriff's offices also serve warrants and civil documents, including eviction notices.

Most states, but not all, have a sheriff for each county. Texas, with 254 counties, has the largest number of sheriffs—one for each county. Alaska, Connecticut, Hawaii, and Rhode Island have no sheriffs, and Delaware has only one sheriff's office. The median number of employees for all sheriffs' offices was eighteen full-time sworn employees in 2008 although a few are extremely large. For instance, the Los Angeles County Sheriff's Office had 9,461 full-time sworn employees.[31]

While sheriffs are elected, police chiefs are hired by the city manager and/or a city council and mayor. Both, however, have notoriously short average tenures, because both positions are lightning rods for public controversy.

Municipal Law Enforcement

When we think of the police, we typically think of the municipal police department. Most towns and cities of any size have their own police department. Small towns may have a police department of only three or four officers, while big-city police forces may number in the thousands, such as New York City with over 34,000 officers. As noted above, most police *officers* work in the larger police departments, even though most police *departments* have fewer than 50 officers.

Larger police departments are typically broken into divisions, such as patrol and investigation. Under the investigation division, there may be further subdivisions, such as homicide, juvenile, and vice. Other departments exist as well, including community relations, internal affairs, training, and research and planning. Some police departments have created special domestic violence teams, police squads specially trained to respond to the mentally ill, and other specialized teams. In smaller departments, of course, patrol officers are expected to be generalists and handle a large variety of calls.

Special Jurisdiction Law Enforcement Agencies

There are also special or limited jurisdiction municipal law enforcement agencies. We've mentioned state-level special jurisdiction agencies above (e.g. state university police departments). Others occur at the municipal level. Some cities have park police and/or transit police. These agencies have the power to arrest, but their jurisdiction is limited to crimes that occur within or in relation to their specific jurisdiction.

Some Native American tribes may have their own tribal police forces that have exclusive jurisdiction on reservations. In fact, there is a completely separate justice system existing on some Indian reservations, complete with tribal police and a tribal court system. Even civil court matters are dealt with by tribal courts, and a state district court has no authority once a matter is deemed to be under the jurisdiction of these tribal courts.

For information about one such tribal police department, go to the website for the Oneida Indian Nation police department at http://oneida-nation.net/police.

Private Law Enforcement

Private security officers are not peace officers. They are paid with private funds rather than public dollars, and their primary duty is to provide protection and

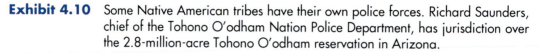

Exhibit 4.10   Some Native American tribes have their own police forces. Richard Saunders, chief of the Tohono O'odham Nation Police Department, has jurisdiction over the 2.8-million-acre Tohono O'odham reservation in Arizona.

Source: Getty

investigative services to the hiring entity, which might be a company, neighborhood, or private individual. We mention private security officers here only because many people misunderstand their power and assume that they have similar powers to those of public peace officers. The other reason that we must mention them is that there may be many more private security officers than police officers. There are probably more than 1.5 million individuals employed in private security, and private security expenditures are on track to be almost double that of public expenditures.

It should also be noted that there is overlap between private and public policing because public police officers are often hired as private employees of security companies. Because police are certified peace officers who can carry a weapon and use their arrest powers even when off-duty, they carry those powers with them into the private position. Otherwise, private security officers have no greater powers of arrest or use of force than an average citizen.

The American Society for Industrial Security (now ASIS International) is the largest professional organization for security professionals. Its website states that it was founded in 1955 and has more than 35,000 members worldwide.[32]

For information about the American Society for Industrial Security, go to http://www.asisonline.org/about/history/index.xml

HOW DID MODERN POLICING EVOLVE?

It may surprise you to know that police agencies are a relatively recent phenomenon in the history of social order, beginning less than 300 years ago. Of course, there has always been a need to control crime and deviance, but that function was largely undertaken by the military, by private watchmen and guards, and by citizens themselves up until the 1800s.

We trace American policing back to the British "bobbie" and the "shire reeve" (sheriff). One of the earliest law enforcement officials was the **shire reeve**, who was responsible for collecting taxes for the king, and keeping the king's peace in the shires (or counties) of England. The modern-day shire reeve is the county sheriff. Another authority figure in early shires was the constable, who was responsible for the administration of shire courts and carrying out the orders of the magistrate. The constable was also responsible for keeping the **gaol** (jail) where prisoners were kept before being punished. There was no organized police force and citizens themselves participated in a watch system.

By the 1800s, this informal system of crime control had become ineffective, especially in major cities like London. Henry Fielding, a magistrate in London, created the **Bow Street Runners** in 1748, which could be considered the first type of organized police force. Their first duties were to enforce warrants from the magistrate's court, but they eventually added crime detection and investigation. Eventually, their reach extended all over England when pursuing criminals. They also provided protection in the Bow Street area of London, especially after a mounted patrol was established by Fielding's successor.

For more information and historical pictures of the London Metropolitan Police Force, see http://www.met.police.uk/history/archives.htm.

In 1829, Robert Peel, the Home Secretary of England, convinced Parliament to pass the Metropolitan Police Act, creating the first police force as we know it today. They eventually became known as "**bobbies**," referencing Peel's role in their creation. By 1839, the Metropolitan Force had absorbed the Bow Street Runners, the Bow Street mounted patrol, and the Wapping Marine Police. The force was initially based in Scotland Yard with five more watch houses and seventeen districts. In 1831, the Special Constables Act was passed, which added more officers to the force.

In the colonies, crime prevention was the responsibility of every citizen. Watch systems existed that were similar to those found in the early English shires. Boston holds the honor of having the first police department in this country, if one uses the date of origin of 1838 (when the first "day police" were hired), and not 1854 (when the police department was created as an agency separate from the constable's office).

New York City's police department was created in 1844. By the early 1800s, New York was overwhelmed with the dual problems of poverty and rising crime. The area of the Bowery, and especially the "Five Points" neighborhood, were the center of the problems that threatened to overrun the city. The power of the immigrant Irish gangs is fancifully portrayed in the hit 2002 movie *Gangs of New York*. Although there was growing support for an organized police force, citizens were suspicious of allowing such a centralized power. Still, by 1845, the Mayor of New York had created a municipal police force with an initial staffing of 900 men.

For an interesting article that compares the *Gangs of New York* movie to the historians' descriptions of the "Five Points" area of New York City and the immigrant gangs of the period, go to http://news.nationalgeographic.com/news/2003/03/0320_030320_oscars_gangs.html

Exhibit 4.11   The Five Points neighborhood was the center of crime and poverty problems that plagued New York in the mid-nineteenth century. The area was the site of the infamous 1857 riot between rival gangs, the Dead Rabbits and the Bowery Boys.

Source: Alamy

New York's police force, like other city police departments, was very much influenced by politics. Police officers received "appointments" for several years and these appointments came through political patronage. Dueling political forces fought over the police department, and in 1857 the Whigs managed to get the state legislature to pass a bill disbanding the municipal police department and creating the Metropolitan Police for the City of New York, Brooklyn, and Westchester County. This led to a brawl between the two police departments in 1857 when the Metropolitan force sought to arrest the mayor. The state militia had to step in and restore order. The police force was returned to municipal control in 1870.[33]

One of the early police commissioners was Theodore Roosevelt. Starting in 1895, he began a series of reforms in the NYPD that included:

- hiring based on skill and aptitude rather than political patronage
- the creation of disciplinary rules and enforcement
- adopting an early form of fingerprinting
- creating a bike squad
- requiring officers to have pistol practice
- instituting physical exams for officers
- hiring the first female police matron to supervise female prisoners (Minnie Gertrude Kelly)
- eliminating the practice of homeless people sleeping in the basements of the precinct offices in horribly unsanitary conditions.[34]

City police departments were slower to emerge in the West and the marshal was often the only law enforcement officer in early Western towns. For instance, a true city police department didn't emerge in Los Angeles until almost 1870. The precursor to the Los Angeles Police Department was the "Los Angeles Rangers," a group of volunteers enlisted to help the county sheriff and marshal in the unruly times of the 1850s. Los Angeles was inundated with immigrants and others who were spurred by "gold fever" to come to the West Coast to make a fortune. The Rangers wore a white ribbon that indicated they served under the authority of the Council of Los Angeles. The "Los Angeles City Guards" succeeded the Rangers and wore the first official uniform. Vigilante justice was commonplace and early authorities were unable to keep order. Evidently, during the 1860s, a group of residents was successful in their request to the French government for protection. For some period of time, French troops were deployed in the city to guard residents![35]

In 1869, six officers were formally hired and paid out of city funds. Led by the city marshal, who also acted as dog catcher and tax collector, this early force was the beginning of the LAPD of today. The mounted patrol began in

For an interesting website that covers the history of the New York City Police Department, go to http://www.nycpolicemuseum.org/

For an interesting description of the early days of the LAPD, go to the official website, http://www.lapdonline.org/history_of_the_lapd/content_basic_view/1107

1875 and existed until 1916. In 1876, the Board of Police Commissioners was formed and a police chief was hired after the marshal was killed by one of his own men. In 1885, the chief of police commanded eighteen men and earned $150 a month. In 1886, two Black officers were hired. In 1889, professional standards emerged with a new chief, John M. Glass, who instituted hiring standards and formalized training.[36]

As the 1800s gave way to the 1900s, cities and towns grew, and most eventually created their own police departments. That process continues today and small towns sometimes make the decision to create a municipal police force, even if it is only a chief and one or two officers, rather than depend on the county sheriff's office for police protection. Sheriff's deputies provide patrol protection and crime investigation to unincorporated areas and small towns that do not have their own police department.

Policing in the Twentieth Century

Early police departments continued to be very influenced by politics through the 1930s. Positions were awarded through political patronage, and sometimes police campaigned in uniform for politicians running for re-election. Of course, if their candidate lost, they would have lost their jobs, and so there may have been, in some situations, more than a hint of coercion and corruption in their involvement with the political process. Police were implicated in coercing votes and stuffing ballot boxes.[37]

Training was minimal, and police were paid very little. Some officers were corrupt and utilized their position for graft. While early police departments were involved in a range of community activities, such as running soup kitchens and pursuing moral reforms such as anti-alcohol campaigns, they were also involved in strike-busting and immigrant control, sometimes through extra-legal and violent means. In some cities with strong political machines, police might have been seen almost as a private security force serving only those in power. The control of the working and "immigrant classes" was not necessarily done with any degree of sensitivity or even legality.[38]

August Vollmer (1876–1955) is credited with beginning the process of professionalizing the police. He was elected marshal of Berkeley, California, in 1905 and later became its first police chief. During his long tenure with the Berkeley Police Department, he was instrumental in a large number of innovations in policing that spread across the country and led to police departments being considered more as professional crime fighters than "hired muscle" for political machines. Interestingly, he is also credited with beginning the first criminal justice department at the University of California at Berkeley, where he taught some of the emerging leaders in the field.

In effect, the "professionalization" of police resulted in a real, or at least perceived, shift of police loyalty from political bosses to the law itself. Professionalization implied objectivity, professional expertise, and specialized training. The professionalization of police probably also led to the emphasis of the crime fighter role over order maintenance in following decades. Professionalization led to more training, hiring standards, and standard operating procedures.

By the 1960s, police were seen as professional crime fighters, but certain factors had combined to drastically change their relationship with the community. They were isolated in patrol cars instead of meeting and interacting with citizens while walking beats, and they had layers of bureaucracy that reduced

Exhibit 4.12   In the 1960s, police were seen responding to peaceful civil rights protests with fire hoses and dogs.

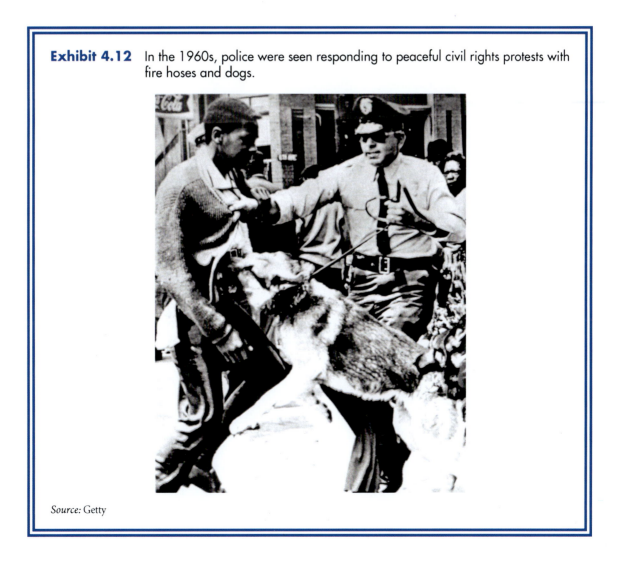

Source: Getty

their discretion when handling community problems. Professionalization may have led to police officers in some cities being seen as well-trained crime fighters, but it also made them seem more like soldiers than public servants.

Then in the 1960s, police departments around the country were faced with civil protests that challenged their ability to maintain public order. When civil rights protests began in the south, police were seen on television news shows using dogs and high-pressure water hoses on peaceful demonstrators.

When race riots broke out in the cities of the north, police were seen by some as an all-White force oppressing an all-Black ghetto. The antipathy one finds between police departments and urban minority communities today has its roots as far back as the late 1800s when police were used to control the immigrant classes, but the more immediate origin is the 1960s race riots. In 1992, after the acquittal of police officers accused of beating Rodney King, Los Angeles erupted in a riot similar to those of the 1960s. The public disturbances in Ferguson, Missouri, and Baltimore, Maryland, and the continuing protests by "Black Lives Matter" groups make it apparent that race relations continue to be problematic for at least some police departments.

Because of the discord and conflict of the 1960s, police departments around the country sought to improve their relationships with minority communities through the recruitment and hiring of minority and female officers. They also created community relations and public information officers. Citizen advisory committees were started in some communities, and other attempts were made to make the relationship between the police department and the community it served more open and cooperative. In the 1990s, these efforts coalesced into an approach called "community policing."

WHAT IS COMMUNITY POLICING?

Community policing is based on a belief that police should partner with communities to prevent and reduce crime. Around the early 1980s, James Wilson and George Kelling developed what came to be called the **"broken windows" theory** of crime. These researchers argued that signs of neighborhood disintegration and deterioration indicated to criminals that no one cared and no one would intervene in criminal acts; therefore, crime is higher in these types of neighborhoods. The more crime, the less community members invest in their neighborhoods, increasing the spiral of disorder, decay, and crime. Markers of such disintegration include abandoned homes, graffiti, loitering youth, drunks and homeless people on the street, and minor offenses like public urination. Herman Goldstein argued that the police had a role in strengthening the community, which would, in turn, increase the community's ability to prevent crime.[39]

Eventually the theory that neighborhood disintegration would lead to crime served as the foundation for community policing, order-maintenance policing, zero tolerance policing, and problem-oriented policing. Depending on the source, these various models of policing are described as the same, similar, or different.

Zero tolerance policing has been mistakenly associated with community policing, but it is conceptually distinct. Zero tolerance policing is associated with William Bratton's term as head of the New York City Transit Police and then as Commissioner of NYPD (1994–96). He also instituted his reforms as Chief of the Los Angeles Police Department (LAPD) (2002–09), and in 2013 returned as NYPD Commissioner. This type of policing, based on "broken windows," deals with all public order crimes, such as graffiti, noise violations, public urination, and aggressive panhandling, with full enforcement. The idea is that you arrest the "little" criminals and it prevents serious crime. There is no necessary partnership with the community to undertake this model of policing and, in fact, eventually the community rebels because police officers become perceived as too intrusive and oppressive as they enforce minor ordinances against everyone.

Critics contend that it is a policing approach that has the risk of biased enforcement against cultural groups that do not fit into the mainstream.[40] Street people, youth, and minorities are affected, but so, too, are "law-abiding" people who violate a city ordinance, such as parking or maintenance of property. In New York City, the zero-tolerance approach taken by the police was touted as the reason crime in the city dropped substantially through the late 1990s and 2000s, but critics contend that the crime rate dropped in other places that did not implement zero tolerance. Further, the rate of citizen complaints during the same time period increased substantially, so there is a cost in citizen–police relations with zero tolerance that may not be justified by any proven link to reduced crime.

Community policing is used as a broad term that encompasses many different types of tactics and programs, all with the goal of officers and community members developing partnerships to solve some of the neighborhood's problems. The purpose of all community policing efforts was to increase the partnership between the community and the police in crime prevention.[41] The programs loosely grouped under a community policing strategy attempted to get community members to assist in crime prevention efforts. These partnerships may have been as simple as "National Night Out," where neighborhood members were encouraged to go outside on a specified night and meet their neighbors, to more elaborate citizen–police partnerships that identified problems in the community and shared the responsibility of fixing them. Community policing efforts have included the following:

- an increase in foot and bike patrols
- storefront police stations
- bilingual crime hotlines
- prevention newsletters and watch programs
- meetings with community members
- citizen police academies
- D.A.R.E. and G.R.E.A.T. programs
- officers with greater responsibility and autonomy dedicated to the neigborhoods they are assigned.

Exhibit 4.13   Community policing seeks to create a partnership between police and residents to solve a neighborhood's problems. These efforts can include increased foot (or Segway) patrols and meetings with community members.

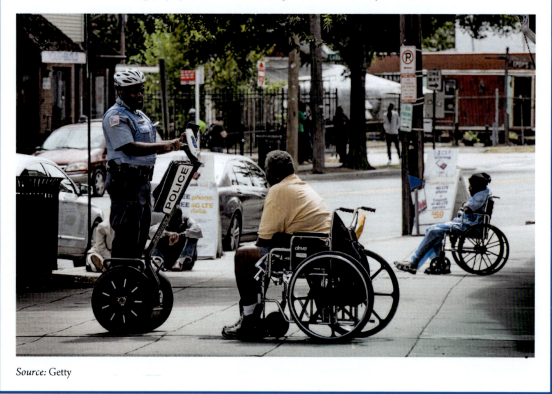

Source: Getty

Community policing efforts also emphasize the decentralization of policing. Neighborhood storefront police stations were given greater autonomy in prioritizing and solving the problems of that particular neighborhood. The police role expanded to include helping citizens get the city to respond to abandoned cars, broken streetlights, overgrown empty lots, and dilapidated houses. Permanent assignments rather than rotating shifts help police officers develop working relationships with citizens and encourage a feeling of responsibility for their assigned community. Exhibit 4.14 displays some of the strategies used in community policing.

Exhibit 4.14 *Community Policing Strategies*

- Direct engagement with the community with greater information about neighborhood problems.
- Freeing community police officers from responding to dispatched crime calls so they can engage in proactive crime prevention.
- More visible police operations.
- Decentralized operations that lead to greater familiarity with specific neighborhoods.
- Encouraging officers to see citizens as partners.
- Moving decision making and discretion downward to patrol officers.
- Encouraging citizens to take more initiative in preventing and solving crimes.

Source: National Institute of Justice, "Community policing in the 1990s." *NIJ Research Bulletin.* Washington, DC: U.S. Department of Justice, 1992, p. 3.

Critics of community policing programs argued that the efforts were ineffective in crime prevention for a variety of reasons. One reason was that they mistakenly assumed "community" could be defined purely geographically. That is, community policing programs might have targeted a particular neighborhood, drawing boundaries by crime rates, voting districts, or through some other means of establishing the border of the "community." However, people may be affiliated more through activity than "place." For instance, a family may not know its neighbors but be very active in a church that is three miles away.[42] More police presence in a particular geographic neighborhood may have deterred some crime, but it may not have been successful in strengthening the community sufficiently to prevent criminal decision making.

Community policing efforts in some locales may have failed because there was no "community" to join with, or because the partnership was nonexistent. The neighborhoods where crime is the highest are also marked by high mobility, low home ownership, few community leaders, and a lack of willingness or ability for volunteering. Such communities may need community policing the most, but they are also the least likely places such partnerships work.

Critics argued that some programs used the community as the "eyes and ears" of police, to gain political support, monetary assistance, and moral support; but they did not involve the community in power sharing or decision making.[43] Further, in some communities, police are seen as the enemy and the antipathy felt toward police overwhelmed any attempts to gain trust. Residents may not have liked criminals, but they liked police even less. In these neighborhoods, any partnerships needed to overcome the residual distrust and dislike before becoming workable.

Evaluations of community policing efforts have been mixed. Evaluations showed that public satisfaction increased when a police department adopted community policing programs, but whether such approaches reduced crime is difficult to say. Some researchers argue that findings indicate the central organization and service delivery of policing never changed that much anyway.[44] Ironically, one of the major hurdles of community policing efforts was that the community police officer emphasized order-maintenance tasks rather than crime-control tasks. This may have been a less desirable role for many officers who preferred to see themselves as "crime fighters," regardless of the effectiveness of community policing efforts.

Problem-oriented policing has been associated with community policing and the approach is certainly consistent with community policing, but it can be removed from the community policing model and still have legitimacy. Generally, problem-oriented policing follows the so-called **SARA model** of problem solving. SARA stands for scanning, analysis, response, and assessment. It refers to how police should approach crime problems. Instead of simply patrolling and reacting to crime calls, police should be constantly scanning for problems by using crime reports and other sources of information to target a particular problem, for instance an increase in burglaries in a particular neighborhood. Then, the analysis phase identifies potential explanations for the crime problem and ways to address the situation to reduce crime. Response involves implementation, which might be increased patrol, targeted enforcement, or some other response. Finally, assessment measures whether the response was successful.

Despite literally thousands of articles and news reports of various problem-oriented programs across the country, there are fairly few rigorous evaluations of its effectiveness, although those that have been done do indicate that problem-oriented policing is effective.[45] In at least one study that evaluated the methods used in responding to identified crime problems, it was found that situational prevention responses were more effective than simple arrest strategies, calling into question the effectiveness of the zero tolerance approach.[46]

The Demise of Community Policing

Many argued that 9/11 marked the beginning of the end of the community policing era. Arguably, it was never accepted wholeheartedly by the majority of officers since it seemingly replaced a crime fighter role with a social worker role by prioritizing community problems. The threat of terrorism spurred a return to traditional policing.[47] Community policing continued to be a term seen in official documents, and the federal government continues to fund the Office of Community Oriented Policing Services (COPS), but the promise of the community policing model was supplanted by the 1033 program where local police departments could purchase for minimal amounts surplus military hardware, the majority of which was desks and other equipment, but also included armored vehicles and even grenade launchers.[48]

It appears that the President's Task Force on 21st Century Policing has spurred a new cycle of reform with police leaders across the country debating the "warrior" versus **"guardian" model**.[49] This conceptual dichotomy recognizes that police officers at times are engaged in crime fighting, but that they should not approach their role as if they are "at war" with the community they serve. They are guardians of the citizenry, and, more importantly, guardians of the law and democracy itself. The hallmarks of the guardian role are public service, promoting relationships with the community through mutual respect, and the use of communication techniques such as de-escalation to prevent the use of force unless absolutely necessary. Others have taken issue with this promotion, arguing that emphasizing a multitude of rules, policies, and best practices that discourage the use of force will endanger police officers. Thus, once again, the debate continues between the primacy of crime fighting versus public service in the police officer role.[50]

SUMMARY

What Is the Function of Policing?

It is common to identify crime control and order maintenance (or community caretaking) as the two major functions of law enforcement. Crime control includes all the tasks associated with preventing crime and arresting criminals. Community caretaking takes up the majority of time and includes everything else police officers do.

What Are the Major Issues Facing Policing Today?

Currently, there is a great deal of scrutiny and criticism directed toward police departments. There is a split between White and minority citizens in this country in how police are perceived, with Black and other minority citizens less likely to trust police or believe that they are accountable. Other issues include whether police officers use their legal powers appropriately. There is also a current concern that attacks on police officers have increased.

How Many Police Officers Are There and Who Are They?

A survey in 2013 reported on 15,388 agencies with 1,045,360 total personnel including 724,690 full-time sworn employees. Most police departments are small (under 100 officers), however, about one-third of all police officers work in the very largest departments (New York City, Los Angeles, Chicago, etc.). About 27 percent of police officers are members of a minority group; about 12 percent are Black and about 11.6 percent are Hispanic. The percentage of female police officers is about 12 percent and has plateaued in recent years.

What Is the Difference between Federal, State, and Local Law Enforcement?

Many federal agencies have law enforcement personnel in addition to the FBI who perform investigative and apprehension functions. State law enforcement includes the highway patrol and other state-level agencies. Municipal law enforcement is the most commonly thought-of type of law enforcement, e.g. NYPD. There are also special jurisdiction agencies (such as university police, park police, transit police and so on).

How Did Modern Policing Evolve?

Modern policing evolved from the British "bobby" and has a history in this country of being tied to politics. In the early 1900s a move toward professionalization removed policing from political patronage and increased the skills required. Policing has always swung between a crime fighter role and a public service function.

What Is Community Policing?

Begun in the 1990s, community policing was an approach that put police officers in partnership with community members to solve neighborhood problems. The idea was that by working as partners, crime could be prevented. The approach was less emphasized after 9/11 when the threat of terrorism eclipsed efforts to improve relations between police agencies and communities. More recently, a similar discussion has emerged in the contrast between the warrior versus guardian role of policing.

Critical Thinking Exercises

1. Research community policing programs in your area (if there are any). Has there been any controversy over the implementation of such programs? If so, what is the controversy, and what facts are needed to help resolve the controversy?

2. Are there any issues with policing in your city or town? Research what they might be (using a search engine for the local newspaper). Are there two sides to an issue? Are there more than two sides? Is there competing data (i.e., data that doesn't seem to be consistent with each other used by either side)? Can you reconcile the data?

NOTES

1 S. Mastrofski, R. Parks, A. Reiss and R. Worden, *Policing Neighborhoods: A Report from Indianapolis*. Washington, DC: National Institute of Justice, 1999.

2 Task Force, *Final Report of the President's Task Force on 21st Century Policing*. Washington, DC: Office of Justice Programs, 2015. Available at: http://www.cops.usdoj.gov/pdf/taskforce/TaskForce_FinalReport.pdf

3 Gallup. Accessed 2/16/2016 from http://www.gallup.com/poll/175088/gallup-review-black-white-attitudes-toward-police.aspx

4 Pew Research Center, accessed 2/16/2016 from http://www.pewresearch.org/fact-tank/2015/04/28/blacks-whites-police/

5 B. Chappell, "Number of police officers killed by gunfire fell 14 percent in 2015, study says." NPR. December 29, 2015. Retrieved 4/15/2016 from http://www.npr.org/sections/thetwo-way/2015/12/29/461402091/number-of-police-officers-killed-by-gunfire-fell-14-percent-in-2015-study-says

6 T. Jackman, "About 10 police officers per year are killed in ambushes, but five already in 2016." *Washington Post*, March 14, 2016.

7 Various news stories, e.g. http://www.cbsnews.com/news/cops-tennessee-shooter-targeted-white-victims-similar-to-dallas-ambush/

8 B. Reaves, *Census of State and Local Law Enforcement Agencies, 2008*. Washington, DC: Bureau of Justice Statistics, 2011, p.3.

9 B. Reaves, *Local Police Departments, 2013: Personnel, Policies, and Practices*. Washington, DC: Bureau of Justice Statistics, 2015.

10 Ibid., p. 2. The 2015 Reaves report does not provide information on special jurisdiction agencies.

11 Reaves, 2011.

12 Reaves, 2015, p. 3.

13 Reaves, 2011, p. 4; Reaves, 2015, p. 14.

14 Reaves, 2015, p. 6.

15 *Houston Chronicle*, retrieved 2/16/2016 from http://work.chron.com/police-officers-starting-salary-6740.html

16 J. Kuykendall and P. Burns, "The black police officer: A historical perspective." *Journal of Contemporary Criminal Justice* 1 (1980): 103–113.

17 Accessed census from http://www.census.gov/quickfacts/table/PST045215/00

18 Reaves, 2015, p. 5.

19 Accessed 2/15/2016: http://www.nytimes.com/interactive/2014/09/03/us/the-race-gap-in-americas-police-departments.html

20 Reaves, 2015, p. 6.

21 S. Martin, *Breaking and Entering: Policewomen on Patrol*. Berkeley, CA: University of California Press, 1980; L. Langton, *Women in Law Enforcement, 1987–2008*. Washington, DC: Bureau of Justice Statistics, 2010, p. 3.

22 A. Kringen, *Understanding Barriers That Affect Recruiting and Retaining Female Police Officers: A Mixed Method Approach* (Doctoral dissertation), 2014. Retrieved from ProQuest Dissertations & Theses Global (3681033).

23 Discussion with Sue Rahr, March 2016.

24 Reaves, 2015, p. 4;

25 M. Hickman and B. Reaves, *Local Police Departments, 2000*. Washington, DC: Bureau of Justice Statistics, 2003, p. 4.

26 Reaves, 2015, p. 5.

27 B. Reaves, *Federal Law Enforcement Officers, 2008*. Washington, DC: Bureau of Justice Statistics, 2012, p. 1.

28 Ibid.

29 B. Reaves and L. Bauer, *Federal Law Enforcement Officers, 2002*. Washington, DC: Bureau of Justice Statistics, 2003, p. 5.

30 Ibid, p. 8.

31 B. Reaves, *Census of State and Local Law Enforcement Agencies, 2008*. Washington, DC: Bureau of Justice Statistics, 2011, p. 6, 18.

32 ASIS International. Retrieved 6/8/2007 from http://www.asisonline.org/about/faqs.xml

33 W. Andrews, *The Early Years: The Challenge of Public Order, from 1845 to 1870*. New York Police Department, 2007. Retrieved from http://www.ci.nyc.ny.us/html/nypd/html/3100/retro.html

34 W. Andrews, *An Era of Corruption and Reform: 1870–1900*. New York Police Department, 2007. Retrieved from http://www.ci.nyc.ny.us/html/nypd/html/3100/retro.html

35 Los Angeles Police Department. Retrieved 4/16/2016, from http://www.lapdonline.org/history_of_the_lapd/content_basic_view/1107

36 Los Angeles Police Department. Retrieved 6/1/2007, from http://www.lapdonline.org/history_of_the_lapd/content_basic_view/1107

37 J. Crank, *Understanding Police Culture*. Cincinnati, OH: Anderson Publishing, 2003.

38 V. Kappeler, R. Sluder and G. Alpert, *Forces of Deviance: Understanding the Dark Side of Policing*. Prospect Heights, IL: Waveland Press, 1994, p. 41; S. Walker, *A Critical History of Police Reform: The Emergence of Professionalism*. Lexington, MA: Lexington Books, 1977.

39 H. Goldstein, *Problem-Oriented Policing*. New York: McGraw-Hill, 1990.

40 C. Kubrin, "Making order of disorder: A call for conceptual clarity." *Criminology and Public Policy* 7 (2) (2008): 203–214.

41 P. McCold and B. Wachtel, "Community is not a place: A new look at community justice initiatives." In J. Perry (Ed.), *Repairing Communities through Restorative Justice*. Lanham, MD: American Correctional Association, 2002, p. 47.

42 Ibid., p. 40.

43 Ibid., p. 43.

44 J. Zhao, N. He and N. Lovrich, "Community policing: Did it change the basic functions of policing in the 1990s? A national follow-up study." *Justice Quarterly* 20 (4) (2003): 697–724.

45 D. Weisburd, C. Telep, J. Hinkle and J. Eck, "Is problem-oriented policing effective in reducing crime and disorder?" *Criminology and Public Policy* 9 (1) (2010): 139–172.

46 A. Braga, "Setting a higher standard for the evaluation of problem-oriented policing initiatives." *Criminology and Public Policy* 9 (1) (2010): 173–195.

47 J. Pollock, *Ethical Dilemmas and Decisions in Criminal Justice*. Belmont, CA: Wadsworth/Cengage. 2016.

48 Apuzzo, M, "Local police gearing up with tools of combat." *The Seattle Times*, June 9, 2014, A4.

49 Rahr, S. and S. Rice, *From Warriors to Guardians: Recommitting American Police Culture to Democratic Ideals* (New Perspectives in Policing Series). Washington, DC: U.S. Department of Justice, National Institute of Justice, 2015. NCJ 248654

50 K. Johnson, "In face of criticism, police officials preaching de-escalation strategies." *USA Today*, October 7, 2015. Retrieved 4/16/2016 from: http://www.usatoday.com/story/news/nation/2015/10/07/police-encounters-violent-baltimore-ferguson/72636622/

POLICE OPERATIONS

5

What makes a good police officer? In this chapter, we will discuss how police departments select, train, and supervise their police officers. In a few cases, selection, training, and supervision fail, and police misconduct occurs. It is important to realize, however, that the vast majority of police officers perform their role, whether it be involving proactive or reactive policing, with integrity and competence. Most of the discussion in this and the following chapter focuses on law enforcement at the local municipal level.

HOW ARE POLICE OFFICERS SELECTED AND TRAINED?

The qualifications for being hired by a police department typically include only a few absolute requirements. One major department, for instance, requires that applicants have the following qualifications:

- be 21 to 44 years old
- have put in 60 hours of college or possess an honorable discharge from the military
- be a U.S. citizen
- be height and weight proportionate
- have a valid driver's license

Chapter Preview

- How Are Police Officers Selected and Trained?
- What Is the Difference Between Proactive and Reactive Policing?
- How Has Technology Affected Policing?
- Is Police Officer Stress a Problem and, If So, What Is the Role of Organizational Justice?
- What Is the Police Subculture?
- What Are Some Types of Police Misconduct?
- Do Police Officers Discriminate Against Minorities?
- What Is the Law and Policy Concerning Police Use of Force?
- Focus On Data: Do Police Officers Abuse Their Power to Use Lethal Force?
- What Were the Recommendations of the 21st Century President's Task Force on Policing?
- Summary
- Critical Thinking Exercises

- have no more than two moving violations within the last eighteen months
- have no felony or class A misdemeanors
- have no class B misdemeanors within the last ten years
- have a stable credit history.

Applicants who meet these qualifications must pass a civil service test that is, to a large extent, basic reading comprehension and writing. The next steps of the hiring process include a preliminary interview, physical fitness test, polygraph test, criminal background check, interview, medical exam (including a drug test), and a psychological exam.[1]

The hiring process is described as a "screening out" process rather than a selection process.[2] In other words, all applicants are, in effect, considered as applicants and then are eliminated when factors indicate they would be inappropriate for policing. Factors that would screen out applicants include a lack of intellectual ability (failing the civil service exam), lack of responsibility (bad credit), lack of honesty (failing the polygraph test), lack of physical fitness (failing the physical test), or lack of mental stability (failing the psychological exam).

The psychological exam utilizes objective personality tests, such as the Minnesota Multiphasic Personality Inventory (MMPI), and a personal interview. The psychologist looks for personality characteristics such as aggressiveness, bias, or anxiety, which would indicate that the candidate is a poor fit for the job. On the other hand, there is no desired personality profile that all police departments use to look for candidates. Little research has been done to explore whether certain personality profiles are more or less successful in policing careers. The Inwald Personality Inventory (IPI) was developed to measure personality characteristics and behavioral patterns specific to fitness for law enforcement. The so-called Big Five personality traits (extroversion, neuroticism, agreeableness, conscientiousness, and openness) have been validated as reliable measures of personality and, of these, conscientiousness seems to predict good performance in other jobs and professions. Conscientiousness is related to the degree of organization, control, and motivation one has, and has been related to being organized, reliable, hard-working, self-governing, and persevering. There has been very little research, however, as to whether the trait accurately measures police performance success. Generally, desirable traits and characteristics for officers include higher education, varied life experiences, cognitive problem-solving skills, communication skills, empathy, and respect for others.[3]

In the past, height and weight requirements excluded women and some minorities from being hired by police departments. Stringent height and weight requirements have been struck down as discriminatory by the courts, so today you may see very short police officers. It is still necessary for applicants to be in good physical shape, however, and requirements that applicants be height and weight proportionate have generally been upheld. Applicants are also typically required to pass some form of physical fitness test. Although these vary from department to department, they usually involve some form of cardiovascular fitness (running), strength, and agility. There is some concern that physical ability tests unfairly exclude women or others who might otherwise make good police officers; however, studies have validated that such tests do measure bona fide occupational qualifications (**BFOQ**) for police officers.[4]

Many, if not most, police departments do not require officers to maintain physical standards once hired however. Some have advocated for years that physical standards be adopted by police departments, much as the military does, with gradations of fitness based on age. Arguably, departments could save money in insurance costs and lost time due to sickness and injury if officers were required to maintain height and weight ratios and cardiovascular fitness. These demands would reduce heart attacks or injuries when carrying out police duties, but most departments have not instituted such standards as mandatory.

One interesting topic that has been explored by researchers is whether there is such a thing as a "police personality" that is attracted to policing. A related question is whether the career attracts people with certain personality characteristics, or whether the career changes people so that they develop such characteristics after working in the field. The so-called police personality has been described as having the traits of cynicism, authoritarianism, and suspiciousness. Some researchers have found police officers to be generally cynical, isolated, alienated, defensive, distrustful, dogmatic, and authoritarian. However, there is conflicting research as to the prevalence of these traits in policing. Research has also not shown whether the traits exist prior to being hired, or whether the job changes officers (e.g., makes them more cynical or suspicious than the general population). Furthermore, it is not clear that any particular traits are associated with undesirable behaviors or less effective officers. These are important research questions and should be addressed.[5]

Training

Early officers had no training and were basically given a uniform and nightstick and told to go do their job. Training has expanded exponentially and today police departments require 600–700 hours or more of academy training. To be certified as a peace officer in most states, one must have graduated from a recognized academy and passed standardized tests that include academic subjects as well as skills training, such as firearms and driving. Police officers receive training in departmental or regional academies. Smaller departments may prefer to hire individuals who have already received certification through attendance at a regional academy, but larger departments have their own academies and require all applicants to attend, even those who may already have certification. Some states have centralized training whereby all or almost all law enforcement officers train at one statewide academy. Recruit training includes law, operations, mental health assessments, communication skills, domestic violence, firearms, physical combat, and driving skills, among other topics.

Look at the website for Washington State's Training Commission at https://fortress.wa.gov/cjtc/www/

Exhibit 5.1   All states now require police officers to graduate from a registered academy and pass standardized tests. Larger cities, like Baltimore, seen here, may run their own academies.

Source: Getty

Field training officer (FTO) programs started in 1972.[6] This last portion of training pairs the new recruit with an **FTO** who supervises the trainee for a period that may range from weeks to months. FTOs are expected to help new academy graduates apply their academy training to real-life problems of the street. FTOs generally work from a checklist of sorts that requires him or her to certify the competence of the recruit in a standard list of tasks. Some FTOs and others convey the idea that what one learns in the academy is irrelevant and now they will teach the recruit the way "it really is." Generally, however, all recognize that the academy cannot possibly teach the recruit everything they need to know and FTOs serve a valuable function in bridging "classroom" and "street" learning. FTOs should be, and usually are, chosen for their ability to teach recruits good practices that will prevent citizen complaints and lawsuits against the department. FTOs submit evaluations of the new recruit that determine whether he or she passes the probationary period.

In-service training hours are required for all police officers to maintain their certification. This in-service training usually has content that is mandated by the state, and also optional training segments that can be selected by the department or individual officer. In Massachusetts, for instance, 40 hours of training is required each year, and includes legal updates, eyewitness identification, defensive tactics skills training, use-of-force concepts and tactics, community interactions, Critical Incidents, firearms training and requalification, CPR recertification and first-aid training.[7]

Police management training has been criticized as non-existent; however, there is very advanced training available for police leaders. Various organizations, such as the Police Executive Research Forum (PERF), provide research and training to improve administration and management. There is also training for police managers available through the Federal Law Enforcement Training Center (FLETC), which also conducts training internationally.

> To learn more about PERF, go to http://www.policeforum.org/, and for FLETC, to http://www.fletc.gov/

WHAT IS THE DIFFERENCE BETWEEN PROACTIVE AND REACTIVE POLICING?

Patrol can be considered both **reactive policing** and **proactive policing**. Typically, patrol officers spend time responding to dispatched calls for service, which is obviously reactive policing; however, they also interact with the citizenry, develop relationships with key community members, and follow up on tips which can be considered proactive policing. The idea that simply patrolling deters crime has been called into question. One of the most famous research projects in policing was the Kansas City Preventive Patrol Study. In this study, part of Kansas City, Missouri, was divided into three different areas. One area had no patrol at all—police only responded to dispatched calls. The second area had increased patrol, roughly five to six times the normal pattern. The third area was the control group, with normal patrols scheduled. Study authors found no significant differences among the three areas in level of crime or citizen satisfaction.[8] This does not mean, of course, that police have no effect on crime; but it does call into question the effectiveness of normal patrols.

While regular patrol may not be noticed or have any effect on crime, **saturated patrols**, meaning that a certain neighborhood or area of town is targeted for frequent, perhaps even constant, patrol presence, has been found to be effective. The "hot spot" is identified through crime reports and the saturated patrol continues for a set period or until the crime reports are reduced to an acceptable level. Research has indicated that saturated patrols do work in reducing crime; there is a **residual effect**, meaning reduced crime continues after the saturated patrol ends; and there does not seem to be a **displacement effect**, meaning that crime merely moves to another area of the city.[9]

Two of the most problematic calls for police officers are those that involve the mentally ill and domestic disturbances. When 911 calls are made, the patrol officers who respond have the goal to solve the immediate issue, e.g., a mentally ill person in the middle of traffic, a person threatening suicide, or a fighting couple. Some officers take a more proactive approach, however, and strive to provide more long-term solutions by referring the individuals to resources in the community that can prevent future incidents.

Some departments have special units or specially trained officers to deal with the mentally ill. The news media periodically report on incidents where police officers responding to a call about a mentally ill person resort to using violent means to subdue the individual and then encounter criticism for doing so. Crisis Intervention Training (**CIT**) helps officers identify the signs of mental illness, teaches communication techniques in how to interact with the mentally ill, and provides contact information for the resources that are available in the community to assist these individuals. More controversial are "**de-escalation**" **policies** that require police officers to use time, distance, and shielding to slow down interactions with the mentally ill. When officers respond to a 911 call of any person, including a mentally ill person, with a weapon, the standard response would be to secure the scene and disarm the individual as soon as possible. As long as someone is not in any immediate danger, de-escalation requires responding officers to utilize strategies to protect themselves by staying further back rather than getting close to the person and talking to them until they relinquish the weapon, sometimes for hours if that is what is necessary. Critics contend that taken to an extreme, such strategies are not feasible because police officers respond to too many calls per day and/or that there is too much danger presented in allowing the individual to control the scene. Proponents argue de-escalation is very similar to the hostage negotiation tactics that have been taught for years and even though "rushing the scene" may have a successful outcome, in some cases it has needlessly resulted in death or injury. Proponents argue that as long as officers have the time and there is no immediate threat, they should practice de-escalation.

Some police departments also have special domestic violence units that respond to calls that involve battered women and/or abused children. These officers receive additional training. Before the 1980s, spousal violence was rarely considered a crime. If the injury was "severe," aggravated assault could be charged and the perpetrator could be arrested, but if the injury was not defined as severe, it was only misdemeanor assault and a police officer could not arrest unless the victim swore out a complaint. That changed in the 1980s when states begin passing "mandatory arrest" statutes that allowed or, in some cases, required officers to arrest without a complainant in cases of domestic violence, even if the injury did not rise to aggravated assault. Domestic violence calls comprise a substantial portion of all calls for service. Due to the heightened emotion and frequency of alcohol, these calls can be dangerous for victims and police officers alike.

In larger departments, officers are promoted to the detective ranks, but it would be incorrect to assume that patrol officers do not conduct investigations. In smaller departments officers may rotate assignments from patrol to detective and back again; and, even in departments where patrol officers are not given the title, they do conduct investigations or pick up information to pass along to investigators. Because patrol officers are the public face of the police department and interact with the community more frequently, they often receive the tips that lead to identifying suspects.

Proactive policing refers to those activities where police take the initiative in uncovering and/or preventing crime. Proactive policing includes undercover operations. In undercover operations, police officers may pretend to be drug dealers, prostitutes, or "johns." "Buy-bust" incidents are when the officer pretends to be a drug user and buys from a street dealer, and moments later an arrest is made. Similar set-ups are done to control street prostitution—policemen routinely pretend that they are "johns," and policewomen dress up as prostitutes. Ethical issues arise in undercover operations, especially when they evolve into personal relationships.[10]

In proactive investigations, the central question is: Who do police target and why? Police operations that provide opportunities for crime change the police role from discovering who has committed a crime to one of discovering who might commit a crime if given the chance. Some argue these activities create crime, but others counter by saying that the criminals would be committing such acts regardless of police involvement. In fact, that is part of the definition of entrapment and the legal test to determine if entrapment has occurred is whether the defendant had a predisposition to commit the criminal act.

Read this news article for an example of a controversial de-escalation incident: http://www.nytimes.com/2016/04/26/health/police-mental-illness-crisis-intervention.html?&moduleDetail=section-news-0&action=click&contentCollection=Health&region=Footer&module=MoreInSection&version=WhatsNext&contentID=WhatsNext&pgtype=Blogs

HOW HAS TECHNOLOGY AFFECTED POLICING?

Policing has changed dramatically in the last 40 years because of technology. The advent of computers, communication technology, and other scientific breakthroughs has provided tools for law enforcement that could only have been dreamed of in the 1960s.

Crime mapping is as old as using push-pins on a wall map, but computers have made the process much more sophisticated. One of the most publicized police management strategies has been the **CompStat program**. This approach was developed in New York City during the tenure of Chief William Bratton. Basically it uses computer-generated crime statistics and daily or weekly meetings

Exhibit 5.2   CompStat uses computer-generated crime statistics to see patterns, allocate resources, and hold managers accountable for crime in their districts. The system was developed in New York City where it is run out of this control room.

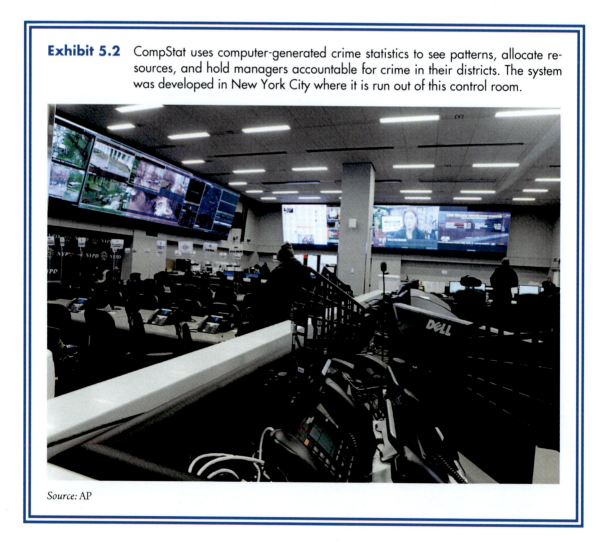

Source: AP

of division heads to hold these managers responsible for the crime in their districts. Immediate feedback, in the form of crime reports, allows higher-level administrators to see who is and who is not successful in reducing crime. Some research has suggested that the format may create pressure to "doctor" crime reports. However, advocates argue that it is an efficient, modern approach to policing that is based on management principles.[11]

In addition to knowing where crimes occur, other technology has made it easier to investigate crime and catch criminals. Patrol car computers provide instant feedback to the officer about a suspect's criminal history, license plate readers provide information about car owners and whether the car has been reported stolen, and cellphones allow citizens to instantly contact officers if they have been provided a phone number. Drones have been used to provide undetected surveillance of marijuana fields, cellphone tracing technology has been instrumental in proving guilt based on a suspect's location, and thermal imaging has helped prove the presence of indoor growing operations as well as assist law enforcement in hostage situations. Officers are becoming adept at utilizing social media to investigate crime as well. Ironically, some individuals have been caught specifically because they boast about their crimes and/or post on social media.

Police departments must have the capacity to use computers because, increasingly, that's where crime occurs. **Cybercrimes** typically refer to computer hacking and the use of computers for identity theft and fraud, but there are other crimes that either target computers or use computers to commit the crime, e.g., sexual solicitation of a minor, pornography, computer-aided voyeurism, sabotage. Now research shows by 2013, half of all state agencies and a quarter of county and municipal agencies had a cybercrimes unit or at least some police officers with primary duties related to cybercrimes. From 2007 to 2012, the FBI reported a 40 percent increase in cybercrime complaints and the number of cybercrimes units in police departments tripled from 9 percent of all agencies to 28 percent.[12]

One study of the use of technology in law enforcement reported that there were issues that prevented the value of technology from being fully utilized. Records software can be cumbersome and not particularly user-friendly and law enforcement officers reported frustration in the user interface that made them less efficient and compromised situational awareness when they spent an inordinate amount of time in their patrol car trying to input data. Further, while officers utilized technology for traditional reactive policing, e.g., finding suspects, they did not utilize technology as readily for proactive policing (e.g., using crime data to determine their patrolling patterns).[13] Some older officers have reported that younger "millennial" officers depend too heavily on their cellphones, texting when they should be having face-to-face meetings with citizens, and showing a lack of ability to engage with citizens because they are more comfortable utilizing social media.[14]

Recently, technology in law enforcement investigations was the issue when the FBI wanted Apple to "hack" into the iPhone of the San Bernadino terrorist Syed Rizwan Farook in order to uncover information about the attack. Apple refused, and the FBI evidently located private parties who were able to do so. This controversy exposes one of the challenges and controversies over the use of technology in law enforcement. Our "surveillance" society is grappling with the situation where technology is outstripping the law and ethics to control it. We live in an age where government can read our texts or emails, facial recognition programs can identify us on the street through a multitude of cameras placed in public places, and real-time satellite images can reach places where cameras don't exist.[15]

Of course, local police don't have access to the most sophisticated equipment available but there is a great deal of overlap between what has been developed and used for international counter-terrorism and local police investigations of garden variety crimes. For instance, the stingray device that "tricks" cellphones into using it as a cellphone tower thereby compromising the user's privacy has been provided to and used by local law enforcement and has led to criminal convictions. The public has only a dim understanding of its presence. Surveillance experts worry about the encroachment of government watchers into our private lives, but even police officers are not immune and are increasingly being filmed themselves by their patrol car dashcams, by body cameras, and by bystanders' ubiquitous cellphone cameras. Research on body cameras so far indicates that their use results in fewer citizen complaints and better behavior by citizens.[16] However, no good answers have emerged over such questions as: Should individual police officers have the discretion to turn the camera off? Should private citizens have the authority to make footage of themselves private; alternatively, should all footage be subject to open records requests? Who should store the unimaginable amount of video footage collected in large cities, and for how long? These questions are only a sample of the many issues with body cameras, and other technology creates similar types of concerns.

IS POLICE OFFICER STRESS A PROBLEM AND, IF SO, WHAT IS THE ROLE OF ORGANIZATIONAL JUSTICE?

Some researchers have concluded that police officers do not experience more stress than those in other occupations, although findings are mixed.[17] One can say with certainty, however, that policing has a few unique stressors not shared by most other occupations—that is, using or being a target of lethal force is not present in most occupations. Research has found that police officers' heart rates increase dramatically when they are going to a serious call. Although heart rates go down after the call, they don't return to normal resting rates immediately. If the officer then receives another call, this raises the heart rate again, without a return to normal resting levels, and so on, so that if an officer is responding to several serious calls during the day, his or her heart rate is constantly elevated.[18]

Interestingly, in some studies officers have reported more stress comes from the organization than from what they experience on the street. Research indicates that officers experience more stress from management over such things as being "second guessed," being punished for minor infractions, and not being rewarded than they do from the "operational" elements of policing (dealing with suspects and danger). In one study on police stress, it was found that officers experienced "organizational stress" (which included perceptions of supervisors being too rigid and oppressive with a corresponding lack of discretion) and that this stress reduced their performance.[19]

Organizational justice refers to the perception that the organization is fair, decisions are made in an equitable manner, and employees are treated with respect. It is related to **procedural justice**, which refers to the idea that individuals may have positive views of what happens to them, even if they don't like the outcome, if the process is deemed as fair.[20] Studies of "organizational justice" indicate that officers have more organizational commitment and are less inclined to commit negative acts when they trust their supervisors and believe the organization is fair.[21] Perceptions of organizational justice by officers are correlated with greater job satisfaction and greater organizational citizenship behaviors (doing things above and beyond the job requirements for the betterment of the organization).

Research has also found that individuals experience the stress of policing differently, and factors such as gender, age, and ethnicity seem to affect the ability to cope with the stressors.[22] Stress is an important issue because it may lead to **burnout**, which is when officers merely "go through the motions" of their job and may be susceptible to corruption. It can also lead to turnover when officers quit or retire early because of stress.

WHAT IS THE POLICE SUBCULTURE?

A **subculture** exists when a group has a different set of values, beliefs, and even language from the dominant culture. In the case of the police subculture, there is research that indicates that in some departments there is a "subculture" of policing that is different from, and in conflict with, formal departmental mission statements. Researchers argue that the reason this subculture exists is the special nature of policing, including the following characteristics:

- Police typically form a homogeneous social group.
- They have a uniquely stressful work environment.
- They participate in a mostly closed social system.[23]

As noted in Chapter 4, police departments are more diverse today than in the past, but the other characteristics of the work life first described in the 1980s still hold true to a great extent. The work life of police officers is marked by shift work and special characteristics (such as dangerousness and stigma). Police officers' social lives tend to include other police officers. The subculture of policing has been described by various researchers as including certain values or themes. **Socialization** is adopting the values and beliefs of one's culture (or subculture). The police subculture has been described as including the following traits:

- stereotypical views of large numbers of citizens as troublemakers
- loyalty to colleagues over citizens or the department
- view that the use of force is acceptable even when not strictly legal
- view that police officer discretion should not be questioned
- view that the truth is relative and subject to protecting officers or crime control.[24]

Another researcher identified the three dominant characteristics of the police culture as cynicism or suspicion (of everyone); the acceptance of the use of force when their authority is threatened; and the perception that they are victims of public misunderstanding and scorn, low wages, and unfair administrators.[25]

The "**blue curtain of secrecy**," an element of the subculture, refers to the alleged tendency of police officers to cover up misconduct by other police officers. It should be noted that recent research indicates that this conspiracy of silence is breaking down.[26] There are interesting contradictions, however, because in a recent survey, while 80 percent of police officers did not think that the "code of silence" was essential for police trust and good policing, fully two-thirds reported that a "whistleblower" would suffer informal punishment from fellow officers. Further, more than half agreed that it was not unusual for police to ignore improper conduct on the part of other officers.[27]

The "blue curtain of secrecy" may not exist in some departments or may exist at varying levels in different police departments. If it does exist, it occurs for various reasons. Officers feel loyalty toward each other. They also may believe that the officer's wrongdoing is not as serious as the discipline he would receive or equal the loss of an experienced officer to the department. There may be egoistic reasons as well, because the officer may believe that he or she has also committed acts that could be disciplined. Loyalty is perhaps stronger in law enforcement than in other professions because police depend on one another, sometimes in life-or-death situations. Loyalty to one's fellows is part of the *esprit de corps* of policing and is an absolutely essential element of a healthy department, but it seems that it can also cause problems when some officers are protected from the consequences of their misconduct.

Most of the research on the police subculture is fairly old, and, although some current research seems to support the continued presence of some aspects of the subculture, it also seems to be the case that it may not be as prevalent or extreme as it once might have been. Factors contributing to the possible weakening of the subculture include: increasing diversity in race, ethnicity, and education of recruits; the formalization of grievance procedures and union advocacy (which negates the need for a subculture); and the threat of civil litigation which makes covering up for someone much more potentially costly. Also, researchers have found that there is substantial variation among officers and differences in their cultural views as well as differences between police departments and even between districts or sub-stations within police departments.[28]

WHAT ARE SOME TYPES OF POLICE MISCONDUCT?

The International Association of Chiefs of Police developed the Law Enforcement Code of Ethics and the Canons of Police Ethics, and many departments have used these or adapted them to their own situations. There are at least four major themes in the International Chiefs of Police Code. Fairness is the single most dominant theme in the law enforcement code. Police officers must uphold the law regardless of the offender's identity. A second theme is that of *service*. The third theme is the *importance of the law*. Police are protectors of the Constitution and must not go beyond it or substitute rules of their own. The final theme is one of *personal conduct*. Police, at all times, must uphold a standard of behavior consistent with their public position. This involves a higher standard of behavior in their professional and personal lives than that expected from the general public.

To read the International Chiefs of Police Law Enforcement Code, go to http://www.lib.jjay.cuny.edu/cje/html/codes/codes-usa-organizational/lece-r.html

Unfortunately, despite the code of ethics, and departmental efforts in selection, training, and supervision to minimize the occurrence of misdeeds on the part of officers, scandals do occur. Examples of widespread corruption occur periodically in the news as well as individual acts of deviance by a few officers.[29] While the vast majorities of officers are honest and perform their job honorably, it is important to understand the structural elements that allow these instances of corruption to occur. It does seem to be the case that the most extreme cases of police corruption occur in large cities. Perhaps this is because there is more anonymity in large departments and it is more difficult to supervise all officers in all divisions and squads. Further, it is harder to develop a cohesive culture of integrity and service in larger departments with thousands of officers.

Corruption can be divided into 1) economic corruption; and 2) abuse of authority. Economic corruption includes graft. **Graft** refers to any exploitation of one's role, such as accepting bribes or protection money. Graft also occurs when officers receive kickbacks from tow truck drivers, defense attorneys, or bail bondsmen for recommending them. **Gratuities** are usually prohibited by departmental policies; they are items of value received by an individual because of his or her role or position, rather than because of a personal relationship with the giver.

A different type of misconduct is abuse of authority. Police abuse of authority comes in three different areas: physical abuse (excessive force, sexual assault), psychological abuse (disrespect, harassment, intimidation), and legal abuse (unlawful searches or seizures or manufacturing evidence).[30] One type of abuse of authority is when officers extort sex from female citizens. Egregious cases in the United States include rapes by officers on duty, and by jailers in police lock-ups. One of the most recent occurred in Oklahoma City where former officer Daniel Holtzclaw was convicted and sentenced to 263 years for raping several women while on duty.[31]

The concept of "**noble cause corruption**" refers to illegal actions or rule violations perpetrated by officers for "noble" reasons, i.e., to get the criminal off the street.[32] Such practices as "**testilying**" (lying in affidavits or when giving testimony) and coercion occur because of **ends-oriented thinking**, which means that the person believes "the end justifies the means" regardless of how bad the means are. Police officers behave this way when they place a high value on crime control, even over due process. The behaviors under the noble cause category are done by those who believe they are fulfilling their oath of protecting the public. Crime lab investigators and prosecutors may also engage in shortcuts and unethical acts in order to convict the perceived guilty. Prosecutors have been known to suppress evidence and allow perjured testimony, so it is not only police officers who feel compelled to break the law in order to further the noble cause of crime control.[33]

There are individual, organizational and societal explanations for police misconduct. *Individual explanations* explain the officer was deviant when hired or became so after hire. Such explanations support better selection procedures and better supervision for reducing the possibility of corruption. *Organizational explanations* point to problems in training or supervision. The concept of organizational justice discussed above might be an organizational explanation of

Exhibit 5.3   Daniel Holtzclaw used his position as an Oklahoma City Police Officer to rape and sexually victimize women while on patrol.

Source: AP

misconduct. Lack of supervision from front-line sergeants, and poor leadership can breed corruption.[34] *Societal explanations* of police deviance focus on the relationship between the police and the public. When societal norms encourage differential application of the law, it supports police graft. As long as the general public engages in illegal activities (like gambling, prostitution, and drug use), it is no surprise that some police officers are able to rationalize not enforcing the law. In another vein, as long as the public relays a message that crime control is more important than individual liberties and rights, then we should not be surprised when some police act on that message and violate the law.

A wide range of suggestions has been offered that may reduce or minimize the chance of police corruption, including those found in Exhibit 5.4.

Exhibit 5.4   Reducing Police Corruption

- Increase the salary of police
- Eliminate unenforceable laws
- Establish civilian review boards
- Improve training, especially ethics training
- Require more education
- Improve leadership
- Set realistic goals and objectives for the department
- Provide a written code of ethics
- Provide a whistleblowing procedure that ensures fair treatment of all parties
- Create more oversight (inspectors' general offices)
- **Integrity testing**
- Perform audits (of overtime or funds paid to informants)
- Have financial disclosure rules
- Improve internal affairs departments
- Rotate staff in certain assignments, e.g., vice
- Have better evidence-handling procedures
- Use video cameras in patrol cars
- Use covert high-technology surveillance
- Decriminalize vice crimes
- Use body cameras for all patrol officers
- Employ early warning systems
- Seek formal prosecutions when appropriate

Source: J. Pollock, *Ethical Dilemmas and Decisions in Criminal Justice.* Boston, MA: Cengage, 2016.

Civilian review/complaint boards are increasingly being called for in communities. Citizens not connected to the police department sit on these committees, commissions, or boards to monitor how police investigate citizen complaints. There are many models for the idea of civilian review, and no one model has been reported to be more effective or better than any other.[35]

Another idea is an **early warning or audit system**. Because research shows that a small number of officers are responsible for a disproportionate share of excessive force complaints and other types of citizen complaints, the idea is to identify these officers early. Early warning systems have been used by New Orleans, Portland, and Pittsburgh. The early warning systems utilize number of complaints, use of force reports, use of weapon reports, reprimands, and other indicators to identify problem officers. Intervention may include greater supervision, additional training, and/or counseling.[36]

Employee behavior is directly influenced by superiors. Even if leaders are not involved in corruption directly, encouraging or participating in the harassment and ostracism that is directed toward whistleblowers supports an organizational culture in which officers may be afraid to come forward when they know of wrongdoing. A different problem may be when certain people in the department do not receive punishment for behaviors that others would receive punishment for. This climate destroys the trust in police leadership that is essential to ensure good communication from the rank and file.[37]

DO POLICE OFFICERS DISCRIMINATE AGAINST MINORITIES?

There is a longstanding, pervasive belief that police treat African Americans, and to a lesser extent, Hispanics, more harshly than Whites. In this section, we will examine the evidence, always with the recognition that one cannot discuss the 12,000 police agencies in the country as a monolithic unit, nor is it fair to assume that a half million police officers are similar on any spectrum, including discriminatory behavior.

Individual prejudices and perceptions of groups such as women, minorities, and homosexuals can influence decision making. The question is whether officers' views of the world affect the way they do their job. The point is not that police officers are more prejudiced than the rest of us; it is that their special position creates the possibility that their prejudices could cause a citizen to be treated differently than others. Essentially, when police act on prejudices while performing their jobs, discrimination takes the form of either enforcing the law differentially or withholding the protections and benefits of the law.

Recent news stories have exposed scandals where officers (e.g., in San Francisco, California; Ferguson, Missouri; Edison, New Jersey; Seattle, Washington; Baton Rouge, Louisiana; and Miami Beach and Fort Lauderdale, Florida) texted racist and homophobic messages, including death threats, calling Black citizens "monkeys," and making jokes about lynching.[38] We know that the Internet is full of racist, sexist, and homophobic rants; however, police officers do not have the same free speech rights as the rest of us to spew such hateful messages when they can be identified as police officers. Departmental policies and codes of conduct require them to meet higher standards of behavior. It is also extremely important to be aware of the power of **implicit bias**.[39] Even if officers do not feel they are treating Blacks or other minorities differently, they may be if their worldview is represented accurately by the racist statements.

Read about implicit bias training for police officers at this website: http://www.fairimpartialpolicing.com/

Recent events indicate, perhaps, that the issue of racism is endemic. There are patterns and practices pervasive in the system of justice that seem to be evidence of unequal treatment. For instance, after the Department of Justice completed their investigation of Ferguson, Missouri, they concluded that Officer Darren Wilson used lawful force in his shooting of Michael Brown; however, the report also documented widespread discriminatory practices directed toward the Black community. The report put into context the violent reaction of the community to the Brown shooting, explaining that there had been years of distrust and resentment because of illegal and unethical practices by the police and justice officials in the town and county. More recently, a task force was created by the Chicago mayor after the Laquan McDonald shooting video sparked widespread protests. The task force issued a scathing report concluding that racism was rampant in the Chicago Police Department based on personal testimony and an examination of police incident reports. It was criticized by the police union and other officials as being one-sided and biased, however, the mayor quickly adopted about half of its recommendations.[40]

Most studies indicate that Blacks express more distrust of police than Whites or Hispanics. Recall from Chapter 4 that a July 2016 *NYT/CBS* poll found that 75 percent of Blacks believed police officers were more likely to use force against Blacks as compared to White residents. In a Pew Research Center public opinion report the percentage of Blacks saying they have "very little" confidence in their local police to treat Blacks and Whites equally has increased, from 34 percent five years ago to 46 percent. The group expressing the most negative views toward police was under-50, Black Democrats.[41] In Exhibit 5.5 below, one can see that the belief that police treat Blacks and Whites equally has decreased over the years.

In Exhibit 5.6, we use the Pew Research Center data to show that about 70 percent of Blacks said police forces across the country did a poor job of holding officers accountable when misconduct occurred, compared with 27 percent of Whites. About six in ten Blacks (57 percent) rated police performance as poor when it came to using the right amount of force for each situation, compared with 23 percent of Whites.[42] The *NYT/CBS* poll that was taken in July 2016 showed even worse percentages so we can assume that the next Pew Research Center poll will also show increased distrust of police by Blacks.

Hispanics also have a more negative view of police than do Whites. A nationwide poll of 1,000 Hispanics, underwritten by the W.W. Kellogg Foundation and reported in the popular press, found that two in three Hispanics fear police use of excessive force, even though 84 percent agreed that police were there to protect them. About 18 percent reported that they had friends or family members who had suffered police brutality.[43]

Academic research supports these findings. In a 33-city sample, it was found that race and age were strong correlates of distrust of police, with the level of distrust of Blacks two to five times higher than Whites across cities. What was interesting about this study was the variation across the cities. For instance, 32 percent of Blacks in New York City as opposed to 7 percent of Whites

Exhibit 5.5 Race Differences in Perceptions of Police

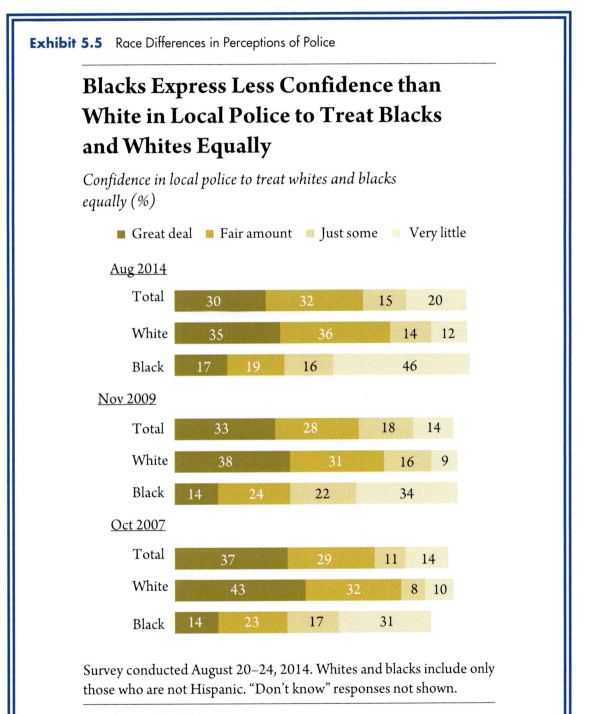

Blacks Express Less Confidence than White in Local Police to Treat Blacks and Whites Equally

Confidence in local police to treat whites and blacks equally (%)

■ Great deal   ■ Fair amount   ■ Just some   Very little

Aug 2014

	Great deal	Fair amount	Just some	Very little
Total	30	32	15	20
White	35	36	14	12
Black	17	19	16	46

Nov 2009

	Great deal	Fair amount	Just some	Very little
Total	33	28	18	14
White	38	31	16	9
Black	14	24	22	34

Oct 2007

	Great deal	Fair amount	Just some	Very little
Total	37	29	11	14
White	43	32	8	10
Black	14	23	17	31

Survey conducted August 20–24, 2014. Whites and blacks include only those who are not Hispanic. "Don't know" responses not shown.

Source: Pew Research Center/USA Today

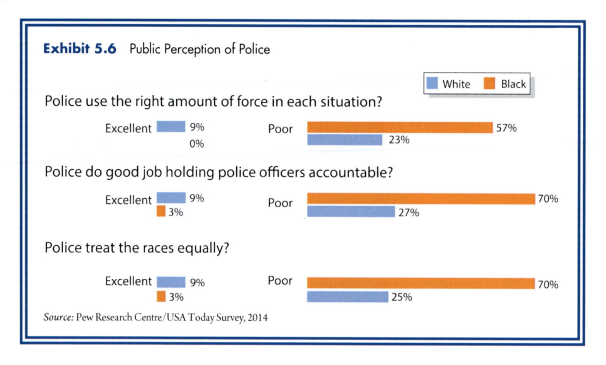

Exhibit 5.6   Public Perception of Police

Legend: White | Black

Police use the right amount of force in each situation?

Excellent — White 9%, Black 0%

Poor — Black 57%, White 23%

Police do good job holding police officers accountable?

Excellent — White 9%, Black 3%

Poor — Black 70%, White 27%

Police treat the races equally?

Excellent — White 9%, Black 3%

Poor — Black 70%, White 25%

Source: Pew Research Centre/USA Today Survey, 2014

expressed distrust of police, but the differences were less pronounced in Birmingham, Alabama, with a much smaller percentage of both Whites and Blacks expressing distrust; 8.9 percent of Blacks compared to 2.08 percent of Whites expressed distrust.[44]

Although there is a wealth of evidence to support the idea that Blacks and, to a lesser extent, other minorities, are more likely to distrust police and believe that police officers discriminate,[45] that is not the same thing as evidence that supports a finding that police officers actually *do* discriminate based on race and/or ethnicity. Discriminatory actions can include decisions to: a) arrest, b) stop and/or search in a discriminatory manner, and c) act disrespectfully toward citizens. Unfortunately, these all pose difficult methodological problems because Blacks are more likely to live in high-crime neighborhoods where police "police" everyone who lives there more aggressively. There is no point in comparing police officer actions in a low-crime suburban neighborhood to a high-crime inner-city neighborhood because police deal with more dangerous people, they go to more calls, and they interact with more individuals with serious criminal records. The reality is that Blacks in this country are more likely than Whites to live in such neighborhoods which complicates what we observe regarding police actions. It may be that police discriminate on the basis of race or ethnicity, but it may also be that police discriminate based on the neighborhood they patrol in.

Decisions to arrest are notoriously difficult to study. Police officer discretion is such that some estimates are that officers don't arrest in about half of the cases where an arrest could be made legally. We do have some glimmer of differential arrest patterns when we look at drug use and drug arrest patterns. Overall, drug use among White and minority groups are about the same; however, Blacks are disproportionally arrested and incarcerated. Exhibit 5.7 below shows cocaine use figures. Whites and Blacks show only a slight difference in use patterns.

Other drugs show slightly different use patterns but the arrest figures show clearly that Blacks are arrested at rates disproportional to their use rates (about one-third of all drug arrests are of Blacks despite comprising only 13 percent of the population). This disparity increases when one looks at prison commitment rates for drug offenses.[46] This disparity could be due to factors other than discrimination; it could be that Blacks are more likely to sell than Whites, more likely to sell in open-air markets, and/or more likely to operate in high-crime neighborhoods that fall under the scrutiny of police. However, it is hard to explain away the extent of the disparity.

Another study done in San Francisco covering the years 2010 to April 2015 showed that African Americans were cited for resisting arrest at a rate eight times higher than Whites. The study reported that of 9,633 arrests for resisting, not accompanied by a felony, Blacks (making up just 6 percent of the population) accounted for 45 percent of the arrests. Suspects can be convicted of resisting arrest, punishable by up to a year in jail and up to a $1,000 fine, even when the underlying offense is minor, such as not complying with an order

Exhibit 5.7   Use of Cocaine by Race and Ethnicity, 2011

	Never Used Cocaine (%)	*Have Used Cocaine (%)*
White	82.9	17.1
Black/African American	90.1	9.9
Native American/ Alaskan Native	78.7	21.3
Native Hawaiian/ Other Pacific Islander	91.9	8.1
Asian	96.4	3.6
Hispanic	89.3	10.7
More than one race	84.3	15.7
Total	85.4	14.6

Source: http://www.icpsr.umich.edu/quicktables/quickoptions.do

to move one's car. Critics of police say the charge is used to cover up cases of police brutality.[47] Note that, without more research, we do not know if these numbers indicate resisting arrest is a charge used in a discriminatory manner, if Blacks are more likely than other groups to resist arrest, or some mixture of the two explanations.

Decisions to stop include both traffic stops and street stops or investigatory detentions based on reasonable suspicion. **Racial profiling** occurs when a police officer makes a stop based entirely on race or ethnicity. When a young Black man is seen, for instance, driving a newer-model, expensive car, police officers suspect that the vehicle is stolen and/or that the man is holding drugs. A "**pretext stop**" refers to the practice of police officers to use some minor traffic offense to stop the individual and in the course of the traffic stop look for other evidence of wrongdoing, specifically by a search, usually a consent search. The Supreme Court has upheld the legality of such stops in *Whren v. U.S.* (1996).[48]

Studies on racial profiling show that minorities may be stopped in numbers greater than their proportion of the population would indicate; however, the methodology of some racial profiling studies is problematic. Comparing stops to simply the percentage of population is not very accurate because it does not take into account the percentage of non-White drivers, the percentage of non-White drivers who engage in traffic offenses, or the percentage of minorities in the geographic area that is being targeted by heavier patrols (which would result in more stops regardless of the race/ethnicity of the driver). Most of the earlier studies used percentage-of-population figures, but other researchers are highly critical of this rough approximation of the base rate. Recently the Texas Department of Public Safety (DPS) was criticized for using percentage-of-population figures for the state to conclude that they did not engage in racial profiling because the percentage of stops that were of Black drivers was lower than their percentage of the population. Critics argued that statewide population figures are irrelevant: Blacks are more likely to be poor and not have a car, and statewide populations and counts of stops mask location-specific patterns. It was also argued that the focus should be on what happens after the stop and earlier studies of DPS statistics showed that Blacks were much more likely to be subjects of a search than Whites.[49]

There is also no clear proof that the stops are due to prejudicial views toward those stopped. Most critics blame the individual officer, but it is important to note organizational influences, especially because studies show that Black officers are just as likely as White officers to stop Blacks in disproportionate numbers.[50]

A Bureau of Justice statistics study utilizing an addendum to the National Crime Victimization Survey showed that more Black drivers than White or

Hispanic (13 percent versus 10 percent) were pulled over for traffic stops, but, interestingly, no difference existed for "street stops" (individuals stopped while walking). Blacks were less likely to believe that police acted appropriately in the stops. This study also found that White drivers were searched and ticketed at a lower rate than Black drivers.[51]

Earlier studies indicated that Blacks were stopped about one and one-half times higher than their percentage of the population.[52] In a later study of what the researchers called "traffic stops" and "investigatory stops," a distinction was made between police stops that occur because the driver commits a clear violation and those where the officer is using the stop for investigatory purposes. The first stop is short and results in a ticket; the second kind of stop is longer and always includes a request for a consent search. There is little racial difference in those stopped for the traffic stop, but there is in the second type. In the study, 60 percent of all stops for Whites were for traffic safety, versus 35 percent for Blacks; however, 52 percent of all stops for Blacks (versus 34 percent for Whites) were for such minor reasons that the stop was coded as investigatory. In these types of searches, individuals are stopped for driving too slowly, broken lights, failure to signal, and other pretexts to initiate a search for drugs.[53] This second kind of stop is proactive policing for crime (mostly drug) control. It is a cost/benefit question as to whether the benefit gained is worth the cost in the antipathy it generates among those who are stopped.[54] Research seems to show that racially based stops may not be very effective anyway. The "hit rate" for finding drugs is lower for African Americans than it is for other racial groups. It is possible that when officers use race in decision making, they become less effective, not more effective, because they do not concentrate on what is important for investigation—behavior, not demographics.[55]

The Department of Justice issued new federal guidelines (mandatory for DOJ agents but only advisory for state law enforcement or other federal agencies) in December 2014. The rules added national origin, gender, gender identity, religion, and sexual orientation to characteristics for which profiling has been prohibited since 2003. Agents are prohibited from using these categories as the sole reason to investigate a target. They also eliminate the broad national security exceptions to profiling restrictions if for terrorism investigations. The new rules arguably were a compromise between the rights of targeted groups (e.g., Muslims) and national security.[56]

Disrespectful treatment by officers can be seen on YouTube videos which have examples of police officers who are rude and abusive to Black citizens. This is *not* a good representative sample of the millions of interactions that take place between police officers and citizens. Academic studies use observers to collect information on all interactions. Earlier studies indicated that residents (both Black and White) are initially disrespectful to police three times as often as police are initially disrespectful to residents (15 percent compared to 5 percent of encounters). Factors associated with being disrespectful include heightened emotion, number of bystanders, presence of intoxicants, being mentally impaired, and being in a disadvantaged neighborhood.[57]

A different methodology is to utilize surveys of citizens about their experiences. In surveys of citizens, Blacks are more than twice as likely to report disrespectful language or swearing by police officers. Minorities that live in metropolitan areas, have less education, less income, are younger, and report more bad experiences with the police, not surprisingly, perceive more police misconduct.[58] Areas of concentrated disadvantage show the least satisfaction with police, and race is still a predictor, even when controlling for neighborhood characteristics.[59] Some research has shown that race was a predictor in the use of verbal and physical coercion by officers.[60] Engel and colleagues, however, after an exhaustive review of prior studies, concluded that being a resident of a disadvantaged neighborhood was a stronger predictor of police "disrespect" to citizens than race.[61]

Thus, what may be happening is that minority citizens, probably partially because they live in high-crime poverty-stricken areas and partially because of implicit bias, are stopped more often for investigatory stops and are more likely to undergo consent searches.[62] Individuals hear of police abuse, see it via social media, or experience it themselves and those experiences may result in non-compliance and disrespect. For instance, minor traffic violation stops of young Black men to search the car for drugs while the driver and passengers are made to sit on the curb, sometimes for long periods of time, are relatively normal occurrences to police officers who probably feel they are just doing their job. However, these events, especially when they happen frequently, are embarrassing and frustrating to the car occupants and appear so to minority residents who see the stops as oppressive and abusive.[63] A pattern of this type of interaction between police officers and minority citizens builds resentment and distrust. Some minority citizens report that even if they were a victim of a crime, they would not call police. This breakdown of the social contract unfortunately may lead to more disorder as vigilantism takes the place of formal social control.

Because of prior bad experiences, minority citizens, especially men, may be non-compliant, disrespectful, and argumentative, which, in turn, triggers heavier-handed police action since police are trained and socialized that, for officer safety, control of the situation is paramount. Officers are taught that their first priority is to "secure the scene" and manage any potential threat. If individuals are arguing, not complying, and engaging in behavior that indicates opposition, then police officers will respond to that resistance as a threat to their safety. In small towns and suburban areas, police officers do not perceive the threat level as very high and so may be more patient and accommodating to non-compliant people; however, police officers in high-crime neighborhoods where violence is frequent and where there have been attacks on the police will respond much more aggressively to non-compliance. Unfortunately, this dynamic can set up a cycle whereby citizen disrespect/non-compliance leads to abuses of police power (or perceived abuses), which lead to even more distrust and hostility from the citizenry, which breeds even more distrust and antipathy between police departments and the citizenry they are sworn to protect.[64]

Hispanics also are more likely to perceive that police officers act in a discriminatory way. In 2012, Sheriff Arpaio in Maricopa County (Phoenix) lost a civil suit brought by the Department of Justice which alleged he and his deputies engaged in a pattern or practice of conduct that deprived persons of rights, privileges, or immunities secured or protected by the Constitution. In June of 2012, the Supreme Court upheld a section of an Arizona law that allowed police officers to check the immigration status of anyone they stopped for some other legal reason if they reasonably suspect the person is not a legal immigrant (*Arizona v. United States*, 2012).[65] Records showed that Hispanic drivers were four to nine times more likely to be stopped, and one-fifth of the traffic stops appeared to be unconstitutional (with no reason to stop) from a review of incident reports. Records indicated that police were dispatched when the report was only that there were "people of dark skin" or "people speaking Spanish" in an area. Findings also indicated that jail officers punished Hispanic inmates for not understanding English, refused to accept forms written in Spanish, and pressured inmates to sign forms waiving rights in English without a translation. Another finding was that there was a general culture of bias against Hispanics, including the use of excessive force against Latinos, a reduction of policing services to the Latino community, and a gender and/or national original bias by failing to adequately investigate sex crimes when the victim was Hispanic. In 2015, Arpaio admitted violating the court order that prohibited the roving patrols that targeted Hispanic-looking drivers, allowing them to continue eighteen months after the judge ordered them to cease.[66]

In cities such as Chicago and Baltimore, the relationship between the police force and the minority community seems to be broken. In other cities, police departments have also been scrutinized as engaging in racially discriminatory practices. It is a very difficult subject to study because of the high emotion on both sides: minority citizens feel they are not treated equally and police officers feel they are being unfairly criticized. Citizen complaints, arrest records, and observation studies help us understand the situation. As with many of the questions raised in this text, the best methodology would be observational studies (ride-alongs) with objective recorders, but although there are some of these studies available, they are very expensive. Body cameras may give us the best source of data for large numbers of interactions with the public and studies are underway that utilize this source.

WHAT IS THE LAW AND POLICY CONCERNING POLICE USE OF FORCE?

The use of force is usually perfectly legal—officers have the right to tackle a fleeing suspect, or use necessary force, including lethal force, when they are defending themselves or the suspect poses an immediate threat to the officer or others. Illegal or excessive force occurs when the officer goes beyond what is necessary to secure a lawful arrest, or has no lawful reason to use force at all. In *Graham v. Connor* (1989),[67] the Supreme Court held that officers have the right to use "reasonable" force in any interaction with the public, as determined by the facts and circumstances. They are not obligated to use the least possible force as long as the force used would be used by a reasonable officer in the same situation. It is very important to remember that force may be legal, even if the police officer's actions might have put him or her into the situation where force had to be used. "Lawful but awful" actions are those that meet the *Graham* standard of reasonableness, but perhaps violate policy because the officer did not follow proper procedures for handcuffing or performing a traffic stop, did not wait for back-up when necessary, or for some other reason helped set up the situation where force was then necessary.

Despite what we see on YouTube or the evening news, force is used very infrequently. Many police officers go through their whole career without ever drawing their weapon on the street. Some may never even experience serious physical altercations with people. In other locales, use of force incidents are more common—this is partly a function of the citizenry whose actions elicit a force response, and possibly a function of the culture of certain police departments which creates a greater likelihood that force will be utilized even when alternatives might be available. Excessive force appears to be more likely when victims challenge police authority—speeding past a patrol car, challenging police officer actions, or intervening in the arrest of another.[68]

In 1994, the Violent Crime Control and Law Enforcement Act was passed requiring the attorney general to acquire data about the use of excessive force by law enforcement officers and publish yearly reports. The annual reports required by Congress in the 1994 law were never produced. More recently, there have been calls to begin a national reporting system with some advocating that the receipt of any federal monies should come with the responsibility to collect and report use of force incidents. Estimates of the use of force come from other sources, such as the Police–Public Contact Survey and single-city studies.[69]

A number of different reports indicate that force is used very infrequently, only in 1 to 2 percent of all encounters with the public.[70] Use of force is more common in arrests, but even with arrest, only 20 percent involve some use of force, and even then it is usually just grabbing and holding.[71] However, use of force seems to vary depending on the city. Garner, Maxwell, and Heraux[72] found in their study that use of force ranged from 12.7 percent of encounters in one city to 22.9 percent of encounters in another city. In addition, a national survey of law enforcement agencies found that the rate of use-of-force events varied by region, with the highest in the South (90 incidents per 100,000), followed by the Northeast (72), the Midwest (68), and the West (50).[73] A recent study also found that use of force seems to be related to use-of-force policies. Those departments that had more stringent administrative force policies had fewer incidents where officers used force than departments where polices were less specific and/or more permissive.[74] It is also important to note that the figures above are describing use of force, not excessive force. Excessive force is estimated to occur in a miniscule portion of total encounters with the public—estimated at one-third of 1 percent.[75]

Characteristics of the target that seem to be correlated with use of force include: race, sex (male), disrespectful demeanor, emotionality, mental illness, intoxication, presence or perception of a weapon, the suspect's violent criminal record (knowledge of), suspect's use of force, gang membership, and socio-economic status.

Situational characteristics correlated with use of force include: the number of citizens present (positive association), the number of police officers present (positive association), and whether the encounter involved a car or foot pursuit.

Characteristics of the officers involved in use of force include sex (male), age (younger), and ethnicity (being Hispanic). Psychological traits of the officer have been identified as well, including lack of empathy, antisocial and paranoid tendencies, inability to learn from experience, a tendency not to take responsibility for actions, and cynicism. Officers who use force have also been found to have a stronger identification with the police subculture. Another factor in the tendency to use force was being involved in a traumatic event or prior injury (thus, use of force would be a type of post-traumatic stress behavior).[76]

It should be emphasized that these studies and the factors identified are associated with the use of force, not necessarily *excessive* force. Also, some studies have reported findings inconsistent with others. Because there is no national database, studies were obtained in various cities and using other datasets that have their own problems (e.g., victim reports, incident reports, and/or newspaper reports).

Even though use of force seems to be rare, and excessive force even rarer, that does not mean that it isn't a problem in some cities. Differences in use of force rates across cities suggest that some cities could do more to reduce use of force. Even one video of excessive force can poison the relationship between a police department and its citizenry.

Other research has shown that a small number of officers are responsible for a disproportionate percentage of the total uses of force. This may be because of their particular assignments, but it could also be because they are too quick to resort to uses of force. As mentioned previously, some studies do find an association between force and race or socio-economic status, but other factors, such as demeanor, seem to be even more influential.[77]

One problematic type of use of force is the use of conducted energy devices (CEDs), commonly known as tasers. Their use has dramatically expanded and proponents of the devices argue that they have resulted in less injury to officers and suspects alike, and officers who use them avoid having to use lethal force. Opponents, such as Amnesty International, argue that they have been responsible for an unacceptable number of deaths. Research indicates that the electricity that is conducted by the devices is not sufficient to seriously harm an individual, but there have been reports of serious injuries caused by falling and deaths occur because of pre-existing conditions. For instance, those who are under the influence of drugs may be more susceptible to injury. Also, if the taser is used multiple times on a person, there is a greater risk of injury.[78]

Some argue that news stories and YouTube videos show tasers being used inappropriately, e.g., when someone is verbally disruptive rather than physically dangerous. Arguments are that the taser should be an alternative to lethal force, not an alternative to physical control tactics. That is, the only time a taser should be used is when the alternative is to use a firearm. Generally, the courts have determined that a reasonableness standard applies to the taser as with any use of force. The officer is not obligated to use the least serious level of force, but he or she is obligated to use only that level of force (including the taser) that is reasonable given the nature of the threat. This means that the officer must feel threatened, and the taser is not appropriate for gaining compliance.

FOCUS ON DATA: DO POLICE OFFICERS ABUSE THEIR POWER TO USE LETHAL FORCE?

In the summer of 2016, Alton Sterling and Philando Castile's deaths at the hands of officers reignited a wave of protest that too many Black men are killed by officers in circumstances that are not legally justified. There is a perception, especially in the Black community, that an unacceptably high number of Black citizens are killed by police officers, and that officers are not held accountable when they engage in illegal uses of lethal force. The killing of Walter Scott (who is Black) by former officer Michael Slager (who is White) is the clearest example of the perception that law enforcement officers abuse their legal authority.

Exhibit 5.8 Walter Scott was attempting to run away from police officer Michael Thomas Slager after a traffic stop in South Carolina when Slager shot and killed Scott. The encounter was caught on video, providing evidence for those who believe police abuse their authority.

Source: AP

In that incident, a traffic stop resulted in Scott running from the officer who shot him in the back as he ran away. The former officer alleged that his shooting was legally justified because Scott had previously struggled with him and attempted to grab his gun. Slager was indicted for murder and faces trial in October 2016. The video of the incident that a bystander recorded is still available on YouTube and other websites. To some, the Walter Scott incident is an example of an endemic problem happening across the country; to others, it is an exceedingly rare event that has served to taint the entire profession unfairly. It is important to, first, ask relevant questions to be answered by data. When is lethal force legally justified? What are accurate statistics of the number of killings, but also the circumstances involved when officers shoot and kill? The second part of the question seems to be missing in many national conversations since it is not enough to simply report the percentage killed who are Black, but, also, what led to the shooting itself since no one argues that if someone is shooting at an officer or engages in conduct that is a clear threat, then the officer has a legal right to use lethal force.

In *Tennessee v. Garner* (1985),[79] the Supreme Court held that a Tennessee officer who shot and killed a teenage burglar who was scaling a fence to get away had engaged in an unconstitutional "seizure." In other words, fleeing felons could no longer be shot and potentially killed to prevent their escape. The Supreme Court held that officers did not have the right to use lethal force when there was no reason to believe that the suspect posed a serious threat. As mentioned previously, the Supreme Court has also said in *Graham v. Connor*, that the use of force must be reasonable, that is, reasonable police officers would have evaluated the situation and decided upon the same action. Thus, police officers have the legal right to use lethal force only if there is a reasonable belief that the target poses a serious threat to the police officer or someone else. If that belief turns out to be mistaken, for instance, if they perceive the suspect has a weapon which turns out to be a cellphone, then that mistake does not invalidate the reasonable belief and the shooting may be ruled justifiable. Further, police officers are not legally required to use lesser means of force—if someone is charging at a police officer and reasonable officers would perceive a serious threat, the police officer is not legally obligated to use a baton or taser first before his or her weapon. The legal analysis is extremely fact-specific because reasonableness is determined by many things; for instance, it is probable that it would not be ruled reasonable to perceive a seventeen-year-old girl charging at officers with only her fists as a serious threat thereby justifying shooting her; however, it might be perceived as a reasonable threat when an enraged 6' 4" 300-pound man charges an officer. Officers must treat every physical assault as weapon-involved because of the potential for their weapon to be taken from them in a fight. It is not reasonable to expect that the officer should allow himself or herself to be physically attacked if the assailant clearly means to do serious harm, and there is a possibility that the officer would be overpowered in the attack and have his or her gun taken by the assailant.

The Supplemental Homicide report of the FBI has a category of "justifiable homicides by law enforcement." These reports show that the number of justifiable homicides was in the 400s in the 1970s, dropped to the 300s in the 1980s, and rose again to averages in the 400s in the 1990s. However, it has been known for quite some time that the number reported is a woeful undercount of the true number of deaths. In 2000, the Deaths in Custody Reporting Act required law enforcement to report any deaths in custody to federal officials to be recorded. "In custody" would include shootings on the street when the individual was shot by law enforcement. The Bureau of Justice Statistics recently did an analysis of homicides from 2003 through 2009 and 2011 and found that of the total number of homicides that should have been recorded in official statistics, this reporting system captured approximately only 49 percent, while the Supplemental Homicide Reports captured only 46 percent. More than one-quarter (28 percent) were not recorded in either system.[80] So, the official number of deaths by police officers is probably less than half of the true number. Some studies now, for instance, put the true number for 2015 at around 1,000.[81] In one study comparing internal reports from the Los Angeles Police Department to FBI numbers, the 184 homicides by police provided to the FBI was 46 percent lower than the 340 uncovered in internal reports.[82] The *Washington Post*[83] and other sources are now tracking police shootings using data sources other than official reports to get more accurate counts and their numbers indicate that there were 980 killings by police officers in 2015 while the official number was 461 in 2013 (the last year available).[84] For this reason, it is probably impossible to state with any certainty whether there is a trend upward or downward in police shootings because we don't have accurate counts for previous years.

The reasons why such undercounting exists remain somewhat obscure. In one investigation of Virginia's justifiable homicide numbers, several killings went unreported because the incidents were not counted as justifiable during the investigation, and then no one went back to record the killing as a justifiable homicide after the investigation was complete. In some cases, departments simply refuse to provide the numbers because they are not legally obligated to do so. In other cases, because there is more than one jurisdiction investigating the killing, confusion results in no agency reporting it.[85]

The second part of the question was what circumstances prompted the officers' actions. Examining either the official reports or the larger set of killings collected from the *Washington Post*, it is clear that the majority of killings are of individuals who have weapons. In some earlier studies, it has been found that at least 80 percent of individuals killed had weapons.[86] In the *Washington Post* final analysis of killings in 2015, only 9 percent of the targets were unarmed. These individuals might have been trying to obtain a weapon or they may be the "mistaken weapon" type of case where an officer sees something in the target's hands, e.g., a cellphone, and misperceives it as a weapon. In three-quarters of the cases, police were actively being attacked or they were defending someone who was under attack. In one-quarter of cases, the target was fleeing. Even though the *Tennessee v. Garner* ruling established the fact that officers cannot legally shoot a fleeing suspect if there is no reason to think he or she poses a threat, if the suspect is armed and/or if there is reason to believe that he or she poses a serious danger to others (e.g., armed, fleeing bank robbers) then lethal force would be legally justified.[87]

About one-quarter of the targets of police shootings in the *Washington Post* analysis were mentally ill. This statistic has spurred efforts to provide **CIT** training to officers in the hope that de-escalation can prevent the need for lethal force. These cases are tragic in that often the police officer has been called by family members because of the erratic and/or threatening behavior of the mentally ill person. The officer arrives at the scene to help and ends up shooting the individual because of a perceived threat, e.g. the person will not relinquish a weapon or charges the officer. Then the officer is criticized for the lethal consequences.[88]

Reports also indicate that Blacks are disproportionately represented in the numbers of individuals shot and killed by police. Black men are only 6 percent of the general population, but in the *Washington Post* analysis, they comprised 40 percent of the unarmed group of those killed by police in 2015.[89] On the other hand, it is a highly misleading statistic to look at percentage of population figures because such shootings are not randomly distributed throughout the population; they are most likely in high-crime neighborhoods and when police feel threatened by the circumstances.

Implicit bias studies determine whether racial biases or stereotypes affect shooting decisions. Contrary to what many expect, researchers find that police officers were *less likely* than civilians to shoot at Black suspects in staged scenarios in laboratory settings, perhaps because they can practice what is called "cognitive control." Studies also show, however that their ability to exercise cognitive control is impeded by high cognitive load, fatigue, fear and high arousal.[90]

A very recent study utilized four different data sets to analyze police officer encounters: 1) the NYPD's records of 5 million stop-and-frisk events; 2) the Police–Public Contact Survey, a nationally representative sample of civilians;

3) event summaries from all incidents in which an officer discharges his weapon at civilians including both hits and misses from three large cities in Texas (Austin, Dallas, Houston), six large Florida counties, and Los Angeles County; and 4) a random sample of police–civilian interactions from the Houston Police Department from arrest codes in which lethal force is more likely to be justified. The study found that the race of the suspect did not influence the likelihood of fatal shootings by police. However, Blacks and Hispanics were 50 percent more likely than Whites to be the targets of all other uses of force. Police were 17 percent more likely to use their hands in encounters with Black residents; 18 percent more likely to push them into a wall, 24 percent more likely to point their weapon, and 25 percent more likely to use pepper spray or a baton against a Black citizen. Researchers said even after controlling for demographics such as age and gender, encounter characteristics such as whether individuals supplied identification or whether the interaction occurred in a high- or low-crime area, the differential treatment of Blacks was still significant.[91] The study has been criticized because much of the primary data used comes from police officer reports, with the assumption that the accuracy of the reports would favor the report writer. Since the data also provided an observed differential use of force in less than lethal situations, the supposition the reports are biased is less persuasive.

Some news reports point to the low number of indictments of police officers (only 54 officers charged between 2005 and 2015) as evidence of a system failing to hold officers accountable. This presentation is misleading, however, without noting that, as indicated above, the majority of shooting incidents show clear legal justification for the shooting. We do not know if this number represents a disproportionally low percentage of the "bad shooting" cases where there were questions about the legal justification for the decision to shoot. It also appears that indictments may be increasing with reports indicating that indictments in 2015 were three times the average of preceding years.[92] Each situation is legally evaluated through the "reasonable officer" standard, but it is what is reasonable at the time with that officer's perception of a serious threat. If that perception is reasonable, even if wrong, there is no abuse of force.

WHAT WERE THE RECOMMENDATIONS OF THE 21ST CENTURY PRESIDENT'S TASK FORCE ON POLICING?

After civil unrest in Ferguson, Missouri, and Baltimore, Maryland, in the summer and fall of 2014, President Obama created the 21st Century President's Task Force on Policing to examine the issues of policing in this country, and, more specifically, the relationship between policing and minority communities. The Task Force was made up of police leaders, academics, and individuals who were affiliated with community groups that had a stake in the issue of police–community relations. They held a series of public commentary meetings where experts, community members, and criminal justice professionals testified and submitted reports about a variety of issues. Their comprehensive report was presented as Six Pillars.

Pillar 1: Building Trust and Legitimacy. The Task Force noted the research on procedural justice—a concept referring to the perception that the processes involved in an individual's interaction with the justice system are fair.[93] Perceptions of procedural justice are said to involve voice (allowing the citizen the chance to speak); neutrality (fairness in decisions); respect (using respectful language and not demeaning the citizen); and trustworthiness (the idea that the actions of the officer are for the public good).[94] Research indicates that those who perceive elements of procedural justice in their interactions with police officers are more likely to comply with orders.[95] The Task Force recommended officers be trained in procedural justice and encouraged programs to build legitimacy in the community.

Pillar 2: Policy and Oversight. The Task Force recommended that all departments work closely with the International Association of Directors of Law Enforcement Standards and Training (IADLEST), including cooperating with the National Decertification Index to remove officers who have been decertified in one state from being hired in another.

Pillar 3: Technology and Social Media. The Task Force recommended that all departments create policies concerning the use of social media and institute research and evaluations of technology.

Pillar 4: Community Policing and Crime Reduction. Community policing concepts were reinforced and recommended by the Task Force.

Pillar 5: Training and Education. The Task Force recommended training in all areas, but emphasized the need for Crisis Intervention Training (CIT) and implicit bias training.

Pillar 6: Officer Wellness and Safety. There was a strong message that the Task Force supported police officers and programs and policies to help them maintain their physical and emotional health, including evaluating shift work and overtime.

The federal COPS office has been encouraging and documenting steps taken across the country that respond to the recommendations of the Task Force's report.

To read the entire report, go to www.cops.usdoj.gov/pdf/taskforce/taskforce_finalreport.pdf; to read about some of the programs that have been implemented, go to http://www.cops.usdoj.gov/policingtaskforce

SUMMARY

How Are Police Officers Selected and Trained?

Police departments use screening tools including civil service tests, physical tests, and psychological tests. Then candidates are subjected to hundreds of hours of training in academies followed by the Field Training Officer (FTO) phase where an experienced officer accompanies the new recruit, and a probationary period. All officers receive annual in-service training.

What Is the Difference Between Proactive and Reactive Policing?

Reactive policing is responding to calls for service and investigating crimes that have already occurred. Proactive policing involves undercover investigations, hot-spot policing, "stings," and other practices where police try to prevent crime rather than respond to calls for service.

How Has Technology Affected Policing?

Computers, cellphones, computers in patrol cars, and other technology have dramatically changed policing. It has made it easier to track criminals, but some technology has had user interface problems, e.g., data software. Cybercrimes units are becoming more common in police departments, no doubt due to the increase in computer-related crimes.

Is Police Officer Stress a Problem and, If So, What Is the Role of Organizational Justice?

A long history of research on police stress shows that stress is a problem, and much of it comes from within the organization. Organizational justice is a concept that indicates officers who believe their organization is fair experience less stress and burnout.

What Is the Police Subculture?

The police subculture is said to be the informal culture in policing that encourages the "blue curtain of secrecy" whereby police officers cover up wrongdoing of fellow police officers, and "noble cause corruption," which includes testilying and other forms of misbehavior that have the goal of gaining a criminal conviction but may violate the law.

What Are Some Types of Police Misconduct?

Acts of corruption can be categorized into acts of economic corruption and abuses of power. Explanations for why some police officers engage in these practices can be categorized into individual explanations, organizational explanations, and societal explanations.

Do Police Officers Discriminate Against Minorities?

Although methodological issues complicate the answer to this question, research seems to support the premise that Black males are more likely to be stopped, searched, and perhaps arrested, at least for drug crimes, than Whites. It is important to realize, however, that much of the different treatment that minorities experience may be due to living in high-crime areas where police "police" more aggressively. There is recent research to indicate that all uses of force (except for lethal force) are more likely to be used in encounters with Blacks and Hispanics.

What Is the Law and Policy Concerning Police Use of Force?

Force, including lethal force, can be used by police officers if it is reasonable. That is, when a reasonable police officer in those circumstances would believe force was an appropriate response. Force is used rarely by officers, despite the media attention to a few instances of abuse.

What Were the Recommendations of the 21st Century Presidents' Task Force on Policing?

There were a multitude of specific recommendations that fell under six "pillars": Building Trust and Legitimacy; Policy and Oversight; Technology and Social Media; Community Policing and Crime Reduction; Training and Education; and, Officer Wellness and Safety.

Critical Thinking Exercises

1. Research and write an update to the Focus on Data section. Is there more recent data on how many people have been killed by law enforcement officers? Has there been recent research on the type of circumstances that exist in such shootings and whether there is evidence that minorities are more likely to be unjustly killed by police officers?
2. Many law enforcement officers reject the 21st Century Panel on Policing and the recommendations that came from it because of a belief that President Obama does not support law enforcement. Research this position and determine whether or not it exists. What are the points of the argument? What exactly about the Panel's recommendations are opposed and why? What evidence exists on either side?

NOTES

1 Houston Police Department. Retrieved 6/1/2007 from www.houstontx.gov/police/img/hr_chart.jpg.

2 B. Sanders, "Using personality traits to predict police officer performance." *Policing: An International Journal of Police Strategies and Management* 31 (1) (2008): 129–147.

3 Ibid.; N. Claussen-Rogers and B. Arrigo, *Police Corruption and Psychological Testing*. Durham, NC: Carolina Academic Press, 2005; G. Cordner and K. Scarborough, *Police Administration*, 7th edn. Burlington, MA: Anderson, 2010, p. 159.

4 G. Anderson, D. Plecas and T. Seeger, "Police officer physical ability testing: Re-validating a selection criterion." *Policing* 24 (1) (2001): 8–32.

5 C. Johnson and G. Copus, "Law enforcement ethics: A theoretical analysis." In F. Schmalleger and R. Gustafson (Eds.), *The Social Basis of Criminal Justice: Ethical Issues for the 80s*. Washington, DC: University Press of America, 1981, pp. 39–83.

6 M. McCampbell, *Field Training for Police: State of the Art*. Washington, DC: National Institute of Justice, 1986.

7 Retrieved 4/16/2016 from http://www.mass.gov/eopss/law-enforce-and-cj/law-enforce/mptc/training-and-academies/annual-professional-development/

8 G. Kelling, T. Pate, D. Dieckman and C. Brown, *The Kansas City Preventive Patrol Experiment: A Summary Report*. Washington, DC: Police Foundation, 1974.

9 L. Sherman and D. Weisburd, "General deterrent effects of police patrol in crime 'hot spots': A randomized, controlled trial." *Justice Quarterly* 12 (4) (1995): 625–648. See also D. Weisburd and L. Green, "Policing drug hot spots: The Jersey City drug market analysis experiment." *Justice Quarterly* 12 (4) (1995): 711–735.

10 J. Pollock, *Ethical Dilemmas and Decisions in Criminal Justice*. Boston, MA: Cengage, 2017; F. Schoeman, "Privacy and police undercover work." In W. Heffernan and T. Stroup (Eds.), *Police Ethics: Hard Choices in Law Enforcement*. New York, NY: John Jay Press, 1985, pp. 133–153; G. Marx, "Police undercover work: Ethical deception or deceptive ethics?" In W. Heffernan and T. Stroup (Eds.), *Police Ethics: Hard Choices in Law Enforcement*. New York, NY: John Jay Press, pp. 83–117; T. Mieczkowksi, "Drug abuse, corruption and officer drug testing." In K. Lersch (Ed.), *Policing and Misconduct*. Upper Saddle River, NJ: Prentice-Hall, 1985, pp. 157–192; M. Baker, *Cops*. New York: Pocket Books, 1985, pp. 139–140.

11 J. Eterno, A. Verma and E. Silverman, "Police manipulations of crime reporting: Insiders' revelations." *Justice Quarterly* (2014). doi. org/10.1080/07418825.2014.980838; M. White, *Current Issues and Controversies in Policing*. Boston: Allyn and Bacon, 2007.

12 D. Willits and J. Nowacki, "The use of specialized cybercrime policing units: An organizational analysis." *Criminal Justice Studies*, 2016: http://dx.doi.org/10.1080/1478601X.2016.1170282

13 C. Koper, C. Lum, J. Willis, D. Woods and J. Hibdon, *Realizing the Potential of Technology in Policing*. Washington, DC: PERF, December 2015.

14 J. Pollock, Jan–July, 2016, unpublished, on-going research.

15 M. Lanier and A. Cooper, "From papyrus to cyber: How technology has directed law enforcement policy and practice." *Criminal Justice Studies*. Doi: http://dx.doi.org/10.1080/1478601X.2016.1170280.

16 R. Wilson, "Police accountability measures flood state legislatures after Ferguson, Staten Island." *Washington Post*, February 4, 2015, http://www.washingtonpost.com/blogs/govbeat/wp/2015/02/04/police-accountability-measures-flood-state-legislatures-after-ferguson-staten-island/; T. Perry, "San Diego police body camera report: Fewer complaints, less use of force." *Los Angeles Times*, March 18, 2015, http://touch.latimes.com/#section/-1/article/p2p-83088560/; T. Farrar, *Self Awareness to Being Watched and Socially Desirable Behavior: A Field Experiment on the Effect of Body Worn Cameras on Police Use of Force*. Police Foundation, 2015. Available via website: http://www.policefoundation.org/content/body-worn-camera

17 J. Storch and R. Panzarella, "Police stress: State-trait anxiety in relation to occupational and personal stressors." *Journal of Criminal Justice* 24 (2) (1996): 99–103.

18 R. McCraty and M. Atkinson, *Resilience Training Program Reduces Physiological and Psychological Stress in Police Officers. Global Advances in Health and Medicine*, 2012. Available at: http://www.heartmath.com/wp-content/uploads/2014/04/police_study_GAHM.pdf; also reported on the Blue Courage website, accessed 4/28/2016 at http://bluecourage.com/

19 J. Shane, "Organizational stressors and police performance." *Journal of Criminal Justice* 38 (4) (2010): 807–818.

20 T.R. Tyler, "Procedural justice, legitimacy, and the effective rule of law." In M. Tonry (Ed.), *Crime and Justice: A Review of Research*, Vol. 30. Chicago, IL: University of Chicago Press, 2003.

21 P. Reynolds, *The Impact of Fairness, Organizational Trust, and Perceived Organizational Support on Police Officer Performance.* Doctoral dissertation, Texas State University, May 2015.

22 R. Haar and M. Morash, "Gender, race, and strategies of coping with occupational stress in policing." *Justice Quarterly* 16 (2) (1999): 303–336.

23 S. Scheingold, *The Politics of Law and Order.* New York, NY: Longman, 1984.

24 J. Van Maanen, "The asshole." In P. Manning and J. Van Maanen (Eds.), *Policing: A View from the Street.* Santa Monica, CA: Goodyear, 1978, pp. 221–240; S. Herbert, "Morality in law enforcement: Chasing 'bad guys' with the Los Angeles Police Department." *Law Society Review* 30 (4) (1996): 799–818; L. Sherman, "Learning police ethics." *Criminal Justice Ethics* 1 (1) (1982): 10–19.

25 S. Scheingold, *The Politics of Law and Order.* New York, NY: Longman, 1984, pp. 100–104.

26 T. Barker, "Ethical police behavior." In K. Lersch (Ed.), *Policing and Misconduct.* Upper Saddle River, NJ: Prentice Hall, 2002, pp. 1–25

27 D. Weiburd and R. Greenspan, *Police Attitudes toward Abuse of Authority: Findings from a National Study.* Washington, DC: National Institute of Justice, U.S. Department of Justice, 2000.

28 E. Paoline, S. Myers and R. Worden, "Police culture, individualism, and community policing: Evidence from two police departments." *Justice Quarterly* 17 (3) (2000): 575–605; also see J. Pollock, *Ethical Decisions and Dilemmas in Criminal Justice.* Boston, MA: Cengage, 2017.

29 J. Pollock, *Ethical Decisions and Dilemmas in Criminal Justice.* Boston, MA: Cengage, 2017.

30 T. Barker and D. Carter, *Police Deviance*, 3rd edn. Cincinnati, OH: Anderson Publishing, 1994.

31 P. Kraska and V. Kappeler, "To serve and pursue: Exploring police sexual violence against women." *Justice Quarterly* 12 (1) (1995): 93–142; D. McGurrin and V. Kappeler, "Media accounts of police sexual violence." In K. Lersch, *Policing and Misconduct.* Upper Saddle River, NJ: Prentice-Hall, 2002, pp. 121–142, 133.

32 J. Crank and M. Caldero, *Police Ethics: The Corruption of Noble Cause.* Cincinnati, OH: Anderson Publishing, 2000/2005.

33 J. Pollock, *Ethical Decisions and Dilemmas in Criminal Justice.* Boston, MA: Cengage, 2017.

34 J. Dorschner, "The dark side of the force." In G. Alpert (Ed.), *Critical Issues in Policing*, 2nd edn. Prospect Heights, IL: Waveland, 1989, pp. 254–274; P. Murphy and D. Caplan, "Conditions that breed corruption." In R. Dunham and G. Alpert (Eds.), *Critical Issues in Policing.* Prospect Heights, IL: Waveland Press, 1989, pp. 304–324.

35 T. Prenzler and C. Ronken, "Models of police oversight: A critique." *Policing and Society* 11 (2001): 151–180.

36 S. Walker and G. Alpert, "Early warning systems as risk management for police." In K. Lersch (Ed.), *Policing and Misconduct.* Upper Saddle River, NJ: Prentice Hall, 2002, p. 224.

37 J. Pollock, *Ethical Decisions and Dilemmas in Criminal Justice.* Boston, MA: Cengage, 2017.

38 J. Pollock, *Ethical Decisions and Dilemmas in Criminal Justice.* Boston, MA: Cengage, 2017.

39 C. Staats, K. Capatosto, R. A. Wright and D. Contractor, *State of the Science: Implicit Bias Review, 2015.* Kirwin Institute for the Study of Race and Ethnicity, 2015.

40 Accessed 4/17/2016: http://www.chicagotribune.com/news/local/breaking/ct-chicago-police-accountability-report-201604 12-story.html

41 Pew Research Center/*USA Today*, "Few say police forces nationally do well in treating races equally." Author, 2014, http://www.people-press.org/2014/08/25/few-say-police-forces-nationally-do-well-in-treating-races-equally/

42 Pew Research Center/*USA Today*, "Few say police forces nationally do well in treating races equally." Author, 2014, http://www.people-press.org/2014/08/25/few-say-police-forces-nationally-do-well-in-treating-races-equally/

43 R. Planas, "Poll reveals widespread fear of police among Latinos." *Huffington Post*, November 12, 2014.

44 E. Sharp and P. Johnson, "Accounting for variations in distrust of local police." *Justice Quarterly* 26 (2009): 157–182.

45 J. De Angelis and B. Wolf, "Perceived accountability and public attitudes toward local police." *Criminal Justice Studies* (2016). http://dx.doi.org/10.1080/1478601X.2016.1158177

46 Human Rights Watch. *Decades of Disparity*, 2009. Accessed at https://www.hrw.org/sites/default/files/reports/us0309web_1.pdf; *Washington Post* infographic, accessed at https://www.washingtonpost.com/news/wonk/wp/2013/06/04/the-black white-marijuana-arrest-gap-in-nine-charts; Drug Policy Alliance, 2016, fact sheet, accessed at http://www.drugpolicy.org/race-and-drug-war

47 E. Green, "African Americans cited for resisting arrest at high rate in S.F." S.F.Gate.com, April 29, 2015. http://www.sfgate.com/bayarea/article/African-Americans-cited-for-resisting-arrest-at-6229946.php

48 *Whren v. U.S.*, 517 U.S. 806, 1996.

49 E. Dexheimer and J. Schwartz, "DPS statistics showing no racial bias in stops are wrong, expert says." *Austin American Statesman*, November 22, 2015, http://www.mystatesman.com/news/news/dps-statistics-showing-no-racial-bias-in-stops-are/npSts/?mc_cid=96fc64421b&mc_eid=890ae5e127

50 M. Smith and G. Alpert, "Searching for direction: Courts, social science, and the adjudication of racial profiling claims." *Justice Quarterly* 19 (2002): 673–703; R. Engel, J. Calnon and T. Bernard. "Theory and racial profiling: Shortcomings and future directions in research." *Justice Quarterly* 19 (2002): 249–273.

51 L. Langton and M. Durose, *Police Behavior During Traffic and Street Stops, 2011*. Washington, DC: Bureau of Justice Statistics, Department of Justice, 2013.

52 S. Mastrofski, M. Reisig and D. McCluskey, "Police disrespect toward the public: An encounter based analysis." *Criminology* 40 (3) (2002): 519–551.

53 C. Epp, S. Maynard-Moody and D. Haider-Markel, *Pulled Over: How Police Stops Define Race and Citizenship*. Chicago, IL: University of Chicago Press, 2014.

54 R. Weitzer and S. Tuch, "Perceptions of racial profiling: Race, class, and personal experience." *Criminology* 40 (2) (2002): 436, 443.

55 D. Cole and J. Lamberth, "The fallacy of racial profiling." *New York Times*, May 13, 2001: A19; D. Harris, *Good Cops: The Case for Preventive Policing*. New York: The New Press, 2005.

56 M. Doyle, "U.S. adds new rules to restrict profiling." *Austin American-Statesman*, December 9, 2014, A10; M. Apuzzo, "Profiling rules said to give F.B.I. tactical leeway." *New York Times*, April 10, 2014, A1.

57 S. Mastrofski, M. Reisig and D. McCluskey, "Police disrespect toward the public: An encounter based analysis." *Criminology* 40 (3) (2002): 534; M. Reisig, J. McCluskey, S. Mastrofski and W. Terrill. "Suspect disrespect toward the police." *Justice Quarterly* 21 (2004): 241–268; W. Terrill and S. Mastrofski, "Situational and officer-based determinants of police coercion." *Justice Quarterly* 19 (2002): 216–248.

58 R. Weitzer, "Citizens' perceptions of police misconduct: Race and neighborhood context." *Justice Quarterly* 16 (4) (1999): 819–846; R. Weitzer, "Racialized policing: Residents' perceptions in three neighborhoods." *Law Society Review* 34 (1) (2000): 129–157; R. Weitzer and S. Tuch, "Reforming the police: Racial differences in public support for change." *Criminology* 40 (2) (2000): 435–456.

59 M. Reisig and R. Parks, "Experience, quality of life, and neighborhood context: A hierarchical analysis of satisfaction with police." *Justice Quarterly* 17(3) (2000): 607–630.

60 W. Terrill, *Police Coercion: Application of the Force Continuum*. New York, NY: LFB Scholarly Publishing, 2001; W. Terrill, E. Paoline and P. Manning, "Police culture and coercion." *Criminology* 41 (2003): 1003–1034.

61 R. Engel, R. Tillyer, C., Klahm and J. Frank, "From the officer's perspective: A multilevel examination of citizens' demeanor during traffic stops." *Justice Quarterly* 29 (2011): 574–643.

62 S. Mastrofski, M. Reisig and J. McCluskey, "Police disrespect toward the public: An encounter-based analysis." *Criminology* 40 (2002): 519–551.

63 S. Whitehead, "The specter of racism: Exploring white racial anxieties in the context of policing." *Contemporary Justice Review*, 2015, DOI: 10.1080/10282580.2015.1025622

64 J. Bouie, "Black and blue: Why more diverse police departments won't put an end to police misconduct." *Slate Magazine*, October 13, 2014, http://www.slate.com/articles/news_and_politics/politics/2014/10/diversity_won_t_solve_police_mis

conduct_black_cops_don_t_reduce_violence.html; J.Bouie, "Brokentaillightpolicing." *SlateMagazine*,April8,2015,http://www. slate.com/articles/news_and_politics/politics/2015/04/north_charleston_shooting_how_investigatory_traffic_stops_ unfairly_affect.single.html

65 *Arizona v. United States*, 567 U.S., 2012

66 S. Parvini, "Sheriff Arpaio admits violating court order in profiling suit." *Los Angeles Times*, March 18, 2015. http://touch. latimes.com/#section/-1/article/p2p-83093795/

67 *Graham v. Connor*, 490 U.S. 386, 1989.

68 V. Kappeler, R. Sluder and G. Alpert, *Forces of Deviance: Understanding the Dark Side of Policing*. Prospect Heights, IL: Waveland Press, 1994, p. 159.

69 M. Doyle, "Data on police shootings is hard to find." Washington Bureau, August 20, 2014. http://www.mcclatchydc.com/ 2014/08/20/237137_data-on-police-shootings-is-hard.html?sp=/99/200/365/&rh=1#storylink=cpy; M. Hickman, A. Piquero and J. Garner. "Toward a national estimate of police use of nonlethal force." *Criminology & Public Policy* 7 (2008): 563–604.

70 R. Worden and S. Catlin, "The use and abuse of force by police." In K. Lersch (Ed.), *Policing and Misconduct*, Upper Saddle River, NJ: Prentice Hall, 2002, 85–120; M.Ducrose, P. Langan and E. Smith, *Contacts Between Police and the Public, 2005*. Bureau of Justice Statistics Report, April 29, 2007.

71 J. Gundy, "The complexities of use of force." *Law and Order* 51 (2003): 60–62.

72 J. Garner, C. Maxwell and C. Heraux. "Characteristics associated with the prevalence and severity of force used by the police." *Justice Quarterly* 19 (2002): 705–745.

73 W. Terrill, "Police use of force: A transactional approach." *Justice Quarterly* 22 (2005): 107–139.

74 W. Terrill and E. Paoline, "The use of less lethal force: Administrative policy matters." *Justice Quarterly*, 2016. Advance pub. http://dx.doi.org/10.1080/07418825.2016.1147593.

75 A. Micucci and I. Gomme, "American police and subcultural support for the use of excessive force." *Journal of Criminal Justice* 33 (2005): 487–500.

76 J. Garner, C. Maxwell and C. Heraux, "Characteristics associated with the prevalence and severity of force used by the police." *Justice Quarterly* 19 (2002): 705–745; G. Alpert and J. MacDonald. "Police use of force: An analysis of organizational characteristics." *Justice Quarterly* 18 (2001): 393–409; G. Alpert and R. Dunham, *Understanding Police Use of Force*. New York: Cambridge University Press, 2004; W. Terrill and S. Mastrofski, "Situational and officer-based determinants of police coercion." *Justice Quarterly* 19 (2002): 216–248; R. Worden and S. Catlin, "The use and abuse of force by police." In K. Lersch (Ed.), *Policing and Misconduct*. Upper Saddle River, NJ: Prentice Hall, 2002, pp. 85–120; W. Terrill, E. Paoline and P. Manning, "Police culture and coercion." *Criminology* 41 (2003): 1003–1034.

77 M. Ducrose, P. Langan and E. Smith, *Contacts between Police and the Public, 2005*. Bureau of Justice Statistics Report, April 29, 2007; J. Garner, C. Maxwell and C. Heraux, "Characteristics associated with the prevalence and severity of force used by the police." *Justice Quarterly* 19(4) (2007): 705–745; J. Pollock, *Ethical Dilemmas and Decisions in Criminal Justice*. Boston, MA: Cengage, 2017.

78 S. Chermak, "Conducted energy devices and criminal justice policy." *Criminology and Public Policy* 8 (4) (2009): 861–864; M. White and J. Ready, "Examining fatal and nonfatal incidents involving the TASER." *Criminology and Public Policy* 8 (4) (2009): 865–891; H. Williams, *Are the Recommendations of the Braidwood Commission on Conducted Energy Weapons Use Sound Public Policy?* Paper presented at the Academy of Criminal Justice Sciences Meeting, February 2010, San Diego, CA.

79 *Tennessee v. Garner*, 471 U.S. 1105, 1985.

80 D. Banks and M. Planty, *Assessment of Coverage in the Arrest-Related Deaths Program*. Washington, DC: Bureau of Justice Statistics, October 2015.

81 M. Hickman, A. Piquero and J. Garner, "Toward a national estimate of police use of nonlethal force." *Criminology and Public Policy* 7 (2008): 563–604; D. Klinger, "On the problems and promise of research on lethal police violence: A research note."

Homicide Studies 16 (2012): 78–96; S. Somashekhar and S. Rich, "Final tally: Police shot and killed 986 people in 2015 with over 900 fatal U.S. police shootings in 2015, a call for retraining." *Washington Post*, January 6, 2016; M. Apuzzo and S. Cohen, "Data on use of force by police across U.S. may prove almost useless." *New York Times*, August 12, 2015, A9; M. Wines and S. Cohen, "Police killings rise slightly." *New York Times*, May 1, 2015, A1.

82 D. Klinger, "On the problems and promise of research on lethal police violence: A research note." *Homicide Studies* 16 (2012): 78–96.

83 S. Somashekhar and S. Rich, "Final tally: Police shot and killed 986 people in 2015 with over 900 fatal U.S. police shootings in 2015, a call for retraining." *Washington Post*, January 6, 2016.

84 FBI website, accessed 7/12/2016: https://www.fbi.gov/about-us/cjis/ucr/crime-in-the-u.s/2013/crime-in-the-u.s.-2013/offenses-known-to-law-enforcement/expanded-homicide

85 M. Bowes, "Untold number of police killings in Va. go unreported or uncounted." *Richmond Times-Dispatch*, February 7, 2015, http://www.richmond.com/news/article_c656c2ba-b51a-5b91-b1c7–6b6cee89b336.html

86 K. Kindy, "Fatal police shootings in 2015 approaching 400 nationwide." *Washington Post*, May 30, 2015, http://www.washingtonpost.com/national/fatal-police-shootings-in-2015-approaching-400-nationwide/2015/05/30/d322256a-058e-11e5-a428-c984eb077d4e_story.html

87 K. Kindy and K. Elliott, *Washington Post* graphic, accessed 4/28/2016 from https://www.washingtonpost.com/graphics/national/police-shootings-year-end/

88 K. Kindy and K. Elliott, *Washington Post* graphic, accessed 4/28/2016 from https://www.washingtonpost.com/graphics/national/police-shootings-year-end/; W. Lowery, "Prosecutors will seek murder charges against Georgia officer who shot an unarmed, naked black man." *Washington Post*, January 7, 2016. Also see D. Kesic, S. Thomas and J. Ogloff, "Use of nonfatal force on and by persons with apparent mental disorder in encounters with police." *Criminal Justice and Behavior* 40 (3) (2013): 321–337.

89 S. Somashekhar and M. Walsh, "The myth of the killer-cop 'epidemic'." *New York Post*, January 2, 2016. http://nypost.com/2016/01/02/myth-of-the-cop-killing-epidemic/

90 J. Correll, S. Hudson, S. Guillermo and D. Ma, "The police officer's dilemma: A decade of research on racial bias in the decision to shoot." *Social and Personality Psychology Compass* 8 (2014): 201–213.

91 R. Fryer, *An Empirical Analysis of Racial Differences in Police Use of Force*. Cambridge, MA: National Bureau of Economic Research, July 2016. Accessed at http://www.nber.org/papers/w22399; Q. Bui and A. Cox, "Surprising new evidence shows bias in police use of force but not in shootings." *New York Times*, July 11, 2016.

92 W. Lowery, "Prosecutors will seek murder charges against Georgia officer who shot an unarmed, naked black man." *Washington Post*, January 7, 2016; K. Kindy and K. Elliott, *Washington Post* graphic, accessed 4/28/2016 from https://www.washingtonpost.com/graphics/national/police-shootings-year-end/

93 T. Jonathan-Zamir, S. Mastrofsky and S. Moyal, "Measuring procedural justice in police-citizen encounters." *Justice Quarterly* 32 (2015): 845–871.

94 T. Tyler and Y. Huo, *Trust in the Law: Encouraging Public Cooperation in the Police and Courts*. New York City: Russell Sage Foundation, 2002; T. Tyler, "Procedural justice, legitimacy, and the effective rule of law." In M. Tonry (Ed.), *Crime and Justice: A Review of Research*, Vol. 30. Chicago, IL: University of Chicago Press, 2002.

95 L. Mazerolle, S. Bennett, J. Davis, E. Sargeant and M. Manning, "Procedural justice and police legitimacy: A systematic review of research evidence." *Journal of Experimental Criminology* 9 (2013): 245–274; J. Gau. "Procedural justice and police legitimacy: A test of measurement and structure." *American Journal of Criminal Justice* 39 (2014): 187–205.

POLICING AND THE LEGAL PROCESS

6

Much of the training that police officers receive in the academy as well as in-service classes relates to the law. The authority of the police officer derives from the law, but the law also sets limits on his or her powers. The case holdings that will be discussed in this chapter have set restraints on the power of the police to stop, detain, search, or question. Some argue that these court decisions have "handcuffed" the police from doing their job. Actually, there is no research to indicate that many cases have been lost or arrests have not been made because of the due process protections recognized and/or created by the Supreme Court.

Chapter Preview

- What is the Source of Our Rights Against Police Power?
- When Can Police "Seize" A Person in Any Way?
- When Can Police Search Without a Warrant?
- Do Police Need a Warrant to Obtain a Blood Sample? Breathalyzer Test? Saliva? Urine? Hair? DNA?
- Do Police Need a Warrant to Obtain a Handwriting Sample? Clothing? Line-Ups or Photo Arrays?
- What Are Our Rights During Interrogation?
- What Is the Exclusionary Rule?
- Focus On Data: Do Gun Control Laws Reduce Gun-Related Violence?
- Summary
- Critical Thinking Exercises

WHAT IS THE SOURCE OF OUR RIGHTS AGAINST POLICE POWER?

The source of our rights against police power comes from the federal Constitution's Bill of Rights, state constitutions, and case holdings that have interpreted these legal documents. Generally, a state can recognize greater rights for its residents than the federal constitution, but cannot take away

For an interesting website about the Bill of Rights, go to http://www.archives.gov/exhibits/charter/bill_of_rights.html

any that the Supreme Court has determined exist by virtue of the federal Bill of Rights. This is why we will focus almost entirely on Supreme Court cases in this chapter—because your particular state may have more stringent controls on police power based on your state constitution and caselaw.

More specifically, we will concentrate on the 4th Amendment, the 5th Amendment, and the 14th Amendment in the following discussion of civil rights. The 4th Amendment states:

> [t]he right of the people to be secure in their persons, houses, papers, and effects, against unreasonable searches and seizures, shall not be violated, and no Warrants shall issue, but upon probable cause, supported by Oath or affirmation, and particularly describing the place to be searched, and the persons or things to be seized.

The 4th Amendment applies whenever law enforcement officers wants to search a person or place, or seize a person or item. Note that the protection does not say that law enforcement must have a warrant, only that the search must be reasonable, and if a warrant is issued, it must be supported by probable cause.

The 5th Amendment has several clauses that provide for different rights. It states:

> No person shall be held to answer for a capital, or otherwise infamous crime, unless on a presentment or indictment of a grand jury, except in cases arising in the land or naval forces, or in the militia, when in actual service in time of war or public danger; nor shall any person be subject for the same offense to be twice put in jeopardy of life or limb; *nor shall be compelled in any criminal case to be a witness against himself*, nor be deprived of life, liberty, or property, without due process of law; nor shall private property be taken for public use, without just compensation. [emphasis added]

The clause that is most relevant to policing is the right against self incrimination. The protection exists to prohibit any practice that might coerce or compel an individual to self incriminate (e.g., when written, the framers were probably thinking of torture).

Due process is defined as those protections designed to protect against governmental error in the deprivation of life, liberty, and property. Note that due process protections are mentioned in the 5th Amendment against federal power. After the Civil War, the 14th Amendment was passed and a due process clause in the 14th Amendment protects individuals against state power as well.

All persons born or naturalized in the United States, and subject to the jurisdiction thereof, are citizens of the United States and of the State wherein they reside. No State shall make or enforce any law which shall abridge the privileges or immunities of citizens of the United States; nor shall any State deprive any person of life, liberty, or property, without due process of law; nor deny to any person within its jurisdiction the equal protection of the laws. [emphasis added]

The 14th Amendment was the basis for the **incorporation** of some of the protections from the 1st, 4th, 5th, 6th, and 8th Amendments to citizens who may be faced with actions by state or local government agents. In other words, through a sequence of court cases, the Supreme Court held that, although when written, the protections only applied to actions by the federal government, the 14th Amendment extended these protections against state and local police actions as well. This clause is the source of recognized protections when it comes to state or municipal law enforcement officers' actions and has been used to "incorporate" 4th and 5th Amendment rights to state citizens against state powers. Without the 14th Amendment, the 4th and 5th Amendments would only apply to federal law enforcement personnel. Not all rights in the Bill of Rights have been judicially recognized in caselaw as applying against state (as opposed to federal) authorities; only those that are considered as essential to fundamental liberties have been incorporated.

For a very useful and interesting website devoted to the Supreme Court, where you can even hear recordings of Supreme Court cases and research case holdings, go to http://www.oyez.org/

WHEN CAN POLICE "SEIZE" A PERSON IN ANY WAY?

When can police stop and question someone? One answer is any time that the person consents to stop and answer their questions. However, the more important question is when can they stop and question someone who doesn't want to be stopped? The answer to that question is when they have *reasonable suspicion* that a crime has been or is about to be committed. We can distinguish four types of stops or "seizures":

- **Consent stops**: individual consents to stay and talk to police officers but could leave at any time.
- **Sobriety checkpoints**: everyone, or some random selection of individuals, is stopped for a very brief check of driver's license and registration to evaluate drivers for intoxication or other impairment.
- **Investigatory detentions**: the police have *reasonable suspicion* that a person is engaged in or about to commit a crime; they can stop that person, ask for identification and question the person, and conduct a superficial search for weapons.

Exhibit 6.1   The Supreme Court requires police officers to have probable cause of a crime or traffic violation to stop a moving vehicle, but make a public safety exception for sobriety checkpoints, like this one in Kansas City, Missouri.

Source: Getty

- **Arrest**: the police have *probable cause* that the person committed a crime or traffic violation; a search may be conducted for weapons and evidence of crime.

Consent Stops

A large number of police–citizen interactions occur because the citizen agrees to stop and talk to police officers. When police stop someone on the street and ask what they are doing, it is a consent stop unless the individual is not free to leave. Similarly, if a police officer asks someone if they can look into their bag, it is a consent search when the person allows the search. When the police ask someone to accompany them to the station for questioning, it is a consent visit unless the person reasonably feels they have no choice. The police do not need any level of suspicion or probable cause to ask people to talk to them or ask to search, but the person can also refuse to comply with such requests.

On the other hand, some courts have held that police can't stop automobile drivers and say that it is a consent stop. The situation of stopping a moving car is different because it affects a person's movement more completely than a pedestrian stop. Therefore, police need at least a reasonable suspicion before they stop a moving automobile (unless it is at a fixed checkpoint). In most cases, they stop a car only after they have seen a traffic violation, however minor. Once the driver has committed a traffic violation, police have probable cause to stop and even arrest (even if only a traffic offense).

Sobriety Checkpoints

The Supreme Court has allowed police departments to engage in "fixed checkpoints" or "sobriety checkpoints" to protect us from drunk drivers. The rationale for allowing such stops is that the inconvenience to the public is minor, the governmental interest in stopping drunk drivers is high, and the stops are not conducted in a way that could be arbitrary and capricious. Every driver must be stopped or police must use some random system for stopping some drivers, if not all drivers. Further, the checkpoints can only occur with supervisory approval. So far, fixed checkpoints have been acceptable only when the goal is to stop drunk drivers. Courts have not allowed such checkpoints to be used to identify drug offenders (away from border areas) or other criminal suspects.[1]

Investigatory Detentions

One of the earliest cases that set the boundaries of the police power to stop was *Terry v. Ohio*[2] in 1968. In this case, a police officer observed Mr. Terry walking around a bank several times and peering in the window. While the officer did not have probable cause to arrest, he did have a reasonable suspicion that Terry was "casing" the building for a robbery or burglary. The officer stopped and searched Terry, and found a gun. Terry was convicted of an unlawful weapons charge. He appealed the conviction, arguing that the gun should have been excluded because the stop and search was unlawful in that there was no probable cause that he had committed a crime. The Supreme Court held that the search was lawful because the stop was lawful. According to the Court, police officers can stop and detain someone briefly to investigate a potential crime if they have reasonable suspicion that a crime had been, or was going to be, committed. Furthermore, police officers had a right to pat down the suspect for weapons to protect themselves while they were conducting a brief investigation. These types of stops are now sometimes called "**Terry stops**" referring to this case.

A Terry stop must be supported by reasonable suspicion. The stop must be brief and not inconvenience the citizen unreasonably. The courts have never created a bright-line test for what a reasonable length of time might be as it depends on the circumstances of the stop and other factors. A police officer's "hunch," without any factual basis, that an individual was going to commit a crime would not be sufficient to justify such a stop. The Supreme Court stopped short in this case of requiring the individual to answer the officer's questions. Justice White said, in his concurring opinion, that the person stopped is not obliged to answer questions and his refusal cannot be used to justify an arrest.

However, 36 years later, in *Hiibel v. Sixth Judicial District Court of Nevada*[3] the Supreme Court upheld a Nevada statute that made it illegal to refuse to give police officers one's name, when they had reasonable suspicion that the detainee was involved in a crime. The Court held that this law did not violate the 4th or 5th Amendments to the federal Constitution. In the *Hiibel* case, the detainee was stopped by police responding to a report that a woman had been assaulted. It turned out that Mr. Hiibel had been in an argument with his daughter, who had gotten out of his car and walked home. When police arrived, he refused to give his name even after they threatened him with arrest. He was subsequently arrested, fined $250, and appealed the conviction all the way to the Supreme Court, arguing that citizens shouldn't have to give their name to police when they have not been arrested. The Supreme Court did not agree. The Court held that as long as police have a reasonable suspicion to stop someone, a state statute that requires an individual to simply give their name does not violate the 4th or the 5th Amendments to the Constitution. You should understand, though, that other states (e.g., Texas) only require an individual to give identification when there is *probable* cause that a crime has been committed—in other words, when police have enough evidence to arrest the suspect.

As noted in Chapter 5, **racial profiling** is when a traffic or investigatory stop is based solely or mostly on the driver's race or ethnicity. An officer cannot seize someone against their will only because of their race—if it is a traffic stop, there must be a traffic violation; if it is a Terry stop, there must be articulable suspicion that a crime has been or is about to be committed and the race or ethnicity of the detained person cannot be the sole basis for the suspicion. However, the Supreme Court has approved traffic stops when the police officer admitted the purpose of stopping the car after observing a traffic violation was to search for drugs. These types of stops are called **pretext stops** because the traffic violation is a pretext for the stop.[4]

New York City has seen the number of Terry stops (or stop-and-frisks) decline dramatically in the last several years due to court challenges that officers were conducting such stops without reasonable suspicion. In 2013, in *Floyd v. City of New York*[5] a federal judge held that the stops were unconstitutional in that in many cases, police officers did not have articulable reasonable suspicion for the stop. Further, the court found that the stops were disproportionally of Black and other minority citizens.

The Second Circuit issued an injunction preventing the judge's opinion from being enforced with the argument that she had shown bias in steering the case to her court and making statements to the press. However, the policy of the NYPD shifted, and the number of stops declined anyway after the ruling, as well as after another case where the NYPD was chastised for using trespass as the reason for stopping individuals from entering or leaving high-crime housing developments. In Exhibit 6.2 below, the pattern of NYPD's stops is presented, which show that the height of the practice was before 2012, and the number of stops dropped dramatically afterwards.

Read a case decision regarding NYPD's stop-and-frisk practices here at http://www.nytimes.com/interactive/2013/08/12/nyregion/stop-and-frisk-decision.html

To read a relevant court holding, see: http://www.nyclu.org/files/releases/CleanHallsRuling_1.8.13.pdf

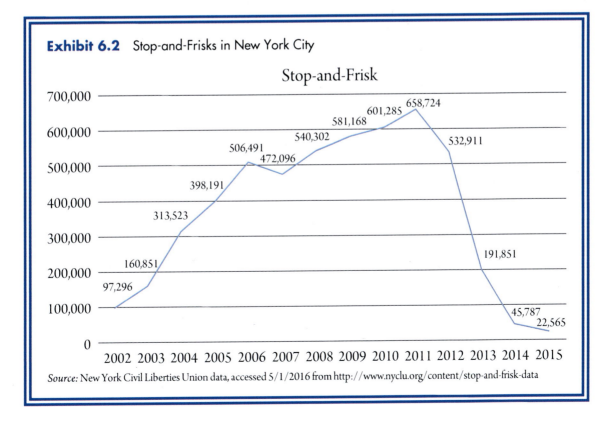

Exhibit 6.2 Stop-and-Frisks in New York City

Stop-and-Frisk

Values plotted by year:
- 2002: 97,296
- 2003: 160,851
- 2004: 313,523
- 2005: 398,191
- 2006: 506,491
- 2007: 472,096
- 2008: 540,302
- 2009: 581,168
- 2010: 601,285
- 2011: 658,724
- 2012: 532,911
- 2013: 191,851
- 2014: 45,787
- 2015: 22,565

Source: New York Civil Liberties Union data, accessed 5/1/2016 from http://www.nyclu.org/content/stop-and-frisk-data

Arrest

Police officers have the legal authority to arrest individuals when they have probable cause to believe that the person has committed a crime. In some states, misdemeanor arrests must be based on an arrest warrant supported by a criminal complaint filed by a victim or a police officer. However, usually if the misdemeanor is committed in the presence of an officer, the police officer can arrest the suspect without a criminal complaint having been filed. It is a misperception to think that police need a warrant to arrest. Officers may arrest without warrants if they have probable cause. However, they do need an arrest warrant if they need to enter a private dwelling to arrest the suspect.[6] The greater intrusion created by an entry requires that police have obtained a warrant (unless they are in hot pursuit).

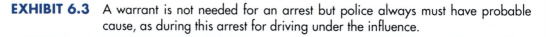

EXHIBIT 6.3   A warrant is not needed for an arrest but police always must have probable cause, as during this arrest for driving under the influence.

Source: AP

Arrest is the power to hold someone against their will. Police officers may be guilty of unlawful arrest only when there is evidence of maliciousness. Otherwise, if the arrest turns out to be invalid or in error, the officer can use a "good faith" defense. Police officers don't necessarily have a legal obligation to arrest. In fact, the decision to arrest is one of the least studied areas of criminal justice. Generally, police officers use their discretion, and in many cases where there is legal authority to arrest, officers choose not to. Even when more serious offenses occur, police may choose not to arrest, unless there is a specific law that compels arrest. For instance, some states have passed "mandatory arrest" laws in domestic violence cases that require police officers to arrest when there is probable cause that future violence will occur.

When has an arrest occurred? If a reasonable person would not feel free to leave, then an arrest has occurred. There are no "magic words" that are required to create the arrest. If a police officer puts handcuffs on an individual and places him or her in a patrol car, that person has been arrested without having to hear the words "you are under arrest." On the other hand, if someone is asked to come in to the police station to talk about a crime, they are not under arrest unless a reasonable person would not feel free to leave. The so-called **Mendenhall test** is that an arrest has occurred when a reasonable person does not feel free to leave.[7]

You may not realize that a traffic ticket is an alternative to a custodial arrest. You have committed a crime and the officer may arrest you and take you into custody; however, in all states, there is enabling legislation that allows the officer, instead, to give you a citation or "ticket to appear," which operates in lieu of a custodial arrest. You still have to appear in court (or admit guilt by paying the fine). The Supreme Court has upheld the right of police officers to utilize full custodial arrests in minor traffic violations, even when the maximum penalty involved is only a fine.[8] The Supreme Court has also held that evidence obtained from a search incident to arrest may still be admitted into evidence even if the arrest itself is invalid because state law does not allow arrests in those particular offenses.[9]

Police are authorized to use force to accomplish an arrest and it is unlawful to resist an arrest (which would be a crime in addition to the original crime). The ultimate "seizure" of course is death. Police cannot use lethal force to catch or subdue a suspect if there is no reason to believe the suspect poses a danger to the officer or others. Recall, from Chapter 5, the case of *Tennessee v. Garner*[10] involved the police shooting of an unarmed teenager who was running away from them after being caught burglarizing a home. The Court held that it was a violation of the 4th and 14th Amendments to shoot at a fleeing suspect if the only reason for the shooting was to stop him or her from escaping and there was no evidence that the suspect would be dangerous to others.

WHEN CAN POLICE SEARCH WITHOUT A WARRANT?

Recall that when it was written, the 4th Amendment protected us as citizens from unreasonable invasions of privacy by federal agents. Indeed, the Bill of Rights (the first ten Amendments to the Constitution) when written only protected us against violations by federal actors, not from the actions of state or local agents. As mentioned above, the 14th Amendment was ratified in 1868 after the Civil War in order to protect the legal rights of newly freed slaves. One hundred years later in the 1960s, the due process clause in the 14th Amendment was used as the vehicle by which the Court extended the protections of the 4th Amendment to individuals against state actors. In *Mapp v. Ohio*[11] the Supreme Court held that city police officers (not just federal law enforcement agents) must obtain a warrant before searching a private home because the protections described in the 4th Amendment were considered "fundamental liberties" and, as such, protected "state citizens" against state actors as well as "federal citizens" against federal officials.

In all 4th Amendment search cases, the guideline for the Court's reasoning is whether there is a reasonable expectation of privacy on the part of the individual. Additionally, the courts balance the individual's right to privacy against the state's right to investigate and prevent crimes (or for other substantial governmental interests). Law enforcement agencies cannot search your house or papers without probable cause, and in many cases probable cause is ensured through the issuance of a warrant.

When police officers need a warrant to search a house, person, or business, they must prove probable cause that they will find contraband or evidence of a crime. They must state what they expect to find and where they expect to find it with specificity. In other words, they cannot make application to a magistrate for a search warrant based on a hunch, a suspicion, or state that they need to look but don't know exactly what might connect the individual to a crime. If they are looking for drugs, they must say so; if they are looking for particular papers, they must say so, and so on. They must prove that they have credible evidence that rises to probable cause to believe that they will find the target of the warrant where they say it will be. There is no bright-line test as to what constitutes probable cause, however, and that decision comes down to a totality of the information provided and whether it is sufficient to create probable cause.[12] A **magistrate** (any judicial figure authorized to issue a warrant) must evaluate the evidence brought to him or her by police officers and if he or she concludes that there is probable cause a search warrant is issued similar to the one in Exhibit 6.5.

On the other hand, there are many exceptions to the warrant requirement. In some situations, what occurs is not defined as a search. The "**plain view**" **doctrine** states that if a law enforcement officer has a right to be somewhere

Exhibit 6.4 Members of the NYPD and FBI execute a search warrant, which is issued by a magistrate if he or she is convinced probable cause exists that fruits or instrumentalities of a specific crime will be found in the place described with specificity in the affidavit for the search warrant.

Source: AP

and then sees something that is clearly a fruit or instrumentality of a crime, then that item can be seized without any warrant requirement. Consent searches do not need warrants. The other major category of searches exempt from warrants is what is called "exigent" (emergency) circumstances. If, for instance, officers hear screaming inside a house, they can enter because someone might be in danger and, if they enter and see fruits or instrumentalities of a crime, then those can be seized. If there is a definite danger of evidence being destroyed, then officers do not need to wait for a warrant to seize the contraband. In Exhibit 6.6 there are descriptions of some types of searches and the legal justification for each type of search.

Exhibit 6.5   Sample Search Warrant

State of Ohio, _____ County, ss:

To the sheriff (or other officer) of said County, greetings:

Whereas there has been filed with me an affidavit, of which the following is a copy (here copy the affidavit).

These are, therefore, to command you in the name of the State of Ohio, with the necessary and proper assistance, to enter, in the daytime (or in the nighttime) into (here describe the house or place as in the affidavit) of the said _____ of the township of _____ in the County aforesaid, and there diligently search for the said goods and chattels, or articles, to wit: (here describe the articles as in the affidavit) and that you bring the same or any part thereof, found on such search, and also the body of _____, forthwith before me, or some other judge or magistrate of the county having cognizance thereof to be disposed of and dealt with according to law.

Given under my hand this _____ day of _____, 2008 _____, Judge, County Court

Source: Ohio Revised Code Annotated § 2933.25. Form of search warrant.

Exhibit 6.6   Warrantless Searches

1. **Search for weapons to protect officers during investigative stops—"pat-downs"**
    On an investigatory detention (Terry stop), the officer has a right to "pat down" the subject for the officer's protection. The search is limited to a tactile search for weapons. If something feels like a weapon, the officer can remove it from a pocket and if other contraband is found during the search, that evidence can be used against the suspect (*Terry v. Ohio*).

2. **Search for weapons and evidence upon lawful arrest**
    When a suspect has been placed under a lawful arrest, officers have the right to search the person and immediate vicinity of the person for weapons and contraband and evidence of the crime. This is to ensure that evidence is not destroyed by the suspect or others. This search is more intrusive than the pat-down search, but is justified by the arrest (*Chimel v. California*).

3. **Exigent circumstances**
    All exigent circumstance exceptions are based on logic and reasonableness. Basically, the exception recognizes that there are some circumstances where getting a warrant is impossible because the suspect will flee, the evidence will be destroyed, or there is some other good

reason to allow the officer to search without a warrant. Note that it is not an exception to probable cause. The officer must still have probable cause that the suspect has engaged in a crime, but it provides an exception to the requirement to obtain a warrant before undertaking a search.

The "**hot pursuit exception**" is a type of exigent circumstances search. It refers to situations where police officers are following a fleeing suspect who has just committed a crime or they have probable cause to believe he has just committed a crime. If waiting for a warrant will result in the escape of the suspect or the destruction of evidence, they may pursue the suspect into a dwelling and search for him or her. If they see contraband or the fruits of the crime during the course of the search for the suspect, they may seize that evidence as well (*Warden v. Hayden*).

Another exigent circumstance is when police have cause to believe someone is in danger. If police officers hear screaming from inside the home, they can enter the home without permission and without a warrant to protect the suspected victim. Even if they turn out to be wrong (e.g., the screaming was coming from the television), the entry is legal; therefore, any contraband seen by the police is subject to seizure and use as evidence against the homeowner. As soon as they are aware that there is no danger to anyone, however, they must exit the premises. Only evidence that is seen during the course of the legitimate entry can be used in any subsequent prosecution.

4. **Automobile searches**

Automobile searches are a type of exigent circumstance, e.g., when there is a real danger that the evidence will be destroyed or taken away. Both of these circumstances exist when an automobile driver is stopped and there is probable cause to believe that there is evidence of a crime or contraband inside the car. Earlier cases distinguished between a car and the trunk, and a car and any containers in the car, but, finally, the Supreme Court held that when a police officer had probable cause to believe a crime had been committed using or within the automobile, then that auto could be searched, along with any containers found inside, including containers (such as purses) owned by passengers. Later, another case expanded that provision to when the probable cause applied only to a container that happened to be in a car. Therefore, when a police officer stops a car because of a minor traffic violation and smells marijuana, or observes any other evidence of a crime that rises to probable cause, he or she may search the car and any bags, purses, or backpacks found in the car (*United States v. Ross*). Another type of automobile search occurs when the driver and/or passengers are arrested. Officers may conduct a search of the automobile under a search incident to arrest because the court has held that anywhere in the automobile may be within reach of the suspect if there may be evidence related to the reason for the arrest. Note that this does not mean officers can search for drugs if there has been an arrest for a traffic offense because there is no evidence of the traffic offense likely to be in the car. The other reason a search during an arrest could occur is when circumstances indicate the officer may be in danger (e.g. multiple suspects and one officer). In these cases, the officer is searching for weapons that might be used against him or her or evidence that could be easily destroyed (*New York v. Belton*). If someone was arrested for a traffic violation and there was nothing to indicate the officer might be in danger, then a search of the car would be unwarranted.

5. **Inventory searches**

    An inventory search is not a search for evidence—it is simply a search to identify and record any possessions, especially valuables, found inside a car or other vehicle that is impounded by a law enforcement agency. If contraband or evidence is found during a routine inventory search, it can be used against the suspect. On the other hand, an inventory search does not include taking the panels off the inside of the car or deconstructing it in any way. If police choose to do this type of search, they should obtain a warrant.

6. **Consent searches**

    If a police officer asks to look into a driver's trunk, and the driver opens it, then the search is legal because the driver has given consent. Similarly, if a police officer asks someone to empty their pockets and they agree to do so, the officer doesn't need probable cause for this type of consent search. Only if the consent is clearly coerced would any contraband or evidence be excluded in this type of situation (*Schneckloth v. Bustamonte*). If there are two residents to a home, if one consents and the other does not, then a warrant must be obtained; however, if the non-consenter leaves the premises (even if he or she is taken away by law enforcement), then police may search with the consent of the remaining party (*Fernandez v. California*).

7. **Plain view seizures (these are not searches!)**

    When an officer has legal authority to be in a particular place, then anything that can be seen with the aided or unaided eye is subject to seizure. This is not considered a search and, therefore, requires no legal justification other than the legal right to be there. For instance, when an officer responds to a domestic disturbance call and is allowed into a home, then anything he or she sees in the home, such as drugs on the table, is subject to seizure and use for prosecution. When an officer is in a public hallway in an apartment building and peers through an uncurtained front window and sees narcotics, this is a plain view situation and he may use this information to get a search warrant. However, if a police officer comes into a yard with "no trespassing" signs posted, onto the porch, and stands on a box to peer into a window, that is considered a search and any evidence or "fruits" of the evidence obtained from such a "search" will be excluded. The **open fields doctrine**, however, states that even when homeowners put up "no trespassing" signs and enclose fields by fences, if the field can be seen from the air, it falls under plain view and officers would not need a warrant to search.

8. **Border searches**

There are greater police powers to search at the borders of this country. The argument, of course, is that there is a great need to protect the country's borders and if people choose to go across a border, they therefore choose to be subject to the greater powers of search by border agents. We are all familiar today with the metal detectors and even pat-downs by TSA officers when traveling through airports. These pat-downs are done without probable cause or even reasonable suspicion because flying isn't a right and one implicitly consents to such searches by choosing to fly. Our bags are sniffed by drug dogs and we may be asked to open our luggage to be searched by customs or border agents.

In cases where officers have reasonable suspicion, they may detain an individual in an airport or at a border for a reasonable period to determine if a crime is being committed. When individuals are suspected of smuggling drugs, they may be detained and searched. They may be asked for consent to an ultrasound of their stomach and, if they refuse, be monitored when they go to the bathroom to see if drugs are being carried in their body. These invasions of privacy are done without warrants only because airports are considered similar to borders and we all have a reduced expectation of privacy when crossing the border. Highway border stops may even be 100 miles inside the border, yet the same justification applies (*United States v. Martinez Fuerte*).

Electronic "Searches"

One typically thinks of only physical searches as being protected by the 4th Amendment, but wiretaps and some forms of electronic surveillance are also treated as searches because they also intrude upon the privacy of citizens. Arguably, before police "bug" your house, tap your phone, or record your actions, they should have some justification for doing so. Crimes against wiretapping by private citizens go back as far as the telegraph in the late 1800s, and restrictions on police using such devices have been in place for decades.[13]

Although there are some exceptions, states generally follow federal law in allowing some wiretapping and eavesdropping; specifically, when there is consent by at least one party, and/or when law enforcement has the proper authorization from the court. Cases involving wiretapping, as in all 4th Amendment cases, involve one's reasonable expectation of privacy. One of the earliest cases was *Katz v. United States*.[14] In this case, the Supreme Court held that police officers must have a warrant before placing a wiretap on a public telephone because people using public phone booths had a reasonable expectation of privacy. On the other hand, individuals talking in a public park do not have a reasonable expectation of privacy if police officers sitting close by can hear without the aid of any electronic listening devices, but officers must obtain a warrant before using any electronic equipment that amplifies sound from distances.[15] Individuals in jails have no reasonable expectation of privacy when they use jail phones, especially when there are signs stating that calls may be monitored and recorded.[16] Thus, any place your expectation of privacy would not be reasonable is fair game for surveillance; however, in your home or place of business you have a reasonable expectation of privacy and are protected by the requirement that law enforcement obtain a warrant before using a listening device or surveillance of any sort. It is important to remember also that only one party has to consent in many states, so in those states if there is a confederate that is involved in the interaction who knows surveillance is taking place, then law enforcement may record without a warrant in those states. While state agents must comply with both the federal minimum standards and any additional restrictions imposed by their state, federal investigators are governed by federal regulations and laws. The USA Patriot Act and federal laws governing law enforcement investigations of terrorists have expanded regular law enforcement accessibility because if federal agents come across evidence of regular criminal activity during a counter-terrorism investigation, they may share such knowledge with local law enforcement.

In *Kyllo v. United States*[17] the Supreme Court held that a thermal-imaging device that was able to measure the amount of heat coming from a house was a "search" and required a warrant. The Court held that individuals had a reasonable expectation of privacy in their own home and a right to expect that police are not using electronics not available to the general public to measure sound, heat, or anything else coming out of their private home. Note that police can use such equipment, but they must develop probable cause first and seek a warrant from a magistrate before "searching" using the equipment.

Police can physically follow suspects without a warrant, but a warrant must be obtained to use GPS-tracking devices on automobiles.[18] The Supreme Court decided that the GPS tracker was a "trespass" because it was affixed to the suspect's car and, as a trespass, it required a magistrate's oversight. Law enforcement may track a suspect's location from personal cellphones in two ways: the first is to triangulate data from cellphone towers used, and the second is when the cellphone is equipped with GPS, which then can provide the cellphone's exact location. Police have used cellphone location information in murder cases to impeach suspects' alibis and to prove a suspect was near the location of the body or place of kidnapping. Police generally have used only court orders, not warrants, to obtain this information. Often months of cellphone records are obtained early in a case investigation in order to build probable cause. Privacy advocates urge courts to require warrants to obtain such information; law enforcement argues against the need for warrants. This is an unsettled area of law. On the one hand, there is an argument that individuals agree to disclose their location to their cellphone provider and, because it is provided to this third party, there is no privacy right to such information at all. On the other hand, privacy advocates argue that cellphone users have a reasonable expectation that their location information should not be shared without a warrant.[19] The Supreme Court has ruled on whether a warrant is required to force access to a cellphone in *Riley v. California*.[20] In that case, as with many others, officers arrested Riley and looked into his cellphone for contacts and texts to determine if he was affiliated with a gang. That information was used to build probable cause for an arrest. He argued that they should not have accessed his cellphone without a warrant and the Supreme Court agreed. The Supreme Court was persuaded by the argument that the cellphone today is like a photo album, banking records, an address book, and a diary. It can carry more information about an individual than pockets, purses, briefcases, and file drawers combined and because of these uses, a warrant is needed to ensure that law enforcement officers have probable cause before invading an individual's privacy.

DO POLICE NEED A WARRANT TO OBTAIN A BLOOD SAMPLE? BREATHALYZER TEST? SALIVA? URINE? HAIR? DNA?

Taking samples of blood, hair, or saliva for forensic examination or DNA are searches and seizures of a sort; therefore, the 4th Amendment applies. It has also been argued that this is a 5th Amendment issue because giving one's blood, for instance, may be akin to giving testimony against oneself. The courts have disagreed with the latter presumption, however, distinguishing physical evidence (such as blood or DNA) from testimonial evidence (confession). One cannot be compelled to confess, but one can be compelled to give a DNA sample. On the other hand, because it does constitute an intrusion, a warrant is usually required.

The approach taken by the courts in these cases is reasonableness. Police may pluck a paint chip off a suspect's clothing during an arrest, but they cannot compel a suspect to give them a sample of any body fluid. Unless there are exigent circumstances, a warrant is required when there is penetration of a body's surface, when blood, urine, saliva, semen, or pubic hair samples are obtained, when there is a manual inspection of a rectal or genital area, or other discomfort or humiliation, or when there might be a risk to health.[21]

Up until recently, law enforcement officers could obtain blood to determine blood-alcohol level if a drunken driver suspect was in the hospital receiving treatment;[22] however, in *Missouri v. McNeely*[23] in 2013, the Supreme Court held that a warrant was required to force a suspect to undergo a blood test in a suspected drunken driving case. The exigent circumstances argument that the alcohol would be metabolized by the body before a warrant could be obtained was rejected since science showed widely divergent estimates of the rate of the metabolization. Law enforcement officers often use the breathalyzer test results to make a case for DWI or DUI. You cannot be compelled to take the breathalyzer test; however, your refusal can result in the suspension of your driver's license. Since driving is a privilege, not a right, the legal justification for compelling cooperation is implied consent; that drivers implicitly agree to such demands by driving. Some jurisdictions employ "no refusal" campaigns where officers are able to access magistrates for instant warrants for a blood alcohol content test if a suspect refuses to take the breathalyzer.

One's privacy interests are drastically curtailed after arrest. In *Maryland v. King*[24] the Supreme Court upheld Maryland's practice of obtaining cheek swabs from all jailed suspects to place in a DNA database and to be used to identify suspects from cold cases. King argued it was a warrantless search and a violation of privacy since the state did not need the DNA to prove the case he was jailed for (his DNA identified him as a suspect in an earlier, more serious crime). The majority of the Supreme Court decided that the intrusion was minimal and the governmental interest strong in identifying those booked into jail, considering obtaining DNA was akin to fingerprinting and photographing. Privacy advocates bitterly argued against this reasoning in that one's DNA provides much more private information than a fingerprint or photograph—it identifies one's racial heritage, one's familial relationships, propensity to disease, and so on.

In the television shows, the actors frequently obtain DNA from discarded soda cans or coffee cups. Although it is questionable that such tricks always will result in usable DNA, the practice does not violate any rights. The analogy would be when someone discards garbage and then police pick up the garbage and find evidence. The Supreme Court has held that there is no reasonable expectation of privacy over one's discarded garbage and, by analogy, none over a discarded soda can.[25]

DNA has become ubiquitous in television dramas and real criminal investigations and prosecutions. Along with the use of DNA, have come crime lab scandals that have exposed shoddy laboratory procedures and possible bias in testimony.[26] In 2009, the National Academy of Sciences issued a 225-page report on forensics and crime labs across the country. It was a highly critical report, incorporating the descriptions of many cases of innocent people convicted because of faulty scientific evidence. The authors concluded that crime labs lacked certification and standards, and that, except for DNA, many forensic disciplines, using pattern recognition (of fingerprints, bite marks, tool marks) was without scientific standards or validation. The report called on Congress to establish a national institute of forensic science to accredit crime labs and analysts.

To read about the report by the National Academy of Sciences on forensic labs, go to http://www.nap.edu/catalog.php?record_id=12589

DO POLICE NEED A WARRANT TO OBTAIN A HANDWRITING SAMPLE? CLOTHING? LINE-UPS OR PHOTO ARRAYS?

If the collection of body evidence is not intrusive (e.g., picture, handwriting or voice exemplar, fingerprint), and the person is already in legal custody, then such items can be obtained without a warrant. The test of reasonableness applies. For instance, if you go out in public, then you have no reasonable expectation of privacy over a picture being taken of you by law enforcement for a photo array. If you interact in a normal way through business and personal relationships, then you have no reasonable expectation of privacy over your voice, therefore no warrant is required to obtain a voice sample as long as the content of the exemplar is not used as testimonial evidence.[27] Similarly, a fingerprint is not private and you leave your fingerprints everywhere you go.

These non-intrusive collections of body evidence are done when the individual is already being lawfully detained; either in an investigatory detention, or after probable cause has been established and the suspect is under arrest. Law enforcement officers could not compel you to provide these items if you were not already being lawfully detained without a court order.

A line-up is when the suspect is placed with other individuals in order for the victim to identify him or her. In *United States v. Wade*[28] the Supreme Court held that the defendant's attorney must be present at a line-up in order to make sure that it was not biased against the defendant. On the other hand, if the line-up occurs at an earlier phase of the investigation and the suspect has not been indicted, then there is no requirement for an attorney to be present.[29]

Other forms of identification procedures include **show-ups** and **photo arrays**. Show-ups are frowned upon and should only occur when circumstances are such that it is unlikely that the victim-witness would make a mistake in identifying the suspect. In the most common example, a victim calls the police and provides a description, the suspect is found nearby and is immediately brought to the victim for identification, that is, "Did this guy take your purse?" Show-ups have the potential for biasing the witness and, therefore, are not used except in circumstances similar to the example given above. In the photo array, a suspect's picture is placed on a page with other pictures of similar-looking men or women. The photo array is, perhaps, the best method of identification to ensure admission of the identification because the array can be admitted into trial as evidence and jury members can see for themselves that the array was not biased and did not unfairly target the suspect as the potential offender. As stated above, a photo does not implicate privacy concerns; therefore, law enforcement officers do not need a warrant to obtain one.

WHAT ARE OUR RIGHTS DURING INTERROGATION?

Recall that one portion of the 5th Amendment to the United States Constitution states, in part:

> No person . . . shall be compelled in any criminal case to be a witness against himself.

The 5th Amendment was written by our founding fathers to prevent courts from using evidence obtained by force, coercion, and torture. Before the twentieth century, the 5th Amendment was interpreted to mean the right not to be forced to speak. Then, in the twentieth century, the Supreme Court developed a broader interpretation of the 5th Amendment that included the right of the individual to remain silent. Furthermore, the choice to remain silent cannot be used against an individual by a prosecutor who might use it to infer guilt. As with the 4th Amendment, the 5th Amendment protects citizens (from being compelled to give testimony against themselves) in *federal* prosecutions, and the right had to be "incorporated" to us as state citizens in state prosecutions.

In *Escobedo v. Illinois*,[30] the Supreme Court recognized that a suspect had a right to an attorney if he/she requested one during interrogation. The Supreme Court in *Miranda v. Arizona*[31] required law enforcement officers to notify suspects of their right to an attorney and the right against self-incrimination. The Miranda warning must be issued before any custodial interrogation. The famous Miranda warning is set out in Exhibit 6.8.

What this means for police is that the Miranda warning must be given before they can conduct an interrogation of a suspect held in custody. The requirement of police to give Miranda warnings is widely misunderstood, however, and in many situations where police are interacting with the public, there is no requirement for the warnings to be given. For instance:

Exhibit 6.7   Ernesto Miranda was arrested and convicted of rape and kidnapping. His conviction was overturned by the Supreme Court in *Miranda v. Arizona* on the grounds that he was not warned of his rights before being interrogated by police officers.

Source: AP

Exhibit 6.8   Miranda Warning

You have the right to remain silent. If you give up this right, anything you say can and will be used against you in a court of law. You have the right to an attorney during questioning. If you cannot afford an attorney, one will be appointed for you by the court. Do you understand these rights?

Source: Miranda v. Arizona

- When police arrive after receiving a crime report, they will question a number of people to get information about the alleged crime. No warnings are required because no one is a suspect and no one is in custody.
- When police ask someone to come into the station house to talk to them about a crime, but the person is not officially in custody (is free to leave), warnings are not required.
- When a suspect is arrested but the police do not question him or her, and the suspect volunteers information about the crime, no warnings are required.
- When police are conducting an investigative detention, Miranda warnings are not required. The officers must have reasonable suspicion to stop, and, at the point where probable cause that a crime has been committed has been established and the questioning turns from information seeking to the goal of collecting evidence for arrest, then Miranda warnings are required.

Interrogations occur when the investigation has narrowed to one or a few suspects and the questioning is directed specifically at uncovering evidence for prosecution or obtaining a confession. Interrogations can occur even if the officer is not asking the suspect specific questions but engages in words or actions designed to elicit a confession.[32] The Supreme Court has considered the use of deception and other mental tricks used by police on suspects in order to get them to confess or provide evidence. While deception is acceptable, police may not threaten a suspect with physical harm, but they can threaten harsher charges or a recommendation for the death penalty if the suspect does not cooperate.

Once the right to an attorney is "invoked," the interrogation should cease until an attorney is present. It should be noted that, after indictment, the right to an attorney comes from the 6th Amendment and is part of the defendant's "trial rights," but the right to an attorney during a pre-indictment interrogation stems from the 5th Amendment. The right to an attorney during interrogation is largely to protect the defendant from coercive methods that overcome his or her 5th Amendment right to remain silent. It is called a "prophylactic" right, meaning that it is largely to prevent the violation of another right—in this case, the right not to be forced to incriminate oneself. Generally, questioning must cease when the suspect requests a lawyer, but, the Supreme Court has held that the suspect must be explicit in his request.[33] In another case, the Court held that questioning can resume after a time even if the suspect has not seen an attorney.[34] The Court has also held that the strict wording of the Miranda warning is not necessary.[35] Finally, Miranda warnings are not required unless the interrogation is being conducted by an agent of the state; generally, queries by citizens do not trigger Miranda warnings.

Observers note that the current Supreme Court seems to be moving in a direction that will dilute the power and practice of the original *Miranda* decision; however, Miranda warnings are now so entrenched in our national culture and police practice that court decisions probably will not change standard police practices at this point.[36]

WHAT IS THE EXCLUSIONARY RULE?

What happens when an officer violates the rights of a citizen by ignoring a warrant requirement, putting the individual in a biased line-up, or using physically coercive or other illegal interrogation tactics? The Supreme Court has held that the court's response to such violations will be to exclude the evidence obtained from the illegal action.

In the 1914 case of *Weeks v. United States*[37] the Supreme Court excluded evidence obtained in violation of the 4th Amendment by federal officers, but the ruling did not bar state or local police from using illegal evidence. Then in 1961, in *Mapp v. Ohio*[38] the Court extended the **exclusionary rule** to state and local police as well. In the *Mapp* case, Dolree Mapp's home was searched by officers looking for explosives or other evidence of revolutionary activity. They said they had a warrant, but they didn't. The officers found no explosives but did find some pornography in her basement and they arrested her for that. In the subsequent court trial and appeal, she argued that the evidence should have been excluded because it was obtained through an illegal search. The Supreme Court agreed, and eliminated the **silver platter doctrine**, whereby state and local officers, who were not bound by the *Weeks* decision, obtained evidence illegally and handed it to federal officers "on a silver platter." The *Mapp* decision extended the exclusionary rule to all law enforcement officers, whether they are federal, state, or local.

Despite the possibility that courts will exclude evidence that is illegally obtained, critics argue the exclusionary rule does not deter law enforcement from violating the rights of individuals. Rarely are law enforcement officers disciplined when a court excludes evidence obtained, and very often, law enforcement officers don't even know what happens to a case at the appellate level.

The Supreme Court has recognized exceptions to the exclusionary rule that allow evidence to be used even if the actions of law enforcement did violate the law. In several cases, the Supreme Court held that there was either minimal harm in the violation or the exclusion would generate more harm than letting in the evidence. In all of these cases, the evidence was admitted despite a constitutional violation.

1. **The "Good Faith" Exception**

   In 1984, the Supreme Court decided in *United States v. Leon*[39] that if the officer relied in good faith on a warrant, and that warrant turned out to be faulty, then evidence obtained under the warrant would still be admitted. In this case, the warrant was faulty because it was granted without meeting the probable cause standard. Therefore, the warrant issued by the magistrate was without legal authority. On the other hand, the court stated that the police officer should not be punished because the magistrate erred, and, therefore, the evidence would be admitted under this "good faith" exception. This good faith exception has been dramatically expanded to include errors made by the law enforcement officer himself. In *Heien v. North Carolina*[40] an officer stopped Heien for a broken brake light and obtained a consent search; however, it turned out that under North Carolina law, only one brake light needed to be working, therefore the stop was unjustified and evidence obtained in the resulting search, arguably, should have been excluded. The Supreme Court said it didn't matter because the officer's error was reasonably made in good faith.

2. **The "Inevitable Discovery" Exception**

   Under this exception, if the state can show that the evidence would have been found anyway without using the illegally obtained evidence, then the information may be admitted as evidence. Basically, the argument here is that the evidence shouldn't be excluded because it would have inevitably been discovered anyway.[41]

3. **"Public Safety" Exception**

   Even though interrogations are supposed to be prefaced by a Miranda warning, in some situations when police officers do not give the warning, the information obtained from questioning can be used as evidence anyway. In *New York v. Quarles*,[42] police officers had cornered a suspect in a grocery store. They demanded to know where he had hidden a gun he had been seen carrying, and they argued that they did so because they were afraid that citizens in the store might find the weapon and be hurt. He pointed out where he had hidden the gun and it was used as evidence against him. When he appealed, arguing that the question was an interrogation for evidence and therefore the gun should be excluded, the Supreme Court held that the officers' question was for public safety reasons, not for evidence collection, and the evidence could be admitted.

4. **The "Attenuation Doctrine" Exception**

   This exception to the exclusionary rule is an opposing argument to the "fruit of the poisonous tree" logic whereby if law enforcement's actions were illegal, then any piece of evidence obtained as a result of that illegality should also be excluded. **Attenuation** means "reduce the size, strength, or density of something, or become thinner, weaker, or less dense"[43] and, as applied here, it means when the linkage between the original illegal action of the officer and the evidence obtained is extremely weak either by time or distance, then the evidence may be allowed. For instance, if officers conduct an illegal interrogation and hear the name of a suspect, but they do not act on the name and, during the course of the investigation, come upon the suspect's name and/or focus on that individual through independent means, then the fact that the suspect's name was originally stated in an illegal interrogation does not mean that all evidence concerning the suspect has to be suppressed.

Arguably, these cases and others show that police and the courts don't have to be adversaries. Law enforcement is ultimately all about law. Generally, case decisions are made by balancing the needs of crime control against individual due process protections. Reasonableness is usually the legal test used when determining legal issues concerning the rights of suspects versus the governmental interest of crime control.

FOCUS ON DATA: DO GUN CONTROL LAWS REDUCE GUN-RELATED VIOLENCE?

There are probably few questions as controversial as whether gun control laws are effective in reducing gun-related violence. The controversy is ignited every time there is a mass shooting, e.g., Sandy Hook Elementary School where twenty children and six adults were killed or the Orlando nightclub massacre where forty-nine patrons were killed. Because the topic is emotional, it is even more important to practice critical thinking in order to avoid presuppositions and biased perceptions. Recall that the first step in critical thinking is to carefully construct the question or questions to be answered.

In this topic area, there is no specificity and no consensus on what is being asked or answered. "Gun control" can include: assault weapon bans, background checks, registration requirements, three-day waiting periods, requirements for concealed carry permits, or other specific laws, such as requiring gun-safes or gun-locks. "Gun-related deaths" usually are interpreted to mean mass shootings or other felonious homicides, but could include suicides and gun-related accidents as well. Since over twice as many gun deaths are suicides as homicides, it is important to consider this fact. Exhibit 6.9 shows the type of gun deaths in 2013.

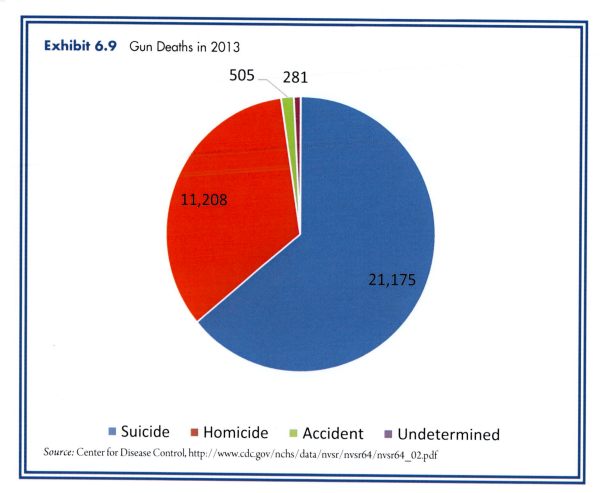

Exhibit 6.9 Gun Deaths in 2013

505 — 281

11,208

21,175

■ Suicide   ■ Homicide   ■ Accident   ■ Undetermined

Source: Center for Disease Control, http://www.cdc.gov/nchs/data/nvsr/nvsr64/nvsr64_02.pdf

Even "gun" is subject to different definitions and any research should specify whether the question is limited to handguns or whether long rifles are included and/or whether the focus is on assault-type weapons, and, if so, what specific type.

The question itself presupposes that gun possession is related to gun-related violence, but even that truism is difficult to measure since no one knows for sure how many guns exist in the United States. Prior research has used data from gun registration jurisdictions and projected those percentages to other jurisdictions, but that number does not include owners who have not registered their gun; surveys have been used asking people if they own a firearm, but validity checks indicate that 10–13 percent of gun owners do not admit to strangers that they possess a gun; proxies such as gun magazine subscriptions or membership in the NRA have been used to estimate ownership, but these are poor measures. In short, it is difficult to measure the effect of gun ownership on gun-related violence when we don't have a very accurate estimate of how many guns there are. Estimates derived from surveys indicate that gun ownership is not evenly distributed; the proportion of households owning guns ranges from 57.8 percent in Alaska and 57.7 percent in Montana to 8.7 percent in Hawaii and 12.3 percent in New Jersey; and, even within these jurisdictions, gun ownership tends to be concentrated in a smaller percentage of the population who own multiple weapons.[44]

The lack of specificity in terms and difficulty of measurement has been exacerbated by a void in good research. In 1996, Congress reduced the funding for the Centers for Disease Control in the amount it had allocated for studying gun-related deaths. Congress also passed an Act prohibiting any funding from being used to promote or advocate gun control; a position that effectively stopped federally funded gun violence research for twenty years. In 2005, the National Academies of Science composed a large panel of well-respected researchers to examine the evidence available at the time on gun violence and control measures and after two years of study, their conclusion was basically that more research was necessary and, even with that finding, they were criticized by some as being partisan.

To read the NAS report, go to http://www.nap.edu/read/10881/chapter/1

It is unfortunate that firearms researchers tend to either be or become strong advocates for or against gun control. Recall that one of the steps of critical thinking is to gather data, but also consider the objectivity of the findings, especially when the research is done by advocacy groups. It doesn't necessarily mean that the findings are biased, but it would be a better approach to obtain data from multiple sources, especially when some sources are clearly advocacy groups.

There is even controversy over basic facts; for instance, whether mass shootings are becoming more frequent or not. As Chapter 2 showed, all crime is at a historic low, including gun-related violent crime. Some argue, however, that mass shootings have increased, but others argue they haven't. The disagreement comes from how mass shootings are counted. One source reports that since 2000 there have been, on average, about 21 mass shootings annually in the United States in which four or more victims were killed by gunfire. Moreover, averages for five-year intervals (19.6 for 2000–04, 22.4 for 2005–09, and 20.8 for 2010–14) reveal no pattern.[45] Another source reports that there were, on average, 16.4 such shootings a year from 2007 to 2013, compared with an average of 6.4 shootings annually from 2000 to 2006.[46] A third source compares three different counts to show that there are discrepancies in how mass shootings are counted.[47] The number of incidents can be counted or the number of victims. In the past thirteen years, 486 people have been killed in mass shootings, with 366 of the deaths between 2007 and 2014, according to one study.[48]

Once we have some fairly accurate estimate of gun ownership and an agreed upon measure of gun-related homicide, then we would look for a **correlation** to determine if more guns equaled more violence. Another important point to note is that there is a perception that gun ownership is evenly distributed and gun violence is evenly distributed across a jurisdiction, but we know that definitely is not true. One study in Boston, for instance, over a 28-year period, found that 74 percent of firearm crimes occurred on only 5 percent of the city's blocks. Fully half of the city's gun homicides could be attributed to 1 percent of the city's population.[49] One of the problematic issues in studying gun violence or the effect of gun control is that, in general, gun ownership is higher in rural areas with less crime and gun violence more often occurs in urban areas.

Some research has found no correlation with gun ownership levels and level of gun-related homicide. In one study of 170 American cities that had populations over 100,000, using five proxy measures for gun ownership, researchers looked at statistical relationships between gun ownership density and six forms of violence: homicide, aggravated assault, robbery, suicide, rape, and fatal gun accidents. The only form of violence that seemed to be related to gun density was suicide; the others showed no correlation with gun density.[50]

A more recent study examined the correlation between firearm ownership and homicide rates over a 33-year period from 1981 to 2013 for all 50 states, controlling for gender, race/ethnicity, region, urbanization, poverty, unemployment, income, education, income inequality, divorce rate, alcohol use, nonviolent crime rate, hate crime rate, suicide rate, and incarceration rate.[51] The researchers found that in states where a greater proportion of the public owns firearms, there are more homicides committed, more firearm-related homicides committed, and, in particular, more non-stranger firearm-related homicides committed. These researchers argued that they controlled for numerous other factors that could cause **spurious associations** (statistical relationships that look causal but are not because of some unknown factor that is affecting both). The percentage of variance in the non-stranger homicide rate explained by firearm ownership was substantially higher for female victims (41 percent) compared with male victims of homicide (1.5 percent). In other words, higher rates of gun ownership was associated with more deaths of females by non-strangers.[52]

Another methodology is to use matched pairs, that is, identify homicide victims and compare them to a matched sample that are similar in demographics and location and determine how many of the victims owned guns compared to those who were not homicide victims. Researchers did find that homicide victims were more likely to be gun owners, but they included homicide victims where the killer used his own weapon. Logically, it doesn't make sense to include these homicides if one is attempting to discover how gun ownership is related to gun violence.[53] However, this finding does tend to support the idea that gun violence is limited to a small segment of the population where individuals are more likely to be both victim and perpetrator.

The real question, however, is whether gun control laws (of any specific kind) *reduce* gun-related violence. The concern for the extreme deadliness of assault weapons prompted the passage of the 1994 Federal Assault Weapons Ban (AWB), which expired ten years later when Congress did not renew the law. Researchers have compared the rate of homicides during the time the AWB was in effect with time periods when it was not. According to one researcher, the monthly counts of mass shooting incidents during 1976 through 2014 was not affected by the AWB during 1994–2004. However, this researcher did not count the number of victims during the time periods, only the number of incidents.[54] Others predicted that the AWB could not have affected gun violence much at all anyway because it was not an outright ban; the law cut off further production, for civilian use, of specific firearms while leaving all existing ones in circulation. The law applied only to certain types of semi-automatic rifles with certain names or certain characteristics, such as a separate pistol grip, a flash suppressor, or a bayonet, but manufacturers were free to market semi-automatics without those features.[55]

To measure the effect of gun control laws, researchers compare jurisdictions with stricter gun control laws to those with looser laws, but the methodology is fraught with problems and most studies have been thoroughly criticized by other researchers. For instance, one study compared Seattle, Washington, and Vancouver, British Columbia, and did find a dramatically different homicide rate between the two cities, but not for 75 percent of the population (recall that gun violence is limited to a small percentage of the population).[56] Another study looked only at cities and specific gun control laws to determine their effect on several specific crimes and suicide, controlling for a range of other factors. Estimates indicated that owner licensing was associated with reduced homicides and possibly a lower number of suicides. Purchase permits also were somewhat related to reduced numbers of homicides. The study also found that handgun bans were correlated with a smaller number of rapes, but not other forms of violence which doesn't seem to be logical. No other correlations were found.[57]

Researchers have also looked at conceal carry permits to see whether those states adopting such laws saw increases in crime. Different researchers, using different methodologies and data sets, find that conceal carry permits decrease homicide, others find increased homicides, and some found no effect on homicides.[58] It is frustrating to not have clear answers to these very important questions, but the problem is that it is difficult, probably impossible, to control for all the other variables that affect crime, thus attempting to construct a study to measure the effect of gun control laws on gun crimes will always be a challenge. We must also remember that gun violence is extremely concentrated in certain segments of society, and gun ownership is also not randomly distributed in the population so studies that look at whole states may be problematic. The strongest evidence indicates that gun control laws that limit access may affect suicide rates and, possibly, domestic homicide. Some research also shows that targeted programs toward those who are more likely to be involved in gun violence are more successful in reducing violence than less directed methods.[59] Mass shootings, even if they are increasing, are still an extremely unusual event so it would be hard to find a correlation between them and any factor, including gun control laws.

To approach this topic, as with all others, the first step is to clearly specify the terms (instead of "gun control," a specific law should be identified; instead of "gun ownership," identifying specific ownership groups would be better, and so on), look for objective research (rather than information published by advocacy groups), and triangulate to determine if findings are replicated by other researchers. Recently, there are indications that federal monies may be available for research, so we may have more information to help us answer these questions in the future.

SUMMARY

What Is the Source of Our Rights Against Police Power?

The government, including federal and local law enforcement officers, are guided and restricted by the Bill of Rights of the federal Constitution and state Constitutions and case law that has interpreted these sources. For criminal suspects, the 4th, 5th, 6th and 14th Amendments act as a limit to state power.

When Can Police "Seize" a Person in Any Way?

Four types of police–citizen interactions are consent stops, sobriety checkpoints, investigatory detentions, and arrest. No proof is necessary for consent stops and sobriety checkpoints. The lowest level of proof necessary for an investigatory detention is "reasonable suspicion" and this stop must be brief. Probable cause is required for an arrest.

When Can Police Search Without a Warrant?

The 4th Amendment requires police officers to have probable cause before they search a person's private papers or home. Some types of searches do not require warrants including pat-downs, searches incident to arrest, exigent circumstance searches, some (but not all) auto searches, inventory searches, consent searches, and border searches. Plain-view seizures are not searches.

Do Police Need a Warrant to Obtain a Blood Sample? Breathalyzer Test? Saliva? Urine? Hair? DNA?

The 4th Amendment protects individuals against intrusive body searches and law enforcement generally must obtain a warrant; however, if the person is already in jail, the Supreme Court has allowed the collection of DNA through cheek swabs.

Do Police Need a Warrant to Obtain a Handwriting Sample? Clothing? Line-Ups or Photo Arrays?

Courts have determined that there is no reasonable expectation of privacy over non-intrusive collections of things like handwriting or voice exemplars. If an individual is lawfully detained, either in an investigatory detention or arrest, then the non-intrusive collection of fingerprints, clothing, photos for photo arrays, or the person him/herself for line-ups does not require a warrant. If the line-up is after the suspect has been indicted, then he or she does have the right to have an attorney present.

What Are Our Rights During Interrogation?

The 5th Amendment gives us the right to be silent when accused of a crime. The Miranda warnings are judicially created procedures to ensure that everyone knows of this and other rights. Miranda warnings must be given before custodial interrogations take place.

What Is the Exclusionary Rule?

The exclusionary rule is the punishment imposed when police violate the rights of the accused—the evidence obtained from the illegal action is excluded from the criminal trial. However, there are exceptions: the good faith exception, the inevitable discovery exception, the public safety exception, and the attenuation doctrine.

Critical Thinking Exercises

1. Look in the penal code for your state (you can probably find it online) and find out if there is a statute that requires a person to give their name to police officers when asked. Do police need *reasonable suspicion* or *probable cause* if there is such a statute?
2. Go to the Oyez website (https://www.oyez.org) that offers audio of Supreme Court arguments and find the recording for the case: *Utah v. Streif* (2016); or you can go directly to the audio recording at https://www.oyez.org/cases/2015/14–1373. Read the case first to determine the legal question which is related to the attenuation doctrine discussed in this chapter: https://www.supremecourt.gov/opinions/15pdf/14–1373_83i7.pdf and then listen to the argument. Which side was more persuasive? Do you agree with the court's holding or not? Why?

NOTES

1 *Mich. Dept. of State Police v. Sitz*, 496 US 444, 1990; *City of Indianapolis v. Edmond*, 531 US 32, 2000.

2 392 U.S. 1, 1968.

3 124 S. Ct. 2451, 2004.

4 *Whren v. US*, 517 U.S. 806, 1996.

5 *Floyd v. City of New York*, 959 F. Supp. 2d 540, 2013.

6 *Payton v. NY*, 445 US 572, 1980.

7 *United States v. Mendenhall*, 446 U.S. 544, 1980.

8 *Atwater v. City of Lago Vista*, 532 U.S. 318, 2001.

9 *Virginia v. Moore*, 553 U.S. 164, 2008.

10 471 U.S. 1, 1985.

11 *Mapp v. Ohio*, 367 U.S. 643, 1961.

12 *Illinois v. Gates*, 462 U.S. 213, 1983.

13 *Berger v. New York*, 388 U.S. 41, 87 S. Ct. 1873, 18 L. Ed. 2d 1040, 1967.

14 *Katz v. United States*, 389 U.S. 347, 1967.

15 *Malpas v. State*, 16 Md. App. 69, 695 A.2d 588, 1997.

16 *United States v. Friedman*, 300 F.3d 111 2d Cir., 2002.

17 *Kyllo v. United States*, 533 U.S. 27, 2001.

18 *United States v. Jones*, 132 S. Ct. 945, 565 U.S. ____ (2012)

19 A. Marimow, "Court asks: Do police need a warrant to track your cellphone for months at a time?" *Washington Post*, March 22, 2016.

20 *Riley v. California*, 573 U.S. ____, 2014.

21 J. Kanovitz, *Constitutional Law*. New York: Routledge (Taylor & Francis), 2015, p.395.

22 *Schmerber v. California*, 384 U.S. 757, 1966.

23 *Missouri v. McNeely*, 133 S. Ct. 1552, 2013.

24 *Maryland v. King*, 133 S. Ct. 1958, 2013.

25 *Greenwood v. California*, 486 U.S. 35, 1988.

26 J. Pollock, *Ethical Dilemmas and Decisions in Criminal Justice*, 9th edn. Boston, MA: Cengage, 2017.

27 *United States v. Dionisio*, 410 U.S. 1, 1973.

28 *United States v. Wade*, 388 U.S. 218 1967.

29 *Kirby v. Illinois*, 406 U.S. 682, 1972.

30 *Escobedo v. Illinois*, 378 US 478, 1964.

31 *Miranda v. Arizona*, 384 U.S. 436, 1966.

32 *Rhode Island v. Innis*, 446 U.S. 291, 1980.

33 *Berghuis v. Thompkins*, 560 U.S. 370, 2010.

34 *Maryland v. Shatzer*, 559 U.S. 98, 2010.

35 *Florida v. Powell*, 130 S. Ct. 1195, 2010.

36 *Dickerson v. United States*, 530 U.S. 428, 2000.

37 *Weeks v. United States*, 232 U.S. 383, 1914.

38 *Mapp v. Ohio*, 367 U.S. 643, 1961.

39 *U.S. v. Leon*, 484 U.S. 897, 1984.

40 *Heien v. North Carolina*, 135 S. Ct. 530, 2014.

41 *Nix v. Williams*, 467 U.S. 431, 1984.

42 *New York v. Quarles*, 467 U.S. 649, 1984.

43 Encarta Dictionary.

44 D. Hardy, "Criminology, gun control and the right to arms." *Howard Law Journal* 58 (2015): 679–690, p. 683.

45 J. Fox and E. Fridel, "The tenuous connections involving mass shootings, mental illness, and gun laws." *Violence and Gender* 3 (1) (2016): DOI: 10.1089/vio.2015.0054

46 M. Schmidt, "F.B.I. confirms a sharp rise in mass shootings since 2000." *New York Times*, September 25, 2014, A19.

47 R. King, C. Bialik and A Flowers, "Mass shootings have become more common in the U.S." Retrieved 7/15/2016 from http://fivethirtyeight.com/features/mass-shootings-have-become-more-common-in-the-u-s/

48 M. Schmidt, "F.B.I. confirms a sharp rise in mass shootings since 2000." *New York Times*, September 25, 2014, A19

49 D. Hardy, "Criminology, gun control and the right to arms." *Howard Law Journal* 58 (2015): 679–690, p. 684.

50 See G. Kleck and E. B. Patterson, "The impact of gun control and gun ownership levels on violence rates." *Journal of Quantitative Criminology* 9 (3) (1993): 249.

51 M. Siegel and E. Rothman, "Firearm ownership and the murder of women in the United States: Evidence that the state-level firearm ownership rate is associated with the nonstranger femicide rate." *Violence and Gender* 3 (1) (2016): DOI: 10.1089/vio.2015.0047

52 See David J. Bordua, "Firearms ownership and violent crime: a comparison of Illinois counties." In J. M. Bryne and R. J. Sampson (Eds.), *The Social Ecology of Crime*. New York, NY: Springer-Verlag, 1986, pp. 156–157.

53 For a review of the weakness of this methodology, see D. Hardy, "Criminology, gun control and the right to arms." *Howard Law Journal* 58 (2015): 679–690.

54 J. Fox and E. Fridel, "The tenuous connections involving mass shootings, mental illness, and gun laws." *Violence and Gender* 3 (1) (2016): DOI: 10.1089/vio.2015.0054

55 D. Hardy, "Criminology, gun control and the right to arms." *Howard Law Journal* 58 (2015): 679–690.

56 For a review of the weakness of this methodology, see D. Hardy, "Criminology, gun control and the right to arms." *Howard Law Journal* 58 (2015): 679–690.

57 See G. Kleck and E. B. Patterson, "The impact of gun control and gun ownership levels on violence rates." *Journal of Quantitative Criminology* 9 (3) (1993): 249.

58 J. LaValle, "'Gun control' vs. 'self-protection': A case against the ideological divide." *Justice Policy Journal* 10 (2013); D. Hardy, "Criminology, gun control and the right to arms." *Howard Law Journal* 58 (2015): 679–690.

59 A. Piquero, "Reliable information and rational policy decisions: Does gun research fit the bill?" *Criminology and Public Policy* 4 (2005): 779–798.

Section 3
THE LAW AS SOCIAL CONTROL

LAW AND SOCIETY

7

We take the law for granted, but it is important to continue our critical thinking stance and take a moment to think about the purpose and origins of law. There is a tendency to believe that the law is objective, neutral, and predictable; is that true? There is a belief that we all agree on what constitutes criminal behavior; is that true? Why are certain behaviors defined as crimes? Who do we excuse from criminal culpability? In this chapter, we will answer these questions and others before moving on to describe in more detail the American court system. As always, it is important to understand the fundamentals before one can discuss current issues.

In the last chapter and this one, many court cases are cited and the law is described as the outcome of a court's legal analysis of the issues, e.g., why some piece of evidence is subject to the exclusionary rule while another is not; why someone is legally culpable for their actions and another is not. Legal analysis is a specific type of critical thinking. Our "Focus on Data" sections ask questions that require empirical analysis; however, we could be asking legal questions that require

Chapter Preview

- What Is the Purpose of Law? What Is the Purpose of Criminal Law?
- What Is the Origin of Our Legal System?
- What Are Some Differences Between Civil and Criminal Law?
- What Are Some Constitutional Challenges to Creating Laws?
- What Are the Elements of a Crime?
- What Are Some Defenses to Criminal Culpability?
- What Are Some Recent Issues in Criminal Law?
- Focus on Data: Is Medical Marijuana Crime or Cure?
- Summary
- Critical Thinking Exercises

legal analysis. In this form of critical thinking, the legal issue or question is addressed by exploring precedent cases, legal rules, and making determinations based on these "facts." *Objective* legal analysis doesn't decide a case and then construct an argument to support one's opinion, but, rather, looks to build and/or extend legal principles by carefully utilizing existing law.

WHAT IS THE PURPOSE OF LAW? WHAT IS THE PURPOSE OF CRIMINAL LAW?

The law serves as a written embodiment of society's norms and morals. It regulates relationships between people in order to ensure fair dealings, e.g., between employer and employee; landlord and tenant, or parties to a contract. It makes business and personal relationships more predictable and, by doing so, creates stability in society. The purpose of criminal law is to:

- define the wrongs that are considered necessary to protect individuals
- define the method of determining guilt or innocence
- designate the type of punishment or treatment following conviction for violating the laws of society.[1]

Why are some behaviors prohibited through law? **Natural law** refers to the belief that some laws exist in the natural world and can be discovered by reason. Natural law theorists equate law with morality—what is immoral is illegal and what is illegal is immoral. In fact, St. Augustine argued that an immoral law is no law at all because law must conform to natural laws of morality. **Positivist law** theorists believe that law is entirely a man-made creation (not part of the natural world) and, thus, law can be, but is not necessarily, relevant to questions of morality. Related to the discussion of natural versus positivist views of law are the concepts of *mala in se* acts (wrong in themselves) which are said to be intrinsically wrong acts; as compared to *mala prohibita* acts that are behaviors prohibited in certain societies, but not necessarily inherently wrong. We can say, for instance, murder is a *mala in se* crime, but not paying your taxes or driving on the wrong side of the road are *mala prohibita* crimes. These acts are wrong only because the law says so, there is nothing inherently evil about the actions.

Positivists would argue that an extremely immoral law (e.g., Jim Crow laws or the Nuremberg Laws of Nazi Germany[2]) are still legitimate laws as long as they were passed according to legal procedures of the time; natural law theorists would argue that such laws are not legitimate because they offend natural laws of morality. This is not just a theoretical or philosophical argument—consider that civil disobedience is premised on the belief that the existing law is wrong and those who commit civil disobedience believe that they have moral authority to contest the law.

Recall, we discussed the **social contract** in Chapter 1, a concept originating with Thomas Hobbes and John Locke in the Age of Enlightenment. The social contract refers to the "contract" individuals make when living in civil society where certain liberties are given up in return for being protected by society. We give up the "right" to steal what we want in return for society's protection against our being victimized by others. We agree to follow the law but, in return, society should impose laws that are minimally intrusive upon our individual liberties. Law can be considered always balancing individual liberty and societal control. According to John Stuart Mill, a famous philosopher, the law should only exist if it protects against harm. There are three forms of harm that criminal law protects against:

- protection from the harm caused by others
- protection from the harm caused by ourselves
- protection of societal morals.

The most obvious protection that the criminal law provides is protection against harm caused by others. Laws against homicide, rape, theft, and arson offer obvious protections. If we are harmed, these laws ensure that the offender will be punished if caught. Some legal writers identify a second set of wrongs that are not harmful but are offensive. Laws against public indecency or public disturbance aren't exactly prohibiting *harmful* behaviors but, rather, behaviors that are offensive to the majority of the population. One might say, then, that these "harm" our sense of order rather than threaten our physical security.

The second form of protection that the law provides is protection against harm caused by ourselves. So-called **paternalistic laws** protect us against our own foolish behavior. Seat belt laws are one example of a paternalistic law. Although you may prefer to drive your car without such a restraint, you will be punished with a fine if you do so. Paternalistic laws exist with the expectation that they will deter most people from doings acts that are not in their best interest.

The third form of protection the law provides is protection of societal morals. We used to have many more laws that protected societal morals. Laws against businesses operating on Sunday, blasphemy, and adultery may all be relics of the past, but some of our current laws (gambling, pornography, prostitution) still have the major purpose of enforcing society's morals. The most controversial court cases, such as challenges to consensual sodomy laws in *Lawrence v. Texas*[3] or same-sex marriage in *Obergefell v. Hodges*,[4] involve arguments between the law's role in protecting society's morals and whether laws should exist to protect individuals' rights to private, consensual behaviors. Laws related to obscenity, pornography, gambling, prostitution, and even drugs are justified by those who support them by legal moralism. Even though legal moralism may be a legitimate justification for laws, privacy rights often conflict with the government's right to enforce morality because we live in a heterogenous society where belief systems about right and wrong conflict.

Exhibit 7.1   Jim Obergefell sued when the state of Ohio refused to recognize his marriage to John Arthur. The Supreme Court weighed the individual's right to make decisions about personal and private matters and equal protection against states' rights to utilize their police power to pass laws defining the parameters of marriage and, in that way, enforce their view of morality. The Court ultimately ruled in his favor and held that states could not ban same-sex marriages and they must recognize same-sex marriages that took place in other states.

Source: AP

In some cases, individuals may agree that a particular action is immoral but at the same time believe that the government should not have the power to restrict an individual's choice. For instance, some who advocate decriminalization of drugs do so because of cost effectiveness or libertarian reasons, not necessarily because they approve of drug use. One other thing to think about is that sometimes the state loses its moral authority to condemn actions; for instance, states have little moral ground to justify laws against gambling when there is a state lottery. Laws that are based on the rationale of moral harm are usually the most controversial of all laws, and they have been, and continue to be, subject to shifts in public opinion and concern.

WHAT IS THE ORIGIN OF OUR LEGAL SYSTEM?

Our criminal law system in the United States is especially complex, because the criminal law is derived from English common law, statutory law, and our own case law tradition, split into 50 different state jurisdictions, the federal system, and thousands of counties and municipalities. We can trace the history of law back to very early codes, such as the Code of Hammurabi (ca. 2000 BCE), which mixed secular and religious rules of behavior. These codes also standardized punishments. However, most of our present-day crimes in the United States have their origins in the so-called **common law**. This was the law that developed in England. William the Conqueror (1066) and his son, Henry I (1100–35), are generally credited with the development of a national court system that involved judges who traveled across England and provided guidance to local magistrates. The effect was a gradual consistency in court decisions that led to the establishment of similar decisions in similar cases, which became known as the "common law." Eventually, judges decided the cases that came before them according to established principles from prior cases. In 1765, William Blackstone published *Commentaries on the Laws of England*.[5] This work was the most comprehensive written source of the common law at the time, and is still cited as a legal source.

Common law became the starting point for American law. Gradually, states passed their own criminal codes that supplanted the common law, but if a particular code was silent on an issue, many courts would fall back to common law principles. For instance, in the 1970 case of *Keeler v. Superior Court*,[6] the defendant was prosecuted for intentionally killing his wife's unborn child by kicking her in the stomach. However, because the California statute in question defined homicide as the killing of a "person," and the common-law definition of person did not include the unborn, Keeler could not be prosecuted for the death of the fetus. This led to California and other states changing their criminal code by redefining "person" to include a fetus, or creating the new crime of feticide. However, the decision in the *Keeler* case had to be made based on common-law definitions because the California Penal Code was silent on the issue.

Today, almost all crimes in all states are "statutory crimes," meaning that the state criminal code defines it as a crime. When a legislative body (federal or state) determines that certain conduct is undesirable and should be forbidden, a bill is prepared describing what conduct should be prohibited. This is introduced in the state house of representatives or the state senate, and is voted upon by the elected members of the legislative body. If both houses of the state legislature approve the bill, it then goes to the governor for consideration and approval. If the chief executive officer signs the legislation, it then becomes a law to be enforced by those involved in the justice process. Even if the chief executive officer refuses to sign (in other words, vetoes the bill), the bill may become law if enough members of the legislative body approve it, overriding the veto. The same process applies at the federal level in the creation of federal crimes. The legislature is permitted to define criminal offenses in any way it chooses, as long as the law is not arbitrary and does not violate state or federal constitutions.

States have primary **police power**, which is the authority to enact and enforce legislation to protect the health, welfare, morals, and safety of the people of the state. The 10th Amendment to the Constitution was added to make clear that the powers not delegated to the United States by the Constitution would remain in the states, respectively, and the people. The 10th Amendment states:

> The powers not delegated to the United States by the Constitution, nor prohibited by it to the States, are reserved to the States respectively, or to the people.

The federal government has no inherent police power. In the federal system, there have never been common-law crimes, because the federal government only has the power that is delegated to it by the Constitution. Certain crimes, such as treason, are federal crimes because the Constitution grants to the federal government the specific right to define and prosecute treason. Congress may also pass laws that are related to one of the express powers granted to the federal government by the Constitution. The enumerated powers granted to the federal government are found primarily in Article I, Section 8 of the Constitution. Federal crimes must be derived from these enumerated powers. For example, under the power to regulate interstate and foreign commerce, Congress has created federal crimes such as transporting stolen vehicles (interstate) and kidnapping (with interstate elements). Counterfeiting is specifically mentioned in Article I, Section 8 as a federal crime. Drug smuggling comes from the federal power to protect our borders, but other drug laws are justified under the power to regulate interstate commerce. In the last 30 years, the number of new federal laws has increased dramatically with attendant increases in the federal law enforcement, judicial, and correctional systems.

To view a few selected state penal codes, go to http://www.statutes.legis.state.tx.us/Index.aspx. (Texas); http://www.legis.state.wv.us/WVcode/code.cfm?chap=61&art=1. (West Virginia); http://www.leginfo.ca.gov/cgi-bin/calawquery?codesection=pen. (California).

To look at the United States Criminal Code, go to http://www.law.cornell.edu/uscode/18/usc_sup_01_18.html

Exhibit 7.2   A federal agent in Los Angeles displays seized counterfeit bills. Counterfeiting is specifically mentioned in Article I, Section 8 as a federal crime.

Source: AP

Cities, counties, townships, and municipal corporations also have limited authority to make and enforce rules and regulations. State legislatures have given these units of government the power to create laws as long as the regulations and ordinances do not conflict with the U.S. Constitution, the state constitution, or the laws of the state. The state may withhold, grant, or withdraw powers and privileges as it sees fit. City ordinances may vary quite a bit and are constantly being updated and revised in response to citizens' concerns.

WHAT ARE SOME DIFFERENCES BETWEEN CIVIL AND CRIMINAL LAW?

Early codes of law did not differentiate between what we might call public wrongs and private wrongs. Today, we have separated criminal law (public wrongs) and civil law (private wrongs). **Criminal law** is the branch or division of law that defines crimes and provides for their punishment. In a criminal case, the state pursues justice to preserve the public peace. On the other hand, in **civil law** a person seeks a remedy against their perceived wrongdoer by bringing a civil, or *tort*, action. **Torts** are personal wrongs. Some examples of torts are assault, defamation, intentional infliction of emotional distress, and arson. *Torts* and *crimes* are not synonyms. While there is a great deal of overlap between crimes and torts, some crimes are not torts, and some torts are not crimes.

With torts, the emphasis is on adjusting the conflicting interests of individuals to achieve a desirable social result. The aggrieved party is the plaintiff and he or she must pay for the cost of the trial, although if he or she wins the court may order the defendant to reimburse the plaintiff for costs incurred. There may also be punitive damages assessed in addition to compensatory damages. For example, if Ann hits Bob, causing him bodily injury, Bob may bring an action in court for recovery of expenses and for compensation for losses incurred. The state may also initiate an action against Ann for assault and prosecute the case in criminal court. You may remember that there was a successful civil suit against O.J. Simpson for wrongful death *after* his acquittal in criminal court. It is entirely possible for a defendant to "win" in one court and "lose" in the other, partially because of the different burdens of proof in civil versus criminal court. Exhibit 7.3 presents some examples of torts and comparable crimes if they exist.

Victims are essentially witnesses in a criminal case, not parties in the action, as they are in a civil case. That is why criminal cases are called "*State v. Defendant*" while in civil cases, the plaintiff is a named party in the case title. It is not correct to say, however, that victims are ignored in criminal prosecutions. Prosecutors will often confer with victims before offering plea bargains and take their wishes into account in terms of charging decisions. Victim witness statements are heard in court before sentencing in most jurisdictions. There is a difference in the goal of criminal and civil justice however. In civil law, the goal is to secure one's compensation for loss or injury and, if appropriate, punitive damages, while the aim of the prosecutor is justice (whatever that might mean).

WHAT ARE SOME CONSTITUTIONAL CHALLENGES TO CREATING LAWS?

The federal government, states, and municipalities have great powers, but they do not have the power to pass a law that violates one of the rights granted by

Exhibit 7.3 Examples of Torts Compared to Crimes

Tort	Definition	Crime
Assault	Intentionally threatening harmful or offensive contact creating reasonable fear	Assault
Battery	Harmful or offensive contact with a person without consent	Assault (assault and battery is combined in criminal law)
False imprisonment	Confinement without legal authority against consent	False imprisonment
Intentional infliction of emotional distress	Intentional conduct that results in extreme emotional distress	n/a
Trespass	Intentional entrance onto the land of another without lawful excuse	Trespass
Conversion	Willful interference with plaintiff's possessory rights of property	Embezzlement
Defamation	Intentional false claim that may harm the reputation of plaintiff	Libel, slander
Invasion of privacy	Intrusion into the personal life of another person without just cause	n/a (although voyeurism, computer crimes, wiretapping, and other crimes address similar behavior)
Breach of confidence	Disclosure of private information conveyed in confidence to detriment of plaintiff	n/a (honest services fraud may address similar behavior)
Fraud	False representation with intention to induce harm or loss to other party	Fraud (criminal law limits to financial loss or injury)
Tortious interference	Intentionally damaging the plaintiff's contractual or other business relationships	n/a
Nuisance	Preventing owners of quiet enjoyment of real property	Public nuisance (somewhat different definition)
Breach of duty of care	Not adhering to a reasonable standard of care while performing acts that could possibly harm others	This would be an attendant circumstance to a crime that resulted in death or serious injury, e.g., involuntary manslaughter

the United States Constitution. As discussed in an earlier chapter, protections are found in the first ten Amendments, which make up the **Bill of Rights**. We are protected against laws that are vague, punish behavior after the fact (**ex post facto laws**), or infringe upon our freedom of expression, association, religion, or right to bear arms. Furthermore, laws that treat people in a discriminatory manner or that unreasonably infringe upon individual privacy rights are prohibited. A summary of some of the rights granted in the Bill of Rights which might give rise to a challenge against a criminal law appears in Exhibit 7.4.

Exhibit 7.4   Bill of Rights

1st Amendment: Freedom of religion, expression, association

2nd Amendment: Right to bear arms

3rd Amendment: Right not to have soldiers quartered in people's homes

4th Amendment: Right to be free from unreasonable governmental search and seizure

5th Amendment: Right to be free from compulsory self-incrimination, federal right to grand jury, protection against double jeopardy, due process

6th Amendment: Right to an impartial jury trial that is speedy and public, with specified due process elements

7th Amendment: Right to trial in suit at common law, jury to be trier of fact

8th Amendment: Right against excessive bail, right to be free from cruel and unusual punishment

9th Amendment: States "The enumeration in the Constitution, of certain rights, shall not be construed to deny or disparage others retained by the people."

10th Amendment: Reserves all other powers not specifically delegated in the Constitution to the states

---

There has been a great deal of press over federal, state, and local attempts to control the sale and/or possession of firearms. This controversy has reignited after the mass killing in an Orlando nightclub in June of 2016 and we explored the research relating to the effectiveness of gun control laws in the last chapter. As you probably know, there are legal challenges to these laws which are based on the 2nd Amendment's right to bear arms and the Supreme Court's interpretation of that right as an individual right in *D.C. v. Heller* (2008) and *McDonald v. Chicago* (2010).[7] Gun control laws range from outright bans (e.g. of some types of weapons or by some groups of people) to background checks before purchases. Each law must be subjected to scrutiny to determine if it unduly interferes with one's 2nd Amendment rights, but it is not correct to assume that a right enumerated in the Bill of Rights cannot be subject to *reasonable* restrictions. For instance, the 1st Amendment gives you freedom of speech, but you cannot defame someone with lies; the 2nd Amendment protects your right to bear arms, but no one argues against laws that prohibit children from buying firearms; even though the 4th Amendment protect your from unreasonable governmental invasion of your home or papers, government agents can still search your home with a warrant; and, in similar ways, all of the rights provided in the Bill of Rights are subject to reasonable restrictions.

Other challenges to the constitutionality of laws are based on at least one of the following arguments:

- vagueness
- ex post facto
- equal protection
- 1st Amendment rights
- right to privacy.

Vagueness. It is a fundamental principle of criminal law that the legislation must not be vague, meaning that there is some reasonable doubt as to the meaning of the law. In vagueness challenges, the law is criticized as being so unclear as to what is prohibited that reasonable people would not have proper notification that some act was wrong.

In *City of Chicago v. Morales*,[8] the Supreme Court struck down an anti-gang law passed by Chicago City Council in order to control gang activity. The law/ordinance prohibited those "believed to be criminal street gang members" from "loitering in any public place." Criticisms of this law centered on the vague nature of identifying who were street gang members and the vagueness of the terms "loitering" and "public place." The majority of the Court objected to the fact that it was solely within the police officer's discretion to define when loitering was occurring. The Supreme Court, in this case, indicated that there may be anti-gang laws that could pass the vagueness test, but they needed to be written in a way that definitely stated what actions would be defined as criminal.

Basically, the right to be free from vague and overbroad laws comes from the 5th and 14th Amendments. Both Amendments provide that an individual should receive "due process of law" before being deprived of life, liberty, or property. The 5th Amendment provision has been interpreted to provide protection against due process violations by federal actors (such as the FBI), and the 14th Amendment provision protects us from due process violations by state governmental actors (such as your municipal police). **Due process** has been defined as the procedures designed to protect against error in the governmental deprivation of life, liberty, and property. Due process includes the right to notice (to know what we are being accused of). Obviously, in order to have notice, a law must be clear and not subject to arbitrary definitions.

In *Skilling v. United States*,[9] Jeffrey Skilling, one of the executives of Enron who ended up in prison after the collapse of the huge energy company, challenged his federal conviction under what is informally called the "honest services" law. The federal law made it a crime to deprive your employer or anyone owed a **fiduciary duty** to your honest services. A fiduciary duty is the requirement to prioritize that person's interests over one's own interests—such as a stockbroker to a client. The federal law was used successfully in many corruption cases and was especially useful to prosecutors when they could not prove specific bribes or kickbacks were received or offered in return for specific acts, although they could prove a pattern of behavior that rose to a level that indicated the "honest services" of the accused were compromised by some inappropriate enrichment. The Supreme Court in June 2010 held that the law was void for vagueness, arguing that a reasonable person would not know when they violated the law. The holding spurred many public corruption defendants to file challenges to their convictions.

Ex Post Facto Laws

The U.S. Constitution and state constitutions specifically prohibit ex post facto laws. The two sections of the federal Constitution that relate to ex post facto laws are Article I, Section 9, which provides that "no bill of attainder or ex post facto law shall be passed," and Section 10, which provides that "[n]o state shall . . . pass any ex post facto law."[10] These provisions were added to the Constitution of the United States and similar provisions have been added to the constitutions of the respective states to prohibit legislative bodies from punishing a person for an act that was neither a crime nor punishable when the act was committed, or from increasing the punishment after the fact. Two critical elements are necessary to establish an ex post facto claim:

- The law must be retrospective—that is, it must apply to events occurring before its enactment.
- It must disadvantage the offender affected by it.[11]

A mere procedural change in the law, not increasing punishment, or not changing the elements of the offense, does not result in a constitutional violation. A law may be invalid as ex post facto toward a particular person who committed an act before its enactment, but that does not affect its validity generally to those who commit the crime after the legislation has passed.

Even though defining an act as criminal and/or punishing an act retroactively violates ex post facto prohibitions, if the governmental action is considered administrative as opposed to punitive, there is no violation. Laws forcing sex offenders to register, even those who were already convicted of a sex crime and serving their sentence, seems as if it is imposing retroactive punishment; however, the Supreme Court decided that it was not a criminal punishment to register, but rather, a regulation or administrative action, and therefore, there was no violation of the ex post facto laws prohibition.[12] Later cases have been decided differently based on state constitutions. A new law that forced convicted sex offenders to register for longer than their original sentence entailed was ruled a violation of the ex post facto prohibition under the Oklahoma constitution.[13] Laws that allow the indefinite commitment of sexually violent predators in mental institutions have also faced ex post facto challenges and, in *Kansas v. Hendricks*,[14] the Supreme Court has ruled that such laws do not violate either ex post factor prohibitions or double jeopardy because commitment to a mental institution is not punishment.

Equal Protection Violations

The 14th Amendment to the Constitution prohibits the government from treating "similarly situated" people differently. That is, if two groups are similar, then they must be treated equally under the law unless there is a substantial governmental objective to be served in treating them differently. The 14th Amendment states:

> No State shall make or enforce any law which shall abridge the privileges or immunities of citizens of the United States, nor shall any State deprive any person of life, liberty, or property, without due process of law, *nor deny to any person within its jurisdiction the equal protection of the laws*. [emphasis added]

The government must have a very good reason for treating different racial, ethnic, or religious groups differently under the law. If a law that is neutral on its face differentially affects only one group of people, it would also be scrutinized.

In 1967, the Supreme Court struck down Virginia's **miscegenation laws**, which made it a crime to marry someone of a different race.[15] The Court held that the state did not have a reason that was sufficiently important to justify treating those who wanted to marry someone from another race and those who married within their own race differently. The holding invalidated all miscegenation laws in not only Virginia, but also the other states that had them.

Exhibit 7.5   Mildred and Richard Loving challenged Virginia's miscegenation laws after they were arrested. In 1967, the Supreme Court ultimately held that the law had "patently no legitimate overriding purpose independent of invidious racial discrimination."

Source: Getty

In the case *In re Michael M.,*[16] a California statutory rape law was challenged. The law made statutory rape a crime that could only be committed by male perpetrators against female victims. The argument was that the law violated equal protection because it treated male and female actions differently by defining the crime in such a way that only men could be perpetrators and only girls could be victims. In this case, the Supreme Court upheld the law because the parties were *not* considered similarly situated, in that only female victims could become pregnant, and the law's imputed purpose was to prevent teenage pregnancy. Through the 1970s and 1980s, however, sexual assault laws were rewritten in most states with gender neutral language so that boys and men can be victims of sexual assault, and girls and women can be prosecuted as perpetrators.

Many laws that treat men and women differently have been struck down, such as laws that had different drinking ages (*Craig v. Boren*[17]). However, in *Rostker v. Goldberg,*[18] the Supreme Court in 1981 upheld the law that only required young men, not young women, to register for the draft. If this legal mandate was challenged today under equal protection grounds, the holding of the current Supreme Court might be different. In equal protection cases, a law that treats groups differently can be upheld if (a) the groups are not "similarly situated," or (b) if the reason for the difference passes the so-called "strict scrutiny" standard, which requires that the government have a substantial and important government purpose and the difference is narrowly tailored to meet that purpose.

1st Amendment Rights

Neither the states nor the federal government can pass a law that *unreasonably* limits 1st Amendment rights. As you know, the 1st Amendment protects our freedoms of speech, association, and religion.

> Congress shall make no law respecting an establishment of religion, or prohibiting the free exercise thereof; or abridging the freedom of speech, or of the press; or the right of the people peaceably to assemble, and to petition the government for a redress of grievances.

The government does have a right to pass laws that do not unduly interfere with these rights. Thus, for instance, if our speech creates an imminent danger to others, it can be prohibited and even punished. One does not have the right to incite a riot, utter a threat, or verbally agree to commit a crime.

When is a threat serious enough to be prosecuted as a crime? Consider the case of Justin Carter. Carter was an eighteen-year-old Texas student who, on a gaming website, was in an argument with another gamer who said that he must be crazy. Carter responded with this statement: "I'm (messed) up in the head alright, I think I'ma SHOOT UP A KINDERGARTEN...AND WATCH THE BLOOD OF THE INNOCENT RAIN DOWN...AND EAT THE BEATING HEART OF ONE OF THEM." A different person took a screenshot of the exchange and sent it to police in Comal County, Texas, and Justin was arrested in 2013 for making a terroristic threat. The Texas law in question defines a criminal threat as:

> A person commits an offense if he threatens to commit any offense involving violence to any person or property with intent to: 4) cause impairment or interruption of public communications, public transportation, public water, gas, or power supply or other public services: 5) place the public or a substantial group of the public in fear of serious bodily injury.

He was jailed with adults and beaten by other jail inmates before being able to make bail. His trial is set to begin sometime in 2016.[19] Although many legal experts contend that his actions do not meet the definition of a terroristic threat, the determination to charge is within the prosecutor's discretion and it will be up to the jury to decide if he is guilty.

In *Texas v. Johnson* (1989), an individual was arrested and punished under a Texas statute that made flag burning illegal. The Supreme Court ruled that the law violated 1st Amendment rights because flag burning was defined as symbolic speech.[20] This case decision is still controversial and a large number of people believe that burning the American flag, even if done as a protest, should be criminalized. In response, Congress has considered a proposal for a constitutional amendment that would criminalize flag burning. This illustrates the dynamic nature of law—what is criminal today may not be tomorrow, or vice versa.

Other constitutional challenges may involve the 1st Amendment protections of religion, speech, or association. Generally, one has the right to speak, associate freely, and practice one's religion without state interference. However, laws can be passed if the behavior in question harms others or intrudes unduly on governmental interests in safety and order. These areas can raise interesting questions in how to balance individual freedoms and societal interests. Should worshipers, for instance, be allowed to sacrifice goats as part of their religion, or should they be bound by animal cruelty laws? Should followers of certain religions be allowed to have multiple wives, or be subject, as everyone else, to bigamy laws? These challenges to created laws are always difficult and are resolved by balancing individual interests against government interests.

Privacy Violations

The right to privacy is not identified specifically in the Constitution, but has been recognized by the Supreme Court in various case decisions. Basically, the Justices' position in these decisions has been that the framers of the Constitution meant that privacy rights should exist, based on their language in certain amendments, such as the 4th Amendment. One of the most important cases that established the protected right of privacy against governmental interference was *Griswold v. Connecticut*.[21] In that case, the Supreme Court struck down Connecticut's criminal law that punished the distribution of information regarding birth control and contraceptives to married couples. According to Justice William O. Douglas, the 1st, 3rd, 4th, 5th, 9th, and 14th Amendments can be read to construe a privacy right that restricts the government from interfering with private decisions of procreation by a married couple. *Griswold* and similar case decisions identifying a right of privacy even though it is not specifically enumerated in the Bill of Rights, were used as the precedent for the *Roe v. Wade*[22] decision which invalidated laws criminalizing all abortions.

The balance between individual liberty and governmental interest in many so-called privacy cases is typically the individual's right to make personal decisions versus protection of society's morals. Laws against drugs, pornography, gambling, and prostitution have been challenged under the privacy rationale, but generally have lost to the argument that the government's interest in societal safety and protection of societal morals justifies such laws. Laws against same-sex consensual sexual intercourse were ruled a violation of the Constitution in *Lawrence v. Texas*.[23] Many commentators believed that the decision in *Lawrence* signaled that other privacy challenges would be successful as well; however, such cases are still being litigated and there may be differences between what is legal and illegal between jurisdictions. For instance, a law in Alabama prohibits the sale of "any device designed or marketed as useful primarily for the stimulation of human genital organs" and it was similar to a law in Texas that prohibited the sale of "obscene devices," defining "with intent to sell" as having more than six devices. In challenges to these laws using *Lawrence* as precedent, the Fifth Circuit (covering Louisiana, Mississippi, and Texas) struck down the Texas law as infringing on privacy, while the Eleventh Circuit (covering Alabama, Florida, and Georgia) upheld Alabama's law.[24] The Supreme Court refused to hear an appeal from the Eleventh Circuit case so, at this point, selling sex toys is illegal in Alabama but not in Texas. Federal Circuit Court decisions are the law in that jurisdiction unless or until they are overturned by the Supreme Court and it is entirely possible to have different holdings regarding points of law, just as it is possible to have different state court decisions so that what is law in one state may not be the same in another.

WHAT ARE THE ELEMENTS OF A CRIME?

If a law is not struck down because it violates one or more constitutional rights, it is enforceable as a crime. All crimes are classified as felonies, misdemeanors, or treason. These classifications are important not only in determining the degree of punishment, but also when determining the authority of justice personnel to take action. For example, in some states, law enforcement officers may not make misdemeanor arrests unless the offense was committed in their presence (or they had an arrest warrant).

According to most authorities, crimes punishable by death or by imprisonment in a state prison or penitentiary are **felonies**. A crime may be made a felony by reference to the punishment attached, or it may be made a felony by a statute that specifically says that it is a felony. When an offense is not designated by statute as either a felony or a misdemeanor, but a specific punishment is prescribed, then the grade, or class, of the offense is determined by the punishment. Generally, felonies are punishable by at least one year in prison.

Misdemeanors are offenses for which the punishment is other than death or imprisonment in a state prison or that have not been designated felonies by statute. A person convicted of a misdemeanor will ordinarily be incarcerated in a local jail or be required to pay a fine, but will not be sent to a state penitentiary. What is defined as a felony in one state may be a misdemeanor in another, except for the most serious crimes, such as murder, robbery, and rape, which are always felonies.

Treason is one of the only crime that is described in the Constitution. Because those who commit treason threaten the very existence of the nation, it is given a higher classification than a felony. According to the Constitution:

> Treason against the United States shall consist only in levying war against them, or in adhering to their enemies, giving them aid and comfort.[25]

Also, the Constitution provides that no person shall be convicted of treason unless on the testimony of two witnesses to the same overt act, or on confession in open court.

Each crime, as defined in a criminal code, must include a specific prohibited act (or omission), a prescribed mental state, and possibly attendant circumstances. A crime, then is composed of the parts as represented in Exhibit 7.6.

The first necessary element to a crime is referred to as the *actus reus*. The law does not punish mere criminal thoughts, nor does it punish a person for who he or she is. Each crime's definition includes a physical act or, in some instances, a failure to act. The physical act must be voluntary, such as pulling

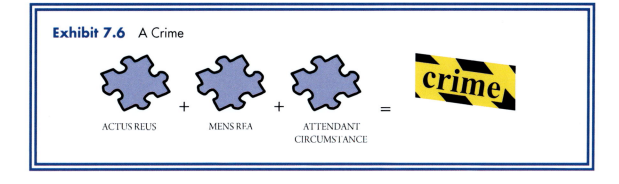

Exhibit 7.6 A Crime

ACTUS REUS + MENS REA + ATTENDANT CIRCUMSTANCE = crime

the trigger of a gun or breaking into a house to commit theft. There have been a few cases in criminal law in which the act was deemed to be not "volitional" or voluntary on the part of the perpetrator. Examples of acts that are not considered voluntary include actions taken during epileptic seizures or spasms, reflexive actions, or actions taken while sleepwalking or in some other form of "unconscious" state.

In some cases, the crime consists of a failure to act, such as a failure to register for the draft or failure to prepare income tax returns. An omission to act can only constitute a crime when there is also a legal duty. Legal duties are created by:

- statute
- relationship
- contract
- voluntary assumption of care.

Examples of statutory duties are, for instance, the duty to file tax returns and the duty (of convicted sex offenders) to register in sex-offender registries. Failure to perform these duties is a crime in itself.

Certain relationships also carry duties. The most obvious and common is the duty of a parent to care for a minor child. Care includes not only feeding and housing your child, but also providing medical care and ensuring that school-age children receive an education. In about twenty-eight states, **filial responsibility laws** exist. These statutes create a duty for adult children to financially provide for one's aged and infirm parents if one is able to do so. In some states, a defense can be offered that the parent abandoned the child before the age of majority. Despite the fact that these state statutes exist, they are rarely enforced; in eleven of these states, *no one* has ever been prosecuted for failing to care for their elderly and infirm parents.[26]

Contractual duties arise when one person receives something of value in exchange for a duty to care for others. If they are negligent in that duty, criminal culpability may be created. Examples of contractual duties exist between the following actors:

- lifeguards to swimmers
- child care providers to those in their care
- doctors to patients.

If a person who has no statutory, relationship, or contractual obligation to render aid chooses to begin administering assistance, then they may create a duty for themselves. For instance, unless a state has a **Good Samaritan law**, there is no statutory duty to stop and render assistance if one sees a traffic accident (unless one is involved in the accident). However, if a passerby does stop and begins to help, then they must not abandon their effort if it would leave the victim in a worse condition than before. If one sees a person in distress on the street, there is no duty to render aid; however, if the passerby helps the person in distress to a park bench or helps them to a doorway, or in any other way moves them away from where they might have received assistance from others, then the duty to continue care has been created. The rationale is that abandoning one's effort would leave the victim in a worse condition than before.

The second necessary element of every crime, in addition to the *actus reus*, is a criminal state of mind, or **mens rea**. Under common law, each crime possessed a *mens rea*, but the language used in old English cases and early state statutes and cases in this country was not uniform; thus, for instance, the necessary intent for homicide was defined as malicious, premeditated, depraved indifference, depraved heart, or wanton disregard. The **Model Penal Code** condensed all the myriad definitions of *mens rea* into only four enumerated mental states. In all states that have adopted the Model Penal Code, statutes clearly specify that the actor must have acted *purposely, knowingly, recklessly,* or *negligently*. Further, the definitions of these terms do not vary state by state; they always mean the same thing. The definitions of these terms are as follows:

- *Purposely:* when the actor intends the act and intends to cause the result.
- *Knowingly:* when the actor is aware of the nature of his conduct and is aware of the practical certainty of the result of his conduct.
- *Recklessly:* when the actor knows of, but consciously disregards, an unjustifiable risk (and the action involves a gross deviation from a reasonable standard of conduct).
- *Negligently:* when the actor is unaware of, but *should have been* aware of, an unjustifiable risk (and the action involves a gross deviation from a reasonable standard of conduct).

One other concept important to criminal *mens rea* is the principle of **transferred intent**. This can be remembered as "bad aim" intent because the classic example is that if the defendant intends to kill victim A, but misses and kills victim B instead, he will be guilty of first-degree murder (for B's death) and attempted murder (for trying to kill A). The intent to kill was transferred to the actual victim.

The third element to a crime is attendant circumstances. For example, if the crime is receipt of stolen property, the attendant circumstance must be that the property is indeed stolen. Lack of consent (of the purported victim) is an attendant circumstance in many crimes. The criminal law must clearly specify all the required elements to any and all crimes.

If you examine any crime in your state's criminal code, you should be able to identify the specific *actus reus* and the *mens rea* required for criminal culpability. In Exhibit 7.7, several serious crimes are given with the *mens rea* and *actus reus* attached. Obviously, these represent only a small portion of the crimes in any

Exhibit 7.7 Crimes and Mental States

Crimes	Mens Rea	Actus Reus
Homicide, first degree	Purposely	An act that resulted in the death of another (and intended the result)
Homicide, second degree	Knowingly	An act that resulted in the death of another either intentionally or with knowing it was an almost inevitable outcome
Voluntary manslaughter	Knowingly	An act that resulted in the death of another (and intended the result *but with provocation*)
Involuntary manslaughter	Recklessly	An act that resulted in the death of another by engaging in behavior where the risk was known to the defendant
Rape/sexual assault	Knowingly	Penetrated the sexual organ of another with the use or threat of force, against the consent of the victim
Robbery	Knowingly	Took something of value from another in their presence with the use or threat of force
Burglary	Purposely/ with intent	Breaking and entering with the intent to commit a felony inside
Theft	Purposely/ with intent	Taking something from another, without consent, with the intent to permanently deprive

jurisdiction. It is important to remember that these definitions may not match exactly your state's definition. Each state's penal code may define the crimes in slightly different ways. If the *mens rea* is not specifically stated, case law usually assumes the legislators meant "knowingly."

WHAT ARE SOME DEFENSES TO CRIMINAL CULPABILITY?

Defenses to the accusation of a crime fall into two main categories: (1) I didn't do it (e.g., alibi); and (2) I did it, but... In the second category of legal defenses, the accused argues various reasons why they are not legally culpable for their actions. These defenses include: "infancy"; insanity or incompetence; duress or compulsion; necessity (choice of evils); self-defense; entrapment; and, ignorance or mistake. One last defense is when the prosecution occurs after the statute of limitations has run.

Infancy

Under this defense, an individual argues that they were too young to understand the consequences of their actions and, therefore, cannot form criminal *mens rea*. Infancy, in the legal sense used here, means only that the child does not have the capacity to determine right and wrong. The age of infancy is set by case law or statute. We also use the term **juvenile** to refer to a child below the age of legal culpability. Under common law, anyone under seven years of age was deemed too young to be legally culpable. Today, states set their age of infancy—the age at which no criminal prosecution would commence (although the youngster would be dealt with in the juvenile court). States also have a "rebuttable" age range—this age range, e.g., seven to fourteen, is when the child is presumed to be too young to be held legally responsible, but that presumption can be rebutted by evidence of maturity. For instance, the state of Washington sets the age of infancy this way:

> Children under the age of 8 are incapable of committing crime. Children of 8 and under 12 years of age are presumed to be incapable of committing crime, but this presumption may be removed by proof that they have sufficient capacity to understand the act or neglect and to know that it was wrong.[27]

A juvenile court may "waive" jurisdiction to an adult court if the crime is serious enough and the court finds the juvenile knew the consequences of their actions. Federal and state statutes define the way legal infancy can act as a defense to criminal culpability. Supreme Court cases have also slowly expanded the parameters of this legal "excuse" for criminal culpability by addressing what punishments are considered "cruel and unusual" and a violation of the 8th Amendment when directed to juveniles. In *Roper v. Simmons* (2015), the Supreme Court held that an individual could not be executed if they committed murder before the age of eighteen.[28] In *Graham v. Florida* (2010),[29] the Supreme Court held that juveniles could not be given sentences of life without parole for non-homicide crimes; then, in *Miller v. Alabama* (2012)[30] they decided that life without parole for juveniles convicted of murder was also too harsh. Juveniles are treated differently under the law because their decision-making capabilities are not fully developed, and they have a greater possibility of rehabilitation. We will discuss these issues more fully in Chapter 13.

Mental Capacity

Mental capacity is relevant in criminal prosecution at (1) the pre-trial stage, (2) the verdict stage, and (3) the sentencing stage. First, one can be found **incompetent to stand trial** which means that there is a decision that the defendant doesn't understand what is happening and cannot assist in their own defense. If there is a determination of incompetence, criminal prosecution cannot move forward. Incompetency can be because of mental illness, mental development, or medical conditions like amnesia. The individual may be held in an institution until such time as they become competent.

The second way mental capacity is relevant is when the accused's defense is that their mental state was the reason they committed the offense. **Insanity** is a legal term, not a medical term. It refers to any mental illness that meets the legal threshold for incapacity. The most common legal test of insanity is the **M'Naghten Test**, from an early English case. If the defendant "was laboring under such a defect of reason, from disease of the mind, as not to know the nature and quality of the act he was doing, or, if he did know it, that he did not know he was doing what was wrong" then he should be acquitted. This has become known as the "right and wrong test." A person is insane if they did not know what they were doing or they did not know what they were doing was wrong. Not all jurisdictions use this test, but the majority use some version of it.

One of the difficulties in applying the test is when the mentally ill person, because of his or her delusion, believes they are saving the world or killing a demon, but they understand they are breaking the law. If they knew that killing was against the law, they could be found sane, not insane, because most jurisdictions instruct the jury that the knowledge requirement relates to *legal* or *societal* definitions, not *moral* definitions. This is a frequent issue because schizophrenics often have religious delusions that they are doing the work of God or that victims are some form of demon or an alien that need to be killed.[31]

Some people are uncomfortable with the mentally ill person being acquitted due to insanity when they have committed a horrific crime. In fact, this might result in a jury finding someone sane when evidence clearly indicates they were under some form of schizophrenic delusion during the crime. As noted before, insanity is a legal term and judges or juries have discretion to determine whether insanity was the cause of the crime. An alternative occurs when insanity is removed as a legal defense. About thirteen states now have adopted the "guilty but mentally ill" concept, which preserves the traditional insanity defense but provides an alternative to it. A jury can choose between a verdict of "not guilty by reason of insanity," which results in acquittal, or a verdict of "guilty but mentally ill," which will result in a sentence for the same term provided for a regular guilty verdict. The sentence, however, would be served in a state mental hospital.[32] In general, these changes in statutes have been upheld against constitutional challenges. For instance, an Indiana court upheld the state statute that permits the jury to find the defendant guilty but mentally ill, agreeing that the statute did not violate the equal protection clause and the statute had a rational relationship to a legitimate state interest in securing convictions and obtaining treatment for defendants who suffer from mental illness.[33] In fact, courts have held that due process does not require states to offer the insanity defense at all.[34]

In some cases, an individual is not pleading insanity, but evidence of diminished capacity may reduce the seriousness of the crime. The argument is that they could not have formed the highest level of intent. Diminished capacity defenses have included the PMS defense (that premenstrual syndrome symptoms include behavioral and emotional incapacitation to the extent that the defendant could not control her actions), PTSD (post-traumatic stress syndrome symptoms caused the individual to commit the criminal act), and the battered woman syndrome (repeated victimization was responsible for the defendant attacking the perpetrator). Alcoholism has never been successful as a defense to a crime although some states allow it to be used to prove the defendant didn't have the highest level of *mens rea*.

Recall in February of 2013, Chris Kyle, the author of the book *American Sniper* which was made into a recent movie of the same name, was shot by Eddie Ray Routh while they were target shooting at a gun range. Routh suffers from PTSD, and Kyle was helping him to recover from his condition brought on by military service in Iraq. Routh, who evidently experienced paranoia, delusions, and sleeplessness, had been under treatment with Veterans Affairs doctors who prescribed a variety of mood-disorder and anti-psychotic medications, but refused to hospitalize him even though he had threatened violence and suicide. The motive for the shooting is unknown, but Routh confessed he killed Kyle and Kyle's friend, Chad Littlefield, at the shooting range. His defense was PTSD but the jury convicted him of first degree murder and sentenced him to life in prison without parole.[35]

Exhibit 7.8   Eddie Ray Routh was convicted of first-degree murder in the killing of Chris Kyle and Chad Littlefield. Routh argued he had diminished capacity due to PTSD after serving in Iraq, but the jury sentenced him to life without parole.

Source: Getty

The third and final way one's mental state might be relevant in criminal prosecution is at the sentencing stage. Even if a defendant does not convince a jury that they were legally insane and not responsible for their actions, relevant evidence may be introduced at the sentencing stage to affect the sentencing decision. Most state prison systems have psychiatric units (or whole facilities in larger states). In fact, it is a sad commentary that there are now more mentally ill individuals in prison than in mental hospitals.[36]

It is important to remember that mental illness and insanity are not synonyms—insanity is a legal term that denotes mental disability to the point where one cannot be held legally culpable while mental illness is a broad term that encompasses many disorders. The Diagnostic and Statistical Manual of Mental Disorders (DSM-V), the definitive guide by the American Psychiatric Association, defines a mental disorder as a behavioral or psychological syndrome or pattern that occurs in an individual that reflects an underlying psychobiological dysfunction with consequences that include clinically significant distress (e.g., a painful symptom) or disability (i.e., impairment in one or more important areas of functioning). The symptom must not be merely an expectable response to common stressors and losses (e.g., depression after the loss of a loved one), caused primarily a result of social deviance or conflicts with society.[37] It is important to remember that one can be mentally ill, but not necessarily legally insane.

Duress

Another defense is called either **duress** or compulsion. Except in the case of homicide, an act that would otherwise constitute a crime may be excused when committed under duress or compulsion that is imminent, and produces a well-grounded fear of death or serious bodily harm.[38] There must be no reasonable escape without committing the crime.[39] This defense cannot be used if the defendant has committed murder; someone holding a gun to your head threatening you does not give you a legal justification to kill an innocent party. It can excuse other crimes, however, like theft. The test as to whether the coercion was enough is reasonableness—was the threat sufficient to overcome the will of a reasonable person? The threat must be imminent—the person making the threat must intend and be prepared to carry out the threat immediately—if someone says, "rob a bank or your family will be killed next week", this does not constitute an imminent threat.

The battered spouse/woman syndrome has been described as a type of diminished capacity, but it could also be placed here under duress. Basically the defense is that the defendant experienced severe abuse that affected the ability to leave the abuser, and, ultimately, the defendant felt the only way to get away from the abuse was to kill the abuser, often not during an active abuse incident but, rather, when the abuser is incapacitated either by sleep or alcohol. Not all courts recognize this defense, however, and some have refused to allow in evidence of prior abuse, as it is not relevant to the immediate crime.

Necessity

Duress and necessity are somewhat similar defenses; however, while duress always involves fear of harm or intimidation, necessity is a broader defense that justifies criminal actions if it is to avoid greater harm. For instance, if you are trapped in a snowstorm on a mountaintop and the choice is to freeze to death or break into someone's cabin, the law allows you to break and enter (as long as there is compensation to the victim). The necessity defense, similar to duress, will not allow one to sacrifice an innocent to save oneself or one's property. The classic necessity case is *Regina v. Dudley and Stephens.*[40] In this case, Dudley and Stephens were tried for the murder of another sailor. All three had been adrift in an open boat for twenty days and were starving. They killed and ate the victim, because he was the youngest and the weakest, and were rescued four days later. The court found that they would have most probably died if they had not committed the act and that the boy would have died before them; however, they were convicted because necessity was not recognized as a defense to murder. They were sentenced to death but the Crown commuted their sentence to six months' imprisonment.[41]

Examples of successful and unsuccessful uses of the necessity defense include: a convicted felon who was legally prohibited from possessing weapons and who grabbed one to defend himself used the defense successfully when charged with "Felon in Possession of a Firearm";[42] a person who stole food argued economic necessity unsuccessfully;[43] and a defendant who kidnapped another to save them from a religious cult was unsuccessful in the use of the necessity defense.[44] Recently, some defendants have tried to use the necessity defense when they have been prosecuted for marijuana possession in the states that do not have medical marijuana legislation, arguing that marijuana is a necessary treatment to an illness or condition. They have not been successful.[45]

Self-defense

Self-defense is as old as common law. The law allows you to protect yourself and others with violence if necessary, but there are certain elements that must be present in order for self-defense to be successful. Other elements vary from state to state. The basic elements of self-defense are: (1) fear of serious harm; (2) the fear is reasonable; (3) the harm is imminent; (4) the defense is proportional; and (5) the defendant did not create the threat. In some jurisdictions (but not all), there is a (6) duty to retreat (but not in one's own home).

The reasonableness of the fear is determined by an objective test; the question asked is not if the defendant was in fear, but whether a reasonable person would have been in fear given the same set of circumstances. The danger must be immediate, and the response must be proportional (in caselaw this is not a very consistent requirement, however, and is quite subjective). For instance, self-defense can be used when someone attacks you, but your response has to be reasonable to the level of the threat. Another element that some states have as a necessary element for self-defense is "clean hands," the idea that you couldn't have started the fight or set up the situation which created the need to use violence to defend yourself. Some states also have the duty to retreat—this means that before using violence to defend oneself you must try and escape the threat. Even in those states that have a duty to retreat element to self-defense, the requirement does not apply when one is at home. You have no duty to retreat in your own home. Other states have no duty to retreat at all.

In some states, **"stand your ground" laws** have expanded the legal right to use lethal force. Florida became the first state to pass such a law in 2005 and now over a dozen states have similar laws. Statistics showed a sharp increase in justifiable homicides after 2005, when Florida and sixteen other states passed the laws. Overall homicide rates in those states stayed relatively flat, however the average number of justifiable homicide cases per year increased by more than 50 percent in the decade's latter half.[46] In Texas and Georgia, such cases nearly doubled, and in Florida, they nearly tripled. Meanwhile, in states that saw no new "stand your ground" laws, justifiable homicides reported to the FBI stayed nearly flat after a slight uptick in the middle of the decade.

In 2012, Florida's law was the center of controversy in the shooting of Trayvon Martin, a teenager shot by a neighborhood watch volunteer who followed him as he was walking through the neighborhood and ended up shooting him when he engaged the youth and a fight ensued. His release without charges set up a national outcry.[47] The Florida statute allows an individual to use force up to lethal force when he or she has a reasonable fear of being harmed. There is no duty to retreat.[48] Another recent analysis of homicides comparing states without "stand your ground" laws to those with such laws[49] found that rates of homicides ruled justifiable were generally significantly higher in states with "stand your ground" laws. The only exception was that there was no difference in the rate of homicides ruled justifiable between a Black perpetrator and White victim in states with "stand your ground" laws and those without. In states without the laws, only 1.13 percent of Black-on-White homicides were ruled justifiable and 1.4 percent of homicides in states with the laws were ruled justifiable—not a significant difference. On the other hand, for White-on-Black shootings, justifiable rulings increased from 9.51 percent of all to 16.85 percent of all homicides in states with "stand your ground" laws. Black-on-Black and

White-on-White homicides showed less dramatic increases. There is no way to interpret these findings with only the numbers available. It is possible, perhaps, that they represent victims who are defending themselves during a criminal event; or, alternatively, they represent a negative outcome of the "stand your ground" law which may allow too much latitude in defining what is a reasonable use of deadly force.

Generally, violent actions have been justified by self-defense only to prevent serious bodily harm. **"Make My Day" statutes** in some states expanded self-defense by allowing individuals to use deadly force against a home intruder in situations where there is no immediate threat from the person who made the unlawful entry, as long as there is a reasonable belief that a crime is intended. Colorado's law, for instance, states that:

> any occupant of a dwelling is justified in using any degree of physical force, including deadly physical force, against another person when that person has made an unlawful entry into the dwelling, and when the occupant has a reasonable belief that such other person has committed a crime in the dwelling in addition to the uninvited entry, or is committing or intends to commit a crime against a person or property in addition to the uninvited entry, and when the occupant reasonably believes that such other person might use any physical force, no matter how slight, against any occupant.[50]

What the Colorado law and similar laws in other states do is expand self-defense from defending oneself or others against physical harm to defending one's property. Not all states have such laws for the public policy reason that property should not be prioritized above life.

If all the required elements of self-defense are proven, the defendant should be found not guilty of a crime, either by a judge as a matter of law or by a jury decision. In some situations, however, not all the elements are proven leading to the "imperfect defense" of self-defense. Generally the effect of an imperfect defense is to reduce the level of *mens rea* and severity of the crime. For instance, if the defendant is in a fight with the victim and he kills him, he may argue self-defense. However, if there is a finding that he started the fight or used disproportional force; in this case, the self-defense facts may go toward reducing the crime from a first or second degree murder to a voluntary manslaughter. Similarly, if an objective test of reasonableness is used and the defendant mistakenly and unreasonably believed he was in danger and used unlawful force, then his defense is imperfect and the use of force will not be justified, although he might be found to have a lesser *mens rea*.

Entrapment

Entrapment did not exist as a defense under common law. It was first recognized in a federal case in the 1930s. In this defense, the defendant is saying, "Yes, I did it, but the police made me do it." The argument is that law enforcement creates the crime by providing too much of a temptation for a person who has no predisposition to crime. Entrapment tends to be used most often in drug cases, although recently it has been used when individuals have plotted to commit terrorist acts with undercover federal agents. Police engage in a wide variety of situations where they provide the opportunity to commit a crime. They may pretend to be:

- individuals offering public officials a bribe in return for special treatment
- drug sellers (or buyers)
- prostitutes (or "johns")
- children in Internet chat rooms offering to meet a predator for sex
- fences encouraging the theft of certain types of automobiles
- hit men who are willing to kill for money
- someone who can provide cable service for free
- a drunk on the street with money sticking out of his pocket.

Generally, the guideline for which of these situations constitutes entrapment is whether the person who succumbs to the temptation had a "predisposition" to commit the crime, basically asking the question: "Would a person with no predisposition to commit that type of crime be tempted by governmental actions to do so?"[51] The test was developed by the federal courts in a federal case, but many states have adopted it as well. For instance, Colorado's statute is as follows:

> **Colo. Rev. Stat. § 18–1–709**
>
> The commission of acts which would otherwise constitute an offense is not criminal if the defendant engaged in the proscribed conduct because he was induced to do so by a law enforcement official or other person acting under his direction, seeking to obtain that evidence for the purpose of prosecution, and the methods used to obtain that evidence were such as to create a substantial risk that the acts would be committed by a person who, but for such inducement, would not have conceived or engaged in conduct of the sort induced. Merely affording a person an opportunity to commit an offense is not entrapment even though representations or inducements calculated to overcome the offender's fear of detection are used.

Merely offering the opportunity to commit a crime is not sufficient for an entrapment defense to be successful. Especially for drug offenders, any past criminal history will probably mean that there will be a presumption the defendant had a predisposition to commit the crime. In a federal case, the Ninth Circuit Court stated that for a defendant to prove the defense of entrapment, he must point to undisputed evidence making it patently clear that an otherwise innocent person was induced to commit the illegal act by trickery, persuasion, or fraud of a government agent.[52]

Ignorance or Mistake

You have probably heard the phrase "ignorance of the law is no excuse," and that is generally true; however, sometimes ignorance of a law is an excuse if the law itself is obscure or a reasonable person would not be presumed to know of it. Also, a mistake about a crime may be a defense. There are two types of mistakes—mistakes about the legality of an action ("I made a mistake thinking that my action was legal") and mistakes about an essential fact ("I made a mistake in that I believed the goods were not stolen"). Mistakes of law are rarely successful defenses; mistakes of fact (if honest and reasonable) may excuse criminal culpability if the mistake is about an element of the offense. The classic example of a mistake of fact defense is when someone mistakenly takes another person's coat from a restaurant thinking it was his or hers. Taking possession of the property of another is ordinarily theft, but since the *mens rea* of theft is *intentionally* taking the property of another, the mistake of fact (thinking it was your coat) means that the *mens rea* requirement of theft is not present. Another example would be when you accept a gift from someone thinking they bought it for you, only to find out from police that it was stolen. You would have a valid defense if you were charged with receipt of stolen property because the *mens rea* for that crime is *knowing* the property is stolen and *intending* to receive stolen goods.

Drug smuggling cases have posed a thorny problem for criminal law when the smuggler is mistaken as to the substance. For instance, if Jack buys white powder in Mexico that he thinks is cocaine and smuggles it across the border by hiding it in a secret compartment of his luggage, has he committed a crime if it turns out to be talcum powder? Before changes in the law, some judges decided that no crime was committed because it is not illegal to smuggle talcum powder. However, federal law and many state statutes are now written in such a way that a mistake as to the actual substance does not change criminal culpability—if one intends to smuggle or sell a controlled substance and acts to do so, then they are still culpable even if the substance turns out not to be a controlled substance.[53]

Statute of Limitations

One last defense is when the time limitation (Statute of Limitations) for prosecution has expired. The rationale for the time limitations is that the defendant should have some substantial safeguards against an erroneous conviction because of the staleness of the evidence and because the defendant is entitled to a speedy trial. Therefore, when the defendant claims that the statutory period has expired, the guilt or innocence of the defendant is not an issue. If the statutory period has expired, the defendant is entitled to an acquittal as a matter of right. As a general rule, the time begins to run when the crime is committed and runs until the prosecution is commenced. Depending upon the provisions of the statute, the running of the time is stopped by the filing of an indictment or information or at the time a complaint is laid before a magistrate and a warrant of arrest is issued.[54] If the defendant leaves the jurisdiction or otherwise prevents prosecution, then the Statute of Limitations does not run during that time period.

WHAT ARE SOME RECENT ISSUES IN CRIMINAL LAW?

As noted above, cases concerning privacy and equal protection continue to be controversial. The reason why confirmation hearings of Supreme Court Justices are so contested is that the law is not a simple math equation and the interpretation of the law, and constitutional rights in particular, are fraught with political influence. For instance, even though *Roe v. Wade*[55] was decided in 1973, it is by no means a settled area of law and cases continue to be heard as states refine and restrict the "right" to abortion. The most recent case continued to utilize the test of "undue burden." In *Whole Woman's Health v. Hellerstedt*, decided in June 2016, the Supreme Court decided that a new law requiring abortion clinics to meet high standards of surgical centers with doctors required to have privileges at local hospitals posed an undue burden to women's right to access abortion services. At this point, it appears the Supreme Court is following the precedent set; however, it is entirely possible that one day the *Roe* decision will be overturned if the composition of Justices shifts to a majority that believed it was wrongly decided.

Even though the Supreme Court decided *Obergell v. Hodges*[56] in June of 2015 affirming that the right to marry someone of the same sex was a fundamental right that could not be infringed upon by state laws, this area of law is clearly not settled either. A recent legal controversy is whether "faith-based" statutes could give business owners the right to refuse services to same-sex couples or transgenders based on their religious objections to such individuals. Ultimately, the question becomes: do the laws violate either group's constitutional

To listen to the arguments in this case, go to http://www.scotusblog.com/case-files/cases/whole-womans-health-v-cole/

rights (either of equal protection, privacy, or some other right embedded in the Bill of Rights).

One need only look in the newspaper to see current legal controversies. Should hate crimes be extended to gender? Should concealed firearms be allowed on college campuses? Should there be a crime that holds owners of dogs that maul victims criminally culpable? Should federal drug laws override state medical marijuana laws? Should marijuana be legalized for recreational use? Should teenagers be prosecuted for pornography for "**sexting**"? The point is that the law affects you every day and it is a dynamic entity. It constantly changes in response to current events and political and social influences. Our focus on data for this chapter discusses one current controversy—whether medical marijuana should be a crime.

FOCUS ON DATA: IS MEDICAL MARIJUANA CRIME OR CURE?

Marijuana is a crime under federal law and the law of most states; however, four states have legalized marijuana for recreational purposes, and 23 states have legalized medical use of marijuana.[57] Recent news indicates that perhaps five states will be voting on legalizing small amounts of marijuana for recreational use in the next election cycle. This is a very interesting legal issue because any possession or sale of marijuana is still illegal under federal law. The federal government has created a "schedule" of controlled substances, which categorizes substances by potential for addiction and whether there are legitimate medical uses. Marijuana was placed in "Schedule 1" along with cocaine, heroin, methamphetamine, and other highly addictive drugs that have no legitimate medical uses.

The Federal Bureau of Investigation reports that there were an estimated 1,663,582 arrests for drug abuse violations in 2009 and 1,120,133 in 2014. In 2014, only about 17 percent of arrests were for sales or distribution, the majority (83 percent) were for possession. Of the possession arrests, 39.7 percent were for marijuana (down from 45 percent in 2009); thus, the majority of drug arrests in this country are for possessing marijuana.[58] The Gallup poll shows that in 2015, 58 percent of Americans were in favor of legalizing marijuana,[59] and an even greater number favor legalizing marijuana for medical use (89 percent).[60]

In some cases, defendants have attempted to use the necessity defense to a marijuana prosecution arguing that medical necessity created the need to violate drug laws.[61] As of this point, medical necessity has not been recognized as a defense by the courts. Some argue that with the increased number of states that have passed medical marijuana laws, the medical necessity defense should be re-examined in those states without medical marijuana laws. However, the Supreme Court as of 2016 has not ruled that those states' laws (utilizing medical necessity or any other legal argument) can usurp or overcome the 1970 Controlled Substances Act; therefore a person may conform to state law in their possession of medical marijuana, but still be in violation of federal drug laws.[62] Proponents argue that the sole Supreme Court case involved distribution, not possession, and that it is possible the Court would be more sympathetic to a case of a seriously ill individual who possessed marijuana for their medical needs. Under the Obama administration, the Department of Justice has shifted its enforcement to de-emphasize marijuana prosecutions in the states that have decriminalized marijuana; however, those individuals could still be prosecuted under federal law.

Proponents argue the time has come to recognize that marijuana (cannabis) presents some health benefits for individuals who cannot ingest other forms of pain medicine. Opponents to such laws argue that there are other safer methods, and that medical marijuana dispensaries are nothing more than legalized drug shops, and they bring an undesirable element to the community and serve as a gateway to other drugs. What are the facts concerning marijuana as a medical treatment?

A growing number of people argue that marijuana is the only effective treatment for symptoms of medical conditions such as glaucoma, cancer (nausea), multiple sclerosis (pain), and AIDS (pain). A barrier to good research has been that mere possession of marijuana has been illegal in all states until fairly recently, thus there has been little scientific research as to marijuana (cannabis) benefits. Scientists do know that the chemicals in cannabis prompt a response in the brain that affects many of the body's functions, such as in the heart, digestive, endocrine, immune, nervous, and reproductive systems. Cannabis has been proven to help manage pain and reduce muscle spasms in patients with multiple sclerosis.[63]

Thus far the medical community has not spoken with one voice in support of whether marijuana poses more risks than benefits in the treatment of certain ailments. As with other issues discussed throughout the book, advocacy and interest groups are not necessarily objective purveyors of facts. The issue has been hampered by the lack of ability to run stringent experimentation on the effects of cannabis in scientific settings. No doubt in the years to come, more data will be available, although it seems clear that the public support for legalization, at least for medical use, continues to grow. At this point the legal position of those who either distribute or possess medical marijuana is precarious since until the federal government changes federal laws, they can still be prosecuted. This is true as well, of course, for those in the few states that have passed laws decriminalizing marijuana for recreational use.

SUMMARY

What Is the Purpose of Law? What Is the Purpose of Criminal Law?

Society has law in order to regulate and guide personal and public interactions. Criminal law is the branch or the division of law that defines crimes, their elements, and provides for their punishment. The protections of law fall into three areas: protection from harm from others, protection from harm from oneself, and protection of society's morals.

What Is the Origin of Our Legal System?

Most present-day crimes in the various states had their origins in the common law of England. This was the law developed in early English court decisions and was modified by English legislative bodies. Common law became the starting point for our criminal law, but has now largely been supplanted by statutory law as found in state and federal criminal codes.

What Are Some Differences between Civil and Criminal Law?

Civil law is concerned with private wrongs (torts). The plaintiff brings the case instead of the state. Crimes can also be torts and a civil action can take place along with a criminal prosecution. Civil law is much broader than criminal law and deals with property law, contract, tax, estate, and other branches of law.

What Are Some Constitutional Challenges to Creating Laws?

Constitutional challenges fall into the areas of vagueness or ex post facto violations; or, the law violates the rights recognized in the 1st, 2nd, or 14th Amendments, or violates privacy rights.

What Are the Elements of a Crime?

Crimes are also classified as felonies, misdemeanors, and treason. Each crime's definition includes a prohibited action (the *actus reus*), the requisite state of mind (*mens rea*), and possibly specified attendant circumstances.

What Are Some Defenses to Criminal Culpability?

Defenses include: "infancy"; insanity or incompetence; duress or compulsion; necessity (choice of evils); self-defense; entrapment; ignorance or mistake; and Statute of Limitations.

What Are Some Recent Issues in Criminal Law?

Law is dynamic and it changes depending on public opinion and shifting public morals. On any given day, one could identify numerous legal issues in the daily newspaper or from an analysis of current events. Today, issues of religious freedom, LGBT rights, gun control, marijuana legalization, and euthanasia all appear in news stories frequently.

Critical Thinking Exercises

1. Find the penal code for your state; you should be able to find a copy online. Find out whether your state uses the Model Penal Code's *mens rea* definitions (purposeful, knowing, reckless, and negligent). Look up specific crimes to see if you can identify the *mens rea*—is the language clear or does it leave room for argument as to the mental state required?
2. Read a newspaper and identify any and/or all legal issues that appear that day. Can you identify natural law positions versus positivist positions in the proponents and opponents of the issue?

NOTES

1 J. Pollock, *Criminal Law*. New York, NY: Routledge, Taylor & Francis, 2015, p. 3.

2 Read about anti-semitic legislation of Nazi Germany at https://www.ushmm.org/outreach/en/article.php?ModuleId=10007695

3 *Lawrence v. Texas*, 539 U.S. 558, 2003.

4 *Obergefell v. Hodges*, 76 U.S. ___, 2015.

5 W. Blackstone, *Commentaries*, vol. 4, 1769.

6 *Keeler v. Superior Court*, 470 P.2d 617 (Cal. 1970).

7 *D.C. v. Heller* (554 U.S. 570, 2008); *McDonald v. Chicago* (561 U.S. 742, 2010).

8 *City of Chicago v. Morales*, 119 S. Ct. 1849, 1999.

9 *Skilling v. United States*, 561 U.S. 358, 2010

10 U.S. Const. Art. I, §§ 9 and 10, Cl. 1.

11 *United States v. Abbington*, 144 F.3d 1003 (6th Cir. 1998); *Myers v. Ridge*, 712 A.2d 791 (Pa. 1998).

12 *Smith v. Doe*, 538 U.S. 84, 2003.

13 *Starkey v. Oklahoma Department of Corrections*, 2013 OK 43, 2013.

14 *Kansas v. Hendricks*, 521 U.S. 346, 1997.

15 *Loving v. Virginia*, 388 U.S. 1, 1967.

16 *In re Michael M.*, 450 U.S. 464, 1981.

17 *Craig v. Boren*, 429 U.S. 190, 1976.

18 *Rostker v. Goldberg*, 453 U.S. 57, 1981.

19 Various news articles, e.g., http://www.expressnews.com/news/local/article/Facebook-threat-case-back-on-track-for-trial-6485258.php.

20 *Texas v. Johnson*, 491 U.S. 397, 1989.

21 *Griswold v. Connecticut*, 381 U.S. 479, 1965.

22 *Roe v. Wade*, 410 U.S. 113, 1973.

23 *Lawrence v. Texas*, 539 U.S. 558, 2003

24 *Williams v. Morgan*, 478 F.3d 1316 (11th Cir. 2007); *Reliable Consultants v. Earle*, 517 F.3d 738 (5th Cir. 2008).

25 U.S. Const. Art III, Sec. 3.

26 See "Caring for our parents in an aging world: Sharing public and private responsibility for the elderly." *N.Y.U. Journal of Legislation and Public Policy* 5 (2001): 563–595.

27 Rev. Code Wash. § 9A.04.050.

28 *Roper v. Simmons*, 543 U.S. 551, 2005

29 *Graham v. Florida*, 130 S. CT. 2011, 2010.

30 *Miller v. Alabama*,132 S. CT. 2455, 2012

31 *State v. Crenshaw*, 659 P.2d 488 (Wash. 1983).

32 730 Ill. Comp. Stat. § 515–2 (1999); Mich. Comp. Laws § 768.36 (1999).

33 *Gambill v. State*, 675 N.E.2d 668 (Ind. 1997).

34 *Ake v. Oklahoma*, 470 U.S. 68, 1985; *State v. Searcy*, 789 P.2d 914 (Idaho 1990).

35 News articles, e.g., http://www.theguardian.com/film/2015/feb/25/american-sniper-trial-eddie-ray-routh-found-guilty-and-sentenced-to-life-in-prison-without-parole

36 http://www.thejha.org/node/54

37 APA, *Diagnostic and Statistical Manual of Mental Disorders-5*. Available at https://www.psychiatry.org/psychiatrists/practice/dsm

38 *United States v. Anthony*, 145 F. Supp. 323 (M.D. Pa. 1956); *Jackson v. State*, 558 S.W.2d 816 (Mo. Ct. App. 1977).

39 *State v. St. Clair*, 262 S.W.2d 25 (Mo. 1953); *Jackson v. State*, 504 S.W.2d 488 (Tex. Crim. App. 1974).

40 14 Q.B.D. 273 (1884).

41 A similar American case was *United States v. Holmes*, 26 F. Cas. 360 (C.C.E.D. Pa. 1842).

42 *United States v. Paolello*, 951 F.2d 537 (3d Cir. 1991).

43 *State v. Moe*, 24 P.2d 638 (Wash. 1933).

44 *People v. Brandyberry*, 812 P.2d 674 (Colo. Ct. App. 1991).

45 *Jenks v. State*, 582 So.2d 676 (Fla. Dist. Ct. App. 1991); *State v. Hanson*, 468 N.W.2d 77 (Minn. Ct. App. 1991), *State v. Ownbey*, 996 P.2d 510 (Ore. App. 2000), *State v. Poling*, 531 S.E.2d 678 (W. Va. 2000), *United States v. Randall*, 104 Daily Wash. L. Rptr. 2249 (D.C. Super. Ct. 1976). For review, see J. Pollock, *Criminal Law*, 11th ed. New York, NY: Routledge, Taylor & Francis, 2016.

46 J. Palazzolo and R. Barry, "More killings called self defense." *Washington Post*, April 2, 2012. Retrieved from http://www.wsj.com/articles/SB10001424052702303404704577311873214574462

47 Various news stories, e.g. http://www.outsidethebeltway.com/federal-civil-rights-charges-against-george-zimmerman-said-to-be-off-the-table/

48 Fla. Stat. 776.012.

49 J. Roman, "Race, justifiable homicide, and stand your ground laws: Analysis of FBI Supplementary Homicide Data." Washington, DC: Urban Institute, 2013.

50 Colo. Rev. Stat. §18–1–704.

51 411 U.S. 423, 1973.

52 *United States v. Mendoza-Prado*, 314 F.3d 1099 (9th Cir. 2002). See also *Matteo v. Superintendent*, SCI Albion, 171 F.3d 877 (3d Cir. 1999).

53 J. Pollock, *Criminal Law*. New York, NY: Routlege, Taylor & Francis, 2016.

54 *Jarrett v. State*, 49 Okla. Crim. 162, 292 P. 888 (1930).

55 *Roe v. Wade*, 410 U.S. 113, 1973.

56 *Obergefell v. Hodges*, 576 U.S. ___, 2015,

57 See http://medicalmarijuana.procon.org/view.resource.php?resourceID=000881

58 FBI, Uniform Crime Reports, Arrest Tables, 2009, 2014. Retrieved 6/15/2016 from https://www.fbi.gov/about-us/cjis/ucr/crime-in-the-u.s/2014/crime-in-the-u.s.-2014/persons-arrested/main

59 J. Jones, "In U.S., 58% back legal marijuana use". Gallup.com, October 21, 2015, http://www.gallup.com/poll/186260/back-legal-marijuana.aspx

60 Quinnipiac University Poll, retrieved 6/17/2016 from http://www.pollingreport.com/drugs.htm

61 *Jenks v. State*, 582 So.2d 676 (Fla. Dist. Ct. App. 1991); *State v. Hanson*, 468 N.W.2d 77 (Minn. Ct. App. 1991), *State v. Ownbey*, 996 P.2d 510 (Ore. App. 2000), *State v. Poling*, 531 S.E.2d 678 (W. Va. 2000), *United States v. Randall*, 104 Daily Wash. L. Rptr. 2249 (D.C. Super. Ct. 1976).

62 *United States v. Oakland Cannabis Buyer's Cooperative*, 532 U.S. 483 (2001).

63 WebMD.com, retrieved 6/17/2016 from http://www.webmd.com/news/breaking-news/marijuana-on-main-street/medical-marijuana-research-web?page=2

CRIMINAL PROSECUTION

8

There are 50 different state court systems (as well as the court systems in Puerto Rico, Guam, and American Samoa), and a parallel federal court system. In this chapter, we will focus specifically on criminal courts, but remember that states may also have civil courts, family courts, probate courts, and a host of other limited jurisdiction courts. Our inquiry will include an objective look at some of the new court processes to see whether these innovations improve the system.

WHAT ARE THE DIFFERENT LEVELS OF COURTS?

Generally, each state has trial courts, intermediate appellate courts, and a supreme court or court of last resort that hears final appeals. Trial courts can be further separated into courts of general jurisdiction and courts of limited jurisdiction.

The names of each level of the court system can vary considerably from state to state. "Supreme" may refer to the court of last resort, or, in some states, this term refers to trial courts. "Circuits" may refer to the

Chapter Preview

- What Are the Different Levels of Courts?
- What Are Specialized Courts?
- Focus on Data: Are Specialized Courts Effective?
- How Do Prosecutors Decide Whether and What to Charge?
- What Are the Duties of a Defense Attorney?
- What Is the Role of a Judge? How Are They Selected?
- What Is the Jurisdiction of Federal Courts?
- How Does Due Process Protect Individuals Against Error in the Criminal Justice Process?
- What Are the Steps of a Trial?
- Summary
- Critical Thinking Activities

intermediate appellate courts or the trial courts. That is why it is best to become familiar simply with the general categories of:

- trial courts (limited jurisdiction and general jurisdiction)
- intermediate appellate courts
- courts of last resort (final appeal).

Courts have subject matter jurisdiction and geographic jurisdiction. **Subject matter jurisdiction** refers to the type of case that can be heard in each type of court; this is defined by legislation. Municipal courts, for instance, can only adjudicate certain types of cases. Courts must also have **geographic jurisdiction** over the case. In criminal cases, this means that the crime must have taken place in the court's geographic jurisdiction. If the prosecutor does not prove this essential fact, the defendant must be acquitted. In California and many other states, the geographic boundary for each court is the county; however, in some states, a district or circuit may encompass more than one county.[1] In larger jurisdictions, there may be many judges, each with their own courtroom, for that jurisdiction. Each of the courts receives incoming cases on a random or rotating basis.

General jurisdiction courts are the courtrooms of television and movies, and they are what most people think of when they think of criminal courts. These courts typically try felonies and have the power to sentence to state prison. General jurisdiction courts also try civil cases, although the courts are usually divided, so that there are civil trial courts and criminal trial courts. These general jurisdiction courts may be called district courts, superior courts, or some other name. **Courts of limited jurisdiction** can be found in all but five states.[2] Their jurisdiction is limited to specific types of cases. For instance, municipal courts may only adjudicate city ordinances and misdemeanors. There may be special traffic courts that only hear traffic violations up to a certain level of seriousness. Justices of the peace exist in some states and may hear minor misdemeanors and ordinance violations as well as civil cases. The judges/magistrates in such courts may also hold first appearances and arraignments for felony cases. The powers of such courts are set by legislation, and their jurisdiction may be limited to a county, part of a county, city, or municipality. In Exhibit 8.1, the criminal court system of New York is presented as an example of one criminal court system.

Trial courts. The trial courts as represented on television may not be what you see if you go into a criminal court, since the majority of time, other things are happening. On any given day in a trial courtroom you may see judges taking pleas, having docket calls, listening to pre-trial motions, or conducting other court business. Trials are not always underway and, in fact, there is tremendous

Exhibit 8.1   Court Structure of New York State

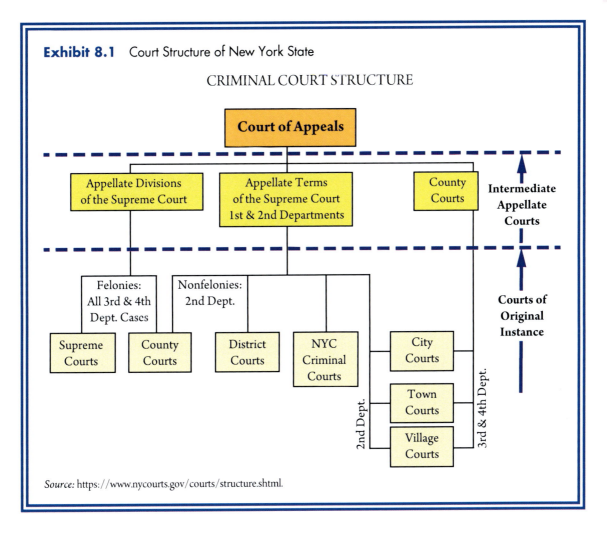

CRIMINAL COURT STRUCTURE

Source: https://www.nycourts.gov/courts/structure.shtml.

variation, even within the same jurisdiction, among judges in how many trials are conducted each year. While some judges may clear up to a dozen cases off their **docket** (cases assigned to their court) each month, others take a more leisurely pace.

Many states now allow cameras and audio equipment in the courtroom, but jury deliberations continue to be held in private. Despite news footage and reality programming, most people's perception of what happens in a courtroom is shaped by the countless television shows and movies that find courtroom drama so compelling.

The combined state and federal criminal trial courts produce convictions from well over one million offenders each year. In 2006, 1,132,290 defendants were convicted of a felony in state trial courts, and 69 percent were sentenced

For an interesting website that provides information about state courts, go to the National Center for State Courts' website at www.ncsc.org/

to jail or prison. Of these, 18 percent were convictions for a violent crime, 28 percent were convictions for a property crime, and 33 percent were convictions for a drug offense. Unfortunately, this seems to be the last year that the Bureau of Justice Statistics has provided statistics of felony processing.[3] In another data series source, it was reported that state prosecutors' offices reported closing 2.9 million cases charged as felonies in 2007 through convictions, acquittals, dismissals, or other dispositions.[4]

Appellate courts. Defendants who are convicted may appeal only if there has been some error in the trial or the process leading up to the trial. If, for instance, police officers interrogated the defendant and obtained a confession without giving him the Miranda warnings, that would be grounds for an appeal. Or, if, during trial, the judge made incorrect legal rulings, or if there was some attempt to improperly influence the jury, that would be grounds for appeal. The defense attorney must "preserve" the error by objecting to it during the trial. If he or she does not object, then in most cases the error will not be able to be used as grounds for an appeal. All defendants have a right to an attorney for the first "direct" appeal. If there are subsequent appeals, then the defendant must pay for the attorney. If there is an alleged violation of the Constitution then, after state appeals are exhausted, there can be an appeal to the Supreme Court. Generally, this is done through the writ of **habeas corpus**, which basically alleges unlawful imprisonment. In some cases, the writ is used when a prisoner believes the prison or the holding facility is operated in a way that is violative of the Constitution, but in other cases, it is used when the allegation is that the person ought not to be held at all because of an error at trial.

The appellate courts evaluate the alleged error and determine whether to take the case and, if they do, both parties will file a written brief and engage in oral argument before the court. If the appellate court does not find for the appellant (defendant), then that decision can be appealed to a higher court up to the state's highest court. If the appellate court does find for the appellant (defendant), then the state can appeal the decision. Sometimes, the appellate court agrees with the appellant but determines that the error was "harmless" and did not affect the outcome of the trial. **Harmless error** means that there was a legal error, but the evidence was so substantial in other ways that even if the error hadn't occurred, the result would have been the same.

In some states, there are several intermediate courts of appeal, distributed geographically across the state. In most states, the intermediate appellate court must review all appeals filed from trial courts (at least in criminal cases). That does not necessarily mean that there is any type of hearing. The court may review the appellate brief and find it is without merit and deny a full hearing.

While the **court of last resort** in any state is usually a very old institution, probably dating back to the beginning of statehood and the state constitution, intermediate appellate courts are more recent additions and serve to reduce the highest court's caseload. About forty states have these intermediate courts.[5] California has the largest number of intermediate courts, divided into nine divisions with more than 100 judges. Most of the time cases are heard by a panel of three judges, rather than the total number of judges in each division.

The highest court in the state, or court of last resort, is often called the state supreme court. Texas and Oklahoma are the only two states that split their court of last resort into two courts, including one that hears criminal appeals (court of criminal appeals), and one that hears civil appeals (supreme court).[6] If appellants also lose at the highest state level, and when there is an issue of constitutionality, the appellate attorney may file a **writ of certiorari** to the United States Supreme Court. The U.S. Supreme Court only hears about 1 percent of cases that are appealed in this way.

A good rule of thumb is that trial courts decide upon facts, and appellate courts rule on points of law. However, this is not completely accurate because trial courts also make rulings on interpretations of law. The most important thing to remember is that an appeal can only be filed because of an error of law. Appellate courts never retry facts. Thus, the guilt or innocence of a defendant is never the issue, only whether there was some legal procedural error, or violation of a state or federal constitutional right, during the proceedings.

WHAT ARE SPECIALIZED COURTS?

There are also a growing number of **community courts**,[7] or problem-solving courts, which may be courts of limited jurisdiction, but more often are courts of general jurisdiction, meaning that they may handle up to and including felony criminal matters. The defining feature of this type of court is a focus on "problem solving." Community courts focus on less serous criminal offenses and attempt to divert offenders from the criminal justice system. The concept fits well with community policing because both are interested in strengthening the community's ability to respond to such problems as delinquency and crime. Typically, community courts use alternative sentencing models to achieve the restorative justice goals. Community courts or problem-solving courts might include drug courts (dealing specifically with drug offenders or offenders who are drug addicted), veteran's courts (dealing specifically with offenders who have served in the military), domestic violence courts (dealing specifically with crimes involving family member victimization), and so on. An important question to ask is if these types of courts are more effective than traditional prosecution and our focus on data section looks at this question.

FOCUS ON DATA: ARE SPECIALIZED COURTS EFFECTIVE?

One type of problem-solving court is the **drug court**, which is typically a court of general jurisdiction but with a specialized caseload of drug cases. Since the first drug court was established in 1989, hundreds of drug courts have been established across the country. The judges in these alternative courts identify first-time drug offenders, sentence them to drug testing and treatment programs, and then monitor the offender's progress through the program. If

Exhibit 8.2　Drug courts in many states offer first-time drug offenders a chance to avoid incarceration by completing drug testing and treatment programs. Here a judge in Los Angeles hugs a defendant at a graduation ceremony for people who have completed the program.

Source: Getty

the offender successfully completes the program, he or she may be diverted from incarceration and their conviction may also be erased.[8] The major goal of drug courts is to break the cycle of drug use rather than simply administer punishment.

Some studies have shown that offenders who go through drug courts are more likely to complete drug treatment programs and have lower recidivism rates than offenders who are sentenced through regular court processes. However, at this point, the research is mixed, with just as many evaluations showing no difference as those that find that drug courts reduce recidivism, as compared to regular court processing.[9] In a study of a Cincinnati drug court, researchers found that drug court participants were more likely to get probation than a comparison group, and the comparison group was more likely to receive intensive supervision probation. While there was no difference in drug arrests between the drug court participants and the control group (30.8 percent versus 37.4 percent were re-arrested), there was a significant difference in theft/property arrests (18.4 percent versus 31.7 percent).[10]

Another study looked at whether biweekly review sessions with the judge had an effect on recidivism. In some drug courts, there is minimal interaction between the offender and the judge, but this study looked at a program where the judge met much more frequently with the offenders. The findings indicated that biweekly hearings reduced recidivism among high-risk offenders, but not low-risk offenders.[11] In a cost-effectiveness study, researchers concluded that cost savings in a drug court in Multnomah County, Oregon, saved taxpayers close to $500,000 for every 100 participants.[12] In one review of several drug court evaluations, the authors concluded that effectiveness would be increased if the courts:

- used objective risk and need instruments
- used behavioral and cognitive treatment strategies
- made sure the level of treatment was matched to the offender
- provided aftercare
- maintained quality control over treatment options.[13]

A more recent study conducted by Urban Institute researchers utilized twenty-three drug courts and six comparison jurisdictions covering eight states in a five-year study that interviewed participants and examined criminal records. They found that drug courts did significantly reduce substance abuse and crime. Offenders in drug court caseloads reported committing half as many crimes as those in regular courts. Researchers also found that positive effects were correlated with perceptions of the judge. Those who perceived the judge treated them fairly and with respect, and allowed them to talk in court, were likely to do better than those without such perceptions. The final analysis showed that drug courts saved the jurisdiction $2.00 for every $1.00 spent.[14]

Domestic violence courts deal with assaults that occur between intimates, either in a spousal (husband–wife), familial (parent/caregiver–child/dependent), or intimate (boyfriend–girlfriend or same-sex partners) relationship. These courts have developed because of the growing awareness of the problem of domestic violence and the system's reaction to it. Mandatory arrest policies, for instance, have led to an increase in prosecutions for domestic assaulters, taxing the courts and filling jails and prisons with offenders. The impetus for domestic violence courts came from the Violence Against Women Act, which created federal funding for the implementation of the courts. Domestic violence courts increase coordination among the courts, police, and social service agencies, and adopt a "therapeutic approach" to justice.[15] The concept of a specialized court recognizes the unique interpersonal issues involved in domestic violence and emphasizes treatment for the batterer and services for the victim. These courts employ both sanctions (punishment) and services for greater effect. Recognizing the unique nature of domestic violence, these courts may also handle restraining or protective orders and even child custody and visitation issues to provide a comprehensive judicial response to the problem of violence in the home.

In the few studies that have been undertaken, domestic violence courts were found to reduce recidivism over traditional court processing. In one study, recidivism in the domestic violence court sample was 6 percent compared to a control sample of 14 percent. On the other hand, another study showed that the creation of a domestic violence court increased the number of arrests for domestic violence. This was explained as the result of law enforcement becoming sensitized to the issue, as well as being more likely to arrest, knowing that the domestic violence court was available as a resource. The study also found that participants in the domestic violence court were significantly less likely to recidivate than those who went through traditional court processing. The conclusion of the study described earlier was that a "coordinated community response" to domestic violence, involving the police, courts, and social services, reduces recidivism.[16] In another study, a court program for domestic violence offenders in Albuquerque, New Mexico, was found to reduce recidivism as compared to a matched sample who did not go through the court program.[17]

Although findings are mixed, specialized problem-solving courts seem to be helpful in reducing recidivism over traditional court processing. The studies that exist seem to indicate that certain elements, e.g., closer judicial supervision, may improve the success of such courts so it would be important to carefully evaluate programs noting differences between them.

HOW DO PROSECUTORS DECIDE WHETHER AND WHAT TO CHARGE?

A district attorney (prosecutor) is usually an elected official (except in Alaska, Connecticut, the District of Columbia, and New Jersey).[18] In all but the smallest jurisdictions, there are also assistant prosecutors who also try cases, but are hired and not elected. In larger jurisdictions, they may number in the hundreds, and the elected district attorney never actually prosecutes a case, but rather acts as the policy director and CEO of the office. There are about 2,330 state court prosecutors' offices, employing 78,000 attorneys, investigators, and support staff. This does not include county or city prosecutors who prosecute in courts of limited jurisdiction.[19]

Our conception of prosecutors' offices is probably shaped by television and movies, which tend to portray large jurisdictions such as New York City and Los Angeles. In reality, most offices are quite small. Most prosecutors' offices receive both state and county funding. Most prosecutors' offices employ ten or fewer people. In some offices, prosecutors serve on a part-time basis, maintaining their own private law practice as well. The role of a part-time prosecutor in a small town is very different from the district attorneys in large cities like New York, Chicago, or Houston, which have hundreds of assistant prosecutors.[20]

In very rare cases, special prosecutors are appointed by the governor or attorney general when it is believed that a local prosecutor has a conflict of interest or the prosecution involves a case that crosses jurisdictional lines. Such special prosecutors can also be found at the federal level. Currently, there is discussion nationwide as to whether special prosecutors should be appointed by state attorneys' general offices when a police officer is charged with a crime. The argument is that local prosecutors' offices have too close of a relationship with police departments to be unbiased in decisions of charging or trial strategy.

To read a news story about this issue, go to http://www.nytimes.com/2015/07/08/nyregion/cuomo-to-appoint-special-prosecutor-for-killings-by-police.html?_r=0

In some larger jurisdictions, the prosecutor's office is divided into divisions. The most common divisions are the misdemeanor division and the felony division. There may also be specialized caseloads, such as sexual assault or domestic violence caseloads. Prosecutors may be attached to a specific court and always appear before the same judge in the same courtroom, following a case from first appearance through sentencing. Alternatively, prosecutors may be assigned different stages of the process, so that they may deal with only preliminary hearings or only first appearances and pass the case on to those who specialize in litigation for the trial portion.

In some states, counties and cities also each have either appointed or elected attorneys who handle cases for these jurisdictions. The majority of their caseloads may be civil, but city attorneys, for instance, may enforce code violations and infractions.

For a website that further describes attorneys general, go to www.naag.org/

To find information on the staffing and salaries of prosecutors, go to the most recent national statistics from the Bureau of Justice Statistics at http://www.bjs.gov/content/pub/pdf/psc07st.pdf

Each state also has an attorney general who is the state's chief legal officer. Attorneys general may have personnel who enforce child support enforcement; they may have lawyers that represent the state's citizens in consumer protection, antitrust, and utility litigation; they enforce federal and state environmental laws and represent the state and state agencies in criminal appeals and statewide criminal prosecutions.

The role of any prosecutor is quite different from that of the defense attorney. While the defense attorney's role is to protect the rights of the accused, the prosecutor has the ethical duty to "seek justice"—and this does not necessarily translate into "get a conviction." Prosecutors must balance office resources, the relative seriousness of the crime, and the desires/needs of the victim and community when making decisions about whether and how to prosecute. Not all cases that begin with arrest are prosecuted. In fact, prosecutors drop many cases without prosecution, and this decision-making ability is one of the least studied areas of the criminal justice system.

A study of prosecutors' discretion in two large counties utilized interviews and a survey that included hypothetical cases. The results were then analyzed to determine the elements of prosecutors' decisions. Research showed that outcomes are affected by legal factors (e.g., strength of the evidence, type and seriousness of the offense, and defendant's culpability), quasi-legal factors (e.g., legally non-relevant though potentially influential factors, such as defendant–victim relationship, victim age, and defendant age), and extra-legal factors (e.g., legally impermissible factors pertaining to defendant and victim, such as race, ethnicity, or gender).[21] Organizational factors also influence prosecutors. Rules, the availability of resources, and personal relationships, perhaps with police officers involved, sometimes are more important than evaluations of the strength of the evidence, the seriousness of the offense, and the defendant's criminal history.

WHAT ARE THE DUTIES OF A DEFENSE ATTORNEY?

Defense attorneys are favorite characters for television and movie script writers. They are portrayed as tireless crusaders for the downtrodden or sleazy "hacks" willing to do anything to help their clients avoid their just punishment. The reality, of course, resembles neither of these two extremes. Defense attorneys, for the most part, help the system work by helping individual defendants navigate the complex and confusing world of the justice system. Clients are more likely to receive due process because of defense attorneys. Criminal law is not a favored specialty of lawyers; less than 10 percent of all lawyers have a full-time criminal practice. Most attorneys who do take criminal cases also carry a general law practice.

The Supreme Court holding in *Gideon v. Wainwright* (1963)[22] recognized a 6th Amendment right to an attorney when a defendant was facing a felony conviction, and later, in *Argersinger v. Hamlin* (1972)[23] the Supreme Court held that all indigent offenders facing incarceration had a 6th Amendment right to counsel (an attorney). This requirement meant that states needed to develop ways of providing defense counsel to all defendants facing jail or prison. The two most common ways are appointed counsel systems and public defender offices. All states except Maine have either a state or county public defender system (although most states also have appointed attorneys to supplement the public defenders).[24]

Appointed counsel systems operate with a list of attorneys approved to be appointed to indigent defendants. Assignments are given on a rotating or other basis. Attorneys get on this list by volunteering or, in a few cases, all attorneys in the jurisdiction are on the list. These attorneys are in private practice and have private clients as well as court appointments.

In public defender systems, the defense attorneys are full-time employees of a public defender office. They may be either county or state employees, or employees of a private nonprofit agency that holds a contract from the state for indigent defense. Public defender systems are more common in urban areas, while appointed counsel systems are more common in suburban and rural areas.[25]

A third form of indigent defense is the contract attorney model. This is similar to the appointed counsel model, except that, instead of distributing cases to all the attorneys on a list, one or two attorneys take all of the indigent cases for a set contract amount. These attorneys may or may not also have a separate private practice, depending on how large is the indigent caseload. This model has proven to be attractive to some jurisdictions because it may be less expensive than the appointed counsel model and is useful in jurisdictions that do not have enough indigent cases to justify a public defender office.

The general thought is that individuals who are defended by a public defender or appointed counsel do not receive the same quality of legal assistance as those who are able to hire their own private attorneys. While the findings of researchers are mixed, it seems to be the case that indigents are more likely to receive a sentence to jail or prison and are more likely to plead guilty when they have counsel provided to them, but they receive shorter terms than those with privately retained attorneys.[26]

Other research indicates that, at least in the federal system, appointed attorneys perform considerably worse than public defenders. They evidently bill for more hours per case, are less qualified, and achieve worse results for their clients. They cost the public, in the aggregate, about $61 million more than

To find information about your own state's method for delivering indigent defense services, go to http://public.findlaw.com/library/state-public-defenders.html

To read an interesting article about a day in the life of a public defender, go to http://www.courier-journal.com/story/news/crime/2015/11/19/kentucky-public-defenders-risks/76046976/?from=global&sessionKey=&autologin=

if public defenders had taken the cases. Suggested reasons for the difference between appointed attorneys and public defenders are that public defenders have more experience in criminal law and have a better relationship with prosecutors.[27] Another study found that about 29 percent of cases with private attorneys resulted in a prison sentence, 32 percent with a public defender did so, but 46 percent of cases with appointed counsel did, indicating that there was a lower standard of representation with appointed counsel.[28]

About 80 percent of all criminal defendants are indigent. **Indigency** requires the provision of publicly funded defense. One study reports that when the federal public defender system began in the 1960s about 30 percent of defendants were indigent and needed services, but now that figure is 90 percent.[29] Unfortunately, the system of public defense has been chronically underfunded.[30] In a 2008 report concerning public defense sponsored by the Department of Justice, the Bureau of Justice Assistance, and the National Legal Aid and Defender Association, it was noted that in the last 30 years there had been substantial improvement in the coverage of public defender programs; however, many indigent defendants do not receive adequate legal aid before pleading because of resource deficits in the states.[31] In a study of how states spent their Byrne Justice Assistance Grant funds from the Department of Justice, it was found that in Fiscal Year 2009, $20.8 million went toward prosecution, and only $3.1 million went to public defense. A total of $1.2 billion was allocated for all programs, meaning that the public defense allocation amounted to roughly 0.25 percent.[32] Costs of criminal defense represent a very small portion of criminal justice costs: about one-twentieth the costs of police and about one-fifteenth the cost of corrections.[33] One study in Tennessee showed that prosecution costs were between $130 and $139 million for the same set of cases for which public defense received $56.4 million.[34] Other countries spend more on public defense than the United States. While the UK spends 0.2 percent of its GNP on public defense, the US spends only 0.0002 percent.[35]

About twenty-two states administer and fund at the state level; eighteen rely primarily on county funding with some state support, and the remaining states have some hybrid system.[36]

To see states' funding for indigent defense, go to a 2016 Bureau of Justice report at http://www.bjs.gov/content/pub/pdf/idsus0812.pdf

In 2012, U.S. Attorney General Eric Holder announced that significant new resources would be directed to indigent aid. A number of private and public advocacy groups (6th Amendment Center, Brennan Center, The Constitution Project, the Gideon at 50 Project, the American Bar Association) have recently brought attention to the fact that indigent legal aid is so overburdened that representation likely falls below constitutional requirements. Studies show that public defender caseloads are often twice what ABA standards indicate they should be. Another source indicated that 79 percent of state public defender

Exhibit 8.3   Public Defender Costs in Tennessee

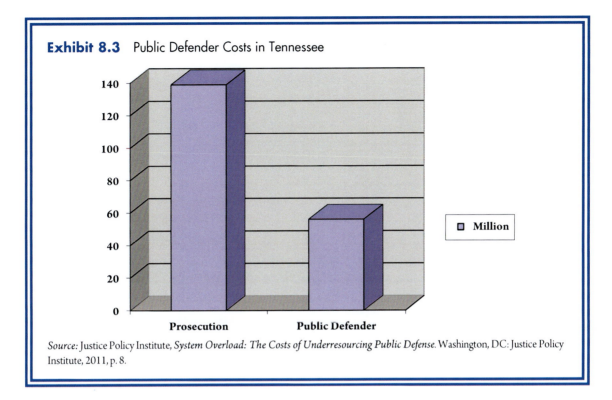

Source: Justice Policy Institute, *System Overload: The Costs of Underresourcing Public Defense.* Washington, DC: Justice Policy Institute, 2011, p. 8.

offices did not have enough attorneys to meet ABA recommended caseload sizes and that public defenders in large cities often handle 2,000 misdemeanor cases a year, which is five times the recommended number.[37] This means that public defenders or appointed counsel meet with their clients sometimes minutes before court appearances, don't have the resources to hire investigators, and miss the opportunity to obtain bail or pre-trial release for their clients. Underresourcing public defenders may result in higher costs to the system because offenders stay in the system longer unnecessarily.

In 2012, the American Bar Association's Standing Committee on Legal Aid and Indigent Defendants and the National Association of Criminal Defense Lawyers completed an examination of indigent defense and produced five core principals to improve indigent defense:

- Reclassify petty and nonviolent offenses to reduce "overcriminalization" that leads to unmanageable caseloads.
- Ensure counsel is provided to defendants at all initial court appearances, particularly when it comes to decisions about bail, to cut down on cost of detaining, especially those charged with minor offenses.

- Ensure access to effective counsel.
- Consult with defense bars before new law enforcement initiative are launched.
- Foster greater private–public involvement in indigent defense under a structured system.[38]

There is currently also interest in creating a more holistic approach to public defense. This involves the participation of other professionals who work with the defense attorney, such as social workers, community outreach workers, and others, who develop a more comprehensive response to the offender rather than merely a legal response to the charge. For instance, social workers may be in court and begin the process of finding a drug treatment program immediately as well as helping the offender with housing and jobs. In the long run this approach may have the potential to reduce the offender's involvement in the criminal justice system by addressing underlying problems, but it is time- and cost-intensive and requires adequate resources to be effective.[39]

WHAT IS THE ROLE OF A JUDGE? HOW ARE THEY SELECTED?

As described earlier, judges may be either trial judges in courts of general jurisdiction or courts of limited jurisdiction, or they may be appellate judges in intermediate courts or the court of last resort in the state (the state supreme court). Judges may be either elected or appointed. About one-third of all state trial judges receive their position through a general nonpartisan election (33.3 percent). Roughly another third (31.4 percent) are chosen through some form of merit selection process. Another 17.6 percent are elected through partisan elections. The rest obtain their judgeships through legislative appointments, gubernatorial selection, or other means.[40]

They typically serve fixed terms, although in a few states their terms are for life or at least until retirement age. The **Missouri Plan** is a merit selection process of appointing judges that involves a nominating process by statewide (for appellate) and local (for trial judges) committees. These committees send the nominees' names to the governor, who makes the appointment. The appointee then faces an election after one year, running against his or her own record. While 37 states use some form of nomination process, the remaining states still use general elections. In some of those states, the elections are partisan (with judges running as Democratic, Republican, or Independent), and in others the elections are nonpartisan.

There is increasing criticism of judges being elected through partisan elections. Critics argue that judges should be guided by the law, not popular

To read about how judges are selected in your state, go to the National Center for State Judges website and click on your state on the map: http://www.judicialselection.us/

opinion and they should not be elected in the same way as other politicians. More importantly, the public is not knowledgeable about the candidates or what should be considered as qualifications, i.e., legal expertise, conscientious or ethical behavior. Even retired Supreme Court Justice Sandra Day O'Connor has weighed in on this important topic and favors a hybrid system whereby a judicial nominating commission presents a recommendation to the governor who appoints the judge, a judicial performance evaluation is then done and publicized followed by a retention election.

To read this report go to http://iaals.du.edu/quality-judges/projects/oconnor-judicial-selection-plan

Trial Judges

Trial judges may preside over courts of general jurisdiction or limited jurisdiction. They may be family court judges, juvenile judges, criminal judges, or civil judges; or, in other jurisdictions, they may try all these kinds of cases in the same courtroom. Judges of limited jurisdiction (county courts, municipal courts, justices of the peace) may sit only part-time. Some of these magistrates may not even need to be lawyers to hold the judicial position (although this is rare). Some jurisdictions may occasionally hire retired judges to help with overloaded dockets.

Trial judges are basically like umpires in the justice process. They make decisions on rules of evidence and procedure. If a defendant decides to plead guilty (as the vast majority of defendants do), the judge must ensure that the confession is voluntary and that there is other evidence, in addition to the confession, upon which to convict the defendant. The judge, in these cases, must decide whether to agree with the prosecutor's recommendation for sentencing. Over 90 percent of all cases are resolved through a **plea bargain**, in which the defendant agrees to plead guilty in return for a favorable sentencing recommendation.

In cases that go to trial, the defendant may choose to have a **bench trial**, which means that there is no jury and the case is tried solely by the judge. The judge not only ensures that rules are followed, but also determines guilt or innocence in these trials. Most felony trials, however, include a jury.

Judges carry great weight with the jury and jurors may be influenced by any obvious bias the judge displays toward either the defense or the prosecution. The judge may be called upon to rule on pre-trial motions, which may include motions to exclude evidence because of alleged 4th Amendment violations by police officers. During the trial, judges rule on objections made by either the prosecution or defense attorney, based on rules of procedure in that jurisdiction. Some of the more common objections made during a trial are that the evidence does not have a proper foundation (meaning that the attorney has not obtained, through questioning witnesses, the proper level of proof that the item is what it is purported to be), the question asks something that is irrelevant or prejudicial, or the attorney was "leading" the witness (meaning that they were answering the question or suggesting the answer to the witness).

Although the jury determines guilt or innocence, the judge does have the power to throw out a guilty verdict if he or she finds that there is not sufficient evidence to support a judgment of guilt, as a matter of law. If a guilty verdict occurs, the judge may also be obliged to sentence the offender; although in some states juries have this function. Judges (or juries) must sentence within the statutory guidelines for sentencing.

If an offender is sentenced to probation, the judge maintains control over the defendant. Probation officers periodically submit progress reports to the court. The sentencing judge will ultimately be the one to close the case, either by revoking probation and sending the person to prison, by agreeing to an early release, or by recognizing that the offender has served the full term of probation.

Appellate Judges

There are about 1,335 appellate judges in the country. Their terms range from four to sixteen years, but Rhode Island judges have a term for life, and judges in Massachusetts and Puerto Rico have terms that last until age 70 (the mandatory retirement age).[41] Appellate judges may not be as newsworthy as their brethren in trial courts, but their decisions are, in some ways, much more powerful. Appellate courts overturn trial verdicts when they recognize errors of law and/or constitutional violations. Much of their caseload consists of civil appeals, but they also hear criminal appeals. Typically, appeals are heard by three-judge panels, and, if the three-judge panel denies relief, the petitioner may appeal to have the case heard **en banc**, meaning with the full number of appellate judges, or, in a state with more than one appellate jurisdiction, with all of the justices in that jurisdiction. It is typically from the ranks of state appellate judges that federal justices are selected.

WHAT IS THE JURISDICTION OF FEDERAL COURTS?

The federal court system is a parallel to what we have described here for state court systems. Exhibit 8.4 illustrates the organization of the federal court system. There are trial courts and appellate courts. Federal trial courts (called federal district courts and magistrate courts) hear criminal cases prosecuting alleged violations of federal laws. If convicted, these federal convictions can be appealed. The federal system has appellate courts (circuit courts) to hear

Exhibit 8.4 Federal Court System

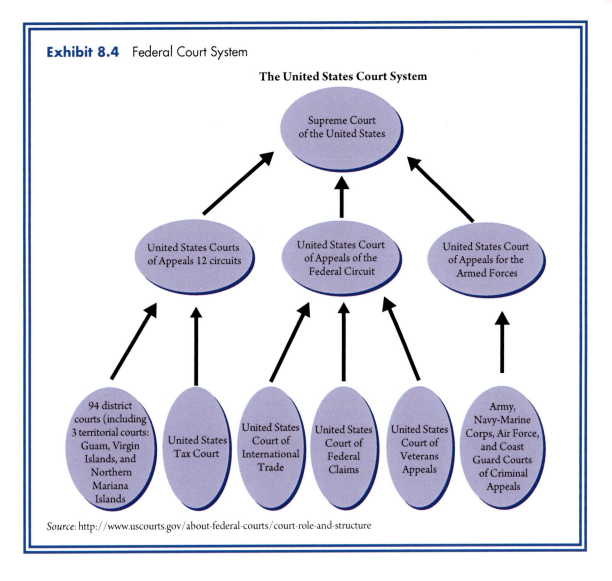

The United States Court System

Source: http://www.uscourts.gov/about-federal-courts/court-role-and-structure

appeals if there have been legal errors or constitutional violations, and, ultimately, these cases may also be appealed to the U.S. Supreme Court.

The United States military has its own judicial system. Each of the branches of the military has its own court of military review. Military law is set out in the Uniform Code of Military Justice. Decisions may be appealed to the United States Court of Military Appeals and, ultimately, to the Supreme Court. Procedures, rules of evidence, and even crimes are different in the military justice system. One of the interesting differences is that the defense and the prosecutor for a case are assigned out of the same office (the adjutant general's office).

The United States attorney is the federal equivalent of a district attorney or state prosecutor. There are about ninety-four U.S. attorneys attached to the ninety-four U.S. federal district courts, which are the federal trial courts.[42] There are also specialized courts that have limited jurisdiction over matters such as tax and patent law. A federal case can be appealed to the court of appeals. The country is divided into twelve circuits, each with its own court of appeals.

All federal judges are nominated by the president after receiving recommendations from the U.S. senators in that jurisdiction. The nominees must go through a confirmation process by the United States Senate. Once confirmed, they may hold their position for life, unless they are impeached by Congress.

The United States Supreme Court is the highest court in the land. The Justices on the Supreme Court hold their position for life. The Supreme Court is the only court that was established by the United States Constitution. Article III states:

For an interesting website on the Supreme Court, go to http://www.supremecourt.gov/

> The judicial Power of the United States, shall be vested in one supreme Court, and in such inferior Courts as the Congress may from time to time ordain and establish. The Judges, both of the supreme and inferior Courts, shall hold their Offices during good Behavior, and shall, at stated Times, receive for their Services a Compensation which shall not be diminished during their Continuance in Office.

Article III also specifies the jurisdiction of the court.

> The judicial Power shall extend to all Cases, in Law and Equity, arising under this Constitution, the Laws of the United States, and Treaties made, or which shall be made, under their Authority;—to all Cases affecting Ambassadors, other public Ministers and Consuls;—to all Cases of admiralty and maritime Jurisdiction;—to Controversies to which the United States shall be a Party;—to Controversies between two or more States;—between a State and Citizens of another State;—between Citizens of different States;—between Citizens of the same State claiming Lands under Grants of different States, and between a State, or the Citizens thereof, and foreign States, Citizens or Subjects.

Article III goes on to specify that, in some cases, the jurisdiction of the Supreme Court shall be original (meaning that the case can be brought directly), but in other cases the jurisdiction is appellate (meaning that the Court can only hear appeals after the case has been litigated in a lower court).

In all Cases affecting Ambassadors, other public ministers and Con-
suls, and those in which a State shall be Party, the supreme Court shall
have original Jurisdiction. In all the other Cases before mentioned, the
supreme Court shall have appellate jurisdiction, both as to Law and
Fact, with such Exceptions, and under such Regulations as the Congress shall make.

The Court rarely exercises original jurisdiction and almost all case decisions
are those that occur when the Court issues a writ of certiorari, which means
to bring the case forward. Because most of the cases appealed to the Supreme
Court fall into the area of discretionary review, the Court does not have to hear
them. When four or more justices agree to hear a case, the Court issues the writ
of certiorari. Typically, the Court receives thousands of appeals each year but
issues written opinions in only a hundred or so cases.

It is important to note that only decisions of the Supreme Court are clearly
and absolutely "the law of the land." In all other legal questions or issues, you
cannot assume that you know the law in your state and jurisdiction unless
you research case decisions in your particular jurisdiction. In textbooks, for
instance, you may read cases from a court opinion from a federal circuit that
does not encompass your state, or the supreme court of another state, or from
a state intermediate court of appeals from a jurisdiction in your state, but one
that does not include your city or town. In these cases, the holding or the principle of law that is set by the court may or may not be the law in your jurisdiction.
The holdings in other jurisdictions are only "persuasive," not "authoritative"
when the same legal issue comes up. The Supreme Court's opinions, however,
apply instantly and absolutely to all jurisdictions in the country. For this reason, these nine individuals on the Court are sometimes called the most powerful people in the country.

When Justice Atonin Scalia passed away in February 2016, the Supreme
Court was reduced to eight from its normal nine members. The current members of the court are:

- Chief Justice John Roberts
- Samuel Alito
- Ruth Bader Ginsburg
- Stephen Breyer
- Clarence Thomas
- Anthony Kennedy
- Sonia Sotomayor
- Elena Kagan.

Exhibit 8.5   Supreme Court nominees are appointed by the President with the advice and consent of the Senate, which typically holds hearings to evaluate the nominee, in this case, Elena Kagan.

Source: Getty

HOW DOES DUE PROCESS PROTECT INDIVIDUALS AGAINST ERROR IN THE CRIMINAL JUSTICE PROCESS?

Recall that due process refers to procedural protections that guard against errors when the government seeks to deprive anyone of life, liberty, or property. Elements of due process include:

- notice of charges
- right of counsel
- right to confront and cross-examine witnesses and evidence
- right to present witnesses and evidence
- right of impartial fact finders

- right to a statement of fact findings
- right of appeal.

Due process is perhaps the most important civil right guaranteed to us by our Constitution. We have certain protections when governmental actors want to take something from us, whether it is life, liberty, or property. These protections don't stop the deprivation, but they do make it more likely that government actors make these decisions in a fair, unbiased, and nonarbitrary manner. Due process applies in other contexts besides the criminal justice system; whenever the government seeks to deprive an individual of some protected liberty interest, due process applies. For instance, denial of social security payments, **eminent domain**, and involuntary mental commitments are all examples where due process protections are in place to protect individuals from governmental power. Due process is not a static concept. What is considered necessary due process depends on the nature of the deprivation. The deprivation of life, for instance, is the most extreme of all deprivations, which is why extreme procedural protections are in place for capital trials. The more serious the deprivation, the more important it is to make sure that no errors are made. Recall that due process clauses exist in the 5th and 14th Amendments, but the 6th Amendment can be considered to provide specific elements of due process and is often called the "trial rights" amendment.

The 6th Amendment states that the accused deserves a speedy and public trial, by an impartial jury. Further, each defendant has a right to be informed of the nature of the charges, to have the opportunity to confront and cross-examine the accusers and witnesses, and to have the assistance of counsel. It should be understood, however, that the 6th Amendment "trial rights" are only an example of due process. The framers of the Constitution evidently thought it necessary to specifically identify the rights of the individual when facing the awesome power of the government in the 6th Amendment.

> In all criminal prosecutions, the accused shall enjoy the right to a speedy and public trial, by an impartial jury of the State and district wherein the crime shall have been committed, which district shall have been previously ascertained by law, and to be informed of the nature and cause of the accusation; to be confronted with the witnesses against him; to have compulsory process for obtaining witnesses in his favor, and to have the Assistance of Counsel for his defence.

Due process applies before and after the trial. Pre-trial diversion, being held before booking, and being arrested implicate due process rights because they involve various types of deprivations. Sentencing and treatment in prison also may implicate due process rights. In fact, due process applies at each step in the justice process from investigatory detentions through release from prison.

Arrest

Due process mandates that **probable cause** must exist before a warrant can be issued or an arrest made. If the police officer does not meet the probable cause standard, then the arrest is an illegal deprivation of liberty. The legal remedy for an improper arrest is that any evidence obtained directly from that arrest can be excluded under the exclusionary rule. If maliciousness can be proven, an individual subject to a false arrest may also pursue a civil judgment against the individual officer, and even the department if there was complicity on the part of superiors. The charging document for an arrest is a "complaint"—which sets out the facts that make up probable cause.

Booking

Booking typically involves transporting the suspect to the lockup or county jail and filling out appropriate paperwork before the individual enters the facility. Booking is a due process step only in the sense that some errors of identity may be discovered at this point when fingerprints are taken. In rare cases, individuals are arrested because of outstanding warrants for others with the same name and birth date. If fingerprints are on file for the true offender, the booking process may be instrumental in discovering this mistake. Individuals may also be kept in **lockups** for a short period. These temporary holding cells are in police stations.

Initial Appearance

Due process requires that every person taken into custody must see a magistrate within a reasonable period. In *Riverside v. McLaughlin*,[43] the Supreme Court ruled that, unless there were special circumstances, the initial hearing must take place within forty-eight hours of arrest. This is in order to ensure that the detention of the individual is legal, that is, that the charging documents are in order, there is probable cause for the arrest, and there is no clear abuse of power.

One of the major functions of the initial appearance is to notify the accused of the charges against him or her. Recall that one of the first elements of due process is notice. It is impossible to defend yourself unless you know what it is you are being accused of. The accused is usually provided with a copy of the complaint or charging document at this point. The magistrate also recites the Miranda warnings again to make sure that the defendant understands them. The hearing magistrate, who may be a judge of any level from municipal court to state district court, will begin to assess whether the accused is indigent and will need an attorney provided by the state. Jurisdictions typically use some form of a questionnaire that asks the defendant to show assets and debts in order to determine indigency, which simply means without appreciable assets. The other major function of the hearing is to assess bail or offer some other **pre-trial release program**.

Bail

Bail or **release on recognizance** allows the accused to spend the time before trial out in the community. The adjudicatory process sometimes takes months or even years to complete. Until it is over, it is obviously important that the suspect/defendant remain in the jurisdiction. For this reason, many are kept in jail until a conviction, dismissal, or acquittal occurs. However, if other means are sufficient to ensure that the individual does not disappear, then pre-trial detention is unnecessary. The bail hearing is the due process designed to minimize error in the decision regarding this deprivation of liberty. The judge determines how likely it is that the defendant will **abscond** (escape the jurisdiction), and then determines whether to offer a pre-trial release option, and/or what level of bail is the lowest necessary to ensure presence at trial. There is no constitutional right to bail, although the 8th Amendment prohibits excessive bail.

> Excessive bail shall not be required, nor excessive fines imposed, nor cruel and unusual punishments inflicted.

The individual pledges money and/or property that is forfeited if they do not appear. More serious crimes carry with them more serious punishments; therefore, bail is set higher because it is assumed that defendants have more reason to run when facing more serious punishments. The amount of bail for each suspect is determined not only by the seriousness of the crime, but also by the characteristics of the defendant. Home ownership, employment, and residential stability indicate that the suspect is a low risk for flight (unless the crime is very serious); however, if the offender is unemployed, has no family in the area, and has no place to stay prior to trial, there is a high probability that he or she will flee. Of course, there is also the high probability that they cannot afford bail either, and so these individuals would probably remain in jail.

To read an interesting *New York Times* article about bail in New York City that describes typical cases and how the process works, go to http://www.nytimes.com/2015/08/16/magazine/the-bail-trap.html

There are a variety of bail/surety alternatives involving the courts and/or private bail bonds providers:

1. Direct/full bail
2. Private bail bonds—secured (requiring collateral) or unsecured
3. Court surety programs—secured (requiring collateral) or unsecured
4. Release on recognizance.

Some defendants may be able to post the full amount of bail; however, most do not have the ability to offer that amount of cash. Most often, defendants or their families contract with bail bonds agents who often demand collateral from the defendant (i.e., house, car, money) in return for the bond agent signing a promissory note to the court. If the defendant does not appear, the bond agent must pay the full amount of the bail. Bond agents receive a fee even if the defendant appears; thus, even if the defendant is acquitted of all charges or the charges are dropped, they still have to pay the bond agent for the right to be released prior to court proceedings. In other instances, bond agents do not require collateral; they take on the risk of having to pay the court the full amount if the defendant absconds. In return for their assumption of this risk, the bond fee may be higher.

Exhibit 8.6   Bond agents will cover a defendant's bail in exchange for a fee.

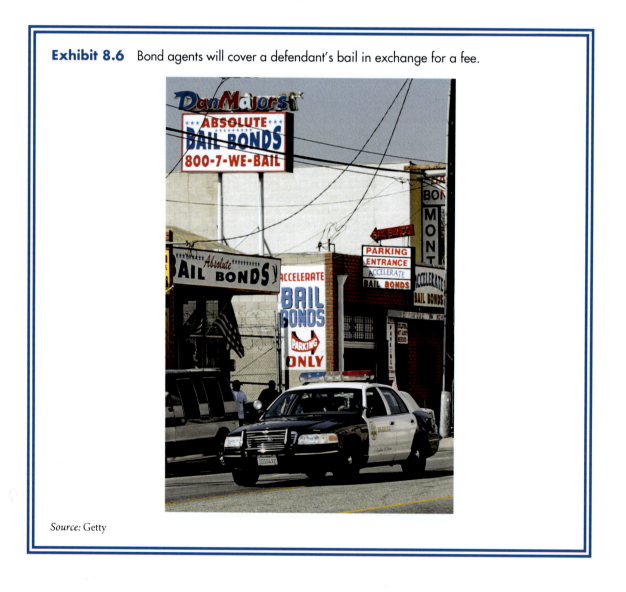

Source: Getty

In some jurisdictions, the court cuts out the private bond agents and allows the defendant to offer the collateral directly to the court, along with a percentage (typically 10 percent) of the full amount of bail. If the defendant does not appear, then the deposit and the property are forfeited. In a very few jurisdictions, courts offer an unsecured bond option where the defendant promises to pay the full amount, but it is unsecured by collateral. In both types of these **court surety programs**, if the defendant does appear, he or she pays only a small administrative fee. These programs, where they exist, save defendants quite a bit of money. Even in the areas where there are court surety programs, private bail bond agents still have a role because defendants typically must meet fairly stringent background characteristics in order to be eligible for the court surety program, and all others who have bail granted must resort to the private vendor if they want to be released prior to trial. The problem is that many defendants do not have any collateral. They do not have financial resources to equal the bail amount and, therefore, are not eligible for programs that require collateral. Thus, it is argued that the poor spend pre-trial time in jail while those who have money do not, regardless of their risk of flight.

In the 1960s, the Vera Institute of Justice funded the Manhattan Bail Project. This was the first formal **release on recognizance** (ROR) program. Defendants who could not afford bail but who seemed to be good risks were identified. In the course of one study period (1961–64), the project evaluated 10,000 defendants for release; 4,000 were recommended for release; 2,195 were released; and only 15 did not show up for a court appearance. In general, ROR programs find that the failure-to-appear rates for those in the program are similar to those on bail.[44]

Current studies are also finding that unsecured bonds can be an effective release mechanism. For instance, one study, utilizing court data from Colorado, found that for low-risk, moderate-risk, and high-risk offenders, unsecured bonds were as effective (in not resulting in new crimes) as secured bonds and unsecured bonds were as effective in ensuring court appearances as secured bonds. The use of unsecured bonds freed up more jail beds by allowing booked defendants to be released and released faster. Another interesting finding of this study was that the cost of the bonds was associated with pre-trial detention (that is, the higher the bond, the less likely the defendant was to pay it and be released), but it was not related to increased court appearance rates.[45] The policy implications of this study and others is that unsecured bonds can reduce jail populations without sacrificing public safety.

In 1984, Congress passed the Federal Bail Reform Act.[46] This bill allowed for the preventive detention of federal defendants. **Preventive detention** is when the individual is incarcerated before trial, not because of a fear that they will abscond, but because of a perceived risk to the public if they are in the community. With the federal preventive detention measure, judges can consider the offense, the weight of the evidence, the history and character of the defendant, ties to the community, drug history, and the nature and seriousness of danger to the community. They may determine that the risk to the public is too great to allow the offender to remain in the community prior to trial, and the offender will be held without bail. This seems to be contrary to the due process concept of "innocent until proven guilty," but there is at least some due process in that there is a separate preventive detention hearing where the magistrate weighs the risk and makes the determination.[47]

Your state probably has similar legislation allowing for the preventive detention of suspects in state prosecutions.

Grand Jury Indictment or Information

Arrests generally are based on criminal complaints issued against the accused, however, before the process goes further, a formal charging document must exist—the two charging documents are an **indictment** issued by a grand jury or an **information** issued by the prosecutor's office. The 5th Amendment guarantees the right of grand jury review to federal defendants, but the right has not been "incorporated" to state citizens (those facing prosecution by states). Only about half of the states use **grand juries**. In some of these states, the right, at least for felony defendants, is guaranteed by the state constitution (New York, Ohio, and Texas). In other states, there is an option to go to the grand jury for indictment; otherwise, the prosecutor will issue the charging instrument.

Many people are confused about the difference between a grand jury and a **petit (or trial) jury**. You will not usually ever see a grand jury. Grand jury members are selected by the presiding or administrative judge and tend to be "good citizens known to the court." They sit for a month, six months, or even a year, for one day or an afternoon a week. The grand jury listens to cases brought before them by the prosecutor. The prosecutor may bring in witnesses to question, or just describe the evidence in the case, and then they determine whether there is probable cause to go forward. If a grand jury decides that there is probable cause, they return an indictment. If they do not believe that the prosecutor has proven probable cause, they will **no bill** the case, meaning that there is no indictment.

Preliminary Hearing

The preliminary hearing may also be called the preliminary examination, probable cause hearing, bindover hearing, or some other term. This type of hearing is sometimes combined with the initial hearing, but more often it takes place several days later. While defendants would not necessarily have an attorney at the initial appearance, they must have one at the preliminary hearing. In the preliminary hearing, a judge rules on the strength of evidence by determining whether the prosecutor has shown that there is probable cause the defendant committed the crimes charged. The defense is not obligated to do anything at a preliminary hearing. If they choose, they can present evidence or witnesses, and they may cross-examine prosecution witnesses, but it is solely the prosecutor's burden to prove that there is enough evidence to go forward with the prosecution.

If the charges are dismissed at this point, the prosecutor is free to continue to try to make a case. **Double jeopardy**—the right not to be tried for the same offense—does not "attach" or become an issue until a jury is empaneled. About half of cases are dismissed before trial, although some are refiled when there is more evidence.[48] If the prosecutor is successful in showing probable cause, then an information is issued, which is the charging document to go forward.

Arraignment and Plea Bargaining

The next step in the proceedings is the arraignment. Here, the defendant is formally notified of the charges against him or her and asked for a plea. If the defendant accepts a plea bargain, the arraignment may become the end of the process with the judge accepting the plea and setting punishment. As you probably know, over 90 percent of criminal defendants plead guilty. Most do so in return for a recommendation for a reduced sentence. Judges are not bound to accept the prosecutor's recommendation for sentencing, but they do so in the vast majority of cases. If a judge takes a plea, typically, the only evidence is an affidavit of the defendant admitting guilt. Attached to this legal document is the prosecutor's recommendation for sentencing. The judge should ensure that the defendant is knowingly and voluntarily agreeing to the plea bargain. If the judge does not agree to the recommendation, the defendant has a right to withdraw the confession. The prosecutor is also barred from agreeing to a sentence and then retracting the agreement once he or she has obtained a confession. On the other hand, the Supreme Court has generally upheld cases where the defendant was forced to choose between a plea bargain and the possibility of the death penalty. Plea bargaining allows the system to dispose of a tremendous number of cases without the expense of further adjudication.

Pre-trial Motions

Typically, after the arraignment, but before the beginning of the trial, if the case isn't plea bargained, there may be a number of pre-trial motions. A **motion** is simply a request that the judge order something to be done or not done. For instance, the defense may file a motion to exclude evidence. The defense attorney would have to show either that the evidence was obtained illegally and should be excluded, or that the evidence is more prejudicial than probative (meaning helpful to prove). Generally, prior prison sentences or prior accusations are excluded because they are highly prejudicial and don't prove that the defendant did this particular crime, although, in some cases such evidence might come in as evidence of a pattern of criminal behavior. The **motion in limine** requests the judge to bar the mention of something that might be prejudicial during the trial, but has no bearing on guilt or innocence in the case, such as a prior prison term.

Another pre-trial motion is a **change of venue**, which is a request for the trial to be moved to another jurisdiction because of a belief that any jurors from the locale where the crime took place would be too biased to render a fair verdict. This is also a motion typically filed by the defense.

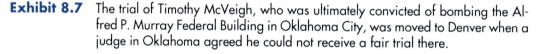

Exhibit 8.7   The trial of Timothy McVeigh, who was ultimately convicted of bombing the Alfred P. Murray Federal Building in Oklahoma City, was moved to Denver when a judge in Oklahoma agreed he could not receive a fair trial there.

Source: AP

Either side might, but rarely does, file a motion for the judge to **recuse** himself (**recusal**). This motion basically argues that the judge is not able to conduct the trial in a fair and unbiased manner because of some conflict of interest. The attorney who files a recusal motion hopes that the judge will grant it and remove him- or herself from the case and give it to another judge.

Brady motions have become well-known because of cases of prosecutorial misconduct in not providing exculpatory evidence to the defense. The motion comes from *Brady v. Maryland*,[49] a case where the Supreme Court held that prosecutors must share with defense when asked for any evidence that might lead to a finding of innocence. In some of the most notorious exonerations where innocent people have been released from prison, it was discovered that prosecutors did not turn over exculpatory information that might have prevented the conviction and incarceration of the innocent person.

Other pre-trial motions judges may be called upon to decide are motions for severance of defendants when two or more defendants are being charged and tried together, but a defense attorney wants to separate out his or her defendant to be tried separately. Another motion is to force discovery, when the defense believes the prosecution has something that they are not sharing and the defense has a legal right to have access to it. Finally, perhaps the most common motion is a motion for continuance when one side or the other requests that the trial date be delayed for some reason. It is not at all uncommon to have a dozen or more continuances delaying the trial for a year or more from its originally scheduled date.

WHAT ARE THE STEPS OF A TRIAL?

If one were to enter a criminal trial court in most states, it would be easy to identify the judge, the prosecutor(s), and perhaps the defense attorney(s). One could also identify the bailiff, who may be either a sheriff's deputy or a court employee. Typically, there is also a court administrator who handles the nonjudicial aspects of the court, including scheduling and caseload processing. The court clerk handles legal filing of court orders, may collect court fees, and schedules the trial docket. In larger jurisdictions where there are many judges, one of the trial judges also serves as a presiding or administrative judge and handles the managerial and the budgetary aspects of the court system in that jurisdiction. Most cases that go to trial are serious crimes such as murder, rape, or another serious crime where the defendant is facing a long prison sentence or perhaps even a death sentence.

In a criminal case, the state has the burden of proving the guilt of the accused beyond a reasonable doubt. That means that the prosecution has the

For an interesting website about famous trials throughout history, go to http://www.law.umkc.edu/faculty/projects/ftrials/ftrials.htm

responsibility to prove each of the elements of the crime with which the accused is charged. For example, the crime of burglary generally has these elements: breaking and entering the dwelling of another with intent to commit a felony therein. If the prosecution fails to prove any element of the crime beyond a reasonable doubt, but proves the other elements, the accused may sometimes be found guilty of a lesser crime. But ordinarily, if the prosecutor is unable to prove all elements beyond a reasonable doubt, the person charged cannot be convicted of the crime. Also, recall that the prosecutor must also prove that the offense took place within the geographic jurisdiction of the court.

In a civil case the degree of proof is a "preponderance of the evidence"; but in a criminal case, the degree of proof is "beyond a reasonable doubt." In some states, the exact wording of the charge to the jury dealing with the standard of proof is stated by statute. In other states, there is no such requirement, and in fact, the judge may not allow the prosecutor's or defense attorney's suggested definitions, preferring the jury to decide themselves what it means. The "beyond a reasonable doubt" standard is a constitutional requirement. In 1970, the Supreme Court left no doubt about the requirement in the holding of *In re Winship*:

> Lest there remain any doubt about the constitutional stature of the reasonable-doubt standard, we explicitly hold that the Due Process Clause protects the accused against conviction except on proof beyond a reasonable doubt of every fact necessary to constitute the crime with which he is charged.[50]

In most cases, the defense has no burden of proof at all, and can merely remain silent and argue that the prosecutor has not proven beyond a reasonable doubt that the defendant committed the crime. In certain cases, however, the defense may argue an **affirmative defense**, such as coercion, self-defense, entrapment, mistake, alibi, or insanity. In these cases, the defendant's attorney must offer proof (usually by a preponderance) before the jury can consider the defense.

Jury Selection

As noted above, there may be pre-trial motions and many continuances before a trial actually starts. The first step in the trial itself is jury selection.

As you know, the 6th Amendment gives criminal defendants the right to a trial by a jury of their peers. This has been interpreted by a line of court cases to mean that the jury pool must be pulled in such a way as to not clearly exclude any particular group, not necessarily that the jury panel represent the demographic characteristics of the defendant.

Typically, jurisdictions use voter registration, driver's licenses, or motor vehicle registration lists to pull jury panels. Once called to perform jury duty, you may or may not actually serve on a jury. Depending on the jurisdiction, you may be on call for a day or a week (perhaps having the option to call in each morning to check to see if you are needed). If a judge in that jurisdiction is starting a trial, he or she will call for a jury panel of up to 50 people (depending on the case, the number of peremptory challenges, and the size of the jury in that jurisdiction).

Most jurisdictions allow for certain exemptions from jury duty. If one has minor children at home, is a full-time student, or is past a certain age, they are generally exempt. Some states have automatic occupation exemptions; others do not. Typically, jury members must be citizens, not have a criminal record, and be of "sound mind."

We tend to think that juries must be twelve individuals who vote unanimously to convict the defendant, but there is no constitutional right to a twelve-person jury.[51] States may require only eight people to be on a jury (Arizona and Utah), or six (Connecticut and Florida), at least in noncapital cases. There is also no constitutional right to have a unanimous verdict. Some states do not require unanimous jury verdicts (Louisiana and Oregon).[52]

After the jury panel has been seated, the defense and prosecuting attorneys have a chance to examine the jury cards that jury panel members have filled out. These provide quite a bit of information about each panel member, including marital status, age, occupation, income, number of children, and so on. The process by which the prosecutor and defense attorney question the jury panel to determine if they need to request any members of the panel be removed is called **voir dire**. A translation of voir dire is something like "to see to say," but it basically means to speak the truth. The first question that is asked is whether jury members know any of the principal players in the trial, such as the victim, the offender, either attorney, or the judge. Then attorneys ask questions relevant to the particular case. For instance, if the defendant was charged with negligent manslaughter because he killed someone in an accident after a night of drinking, the defense attorney is going to want to know the drinking habits of the prospective jurors and whether any of them had a relative who had been killed by a drunk driver. Attorneys may ask any questions that may uncover any biases that prospective jurors may have either for or against the defendant.

State statutes set the number of **peremptory challenges** for the prosecutor and the defense attorney. Peremptory challenges allow the attorney to reject the juror without having to show a particular reason. However, the attorney cannot use race as a reason to reject someone. The Supreme Court said in *Batson v. Kentucky*[53] that attorneys who used race as a reason to reject prospective jurors violated the equal protection clause of the 14th Amendment. In subsequent cases, the Court also rejected the use of race by the defendant (as opposed to the prosecutor as in *Batson*) and gender. **Challenges for cause** are unlimited, but there must be a reason why the juror would be biased in the trial. The attorney has to state what the objection is, and the judge will consider the challenge and agree and dismiss the juror, or disagree and allow the juror to remain.

After each attorney has identified the jurors he or she has rejected under the peremptory challenges, and the judge has dealt with any requests to strike jurors for cause, the remaining jurors are called up one at a time to the jury box until it is filled with the appropriate number and, in some instances, alternates. Once the jury is seated, the trial can begin.

Opening Statements

The opening statements are the attorneys' opportunity to address the jury as to what they should be looking for in the presentation of evidence. Each attorney seeks to educate the jury as to his or her version of the events. They need to convince the jury of their version through evidence that consists either of witnesses who testify to what they have seen, heard, or experienced, and/or expert witnesses who can offer opinions and judgments, at least within the confines of their expertise. The opening statement gives the attorney a chance to talk directly to the jury and tell them what they are going to hear. The defense often asks that their opening be deferred to the beginning of the defense's case.

Presentation of Evidence

You have probably seen innumerable trials on television shows and movies. Some are fairly accurate and some are not. The prosecution presents the state's case first. Witnesses are put on the stand, and the prosecutor goes through a **direct examination**, which is the questioning of his or her own witness. The questions cannot be leading (telling the witness the answer or making a statement); they cannot ask for an opinion, they cannot ask for **hearsay** (something that the witness did not hear, see, or experience directly), although there are many exceptions to this rule. They also cannot ask for something that would be unduly prejudicial or otherwise not be allowed into evidence.

After the prosecutor has finished questioning a witness, the defense may cross-examine the witness. These questions have pretty much the same rules, but there is the opportunity to ask leading questions, such as, "Isn't it true that on the night of July 15, you had so much to drink that you were not able to see the defendant clearly across the parking lot of the bar?" After the defense has finished the cross-examination, the prosecutor has the opportunity to question the witness again over any material that was brought up in the cross-examination. This process continues until all witnesses have been examined. Then, the prosecutor has the chance to present any rebuttal witnesses that might be appropriate. This might occur if the defense has elicited some information from one of the witnesses that the prosecutor can show is irrelevant or untrue or just to shed additional light on the information. Rebuttal witnesses respond directly to the facts already in evidence.

The presentation of the defense's case comes next, beginning with the opening statement if the attorney reserved the right to give one. The direct examination, cross-examination, and rebuttal witnesses occur in the same order, only this time the witnesses are defense witnesses and the prosecutor cross-examines. After all witnesses are finished testifying, there are closing arguments.

Closing Arguments

An instance where the prosecutor has an advantage over the defense is that they are allowed to have the first closing statement and then are able to speak to the jury again after the defense's closing statement. This is because prosecutors have the burden of proof in a trial. In the closing, each side summarizes the evidence in a way that supports their version of the case. They emphasize certain portions of the evidence, and they comment on the weight of the evidence. Attorneys cannot mention any facts not in evidence.

Jury Instructions

After the closing, the judge reads to the jury an instruction. The instruction to the jury is written by the judge with both attorneys suggesting text. It may include definitions of legal terms. It may ask them to choose between two or more different levels of culpability. For instance, in a homicide case, the instructions may give the jury the choice between finding the defendant guilty of murder in the first degree, second degree, or even manslaughter. The rules for instructions are different among the states, but it is basically the guidelines, rules, or verdict available for the jury to follow in their deliberation.

Jury Deliberation

You may have seen movies where the jury is sequestered, meaning that they stay in hotel rooms until they reach a verdict. Ordinarily, they are allowed to go home in the evening until the verdict is reached although they are instructed not to watch news or discuss the case. If the jury cannot reach a verdict, it is called a "hung jury" and the prosecutor may decide to try the case again. This would not be double jeopardy because the trial is not officially over yet. If the jury comes back with an acquittal, it does not mean the jury members necessarily believe the defendant is innocent, it means that they did not believe the prosecutor proved the case beyond a reasonable doubt. If the jury comes back with a guilty verdict, the next step is sentencing.

Exhibit 8.8   After closing arguments in the O.J. Simpson murder trial, Judge Lance Ito reads instructions to the jury.

Source: Getty

Sentencing

Depending on the state, judges or juries may sentence convicted felons and misdemeanants. In both cases, statutory guidelines limit the discretion of the judge or jury in what type of sentence can be imposed, and how long the sentence may last. A sentencing hearing is a "critical stage" of the trial process, meaning that the courts have held that a defendant must have an attorney present if they are facing the possibility of a jail or prison sentence. There are, however, relaxed rules of evidence. Hearsay may be admitted, as when people testify about the character of the offender. Victim statements may be read, which allow the victim or the victim's family to state how the crime has affected them.

In most states, pre-sentence reports are also used in order to give the judge or the jury more information about the offender before a sentence decision is made. A pre-sentence division in a probation agency conducts pre-sentence investigations, and they provide information on the offender's criminal, educational, family, and work history. Sentencing can be considered the last step of the trial process and the first step in the corrections process.

SUMMARY

What Are the Different Levels of Courts?

State systems typically involve state trial courts of general and limited jurisdiction, intermediate appellate courts, and state courts of last resort. Specialized courts exist, such as family or juvenile court, community courts, drug courts, and domestic violence courts.

What Are Specialized Courts?

Specialized, community or problem-solving courts refer to courts that have specialized caseloads and their objective is not to simply administer a verdict and punish, but to address the underlying causes of the defendants' criminality, e.g., drug addiction, PTSD, or some other issue.

How Do Prosecutors Decide Whether and What to Charge?

District attorneys (prosecutors) are usually elected, but their assistant prosecutors are not. Most prosecutors' offices employ less than ten people, but some large cities have hundreds of prosecutors. Prosecutors are not legally obligated to bring charges and do so typically on the basis of the strength of the evidence, although other factors also play a part, such as victims' wishes.

What Are the Duties of a Defense Attorney?

Defense attorneys for indigents are provided through a public defender system, an appointment system, or by contract attorneys. Their duty is to zealously pursue the interests of their client without subverting the legal process.

What Is the Role of a Judge? How Are They Selected?

Judges may be elected or appointed. If appointed, typically a form of the Missouri Plan is utilized. The role of a judge is somewhat like an umpire. He or she rules on pre-trial motions and trial objections, and ensures the legal process proceeds without error. In bench trials, the judge decides guilt or innocence because there is no jury.

What Is the Jurisdiction of Federal Courts?

The federal court system operates in parallel to state systems, and federal crimes (and civil matters relevant to federal laws or that cross state lines in jurisdiction) are prosecuted in these courts. There are 94 federal districts, each with their own trial court and a U.S. attorney (and assistants) to prosecute federal crimes. Federal cases (and some state cases that allege constitutional issues) can be appealed to federal courts of appeals and, ultimately, to the Supreme Court. The Supreme Court hears only a small fraction of the cases that are appealed to it. When the Court chooses to hear a case, a writ of certiorari is issued.

How Does Due Process Protect Individuals Against Error in the Criminal Justice Process?

Due process protections come to us through the 5th and 14th Amendments. The 6th Amendment gives us specific due process rights when faced with criminal prosecution, including a right to a jury of peers, and counsel. It is important to remember, however, that our due process rights go far beyond the Sixth Amendment, and are implicated any time the government attempts to deprive us of life, liberty, or property. The steps of the criminal process begin with arrest and booking, continue through initial appearance, preliminary hearing, indictment or information, arraignment, and trial and sentencing. At each step, the process is designed to minimize or eliminate any errors that the government may make.

What Are the Steps of a Trial?

A trial includes pre-trial motions, jury voir dire, opening statements, direct examinations, cross-examinations, rebuttal witnesses, and closing statements. A sentencing hearing follows if the defendant is convicted.

Critical Thinking Exercises

1. Utilize any movie or television show that portrays a criminal prosecution through trial. Try to identify as many errors as you think the scriptwriters commit after reading this chapter.
2. Plea bargaining continues to be a controversial element of our criminal justice system. Do some research and construct an argument for plea bargaining and an argument against it.

NOTES

1 D. Rottman and S. Strickland, *State Court Organization*. Washington, DC: Bureau of Justice Statistics, 2006, p. 4.

2 R. Malega and T. H. Cohen, *State Court Organization, 2011*. Washington, DC: Bureau of Justice Statistics, 2013, p. 4.

3 S. Rosenmerkel, M. Durose and D. Farole, *Felony Sentences in State Courts, 2006, Statistical Tables*. Washington, DC: Bureau of Justice Statistics, 2009.

4 S. Perry, D. Banks, *Prosecutors in State Courts, 2007—Statistical Tables*. Washington, DC: Bureau of Justice Statistics, 2011, p. 1.

5 R. Malega and T. H. Cohen, *State Court Organization, 2011*. Washington, DC: Bureau of Justice Statistics, 2013, p. 4.

6 D. Rottman and S. Strickland, *State Court Organization*. Washington, DC: Bureau of Justice Statistics, 2006.

7 P. Casey and D. Rottman, *Problem Solving Courts: Models and Trends*. Washington, DC: National Center for State Courts, 2003.

8 J. Petersilia, *Reforming Probation and Parole*. Lanham, MD: American Correctional Association, 2002, p. 4; S. Listwan, J. Sundt, A. Holsinger and E. Latessa, "The effect of drug court programming on recidivism: The Cincinnati experience." *Crime and Delinquency* 49 (3) (2003): 389–411.

9 J. Petersilia, *Reforming Probation and Parole*. Lanham, MD: American Correctional Association, 2002, p. 5.

10 S. Listwan, J. Sundt, A. Holsinger and E. Latessa, "The effect of drug court programming on recidivism: The Cincinnati experience." *Crime and Delinquency* 49 (3) (2003): 389–411.

11 D. Marlow, D. Festinger, P. Lee, K. Dugosh and K. Benasutti, "Matching judicial supervision to clients' risk status in drug court." *Crime and Delinquency* 52 (1) (2006): 52–76.

12 M. Carey and W. Finigan, "A detailed cost analysis in a mature drug court setting." *Journal of Contemporary Criminal Justice* 20 (3) (2004): 315–338.

13 S. Johnson, D. Hubbard and E. Latessa, "Drug courts and treatment: Lessons to be learned from the 'what works' literature." *Corrections Management Quarterly* 4 (4) (2000): 70–77.

14 S. Rossman, J. Roman, et al., *A Multi-site Adult Drug Court Evaluation*. Washington, DC: Urban Institute, 2011.

15 A. Gover, J. MacDonald and G. Alpert, "Combating domestic violence: Findings from an evaluation of a local domestic violence court." *Criminology and Public Policy* 3 (1) (2003): 109–132. Also see L. Levy, M. Steketee and S. Keilitz, *Lessons Learned in Implementing an Integrated Domestic Violence Court*. Williamsburg, VA: National Center for State Courts, 2001.

16 A. Gover, J. MacDonald and G. Alpert, "Combating domestic violence: Findings from an evaluation of a local domestic violence court." *Criminology and Public Policy* 3 (1) (2003): 111.

17 W. Pitts, E. Givens and S. McNeeley, "The need for a holistic approach to specialized domestic violence court programming: Evaluating offender rehabilitation needs and recidivism." *Juvenile and Family Court Journal* 60 (3) (2009): 1–22.

18 C. DeFrances, *Prosecutors in State Courts*. Washington, DC: Bureau of Justice Statistics, 2001.

19 S. Perry and D. Banks, *Prosecutors in State Courts, 2007—Statistical Tables*. Washington, DC: Bureau of Justice Statistics, 2011, p. 1.

20 D. Rottman and S. Strickland, *State Court Organization*. Washington, DC: Bureau of Justice Statistics, 2006.

21 B. Frederick and D. Stemen, *The Anatomy of Discretion: An Analysis of Prosecutorial Decision Making—Technical Report*. Washington, DC: National Institute of Justice, OJP, 2012.

22 *Gideon v. Wainwright*, 373 U.S. 335, 1963.

23 *Argersinger v. Hamlin*, 407 U.S. 321, 1972.

24 L. Langton and D. Farole, *State Public Defender Programs*. Washington, DC: Bureau of Justice Statistics, 2010.

25 Justice Policy Institute, *System Overload: The Costs of Underresourcing Public Defense*. Washington, DC: Justice Policy Institiute, 2011.

26 C. Harlow, *Defense Counsel in Criminal Cases*. Washington, DC: Bureau of Justice Statistics, 2000.

27 A. Liptak, "Study reveals gap in performance of public defenders." *Austin American-Statesman*, July 14, 2007, A9.

28 T. Cohen, "Who's better at defending criminals? Does type of defense attorney matter in terms of producing favorable case outcomes." Social Science Research Working Paper series, 2011. Available at: https://nationalcdp.org/docs/defense-counsel-and-ajudication.pdf

29 National Association of Criminal Defense Lawyers. *Federal Indigent Defense, 2015: The Independence Imperative*. Washington, DC: NACDL, 2015.

30 K. Goetz, "Ky public defenders: Thin ranks, high risks." *St Louis Courier*, November 22, 2015. Retrieved from: http://www.courier-journal.com/story/news/crime/2015/11/19/kentucky-public-defenders-risks/76046976/?from=global&sessionKey=&autologin=

31 Bureau of Justice Assistance, *Public Defense Reform since Gideon: Improving the Administration of Justice by Building on Our Successes and Learning from Our Failures.* Washington, DC: Bureau of Justice Assistance, 2008.

32 N. Mariano, "Justice denied: The high price of justice." TheSouthern.com, April 19, 2015, http://thesouthern.com/news/local/justice-denied/the-high-price-of-justice-sixth-amendment-guarantee-deteriorating-under/article_2992e476-c4ca-5124-a433-23a025a26bf8.html

33 Justice Policy Institute, *System Overload: The Costs of Underresourcing Public Defense.* Washington, DC: Justice Policy Instititue, 2011, p.7.

34 Quoted in Justice Policy Institute, *System Overload: The Costs of Underresourcing Public Defense.* Washington, DC: Justice Policy Institute, 2011, p. 8.

35 Quoted in Justice Policy Institute, *System Overload: The Costs of Underresourcing Public Defense.* Washington, DC: Justice Policy Institute, 2011, p. 7.

36 N. Mariano, "Justice denied: The high price of justice." TheSouthern.com, April 19, 2015, http://thesouthern.com/news/local/justice-denied/the-high-price-of-justice-sixth-amendment-guarantee-deteriorating-under/article_2992e476-c4ca-5124-a433-23a025a26bf8.html. Note that another source (Justice Policy Institute, note 33) reported 30 public defender systems were state funded, 18 were county and state funded, and only 1 state—Pennsylvania—was entirely county funded.

37 Quoted in Justice Policy Institute, note 33, p. 11.

38 Quoted in N. Mariano, note 35.

39 Justice Policy Institute, note 33.

40 American Judicature Society, *Judicial Selection in the States.* Des Moines, IA: American Judicature Society, 2004.

41 Bureau of Justice Statistics. Retrieved 6/1/2007 from http://www.ojp.usdoj.gov/bjs/.

42 U.S. Department of Justice, United States Attorneys. Retrieved 6/1/2007 from http://www.usdoj.gov/usao/offices/usa_listings2.html#n.

43 *Riverside v. McLaughlin*, 500 U.S. 44, 1991.

44 S. Maxwell, "Examining the congruence between predictors of ROR and failures to appear." *Journal of Criminal Justice* 27 (2) (1999): 127–141. Also see, T. Cohen and B. Reaves, *Pretrial Release of Felony Defendants in State Courts.* Washington, DC: Bureau of Justice Statistics, 2007.

45 M. Jones, *Unsecured Bonds: The As Effective and More Efficient Release Option.* Pretrial Justice Institute, 2013. file:///C:/Users/jp12/Desktop/INTRO3RD/COURTS/Unsecured+Bonds,+The+As+Effective+and+Most+Efficient+Pretrial+Release+Option+-+Jones+2013.pdf

46 18 U.S.C.A. § 3141 et seq. 1996.

47 See *United States v. Salerno*, 481 U.S. 739, 1987.

48 B. Boland, P. Mahanna and R. Sones, *The Prosecution of Felony Arrests, 1988.* Washington, DC: Bureau of Justice Statistics, 1992.

49 *Brady v. Maryland*, 373 U.S. 83, 1963

50 *In re Winship*, 397 U.S. 358, 1970.

51 *Williams v. Florida*, 399 U.S. 78, 1970.

52 *Apodaca v. Oregon*, 406 U.S. 404, 1971.

53 *Batson v. Kentucky*, 476 U.S. 79, 1986.

CRIMINAL SENTENCING

9

A criminal trial that ends with a conviction is followed by a sentencing hearing. Depending on the state, judges or juries may sentence convicted felons and misdemeanants. In both cases, statutory guidelines limit the **discretion** of the judge or jury in what type of sentence can be imposed, and how long the sentence may last. Remember, however, that the vast majority of cases are plea-bargained which means that there is no sentencing hearing. In over 90 percent of criminal cases, the defendant agrees to plead guilty and is offered a specific sentence in return for a guilty plea, thus, there is no trial and no sentencing hearing. Plea-bargained sentences must still fall within statutory guidelines.

Disparity refers to different sentences for similar offenders. When the individual's criminal history and background is similar, and the criminal event is similar, sentencing should be roughly similar. If it is not, then that is said to be sentencing disparity. Disparity may occur between judges (different judges sentence similar offenders to significantly

Chapter Preview

- What Happens in a Sentencing Hearing?
- What Are the Goals of Sentencing?
- What Are the Types of Sentences That Might Be Given to Criminal Offenders?
- What Are Three-Strikes Sentencing Laws?
- What Is the Most Common Sentence?
- What Is the Criticism Regarding Fines and Fees?
- What Recent Events Have Occurred with Federal Drug Sentencing?
- What Is Restorative Justice?
- What Are the Legal Arguments Against the Death Penalty?
- Focus On Data: Is There Racial Disparity in Sentencing?
- Summary
- Critical Thinking Exercises

different sentences), between jurisdictions, or it could occur between groups, e.g., women are observed to receive, on average, shorter sentences than men. One of the most researched issues is whether Blacks receive, on average, harsher sentences than Whites. This is the subject of our Focus on Data section in this chapter.

WHAT HAPPENS IN A SENTENCING HEARING?

A sentencing hearing is a "critical stage" of the trial process, meaning that the courts have held that a defendant must have an attorney present if they are facing the possibility of a jail or prison sentence.[1] There are, however, relaxed rules of evidence. **Hearsay** (testifying about what other people might have said) may be admitted and character evidence is admitted (witnesses who testify about the good or bad things the defendant has done in his or her life). Victim statements may be read, which allow the victim or the victim's family to state how the crime has affected them.[2]

In most states, pre-sentence reports are also used in order to give the judge or the jury more information about the offender before a sentence decision is made. A pre-sentence division in a probation agency conducts pre-sentence investigations, and they provide information on the offender's criminal, educational, family, and work history.

In the summer of 2016, many people became very interested in the process of sentencing when a jury convicted a Stanford University swimmer of sexually assaulting an extremely intoxicated unconscious woman he had evidently led away from a fraternity party. Witnesses stopped his assault and prevented him from running away. The victim read an impassioned fourteen-page letter in the sentencing hearing which quickly went viral and millions of people read it online. The statutory maximum punishment was a fourteen-year prison term, and the prosecutor recommended six years of imprisonment, but the judge followed the pre-sentence recommendation of the probation department and sentenced the nineteen-year-old to six months in jail followed by probation and the obligation to be on a sex offender registry for the rest of his life. Social media erupted with disgust and anger over the lenient sentencing and a petition to impeach the judge began. Was the judge's sentence unjust to the victim? Was a lifetime of being labeled a sex offender unfair to the young man? What is a just and fair punishment is a matter of philosophy, but whether some people get either harsher or more lenient punishment than others can be studied empirically.

To read the victim's letter, go to https://www.buzzfeed.com/katiejmbaker/heres-the-powerful-letter-the-stanford-victim-read-to-her-ra?utm_term=.ifdq2nQOA#.mlRezYVKm

WHAT ARE THE GOALS OF SENTENCING?

We have a system in which there are several concurrent goals of sentencing. They include:

- *Punishment*: we believe that criminals must be punished because they deserve it.
- *Deterrence*: we believe that what we do to offenders will make others decide not to commit crime and will also encourage the offender not to commit additional crime.
- *Rehabilitation*: we believe that programs and what is done to the offender in the system may create some internal change that will make him or her become more law-abiding.
- *Incapacitation*: if nothing else, we believe that we should hold the offender in a manner that will prevent him or her from committing any crimes, at least for that period of time.

Theoretically every sentence should achieve one or more of these goals. Practically, we note that there are sometimes conflicts between the goals, e.g., between rehabilitation and punishment.

WHAT ARE THE TYPES OF SENTENCES THAT MIGHT BE GIVEN TO CRIMINAL OFFENDERS?

The most important sentencing decision is whether the offender receives a sentence of incarceration in prison (or jail) or receives probation. All sentencing is governed by state sentencing statutes that identify the parameters of what type of sentence may be given. Probation almost always comes with conditions (rules) and violations of these conditions can result in having probation revoked and being sent to prison. Fines and fees may be given with or without a probation or prison sentence.

In the 1980s, **split sentencing** was introduced, sometimes called shock probation, shock incarceration, or another term. The idea was to be able to sentence offendees to a short period in jail or prison, and then put them on probation, thereby allowing the judge to keep control over the offender through the entire period of supervision. In this type of sentence, the average jail sentence length is six months and the probation supervision length is 40 months.[3]

States may have indeterminate, determinate or hybrid sentencing systems. When the sentencing system allows for **indeterminate sentences**, the release date is unknown. The judge sets a period as provided for by statute, such as five to fifteen years. How much of that is served depends on another agency, typically a paroling authority. This group of decision makers looks at the offender's behavior in prison. An offender may serve a small portion or the majority of the range of years, depending on the parole board (or paroling authority) decision. A **determinate sentence** is when the release date is fixed, i.e. a five-year sentence. Determinate sentencing systems set the amount of punishment for each crime by statute. The judge has little flexibility and, once there is a conviction and decision to send to prison, the judge must use the sentence specified by the statute. There is often a very small range (i.e., a year more or less) for the judge to adjust the sentence by making it shorter or longer.

Indeterminate sentences have been around since the early reformatories in the late 1800s and early 1900s. They were the most prevalent sentencing structure in the 1960s and 1970s. However, critics argued that indeterminate sentences were unfair; conservatives claimed offenders were getting out of prison too early, and liberals complained that there was no accountability or predictability in who was getting out in what amount of time. Beginning in the late 1970s and 1980s, various forms of determinate or structured sentencing replaced indeterminate sentencing statutes in many states. The goals of structured sentencing have been listed as:

- to increase fairness in sentencing
- to reduce unwarranted disparity in decisions to imprison or sentence length
- to establish truth in sentencing
- to balance sentencing policy with limited correctional resources.[4]

Even in those states which kept their indeterminate sentencing statutes, some may have passed **mandatory minimum sentence** statutes that are simply added to a state's indeterminate sentencing structure. These statutes are passed to control sentencing discretion for certain specific crimes, usually because the crimes are heinous or have captured public attention. For instance, in a state that has an otherwise indeterminate sentencing system, there may be a mandatory jail sentence for third-conviction DUIs, or there may be a mandatory prison term for violent felonies that involve the use of a weapon. All fifty states have at least one type of mandatory sentence.

WHAT ARE THREE-STRIKES SENTENCING LAWS?

About half of all states have some form of **three-strikes** (habitual felon) sentencing statutes.[5] These sentencing statutes allow prosecutors the discretion to charge offenders as three-strike offenders when they have committed qualifying felonies, i.e. a third felony. Three-strike charges are discretionary on the part of the prosecutor; he or she may choose to charge a defendant with the "third strike" felony or simply charge the felony itself. If the defendant is convicted, a much longer prison sentence will be received; in some cases, a life sentence is mandatory regardless of the underlying third felony, as long as it was a qualifying felony. Two-strike legislation, if it exists in a state, captures even more offenders in long sentences that are much more severe than the statutory sentence for the qualifying second felony.

California's three-strike and two-strike legislation was considered the harshest in the nation because the qualifying felony was not limited to violent crimes. Thus, someone who stole golf clubs as a third felony could be sentenced to twenty-five years to life in prison. Passed in 1994, it survived several Supreme Court challenges;[6] however, in 2012, Proposition 36 passed with about 69 percent of voters approving a change to the harsh sentencing law. The amendment

Exhibit 9.1   Three children whose father was incarcerated under California's three strikes law attend a protest. The law was softened in 2012.

Source: AP

reduced the types of felonies that could be considered qualifying felonies for three-strikes charging, eliminating the possibility, for instance of shoplifting or drug possession charges as being the third felony for a 25-years-to-life sentence. The legislation also allowed for review of those offenders who had previously received life sentences for relatively minor crimes.[7]

WHAT IS THE MOST COMMON SENTENCE?

There is a widespread belief that most criminal offenders get probation or lenient sentences. In the last several decades, probation has been surpassed by prison or jail as the most frequent sentence handed down in felony courts. According to national statistics, 69 percent of those convicted in 2006 were sentenced to incarceration, either to jail or prison. About 27 percent received probation, and about 4 percent received a fine or something other than probation or incarceration as the sole method of punishment. Of those sentenced to some form of incarceration, the average sentence was four years, eleven months. Drug offenders received a prison sentence of, on average, seven years,

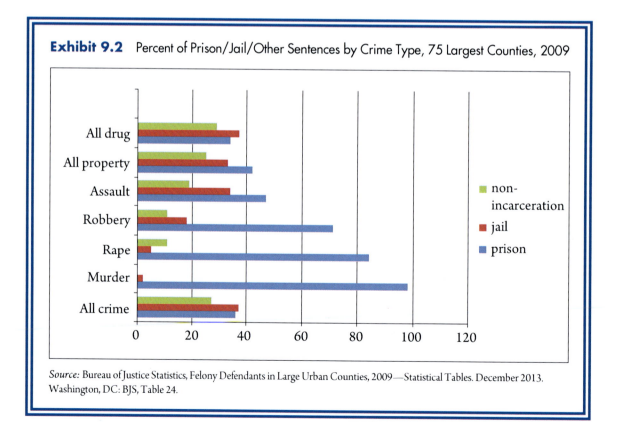

Exhibit 9.2 Percent of Prison/Jail/Other Sentences by Crime Type, 75 Largest Counties, 2009

Source: Bureau of Justice Statistics, Felony Defendants in Large Urban Counties, 2009—Statistical Tables. December 2013. Washington, DC: BJS, Table 24.

three months if they were federal defendants, and two years, seven months if they were state defendants.[8] The Bureau of Justice Statistics has not published updated figures for all felony defendants, but they have provided summary statistics for sentences handed out in 2009 in the seventy-five largest counties. Sentences for selected crimes are presented in Exhibit 9.2, which shows that when you combine prison and jail, the most common sentence is some type of incarceration. The average sentence for all crimes was four years and four months; for violent crimes was seven years, seven months; and, for both all property crimes and all drug crimes, the average sentence was three years, four months.[9]

A study of federal drug offenders revealed that of the 95,305 offenders incarcerated in federal prisons for drug offenses, three-fourths were determined to have no serious history of violence and over half (56 percent) had no history of violence. Only 14 percent of those sentenced were managers, supervisors, or leaders in the drug business. About 78 percent of federal drug offenders were sentenced under mandatory minimums (the type of sentence in which judges have no discretion to change the length of time). This study showed that the average length of time of those sentenced under mandatory minimum sentences was eleven years compared to those who were not who averaged six-year sentences.[10]

WHAT IS THE CRITICISM REGARDING FINES AND FEES?

Recently, there has been concern that the continual increase in fees, fines, and court costs in the last thirty years is detrimental to the goals of deterrence and re-entry.[11] What occurs is that a two-tiered system is created: those who have financial resources pay their fees and fines and move on with their lives, but the poor who cannot are trapped in a cycle of non-payment, additional charges for late fees, contempt and, often, incarceration because of non-payment. This has come to be called the "poverty penalty."[12]

To read one report on the problem, go to https://csgjusticecenter.org/courts/publications/the-debt-penalty-exposing-the-financial-barriers-to-offender-reintegration/

The charges have increased even more when private companies that provide probation or prison services are involved.[13] Today, offenders may have debts of thousands of dollars stemming from court costs, arrest fees, warrant fees, prosecution fees, and even fees for applying for a public defender. They may also be assessed for jail fees and, in prison, fees for health care and even hygiene supplies. By the time they are released, they may owe the system thousands of dollars and non-repayment is considered a violation of their parole even if they are unemployed.[14] It is not surprising, therefore, that parole violation rates are sometimes over 50 percent.

Historically, debtors' prisons existed to incarcerate people who owed money to others. The debtor would be incarcerated until he or his family paid off the debt. Gradually this practice ended and statutory or constitutional provisions prohibiting imprisonment for debt exist in every state.[15] Debt owed to the government, however, is treated differently. Debt occurs when the offender cannot pay fines or fees. Fines are a very common type of punishment—they are almost the sole punishment for traffic offenses and some other misdemeanors. In other offenses, fines are inflicted in addition to incarceration and probation. According to one source, fines are imposed in 42 percent of general jurisdiction convictions and in 86 percent of limited jurisdiction court convictions.[16] A Washington state study found that using the median criminal justice debt amount of $7,234, a defendant paying $100 per month, representing 15 percent of his expected monthly earnings, would—based on the accrual of interest charges—still owe nearly $900 after ten years.[17]

Fees of some sort are almost always attached to a criminal conviction. They may be attached to pre-sentence and investigatory reports, court costs and fees for reimbursement for the public defender and/or the prosecutor. Fees are increasingly being used to fully fund crime stopper programs, courtroom technology, and other services unrelated to the offender's criminal charges.[18] In jail and prison, offenders accumulate charges for room and board, health care, haircuts, telephone, and work-release programs. Almost half of all states (43) allow charges for room and board, and in thirty-five states prisoners may be charged for medical care. Telephone charges have become a significant source of profit for telephone companies who charge exorbitant rates and, in effect, funnel back to the prison system a "kickback" of a portion of profits.

Probationers may have the fines and fees from their conviction to pay back in addition to monthly accruing charges for probation supervision, drug test fees, electronic monitoring fees, drug treatment fees and other charges. Probation officers have become more akin to debt collectors than anything else and a probationer may have their probation revoked for non-payment, even if they have not committed any other crime or violation. Monthly charges may range from $180 to $360.[19] In Exhibit 9.3, the number of states with fees are shown, along with how many have increased their fees since 2010.

The Supreme Court has held that a person's constitutional rights are violated when they are incarcerated solely because they cannot pay a fine. The Court invalidated the practice of jailing someone because they couldn't pay the fine in a fine-only traffic offense.[20] In a later case, the Supreme Court held that a probationer could not be sent to prison solely because he couldn't pay his fines and fees.[21] These holdings have not prevented incarceration of individuals for non-payment, however, because the Court held open the possibility of imprisonment when someone refused to pay as opposed to was unable to pay. The Court required a finding of indigence, but, in practice, the

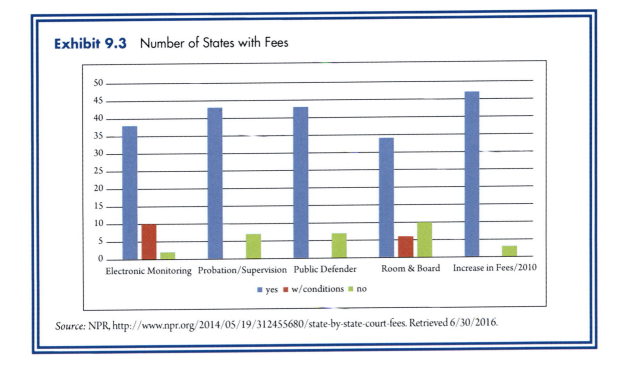

Exhibit 9.3 Number of States with Fees

yes *w/conditions* *no*

Electronic Monitoring Probation/Supervision Public Defender Room & Board Increase in Fees/2010

Source: NPR, http://www.npr.org/2014/05/19/312455680/state-by-state-court-fees. Retrieved 6/30/2016.

individual's ability to pay is often not considered when assessing fines, nor is it seriously evaluated in decisions to revoke probation or parole for non-payment. A 2015 class action suit in Ferguson, Missouri successfully showed that poor people, mostly people of color, were charged non-payment penalties for unpaid fines and fees without evaluating ability to pay. Some argued that the city's criminal justice system had become a revenue generator rather than a system of social control.[22]

Even those sent to prison may have fines and fees hanging over their head and then accumulate charges while in prison for everything from medical care to haircuts. The Brennan Center analyzed state statutes from all fifty states and found that as of 2015, at least forty-three states authorize room and board fees and at least thirty-five states authorize medical fees.[23] Critics argue that some fees, such as for medical care, should be abolished as not in keeping with the fair application of justice. Further, only civil penalties should apply when fees cannot be paid. As for fines, incarceration should only be permitted if a court fairly determines that the individual is able to but chooses not to pay, and should never occur when there is an inability to pay or payment would impose a hardship on the family. It would also help if fines and fees were based on income and adjusted to accommodate changing financial circumstances.

WHAT RECENT EVENTS HAVE OCCURRED WITH FEDERAL DRUG SENTENCING?

Sentencing guidelines were introduced in several states in the early 1980s as a measure to reduce sentence disparity. Federal sentencing guidelines were created in 1987.[24] By 1992, federal parole was phased out in favor of the guidelines' determinate sentencing structure, although the federal system still included time off for good behavior, and allowed for a small downward or upward movement in sentence length depending on specified mitigating or aggravating factors.

Sentencing guidelines offer a presumptive or advisory sentence length for any given criminal/crime in a grid. Along one axis is the criminal risk score (made up of factors that have been statistically correlated with recidivism such as age at first offense) and on the other axis is the seriousness of crime. The amount of time an offender should serve in prison is then presented using these two factors. In some jurisdictions, like the federal system, the guidelines were mandatory, not advisory like in some states. As of 2008, twenty-one states had some form of sentencing guidelines.[25]

To read about sentencing guidelines, go to http://www.ncsconline.org/csi/PEW-Profiles-v12-online.pdf

In a series of court cases, the Supreme Court, in effect, eliminated the mandatory nature of the guidelines as violations of due process. The first case dealt with the state of Washington's mandatory guidelines. In 2004, in *Blakely v. Washington*,[26] the Court invalidated the use of the guidelines to determine sentence length when elements not introduced and proven in court were used, such as number of prior offenses or use of a weapon. As expected, the U.S. Sentencing Commission Guidelines, used with federal offenders, was challenged next. In *United States v. Booker*,[27] the Supreme Court ruled that federal sentencing guidelines could only be advisory and not consider facts "not in evidence" to determine sentence length. The reason for this is that due process rights require the government to prove the elements it uses to determine a sentence. Many of the elements in a sentencing guidelines structure are not entered into the record, the defendant does not get a chance to refute them, and they do not have to meet any burden of proof. Consequently, the Supreme Court decided that the due process rights of an offender were violated when the sentences in the guidelines were considered to be mandatory rather than advisory.

In *Gall v. United States*,[28] the Supreme Court ruled that judges who sentenced outside of guideline-designated sentence lengths did not have to show extraordinary circumstances; thus, in effect, giving the judges back the discretion for sentencing that existed before the guidelines creation.

One of the most contested elements of federal sentencing guidelines was an almost 100:1 differential between sentences for crack cocaine and powder cocaine; that is, a person with a given amount of crack cocaine would receive

100 times the sentence length as someone with the same amount of powder cocaine. This differential was criticized as having a disparate impact on minority offenders who were more likely to be charged with offenses involving crack cocaine (which is a distillate of powder cocaine) while powder cocaine was more likely the drug of choice for White offenders. Although commentators and even some federal justices argued against the disproportional punishments mandated by sentencing guidelines, only Congress could change the sentence lengths specified in the guidelines. Finally, in 2010, in the Fair Sentencing Act, Congress reduced the punishment differential to 18:1 between the two forms of cocaine, however, by that time the Supreme Court had already eliminated the mandatory nature of the guidelines through case decisions.

One study analyzed the criminal history of federal prisoners and found that almost half (45 percent) of the 95,305 individuals in federal prison for drug offenses are in the lowest two criminal history categories, indicating minimal prior convictions and a low risk of recidivism. In fact, over one-quarter (26 percent) have no prior criminal history. Over three-quarters of all individuals in federal prison for drug offenses have no serious history of violence before the current offense. More than half have no violent history, and nearly one-quarter have only minor histories of violence, such as a simple assault and other crimes that do not typically lead to serious injury.[29] Of course it is important to remember that crimes of conviction are not necessarily an accurate indicator of what the person actually did since many crimes are plea-bargained down several degrees of seriousness or dropped altogether in a plea deal.

The large number of federal prisoners who had been sentenced under earlier, harsher laws and were serving twenty-year or life terms under mandatory minimum sentences have been allowed to petition for **clemency** or **commutation** of their sentences, allowing them to go free. Some reports indicated that 33,000 (roughly 15 percent of the entire federal prison population) applied for clemency.[30] As of June 2016, President Obama commuted the sentences of 342 federal drug offenders, but that is a small sliver of the thousands who are eligible and waiting to have their cases reviewed.

The White House guidelines for who is eligible for clemency consideration include:

- a federal prisoner who has served at least ten years of their sentence and would have received a substantially lower sentence if convicted of the same offense(s) today
- with no significant ties to gangs, organized crime or cartels, and no significant criminal history or history of violent crime, and
- who has demonstrated good conduct in prison.

Read about the process on a White House webpage at https://www.whitehouse.gov/blog/2016/03/30/president-obama-has-now-commuted-sentences-348-individuals

Exhibit 9.4   In 2015, President Obama visited El Reno Federal Correctional Institution in Oklahoma, where he spoke about reducing sentences for non-violent offenders.

Source: AP

To read about The Clemency Project 2014, go to https://www. clemencyproject2014.org/

Thousands of prisoners in federal prisons were eligible for consideration and The Clemency Project 2014 is an effort to utilize the volunteer services of hundreds of attorneys who prepare case files for the federal prisoners, showing that they meet the above criteria.

By May of 2016, the project had reviewed, prepared, and submitted over 1,000 clemency petitions to the Office of Pardon Attorney.[31] However, law professors and advocates argue that the process has been too slow, and because of the slow pace of review, there are over 10,000 still waiting for their cases to be reviewed.[32]

In 2015, the U.S. Sentencing Commission changed federal sentencing guidelines to retroactively make more than 40,000 drug offenders eligible for an average two-year reduction if a judge, in each case, found that they were not

Exhibit 9.5   Presidential Commutations

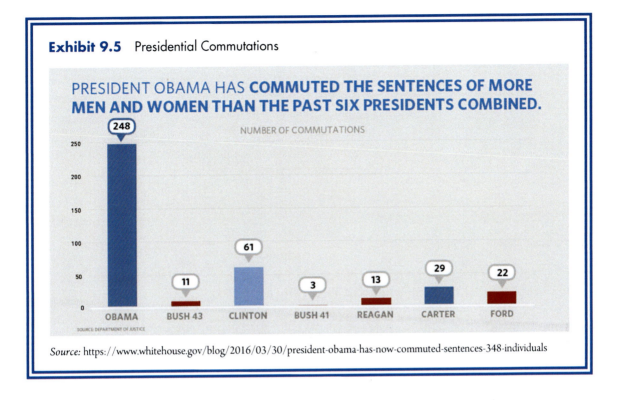

PRESIDENT OBAMA HAS **COMMUTED THE SENTENCES OF MORE MEN AND WOMEN THAN THE PAST SIX PRESIDENTS COMBINED.**

NUMBER OF COMMUTATIONS

SOURCE: DEPARTMENT OF JUSTICE

Source: https://www.whitehouse.gov/blog/2016/03/30/president-obama-has-now-commuted-sentences-348-individuals

a public safety risk. In October of 2015, 6,000 federal inmates were released with thousands more to follow.[33]

Only legislation repealing or reducing mandatory minimums can dramatically affect the number of federal drug prisoners, and there has been recent bipartisan attempts to pass sentencing reform bills. Opponents to such reforms, such as one organization purporting to represent one-third of all federal prosecutors, argue that federal drug offenders cannot be characterized as non-violent since drug markets are by nature violent, and reducing federal drug sentences would increase crime.[34] This is a topic that is clearly in need of stringent research. For instance, proponents of reducing the long, mandatory sentences for drug offenders argue that states that have eliminated or reduced state mandatory minimum sentences have not seen a crime increase. Another research question would be what the recidivism rate has been for those whose drug sentences have been commuted and whether they have engaged in violent crime.

Federal sentencing reform has stalled in the latter portion of 2016 and no one expects much to happen until after the 2016 presidential election at this point. In Exhibit 9.6, a proposed bill is presented that attempted to address a wide range of issues that affects the number of federal offenders prosecuted and imprisoned. Some of the issues addressed include the perceived "over-criminalization" of federal law (too many regulatory wrongs defined as criminal with criminal penalties attached), no-bond pre-trial release to reduce number of defendants in jail, support for Innocence Project-type activities to protect against federal false convictions, and a reduction in the number of people the federal mandatory minimum sentences can be applied to. The bill never emerged out of committee so was not considered by the House of Representatives. Supporters hope that the bill will be reintroduced in 2017.

Exhibit 9.6 H.B. 2944

The Sensenbrenner-Scott Over-Criminalization Task Force Safe, Accountable, Fair, Effective (SAFE) Justice Reinvestment Act of 2015

Title I—Identifying and Reducing Over-Federalization and Over-Criminalization by Respecting the Balance of Powers Among the States and the Federal Government

Sec. 101—Compilation and Publication of Criminal Offenses to Provide Fair Notice to Address Over-Federalization

Requires federal agencies, to compile and publish all federal offenses that carry criminal penalties on a publically available website and to obtain the approval of the Attorney General before adding any criminal penalties to agency regulations. Also adds a sunset provision of five years for any penalty.

Sec. 102—Procedures to Reduce Over-Federalization

Requires the Attorney General and federal agencies to consider whether civil sanctions are more appropriate than criminal charges, and if criminal charges, whether diversion would be most appropriate. Also requires federal prosecutors to coordinate with state prosecutors to reduce duplicative prosecutions at the state and federal level.

Also requires the Inspector General to issue a report on the number of cases accepted for federal criminal prosecution that could have been handled civilly by a federal agency or prosecuted by state or local law enforcement, the estimated federal correctional costs associated with those cases, the number of cases declined for federal criminal prosecution, and the estimated federal correctional savings.

Sec. 103—Procedures to Reduce Pre-Trial Detention

Requires considering a summons rather than arrest warrant and alternatives to pre-trial detention because of inordinate impact of pre-trial detention on the poor, especially in regard to employment and housing. Requires the Inspector General to issue a report and recommendations.

Sec. 104—Creation of a Citizen Complaint Process

Requires the Attorney General to create a secure and confidential online complaint system to the Office of Professional Responsibility for individuals who believe their case is being mishandled by prosecutors. Requires that the Office of the Inspector General to conduct an annual review of the citizen complaint process to determine whether the OPR has taken appropriate disciplinary measures against prosecutors who have mishandled cases or engaged in misconduct, and to report all cases in which any judge or court has substantively discussed allegations that a prosecutor or law enforcement officer engaged in misconduct, whether or not such a finding resulted in reversal of a conviction or sentence.

Sec. 105—Exclusion of Acquitted Conduction and Discretion to Disregard Manipulated Conduct from Consideration During Sentencing

Bars the use of acquitted crimes in sentencing and allows the judge to disregard any conduct or possession not charged or convicted of. Permits courts to disregard any chargeable conduct or possession in cases of "reverse stings and fictitious stash-house robberies" in which law enforcement solicited the defendant for the offense and determined the quantity and type of drugs, firearms, or ammunition. Directs the Sentencing Commission to review and amend its guidelines accordingly.

Sec. 106—Focusing Federal Criminal Penalties for Simple Possession to Places of Special Federal Interest in Recognition of the Balance of Power Between the Federal Government and the States

Limits the jurisdictions in which federal authorities can prosecute simple possession of controlled substances to those areas exclusively under federal control, such as military bases and national parks.

Title II—Addressing Information Disparity and Accuracy in Criminal Prosecutions to Protect Innocence More Robustly and Reduce the Number of Wrongful Convictions

Sec. 201—Findings and Declarations

Acknowledges statistics on wrongful convictions and the practices that increase the risk of wrongful conviction.

Sec. 202—Reauthorization of the Innocence Protection Act of 2001

Reauthorizes the Innocence Protection Act of 2001 from 2016 to 2021. That Act provides services that exonerate the innocent through DNA testing, ensure competent legal services in capital cases, respect the balance of power between the states and federal government in capital cases, and provide increased compensation to victims of wrongful conviction in capital and non-capital cases.

Sec. 203—Accuracy and Reliability of Evidence in Criminal Cases and Addressing Information Disparity in Criminal Cases

Requires the Attorney General, in consultation with bar associations and defense organizations, to identify and implement best practices in evidence, discovery, and interrogation.

Requires the Attorney General to adopt an "open file" discovery policy that permits the timely and continued obligation of disclosure to the defense of the full contents of all investigative and case files, excepting only privileged material or attorney work product.

Sec. 204—Notification Relating to Forensic, Prosecutorial, or Law Enforcement Misconduct

Requires the Attorney General to notify all defendants whose cases involved technicians, facilities, prosecutors, or law enforcement officers who were found to have provided flawed forensic analysis or engaged in misconduct. Provides remedial measures for affected defendants to have their evidence retested, to examine the investigative and case files, or petition for appropriate judicial relief.

Sec. 205—Remedies

Instructs Attorney General to use his existing power to discipline federal prosecutors for failing to follow procedures and utilize the exclusionary rule for illegally obtained evidence.

Sec. 206—Toolkits for State and Local Government

Directs the Attorney General to provide toolkits regarding training in best practices developed under this title to state and local governments and to encourage them to adopt these practices.

Title III—Encouraging Greater Use of Sentencing Alternatives for Lower-Level Offenders

Sec. 301—Eligibility for Pre-Judgment Probation

Allows probation for offenders with prior possession and low-level retail convictions, while continuing to exclude those with prior state or federal high-level drug trafficking convictions.

Sec. 302—Presumption in Favor of a Sentence of Probation in Limited Circumstances

Creates a presumption in favor of probation in limited circumstances in which the defendant is a first-time low-level non-violent offender who is capable of being supervised by probation and has not been convicted of a crime of violence or an otherwise serious enumerated offense.

Sec. 303—Directive to the Sentencing Commission Regarding Use of Probation

Directs the Sentencing Commission to amend its guidelines to allow for expanded use of probation and pre-judgment probation for first-time low-level non-violent offenders.

Sec. 304—Establishment of Problem-Solving Court Programs and Creation of Performance Measures

Provides for the creation of federal problem-solving court programs that incorporate the available research and best evidence-based practices in the field. Provides for periodic evaluations of the success of federal problem-solving court programs. Problem-solving court programs may include drug, mental health, veterans', employment, and re-entry court programs.

Title IV—Concentrating Prison Space on Violent and Career Offenders

Subtitle A—Restoring Original Congressional Intent to Focus Federal Drug Mandatory Minimums Only on Managers, Supervisors, Organizers, and Leaders of Drug Trafficking Organizations and to Avoid Duplicative Prosecution with States

Sec. 401—Focusing the Application of Mandatory Minimums for Certain Drug Offenses to Restore Original Congressional Intent Respecting the Balance of Power Between the Federal Government and the States While Preserving the Availability of Other Federal Drug Charges

Provides that, for the purposes of the five- and ten-year drug trafficking mandatory minimums, offenders must meet the existing weight thresholds, *and, additionally, be designated as a leader or organizer of a drug-trafficking organization comprised of five or more participants.* Does not exclude possibility of life in prison for subsequent offenses and/or cases which result in death or serious bodily injury.

WHAT IS RESTORATIVE JUSTICE?

Restorative justice has been called a philosophy, a justice mechanism,[35] a program, and an alternative type of justice. It is a term that was offered by some as no less than an alternative justice system whereby victims would become the major emphasis of the system and offenders would not be punished as much as become responsible for restoration (in effect, fixing the damage they had done).

The term came to broadly include sentencing programs that focused on repairing the damage a criminal offense caused to the victim, the community, and, in some cases, the offender. From its beginnings in 1978, restorative justice has become quite prevalent. Exhibit 9.8 shows how many states have legislation that either creates restorative justice programs (by enabling legislation and funding), or is supportive of it without providing funding.

The idea behind restorative justice is that traditional criminal justice sentencing tends to shame the offender in a negative way and often includes banishment from the community.[36] Restorative justice promotes the idea that the offender should recognize and make whole the damage done to the victim, but should be considered a part of the community and, therefore, the immediate community of the offender and victim is the best source of decision-making for sentencing—not criminal justice system actors. Sentencing, therefore, is often done through victim–offender conferencing or sentencing practices whereby the offender, victim, and stakeholders (offender's relatives, community members) communicate together to determine the best response to the criminal offense. These programs are most often designed for juvenile offenders and/ or minor offenders.[37]

Exhibit 9.7 An inmate at the Columbia Correctional Institution in Wisconsin receives his diploma upon graduation from the prison's 25-week restorative justice program, which aims to address the harm done by each inmate's crime.

Source: AP

A few types of restorative justice models related to criminal justice sentencing and corrections are:

Victim–offender mediation. This is the most common program and is more than twenty years old. Some programs are called victim–offender reconciliation programs or dialog programs. There are more than 320 programs in the United States and many more in Europe. They involve the victim and offender meeting and discussing the event and coming to an agreement about restitution and reparation. The idea is to promote healing on the part of the victim and responsibility on the part of the offender. The program may be implemented as a diversion from prosecution or as a condition of probation. Research has found that victims are more satisfied when they have an opportunity to go

Exhibit 9.8   Restorative Justice Legislation

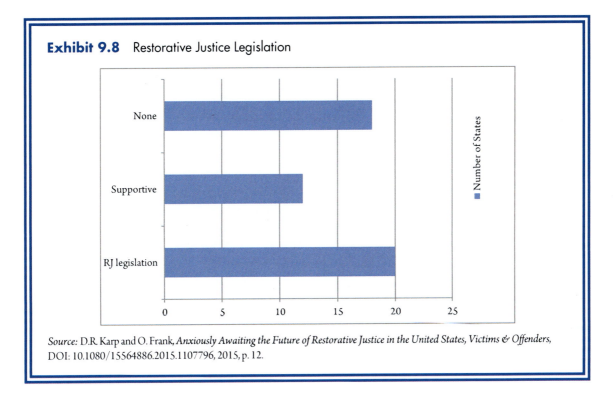

Source: D.R. Karp and O. Frank, *Anxiously Awaiting the Future of Restorative Justice in the United States, Victims & Offenders,* DOI: 10.1080/15564886.2015.1107796, 2015, p. 12.

through these programs. Victims were also significantly less fearful of being victimized. Offenders were more likely to complete their restitution and recidivism was lower for those who went through mediation as compared to traditional sentencing.

Community reparative boards. This model has been more common in the juvenile system and has been in use since the 1920s. It re-emerged with greater popularity in the 1990s and may be called youth panels, neighborhood boards, or community diversion boards. The goals of the program are to promote citizen ownership of the sentencing process, and provide an opportunity for victims and community members to confront the offender in a constructive manner. The idea is also to reduce dependence on formal justice processing. Basically, citizens are involved in a sentencing decision and the experience is more of a dialogue between the offender and the board, who look at long-term solutions rather than retribution.

Family group conferencing. This type of program comes directly from the dispute resolution tradition of the Maori. In fact, it was adopted into national legislation in New Zealand in 1989. In these models, police (or another agency) set up a conference of the offender, victim, and the families of both, as well as others involved. The goal is to have everyone participate, to have the offender come to a greater understanding of how the crime affected others, and to allow others to help make sure that the collective decision is carried out. Participants generally report higher levels of satisfaction than those who go through traditional justice models.[38]

There are criticisms and potential problems with the restorative justice concept. Some argue that it is not an appropriate response for serious violent crimes. Some argue that victims may not want to participate, or that they may feel pressured to forgive the offender or feel "ganged up" on by the offender's family and friends. Generally, however, research indicates that victims are more satisfied when the focus is on their needs and when the offender takes responsibility for and makes right the offense.[39] For instance, a juvenile burglar might meet with the homeowner-victims and over the course of one meeting or several, the victims explain their loss and what would make them whole. It might be simple monetary restitution, but sometimes it could include the offender helping the homeowner fix a lock or repair a door. A storeowner, for instance, might agree that an offender who shoplifted pay back the goods with time, providing janitorial service to the storeowner or some other service. When they are successful, these programs bolster community ties and encourage cohesion among community members.

Over the last thirty years, many different types of programs have been developed and implemented under the restorative justice mantle. Critics warn that by enlarging the scope of the term there is a danger of diluting the meaning. Restorative justice programs, for instance, now may include any type of community service—even if it is by prisoners in a prison. These programs may not conform to the original ideas of restorative justice which emphasized the inclusion of the offender in the decision-making process and the importance of keeping the offender in the community.[40]

Research on restorative justice has looked at satisfaction (of the offender and victim), procedural justice perceptions (whether a participant thought the program was fair), recidivism, and other measures of success with mixed findings. Although many studies showed positive responses from participants, there has also been a thread of findings that indicated victims felt pressured to participate and felt the program was more oriented toward offenders than victims. There is also a concern that programs have resulted in "**net-widening**" so that minor offenders become more engaged in the criminal justice system than they would have otherwise for very minor offenses.[41] One other criticism of restorative justice programs is that they tend to ignore the structural and economic factors of criminal causation and there is some evidence that White offenders are disproportionally diverted to such programs as compared to minority offenders.[42] On the other hand, the positive emphasis on integration, community involvement, and victim satisfaction that is present in such programs are strong reasons why they should be stringently evaluated to determine if they are more, less, or as effective in reducing recidivism and increasing citizens' faith in the justice system.

WHAT ARE THE LEGAL ARGUMENTS AGAINST THE DEATH PENALTY?

The death penalty is a controversial subject and strong feelings exist on both sides of the discussion as to whether capital punishment should exist or not. One of the benefits of the critical thinking process is the development of being able to recognize the types of arguments used to support or oppose capital punishment. The arguments include philosophical and legal rationales. Some of the philosophical rationales for the death penalty involve the emotional sentiment that underlies retributive punishment. In other words, the death penalty is right because the offender *deserves* it. With that rationale, there is no point to discuss whether the death penalty deters, or whether it is more cost-effective to sentence an offender to life in prison, because the rationale is not based on empirical arguments but on the visceral emotion of revenge/retribution.

We will limit this discussion to legal arguments and the history of legal case decisions regarding the use of capital punishment in this country. Death-penalty-relevant law is based on philosophical rationales, pragmatic concerns, the interpretation of rights, and case law precedent. In 1972, in *Furman v. Georgia*,[43] the Supreme Court held that the procedure used for capital punishment sentencing was arbitrary violating the 8th Amendment's prohibition against cruel and unusual punishment. It did not rule that executions were, by their nature, unconstitutional. It was a 5–4 decision and the plurality of Justices were concerned with the process of administering the death penalty and the fact that existing practices were likely to result in arbitrary decisions because juries were not given guidance in who should receive the most severe sentence. In response, states changed their sentencing statutes to include more due process in capital cases. For instance, juries were required to deliberate and decide on specific findings in order to assess the penalty (e.g., future dangerousness). A few states removed all discretion by making capital punishment mandatory for those convicted of capital crimes. This practice was held unconstitutional by the Supreme Court because it did not allow for consideration of individual differences among defendants.[44] Georgia changed its sentencing process to include a separate sentencing hearing after a guilty verdict, the jury had to find at least one aggravating circumstance beyond a reasonable doubt, and automatic appeals occurred for every death sentence. The Supreme Court approved this sentencing process in 1976 in *Gregg v. Georgia*[45] and executions, which had been suspended across the country since *Furman*, resumed.

Since that time, the Supreme Court has been called upon to decide many challenges to the death penalty. In *McCleskey v. Kemp*,[46] the challenge was that a statistical analysis showed a pattern of racial disparities in who received the death penalty (those who killed White victims were 4.3 times more likely to receive the death penalty than those who killed African Americans), evidence that the punishment was applied in an unequal, and, therefore, unconstitutional manner. The Supreme Court disagreed arguing that intentional racial discrimination in that individual case was not proven.

Other challenges have involved who is sentenced to death. Supreme Court cases have ruled that death is a disproportional sentence for rape,[47] even rape of a child.[48] However, the Court did agree that capital punishment was not in violation of the 8th Amendment when handed down to someone who was convicted of felony murder. **Felony murder** is a type of murder where evidence shows the person was involved in a felony which resulted in a homicide, but was not the person who committed the homicide. The Supreme Court held in *Tison v. Arizona*[49] that if the perpetrator was a major participant in the felony and showed a reckless indifference to human life, capital punishment was not a disproportional sentence to that crime even if the offender did not kill or intend to kill the victim.

The Supreme Court has held that the death penalty is cruel and unusual when the sentence is given to juveniles. The Supreme Court first prohibited the use of capital punishment against offenders who committed their crimes at or below the age of sixteen.[50] Then, in *Roper v. Simmons*,[51] the Court overturned prior case decisions to conclude that capital punishment was unconstitutional when imposed on someone who committed the crime before the age of eighteen. This 5–4 decision invalidated sentencing statutes in 25 states that had the penalty available for those offenders.

The Supreme Court has also ruled that capital punishment is unconstitutional when the offender is mentally handicapped.[52]

Cases continue to be heard challenging the states' methods of determining how to evaluate intellectual capacity and the level at which lack of capacity should create immunity from the death penalty.[53] In both of these challenges, the legal position taken by the majority of the justices was that execution was a disproportional punishment for juveniles or the mentally disabled because of their inability to completely appreciate the gravity of their crimes (either because of youth or because of mental disability). The ultimate sentence of

Exhibit 9.9   Daryl Atkins was convicted of murder and sentenced to death, despite an intellectual disability. He appealed his case and the Supreme Court eventually decided that capital punishment is unconstitutional for those with mental handicaps.

Source: AP

death was inappropriate because, compared to other murderers, they could not be determined to be the worst of all offenders; juveniles may be amenable to treatment and maturity may change them, and the mentally disabled are not capable of understanding the gravity of their offense.

Mental illness has also been the subject of challenges and even common law frowned on the execution of the mentally ill. The Supreme Court has ruled

Exhibit 9.10   Public Support for Death Penalty

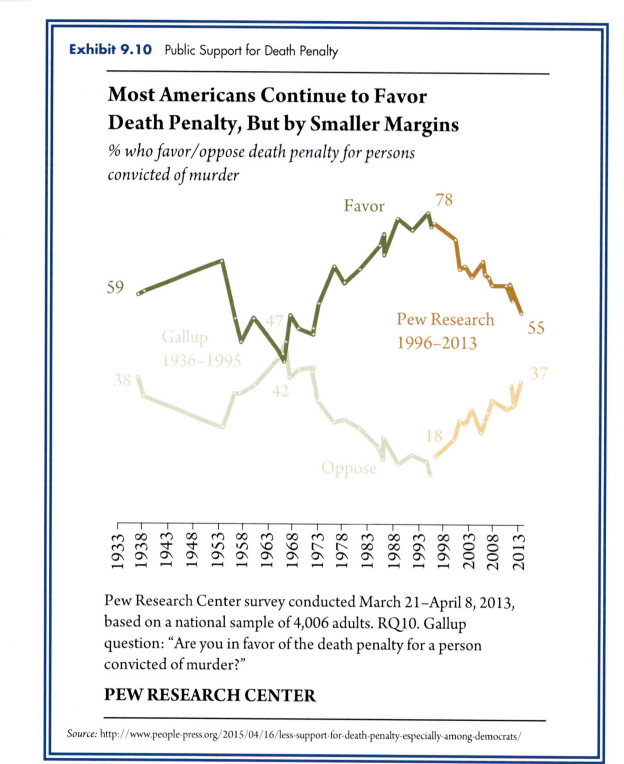

Most Americans Continue to Favor Death Penalty, But by Smaller Margins

% who favor/oppose death penalty for persons convicted of murder

Pew Research Center survey conducted March 21–April 8, 2013, based on a national sample of 4,006 adults. RQ10. Gallup question: "Are you in favor of the death penalty for a person convicted of murder?"

PEW RESEARCH CENTER

Source: http://www.people-press.org/2015/04/16/less-support-for-death-penalty-especially-among-democrats/

that the mentally ill, if their illness is such that they do not understand what is happening to them or why, should not be executed.[54] The legal argument for the mentally ill is that because they do not know what they are doing or why it is wrong, the goals of punishment (retribution and deterrence) are not met by a death sentence. Court challenges continue in how states determine mental illness. It is telling, however, that California has opened a forty-bed psychiatric unit for its death row prisoners.[55]

The most recent area of legal challenge has been toward the method of death. The Supreme Court has recently upheld the lethal drug protocols used by states against appeals that argued that the use of these particular drugs was cruel and unusual.[56] This issue may become even more legally problematic, however, as pharmaceutical companies have begun to withhold the drugs used in lethal injections, forcing states to develop alternative death injection drug combinations.

The majority of Americans are in favor of the death penalty, but the percentage in favor and against capital punishment seems to go up and down as seen in Exhibit 9.10. A series of polls utilized by the Pew Research Center showed that, despite interim increases and decrease, the American public seems to be currently in about the same place regarding the death penalty as it was in 1933 with about 55 percent favoring it and 37 percent opposing it.

Exhibit 9.11   Death Sentences

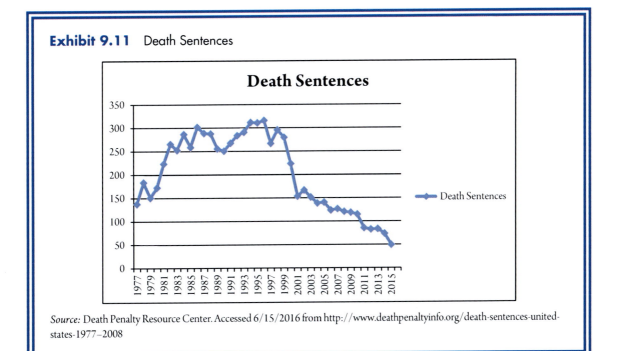

Source: Death Penalty Resource Center. Accessed 6/15/2016 from http://www.deathpenaltyinfo.org/death-sentences-united-states-1977–2008

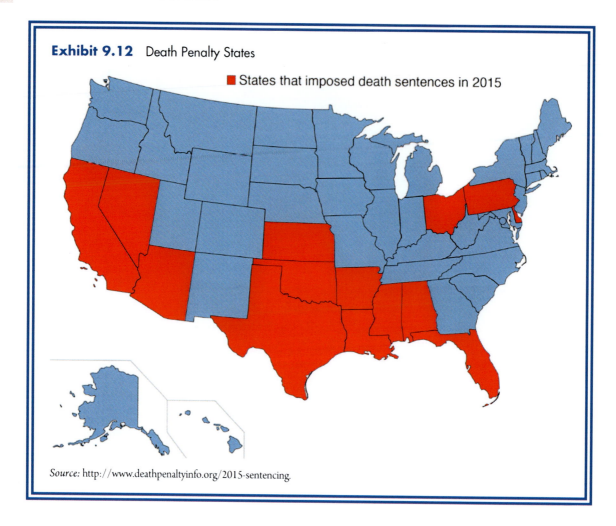

Exhibit 9.12 Death Penalty States

■ States that imposed death sentences in 2015

Source: http://www.deathpenaltyinfo.org/2015-sentencing.

For whatever reason, the number of executions has seen a fairly dramatic decline and recent years have seen all-time lows in the number of executions across the country. Exhibit 9.11 shows the decline from a high in the mid-1990s. Exhibit 9.12 shows that executions are not evenly distributed and most take place in Southern states.

FOCUS ON DATA: IS THERE RACIAL DISPARITY IN SENTENCING?

Some argue that there is evidence that there is racial disparity in sentencing and that minorities (Blacks and Hispanics) receive harsher sentences than Whites on average. If true, competing explanations exist: it may be that sentence decision makers (prosecutors, judges, juries) do sentence minorities differently for "extra-legal" reasons, or there are systemic sentencing policy differences that produce disparity, e.g., minorities are more likely than Whites to commit crimes that trigger long sentences, crimes that trigger mandatory minimums, or sentencing guidelines utilize factors for determining punishment that affect White and minority offenders differently.

It is important to be aware of the methodological problems of answering this question definitively. Most studies begin at the point of a criminal conviction and look at (1) the sentence (incarceration in prison/jail *or* non-incarceration) and (2) length of prison term. Obviously there are factors which affect the sentencing decision and studies should, and do to varying degrees, control for such things as: criminal history, level of participation in crime, extent of injury or loss to victim, and use of weapon. Other factors may play a role also such as remorse and motivation for crime, but these factors are less likely to be controlled for because most studies use existing file information which does not include these items. Unless all factors that affect the sentencing decision are controlled for, then any differences found in sentences between racial or ethnic groups may not be due to race/ethnicity, but, rather, those uncontrolled for factors, whatever they might be.

Another important point to consider is that simply looking at the sentence for the crime of conviction masks any race or ethnicity-based differential treatment that might have occurred at an earlier point in the process. Prosecutors decide whether and what to charge—that decision affects what happens "downstream" (at the point of guilty plea or conviction). Even decisions about bail and/or pre-trial release may be important factors in what conviction rates show because individuals who spend pre-trial time in jail may be more likely to plead guilty or accept less lenient plea bargains. One plea-bargaining study, for instance, found that Black offenders were less likely than White offenders to receive charge reduction offers from prosecutors, and both Black and Hispanic offenders were more likely than Whites to receive a plea offer that included a prison term. Even though the plea differences were largely explained by legal factors such as evidence and arrest history, even after controlling for these factors, some difference remained.[57]

Meta-analyses are studies that combine a large number of previous studies over a topic to see what findings are generally consistent. In meta-analyses of race and sentencing, researchers find that there is mixed evidence that race plays a role in prosecutorial decision making.[58] In one review of twenty-four studies of prosecutorial charging decisions, fifteen of the twenty-four studies found no effect of race on charging decisions.[59] Another meta-analysis found a slight majority of studies showed racial bias in sentencing.[60] Other researchers have found that prosecutors were almost twice as likely to seek mandatory sentences against Hispanic defendants as White defendants,[61] and Black defendants were more likely to be charged with and receive third-strike sentences than White defendants, particularly for offenses known as "wobblers," which can be prosecuted either as a felony or a misdemeanor.[62]

One study of criminal sentencing in Florida found that Black offenders were about 2.3 percent more likely to go to prison than Whites, and Hispanics were 1.3 percent more likely than Whites to go to prison. The largest effect was sex, however, with males 5 percent more likely to go to prison than female offenders. These researchers found that sentencing differences were greatest with serious offenses at the highest end of sentence length. The study results also showed that Black offenders received sentences that were, on average, 4.76 months longer than Whites and Hispanic offenders received 1.65 months longer than Whites. Men received 6.75 months longer prison sentences than female offenders. Sentence length differences were much more extreme at the highest level of crime seriousness with Blacks receiving sentences that were thirty-five months longer than Whites but Hispanics received sentences that were eighteen months shorter than Whites.[63] It is important to note that single state studies or studies that cannot control for all sentencing factors should be interpreted with caution.

Studies that examine the interaction among race, age, and gender find that the combination of these variables affects sentencing patterns more than any one individually. For instance, older Black men are less likely to receive disproportionately severe sentences than young Black men. Women, on the other hand, are sentenced fairly uniformly regardless of age. Race is less important as a factor in sentencing older rather than younger offenders, and for men rather than women. Steffensmeier and his colleagues[64] have examined the interplay of these variables in several studies and find that race does seem to affect sentencing, but it influences sentencing mostly for young men.

The federal system offers an interesting opportunity to observe what happens when judges are given more discretion. Recall from an earlier discussion that federal sentencing guidelines were created in 1987 and were mandatory; judges were required to sentence to the amount of time specified in the guidelines whether they agreed with the sentence or not for that particular offender. The Supreme Court, in a series of cases,[65] ruled that the guidelines must be advisory, not mandatory, thus increasing the discretion judges had to sentence federal offenders. Several studies have occurred since then to determine if sentencing disparity increased, especially between the sentences of White and Black federal offenders. Findings indicated that, once judges had the power to go outside the guidelines, disparity did increase between the sentences of Black and White offenders, and between the sentences of male and female offenders.[66]

The disparity seemed to increase significantly after *Booker*, but then leveled off and stopped increasing. One study found that disparity increased by 4 percent, and also that disparity between judges increased.[67] Some research found that it wasn't that sentences for Black offenders increased, but, rather, that sentences for White offenders decreased more than those for Black offenders, thus increasing the disparity between the two groups.[68] Another finding was that Blacks were more likely to reside in federal circuits where judges sentenced everyone harshly. Disparity between judges was marked, with some sentencing everyone more harshly than judges in other circuits who sentenced everyone more leniently. This factor would affect the overall disparity of sentences for Black and White offenders.[69]

Yet another study[70] examined both a federal sample of sentences after the guidelines became advisory (2005–09) and a sample of cases from Pennsylvania which also used guidelines which were more flexible than the federal guidelines. These researchers examined departures from guidelines and legally relevant (e.g., criminal history) and extra-legal variables (e.g., age, education) they had data for to see if the departures could be explained. The federal sample also included citizenship and education variables.

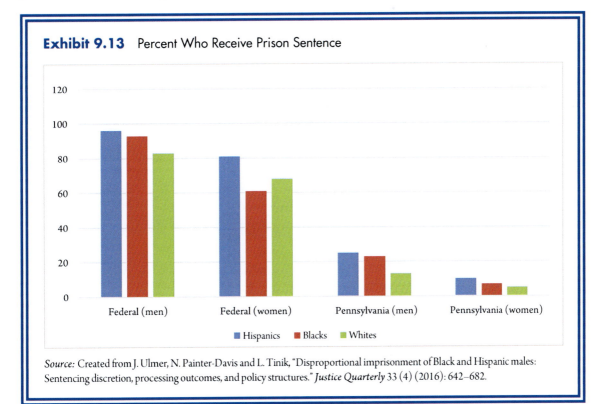

Exhibit 9.13   Percent Who Receive Prison Sentence

Source: Created from J. Ulmer, N. Painter-Davis and L. Tinik, "Disproportional imprisonment of Black and Hispanic males: Sentencing discretion, processing outcomes, and policy structures." *Justice Quarterly* 33 (4) (2016): 642–682.

In the federal data, 93 percent of Black males and 96 percent of Hispanic males are imprisoned, compared to 83 percent of White males, 81 percent of Hispanic females, 68 percent of White females, and 61 percent of Black females.

The other type of potential disparity is sentence length and the data from this study showed that Black males were more likely to receive longer sentences than any other group. Note the longer sentences for federal prisoners, which was probably due to federal mandatory minimum sentencing.

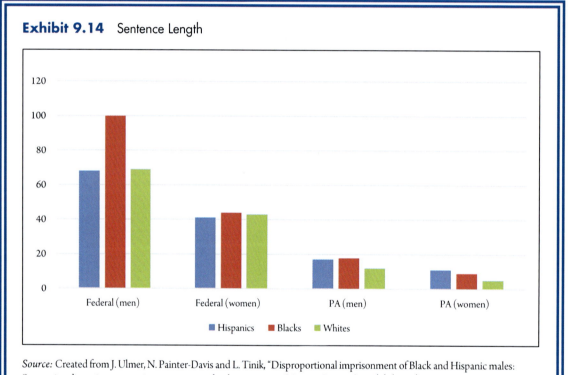

Exhibit 9.14   Sentence Length

Source: Created from J. Ulmer, N. Painter-Davis and L. Tinik, "Disproportional imprisonment of Black and Hispanic males: Sentencing discretion, processing outcomes, and policy structures." *Justice Quarterly* 33 (4) (2016): 642–682.

The researchers found that a great deal of disproportionality is explained by sentencing policy structures; that is, variables such as criminal history and type of offense triggered presumptive sentences and mandatory minimums that occurred more often with Black and Hispanic offenders. In addition, some legally relevant variables (such as criminal history and offense type) also explained differences over and above guidelines. What this presumably means is that judges considered those variables again to increase sentence length above guideline-suggested sentences. Researchers also noted, however, that while about 90 percent of the race/ethnic variation between-courts in *sentence length* in Pennsylvania courts was explained by the legal variables they measured, none of the between-county variation in the *non-incarceration vs. incarceration* was explained by these variables. They also noted that the application of mandatory minimums is almost entirely a product of prosecutorial discretion in Pennsylvania.[71] In other words, because prosecutors get to decide whether to pursue mandatory minimums, incarceration caused by mandatory minimum statutes does not seem to be explained by any legal factors.

The question of whether there is unfair racial/ethnic disparity in sentencing is a very controversial subject and, unfortunately, as with many of the topics discussed in this text, one that requires stringent research methodology with sophisticated statistical tests. Even with the best intentions, it is likely that such research cannot control for all variables that affect sentencing; however, the weight of the evidence seems to indicate that at least some of the racial disparity in sentencing is due to extra-legal (non-relevant) factors.

SUMMARY

What Happens in a Sentencing Hearing?

A sentencing hearing is considered a "critical stage" of the trial process, and the defendant has a 6th Amendment right to an attorney if they are facing the possibility of a jail or prison sentence. Evidence is introduced on both sides that includes culpability, character evidence, and impact on the defendant's family. Victim impact evidence is also introduced. Pre-sentence reports may be introduced. It is important to remember, however, that the vast majority of sentences are determined by plea-bargaining.

What Are the Goals of Sentencing?

The goals of sentencing are punishment, deterrence, rehabilitation, and incapacitation.

What Are the Types of Sentences That Might Be Given to Criminal Offenders?

Criminal sentences can include one or a combination of: fines, fees, informal supervision, probation with or without conditions (rules), split sentences (combining incarceration and probation), jail sentence, prison sentence, death.

What Are Three-Strikes Sentencing Laws?

Three-strikes sentencing are habitual sentencing laws. The baseball analogy refers to a third-strike felony which triggers a much longer sentence (sometimes 25 years to life) than the felony would ordinarily receive.

What Is the Most Common Sentence?

The most common sentence today is some form of incarceration—jail/prison.

What Is the Criticism Regarding Fines and Fees?

There is some evidence to indicate that onerous fees and fines are the reason some offenders have their probation revoked or are unable to earn their freedom from correctional supervision. Fees are assessed for many elements of the criminal justice system such as probation supervision and even public defender costs.

What Recent Events Have Occurred with Federal Drug Sentencing?

Federal sentencing guidelines and mandatory minimums resulted in federal drug offenders serving much longer sentences than other criminal offenders or drug offenders in state courts. Recently, the crack to powder cocaine disparity was reduced from 100:1 to 18:1, and mandatory guideline sentence lengths are now advisory. There is a project underway to review and consider commuting the sentences of those sentenced under much harsher laws.

What Is Restorative Justice?

Restorative justice has been called a philosophy, a justice mechanism, a program, and an alternative type of justice. It refers to types of programs where victims are the major focus and offenders are tasked with repairing the harm they have done. The goal is to restore rather than punish and the offender is considered a part of the community, not banished.

What Are the Legal Arguments Against the Death Penalty?

Case law has considered a sequences of challenges to capital punishment including: the process (due process must exist to prevent arbitrary and capricious decisions); types of crimes (only murder has been accepted as a crime equal to the death penalty); type of offender (juveniles, the mentally challenged, and the mentally insane cannot be punished with death), and method of execution. At this point the Supreme Court majority has continued to agree that there is no violation of the 8th Amendment if a state chooses to utilize capital punishment.

Critical Thinking Exercises

1. Go to the *Washington Post* story that provides the names and crimes of 58 people whose sentences were commuted by President Obama (https://www.washingtonpost.com/news/post-nation/wp/2016/05/05/here-are-the-58-people-whose-sentences-president-obama-just-commuted/?utm_term=.14c95d3d8e25). Find out more about a sample of commutation cases (for another webpage describing those who received commutations, go to http://famm.org/tag/federal-prisoners/). Make sure you check your facts with multiple sources. Determine how long the individuals were incarcerated. Determine, through your review of sentencing guidelines in other states (e.g. Pennsylvania), how long a prison sentence the individual might have served.

2. There is a huge body of literature on capital punishment. Construct a table of arguments with supporting data for and against capital punishments, with sources noted.

NOTES

1 *Mempa v. Rhay*, 389 U.S. 128, 1967.

2 *Payne v. Tennessee*, 501 U.S. 808, 825, 1991.

3 J. Petersilia, *Reforming Probation and Parole*. Lanham, MD: American Correctional Association, 2002, p. 29

4 National Center for State Courts, *State Sentencing Guidelines: Profiles and Continuum*. Retrieved 10/10/2010 from http://www.ncsconline.org/csi/PEW-Profiles-v12-online.pdf, 2008

5 J. Travis and J. Petersilia, "Reentry reconsidered: A new look at an old question." *Crime and Delinquency* 47 (3) (2001): 294.

6 E.g., *Ewing v. California*, 538 U.S. 11 (2003).

7 J. Leonard and M. Dolan, "Softer 3-strikes law has defense lawyers preparing case reviews." *Los Angeles Times*, November 8, 2012.

8 S. Rosenmerkel, M. Durose and D. Farole, *Felony Sentences in State Courts, 2006—Statistical Tables*. Washington, DC: Bureau of Justice Statistics, 2009.

9 B. Reaves, *Felony Defendants in Large Urban Counties, 2009—Statistical Tables*. Washington, DC: Bureau of Justice Statistics, December 2013.

10 Charles Colson Task Force, *Who Gets Time for Federal Drug Offenses? Data Trends and Opportunities for Reform*. Washington, DC: Urban Justice Institute, 2015.

11 D. Evans, *The Debt Penalty—Exposing the Financial Barriers to Offender Reintegration*. New York, NY: Research and Evaluation Center, John Jay College of Criminal Justice, 2014.

12 A. Bannon, M. Nagrecha and R. Diller, *Criminal Justice Debt: A Barrier to Reentry*. Washington, DC: Brennan Center, 2010. Available at: http://www.brennancenter.org/sites/default/files/legacy/Fees%20and%20Fines%20FINAL.pdf

13 Human Rights Watch. *Profiting from Probation: America's Offender Funded Probation Industry*. Accessed at: http://www.hrw.org/sites/default/files/reports/us0214_forupload_0.pdf

14 D. Evans, *The Debt Penalty—Exposing the Financial Barriers to Offender Reintegration*. New York, NY: Research and Evaluation Center, John Jay College of Criminal Justice, 2014.

15 B. Vogt, "Note, State v. Allison: Imprisonment for Debt in South Dakota." 46 *South Dakota Law Review* 334 (2001): 338–340.

16 R.B. Ruback, "The abolition of fines and fees: Not proven and not compelling." *Criminology and Public Policy* 10 (2011): 569–587; R.B. Ruback and M.H. Bergstrom, "Economic sanctions in criminal justice: Purposes, effects, and implications." *Criminal Justice and Behavior* 33 (2006): 242–258.

17 A. Harris, H. Evans and K. Beckett, "Drawing blood from stones: Legal debt and social inequality in the contemporary United States." *American Journal of Sociology* 115 (6) (May 2010): 1753–1799.

18 K.D. Levingston and V. Turetsky, "Debtors' prison—prisoners' accumulation of debt as a barrier to reentry." *Clearinghouse Review: Journal of Poverty Law and Policy* 41 (2007):187–188.

19 A. Harris, H. Evans and K.Beckett, note 17.

20 *Tate v. Short*, 401 U.S. 395, 1971.

21 *Bearden v. Georgia*, 461 U.S. 660, 1983.

22 Ferguson Complaint, *Jenkins v. City of Jennings*, No. 14:15-cv-00252 (E.D. Mo. Feb. 8, 2015), accessed from http://equaljusti ceunderlaw.org/wp/wpcontent/uploads/2015/02/Complaint-Jennings-Debtors-Prisons-FILE-STAMPED.pdf

23 L. Eisen, *Charging Inmates Perpetuates Mass Incarceration*. Washington, DC: Brennan Center for Justice, 2016.

24 Federal Sentencing Reform Act of 1984 (effective 1987), 1 U.S.C. €3553(a).

25 J. Travis and J. Petersilia, "Reentry reconsidered: A new look at an old question." *Crime and Delinquency* 47 (3) (2001): 294.

26 *Blakely v. Washington*, 542 U.S. 296, 2004.

27 *U.S. v. Booker*, 543 U.S. 220, 2005.

28 *Gall v. United States*, 552 US 38, 2007.

29 Charles Colson Task Force, *Who Gets Time for Federal Drug Offenses? Data Trends and Opportunities for Reform*. Washington, DC: CCTF, Urban Institute, 2015.

30 S. Horwitz, "Struggling to fix a 'broken' system: For many drug offenders, their only hope is President Obama's clemency power. And his time is running out." *Washington Post*, December 5, 2015.

31 American Bar Association, "Clemency Project 2014 surpasses 1,000 clemency petitions." *ABA News*, May 16, 2016.

32 Law blog, June 21, 2016. http://sentencing.typepad.com/sentencing_law_and_policy/clemency_and_pardons/. Also, see G. Korte, "Experts warn White House that time is running out for clemency initiative." *USA Today*, June 21, 2016.

33 S. Horwitz, note 30.

34 S. Nelson. "Prosecutors rally against sentencing reform, say build more prisons." *US News and World Report*, July 17, 2015.

35 See K. Daly, "What is restorative justice? Fresh answers to a vexed question." *Victims & Offenders*, 2016. DOI: 10.1080/15564886.2015.1107797

36 J. Braithwaite, *Crime, Shame and Reintegration*. Cambridge, UK: Cambridge University Press, 1989.

37 G. Bazemore and M. Schiff, *Juvenile Justice Reform and Restorative Justice: Building Theory and Policy from Practice*. Devon, UK: Willan Publishing, 2005.

38 J. Braithwaite, "Linking crime prevention to restorative justice." In J. Perry (Ed.), *Repairing Communities through Restorative Justice*. Lanham, MD: American Correctional Association, 2002, pp. 55–66.

39 J. Braithwaite, "Linking crime prevention to restorative justice." In J. Perry (Ed.), *Repairing Communities through Restorative Justice*. Lanham, MD: American Correctional Association, 2002, p. 85.

40 W. Wood and M. Suzuki, "Four challenges in the future of restorative justice." *Victims & Offenders*, 2016. DOI: 10.1080/15564886.2016.1145610.

41 Op. cit., p. 7.

42 D.R. Karp and O. Frank, "Anxiously awaiting the future of restorative justice in the United States." *Victims & Offenders*, 2015. DOI:10.1080/15564886.2015.1107796

43 *Furman v. Georgia*, 408 U.S. 238, 1972.

44 *Woodson v. North Carolina*, 428 U.S. 280, 1976.

45 *Gregg v. Georgia*, 428 U.S. 153, 1976.

46 *McCleskey v. Kemp*, 481 U.S. 279, 1987.

47 *Coker v. Georgia*, 433 U.S. 584, 1977.

48 *Kennedy v. Louisiana*, 554 U.S. 407, 2008.

49 *Tison v. Arizona*, 481 U.S. 137, 1987.

50 *Stanford v. Kentucky*, 492 U.S. 361, 1989.

51 *Roper v. Simmons*, 543 U.S. 551, 2005.

52 *Atkins v. Virginia*, 536 U.S. 304, 2002.

53 *Hall v. Florida*, 572 U.S. ___ , 2014.

54 *Ford v. Wainwright*, 477 U.S. 399, 1986.

55 H. Minitz, "San Quentin: Inside California's death row." *Mercury News*, December 29, 2015. Accessed 6/15/2016 from: http://www.marinij.com/article/ZZ/20151229/NEWS/151225744

56 *Glossip Et Al. v. Gross Et Al.*, Argued April 29, 2015—Decided June 29, 2015, No. 14–7955.

57 B.L. Kutateladze, N.R. Andiloro and B.D. Johnson, "Opening Pandora's box: How does defendant race influence plea bargaining?" *Justice Quarterly* 33 (2016): 398–426, DOI: 10.1080/07418825.2014.915340

58 B. Frederick and D. Stemen, *The Anatomy of Discretion: An Analysis of Prosecutorial Decision Making—Technical Report*. New York, NY: Vera Institute of Justice, 2012.

59 M. Free, "Race and presentencing decisions in the United States: A summary and critique of the research." *Criminal Justice Review* 27 (2002): 203–232.

60 B. Kutateladze, B. Lynn and E. Liang, *Do Race and Ethnicity Matter in Prosecution?* Vera Institute of Justice, 2012. Retrieved October 29, 2013, from the Vera Institute of Justice website: http://www.vera.org/pubs/do-race-and-ethnicity-matter-prosecution-review-empirical-studies

61 J.T. Ulmer, M.C. Kurlycheck and J.H. Kramer. "Prosecutorial discretion and the imposition of mandatory minimum sentences." *Journal of Research in Crime and Delinquency* 44 (2015): 427–458.

62 E.Y. Chen, "The liberation hypothesis and racial and ethnic disparities in the application of California's Three Strikes Law." *Journal of Ethnicity in Criminal Justice* 6 (2008): 83–102.

63 W. Hauser and J.H. Peck, "The intersection of crime seriousness, discretion, and race: A test of the liberation hypothesis." *Justice Quarterly* 2016. Accessed from: http://dx.doi.org/10.1080/07418825.2015.1121284

64 D. Steffensmeier, J. Ulmer and J. Kramer, "The interaction of race, gender, and age in criminal sentencing: The punishment cost of being young, black and male." *Criminology* 36 (4) (1998): 763–797. Also see C. Harris, D. Steffensmeier, J. Ulmer and N. Painter-Davis, "Are blacks and Hispanics disproportionately incarcerated relative to their arrests? Racial and ethnic disproportionality between arrest and incarceration." *Race and Social Problems* 1 (2009): 187–199.

65 *Booker v. United States*, 543 US 220, 2005; *Gall v. United States*, 552 US 38, 2007.

66 Studies reviewed in W. Rhodes, R. King, J. Luallen and C. Dyous, *Federal Sentencing Disparity: 2005–2012*. Cambridge, MA: Abt Associates, 2015.

67 C. Yang, *Free at Last? Judicial Discretion and Racial Disparities in Federal Sentencing*. Chicago: Coase-Sandor Institute for Law and Economics Working Paper No. 661, The University of Chicago Law School, 2013.

68 S. Starr and M. Rehavi, "Mandatory sentencing and racial disparity: Assessing the role of prosecutors and the effects of booker." *Yale Law Journal* 123 (1) (2013): 2–80; C. Yang, *Have Inter-Judge Sentencing Disparities Increased in an Advisory Guideline Regime? Evidence from Booker*. Coase-Sandor Institute for Law and Economics, Research Paper No. 662, 2014.

69 W. Rhodes et al., note 66.

70 J. Ulmer, N. Painter-Davis and L. Tinik, "Disproportional imprisonment of Black and Hispanic males: Sentencing discretion, processing outcomes, and policy structures." *Justice Quarterly* 33 (4) (2016): 642–682.

71 Op. cit., p. 675, 677.

Section 4

CORRECTIONS AS SOCIAL CONTROL

COMMUNITY CORRECTIONS AND CORRECTIONAL CLASSIFICATION

10

Chapter Preview

- What Are the Goals of Corrections? What Was the "Rehabilitative Era"?
- How Do Theories of Crime Relate to What We Do to Criminals?
- What Is Probation and How Is It Different from Parole? How Is It Different from Pre-Trial Diversion?
- What Is the History of Probation?
- What Are Some Typical Conditions for a Probationer?
- What Is the Profile of Offenders Under Correctional Supervision?
- Do Women On Probation Have Different Backgrounds and Needs Than Men; If So, What Are They?
- Many Drug Offenders Are Under Correctional Supervision? What Are Their Issues?
- What Are Some Current Issues of Probation Supervision?
- What Is Revocation? How Many Probationers Fail?
- What Is Classification? What Is Third-Generation Classification?
- Focus on Data: Does R/N/R Classification Result in Reduced Recidivism?
- Summary
- Critical Thinking Exercises

In this chapter we begin our exploration of corrections. Interestingly, we use the term corrections and punishment almost interchangeably. We can punish without any goal of correcting the errant behavior; and we can engage in correctional programming without any pain or discomfort to the offender. States typically refer to the "correctional facilities" in their "corrections" system, and we will follow standard terminology when discussing correctional goals, but, clearly, the goal of the system is also punishment. A critical thinking approach to corrections is to, first, step back and examine what it is we think we want to do (what are our goals?) and whether what we are doing in our "correctional system" is effective at meeting those goals. Also in this chapter, we critically examine the research related to prediction in correctional classification.

Punishment is (a) pain or discomfort inflicted (2) because of some wrong committed, (3) determined and administered by a legitimate and credible authority. State-sponsored punishments have been around as long as there have been organized communities. Humans have been incredibly creative in inventing ways to inflict pain on our enemies or those who have broken societal covenants. At various times in history, we have employed punishments that included crucifying, drawing and quartering, boiling in oil, whipping, penal colonies, enslavement, forfeiture of all property, stocks and pillories, banishment, and many others. Most of these earlier forms of punishment are gone now and criminal offenders today face one of the following or a combination of them: fines, probation, jail or prison (followed by parole for some).

WHAT ARE THE GOALS OF CORRECTIONS? WHAT WAS THE "REHABILITATIVE ERA"?

Historically, the goal of punishment was simply **retribution**, which basically means inflicting punishment proportional to the harm caused. However, **deterrence** has also been a goal, including **specific deterrence** (what is done to an individual to deter him or her from future offending) and **general deterrence** (what is done to an individual to discourage others from future offending). **Incapacitation** simply means to render incapable, and in corrections it means to make the offender incapable of committing crime. Also, in more recent eras, we have added the goal of **rehabilitation** (or reform), which means to change the individual in terms of values, attitudes, beliefs, and behaviors. Thus, the four goals of corrections are:

- retribution
- deterrence
- incapacitation
- rehabilitation/reform.

   The earliest eras of correctional history were strictly *retributive*. Very early forms of justice, such as the Code of Hammurabi, detailed specific punishments for specific crimes and employed a harsh system of corporal and capital punishments. Early punishment systems employed a proportional "eye for an eye" (*lex talionis*) form of punishment. In some societies, offenders were ordered to pay compensation, and only when they could not or would not, would corporal punishment be employed. Very serious crimes warranted banishment.

   Deterrence can also be considered a goal of early punishments, especially those which were public in nature. Exhibit 10.1 shows some of the types of public punishments that were used in early American colonies. If the shame of these punishments did not deter future offending, repeat offenders were banished from the colony and/or branded to discourage them from living in other communities. Banishment from the colonies often meant death because it was hard to survive in the wilderness alone without the protection of the community.

Exhibit 10.1   Forms of Public Punishment

Ducking stool: Typically for women charged with being a "common scold" or, sometimes, for those accused of witchcraft. It was a board with a chair on one end, dunked in the river or other body of water.

Branks: Metal headgear, sometimes with a sharp spike that went under the tongue. Used for those accused of blasphemy or "common scolds."

Exhibit 10.1a   Ducking Stool

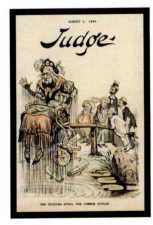

Source: Getty

Exhibit 10.1b   Branks

Source: Alamy

Stocks: The offender's head (and sometimes hands and feet) were secured in this wooden device in the town square. The public would participate by throwing vegetables, jeering, and scolding the offender.

Exhibit 10.1c   Stocks

Source: Getty

Incapacitation is not, strictly speaking, punishment because it does not necessarily involve pain or discomfort. One of the goals of imprisonment is to incapacitate offenders so that they cannot victimize us, at least as long as they are imprisoned. The origins of the penitentiary in this country can be traced to the Walnut Street Jail and the Eastern State Penitentiary in Pennsylvania. We will discuss penitentiaries in greater detail in Chapter 11.

Reform/rehabilitation came into focus as a goal as early as the 1800s. Penitentiaries and reformatories were developed with multiple goals (retribution, deterrence, and incapacitation) that also included reform, hence the name reformatory. There was a clear goal of offender change through religion and good habits formed in the institution. In this country, the **Progressive Movement**, from 1890 through the early 1900s, saw a great deal of activity in the growth of private charities designed to deal with the problems of the poor in Northeastern cities. There was an underlying belief that social problems that existed with a growing urban, immigrant population could be addressed and solved. At the same time, prisons and other institutions (such as orphanages and mental hospitals) were increasingly being used, supplanting earlier responses to crime and other social needs.[1]

Indeterminate sentences and early release based on good behavior was begun as early as the late 1800s, and some historians have called the early 1900s the **reformatory era** because of the increased numbers of reformatories which were aimed at younger and more "reformable" inmates. However, it was after the 1960s when rehabilitation came to the forefront of the correctional mission; the period of the 1960s through 1975 has been called the **rehabilitative era**. It was during this time that many prisons were renamed correctional institutions, and guards were renamed correctional officers. Funding was available for a wide range of prison treatment programs.[2] There also developed a groundswell of support for community alternatives to prison.

Part of this period can also be called the **reintegration era**. The term was coined to discuss the issue of inmates returning to the community and the problems they encountered. Philosophically, the approach adhered to the belief that the community was the best place to deal with most offenders and, if the offender had to be sent away to prison, then it should be for as short a time as possible. After release, the offender has trouble reintegrating into society and, in the reintegrative era, a number of programs were created to help ex-convicts in their re-entry. Some of the popular programs of this era included:

- prerelease programs
- halfway houses to transition back into the community
- work furloughs/release programs

- school-release programs
- service-enriched parole.

This period was also marked by the deinstitutionalization of other groups, such as the mentally ill and juvenile offenders. There was an emphasis on "grassroots development," community empowerment, and a belief that institutions were the least desirable societal response to social deviants.[3] Communities were enticed and encouraged to keep offenders in the community through grants and subsidies that paid counties a per diem for each offender who otherwise would have been sent to prison. Criminal Justice Partnership Acts gave financial incentives to counties to develop programs and partnerships among probation, jail, and other local agencies.

By the beginning of the 1980s, the rehabilitative/reintegration era was over. States were passing determinate sentencing statutes, some states eliminated parole, furloughs and work release programs were being drastically curtailed, and incarceration rates had begun their explosive growth. Probation, which had emerged in the earlier part of the 1900s, continued, of course, but the philosophy shifted to surveillance rather than service. Intensive probation programs originated in the early 1980s as a way to "beef up" this sentencing option and make it more palatable for judges who would otherwise send the offender to prison. The 1980s also saw the emergence of boot camps, created to provide tough incarceration experiences for young adults. Waivers to adult courts for juvenile offenders increased. Mandatory minimum sentence laws for drug offenders were passed in many states and in the federal correctional system; consequently, prison populations surged with drug offenders. In the 1990s, three-strikes sentencing laws became more popular. By the beginning of the new millennium, correctional policy bore only the faintest resemblance to the rehabilitative era of the early 1970s.

There are signs that we have entered into a new correctional era that returns to the emphasis of reform over retribution and alternatives to prison. This shift may be occurring perhaps due to the dramatic decline of crime since the mid-1990s. Another possible reason that there is greater willingness to look for ways to reduce the correctional population may be the crippling economic costs of keeping so many people under correctional supervision. Related to this is the growing awareness of the public that our incarceration rate (the number of residents incarcerated for every 100,000 people) is dramatically higher than any of our peer countries (e.g., Great Britain, France, Canada).[4]

Federal initiatives such as Justice Reinvestment and the Second Chance Act, which will be described in Chapter 12, bear striking similarities to the programs and goals that were present in the rehabilitation/re-entry era. The rollback of mandatory minimums and willingness to use **commutation** (at least on the federal level) are attempts to mitigate the effects of the draconian sentences that were written into sentencing statutes in the 1980s. While many applaud this return to a more reform-minded focus in corrections after 40 years of retribution eclipsing all other goals of correction, others warn that we may be creating the elements necessary for a return to the high crime rates of the mid-1990s. Before we can examine current issues, we need to understand the rationale for correctional programming.

HOW DO THEORIES OF CRIME RELATE TO WHAT WE DO TO CRIMINALS?

It is an interesting reality that in the academic field of criminal justice, criminology (theories of crime) seems to be divorced from corrections (what we do to criminals to induce change). Logically, the two should be very connected; in fact, most of what we do in the area of crime prevention is based explicitly or implicitly on one or more of the theories discussed in Chapter 3. Some people argue for more police and incarceration (deterrence theory), while some argue for more poverty programs and early childhood education (learning theory, general strain and strain/opportunity theory). In corrections, vocational programming and education have support from professionals and the public (strain/opportunity theory).

It seems clear that most theories support the idea of full employment and strengthening the family unit to ensure that all children grow up in stable homes where parents are able to discipline and monitor their behavior through strong, loving attachments. Whether this can ever be accomplished is a difficult question. The answer to why people commit crime and how we can reduce crime, in fact, goes far beyond the criminal justice system unless you believe in solely deterrence as the answer to crime prevention. The criminal justice system is the social control institution that steps in when others (family, church, school) fail. If those institutions could be made stronger, there would be less need for the criminal justice system components, because there would be less crime.

In Exhibit 10.2, many policies and programs that are consistent with the major categories of crime theories are offered. A few points should be emphasized. Some argue against biological theories because, some argue, the policy implication is eugenics or sterilization. That is a false assumption; note the policy implications here recognize that some factors may predispose individuals to criminal choices and offer ways to neutralize the predisposition in the same way that one might neutralize genetic predispositions to medical conditions. Policies based on psychological theories also address individual differences by offering early identification and intervention before criminality is established. Sociological theories address both the individual and society. Some programs are consistent with a number of theories and many programs can be adapted from preventative programs to correctional programs; that is, they can be used in the community or in institutions for correctional clients.

Exhibit 10.2   Crime Theories and Policy Implications

Biological theories: Early intervention in schools for learning disabilities; "healthy start" programs that identify high-risk pregnant women and link them to nurses for pre-natal and post-natal medical assistance and parenting training; lead abatement programs; lunch programs that provide nutritious meals for children for healthy development; comprehensive health care to address childhood disease and medical conditions that might predispose individuals to addiction; comprehensive health care for correctional populations to address chronic and serious issues that may affect ability to work or propensity to addiction; "wrap-around" care for prison and jail releasees that continue needed medications once outside of facility; more comprehensive and accessible mental health care that includes residential and community options.

Psychological theories: Early diagnosis and intervention for antisocial personality disorder; early recognition and assistance to model behavior utilizing pro-social role models rather than antisocial (parenting and Big Brother/Sister programs); changing rewards to encourage pro-social behaviors ("stay in school" awards); foster parent or adoption programs to help high-risk children secure stable and loving home lives; psychological and psychiatric screening for correctional populations to address pre-existing problems, placement of mentally ill in jails and prisons in psychiatric units or diversion to treatment facilities; more comprehensive and accessible mental health care that includes residential and community options; cognitive therapy programs that help correctional clients address "thinking errors" that affect decision making; medically supervised drug treatment.

Sociological theories: Poverty programs that help with employment and housing; "target hardening" programs that reduce criminal opportunity or saturation patrols that would deter criminality because of pervasive police presence; decreasing influence of subcultures such as gangs by arresting gang members or making it easier to refuse gang membership; increasing social efficacy of neighborhoods by providing resources (e.g., parks, community centers, neighborhood associations, and other mechanisms to strengthen social bonds); school programs that encourage stronger ties to school (interest-based after-school groups, tutoring, or truancy programs); parenting programs that help parents teach children self-control (also have such programs in prisons and jails since inmates are likely to be parents); increase perception of procedural justice by teacher and police officer training and programs that encourage fair and respectful interactions between authorities and residents.

WHAT IS PROBATION AND HOW IS IT DIFFERENT FROM PAROLE? HOW IS IT DIFFERENT FROM PRE-TRIAL DIVERSION?

While many of the programs above exist, typically, the way to encourage attendance and participation on the part of criminal offenders is probation. Probation acts as a stick or carrot to encourage the offender to participate in drug treatment, parenting programs, GED programs, or other beneficial services. **Community corrections** refer to any form of correctional alternative that does not involve incarceration in prison. The term includes pre-trial, post-trial, or post-prison supervision. **Probation** is a type of community correction and is basically supervised release in the community. Probation is a Latin word meaning "period of proving" or "trial." Probation is both the sentence and a status. A criminal defendant may receive a sentence of probation, and, once on probation, it becomes a legal status of reduced liberty. Probation may be granted by a judge, jury, or as a result of plea bargaining. Most states have statutes that restrict who can be sentenced to probation. Typically, serious offenders who have committed murder or kidnapping are specifically excluded from receiving a probation sentence. Probation is often confused with parole, but is very different. Typically, an offender is sentenced to probation supervison *instead of* a jail or prison sentence while **parole** always comes after some portion of a prison sentence is served.

Probation, indeed all the forms of diversion, "divert" the offender from the system because of a belief that it is better for the offender and better for the system. It is better for the offender because he or she will suffer less stigma and disruption to work and family. It is better for the system because scarce resources (such as jail and prison beds) can be used for more serious offenders. State statutes set the maximum length of probation. In most states, there is a provision for early discharge. If the probationer has successfully completed a period of supervision and met all requirements, then the probation officer has the discretion to ask the judge to grant an early discharge.

Probation is not the same as **pre-trial diversion programs**, such as deferred adjudication. In Chapter 8 we discussed **pre-trial release** programs, such as release on recognizance (ROR) or court surety programs, which are simply a means by which suspects may avoid having to pay bail before their adjudication. Pre-trial diversion is different in that it takes the place of further prosecution entirely. For instance, a deferred adjudication program, successfully completed, eliminates formal findings of guilt/innocence and sentencing. Probation officers may supervise those who have been placed in **deferred adjudication** or other types of pre-trial diversion in addition to their probationer caseload. This type of diversion requires enabling legislation and usually comprises:

- an evaluation of eligibility by pre-trial services staff (looking at crime, prior record, drug history, employment, residential stability, evidence of mental illness, etc.)
- a contract that clarifies exactly what the defendant must do for successful completion
- a mechanism by which the defendant's case is disposed of, usually through a court order that disposes of the case without a conviction

Pre-trial diversion such as deferred adjudication comes before any finding of guilt. Offenders who successfully complete a deferred adjudication program may honestly say they have never been convicted of a crime, because they haven't. In contrast, probationers have been convicted and are serving their sentence. Despite these very different legal statuses, the supervision experience and the conditions attached may look quite similar.

WHAT IS THE HISTORY OF PROBATION?

There have always been some forms of diversion from harsh punishment. For instance, descriptions of The Bay of Sanctuary in Hawaiian society indicate that those accused of crimes could escape punishment by swimming across and remaining on the other side of the bay. In early Europe, the "**benefit of clergy**" was provided to those who could prove they were members of the clergy. Individuals who were facing trial and punishment in secular courts could have their cases dismissed with the expectation that ecclesiastical courts would take over and punish the clergy member. However, as time went on, the benefit became available to anyone who could read Psalm 54. It became, in effect, a type of diversion for those who, for whatever reason, the court chose to give the benefit of clergy.

The standard history of probation begins with the work of John Augustus. He was a Boston bootmaker who was in court one day in 1841 and decided to intervene in the case of a drunk who was being sent to jail. A strong believer in the temperance movement, he decided to post bail for the man, who was charged with being a common drunk. Augustus asked the judge to defer sentencing for three weeks and release the man into his custody because he thought that he could help the man get his life in order. For the next eighteen years, from 1841 until his death in 1859, he bailed out more than 1,800 adults and children. He selected carefully and only chose first-time offenders. Once released, he helped them find employment or a place to live and reported their progress to the court. Most of the offenders released into his custody were charged with violations of vice or temperance laws.[5] His work continued and spread after he died and, in 1878, Massachusetts hired its first probation officer. In 1901, New York passed a statute authorizing probation for adults. Volunteers or police officers supervised probationers. Early probation officers were usually retired sheriffs and policemen who worked directly for the judge. In 1925, the federal government created an enabling statute for federal probation. There was a very slow increase in the number of federal probation officers, with only 62 officers in 1931. It was not until 1956 that all states had enabling legislation that allowed for probation sentences to be handed out by judges.[6]

Probation suffered the same fate as all "rehabilitative" programs in the 1980s, when politics and public sentiment moved toward a more punitive approach with offenders. Although probation never went away, the major innovation in these decades was intensive supervision, which involved more intensive supervision, not necessarily more intense programming. The number of people sentenced to probation instead of prison declined over time.

Probation has developed most often as a combined model of state and local influence. Most commonly, state executive agencies provide hiring and procedural standards but probation officers are county employees and the progress reports and violation reports they write on probationers are submitted to a local judge. Counties vary in their ability to fund probation and so there may be wide disparities in the quality of supervision. Centralized systems can standardize budgets and provide consistency in employees and procedures. Legislation can provide incentives to counties to keep offenders in the community by funding local sentences (jail or probation instead of prison).[7]

WHAT ARE SOME TYPICAL CONDITIONS FOR A PROBATIONER?

Conditions are almost always attached to probation and include general conditions that apply to everyone. Standard or general conditions include reporting requirements and prohibitions against associating with known criminals. Exhibit 10.3 displays some general conditions.

Special conditions are directed to particular offenders because of their crime or because of their personal issues. Conditions may include participation in a particular type of supervision (e.g., electronic monitoring), a particular program (e.g., drug addiction therapy), or some form of restitution (e.g., paying back the victim). Many of the programs displayed in Exhibit 10.4 are used with both pre-trial diversion clients and probationers. These programs may also become **intermediate sanctions**, because they sometimes are added to a regular

---

Exhibit 10.3   *Standard Conditions of Probation*

- Obey all laws.
- Do not possess firearms.
- Report as directed to probation officer.
- Permit home visits and searches.
- Avoid alcohol and illegal drug use.
- Maintain suitable employment.
- Notify address changes.
- Do not associate with known criminals.
- Pay all fines and fees.

---

probation sentence if the probationer receives a violation report, serving as a "mid-way" punishment to revocation. Recall from Chapter 9 that there is growing concern that conditions related to paying fees and fines are keeping large numbers of people on probation who are otherwise law-abiding.

Recidivism is the term we use to describe when an offender fails to remain law-abiding. It is the measure of success in probation and parole and any correctional program; ideally we want to reduce the rate of recidivism. There are different ways to measure recidivism. It can be either or a combination of the following: re-arrest, reconviction, or revocation. Re-arrest or revocation for **technical violations** result in the largest recidivism rates (since offenders on some form of correctional supervision may be more likely to be arrested even if charges are later dropped). Reconviction and return to prison on a new sentence as measures of recidivism result in smaller recidivism rates.

About 65 percent of all probationers successfully complete their probation and are discharged from probation. The rest have their probation revoked and are sent to prison (16 percent), continue with new conditions, abscond (which means they leave supervision and cannot be located) (3 percent), are revoked without incarceration, or have unspecified reasons, such as death, for leaving probation supervision.[8]

Other conditions besides those briefly described in Exhibit 10.3 include getting tested for drug use, attending therapy, going back to school, writing a letter of apology, and many others. As long as the condition is reasonably related to the goal of rehabilitation and is not violative of the 8th Amendment by being a cruel and unusual punishment, the judge has wide discretion in what conditions to apply. Only judges can impose conditions, and only judges can drop or change conditions. Probation officers file violation reports with the court when the probationer is not compliant.

Exhibit 10.4 Probation and/or Pre-trial Diversion Programs

Day Reporting Centers

Probationers or pre-trial releasees may be required to "check in" to day reporting centers as a condition of their supervision. These centers offer both supervision and services; usually an array of job counseling and placement, educational, and social services are accessed at the sites. The center may be publicly or privately operated, and provide services to probationers and/or pre-trial diversion clients. In a survey of 54 centers, Parent found that centers reported an average "negative termination" rate of about 50 percent; however, the range was from 14 percent to 86 percent. Negative termination included rule violations as well as new arrests. Because the studies show such a range of outcomes, it is difficult to make generalizations about the effectiveness of such centers.[9]

Electronic Monitoring

Electronic monitoring (EM) emerged in the mid-1980s as a supplement to traditional probation or parole supervision, or house arrest. Electronic monitoring basically uses an electronic device strapped to the ankle or wrist of the offender. The monitor operates in such a way that an alarm sounds when the offender is too far away from a transmitting detector, often located in the offender's telephone. The program can be set up so that the offender can travel from home to work and back again, but an alarm sounds if he or she is not home by a certain time. Such programs always cost less than prison or jail; however, cost savings are moderated by the fact that judges may be more likely to give longer community supervision sentences than jail sentences. Further, such cost comparisons typically do not include treatment services that seem to be an essential part of any community sanction. Even accounting for these factors, however, researchers have found that EM programs offer significant savings over incarceration. The research on EM is mixed with some studies finding no difference in recidivism, some studies finding EM programs had higher recidivism, and other studies finding lower recidivism between program participants and those supervised in regular caseloads. The new generation of EM employs global positioning to not only monitor whether an offender returns home when he or she is supposed to, but also to track the offender's movements throughout the day. The extra cost of GPS monitoring may be justified if the alternative is a prison sentence, but not if the alternative would be regular supervision in a diversion program or a regular probation sentence.[10]

Restitution

Restitution is an order by the court that requires the offender to compensate the victim for the injury or the loss suffered in the crime. In 1984, the Victims of Crime Assistance Act and the Federal Comprehensive Crime Control Act ordered courts to consider restitution to victims as part of a criminal sentence. States followed with their own state legislation, enabling judges to set restitution amounts as part of a criminal sentence. Today, every state has enabling legislation and 29 states mandate restitution unless there are compelling reasons not to do so. **Victim-centered restitution** includes the victim in the determination of the amount to be compensated. The offender either pays the victim directly or through the court, but there is a direct link between the offender and his or her victim. In other forms of restitution programs, the victims are not involved in the process and/or the money is paid to a state victim compensation or restitution fund. This form of restitution may be considered not much more meaningful than a fine. It certainly does not encourage the offender to think about the victim. One study found that restitution orders were more commonly imposed on female offenders, property offenders, those with no prior record, and White offenders. Studies indicate that restitution orders are difficult to enforce. One study indicated that only about one-third of the total restitution ordered in a Chicago court was ever paid over a three-year period. Enforcement practices such as registered letters or telephone solicitations threatening adverse action raised the percentage of compliance substantially, as did declaring "amnesty days," where accrued interest would be deducted from the amount owed.[11]

Fines or Day Fines

Criminal fines may be set by statute, case law, or office policy but, in general, are proportional to the seriousness of the crime. Usually, fines may be used to punish property crimes and public order crimes, but not violent crimes, which are considered too serious. In Europe, even violent crimes are likely to be resolved through the use of fines. The trouble with set fines is that any amount is experienced quite differently depending on one's economic situation. Therefore, **day fines** are common in Europe and are also used in some jurisdictions in the United States. Day fines are set by the amount of income the offender has—that is, if the offender is making minimum wage, his daily earnings would be about $42; therefore, a fine of ten days would be about $420. However, a professional may earn $416 a day and his fine would be $4,160. The theory is that each amount would be experienced in the same way by the two offenders. Day fine schedules sometimes also take into account number of dependents. In a U.S. Department of Justice study of day fines, it was found that collection was sometimes a problem, but most professionals working in the criminal justice system liked the concept.[12]

Community Service

Community service might be considered symbolic restitution. It can also be used in place of a fine, especially for those who have no financial resources to pay any type of fine, even a day fine, because they have no income. Restorative service programs attempt to connect the offender to the victim through some process of recognizing the harm and injury done to the specific victim and arriving at an agreement between the offender and the victim as to the appropriate action. For instance, the offender may repair the damage he caused or provide some other type of service to the victim. More often, the service is to a class of victims rather than the offender's specific victim, but it is still meaningful and related to the offense. For instance, an offender who committed fraud against an elderly victim may provide volunteer services to a nursing home. A doctor who committed Medicare fraud may be required to serve in a free or low-cost health clinic. A college student who pleads guilty to DWI may be required to assist in a high-school alcohol awareness program. Punitive service may not be linked to the victim at all, nor have any relationship to the crime. For instance, washing police cars, picking up trash on the side of the road, and clearing vacant lots for the city are examples of community service orders, but they hold little meaning for the offender other than deterrence. Some of the issues that have been discussed in relation to community service as a sanction include: charging poor offenders for being in the program, whether offenders are appropriately placed in some non-profit organizations with vulnerable populations, liability if the offender is injured or if the offender injures someone else, and whether the offender can reasonably meet the hours required if they also have a job.

Scarlet Letter Conditions

Sometimes judges create "**Scarlet Letter**" conditions designed to humiliate or call attention to the wrongdoing of the offender. Some argue that these types of conditions subject the offender and his or her family to needless humiliation; others argue that the tailored conditions mean more than standard punishments. Some of the more unusual conditions include requiring sex offenders to post signs in their front yard warning people away, requiring DWI felons to put bumper stickers on their car identifying themselves as drunk drivers, requiring an individual to seek the forgiveness of his church, and so on.[13]

As mentioned in the last chapter, many states have instituted fees for probation and payment of these fees is added as a condition to the probation sentence. Probationers are charged anywhere from $10 to $40 per month to be on probation and may also have to pay for drug testing, therapy, or electronic monitoring. These fees can be onerous requirements for low-income probationers and often non-payment is the only thing that prevents the probationer from being released early from supervision after a number of successful years of compliance.

WHAT IS THE PROFILE OF OFFENDERS UNDER CORRECTIONAL SUPERVISION?

In 1980, there were 1,842,100 individuals under some form of correctional supervision (probation, jail, prison, or parole). In 2014 (the most recent year statistics are available for) there were about six time more people under

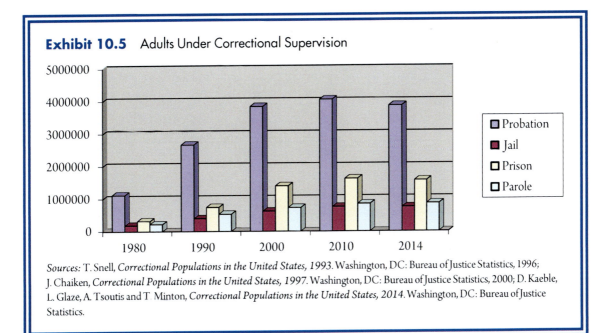

Exhibit 10.5   Adults Under Correctional Supervision

Sources: T. Snell, *Correctional Populations in the United States, 1993.* Washington, DC: Bureau of Justice Statistics, 1996; J. Chaiken, *Correctional Populations in the United States, 1997.* Washington, DC: Bureau of Justice Statistics, 2000; D. Kaeble, L. Glaze, A. Tsoutis and T. Minton, *Correctional Populations in the United States, 2014.* Washington, DC: Bureau of Justice Statistics.

supervision (6,851,000) than there were in 1980.[14] The number under supervision has actually declined in recent years. For instance, in 2009 the total number under correctional supervision was 7,225,800 individuals.[15]

Of course, the national population has increased as well, but even the rate per 100,000, which holds the population constant, shows that the likelihood of correctional supervision has increased in dramatic ways. In 1980, the rate for *any form* of correctional supervision was 1,132 per 100,000. By 1990, that rate had doubled to 2,348 per 100,000, and by 2000, it had increased again to 3,072 per 100,000. Then it began to decline and in 2010, 3,000 citizens of every 100,000 were under some form of correctional supervision, and in 2014 it declined again to 2,780 per 100,000. About 1 in every 32 adults was either in prison or under some other form of correctional control in 2009; but by 2014, the number of adults under correctional supervision had dropped to 1 in every 52 adults.[16]

Of those on correctional supervision, at year end 2014, about 3,864,100 people were on probation, a slight decrease from the year before. Although the population on probation has declined for the last seven years, it is still by far the largest population of the four correctional populations (probation, parole, jail, prison). The Bureau of Justice Statistics reports that in 2006 (the last year for which data is available) only about 27 percent of felony offenders who are

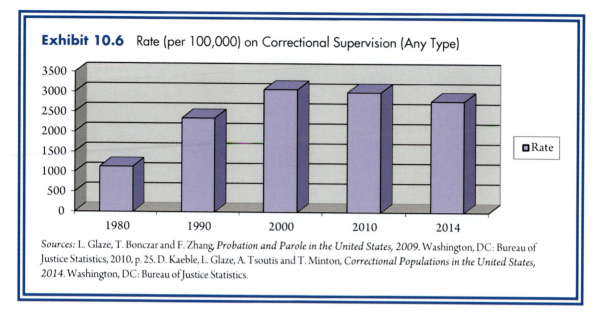

Exhibit 10.6   Rate (per 100,000) on Correctional Supervision (Any Type)

Sources: L. Glaze, T. Bonczar and F. Zhang, *Probation and Parole in the United States, 2009.* Washington, DC: Bureau of Justice Statistics, 2010, p. 25. D. Kaeble, L. Glaze, A. Tsoutis and T. Minton, *Correctional Populations in the United States, 2014.* Washington, DC: Bureau of Justice Statistics.

convicted receive probation, and 69 percent receive either a sentence of prison or jail. The reason there are so many more people on probation than in jail or prison is that the probation sentence tends to be longer. For those who do receive probation, the average sentence is about three years.[17] Even though probation receives less than 10 percent of state and local government expenditures, it deals with almost 60 percent of all offenders.[18]

The number of people on probation varies tremendously from state to state, as does the rate per population. For instance, in 2014, Texas had 388,101 probationers, but North Dakota only had 5,585. Of course, the two states' populations are very different, but even rates, which standardize by population, show extreme variations. For instance, while the state of New Hampshire has a probation supervision rate of 368 (per 100,000), Georgia has a supervision rate of 6,161 (per 100,000). This means that seventeen times more Georgia residents are on probation than New Hampshire residents. The average rate for the United States as a whole was 1,568 in 2014.[19] According to the Bureau of Justice Statistics, in 2014:

- About 25 percent of probationers were women.
- About 54 percent of probationers were White, 30 percent were Black, and 13 percent were Hispanic.
- About 56 percent are on probation for felony sentences (and the rest for misdemeanors).

- About 25 percent were drug offenders, 28 percent were property offenders, 19 percent were violent offenders, 16 percent were public order offenders, with 11 percent recorded as "other".[20]

DO WOMEN ON PROBATION HAVE DIFFERENT BACKGROUNDS AND NEEDS THAN MEN; IF SO, WHAT ARE THEY?

Research indicates that women are less likely to reoffend than men.[21] Women, many researchers argue, follow different pathways to crime and they require **gender-specific programming**, which matches prison and community correctional programs to women's specific needs and pathways to crime. These researchers and practitioners argue that women and men are different, and that, typically, corrections systems ignore their differences or do not respond to the differences in an appropriate way. The following are some of the differences noted between male and female offenders:

- Women are more likely to be primary caregivers of young children.
- They are more likely to have experienced childhood physical and/or sexual abuse.
- They are more likely to report physical and sexual abuse victimization as adults.
- They are more likely to have drug dependency issues.
- They are less likely to be convicted of a violent crime.
- They are less likely to have any stable work history.
- They are more likely to indicate psychosocial problems.
- They are more likely to have an incarcerated parent.
- They are more likely to come from a single-parent household.
- They are more likely to suffer from serious health problems, including HIV/AIDS.[22]

Prior victimization (both physical and sexual) sets women apart from their male counterparts. While both male and female offenders are more likely than the general population to have been abused as children, women are more likely to experience abuse continuing into adulthood. Researchers argue that these experiences of victimization contribute to the multiple problems female offenders have in adulthood, including an inability to cope with stress, suicide, abuse of alcohol and drugs, sensation-seeking and antisocial traits, lower levels of self-esteem, and the lack of a sense of control. Research also shows that gender *and* race/ethnicity create different life experiences so that it is not just enough to consider one or the other when understanding life events that lead to criminal choices.[23]

Risk factors for recidivism for women are probably similar to those for men; for instance, researchers find the following factors are associated with recidivism:

- marital status
- suicide attempts
- family structure of childhood home
- childhood abuse, depression, and substance abuse
- single parenting and reliance on public assistance
- dysfunctional relationships
- victimization.

However, the special needs of women also affect recidivism and may include childcare, victimization trauma counseling, self-esteem counseling, financial assistance, health care, and mental health care. Research shows that programs generally are not gender-specific in that they do not address women's unique issues.[24] One major difference between female and male offenders is their relationship with children. Female offenders are more likely to be custodial parents, and the financial and emotional strain of raising young children has an impact on their ability to stay crime- or drug-free while on some form of community correction status.

There have also been laws passed that have complicated the potential for success. The Personal Responsibility and Work Opportunity Reconciliation Act (PRWORA) of 1996 replaced Aid to Families with Dependent Children (AFDC) with a state block grant system that made it more difficult for single women as heads of households to receive state aid. Another section of the same Act created a lifetime ban on providing any federal assistance to those who were convicted of a state or a federal felony offense involving the use or sale of drugs. This draconian law affects only drug offenders, not those convicted of murder, robbery, or any violent crime. States may opt out of the program, but to do so means losing federal funding.

Barbara Bloom and Barbara Owen, as well as others, have recommended that decision makers approach the issue of correctional supervision for female offenders with the following objectives:

- Enhance supervision and treatment.
- Validate assessment instruments on female samples.
- Use single-gender caseloads.
- Create policies and practices that acknowledge female offenders' special relationships with children, families, and significant others.

- Create policies and practices that provide culturally relevant services and supervision to address substance abuse, trauma, and mental health.
- Provide services appropriate to women's socio-economic status.
- Promote partnerships with other social service agencies.[25]

HOW MANY DRUG OFFENDERS ARE UNDER CORRECTIONAL SUPERVISION? WHAT ARE THEIR ISSUES?

The incredible rise in correctional populations has been fueled to a large degree by enforcement patterns against drug offenders. Most research indicates that the drug–crime connection goes beyond simply arresting for drug offenses. Drug use and criminality are correlated. One source of data on drugs and criminality is the Arrestee Drug Monitoring Program (ADAM II). This federal survey obtains urine samples and interviews all arrestees on their drug use in a few sample jurisdictions. In these jurisdiction, the proportion of arrestees testing positive for any of the ten drugs tested for ranged from 63 percent to 83 percent. Marijuana remained the most commonly detected drug in urine testing and cocaine use continues to decline. There was a significant increase from 2000 to 2013 in the percentage of arrestees testing positive for opiates (about 8 percent), and an increase in some sites in the use of methamphetamines. Other findings included that arrestees were likely to be unemployed, with drug users significantly less likely to be working (43 percent percent to 69 percent) Only one-quarter or fewer of the arrestees had ever participated in any outpatient drug or alcohol treatment and less than 30 percent had ever participated in any inpatient drug or alcohol treatment.[26] It is important to note the issues with this type of methodology. Since arrestees are being sampled, findings are influenced by the enforcement pattern of local police, e.g., if there is a crackdown on methamphetamine markets, then the arrestees will no doubt show higher use figures than in other locales.

According to SAMHSA's National Survey on Drug Use and Health (NSDUH), approximately 23.1 million Americans aged twelve or older needed treatment for an alcohol or illicit drug problem in 2010, yet only 2.6 million received treatment that year.[27] Other research shows that a much higher percentage of those under correctional supervision have drug dependency or abuse issues. About 68 percent of jail inmates reported symptoms consistent with alcohol and/or drug use disorders in one study.[28] In U.S. Department of Justice and SAMHSA surveys, 35 percent of parolees and 40 percent of probationers had drug or alcohol dependence or abuse "in the past year."[29] Another study indicated that 53 percent of state prisoners and 46 percent of federal prisoners in the year prior to their arrest met the DSM-V criteria for substance dependence or abuse. Sixty percent of women in state prison have been estimated to be dependent on or abusing drugs.[30] These percentages seem very high because they are using self-reports from inmates; however, even formally diagnosed drug dependency figures are several times higher in correctional populations than in the general population.

WHAT ARE SOME CURRENT ISSUES OF PROBATION SUPERVISION?

Probation encompasses two major functions: pre-sentence investigations/recommendations and probation supervision. In larger jurisdictions, these functions are separated and assigned to different offices or divisions within the agency. In smaller jurisdictions, the same officer may perform both functions.

The pre-sentence function includes gathering information about offenders before sentencing. This begins with an interview with the offender, often in jail, if the offender is detained. The offender answers a series of questions relating to their past and current situation and then the officer checks the facts. The probation officer writes up the finding and makes a sentencing recommendation to the court. Information in a pre-sentence report (PSR) may include: risk (typically through a scoring instrument), circumstances (work, family, education), what options are available, and a recommendation. About half of all states require a pre-sentence investigation in all felony cases. Another sixteen states define the investigations as discretionary. In only two states are pre-sentence investigations required prior to misdemeanor sentencing.[31]

One of the legal issues that occurs with PSRs is confidentiality. In an early case, the Supreme Court held that information in the PSR could not be kept from the offender if he or she had been sentenced to death. Due process required that the offender be able to know the information in the report in order to contest it as inaccurate or misleading.[32] So far, however, the Court has refused to extend this reasoning to any sentence other than death; thus, whether the report is available to the defense is based on the law and procedural rules of the jurisdiction. The Federal Rules of Criminal Procedure, for instance, require that the PSR be made available to the defendant unless it might "disrupt rehabilitation," when the information was obtained with a promise of confidentiality, or when harm may result to any person because of the disclosure.[33]

The probation officer is not legally liable for any harm that comes from the sentencing recommendation because it is considered a quasi-judicial function. Thus, he or she is able to recommend probation without fear of being sued if the offender subsequently commits a crime, much in the same way that judicial immunity operates. Furthermore, the defendant cannot sue the probation officer (or court service officer) who prepares the pre-sentence report for mistakes or false information. It should be noted that this type of immunity only applies to the quasi-judicial functions of the position (decisions related to sentencing recommendations); however, how the probation officer conducts supervision can be the basis for a lawsuit. For instance, a probationer may sue under Section 1983 for alleged violations of constitutional rights by the probation officer, or third parties may sue under some cause of action such as wrongful death if the officer's gross negligence in supervision resulted in the death of someone at the hands of the probationer. These cases are rare, however, because the standard of negligence is set fairly high.

In addition to conducting pre-sentence investigations and writing pre-sentence reports for the sentencing judge, the other major function of probation is supervision of probationers. Probation has followed a casework approach

Exhibit 10.7   Probation officers often check on probationers by conducting monthly visits to their homes or workplaces or, as in this photo, at a sober living facility.

Source: Getty

to service delivery. The **casework model** is typical of social work and involves the professional interacting with each "client" individually, serving as the primary and, sometimes, only service provider. Most often, probation supervision involves a contact once a month when the probationer comes into the probation office to see the officer and fill out a report, and a "field contact" once a month, where the officer meets the offender in his or her own home or workplace.

In these contacts, the officer checks to see if conditions are being met, whether the offender is still employed, and whether court costs are being paid. Offenders may also be required to submit to urine analysis and the probation officer monitors those test results as well. Probation officers also make "collateral contacts," which are meetings with family members, neighbors, and employers to gather more information about the probationer. Using information obtained from these contacts, the officer periodically writes a progress report to the sentencing judge.

One issue that has arisen concerns the power of the probation officer to search. Typically, to search a home, a government agent must have a warrant that specifies with clarity what is being sought. Part of the probation order always requires the probationer to submit to periodic searches of one's home and/or person by the probation officer. This intrusion would never be justified toward a free person, but probationers do not have all the rights of free people. Courts have generally upheld the right of the probation officer to search without a warrant.[34]

To visit a webpage for probation professionals, go to http://www.appa-net.org/

WHAT IS REVOCATION? HOW MANY PROBATIONERS FAIL?

Sometimes the probationer violates one or more conditions; for instance, by not paying restitution and court costs, having a dirty urine test, or not attending drug treatment. The probation officer may work with the offender to resolve the issue, but sometimes even these technical violations (violations of rules rather than new crimes) may result in a violation report, written by the probation officer and sent to the sentencing judge. If the probation officer learns that the probationer has been arrested for a new crime a violation report is usually always filed. The prosecutor's office may file a "motion to revoke probation" and a revocation hearing is held. The judge decides whether to continue on probation, continue on probation but with modified conditions (i.e., imposing curfew, treatment, intermediate sanction, more conditions), or revoke probation and send the person to jail or prison.

Depending on the state, the time spent on probation may not be counted at all toward the completion of the sentence. In this case, an offender may have already served four years on a probation sentence, but upon revocation must serve the original five-year prison sentence with no credit for time served on probation. In some states, the judge has the discretion to consider time served or not.

The probationer deserves some due process before being deprived of probation. In one Supreme Court case about 50 years ago, the Court ruled that the state of Washington must provide an attorney before revoking probation because the state used **deferred sentencing** where the possible prison sentence is not established. Therefore, the revocation hearing becomes a sentencing hearing which requires a 6th Amendment right to counsel.[35] States now use **suspended sentences**, in which the judge actually hands down a prison sentence, but then suspends it, pending successful completion of probation. If probation is revoked, the suspended sentence would be imposed. The revocation hearing in this instance is more like an administrative hearing, not a sentencing hearing. This means that there is no 6th Amendment right to counsel, but due process still applies. The rights of a probationer before his or her probation is revoked include: the notice of alleged violations of probation and evidence, an opportunity to appear and to present evidence and witnesses, the right to confront adverse witnesses, a neutral decision maker, a written report, and a *conditional* right to counsel when there is a question of guilt or innocence or the individual is not likely to understand the proceedings.[36]

In 1986, 74 percent of probationers successfully completed their term. In 1992, 67 percent were successful, but by 1998, only 50 percent successfully completed probation. In 2008, about 48 percent of probationers were successfully discharged (but for almost one-quarter of discharges the information was unknown).[37] One study found that most probationers failed within the first three months of probation and they failed because of technical violations, not new crimes.

In this study, it was found that Michigan probationers were likely to fail because of such violations as:

- failed drug tests
- failure to attend or successfully complete programming
- failure to perform community service.[38]

There are obvious factors that influence whether offenders will succeed on probation or commit a new crime. If they have no job, no money, no place to live, and continue to associate with criminals, it seems fairly predictable that

Exhibit 10.8   Failed drug tests are among the most common causes of failed probation

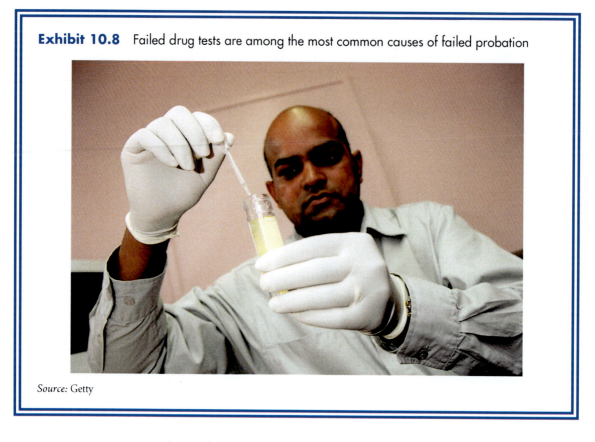

Source: Getty

they will reoffend. Joan Petersilia identified the following factors as associated with recidivism:

- type of crime (burglary and property crime have higher rates)
- extent of prior record
- income at arrest (high unemployment is associated with high recidivism)
- household composition (those who live with spouse and children have lower recidivism)
- age (younger offenders have higher recidivism rates)
- drug use (drug users have higher recidivism rates)
- program participation.[39]

Another study reviewed the findings of prior research to conclude that the following factors may be related to failure:

- sex (women are less likely to recidivate)
- age (mixed findings; older offenders are more likely to be arrested for serious felonies, but in general, younger offenders more likely to reoffend)
- race (mixed findings)

- education (higher levels are associated with success)
- marital status (mixed, but most find marriage is related to success)
- employment (associated with success on probation)
- prior criminal history (associated with failure, especially property offenders).[40]

Intensive supervision programs, popularized in the 1980s, were supposed to reduce recidivism, but the results of evaluations were mixed and, after many evaluations across the country, evaluators concluded that there was little difference in the outcomes between these programs and regular probation.[41]

On the other hand, there are some encouraging recent findings that indicate probation recidivism rates can be lowered. Hawaii began a probation program in 2004 called Hawaii's Opportunity Probation with Enforcement (H.O.P.E.). The program involved rapid and frequent "warning" hearings with judges when probationers were in danger of having violation reports written, and random, frequent, and unannounced drug tests. In the program, judges used short jail sentences as punishment for violations in place of revocation and prison in many instances where offenders failed. There was also drug treatment and mental health counseling for probationers who needed the services. An evaluation of the program showed that H.O.P.E. probationers spent about the same number of days in jail as a control group but in shorter and more frequent time periods. The most encouraging finding, however, was that the recidivism rate for program participants was half that of other probationers in the one-year time period of the study (7 percent compared to 15 percent), and the percentage of H.O.P.E. participants who tested positive for drugs was less than one-third of other probationers (13 percent compared to 46 percent). Finally, program participants were half as likely to be re-arrested (21 percent compared to 47 percent).[42]

WHAT IS CLASSIFICATION? WHAT IS THIRD-GENERATION CLASSIFICATION?

Among the most important activities of correctional professionals are classification and risk assessment. We want to know which offenders are more likely to reoffend, especially by committing violent crime. Once an offender has been sentenced, "client assessment" is concerned with two basic elements: risk (of committing future crimes) and need (personal deficiencies or needs of the offender).

The difficulty inherent in any type of prediction device is the high number of **false positives** (errors involving predictions of recidivism that do not occur). There are likely many more false positives than **false negatives** (errors failing to predict recidivism that does occur), because program staff are more inclined to err on the side of caution. The level of risk willing to be taken determines the cutoff scores that are used for classification purposes. If you are worried about making false positives, then you will lower the cutoff score for high-risk offenders and assign more offenders to high-risk categories. This may make sense if one is dealing with violent offenders and makes no sense at all if one is dealing with low-level minor offenders because the cost would be greater to provide supervision than to accept a higher level of risk.[43]

Prediction/assessment may be clinical, actuarial, or a combination of the two. The **clinical approach** is when psychologists or psychiatrists employ interviews, social histories, and psychological tests to make predictions on future offending. The **actuarial approach** uses patterns of behavior and predicts risk based on prior behavior of those with similar characteristics. For instance, the U.S. Parole Commission developed the Salient Factor Score. This instrument classified parolees (although it could presumably be used for probationers as well) into high, medium, and low levels of risk of reoffending based on the following factors:

- prior convictions/adjudications
- prior commitment(s) greater than thirty days
- age at current offense
- commitments during past three years
- status on probation/parole
- correctional escape
- heroin/opiate dependence.[44]

In general, actuarial approaches are better predictors of recidivism than are clinical assessments. For instance, in one study of 2,850 probationers, the best predictors were found to be stability of employment, marital status, and number of past convictions.[45] Similarly, another study of 266 felony probationers found that the best predictors of recidivism were gender, employment, and prior record.[46] A study that compared the two approaches' ability to predict recidivism among sex offenders showed that the actuarial approach outperformed clinical assessments by a wide margin.[47]

As long ago as 1960, the federal probation system assigned probationers to supervision levels based on crime and risk level. Most were assigned a medium classification level and they were supervised in fifty-person caseloads. Those who posed a minimal risk to the public were placed in caseloads of 70 to 130 cases. However, those who had higher-risk level scores were placed in intensive caseloads of only twenty offenders per officer. This form of classification continues today, and probationers generally are classified as high to low risk and this classification determines the level of supervision. Typically, a probation officer has a general or a specialized caseload and may supervise anywhere from twenty-five (in intensive or specialized caseloads) to more than 100 offenders, with the average at about 130.[48] The number of contacts made each month with probationers depends on their classification level. While intensive supervision probationers might be seen as often as nine times a month with three field contacts, regular probationers may only be seen once, and those on a "mail in" status never see a probation officer—they just mail in or call in their report.

The so-called **third-generation classification** combines the clinical and actuarial approaches. This classification uses risk measures that are stable and don't change (e.g., demographic, file, and historical information). The classification also includes dynamic, changeable items (i.e., personality tests and clinical interviews). The types of information collected include physical health, vocational/financial situation, education, family and social relationships, residence and neighborhood, alcohol use, drug abuse, mental health, attitude, and past and current criminal behavior. This approach tracks changes in the offender during the course of the supervision period because education, mental health, attitude, and drug use will change over time, affecting the offender's risk level (likelihood of reoffending). There are several instruments that are considered "third generation," including the Wisconsin Risk and Needs Assessment Instrument, the Community Risk-Needs Management Scale, and the Level of Service Inventory-Revised (LSI-R).

The LSI-R is a fifty-four risk–need assessment instrument that captures both static and dynamic risk factors. The theoretical base of the LSI-R comes from the work of Don Andrews, James Bonta, Paul Gendreau, and others (sometimes referred to as the "Canadian school" of correctional intervention) and it is largely a social learning approach. Risk factors for criminality in this approach include antisocial attitudes, family functioning, and association with criminal peers.[49] It could also be called the "Cincinnati School" approach since the major applications and tests of the LSI-R have come from professors and students from the University of Cincinnati's School of Criminal Justice. This instrument has enjoyed widespread use that includes an approach toward treatment programming as well called Risk/Needs/Responsivity (R/N/R).

FOCUS ON DATA: DOES R/N/R CLASSIFICATION ACCURATELY PREDICT RECIDIVISM?

There has been a great deal of research on the LSI-R and the R/N/R model that evaluated how well it successfully predicts probationer (or parolee) risk and whether the R/N/R principles are accurate and effective. To reiterate the R/N/R model: the acronym stands for Risk/Need/Response. The *Risk Principle* identifies factors associated with recidivism. Classification for risk includes both static factors that do not change over the life span (e.g., age at first arrest) and dynamic factors that should be re-examined periodically (e.g., unemployment). The *Need Principle* emphasizes targeting only criminogenic needs—those dynamic factors that have been correlated with reoffending (see Exhibit 10.6). Research indicates that responding to criminogenic needs can lower recidivism. Proponents argue that childhood victimization may cause crime, but it does so through the "Big Four" (criminal history, criminal thinking, personality attributes, and criminal peers) and it is these need factors that should be addressed in correctional programming. The *Responsivity Principle* highlights targeting treatment to criminogenic needs and the problem of barriers to treatment. General responsivity refers to the most effective techniques of change which have been shown by research to be behavioral and cognitive-behavioral techniques. Specific responsivity refers to variations among offenders in how they respond. Proponents emphasize the importance of addressing learning styles, reading abilities, cognitive impairments, and motivation when designing supervision and service strategies. The presence of a mental illness, for example, may prevent the offender from engaging fully in a cognitive-behavioral program.[50]

Criticism of the LSI-R

While the LSI-R has been used in numerous states and with tens of thousands of offenders,[51] critics note that the assessment instrument ignores other factors that may affect recidivism. The conclusion that only "criminogenic" needs should be addressed has been criticized as inhumane and unjust. Critics especially target the absence of any recognition of economic need factors, e.g. job skills or unemployment assistance, although these have been added in later revisions of the R/N/R model. Interestingly, more recently, proponents of the R/N/R model mention these factors in the context of Responsivity; specifically that issues such as housing stability and employment can affect the offender's readiness for change.[52] Others have questioned why the model does not address the issue of motivation since there is a growing literature in the area of why and when offenders are motivated to change.[53]

Researchers have found the instrument and approach to be effective across settings (probation, parole, and prisons and jails) and offender populations (including individuals of diverse age, race/ethnicity, and gender) in predicting risk.[54] However, almost all research on the LSI-R and R/N/R has been by those associated with it. Very little independent research exists.

The R/N/R approach then targets treatment and supervision services to address criminogenic risk and need. Interventions are designed to improve

Exhibit 10.9   Need Factors

1. Presence of Antisocial Behavior—early and persistent negative behaviors.
2. Antisocial Personality—adventurous, pleasure-seeking, weak self-control, restlessly aggressive.
3. Antisocial Cognition Attitudes—values, beliefs, and rationalizations supportive of crime; displays of anger, resentment, and defiance; negative attitudes toward the law and justice systems.
4. Antisocial Associates—association with criminals rather than law-abiding individuals.
5. Family and/or Marital—poor relationship quality with little mutual caring or respect; poor nurturance and caring for children.
6. School and/or Work—poor interpersonal relationships within school or work setting; low levels of performance.
7. Leisure and/or Recreation—low levels of involvement and satisfactions in prosocial activities.
8. Substance Abuse—abuse of alcohol and/or other drugs—tobacco excluded.

Source: Adapted from D.A. Andrews, J. Bonta, and R.D. Hoge, "Classification for effective rehabilitation: Rediscovering psychology." *Criminal Justice and Behavior* 17 (1) (1990): 19–52.

an individual's problem-solving skills, reduce his or her criminal thinking, and help limit his or her interactions with antisocial peers. Research shows that prioritizing supervision resources for individuals at moderate or high criminogenic risk can lead to significant reductions in recidivism. Intensive supervision interventions alone can result in higher recidivism rates for low-risk individuals. In fact, research shows that high-intensity programming for low-risk individuals results in negative outcomes.[55] One of the pervasive findings of these evaluations is that intensive treatment is not recommended for all offenders. It seems to be the case that high-risk offenders are more likely to benefit than low-risk offenders when both participate in intensive treatment programs, such as halfway houses or intensive probation. In fact, correctional supervision interventions have been shown to result in *increased* recidivism among low-risk offenders as compared to control samples.[56]

Proponents argue that it is important to classify and match offenders to the type of treatment they need, not only because it is a waste of resources to do otherwise, but also because the treatment program may actually influence a low-risk offender to recidivate. Why would low-risk offenders be more inclined to recidivate when exposed to a correctional intervention? It might be that low-risk offenders would have naturally avoided making any more criminal choices, but that correctional supervision brings them into contact with other criminal offenders. It could also be that being monitored identifies behaviors that are violations, but these behaviors would not have entered the radar screen of the criminal justice system except for the correctional supervision.

Some caution that factors such as poverty may be predictive of recidivism and, therefore, the "need" becomes a "risk" and increases an offender's risk score and that, in turn, increases the level of social control. The problem with this is that someone's status, not behavior, influences the level of punishment one endures, and second, the level of control is often related to the risk of recidivism (the more closely an offender is monitored, the more likely infractions will be found). This is not a criticism unique to R/N/R, however, since all classification risk instruments look at such things as housing stability, unemployment, and drug dependency. There is a real concern that the risk instruments become used to perpetuate racial disparity in the criminal justice system; however, the R/N/R model supposedly would address the problematic needs with intervention, leading to an exit from the criminal justice system. Researchers are also looking at the correctional program itself. The Correctional Program Assessment Inventory measures how well a program adheres to the principles of risk, need, and responsivity as described earlier. Studies have shown that higher scores for the programs are associated with better success rates for offenders in the programs.[57]

Female Offenders

There is a question whether the risk instruments developed with and for male offenders accurately predict risk for female offenders because there are so few women in the system. Earlier studies indicated that classification systems in use in prisons that were developed and validated with samples of male offenders "overclassified" female prisoners, meaning they indicated that women needed more secure settings than probably were necessary.[58] In the few studies that have examined the predictive ability of classification instruments for female offenders, findings were mixed.[59] Regarding the third-generation classification instruments, and LSI-R specifically, critics argued that the instrument ignored special issues of women, primarily because women become "lost" in the much larger numbers of men during statistical analysis. Other research indicated that such things as past victimization, drug use, mental health indices, abusive adult relationships and other factors are more predictive for women.[60] Women's risk factors might also include, for instance, suicide attempts, family structure of childhood home, depression, single parenting, reliance on public assistance, dysfunctional relationships, and adult victimization.[61] Researchers tested the LSI-R classification tool on female offenders along with a gender-specific "trailer" which utilized measures related to specific factors for women, such as self-efficacy, self-esteem, parenting, relationships, and abuse and concluded that gender-neutral models do predict recidivism for women, but the addition of gender-specific factors creates more powerful prediction tools. Some of the items in the LSI-R, such as criminal thinking, were weak predictors for women. For predicting recidivism of women, more important factors were substance abuse, economic and educational factors, and mental health factors. For prison samples (predicting misconduct), it appeared that past histories of trauma, dysfunctional relationships, and mental health concerns were predictive.[62]

SUMMARY

What Are the Goals of Corrections? What Was the "Rehabilitative Era"?

The goals of corrections are retribution, deterrence, incapacitation, and reform/rehabilitation. The rehabilitative era was a short period of time in the late 1960s and 1970s where the focus in corrections was on rehabilitation and there was a wide range of treatment programs.

How Do Theories of Crime Relate to What We Do to Criminals?

Theories of crime seem to be divorced from corrections. However, many policy choices have either implicit or explicit foundations in theory. More police and incarceration depends on deterrence theory, poverty programs and early childhood education are supported by learning theory, general strain and opportunity theory, and so on.

What Is Probation and How Is It Different from Parole? How Is It Different from Pre-Trial Diversion?

Probation is supervised release in the community instead of a jail or prison sentence. Pre-trial diversion may take the place of a criminal conviction (deferred adjudication) when successfully completed but probation comes after a criminal conviction.

What Is the History of Probation?

John Augustus in the 1800s is credited with being the first to supervise offenders in the community to replace a jail or prison system. For many years, probation officers were volunteers. It was not until 1956 that all states had enabling legislation.

What Are Some Typical Conditions for a Probationer?

General conditions are for all probationers, e.g. report monthly, pay court costs and fees, do not engage in criminal activity. Specific conditions are tailored to the offender, e.g. drug treatment, completing a GED, and so on.

What Is the Profile of Offenders Under Correctional Supervision?

In 2014, 3,864,100 people were on probation. About 25 percent of probationers were women, about 54 percent of probationers were White, 30 percent were Black, and 13 percent were Hispanic, about 56 percent are on probation for felony sentences (and the rest for misdemeanors). About 25 percent were drug offenders, 28 percent were property offenders, 19 percent were violent offenders, 16 percent were public order offenders, with 11 percent recorded as "other."

Do Women on Probation Have Different Backgrounds and Needs Than Men; If So, What Are They?

Yes; women are more likely than men on probation to have mental health and drug issues. They come from more disordered backgrounds, are more likely to have been victimized, and have worse employment histories.

How Many Drug Offenders Are Under Correctional Supervision? What Are Their Issues?

Estimates range widely (depending on if one is measuring drug addiction, drug abuse, drug use, or drug crimes), but it probably seems safe to say that drugs are a problem for at least 40 percent of offenders in the correctional system. The major issue is lack of treatment options.

What Are Some Current Issues of Probation Supervision?

Probation officers may be involved in pre-sentence investigations/recommendations and probation supervision. Regarding pre-sentence investigations and recommendation, there is the issue of confidentiality and the probation officer's liability. Regarding supervision, a current issue is the probation officer's right to search.

What Is Revocation? How Many Probationers Fail?

Estimates range but about half of probationers may be revoked, the majority for technical violations, not necessarily new crimes. Factors associated with recidivism include: type of crime, extent of prior record, unemployment, household composition, age, drug use, and program participation.

What Is Classification? What Is Third-Generation Classification?

Classification is using information about the offender and predictive instruments to determine the level of custody (or supervision). Third-generation classification uses static factors that do not change (e.g. age at first arrest) and dynamic factors (e.g., criminal thinking) to determine classification and program needs.

Critical Thinking Exercises

1. Do a newspaper search and collect a "convenience sample" of ten male offenders and ten female offenders (this is merely an educational exercise—it would not meet the standards of publishable research!). Determine the factors of the crime for both groups and determine whether or not you can identify any differences in types of crimes, motivation, criminal history, presence of drug/alcohol abuse, or any other relevant factors that stand out.
2. Find out how many drug treatment beds for offenders are available in your state. Now try to find out how many offenders are drug dependent. (Use websites for corrections departments, newspaper searches, or the Bureau of Justice Statistics.)

NOTES

1 See D. Rothman, *The Discovery of the Asylum*. New York, NY: Scott Foresman, 1971.

2 J. Pollock, N. Hogan, E. Lambert, J. Ian Ross and J. Sundt, "A utopian prison: Contradiction in terms?" *Journal of Contemporary Criminal Justice* 28 (2011): 60–76.

3 R. McCorkle and J. Crank, "Meet the new boss: Institutional change and loose coupling in parole and probation." *American Journal of Criminal Justice* 21 (1) (1996): 1–25.

4 M. Mauer, *Comparative International Rates of Incarceration: An Examination of Causes and Trends*. Washington, DC: The Sentencing Project, 2003.

5 L. Friedman, *Crime and Punishment in American History*. New York, NY: Basic Books, 1993, p. 18.

6 L. Friedman, note 5.

7 J. Petersilia, *Reforming Probation and Parole*. Lanham, MD: American Correctional Association, 2002, p. 38.

8 More recent statistics do not seem to be available. L. Glaze, T. Bonczar and F. Zhang, *Probation and Parole in the United States, 2009*. Washington, DC: Bureau of Justice Statistics, 2010, p. 3.

9 D. Parent, J. Byrne, V. Tsarfaty, L. Valade and L. Esselman, *Day Reporting Centers: Issues and Practices in Criminal Justice*, vol. 1. Washington, DC: National Institute of Justice, 1995; R. Jones and J. Lacey, *Evaluation of a Day Reporting Center for Repeat DWI Offenders*. Washington, DC: National Highway Traffic Safety Administration, 1999; D. Parent, "Day reporting centers: An evolving intermediate sanction." *Federal Probation Journal* 60 (4) (1996): 51–54.

10 A. Gibbs and D. King, "The electronic ball and chain? The operation and impact of home detention with electronic monitoring in New Zealand." *Australian and New Zealand Journal of Criminology* 36 (2003): 1–17; J. Bonta, S. Wallace-Capretta and J. Rooney, "Can electronic monitoring make a difference? An evaluation of three Canadian programs." *Crime and Delinquency* 46 (1) (2000): 61–75; P. Gendreau, C. Goggin, F. Cullen and D. Andrews, "The effects of community sanctions and incarceration on recidivism." *Forum* 12 (2) (2000): 10–13; M. Renzema and E. Mayo-Wilson, "Can electronic monitoring reduce crime for moderate to high-risk offenders?" *Journal of Experimental Criminology* 1 (2005): 1–23.

11 R. Ruback, G. Ruth and J. Shaffer, "Assessing the impact of statutory change: A statewide multi-level analysis of restitution orders in Pennsylvania." *Crime and Delinquency* 51 (3) (2005): 334; A. Lurigio and A. Davis, "Does a threatening letter increase compliance with restitution orders?" *Crime and Delinquency* 36 (4) (1984): 537–548.

12 Bureau of Justice Assistance, *How to Use Structured Fines as an Intermediate Sanction*. Washington, DC: U.S. Department of Justice, 1996.

13 J. Ginzberg, "Compulsory contraception as a condition of probation: The use and abuse of Norplant." *Brooklyn Law Review* 58 (1992): 979–1019.

14 D. Kaeble, L. Maruschak and T. Bonczar, *Probation and Parole in the United States, 2014*. Washington, DC: Bureau of Justice Statistics, 2015.

15 L. Glaze, T. Bonczar and F. Zhang, *Probation and Parole in the United States, 2009*. Washington, DC: Bureau of Justice Statistics, 2010; D. Kaeble, L. Maruschak and T. Bonczar, *Probation and Parole in the United States, 2014*. Washington, DC: Bureau of Justice Statistics, 2015.

16 L. Glaze, T. Bonczar and F. Zhang, *Probation and Parole in the United States, 2009*. Washington, DC: Bureau of Justice Statistics, 2010, p. 25.

17 S. Rosenmerkel, M. Durose and D. Farole, *Felony Sentences in State Courts, 2006—Statistical Tables*. Washington, DC: Bureau of Justice Statistics, 2009, p.2.

18 L. Glaze, T. Bonczar and F. Zhang, *Probation and Parole in the United States, 2009*. Washington, DC: Bureau of Justice Statistics, 2010, see Table 3, p. 3, for completion rates; also, Table 5, p. 26; L. Glaze and T. Bonczar, *Probation and Parole in the United States, 2005*. Washington, DC: Bureau of Justice Statistics, 2006.

19 D. Kaeble, L. Maruschak and T. Bonczar, *Probation and Parole in the United States, 2014*. Washington, DC: Bureau of Justice Statistics, 2015, p. 17.

20 D. Kaeble, L. Maruschak and T. Bonczar, *Probation and Parole in the United States, 2014*. Washington, DC: Bureau of Justice Statistics, 2015, p. 17.

21 M. Gray, M. Fields and S. Maxwell, "Examining probation violations: Who, what, and when." *Crime and Delinquency* 47 (4) (2001): 537–557.

22 J. Pollock, *Women's Crimes, Criminology and Corrections*. Prospect Heights, IL: Waveland, 2014; B. Bloom, "Women offenders in the community: The gendered impact of current policies." *Community Corrections Report on Law and Corrections Practice* 12 (1) (2004): 3–6; M. Chesney-Lind, "Women and the criminal justice system: Gender matters." In *Topics in Community Corrections: Responding to Women Offenders in the Community*. Washington, DC: National Institute of Corrections, 2000, pp. 7–11.

23 C. Widom, "Childhood victimization and the derailment of the girls and women to the criminal justice system." In National Institute of Justice, *Research on Women and Girls in the Criminal Justice System*. Washington, DC: National Institute of Justice, 2000, pp. 27–35; Z. Henriques and N. Manatu-Rupert, "Living on the outside: African American women before, during, and after imprisonment." *Prison Journal* 81 (1) (2001): 6–19; B. Ritchie, *Compelled to Crime: The Gender Entrapment of Battered Black Women*. New York, NY: Routledge, 1996.

24 K. Holtfreter and M. Morash, "The needs of women offenders: Implications for correctional programming." *Women and Criminal Justice* 13 (2003): 137–160; P. Van Voorhis, "Classification of women offenders: Gender-responsive approaches to risk/needs assessment." *Community Corrections Report on Law and Corrections Practice* 12 (2) (2005): 19–20.

25 B. Bloom, "Women offenders in the community: The gendered impact of current policies." *Community Corrections Report on Law and Corrections Practice* 12 (1) (2004): 3–6; B. Bloom, B. Owen and S. Covington, *Gender-Responsive Strategies: Research, Practice and Guiding Principles for Women Offenders*. Washington, DC: National Institute of Corrections, 2003.

26 Office of National Drug Control Policy, *ADAM II, 2013 Annual Report*. Washington, DC: ONDCP, 2014. Retrieved 6/28/2016 from https://www.whitehouse.gov/sites/default/files/ondcp/policy-and-research/adam_ii_2013_annual_report.pdf

27 Substance Abuse and Mental Health Services Administration, *Results from the 2010 National Survey on Drug Use and Health: Summary of National Findings*. Rockville, MD: Substance Abuse and Mental Health Services Administration, Center for Behavioral Health Statistics and Quality, 2011.

28 J. Karberg and D. James, *Substance Dependence, Abuse, and Treatment of Jail Inmates, 2002*. Washington, DC: Bureau of Justice Statistics, 2005.

29 T. Feucht and J. Gfroerer, *Mental and Substance Use Disorders among Adult Men on Probation or Parole: Some Success against a Persistent Challenge*. Rockville, MD: Substance Abuse and Mental Health Services Administration, Center for Behavioral Health Statistics and Quality, 2011.

30 C. Mumola and J. Karberg, *Drug Use and Dependence, State and Federal Prisoners, 2004*. Washington, DC: Bureau of Justice Statistics, 2005.

31 J. Petersilia, *Reforming Probation and Parole*. Lanham, MD: American Correctional Association, 1998, p. 25; S. Walker, *Popular Justice: A History of American Criminal Justice*, 2nd edn. New York: Oxford University Press, 2002, p. 25.

32 *Gardner v. Florida*, 430 U.S. 349, 1977.

33 Federal Rules of Procedure 32(c)(2)(A-D). See *Julian v. U.S. Department of Justice*, 806 F2d. 1411 (9th Cir. 1986).

34 *Griffin v. Wisconsin*, 483 U.S. 868, 1987.

35 *Mempa v. Rhay*, 389 U.S. 128, 1967.

36 *Gagnon v. Scarpelli*, 411 U.S. 778, 1973

37 T. Bonczar and L. Glaze, *Probation and Parole in the United States, 1998*. Washington, DC: Bureau of Justice Statistics, 1999, p. 6; L. Glaze, T. Bonczar and F. Zhang, *Probation and Parole in the United States, 2009*. Washington, DC: Bureau of Justice Statistics, 2010.

38 M. Gray, M. Fields and S. Maxwell, "Examining probation violations: Who, what, and when." *Crime and Delinquency* 47 (4) (2001): 537–557.

39 J. Petersilia, *Reforming Probation and Parole*. Lanham, MD: American Correctional Association, 2002, p. 58.

40 M. Gray, M. Fields and S. Maxwell, "Examining probation violations: Who, what, and when." *Crime and Delinquency* 47 (4) (2001): 537–557.

41 F. Taxman, "No illusions: Offender and organizational change in Maryland's proactive community supervision efforts." *Criminology and Public Policy* 7 (2) (2008): 279.

42 P. Bulman, "In brief: Hawaii HOPE." *National Institute of Justice Journal* 266 (2010). Retrieved 9/14/2010 from http://www.ojp.usdoj.gov/nij/journals/266/hope.htm

43 K. Auerhan, "Conceptual and methodological issues in the prediction of dangerous behavior." *Criminology and Public Policy* 5 (4) (2006): 771–778.

44 P. Van Voorhis, "An overview of offender classification systems." In P. Van Voorhis, M. Braswell and D. Lester (Eds.), *Correctional Counseling and Rehabilitation*, 6th edn. Newark, NJ: LexisNexis/Matthew Bender, 1997, p. 139.

45 R. Sims and M. Jones," Predicting success or failure on probation: Factors associated with felony probation outcomes." *Crime and Delinquency* 43 (3) (1997): 314–327.

46 K. Morgan, "Factors associated with probation outcome." Journal of Criminal Justice 22(4) (1994): 341–353.

47 R. Hanson and M. Bussiere, "Predicting relapse: A meta analysis of sexual offender recidivism studies." *Journal of Consulting and Clinical Psychology* 66 (3) (1998): 348–362.

48 P. Hoffman, "History of the federal parole system: part 2 (1973–1997)." *Federal Probation* 61 (4) (1997): 49–57; G. Camp and C. Camp, *The Corrections Yearbook*. Middletown, CT: Criminal Justice Institute, Inc., 2001, p. 3.

49 P. Smith, F. Cullen and E. Latessa, "Can 14,737 be wrong? A meta-analysis of the LSI-R and recidivism for female offenders." *Criminology and Public Policy* 8 (2009): 183–208.

50 P. Smith, F. Cullen and E. Latessa, "Can 14,737 be wrong? A meta-analysis of the LSI-R and recidivism for female offenders." *Criminology and Public Policy* 8 (2009): 183–208; G. Bourgon and J. Bonta, "Reconsidering the responsivity principle: A way to move forward." *Federal Probation* (September 2014): 3–11.

51 P. Smith, F. Cullen and E. Latessa, "Can 14,737 be wrong? A meta-analysis of the LSI-R and recidivism for female offenders." *Criminology and Public Policy* 8 (2009): 183–208.

52 J. Byrne and F. Taxman, "Crime (control) is a choice: Divergent perspectives on the role of treatment in the adult corrections system." *Criminology and Public Policy* 4 (2005): 291–310; F. Taxman, "Second generation of RNR: The importance of systemic responsivity in expanding core principles of responsivity." *Federal Probation* (September 2014): 32–41.

53 D. Polaschek, "An appraisal of the Risk-Need-Responsivity (RNR) model of offender rehabilitation and its application in correctional treatment." *Legal and Criminological Psychology* (2012): 17, 1–17.

54 D. Andrews, J. Bonta and R.D. Hoge, "Classification for effective rehabilitation: Rediscovering psychology." *Criminal Justice and Behavior* 17 (1) (1990): 19–52; D. Andrews, "The Risk-Need-Responsivity (RNR) model of correctional assessment and treatment." In J.A. Dvoskin, J.L. Skeem, R.W. Novaco and K.S. Douglas (Eds.), *Using Social Science to Reduce Offending*. New York, NY: Oxford University Press, 2012.

55 D. Andrews, J. Bonta and R. Hoge, "Classification for effective rehabilitation: Rediscovering psychology." *Criminal Justice and Behavior* 17 (1) (1990): 19–52; D. Andrews, "The Risk-Need-Responsivity (RNR) model of correctional assessment and treatment." In J.A. Dvoskin, J.L. Skeem, R.W. Novaco and K.S. Douglas (Eds.), *Using Social Science to Reduce Offending*. New York, NY: Oxford University Press, 2012; C. Lowenkamp, E. Latessa and A. Holsinger, "The risk principle in action: What have we learned from 13,676 offenders and 97 corrections programs?" *Crime and Delinquency* 52 (2006): 77–93; D. Andrews, J. Bonta and S. Wormith, "The recent past and near future of risk and/or need assessment," *Crime and Delinquency* 52 (2006): 7–27; D. Andrews and J. Bonta, "Rehabilitating criminal justice policy and practice." *Psychology, Public Policy, and Law* 16 (2010): 39–55; F. Taxman and D. Marlowe, "Risk, needs, responsivity: in action or inaction?" *Crime and Delinquency* 52 (2006): 3–6.

56 C. Lowenkamp and E. Latessa, "Increasing the effectiveness of correctional programming through the risk principle: Identifying offenders for residential placement." *Criminology and Public Policy* 4 (2) (2005): 263–290; D. Andrews, J. Bonta and J. Wormith, "The recent past and near future of risk and/or need assessment." *Crime and Delinquency* 52 (1) (2006): 7–27; C. Lowenkamp, E. Latessa and A. Holsinger, "The risk principle in action: What have we learned from 13,676 offenders and 97 correctional programs?" *Crime and Delinquency* 52 (1) (2006): 77–93.

57 D. Andrews, J. Bonta and J. Wormith, "The recent past and near future of risk and/or need assessment." *Crime and Delinquency* 52 (1) (2006): 7–27.

58 P. Van Voorhis and L. Presser, *Classification of Women Offenders: A National Assessment of Current Practices*. Washington, DC: National Institute of Corrections, 2001; P. Van Voorhis, "Classification of women offenders: Gender-responsive approaches to risk/ needs assessment." *Community Corrections Report on Law and Corrections Practice* 12(2) (2005): 19–20.

59 G. Coulson, G. Ilacqua, V. Nutbrown, D. Giulekas and F. Cudjoe, "Predictive utility of the LSI for incarcerated female offenders." *Criminal Justice and Behavior* 23 (1996): 427–439;. C. Lowenkamp, A. Holsinger and E. Latessa, "Risk/need assessment, offender classification, and the role of childhood abuse." *Criminal Justice and Behavior* 28 (5) (2001): 543–563; K. Holtfreter, M. Reisig and M. Morash, "Poverty, state capital, and recidivism among women offenders." *Criminology and Public Policy* 3 (2) (2004): 185–208.

60 M. Reisig, K. Holtfreter and M. Morash, "Assessing recidivism risk across female pathways to crime." *Justice Quarterly* 23 (2006): 384–403.

61 P. Van Voorhis, "Classification of women offenders: Gender-responsive approaches to risk/needs assessment." *Community Corrections Report on Law and Corrections Practice* 12 (2005): 19–20; K. Blanchette and S. Brown, *The Assessment and Treatment of Women Offenders: An Integrative Perspective*. New York, NY: Wiley, 2006.

62 P. Van Voorhis, E. Wright, E. Salisbury and A. Bauman, "Women's risk factors and their contributions to existing risk/needs assessment: The current status of a gender-responsive supplement." *Criminal Justice and Behavior* 37 (2009): 261–288. Also see, E. Salisbury and P. Van Voorhis, "Gendered pathways: A quantitative investigation of women probationers' paths to incarceration." *Criminal Justice and Behavior* 36 (2009): 541–566.

CONFINEMENT | 11

Jails and Prisons

For most of us, our perceptions of prison are shaped by movies, television dramas, and, increasingly, reality shows. Some of these portrayals have been realistic, some sensationalistic, and some ridiculous. Scriptwriters may never get it right because prison is an abnormal environment that becomes normal for the persons who live and work there. Reality shows aren't realistic in that they record thousands of hours of footage to show a very small sliver of what it is like in prison on a daily basis. Prison has become ubiquitous in American society to the point that people's first thought of punishment is usually a prison sentence. It was not always this way and a critical approach to prisons would address whether a prison sentence should be used as often as it is for criminal offenders.

Chapter Preview

- How Many People Are Incarcerated in Jails and Prisons in the United States?
- What Rights Do Prisoners Have?
- What Is Prison Like Today Compared to Previous Eras?
- Who Are the Prisoners in State and Federal Prisons?
- What Are the Elements of the Prisoner Subculture?
- Is Sexual Assault in Prison a Problem?
- What Are the Issues Concerning the Mentally Ill in Jails and Prisons?
- Why Are Some Prisons and Jails Privately Run? Are Private Prisons Less Expensive?
- What Are the Differences and Similarities of Jails and Prisons?
- Focus On Data: Did The Increase in Incarceration Reduce the Crime Rate between 1995 and 2010?
- Summary
- Critical Thinking Exercises

HOW MANY PEOPLE ARE INCARCERATED IN JAILS AND PRISONS IN THE UNITED STATES?

There are currently more than two million people incarcerated in prisons and jails. The United States' incarceration rate is the highest of the Western nations. It is hard not to be aware of this nation's "mass incarceration" problem since it has moved into the forefront of issues targeted by journalists, advocacy groups, and even some politicians. While academics have argued for years that using incarceration as the first choice instead of last choice for punishment is not in the best interest of society, recently many disparate groups from the entire political spectrum have discovered the issue and have been calling for a reappraisal of the large numbers of offenders who are sentenced to jails and prisons.[1]

In 2014, the total incarcerated population in America (including prisons and jails) was about 2.2 million. About two-thirds (1,561,500) of this number were in prison, and 744,600 were incarcerated in jails. The prison population alone grew about 93.5 percent from 1990 to year-end 2005—from 743,382 to 1,438,701 prisoners in just 15 years.[2] From 2005 to 2014 the rate of increase (1,525,900 to 1,561,500) slowed considerably to 2.33 percent. Our prison population is determined by four variables: the crime rate, the clearance rate (how many crimes result in arrest), the share of convicted felons sent to prison (instead of prison alternatives such as probation), and the average length of prison sentences. We know that felons are more likely to be sentenced to prison today than before the 1980s, and they are likely to serve longer sentences. The average sentence for those convicted of violent crimes increased 38 percent from 1990 to 2009; for property offenders, the average sentence increased 25 percent, and drug offenders served a sentence that was 35 percent longer in 2009 than in 1990.[3]

To better understand the increased use of imprisonment, rates per 100,000 should be used. Rates allow us to compare incarceration numbers between different populations; therefore, we know, when comparing two different years or two different states, that the increase or decrease in prison population is not due to population fluctuations. In Exhibit 11.1 the incarceration rates since 1850 are displayed, and we see that the use of prisons has increased dramatically only after the 1980s. In 2014 (the last year for which statistics are available) the rate was 470 per 100,000 so the chart would show a slight decline from 2010's rate of 500.[4]

There is confusion over incarceration rates and imprisonment rates. It is important to be consistent when constructing rate graphs. **Imprisonment rates** include only state and federal prison populations, while **incarceration rates** include state and federal prisons *and* jails. It is also important to know what the population base is. While the rates displayed in the Exhibit 11.1 are constructed using a total population (all ages), clearly that is not as helpful as knowing what the rate is for adults (since juveniles are rarely sentenced to prison). Exhibit 11.2 shows the difference in rates when using census figures of over eighteen-year-olds compared to rates when using the total population.

Exhibit 11.1 Incarceration Rates

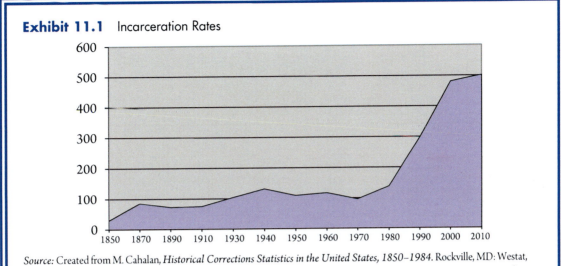

Source: Created from M. Cahalan, *Historical Corrections Statistics in the United States, 1850–1984.* Rockville, MD: Westat, Inc., 1986; B.J.S., *Sourcebook of Criminal Justice Statistics.* Washington, DC: Department of Justice, 1997; B.J.S., *State and Federal Prisoners,* June 30, 1998. Washington, DC: Department of Justice; P. Harrison and J. Karberg, *Prison and Jail Inmates at Midyear 2002.* Washington, DC: Department of Justice, 2003; H. West, W. Sabol and S. Greenman, *Prisoners in 2009.* Washington, DC: Department of Justice, 2010.

Exhibit 11.2 Imprisonment Rates—Rounded

Year	Imprisonment Rate—Over 18	Imprisonment Rate—All Ages
2004	730	490
2014	690	470

Source: D. Kaeble, L. Glaze, A. Tsoutis and T. Minton, *Correctional Populations in the United States, 2014.* Washington, DC: Bureau of Justice Statistics, 2015, p. 4.

If you see different rates in discussions of the prison population, it is likely some of these factors are the reason for the different numbers.

Rates also allow us to compare the United States to other countries. In Exhibit 11.4 we see that the United States uses incarceration as a punishment completely out of step with similar countries. Only a few countries have rates similar to the United States, and most of our "sister" countries, such as the UK, Canada, France, and Germany, have much lower incarceration rates.

Exhibit 11.3   Incarceration Rates, 2014—States

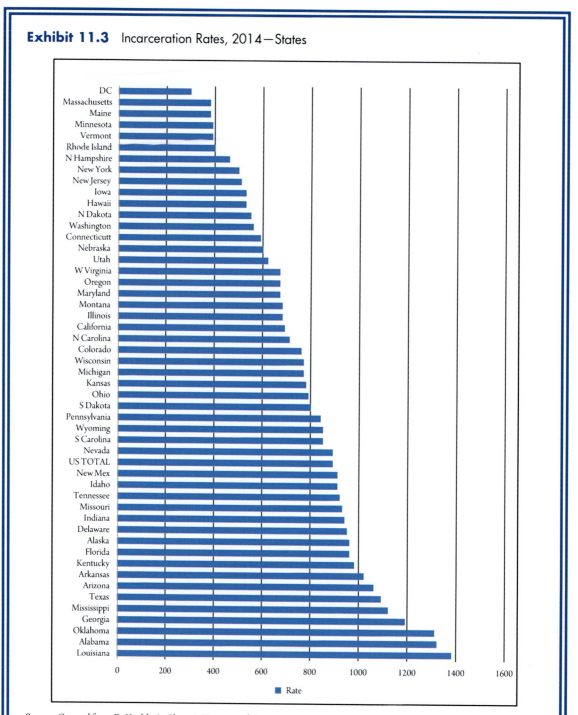

Source: Created from D. Kaeble, L. Glaze, A. Tsoutis and T. Minton, *Correctional Populations in the United States, 2014.* Washington, DC: Bureau of Justice Statistics, 2015.

Exhibit 11.4 International Comparison

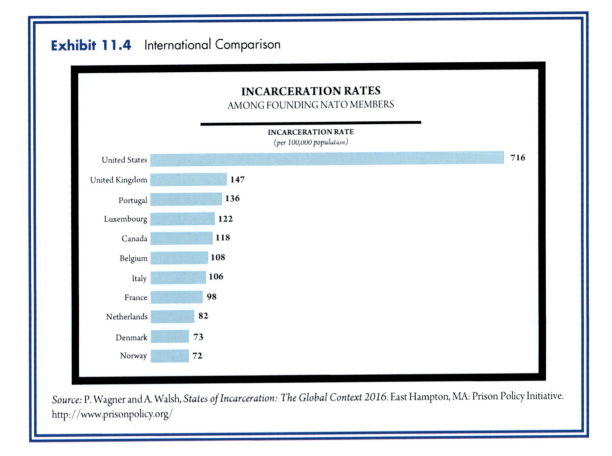

INCARCERATION RATES
AMONG FOUNDING NATO MEMBERS

INCARCERATION RATE
(per 100,000 population)

United States	716
United Kingdom	147
Portugal	136
Luxembourg	122
Canada	118
Belgium	108
Italy	106
France	98
Netherlands	82
Denmark	73
Norway	72

Source: P. Wagner and A. Walsh, *States of Incarceration: The Global Context 2016.* East Hampton, MA: Prison Policy Initiative. http://www.prisonpolicy.org/

The prison population of the United States also contains disproportionate numbers of racial minorities relative to their proportion of the general population. The imprisonment rate for Black men is an amazing 2,724 (down from 3,119 in 2009), which is still almost six times higher than that of White men, whose rate was 487 in 2008. In Exhibit 11.5, we can see the relative rates of imprisonment (which is prisons only, not including jails) across race/ethnicity and gender groups.

Men's incarceration rates are about sixteen time higher than women's. Women's rates, while much lower, have risen at a faster rate than men's. The actual number of women in prison is still low (7 percent of the total prisoner population) but for many decades it was 5 percent of the total. In 1976, there were 11,000 women in prison; in 2014 there were 106,200.[5] Although the total number of women in prison is dwarfed by the number of men in prison, the *percentage increase* of women sentenced to prison has usually been higher than the rate for men. Between 1990 and 2001, the average annual growth rate was

Exhibit 11.5   Imprisonment Rates by Race/Ethnicity/Sex

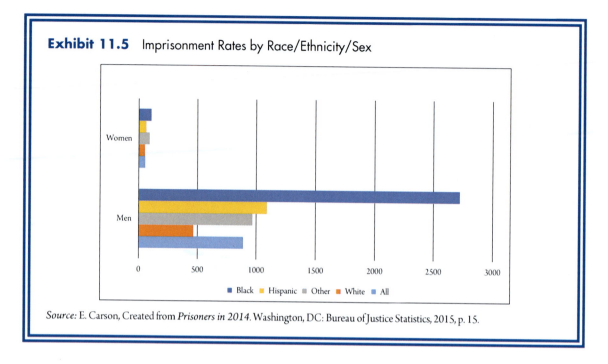

Source: E. Carson, Created from *Prisoners in 2014*. Washington, DC: Bureau of Justice Statistics, 2015, p. 15.

5.7 percent for men and 7.5 percent for women.[6] Between 2004 and 2014, the number of women in prison increased from 95,998 to 106,232, about an 11 percent increase. The number of men in prison increased from 1,337,730 to 1,402,404, a 5 percent increase.[7] Of course, part of the reason women's percentage increase is so much higher is that the numbers are much smaller and percentage increases are influenced by the base number.

Interestingly, the rate of imprisonment for Black women has been declining, even when the rate for White and Hispanic women increased. Exhibit 11.6 displays the imprisonment rates (per 100,000).

The imprisonment rate for Black women is still over double that of White women, but it is significantly lower than it was in 2000 when it was about six times the rate of White women.[8] The rate for Black women declined by 30 percent between 2000 and 2009. During that same time period, the rates for Whites doubled and Hispanics' rate increased by 23 percent.[9] Between 2009 and 2014, rates for all groups declined, 20 percent for Whites, 23 percent for Blacks, and 14 percent for Hispanics.[10]

It is not clear why the rate of incarceration for Black women has decreased so dramatically as compared to Whites and Hispanics. There is a wide disparity in ratios of imprisoned Blacks to Whites between the states from 15:1 in one state to a low of 2:1[11] (meaning fifteen Black women are incarcerated for

Exhibit 11.6 Imprisonment Rates for Women

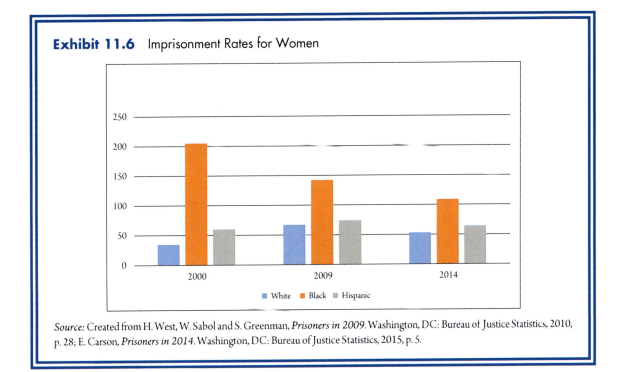

Source: Created from H. West, W. Sabol and S. Greenman, *Prisoners in 2009.* Washington, DC: Bureau of Justice Statistics, 2010, p. 28; E. Carson, *Prisoners in 2014.* Washington, DC: Bureau of Justice Statistics, 2015, p. 5.

every one White woman in the first state to a ratio of two Black women to one White woman in the second state); therefore, there may be different explanations relevant to different states. One source suggested that it may be because Black women are less likely to be involved in drug and violent crimes today, combined with the fact that methamphetamine arrests are rising and White and Hispanic women are more likely to be involved in this type of drug crime.[12] It could also be that determinate sentencing changes reduced any race effects that may have operated to increase the likelihood of prison sentences for Black women. There is very little attention paid to these sentencing patterns since the numbers are so small compared to men's incarceration rates.

Imprisonment rates and numbers in prisons have slowed and, in some states, decreased. Recent figures indicate that twelve states have created double-digit declines between 1999 and 2014. New Jersey's prison population decreased 31 percent since 1999, New York's 28 percent since 1999, Rhode Island's 25 percent since 2008, and California's 22 percent since 2006. These reductions have come about because of court decisions (e.g., California), but also through changes in policies and practices. Research indicates that the states with the most substantial reductions have not seen any increased risk to public safety.[13] It is possible we have seen the peak of incarceration rates and prison populations and the next era will be characterized by policies that emphasize diversion. We will return to this discussion in Chapter 12.

WHAT RIGHTS DO PRISONERS HAVE?

Prior to the 1960s, prisoners had very few rights. In fact, the so-called **hands-off era** (1900–60) referred to the fact that federal and state courts rarely agreed to hear legal challenges brought forward by prisoners. In *Ruffin v. Commonwealth* (1878),[14] a Virginia court basically said that a prisoner was a "slave of the state." State and federal courts rejected prisoner appeals for the following reasons:

1. Deferral to the expertise of administrators: they believed that management of a prison should be left to the experts.
2. "Slave of the state" argument: they believed that prisoners only had privileges (that could be taken away) rather than rights.
3. Federalism: federal courts hesitated to interfere with the business of the state prison.
4. "Opening the door": judges didn't want to open the door to an increase in such prisoner rights litigation.[15]

During the prisoner rights era (1960–80), prisoner petitions increased tremendously and several groundbreaking cases during the Warren court era (when the chief justice was Earl Warren) advanced the legal rights of inmates. However, after 1980, the Supreme Court moved into what was called the due deference era (1980–today), and judges became more likely to give "due deference" to the expertise of prison administrators when faced with prisoner litigation. In 1996, Congress passed the Prison Litigation Reform Act (**PLRA**),[16] which significantly reduced prisoner petitions through a number of measures, including limiting attorney fees, punishing those who file "frivolous" lawsuits, and restricting federal courts from interfering with prison policies unless absolutely necessary.

Generally, prisoners' rights lawsuits allege violations of the 5th or the 14th Amendment (due process), the 8th Amendment (cruel and unusual punishment), and the 1st Amendment (freedom of religion and expression). Prisoners, along with the rest of us, still have the protection of due process whenever faced with a governmental deprivation of a protected liberty interest. Under the due process clauses of the 5th Amendment (covering federal prisoners) and the 14th Amendment (covering state prisoners), prisoners have the right to access the courts. In the past, prison authorities would confiscate letters and legal documents and prevent inmates from having their grievances relayed to the courts. In a series of cases, the U.S. Supreme Court and other courts prohibited prison officials from blocking the inmates' access to the court system.[17] The Supreme Court also made it clear that inmates should have meaningful assistance to access the courts, even if it had to take the form of **jailhouse lawyers**, inmates who help other inmates file petitions for a fee, or law students. The Court also held that legal mail could not be censored, and that prisoners should have access to either law libraries or legal services.[18] However, in more recent decisions, the United States Supreme Court has restricted the right of access to the courts and/or the ability to seek damages if the prison does not provide meaningful access by making it harder to prove that the absence of such assistance resulted in a negative impact for the inmate.[19]

Prisoners have the right to some minimal due process before being punished in prison. One earlier case gave prisoners the right to a notice of charges and a hearing before being punished by segregation or loss of good time.[20] Later cases reduced due process rights solely to when they faced a potential loss of good time as punishment, and curtailed the level of proof required before punishment could be administered.[21] Prisoners never received the right to any due process protections before being transferred, even if it was to a prison far away or to a higher-security classification. Prisoners do not have the right to be incarcerated in the state in which they were convicted. Many prisoners now are housed in states far away from their home in "for-profit" prisons under contract with their sentencing state.[22]

Prisoners have the right to live in conditions that are not unreasonably harmful and dangerous. The 8th Amendment prohibits cruel and unusual punishment and has been the basis for outlawing **corporal punishment** (whipping) in prisons[23] and any practices that result in needless harm. Under the 8th Amendment, prisoners have the right to basic medical care (although not necessarily good medical care). A deliberate withholding of medical care that constitutes an unnecessary and wanton infliction of pain can be a violation of the 8th Amendment, but medical negligence does not constitute a constitutional violation.[24]

Later, **totality of circumstances** cases involved multiple conditions of confinement that, as a whole, constituted cruel and unusual punishment. Conditions that were cited in these cases included high levels of violence (either or both inmate-on-inmate or officer-on-inmate), lack of medical care, lack of sanitation, little or no programming, no assistance for the mentally ill or mentally challenged, and overcrowding. In some of the most egregious cases, prisoners won.

In *Brown v. Plata* (2011)[25] the Supreme Court agreed with a lower federal court that California's prison system violated the 8th Amendment due to overcrowding and lack of medical services. They ordered the state to improve conditions or release prisoners to capacity levels (prison populations were dramatically over rated capacities) and the result was that California went from having a prison population with the highest population of 173,000 in 2006[26] to one substantially lower. California was similar to Texas in 2010 (163,000 to Texas' 166,713); however, in 2014, California's prison population had declined to a population of 135,981 compared to 168,280 in Texas.[27] The large reduction in prisoner population was accomplished by early release and greater use of community corrections. The state is still under a court monitor until they meet compliance with court-ordered standards of care.

The 8th Amendment has also been used to challenge prison treatment programs that involved the infliction of pain. Prisoners have the right to withdraw consent if it was not free and voluntary, or if a treatment program is designated as experimental or involves pain.[28] However, prisoners do not have the right to refuse anti-psychotic drugs if it is determined that it is necessary for the safety of the inmate or the institution.[29]

Prisoners do not have the same 1st Amendment rights as the rest of us, but any censorship or surveillance of mail and communication must be related to the safety and security of the institution or rehabilitative goals, not simply to suppress criticism of the prison or prison officials. Prison officials can read inmates' mail, but they cannot censor it unless there is a threat to safety or security. Prisoners may not receive magazines or other communications that are considered a threat to institutional security, order, or rehabilitation.[30] Prisoners do not have the right to correspond with other inmates.[31]

As would be expected, courts have never been very sympathetic to freedom of speech claims by prisoners. Prison authorities have the right to punish prisoners for angry racial comments, work stoppages, and protests. Prisoners have virtually no rights of association. Numerous cases have categorized visitation as a *privilege* that may be curtailed or denied for just cause, not a *right*. The Supreme Court approved rigorous restrictions on visitation in a Michigan prisoner's challenge.[32]

Prisoners have the right to practice their religious beliefs as long as they do not impinge upon the state's interest in safety, security, and order. Courts use the **rational relationship test** to balance the individual's interest against the state's interest in safety and security. As long as the state's rule or procedure is rationally related to a legitimate state interest, the state will win any challenge to regulations that prohibit an inmate from practicing his or her religion. On the other hand, if the inmate's religious practice does not seem to implicate any security or order concerns, then the 1st Amendment and the Religious

Land Use and Institutionalized Persons Act of 2000 (passed by Congress) protects religious freedoms.[33]

Generally, jail inmates have similar rights to prisoners. One might think that pre-trial detainees (who have not been found guilty of a crime) should have more rights than the convicted, but the Supreme Court has deferred to jail officials' right to run a safe and secure institution accepting that there is no easy way to differentiate between detainees and the convicted when implementing jail policies.[34] Obviously, prisoners' rights are not the same as those of free people. Any right must be balanced against the state's right to run a safe and secure prison.

WHAT IS PRISON LIKE TODAY COMPARED TO PREVIOUS ERAS?

The **penitentiary** in America began with the Walnut Street Jail in Philadelphia.

Exhibit 11.7   The Walnut Street Jail in Philadelphia was the first penitentiary in America.

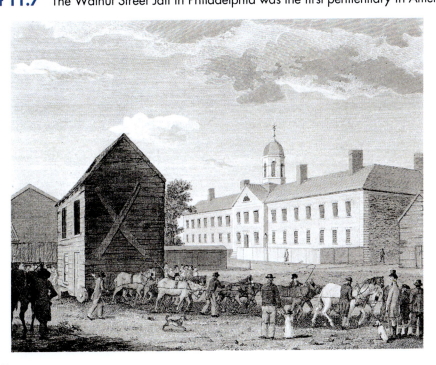

Source: Getty

In 1790, the Society for Alleviating the Miseries of Public Prisons was able to get legislation passed that reformed the Walnut Street Jail. For the first time, women were segregated from men, the sick were separated from healthy prisoners, and the worst offenders were segregated from others. Food, clothing, and medical care were provided by the Society. Most important, the mission of the institution changed from mere incapacitation to reform. Inmates were expected to contemplate their evil ways in their solitary cells and reform themselves through penitence. By the 1800s, the Walnut Street Jail was extremely overcrowded and conditions had deteriorated to the point where the Eastern State Penitentiary was built on the outskirts of Philadelphia to replace the jail. Here, the solitary system was pursued to an even greater degree, and this institution became one of the models for the penitentiary system.[35] The penitentiary was designed to isolate criminals from the contagion of the corrupt influences of the city. Prison advocates argued that prisoners would experience solitude, work, and penitence, and that this experience would transform them into good, sober citizens.

For more information about Eastern State Penitentiary, which is now a tourist attraction, go to http://www.easternstate.org/

Two distinct versions of the penitentiary emerged in the 1800s: the *separate* and the *congregate* systems. The **separate system** originated in Philadelphia at the Walnut Street Jail (1790) and later at the Eastern State Penitentiary (1829). This system is sometimes called the Philadelphia or **Pennsylvania system**. The regimen was one of solitary confinement and manual labor. Prisoners were kept in their cells at all times. The **congregate system** was first introduced at Auburn Prison in New York (1817), and is often called simply the **Auburn system**. Prisoners of this system slept in solitary cells, but worked and ate together. Silence was strictly enforced, however, to prevent them from being corrupted by each other. Regimentation and harsh punishment were used to control inmates, but also to reform them to become obedient and sober workers.

Separation, obedience, and labor became the "trinity" around which officials managed the penitentiary. Convicts were "men of idle habits, vicious propensities, and depraved passions," who had to be taught obedience as part of their reformation. The **lockstep march** was an iconic image of these prisons where prisoners shuffled together, bound by one hand on the opposite shoulder of the man in front. This was the only exercise available to inmates until the 1900s—it was eventually abolished in the early decades of the twentieth century.[36]

The Auburn system became the model for other prisons, largely because it allowed factory work to partially offset the costs of imprisonment. Ironically, the separate system became a more common model for prison building in

Exhibit 11.8 The lockstep march required prisoners to walk in a tight line, with one hand on the shoulder of the person in front. It was abolished in the early twentieth century.

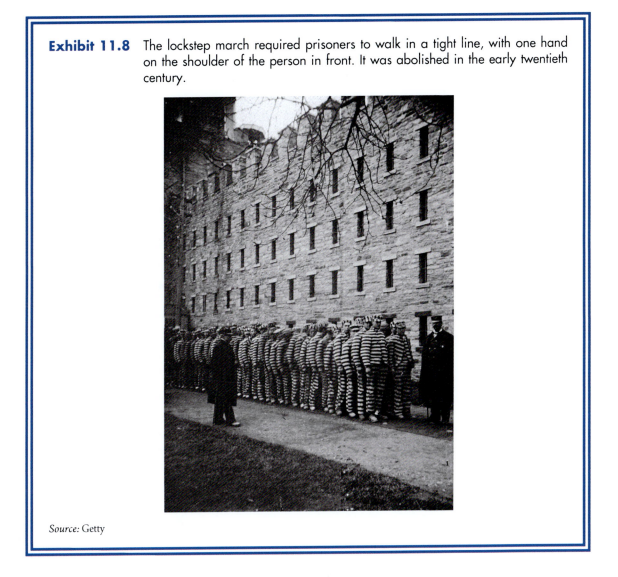

Source: Getty

Europe. In these early penitentiaries there were few women. Those who were confined to penitentiaries were often caged in attics, left unsupervised, and subjected to sexual abuse.[37] Early prisons also did not house many Blacks, at least until after the Civil War, because they more often were punished by slave owners.

In the late 1800s, the **reformatory era** brought new ideas to the philosophies of imprisonment. Elmira Reformatory, dating from 1870, was created for young men and had a mission of reform through education and strict discipline. Reformatories for women followed. While reformatories for men utilized militaristic drills and staffing, reformatories for women sought to recreate home-like environments through the use of cottages.[38] In prisons of the early to mid 1900s, prisoners worked, sometimes in meaningless labor, such as the infamous rock pile. There was no purpose, and no institutional mission, other than incapacitation and punishment. Early prisons in Southern states were more likely to follow an agricultural model, rather than an industrial or a factory model. Landowners leased prisoners' labor and the **lease-labor system** was characterized by brutal conditions for prisoners.[39]

Until about the 1960s, prisons were racially segregated by policy. Early sociological discussions of prisons did not mention Black prisoners at all. Gresham Sykes' classic study, *The Society of Captives* (1958/1966), describes Trenton State Prison in 1950. The prison society, as Sykes described it, was a world where the strong preyed upon the weak. A few prisoners were able to obtain a range of goods, including alcohol and sex, by barter or money from the outside. Prisoners were expected to "do their own time" and ignore the victimization of their fellow inmates.

As early as the 1950s, the penitentiaries of old were beginning the transition to **correctional institutions**. Gradually, prisons began to offer prisoners more privileges, such as yard and recreational privileges, more liberal mail and visitation policies, and occasional movies or concerts. The more important development, however, was the beginning of educational, vocational, and therapeutic programs. By the end of the 1960s and into the 1970s, during the **rehabilitative era**, there were many programs in some institutions, although the South lagged behind the West and the Northeast in innovative programming. Inmates were released through a variety of work and educational release. Women's correctional institutions also followed the mission of reform. Some women's prisons experimented with having apartment-like minimum-security buildings, where female inmates could go out to work in the community, returning to the prison-based apartment at night.[40]

Promises of reform never matched the reality and, arguably, the riots that erupted in the 1970s (most notably the Attica Riot in 1971) occurred because of the disparity between reform rhetoric and reality.

Another important element to the riots, however, was the greater politicization of inmates, especially minority inmates, who often had been involved in organizations such as the Black Panthers on the street. The Black Awareness movement of the 1960s and 1970s spurred the prisoners' rights movement, and it also dramatically changed prison subculture. Prison, although becoming

Exhibit 11.9   On September 9, 1971, prisoners rioted in Attica prison in New York, taking 42 staff hostage and holding them for four days before the state took back control of the prison. The riot resulted in 33 inmates and 10 correctional officers and employees being killed; all but one killing occurred during the retaking of the prison.

Source: Getty

officially desegregated via judicial decisions, became increasingly self-segregated along racial and ethnic lines.[41] Drugs began to affect the prison subculture and raised the stakes of the prison black market economic system.

In the 1980s, increasing numbers led to what has been called the **warehouse prison** of today.[42] Rehabilitative programs were cut and prison administrators struggled to find beds for ever-increasing numbers of prisoners. Even women's prisons have changed. Women were told they were going to be treated like inmates rather than women, and the unique characteristics of women's prisons were systematically eliminated.[43]

Exhibit 11.10   Beginning in the 1980s, women's prisons have become more like men's, as at the Utah State Correctional Facility.

Source: AP

For more information about the American Correctional Association, go to http://www.aca.org/pastpresent future/

Race-based violence escalated dramatically in some prisons. The contemporary prison provides a much better life for prisoners than at earlier times in history; however, because of the crushing burden of numbers, reform or rehabilitation is not a central mission. Most prisoners are simply housed and fed until release. Some state systems are better than others. The goal and mission of correctional systems is to maintain a safe and secure institution and to facilitative proactive change among inmates, but the reality is that the prisoner subculture, the lack of committed staff members, and the oppressive, negative environment of prisons can act to subvert those goals.

WHO ARE THE PRISONERS IN STATE AND FEDERAL PRISONS?

Many prisoners are young (44 percent are under 34), members of a minority group (only about 40 percent of prisoners are White), under-employed (before prison), and undereducated.[44] About half of prisoners are violent offenders as shown in Exhibit 11.11. It is important to note that this is not because half of all sentenced offenders are violent; in fact, violent offenders comprise less than 30 percent of all sentenced felony offenders. However, because violent offenders face longer sentences and serve longer proportions of their sentence than property or public order offenders, they "stack up" in prison, which is why they represent half of all prisoners when presenting crime of conviction percentages for the daily prisoner population.

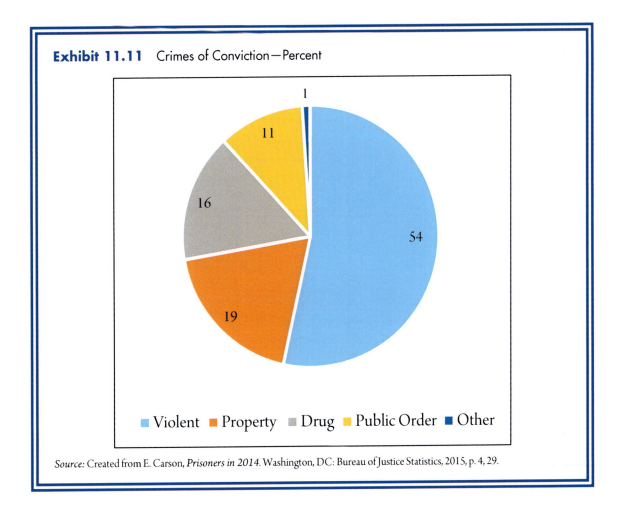

Exhibit 11.11   Crimes of Conviction—Percent

Violent   Property   Drug   Public Order   Other

Source: Created from E. Carson, *Prisoners in 2014.* Washington, DC: Bureau of Justice Statistics, 2015, p. 4, 29.

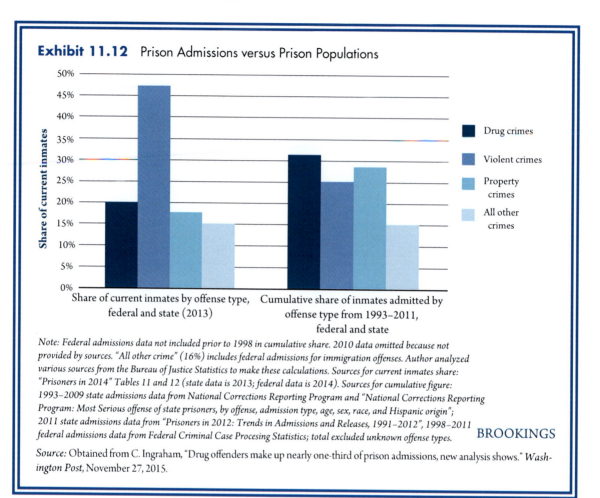

Exhibit 11.12   Prison Admissions versus Prison Populations

Note: Federal admissions data not included prior to 1998 in cumulative share. 2010 data omitted because not provided by sources. "All other crime" (16%) includes federal admissions for immigration offenses. Author analyzed various sources from the Bureau of Justice Statistics to make these calculations. Sources for current inmates share: "Prisoners in 2014" Tables 11 and 12 (state data is 2013; federal data is 2014). Sources for cumulative figure: 1993–2009 state admissions data from National Corrections Reporting Program and "National Corrections Reporting Program: Most Serious offense of state prisoners, by offense, admission type, age, sex, race, and Hispanic origin"; 2011 state admissions data from "Prisoners in 2012: Trends in Admissions and Releases, 1991–2012", 1998–2011 federal admissions data from Federal Criminal Case Procesing Statistics; total excluded unknown offense types.   BROOKINGS

Source: Obtained from C. Ingraham, "Drug offenders make up nearly one-third of prison admissions, new analysis shows." Washington Post, November 27, 2015.

Exhibit 11.12 presents another display that shows more clearly how prison admissions (the bars on the right) are different than prison populations, most notably in the percentage of violent offenders.

The racial and ethnic breakdown of state and federal prisons is displayed in Exhibit 11.13. Blacks and, to a lesser extent, Hispanics, are disproportionally represented based on their percentage of the general population. This is true for female prisoners as well. Exhibit 11.13 shows that the percentage of Blacks has declined slightly in the last ten years and the percentage of Hispanic prisoners has increased very slightly. The remaining prisoners either did not indicate a race/ethnicity or the data is missing.

Exhibit 11.13   Prison Inmates' Race/Ethnicity—Percent

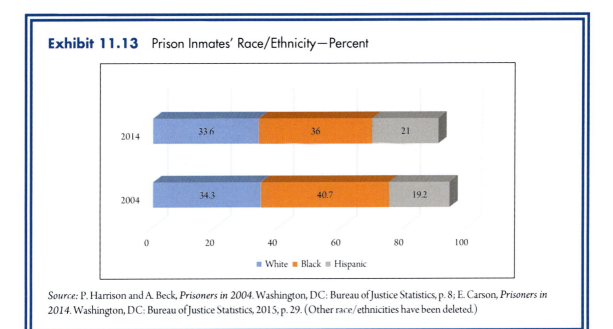

Source: P. Harrison and A. Beck, *Prisoners in 2004*. Washington, DC: Bureau of Justice Statistics, p. 8; E. Carson, *Prisoners in 2014*. Washington, DC: Bureau of Justice Statistics, 2015, p. 29. (Other race/ethnicities have been deleted.)

WHAT ARE THE ELEMENTS OF THE PRISONER SUBCULTURE?

The prisoner subculture has been studied since the 1940s. Researchers have argued whether the prisoner subculture is more influenced by the unique deprivations of prison life (the **deprivation theory**),[45] or by the street subculture that is "imported" to the prison from outside (the **importation theory**).[46] Deprivations that have been said to create subcultural elements include liberty, goods and services, heterosexual relationships, autonomy, and security.[47] Research provides support for both of these explanations of the prisoner subculture.[48] **Prisonization** is the process of being socialized to the prison subculture and all prisoners are more or less prisonized to the subculture with those serving long sentences becoming the most prisonized. The prisoner subculture can be described as including the inmate code, the prison value system, and prison **argot** (language).

The "**inmate code**" is described as a *sub rosa* (subcultural) set of rules by which prisoners "should" run their lives in the prison setting. Early descriptions of the inmate code portrayed a world where convicts "did their own time," shunned guards, and never lost their "cool," even in the face of extreme provocation. The prisoner who followed the code valued loyalty, autonomy, and strength. Violence is often rational, directive, and useful as it indicates tough-ness, strength, and the ability to "take care of business." Snitching may be the most heinous prison "crime." There are a disproportionate number of names for a snitch in the prison setting, including "rat," "squealer," "snitch," "cheese-eater," and "stoolpigeon." Officials and inmates alike often scorn the person identified as a snitch. Ironically, officials indicate that they could not run the prison without informers.

The female prisoner subculture has never been studied as intensely as men's, but some research has found that women do not value "do your own time" as much as men. Women are more likely to confide in each other and have more interactions with staff. Snitching is present in both female and male subcultures, but subcultural sanctions against this behavior are more serious in prisons for men. Different themes exist in the women's subculture which revolve around the "mix"—the subcultural immersion in homosexual rela-tionships, drug dealing, gambling, and the use of violence to obtain economic goods.[49]

The male and female inmate codes have changed from when early research-ers in the 1950s began writing about prisoner subcultures. Inmate solidarity has eroded considerably, if it ever existed at all. Younger and more violent offenders entering prisons have ignored the old-timers' admonitions to stay loyal and keep a low profile. Younger prisoners arguably had little respect for the inmate code, were ready to use violence in any situation, on any inmate, at any time, for even the slightest provocation.[50] The status hierarchy that charac-terized earlier eras was less pervasive as prison gangs upset the power structure. Violence or the fear of violence is ever-present in maximum security prisons for men. Violence stems from racial conflict, gambling or drug debt, sexual exploitation, retaliation for snitching or perceived disrespect. Not all male inmates cope with threats or victimization with violence, but large percentages feel they must.[51] There is also violence in women's prisons, and it is more prev-alent than earlier studies indicated. Most violence in women's prisons occurs when partners become jealous, or is due to debts, retaliation for gossip, or as a tool of economic manipulation.[52]

Today, race is an extremely central issue in prisons. Blacks, who comprise less than 13 percent of the American population, have become the majority in some prisons for men. In fact, it has been said that it is the one place in society where their power is clear: "I was in jail, the one place in America that Black men rule."[53] Racial gangs exist in every state to greater or lesser degrees. Proba-bly the best-known gangs were formed in Illinois, California, and Texas. In Illi-nois and California, prison gangs were imported from the streets in the 1960s and 1970s. They usually control the drug and black market of other contraband in the prison. Some research indicates that gangs among female prisoners are growing, whereas others have found little evidence of this phenomenon.[54] Perhaps the comparative lack of gang membership among female prisoners may be related to social groupings that cross racial lines and provide protection, services, and a feeling of belonging in similar ways to gang membership.

While the most obvious social grouping in prisons for men is the gang, female prisoners are more likely to group in loose associations known as **pseudofamilies**. Pseudofamilies are make-believe family systems that include all the familial roles including fathers, mothers, daughters, sisters, cousins, and so on. Women relate to each other more or less consistently with these roles. These types of relationships are less frequent today than what existed in the past, perhaps because of more liberal visitation policies that allow closer contact with real families.[55]

Prison slang, or prison argot, is the language of prisoners and thought to be an important part of the prison subculture. Ironically, correctional officers learn the prison argot and use it as adeptly as inmates. Argot terms include "fish," slang for a new inmate; "dawg," for a friend or associate; "toads," a derogatory name for White inmates; and "fishcops," new correctional officers. "Shit," "smack," "crap," "H," and "brown" are some of the many names for heroin. Argot for marijuana may be the most numerous with traditional names from "Mary Jane," "grass," or "Aunt Mary," to less recognized names such as "lubage," and "mutha." Slang for drugs in general includes the term "junk."[56] Argot terms for drugs are so numerous that every conceivable combination and potency of a drug may have several different names.[57] Argot by its nature keeps changing because as the language migrates to the dominant culture, the subculture invents new words.

Prisoner roles (or **argot roles**) serve to classify and describe inmates based on their behavior before prison, as well as what they do in prison. Clarence Schrag's (1944) roles have perhaps become the most well known. He described prisoner roles such as the square john, right guy, con politician, and outlaw. The "square john" was the type of inmate who did not have an extensive criminal record and identified more with prison officers than other inmates. Other inmates did not trust him. The "right guy" is characterized as the old-style convict. He was respected as a professional criminal, usually being a thief, bank robber, or a member of an organized crime group. He was respected as a leader in the yard and was not afraid of violence, but used it sparingly and selectively. The "con politician" was a title ascribed to inmates who held the most formal leadership roles in prison, for example, as a representative of the inmate council, and were very visible in interaction with the prison administration. The "outlaw" inmate was characterized as one who did not follow any code of behavior, even the inmate code.[58] There has not been as much research on female role types. In one study, numerous social roles among female prisoners including snitchers (informers), inmate cops (affiliated with correctional officers), squares (square john equivalents), jive bitches (those who stirred up trouble), rap buddies or homies (friends), boosters (shoplifters), pinners (a trusted inmate who serves as a lookout when illicit activities are undertaken), and a number of roles associated with homosexuality—penitentiary turnouts, butches, lesbians, femmes, stud broads, tricks, commissary hustlers, chippies, kick partners, cherries, punks, and turnabouts.[59] Much of the academic research on prisoner subcultures is dated and we know less about what happens inside the prison today, except for issues that are addressed by prisoner surveys, such as sexual assault.

IS SEXUAL ASSAULT IN PRISON A PROBLEM?

Sexual assault in prison occurs and fear of sexual assault is pervasive among new inmates. The actual reality of it is more complicated. Homosexuality in men's prisons is characterized by violent assaults and coercion where older and more experienced convicts (wolves) offer protection to younger inexperienced inmates (punks) for sexual favors and commissary articles. There is little distinction between those who are forced into such a role and those who were homosexual before prison.[60] Sexual assault in women's prisons has been described as rare and sexual relationships between inmates as consensual. In the 1990s more male correctional officers appeared in prisons for women, and sexual misconduct, up to and including rape, by male correctional officers against female inmates emerged as a problem and target of lawsuits.

Sexual victimization in prisons for both men and women came to the attention of Congress, which passed the Prison Rape Elimination Act (**PREA**) in 2003. The Act's provisions included making the prevention of prison rape a top priority for state prison systems; developing and maintaining a national standard for the detection, prevention, reduction, and punishment of prison rape; increasing the available data and information on the incidence of prison rape through national surveys of adult and juvenile facilities; standardizing the definitions used for collecting data on the incidence of prison rape; and increasing the efficiency and effectiveness of federal expenditures through grant programs dealing with social and public health issues.[61] The latest PREA prisoner survey data available is for 2011. Inmates were randomly selected for participation from 233 prisons, 358 jails, and 15 special detainment facilities; 44 of the prisons housed women (7,141 female prisoners participated), and

4 of the jails housed women. This survey defines "non-consensual sex acts" as oral, anal, or vaginal penetration, masturbation, and other sexual acts. "Abusive sexual contacts" is defined as unwanted contact involving touching of buttocks, thigh, penis, breasts, or vagina in a sexual way. "Sexual victimization" includes both categories.

In the survey results, more women than men in prison reported any type of sexual victimization by other inmates (6.9 percent compared to 1.7 percent). About equal numbers of women and men in prison reported staff sexual misconduct of any type (2.3 percent of women compared to 2.4 percent of men). This survey also was administered in jails. About 3.6 percent of female jail inmates reported any type of sexual victimization by other inmates (compared to 1.4 percent of males); and 1.4 percent of female jail inmates reported sexual misconduct by guards (compared to 1.9 percent of males). Survey results indicated that the most vulnerable inmates were those who reported having mental health issues, were committed for sex offenses, and were homosexual or bisexual (these results are from the combined pool of male and female inmates). Juveniles were not statistically more likely to report victimization than adults. It's important to realize that these national averages mask quite extreme differences between facilities. The report identifies "high"-reporting institutions and "low"-reporting institutions.[62]

One of the important findings of the study was that sexual assault (rape) was fairly rare, but more inmates experience other forms of sexual victimization involving unwanted touching and sexual harassment. Some state systems have instituted programs to address the issue of sexual victimization in response to these findings. The other major finding was the prevalence of sexual victimization in women's facilities; even though such victimization was not often physical rape but, rather, unwanted touching and sexual harassment. Further, female inmates were more likely to be victimized by each other rather than by a staff member, as was previously thought. Some researchers had already noted that female inmates were more likely to report inmate-on-inmate sexual victimization than male inmates. One study, for instance, reported that the rate of inmate-on-inmate sexual victimization in the previous six months was four times higher (212 compared to 43 per 1,000) and staff-on-inmate sexual violence was about one and one-half times higher (53 compared to 34 per 1,000) in women's prisons than in men's.[63] Thus, sexual assault in prison (genital rape) is fairly rare, but sexual victimization is more frequent. The range of prisoners who report some type of victimization ranges dramatically across facilities, however, with some prisons having fairly high levels and others fairly low levels.

WHAT ARE THE ISSUES CONCERNING THE MENTALLY ILL IN JAILS AND PRISONS?

The unfortunate fact is that jails and prisons have become de facto mental institutions in the United States. Media reports indicate that jails, especially, are becoming the most likely institutional setting for people with serious mental illnesses.[64] In the 1970s, the deinstitutionalization of the mentally ill occurred when court cases such as *Wyatt v. Stickney*[65] resulted in laws which allowed holding the mentally ill against their will only if it could be shown they posed a danger to self or others. The original intent was that community mental health centers would be better places to serve the mentally ill than housing them in large mental hospitals. Unfortunately, the promise of community mental health care has not been fulfilled to the degree that many advocates had hoped; thus, many mentally ill individuals "slip through the cracks"; they are not sick enough to be institutionalized, but not well enough to fully function in today's society.

Various studies indicate the percentage of correctional clients who have a mental health issue. Percentages vary because of the definition used and the way data is collected. Larger percentages are reported when information is from self-reports of symptomology and the broader term of mental health disorder is used; smaller percentages are reported when only formally diagnosed illnesses or stays in mental health institutions are counted. A mental disorder is "a syndrome characterized by clinically significant disturbance in an individual's cognition, emotion regulation, or behavior that reflects a dysfunction in the psychological, biological, or developmental processes underlying mental functioning."[66]

According to the Bureau of Justice Statistics, an estimated 56 percent of state prisoners, 45 percent of federal prisoners, and 64 percent of jail inmates have a mental health disorder.[67] In one older study, 16 percent of state prisoners were estimated to have a mental illness.[68] Other studies indicate that 9 percent of individuals on probation and 7 percent of individuals on parole were estimated to have a "serious" mental illness.[69] Jail studies have estimated that over 60 percent of jail inmates have some type of diagnosed mental illness which is four times higher than the general population and the rate of substance abuse is four to seven times higher.[70]

Women, Whites, and young inmates were more likely to exhibit mental health problems in one national jail survey. About 75 percent of women in jails exhibited mental health problems compared to 63 percent of male inmates. About 71 percent of Whites, 63 percent of Blacks, and 51 percent of Hispanics were found to have a mental health problem. Jail inmates with mental health problems are more likely to have had past incarcerations, used drugs, have experienced homelessness, have experienced past physical or sexual abuse, have parents who abused drugs or alcohol, and are more likely to violate facility rules.[71] Other studies also show that female jail and prison inmates have more severe problems with drugs and with mental health problems than do their male counterparts.[72]

In another study of more than 20,000 adults booked into five U.S. jails, 14.5 percent of men and 31 percent of women met criteria for a serious mental illness—prevalence rates at least three times higher than those found in the general population.[73] These percentages are much lower than other studies because the definition of "serious" mental health disorder is more restrictive.

Exhibit 11.14 displays the types of mental disorders reported among those in the criminal justice system. Depression is the most common diagnosis, but other disorders are represented as well.

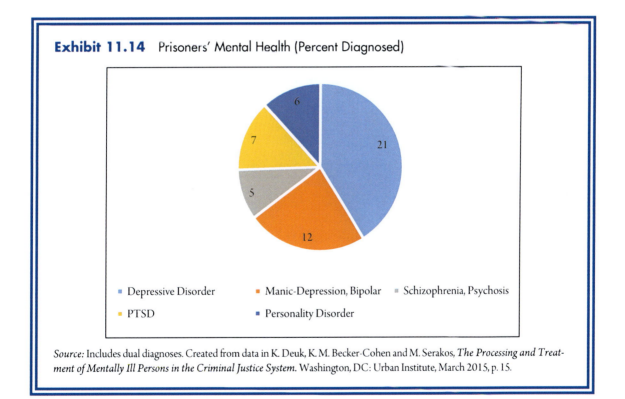

Exhibit 11.14   Prisoners' Mental Health (Percent Diagnosed)

- Depressive Disorder
- Manic-Depression, Bipolar
- Schizophrenia, Psychosis
- PTSD
- Personality Disorder

Source: Includes dual diagnoses. Created from data in K. Deuk, K. M. Becker-Cohen and M. Serakos, *The Processing and Treatment of Mentally Ill Persons in the Criminal Justice System.* Washington, DC: Urban Institute, March 2015, p. 15.

Co-occurring disorders refers to when an individual with a mental health disorder also is drug addicted or dependent. Co-occurrence of mental health and substance use disorders is common. In jails, of the approximately 17 percent with serious mental illness, an estimated 72 percent had a co-occurring substance use disorder. Approximately 59 percent of state prisoners with mental illnesses had a co-occurring drug or alcohol problem.[74] Another study found that individuals suffering from schizophrenia were more than four times more likely to have had drug dependency issues than others; those with bipolar disorder were more than five times as likely to have had such a diagnosis.[75] Exhibit 11.15 shows the prevalence of mental health and drug abuse among correctional populations.

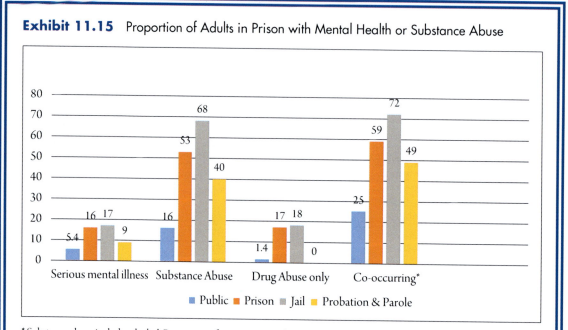

Exhibit 11.15   Proportion of Adults in Prison with Mental Health or Substance Abuse

* Substance abuse includes alcohol. Percentage of co-occurring is the percentage of those with a diagnosed mental health disorder that also has a drug dependency/abuse problem.

Source: Created from F. Osher, D. D'Amora, M. Plotkin, N. Jarrett and A. Eggleston, *Adults with Behavioral Health Needs under Correctional Supervision: A Shared Framework for Reducing Recidivism and Promoting Recovery.* New York, NY: Council of State Governments Justice Center, 2012, p. 6.

Unfortunately, correctional clients, whether on probation, parole, or in jail or prison do not necessarily receive appropriate treatment. Only one in three state prisoners and one in six jail inmates reported having received mental health treatment since their admission.[76] Even so, those with mental health disorders are more expensive to incarcerate. One study reported, for instance, that the overall annual per-inmate health cost was estimated at $4,780, while health costs at the corrections facility for inmates with serious mental illness were $12,000. Another study reported that the daily jail inmate cost was $78, but $125 per day for jail inmates with mental illness.[77]

Jail inmates and state prisoners with mental health disorders have higher rates of misconduct, accidents, and victimization. They are also more likely to recidivate when compared to others. Inmates with any major psychiatric disorder were found to be 2.4 times more likely to have four or more repeat incarcerations than inmates with no major psychiatric disorder. Those with bipolar disorder were 3.3 times more likely to be reincarcerated.[78]

Model programs across the country typically partner corrections and mental health staff who work together to provide mentally ill prisoners with care management and coordinated services before and after their release. Studies show that treatment services are correlated with reducing recidivism in jail releasees with mental health issues.[79] Research indicates that mental health treatment, drug treatment, and correctional rehabilitation are intertwined. It is difficult to address risk factors identified by prediction instruments like the R/N/R model described in Chapter 10 before addressing drug or mental health issues. Even though depression, for instance, is not a risk factor in prediction instruments, it should be addressed before targeting identified risk factors such as antisocial thinking patterns. For those with co-occurring mental health and addiction issues, integrated service models are necessary which address both problems.[80]

Finally, it should be noted that the vast majority of people with mental illnesses are not violent and do not commit crimes;[81] however, those with mental health disorders who do enter the criminal justice system are an especially problematic population. While in the system, they are more likely to have behavioral problems and higher rates of victimization; and, are more likely to be recidivistic.

WHY ARE SOME PRISONS AND JAILS PRIVATELY RUN? ARE PRIVATE PRISONS LESS EXPENSIVE?

The increased use of private prisons has occurred as a cost-savings measure by counties, states, and the federal government. Although various types of private–public models have been in place since the beginning of the penitentiary, such as the lease-labor system in the South, only in the last several decades have private companies been in the business of building and managing prisons under state and federal contracts. The number of prisoners in private facilities continues to grow. Since 1999, the size of this population has grown 90 percent, from 69,000 prisoners at year-end 1999 to 131,300 in 2014.[82] There was actually a decrease in the number of prisoners in private facilities from 2013 to 2014. Idaho, for instance, took back a facility from a private corrections company and so reduced their number of private prison beds by 77 percent.[83] At the federal level, private facilities house almost half of immigration detainees.

Two of the largest companies are CoreCivic (formerly Corrections Corporation of America) and GEO Group (formerly Wackenhut Corporation). There continues to be controversy about whether private prisons are more cost-effective than state-run institutions. There are many different ways of measuring costs (e.g., capital construction costs versus only using per diem costs of running an institution; average cost versus highest costs; counting public tax breaks and incentives, and so on). What is counted obviously makes a difference in the determination of whether private prisons are more cost-effective than public prisons. There are also vested interests involved; for instance, it is not surprising that studies funded by private companies and think tanks that support privatizing government functions show that private prisons are cost-effective, whereas critics show the opposite. Most studies show that there is very little cost savings when using private providers, although a few studies did find some savings.[84] A 2007 meta-analysis of previous privatization studies by University of Utah researchers found: "Cost savings from privatization are not guaranteed and quality of services is not improved. Across the board effect sizes were small, so small that the value of moving to a privately managed system is questionable."[85] Others have researched whether communities really do gain economic benefit when they agree to partner with a private corrections company to have a prison or jail facility built.[86] A 2010 study examined data from 1960 through 2010 and reported that partnering with a private corrections company was not a good investment for the rural communities that had hosted private prisons or jail facilities. Other studies have reported similar results.[87]

Studies have also examined recidivism and discovered that there is no significant difference between the recidivism of releasees from private and public prisons.[88] There are conflicting reports on whether private prisons have more incidents of violence than state or federally run prisons. One of the problems with studies is that sometimes there is no similarity between the populations of private prisons and other prisons (e.g., private prison contracts may specify no mentally ill and no violent offenders) or the private prison is compared to the state prisoner population as a whole, which is not a good comparison.[89]

It is reported that private corrections companies have a combined $3.3 billion in annual revenue and those resources carry some influence to state legislatures. A concern of many is that private prison officials engage in lobbying in states and seem to be involved in decisions about criminal justice policies. The largest private prison organizations contribute millions of dollars to political campaigns and lobbyists have even helped legislators write sentencing laws. Further, there is a "revolving door" whereby officials with private corrections firms become government employees, either attached to legislators, or as professionals in the state corrections departments; and, vice versa, state or federal correctional officials have moved to the private sector.

Because their profits are tied to increased numbers in prisons, there is a justifiable concern that private corrections firms and their officials and lobbyists are more concerned with shareholder profits than the public good. One of the pernicious elements of private contracts is that many require the state to guarantee an occupancy rate of, for instance, 90 percent. This means that even if the state instituted policies that reduced the number incarcerated, the state would still have to pay the private corrections company for unfilled beds.

One other issue is that prisoners housed in private prisons cannot utilize the courts to protect their constitutional rights. In *Minneci v. Pollard* (2012)[90] the Supreme Court decided that prisoners in a private prison could not utilize federal courts to allege constitutional violations since prison employees were private employees. The Justices argued that there were state tort remedies available, but opponents argued this creates an equal protection issue between prisoners housed in private prisons compared to prisoners in state or federally run prisons. Another legal issue is that private prisons seem to be exempt from open records laws. Under the Freedom of Information Act (FOIA), members of the public can request documents from federal prisons and immigration detention facilities—but private prisons are exempt from FOIA requests under both federal and state laws.[91]

For an interesting story from a journalist who was a private prison guard for four months, go to http://www.motherjones.com/politics/2016/06/cca-private-prisons-corrections-corporation-inmates-investigation-bauer

WHAT ARE THE DIFFERENCES AND SIMILARITIES OF JAILS AND PRISONS?

Jails and prisons are often confused, but they are very different institutions. The differences are in:

- location—jails are usually in urban areas close to courthouses, many prisons are in rural areas
- management—jails are usually run by the county sheriff while prisons are state institutions
- size—most jails are very small, although there are some that are as large as the largest prisons
- programming—there is less programming in jails than in state prisons
- history—jails are older
- population movement—jails have a more transitory population
- types of inmates—jails house a wider variety of inmates including pre-trial detainees who have not been convicted.

Jails are local detention facilities that house pre-trial detainees and misdemeanants, as well as a variety of other detainees. Most jails are run by the county sheriff and are located in the county seat. There are also state jails that house both felons and misdemeanants and regional jails that serve several counties and are run by administrators, not sheriffs. More Americans see the inside of a jail than a prison, and the time spent in jail is, for the most part, shorter; however, the jail experience is still disruptive and traumatic to many prisoners. Suicide is a real problem in jails, as are other medical emergencies such as drug withdrawals or overdoses. The rate of suicide in jail is five to six times higher than for comparable individuals outside of jail.[92] Jail personnel must deal with all these issues, perhaps without knowing the history of the individual; thus, insulin shock may look like an alcoholic stupor, or a defendant complaining of pain may be suffering mild drug withdrawal or life-threatening appendicitis. Inmates are often housed for short periods in "bullpens" or large cells. This raises the risk of victimization and creates a sanitation problem when too many people are housed in a small space, especially when some are intoxicated. Unpleasant smells, unremitting noise, and fear of the unknown characterize many individuals' first experience in jail.

Another difference between jails and prisons is that jails are a much older institution. Before the 1700s, jails (or **gaols**) were usually horrific places of confinement that housed the sick along with the healthy, women with men, and children with adults. The so-called **fee system** meant that prisoners had to pay for their room and board. Typically, stays in jails were short. The individual was held only until corporal punishment could be carried out, whether that was by whipping, the stocks or pillory, or hanging. In many cases, individuals were held for debt. In those cases, the person could be held indefinitely until he or his family could pay his debts. If they were unable, then the individual might be subject to **transportation**, which meant the person was sent to the colonies as an indentured servant.

Houses of corrections and bridewells sometimes took the place of the jail to confine the itinerant and poor. These institutions, such as St. Brigid's Well, first established in 1553, required inmates to earn their keep with labor.[93] The idea was that the poor, petty criminals, and orphaned children should learn a trade and become productive. Arguably, this was an improvement over the gaols. In 1777, Sheriff John Howard wrote about his findings after traveling around England visiting gaols. He recommended major reforms in the way jails were run, including classification, segregating women and children, individual cells, eliminating the fee system, and providing religious instruction.[94] The fee system was also in use in this country. Like England, the imprisoned inmates were held only until they were acquitted at trial or punished. Minor offenders and debtors may have stayed longer, but the early history of the jail was simply as a temporary holding facility until punishment could be carried out. Historical records show that there were very few women held in jails and the majority of inmates were White men. Common crimes included everything from theft to murder. While hanging was the punishment for more than 200 crimes in England, the colonies were less likely to impose capital punishment, probably because laborers were in short supply.[95]

Jails house a more transitory population than prisons. There were 11.4 million persons who entered jail during the twelve-month period ending June 30, 2014, a decrease from the peak of 13.6 million in 2008. Note that the daily population of jail is around 744,000. Most people have short sentences so jails have a much greater rate of entry and exits than do prisons. Recall from Chapter 9 that about one-third of all felony sentences are to local jails.

Jails house a higher percentage of females than prisons and a higher percentage of Whites. The number of females in jails increased by 18 percent between 2010 and 2014, while the male population declined about 3 percent during the same period. Women, who had comprised about 11 percent of the jail population in 2000, now comprise almost 15 percent. In 2014, the total jail population was 47 percent White, 35 percent Black, and 15 percent Hispanic. Between 2010 and 2014, the number of White inmates increased by 21,200; the number of Black inmates decreased by 19,400; and the number of Hispanic inmates declined by 7,500 as displayed by percentages in Exhibit 11.16.

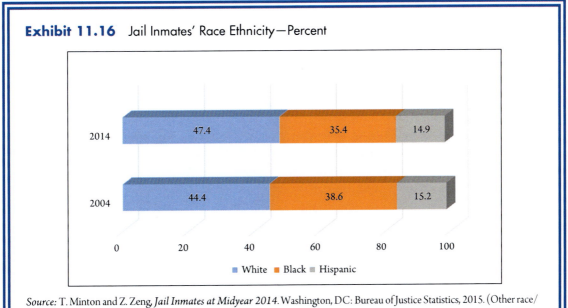

Exhibit 11.16   Jail Inmates' Race Ethnicity—Percent

Source: T. Minton and Z. Zeng, *Jail Inmates at Midyear 2014.* Washington, DC: Bureau of Justice Statistics, 2015. (Other race/ethnicities have been deleted.)

In 2014 about 4,200 juveniles age seventeen or younger were held in local jails at midyear 2014; this is a decrease from 2000. About 60 percent of jail inmates are detainees and not convicted. Since 2000, 95 percent of the growth in the overall jail inmate population (up 123,500) was due to the increase in the unconvicted population (up 117,700 inmates).[96] Recall from Chapter 9 that most arrestees are poor and cannot make bail, which may account for the increase in the number of detainees.

Many jails hold less than fifty inmates. On the other hand, there are extremely large jails that hold thousands of inmates. In 2014, jails housing over 1,000 inmates accounted for only 6 percent of the jurisdictions but held 47 percent of inmates. The largest jail system in the country is Los Angeles County, with a daily population average of over 19,000 inmates. New York City, Harris County (Houston), and Cook County (Chicago), all have close to or over 10,000 inmates.[97]

One of the major differences between prisons and jails is that jails hold a greater variety of types of prisoners, and many have not been convicted or sentenced. Some of the types of inmates include: defendants pending arraignment, trial, or sentencing, probation, parole, bail-bond violators, absconders, juvenile detainees, mentally ill people (pending transfer to mental institution), military violators (pending transfer to military facilities), contempt violators, material witnesses, state prisoners awaiting transfer, and misdemeanants serving sentence.

It may come as a surprise to many that as many as two-thirds of jail inmates were employed prior to their arrest. Unfortunately, many will lose their job before they are released. In surveys of prisoners, about 70 percent used drugs regularly before incarceration and about half had used in the month prior to their arrest.[98]

Because the jail is considered a temporary correctional facility, there is less emphasis on programs. Some of the larger jails may have programs such as work-release and GED tutoring. They may also have parenting classes and other life skills training. However, other jails have virtually nothing to occupy the time of the inhabitants, so inmates often spend all day watching television and playing cards.

Jails now often conform to standards promulgated by the state or the American Jail Association, and may be accredited by the American Correctional Association. Standards cover everything from sanitation to staffing to programming. The adoption of standards, however, has been slow and very few jails are accredited. The major problem, of course, is funding. Jails are a low priority for counties when budgets are written, and because many jails are small it is more difficult for them to meet the standards because it is more costly on a per-prisoner basis.

For more information on the American Jail Association, go to its website at http://www.aja.org/

FOCUS ON DATA: DID THE INCREASE IN INCARCERATION REDUCE THE CRIME RATE BETWEEN 1995 AND 2010?

The most important question to ask regarding prisons and jails is whether the incredible increase in the number of people incarcerated led to the substantial decrease in crime that we have experienced since the mid-1990s. It seems logical to assume that it did since the rise in prison populations occurred as crime decreased, as Exhibit 11.17 illustrates.

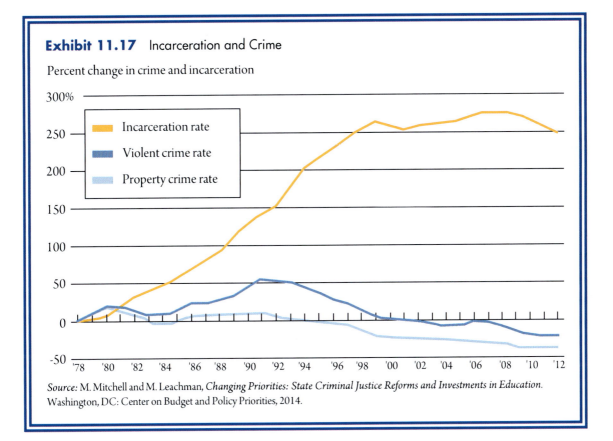

Exhibit 11.17 Incarceration and Crime

Percent change in crime and incarceration

Source: M. Mitchell and M. Leachman, *Changing Priorities: State Criminal Justice Reforms and Investments in Education.* Washington, DC: Center on Budget and Policy Priorities, 2014.

The question of whether the dramatic increase in imprisonment was substantially responsible for the decrease in crime has been the target of study by many researchers. In this discussion, we will utilize the comprehensive reports by the National Academies of Science[99] and a similarly exhaustive study by researchers for the Brennan Center for Justice.[100]

First, the idea that increasing the number of people sent to prison will affect crime rates is based on the idea that prison will (a) deter individuals and others from committing crime; and (b) that it will incapacitate at least the sentenced offender for the time he/she is in prison; thereby reducing the number of criminal events. How to determine statistically whether the increase in numbers of offenders in prison and/or an increase in the length of sentences reduces crime is extremely difficult because there are so many variables involved. For instance, one difficulty is that incarceration rates and crime rates are not separate. They are intertwined, i.e., if crime increases, those arrested and sentenced to prison would also increase. This is called **endogeneity** when the two factors are bi-directional—crime rates may affect incarceration rates even as incarceration rates affect crime rates. This statistical problem must be adjusted for or else estimates of the effect of incarceration will underestimate the degree to which imprisonment reduced crime.[101]

Another issue is that what is being studied is also crime that doesn't happen in the future; researchers want to study the "lagged" effects of incarceration on crime, i.e., future behavior. Are people who have served time in prison less likely to commit future crime because the experience of incarceration has deterred them or are they likely to be more involved in crime after prison because of prison's negative effects?

Models also estimate how much crime did not occur because of a person's incarceration to determine the effect of incarceration on crime. To do this, there has to be some estimate of how much crime individuals commit. Statistical analyses typically use an average of crimes per year (or month) for all offenders, but we know that this is not realistic. Some offenders commit many more crimes than others. Further, offenders don't commit crimes at the same rate throughout their lives; they "mature" out of crime and commit less crime in later years. Earlier studies used crime numbers that were unreasonably high because they estimated from incarcerated populations which include recidivists; this would overestimate the number of crimes per offender. By using higher average number of crimes in the analysis, the effect of incarceration on crime rates was overestimated.

This also illustrates why researchers have found declining effect sizes for greater and greater increases in incarceration rates, sometimes called the law of diminishing returns. Active offenders would be the first caught and imprisoned. What happens when more and more offenders are sent to prison is that the prison population includes more "casual" offenders—those who do not frequently commit crime—reducing the effect size of incarceration. In reverse, there can be substantial releases of prisoners without any increase in crime if the release decisions begin with less serious offenders because they are less likely to commit crime. However, if the incarceration rate is low, then only serious and recidivistic offenders would be released with an immediate impact on crime rates.[102]

Studies that have estimated the effect of incarceration on the crime drop which began in the 1990s have estimated that incarceration reduced crime rates from 0 to 58 percent for the violent crime drop and 6 to 41 percent of the property crime decline.[103] Obviously, there is no consensus in these studies. Some of the studies did not control for other factors that may have also impacted crime, e.g., increase in police. The most problematic issue, however, was that some of these studies were looking at the very beginning of the increase in imprisonment when the incarceration rate was low compared to today and, arguably, serious offenders were being incarcerated. As incarceration rates rose, the law of diminishing returns would presumably take effect, and these studies did not control for this.

More recent studies have reported much smaller effect sizes. One simulation study predicted that a 1 percent increase in imprisonment rates results in a crime reduction of 0.05 to 0.7 percent; another study reported a 0.1 to 0.3 percent crime reduction for a 1 percent increase.[104] The Brennan Center analysis concluded that increased incarceration accounted for approximately 6 percent (estimate range of 0 to 12 percent) of the reduction in property crime in the 1990s; and, increased incarceration accounted for less than 1 percent of the decline of property crime in the 2000s. The researchers also concluded that increased incarceration had no observable effect on the violent crime decline in the 1990s or in the 2000s.[105]

Another problem in estimating the effect of imprisonment on crime rates is that simply removing an offender does not necessarily mean that there is a net reduction in crime because of "replacement," meaning that another person may commit the crime instead. This seems to be especially true in drug markets where dealers are easily replaced.[106]

The studies described thus far attempted to estimate the effects of incarceration on crime using panel state-level data from the 1970s to later time periods with high incarceration with sophisticated statistical techniques to construct models to estimate **effect size** (the size of the correlation between the two variables, e.g., incarceration rate and crime rate). Newer research compares states that have substantially reduced their incarceration rates to see if crime rates increased. The Sentencing Project reported that New York and New Jersey achieved a 26 percent reduction in their incarceration rate from 1999 to 2012, and California experienced a 23 percent decline from 2006 to 2012. During this time frame, crime rates were declining nationally, and, in comparison, these three states generally achieved greater reductions in violent and property crimes than national averages.[107]

Other researchers have also reported findings that indicate states have reduced their incarceration rates without experiencing crime increases. For instance, a recent study reported that over the last ten years, twenty-seven states have decreased both crime and imprisonment. Nationally, imprisonment rates and crime have fallen together, 7 percent and 23 percent respectively since 2006. Many states with the most dramatic crime drops also shrank their incarcerated populations. Large states, such as California (27 percent), New York (18 percent), and Texas (15 percent) experienced some of the most significant reductions in incarceration while also experiencing crime drops of over 15 percent each. South Carolina saw a 38 percent drop in violent crime, the largest in the nation. It also saw a substantial 18 percent drop in its prison population.[108]

In Exhibit 11.18 we display crime rates and imprisonment rates to show that there is no pattern at all: states that have reduced the number of people in prison have seen crime declines (and increases). States that have increased the numbers of people in prison have also seen increased and decreased crime rates.

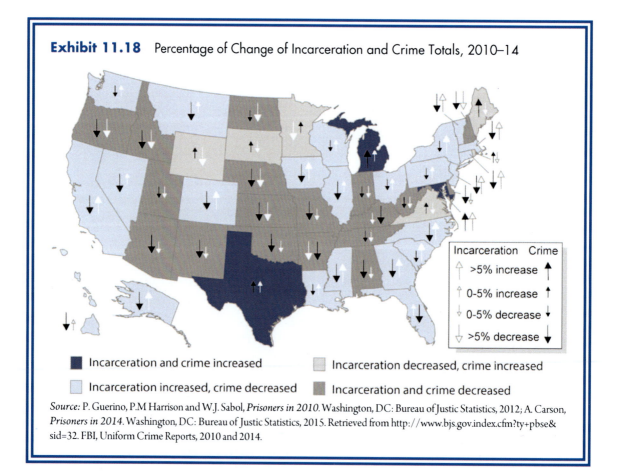

Exhibit 11.18   Percentage of Change of Incarceration and Crime Totals, 2010–14

Incarceration   Crime
- ⬆ >5% increase ⬆
- ↑ 0-5% increase ↑
- ⬇ 0-5% decrease ⬇
- ⬇ >5% decrease ⬇

- ■ Incarceration and crime increased
- □ Incarceration decreased, crime increased
- □ Incarceration increased, crime decreased
- ■ Incarceration and crime decreased

Source: P. Guerino, P.M Harrison and W.J. Sabol, *Prisoners in 2010.* Washington, DC: Bureau of Justic Statistics, 2012; A. Carson, *Prisoners in 2014.* Washington, DC: Bureau of Justic Statistics, 2015. Retrieved from http://www.bjs.gov.index.cfm?ty+pbse& sid=32. FBI, Uniform Crime Reports, 2010 and 2014.

The conclusion of the National Academy of Sciences commission, which reviewed all studies on the relationship between incarceration and crime, was that changes in punishment policies were the main and proximate drivers of the growth in incarceration. Prosecutors and judges became harsher in their charging and sentencing. However, over the four decades of steadily increasing incarceration rates, the rate of violent crime rose, then fell, rose again, then declined. Most studies indicate that if incarceration has had an effect on the crime decline, it has been fairly small. Further, longer sentences seem to have incrementally less effect because recidivism rates decline with age (i.e., many older inmates probably would not have committed further crime even if released).[109] The conclusion of the Brennan Center's researchers is consistent with these findings, adding that there was probably a modest (6 percent) effect size for property crime in the 1990s but that the law of diminishing returns (incarcerating less serious criminals) has reduced the effect of imprisonment on crime rates to the point that some studies are now showing a positive effect. In other words, imprisonment is causing more crime (because of the negative effects of a prison sentence).[110]

SUMMARY

How Many People Are Incarcerated in Jails and Prisons in the United States?

There are currently more than two million people incarcerated in prisons and jails. About two-thirds (1,561,500) of this number were in prison, and 744,600 were in jails. Incarceration rates were stable until the 1980s and then escalated dramatically, only slowing recently. In 2014, the rate of incarceration was 470 per 100,000, which is about five times what it was before 1980 and about five times the rate of many other Western nations.

What Rights Do Prisoners Have?

Prisoners do not have the same rights as free people. They do have the right to access courts without interference, minimal due process if they face the loss of good time, the right to be free from corporal punishment and conditions that cause needless pain or harm, and the right to practice their religion unless doing so will compromise the safety and security of the institution.

What Is Prison Like Today Compared to Previous Eras?

The separate system (solitary confinement) originated in Philadelphia at the Walnut Street Jail (1790) and Eastern State Penitentiary (1829). The Auburn Prison in New York (1817) became the model for prisons and utilized solitary cells but inmates worked and ate together under strict controls. The reformatory era of the 1890s focused on young offenders. The 1900s was a time when prisons were highly regimented and inmates engaged in meaningless work. The rehabilitative era of the 1960s to 1970s gave way to the warehouse prison of the 1980s as the number of prisoners increased dramatically.

Who Are the Prisoners in State and Federal Prisons?

Many prisoners are young (44 percent are under 34 years old), members of a minority group (only about 40 percent of prisoners are White), under-employed (before prison), and undereducated. About half of prisoners are violent offenders but that is because they "stack up" in prison with long sentences. About one-third of prison admissions are for violent crimes. Only about 7 percent of prisoners are women.

What Are the Elements of the Prisoner Subculture?

The prisoner subculture has been explained by the deprivation theory and the importation theory. It can be described as including the inmate code (the set of informal rules in the prison), the prison value system (which emphasizes toughness and doing your own time, which means not getting involved with others), and prison argot (slang). Men's and women's prisoner subcultures are different.

Is Sexual Assault in Prison a Problem?

In the latest survey (which sampled prisons and jails) more female prisoners and jail inmates report sexual victimization by other inmates than male prisoners. About equal numbers of women and men in prison reported staff sexual misconduct of any type. Survey results indicated that the most vulnerable inmates were those who reported having mental health issues, were committed for sex offenses, and were homosexual or bisexual (these results are from the combined pool of male and female inmates).

What Are the Issues Concerning the Mentally Ill in Jails and Prisons?

There are now estimated to be more mentally ill in prisons and jails than in mental health institutions. Although estimates vary, up to 20 percent of prison and jail inmates are said to have some form of mental disorder and closer to 40–50 percent of jail and prison inmates have drug dependency issues. Inmates with mental disorders are more likely to have discipline infractions, be victimized by other inmates, and have higher recidivism than other inmates.

Why Are Some Prisons and Jails Privately Run? Are Private Prisons Less Expensive?

Private prisons are always presented as a cost-saving measure for states and the federal government. Many studies dispute that they do result in cost savings to taxpayers. Studies are often done by advocates of one side or the other making it difficult to determine the facts.

What Are the Differences and Similarities of Jails and Prisons?

The differences between jails and prisons include: location (jails are usually in urban areas close to courthouses; many prisons are in rural areas), management (jails are usually run by the county sheriff while prisons are state institutions), size (most jails are very small, although there are some that are as large as the largest prisons), programming (there is less programming in jails than in state prisons), history (jails are an older institution), population movement (jails have a more transitory population), and types of inmates (jails house a wider variety of inmates including pre-trial detainees who have not been convicted).

Critical Thinking Exercises

1. Read the court case *Brown v. Plata* (2010) and then listen to the oral argument from the Oyez website (https://www.oyez.org/cases/2010/09–1233). List the arguments made by the opposing attorneys and how the Justices decided them in the written holding.
2. Do an Internet search of private prisons and list and describe the positive and the negative things you found about them. Who is promoting privatization in corrections? Who is opposing privatization? Write a "Focus on Data" section on whether private prisons are good for a state.

NOTES

1 J. Pollock, S. Glassner and A. Krajewski, "Examining the conservative shift from harsh justice." *Laws* 4 (2015): 107–124.
2 P. Harrison and A. Beck, *Prison and Jail Inmates at Midyear 2005*. Washington, DC: Bureau of Justice Statistics, 2006; P. Harrison and A. Beck, *Prison and Jail Inmates at Midyear 2002*. Washington, DC: Bureau of Justice Statistics, 2006.
3 Pew Center on the States, *Time Served: The High Cost, Low Return of Longer Prison Terms*. Washington, DC: Pew Center on the States. Available at www.pewstates.org/publicsafety
4 D. Kaeble, L. Glaze, A. Tsoutis and T. Minton, *Correctional Populations in the United States, 2014*. Washington, DC: Bureau of Justice Statistics, 2015.
5 Bureau of Justice Statistics, *Prisoners in 1988*. Washington, DC: Bureau of Justice Statistics, 1989; E. Carson, *Prisoners in 2014*. Washington, DC: Bureau of Justice Statistics, 2015, p. 1.
6 P. Harrison and A. Beck, *Prisoners in 2001*. Washington, DC: Bureau of Justice Statistics, 2002, p. 5.
7 E. Carson, *Prisoners in 2014*. Washington, DC: Bureau of Justice Statistics, 2015, p. 5.
8 H. West, W. Sabol and S. Greenman, *Prisoners in 2009*. Washington, DC: Bureau of Justice Statistics, 2010, p. 28; E. Carson, *Prisoners in 2014*. Washington, DC: Bureau of Justice Statistics, 2015, p. 5.
9 M. Mauer, *The Changing Racial Dynamics of Women's Incarceration*. Washington, DC: The Sentencing Project, 2013, p. 3.
10 E. Carson, *Prisoners in 2014*. Washington, DC: Bureau of Justice Statistics, 2015, p. 5.
11 Mauer, note 9, p. 6.
12 Mauer, note 9.

13 Sentencing Project, *U.S. Prison Population Trends 1999–2014: Broad Variation among States in Recent Years*. Washington, DC: The Sentencing Project, 2014.

14 *Ruffin v. Commonwealth*, 62 Va. 790, 1871.

15 National Advisory Commission on Criminal Justice Standards and Goals Report on Corrections. Washington, DC: U.S Government Printing Office, 1973, p. 18.

16 42 U.S.C. § 3626.

17 *Ex parte Hull*, 61 S. Ct. 640, 1941. *Cooper v. Pate*, 378 U.S. 546, 1964.

18 *Johnson v. Avery*, 89 S. Ct. 747, 1969; *Bounds v. Smith*, 430 U.S. 817, 1977; *Procunier v. Martinez*, 94 S. Ct. 1800, 1974.

19 *Lewis v. Casey*, 116 S. Ct. 2174, 1996, *Shaw v. Murphy*, 121 S. Ct. 1475, 2001.

20 *Wolff v. McDonnell*, 94 S. Ct. 2963, 1974.

21 Superintendent, Massachusetts Correctional Institution, *Walpole v. Hill*, 105 S. Ct. 2768, 1985, *Sandin v. Conner*, 115 S. Ct. 2293, 2303, 1995.

22 *Meachum v. Fano*, 96 S. Ct. 2532, 1976; *Olim v. Wakinekona*, 103 S. Ct. 1741, 1983.

23 *Jackson v. Bishop*, 404 F.2d 571 (8th Cir. 1968).

24 *Estelle v. Gamble*, 97 S. Ct. 285, 1976.

25 *Brown v. Plata*, 563 US 493, 2011.

26 *The Future of California Corrections Executive Summary*. California Department of Corrections and Rehabilitations (CDCR), accessed December 1, 2012, http://www.cdcr.ca.gov/2012plan/docs/plan/exec-summary.pdf.

27 P. Guerino, P. Harrison and W. Sabol, *Prisoners in 2010*. Washington, DC: Bureau of Justice Statistics, p. 4; E. Carson, *Prisoners in 2014*. Washington, DC: Bureau of Justice Statistics, 2015, p. 5.

28 *Knecht v. Gillman*, 48 F.2d 1136 (8th Cir. 1973).

29 *Washington v. Harper*, 494 US 210, 1990.

30 *Pell v. Procunier*, 94 S. Ct. 2800, 1974; *Procunier v. Martinez*, 94 S. Ct. 1800, 1974; *Thornburgh v. Abbot*, 109 S. Ct. 1874, 1989;

31 *Turner v. Safley*, 107 S. Ct. 2254, 1987.

32 *Shaw v. Murphy*, 532 U.S. 223, 2001; *Overton v. Bazzetta*, 123 S. Ct. 2162, 2003.

33 *O'Lone v. Estate of Shabazz*, 107 S. Ct. 2400, 1987; *Holt v. Hobbs*, 135 S. Ct. 853, 2015.

34 *Bell v. Wolfish*, 441 US 520, 1979; *Florence v. Board of Chosen Freeholders*, 566 U.S. ____, 2012.

35 L. Zupan, *Jails: Reform and the New Generation Philosophy*. Cincinnati, OH: Anderson Publishing, 1991.

36 C. Crosley, *Unfolding Misconceptions: The Arkansas State Penitentiary, 1836–1986*. Arlington, VA: Liberal Arts Press, 1986; D. Rothman, *The Discovery of the Asylum: Social Order and Disorder in the New Republic*. Boston, MA: Little, Brown, 1971; R. Johnson, *Hard Time*. Belmont, CA: Wadsworth/ITP, 2002.

37 N.H. Rafter, *Partial Justice: Women, Prisons, and Social Control*, 2nd edn. Boston, MA: Northeastern University Press, 1990, p. xxvi.

38 Rafter, note 37; E. Freedman, *Their Sisters' Keepers: Women's Prison Reform in America, 1830–1930*. Ann Arbor, MI: University of Michigan Press, 1981.

39 R. Johnson, note 36; B. Crouch and J. Marquart, *An Appeal to Justice: Litigated Reform of Texas Prisons*. Austin, TX: University of Texas Press, 1989; Rafter, note 37.

40 J. Pollock, *Prisons and Prison Life: Costs and Consequences*. Boston, MA: Oxford Press, 2012; J. Pollock, *Women's Crimes, Criminology and Corrections*. Prospect Heights, IL: Waveland, 2014.

41 L. Carroll, *Hacks, Blacks and Cons: Race Relations in a Maximum Security Prison*. Lexington, MA: Lexington Books, 1974.

42 J. Irwin, *The Warehouse Prison: Disposal of the New Dangerous Classes*. Los Angeles: Roxbury Press, 2004.

43 A. Rierden, *The Farm: Life Inside a Women's Prison*. Amherst, MA: University of Massachusetts Press, 1997; J. Pollock, note 40.

44 E. Carson, *Prisoners in 2014*. Washington, DC: Bureau of Justice Statistics, 2015, p. 4, 29.

45 G. Sykes, *The Society of Captives*. Princeton, NJ: Princeton University Press, 1958, 2010, p. 1.

46 J. Irwin and D. Cressey, "Thieves, convicts, and the inmate cultures." *Social Problems* 10 (Fall) (1962): 142–155.

47 G. Sykes, *The Society of Captives*. Princeton, NJ: Princeton University Press, 1958, p. 78.

48 J. Pollock, note 40.

49 B. Owen and D.L. MacKenzie, "The mix: The culture of imprisoned women." In M. Stohr and C. Hemmens (Eds.), *The Inmate Prison Experience*. Upper Saddle River, NJ: Pearson, 2004, pp. 152–172; R. Giallombardo, *Society of Women: A Study of a Women's Prison*. New York, NY: Wiley, 1966; J. Pollock, *Women, Prison, and Crime*, 2nd edn. Belmont, CA: Wadsworth, 2002; L. Girshick, *No Safe Haven: Stories of Women in Prison*. Boston, MA: Northeastern University Press, 1999; B. Owen, *"In the Mix": Struggle and Survival in a Women's Prison*. Albany, NY: State University of Albany Press, 1998; J. Pollock, note 40.

50 J. Irwin, *Prisons in Turmoil*. Boston, MA: Little, Brown, 1980; V. Hassine, *Life without Parole: Living in Prison Today*. Los Angeles, CA: Roxbury, 1999.

51 L. Leban, S. Cardwell, H. Copes and T. Brezina. "Adapting to prison life: A qualitative examination of the coping process among incarcerated offenders." *Justice Quarterly* 2015, DOI: 10.1080/07418825.2015.1012096.

52 B. Owen, J. Wells, J. Pollock and B. Muscat, *Gendered Violence and Safety: A Contextual Approach to Improving Security in Women's Facilities*. Washington, DC: NIJ; J. Wooldredge and B. Steiner, "Assessing the need for gender-specific explanations of prisoner victimization." *Justice Quarterly* 2014. DOI:10.1080/07418825.2014.897364

53 J. Jacobs, *Stateville: The Penitentiary in Mass Society*. Chicago: University of Chicago Press, 1977; L. Carroll, *Hacks, Blacks and Cons: Race Relations in a Maximum Security Prison*. Lexington, MA: Lexington Books, 1974; N. McCall, *Makes Me Wanna Holler: A Young Black Man in America*. New York, NY: Vintage, 1995, p. 149.

54 S. Mahan, "Imposition of despair: An ethnography of women in prison." *Justice Quarterly* 1 (1984): 357–385; K. Greer, "The changing nature of interpersonal relationships in a women's prison." *Prison Journal* 80 (2000): 442–468; J. Pollock, note 40.

55 J. Pollock, note 40.

56 C. Trulson, "The social world of the prisoner." In J. Pollock (Ed.), *Prisons Today and Tomorrow*. Sudbury, MA: Jones and Bartlett Publishers, 2005, pp. 79–124.

57 J. Hargan, "The psychology of prison language." *Journal of Abnormal and Social Psychology* 30 (1934): 359–361; J. Lerner, *You Got Nothing Coming: Notes from a Prison Fish*. New York, NY: Broadway Books, 2002; G. Sykes and S. Messinger, "The inmate social system." In R. Cloward (Ed.), *Theoretical Studies in the Social Organization of the Prison*. New York, NY: Social Science Research Council, 1960, pp. 6–10.

58 C. Schrag, "Leadership among prison inmates." *American Sociological Review* 19 (1961): 37–42.

59 R. Giallombardo, *Society of Women: A Study of a Women's Prison*. New York, NY: Wiley, 1966, pp. 105–123.

60 R. Hanser and C. Trulson, "Sexual abuse of men in prison." In F. Reddington and B. Kreise (Eds.), *Sexual Assault: The Victims, the Perpetrators, and the Criminal Justice System*. Durham, NC: Carolina Academic Press, 2004.

61 Prison Rape Elimination Act of 2003, Public Law (2003) 108–179.

62 R. Rantala, J. Rexroat and A. Beck, *Sexual Victimization Reported by Adult Correctional Authorities, 2009–11* (NCJ 243904). Washington, DC: Bureau of Justice Statistics, 2014.

63 N. Wolff, C. Blitz, J. Shi, R. Bachman and J. Siegel, "Sexual violence inside prison: Rates of victimization." *Journal of Urban Health* *3 (2006): 835–848; also see N. Wolff, J. Shi and R. Bachman, "Measuring victimization inside prison: Questioning the questions." *Journal of Interpersonal Violence* 23 (2008): 1343–1362.

64 National Public Radio Staff, "Nation's Jails Struggle with Mentally Ill Prisoners," National Public Radio, September 4, 2011. Available at http://www.npr.org/2011/09/04/140167676/nations-jails-struggle-with-mentallyill- prisoners. (Highlighting that "the three largest in-patient psychiatric facilities in the country are jails: Los Angeles County Jail, Rikers Island Jail in New York City, and Cook County Jail in Illinois.")

65 *Wyatt v. Stickney*, 325 F. Supp. 781 (M.D. Ala. 1971).

66 American Psychiatric Association, Diagnostic and Statistical Manual of Mental Disorders, 5th edn. Arlington, VA: American Psychiatric Association, 2013. http://dsm.psychiatryonline.org/book.aspx?bookid=556.

67 D. James and L. Glaze, Mental Health Problems of Prison and Jail Inmates. Washington, DC: Bureau of Justice Statistics, 2006.

68 P. Ditton, Mental Health and Treatment of Inmates and Probationers. Washington, DC: Bureau of Justice Statistics, 1999.

69 T. Feucht and J. Gfroerer, Mental and Substance Use Disorders among Adult Men on Probation or Parole: Some Success against a Persistent Challenge. Rockville, MD: Substance Abuse and Mental Health Services Administration, Center for Behavioral Health Statistics and Quality, 2011.

70 A. Bell, N. Jaquette, D. Sanner, C. Steele-Smith and H. Wald, "Treatment of individuals with co-occurring disorders in county jails." Corrections Today 67(3) (2005): 86–91; L. Teplin, K. Abram and G. McClelland, "Prevalence of psychiatric disorders among incarcerated women: Pretrial jail detainees." Archives of General Psychiatry 53 (1996): 505–512; P. Harrison and A. Beck, Prison and Jail Inmates at Midyear 2005. Washington, DC: Bureau of Justice Statistics, 2006, p. 8.

71 D. James and L. Glaze, Mental Health Problems of Prison and Jail Inmates. Washington, DC: Bureau of Justice Statistics, 2006.

72 B. Veysey, K. DeCou and L. Prescott, "Effective management of female jail detainees with histories of physical and sexual abuse." American Jails (May/June) (1998): 50–63.

73 H. Steadman, F. Osher, P. Robbins, B. Case and S. Samuels, "Prevalence of serious mental illness among jail inmates." Psychiatric Services 60 (6) (June 2009): 761–765.

74 P. Ditton, Mental Health and Treatment of Inmates and Probationers. Washington, DC: Bureau of Justice Statistics, 1999.

75 D. Regier, M. Farmer, D. Rae, B. Locke, S. Keith, L. Judd and F. Goodwin, "Co-morbidity of mental disorders with alcohol and other drug abuse." Journal of the American Medical Association 264 (19) (1990): 2511–2518.

76 D. James and L. Glaze, Mental Health Problems of Prison and Jail Inmates. Washington, DC: Bureau of Justice Statistics, 2006.

77 Studies reported in F. Osher, D. D'Amora, M. Plotkin, N. Jarrett and A. Eggleston, Adults with Behavioral Health Needs under Correctional Supervision: A Shared Framework for Reducing Recidivism and Promoting Recovery. New York, NY: Council of State Governments Justice Center, 2012.

78 Reported in K. Deuk, K. M. Becker-Cohen and M. Serakos, The Processing and Treatment of Mentally Ill Persons in the Criminal Justice System. Washington, DC: Urban Institute, March 2015, p. 18.

79 R. Arnold-Williams, E. Vail and J. MacLean, Mentally Ill Offender Community Transition Program: Annual Report to the Legislature, December 1, 2008. Olympia, WA: Washington State Department of Social and Health Services, Health and Recovery Services Administration, Mental Health Division—MIOCTP Program; J. Morrissey, Medicaid Benefits and Recidivism of Mentally Ill Persons Released from Jail. Report No. 214169. Washington, DC: National Institute of Justice, Office of Research and Evaluation, Justice System Research Division, 2004.

80 F. Osher, D. D'Amora, M. Plotkin, N. Jarrett and A. Eggleston, Adults with Behavioral Health Needs under Correctional Supervision: A Shared Framework for Reducing Recidivism and Promoting Recovery. New York, NY: Council of State Governments Justice Center, 2012.

81 H. Steadman, E. Mulvey, J. Monahan, P. Robbins, P. Appelbaum, T. Grisso, L. Roth and E. Silver, "Violence by people discharged from acute psychiatric inpatient facilities and by others in the same neighborhoods." Archives of General Psychiatry 55, 5 (May 1998): 393–401.

82 E. Carson, Prisoners in 2014. Washington, DC: Bureau of Justice Statistics, 2015, p. 13.

83 E. Carson, note 82.

84 G. Gaes, "Cost, performance studies look at prison privatization." NIJ Journal (2010), modified. Retrieved 9/14/2010 from http://www.ojp.usdoj.gov/nij/journals/259/prison-privatization.htm. H. Lapp et al., United States Department of Justice, Evaluation of the Taft Demonstration Project: Performance of a Private-Sector Prison and the BOP, 2005; R.A. Oppel, Jr., "Private prisons found to offer little in savings." New York Times, May 18, 2011.

85 B. Lundahl et al., *Prison Privatization: A Meta-Analysis of Cost Effectiveness and Quality of Confinement Indicators*. Salt Lake City: Utah Criminal Justice Center, 2007.

86 J. Greene, "Bailing out private jails." *American Prospect*, September 9, 2001; K. Pranis, *Private Correctional Institutions, Cost-Saving or Cost-Shifting: The Fiscal Impact of Prison Privatization in America 8* (n.d.). Tallahasee, FL: Private Corrections Institute. Available at http://www.prisonpolicy.org/scans/AZ_PP_Rpt_v4.pdf

87 C. Mosher, G. Hooks and P.B. Wood, "Don't build it here: The hype versus the reality of prisons and local employment." In T. Herivel and P. Wright (Eds.), *Prison Profiteers: Who Makes Money From Mass Incarceration*. New York, NY: New Press, 2007.

88 W. Bales, L. Bedard, S. Quinn, D. Ensley and G. Holley, "Recidivism of public and private state prison inmates in Florida." *Criminology and Public Policy* 4 (1) (2005): 57–82; S. Sharp, "Inmate recidivism as a measure of private prison performance." *Crime and Delinquency* 54 (2008): 482–489.

89 D. Perrone and T.C. Pratt, "Comparing the quality of confinement and cost-effectiveness of public versus private prisons: What we know, why we do not know more, and where do go from here." *Prison Journal* 83 (2003): 301–309.

90 *Minneci v. Pollard*, 132 S. Ct. 617, 2012.

91 M. Cohen, "How for-profit prisons have become the biggest lobby no one is talking about." *Washington Post*, April 28, 2015; American Civil Liberties Union, *Banking on Bondage: Private Prisons and Mass Incarceration*. New York, NY: ACLU, 2011.

92 L. Hayes, "Suicidal signs and symptoms." *Correct. Forum* 14 (6) (2005): 36.

93 American Correctional Association, *The American Prison: From the Beginning*. Lanham, MD: ACA, 1983.

94 N. Morris and D. Rothman, *The Oxford History of the Prison*, New York, NY: Oxford University Press, 1995.

95 J. Moynahan and E. Stewart, *The American Jail: Its Development and Growth*. Chicago: Nelson-Hall, 1980.

96 T. Minton and Z. Zeng, *Jail Inmates at Midyear 2014*. Washington, DC: Bureau of Justice Statistics, 2015.

97 T. Minton, *Jail Inmates at Midyear 2009, Statistical Tables*. Washington, DC: Bureau of Justice Statistics, 2010, p. 12.

98 "Percent of Jail Inmates Reporting Drug Use." *Sourcebook of Criminal Justice Statistics* 2003, Table 6.21. Retrieved from http://www.albany.edu/sourcebook/pdf/t621.pdf; P. Harrison and A. Beck, *Prison and Jail Inmates at Midyear 2004*. Washington DC: Bureau of Justice Statistics, 2005.

99 J. Travis, B. Western and S. Redburn, "The growth of incarceration in the united states: Exploring causes and consequences." Washington, DC: National Research Council of the National Academies of Sciences, 2014.

100 O. Roeder, L. Eisen and J. Bowling, *What Caused the Crime Decline?* Washington, DC: Brennan Center for Justice, 2015.

101 J. Travis, B. Western and S. Redburn, *The Growth of Incarceration in the United States: Exploring Causes and Consequences*. Washington, DC: National Research Council of the National Academies of Sciences, 2014, p. 149.

102 O. Roeder, L. Eisen and J. Bowling, *What Caused the Crime Decline?* Washington, DC: Brennan Center for Justice, 2015, p. 18.

103 Reviewed in O. Roeder, L. Eisen and J. Bowling, *What Caused the Crime Decline?* Washington, DC: Brennan Center for Justice, 2015, p. 22.

104 J. Travis et al., note 101, p. 14

105 O. Roeder, note 100, p. 23.

106 J. Travis et al., note 101, p. 141

107 M. Mauer and N. Ghandnoosh, "Can we reduce the prison population by 25%?" *The Crime Report*, August 5, 2014.

108 L. Eisen and J. Cullen, *Update: Changes in State Imprisonment*. Washington DC: Brennan Center for Justice, 2016.

109 J. Travis, note 101, p. 5.

110 O. Roeder, note 100.

RE-ENTRY AND RECIDIVISM | 12

It is an uncontroverted fact that almost all people who are incarcerated eventually return to the community (650,000 or more individuals each year from state prisons alone, and more than nine million individuals from jail). One way to reduce the number of people in prisons and jails is to reduce **recidivism**. A critical approach to the issue of re-entry must consider the factors associated with recidivism, but, also, consider whether a better approach is to refrain from sending so many people to prison in the first place. We examine the approach of "realignment" and "re-investment" which shift correctional populations from state prisons to community placements. As many states begin to decrease their incarceration rates, it becomes essential to determine whether or not such shifts lead to more crime in the community.

WHAT IS THE HISTORY OF PAROLE?

Parole comes from French word *parol* (*parole d'honneur*) referring to "word" as in giving one's word of honor.[1] The idea of releasing prisoners

Chapter Preview

- What Is the History of Parole?
- Who Is on Parole?
- What Are the Problems of Re-Entry?
- What Are Collateral Consequences of a Criminal Conviction?
- What Is the Second Chance Act?
- What Is the Process for Parole Revocation?
- How Many Offenders Recidivate and Who Is Most Likely to Recidivate?
- Focus on Data: What Is the "Justice Reinvestment Initiative" and "Justice Realignment"? Have These Approaches Increased Crime?
- Summary
- Critical Thinking Exercises

from incarceration under some form of community supervision can be traced all the way back to the punishment of **transportation**, which involved sending prisoners from England to the colonies and, after the American Revolution, to Australia. These prisoners were not paroled in the sense that we think of today, but they were released from confinement into the community, and leased to a landowner who used their labor. The last shipment of convicts to Australia was as late as 1868.[2]

Alexander Maconochie (1787–1860) developed an early form of parole on Norfolk Island, a prison colony 1,000 miles off the coast of Australia. Maconochie's **mark system** consisted of stages of increasing responsibility. At the highest stage of responsibility, the offender could live almost independently, albeit on the island, and the final stage was a form of early release. Sir Walter Crofton (1815–97) developed a concept in Ireland more similar to today's parole. His **ticket of leave**, implemented around 1853, was a form of the mark system. Offenders were released early from prison upon going through graduated stages of responsibility and earning marks along the way for good behavior. When the offender had earned enough marks, he received his "ticket to leave" prison and returned to his community. The offender was required to report to police and, supposedly, a police inspector helped find the offender a job and supervised his release. His "ticket to leave" program was picked up by American prison reformers and included in the "Declaration of Principles" at the 1870 Prison Congress.[3]

Zebulon Brockway (1827–1920) was appointed superintendent of Elmira Reformatory in New York in 1877 and instituted a form of indeterminate sentencing and parole release. Inmates of Elmira were young men (16 to 30) who were placed in "second grade," which was the highest form of custody. After six months of good conduct, they were promoted to "first grade." Continued good behavior would earn an early release. Offenders were released to six months of supervision, supervised by volunteer guardians. It wasn't until many years later that parole was implemented with paid employees.[4] Gradually throughout the late 1800s and early 1900s, states adopted some form of early release or parole, but it may not have included any concept of supervision, or supervision was provided haphazardly, or by volunteers. In 1907, New York became the first state to implement parole with the elements we consider associated with modern parole:

- an indeterminate sentence
- a system for granting early release
- postrelease supervision by paid employees
- the possibility of revocation and return to prison.

By 1942, all states had a parole system, although some continued to use volunteer parole officers.[5] The federal system of parole was fully implemented by 1932.

In the **rehabilitative era** of the 1970s, the majority of inmates were released on parole. For instance, in 1977, 72 percent of all prisoners were released via parole. However, along with an increased use of prison and more punitive approach to all offenders, the use of parole declined dramatically in the 1980s and 1990s and, by 1997, only 28 percent of all prisoners were released via parole. At the federal level, the Comprehensive Crime Control Act of 1984 created the U.S. Sentencing Commission, which established sentencing guidelines that specified fixed terms. Federal parole was abolished and replaced with mandatory postrelease supervision. By 2002, fourteen states had abolished parole (Arizona, Delaware, Illinois, Indiana, Kansas, Maine, Minnesota, Mississippi, New Mexico, North Carolina, Ohio, Oregon, Virginia, Washington), and just fifteen states still had full parole discretion (Alabama, Colorado, Idaho, Kentucky, Montana, Nevada, New Jersey, North Dakota, Oklahoma, Pennsylvania, Rhode Island, South Carolina, Utah, Vermont, Wyoming).[6] The remaining 21 states allow parole for only some types of prisoners. Most states that abolished parole have a form of mandatory supervision after release that is based on a percentage of time served and good time awarded. The offender is subject to revocation and return to prison until the full expiration of the original sentence.

> For more information on parole, go to the National Parole Resource Center at http://nationalparoleresourcecenter.org and the Association of Paroling Authorities International at http://www.apaintl.org/

Today parole is usually a division under the state's department of corrections, but can also be a separate agency, or a variation of these two models.[7] In some states, only the parole board is separate from the department of corrections, but parole officers and all employees related to supervision are part of the corrections department. This removes the discretionary release decision makers from the auspices of the agency, but not the supervising officers.

> For an interesting website, go to the National Institute of Corrections where you can browse on a range of topics in corrections: http://nicic.gov/

WHO IS ON PAROLE?

In states that have retained discretionary parole, the inmate is eligible for parole according to statute; typically, when one-half or two-thirds of the sentence has been served. Just because an inmate is eligible for parole does not mean that he or she receives it. The parole board or authority decides if and when an eligible inmate will be released (and in some states also has the power to make recommendations to the governor on **pardons**). The board members are typically political appointments and consist of no more than ten members who may come from a variety of backgrounds, including law enforcement, education, and business.

The appointment is typically a term lasting from three to six years; however, in some states, the appointment is indefinite. Depending on the state, these members may have the power to grant parole, set parole decision dates, rescind parole, issue warrants and subpoenas, set conditions, restore offenders' civil rights, and grant final discharges. Some or all of these duties may be delegated.

Exhibit 12.1 In states that have parole, eligible inmates are typically considered by a panel of three members of the full board, which can have as many as ten politically appointed members.

Source: AP

Even in states that have abolished parole, there may still be discretionary parole for inmates who were sentenced before the state legislature abolished discretionary parole, and most states also have mandatory supervision for all released inmates with the potential for revocation and return to prison.

The Supreme Court has held that parole release is not a right; therefore, states do not have to follow strict due process guidelines in parole release hearings.[8] This means that states can set up any type of procedure deemed expedient in the decision to grant parole, or eliminate the privilege entirely as some states have.[9] For discretionary parole decisions, only a subset of the full board holds release hearings. Parole hearings last an average of twelve to fifteen minutes. In some states, the board may not meet personally with the offender at all. The board may or may not allow the offender to appear personally and/ or present witnesses and evidence in support of his or her release. The board considers a variety of factors in their release decision, including the seriousness of the offense, the amount of time served, the offender's age, juvenile history, criminal history, number of prison infractions, other arrests, participation in programs, and letters of support or protest.

The ability of parole board members to accurately judge when an offender is no longer a risk to the community has always been questionable. Studies show that board members pay most attention to the severity of the crime in making the release decision, not what the offender has done in prison. Other factors that weigh in the decision include prior criminal record, attitude toward family responsibilities, attitude toward authority, and attitude toward the victim.[10] Many states allow victim impact statements and letters from the district attorney to be read at the parole hearing. Research has found that when victims attend the hearing or send letters, offenders are less likely to receive parole.[11]

There is no doubt that fewer individuals are receiving discretionary parole today than in the past. Exhibit 12.2 shows the percentage of prisoners who "**maxed out**," meaning they served their full term with no early release and

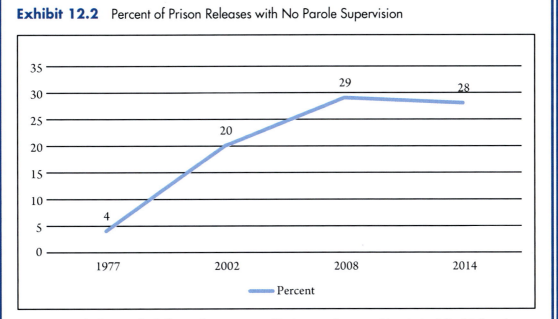

Exhibit 12.2   Percent of Prison Releases with No Parole Supervision

Source: J. Petersilia, "Meeting the challenges of prisoner reentry." In *American Correctional Association, What Works and Why: Effective Approaches to Reentry.* Lanham, MD: American Correctional Association, 2005, p. 179; W. Sabol, H. West and M. Cooper, *Prisoners in 2008.* Washington, DC: Bureau of Justice Statistics, 2009, p. 34; E. Carson, *Prisoners in 2014.* Washington DC: Bureau of Justice Statistics, p. 20.

no supervision after release. We see that in the 1970s, very few inmates were released outright and almost all inmates were released to parole supervision, but today almost one-third of prison releasees are released with no supervision. The rate of parole (the ratio of offenders who receive parole to those who are eligible) fluctuates widely between states and sometimes within a state over different time periods or different regions.

According to the Bureau of Justice Statistics, there were 856,900 people on parole in 2014. The numbers on parole have been increasing as we can see in Exhibit 12.3, but the rate of parole per capita has decreased. There were 350 persons on parole for every 100,000 in 2013 and 348 persons on parole for every 100,000 in 2014. This is substantially down from the peak in 2007.[12]

Most parolees are men (88 percent). About 8 percent of parolees were women in 1990, about 10 percent were women in 1995. By 2000, the figure was 12 percent of the total number of parolees and since then, their percentage has remained stable at about 12 percent.[13] In 2014, the crimes of convictions for parolees was fairly evenly split between drugs and violent crimes. Recall that violent offenders "stack up" in prison because of longer sentences. Exhibit 12.4 shows the percentages of parolees' crimes in 2014.

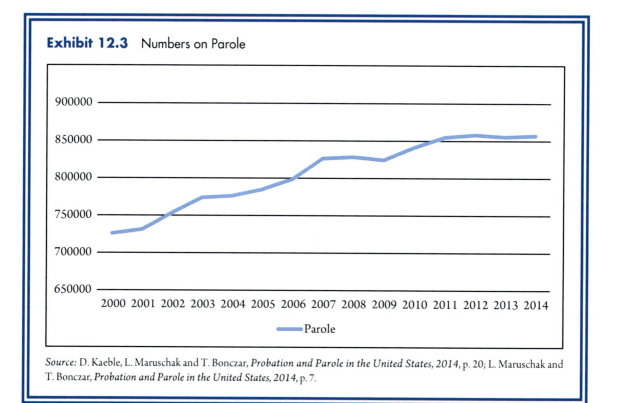

Exhibit 12.3   Numbers on Parole

Parole

Source: D. Kaeble, L. Maruschak and T. Bonczar, *Probation and Parole in the United States, 2014*, p. 20; L. Maruschak and T. Bonczar, *Probation and Parole in the United States, 2014*, p. 7.

Exhibit 12.4   Parolees' Crimes—Percentage of Total

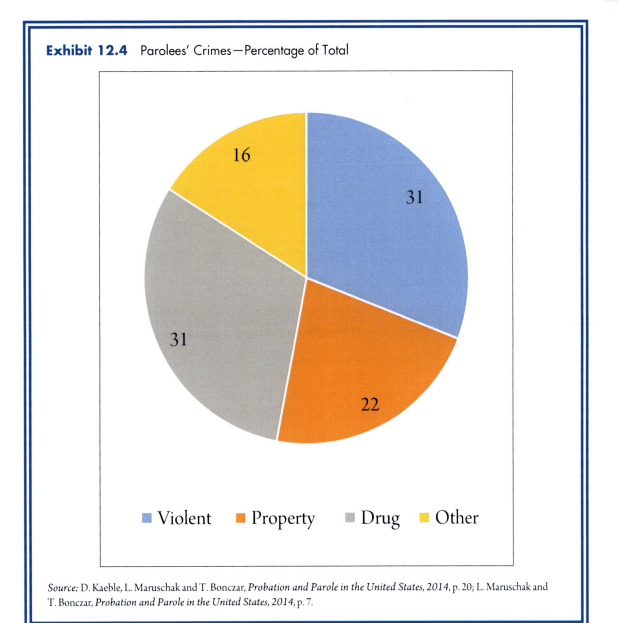

Source: D. Kaeble, L. Maruschak and T. Bonczar, *Probation and Parole in the United States, 2014*, p. 20; L. Maruschak and T. Bonczar, *Probation and Parole in the United States, 2014*, p. 7.

The Bureau of Justice Statistics reports that as a percentage of the total, Blacks decreased from 45 percent of all parolees in 1995 to 39 percent in 2008; that percentage remained stable at 39 percent in 2014 also. The percentage of Whites increased from 34 percent in 1995 to 43 percent in 2014 and Hispanics declined from 21 percent to 16 percent.[14]

WHAT ARE THE PROBLEMS OF RE-ENTRY?

As you might expect, jobs, housing, and avoiding criminal temptations are the problems cited as re-entry difficulties. For offenders who have drug dependency issues, maintaining sobriety is a challenge. Releasees, especially those who have served long sentences, also note the difficulties of adapting to life on the outside as a re-entry problem.

Jobs are key to success on parole, but parolees have major barriers to overcome. Many have very poor job histories and few or no skills. The stigma of being an ex-felon is a tremendous barrier to finding quality employment, even if the offender has a marketable skill. Less than half of offenders have a job waiting for them upon release.[15] Studies show men with a felony drug conviction are 50 percent less likely than men without a record to get a callback or job offer for an entry-level job and Black applicants are half again as likely as White applicants with records to get a callback.[16] Studies have found that between 60 percent and 75 percent of ex-offenders are jobless up to a year after release.[17] The "banning the box" movement refers to encouraging employers to stop asking about prior arrests and/or convictions, or at least stop asking if an applicant "has ever been arrested" since the arrest may have happened years before.

Issues that must be overcome in order to obtain decent employment in addition to lack of a job history and few skills include drug abuse, lack of transportation, restrictions imposed by parole (i.e., curfews and reporting requirements), statutory exclusions for licenses and certifications, and a lack of socialization to workplace culture. Even if a job is secured, keeping it is a problem as parolees have difficult life situations that involve losing homes, transportation difficulties, and other challenges to maintaining good employment habits.

Transitional jobs are those that the offender may obtain immediately upon release. These are important even if they provide no long-range future. Such jobs, to be adequate, must be relatively low skilled, with frequent pay periods, providing close supervision and mentoring, perhaps some subsidies to help the parolee begin life on the outside, and some training for more lucrative employment.[18] Some programs operated by community corrections departments meet most of these elements either through a partnership with a private employer or a community work project employing ex-offenders.

Housing is another issue for newly released prisoners. Federal law prohibits anyone with a drug conviction from living in federally subsidized housing (although states can opt out of this prohibition). Prisoners with drug convictions risk subjecting their family to eviction if they return home. There are very few transitional housing beds in most states even though a substantial number of prisoners who are released are, essentially, homeless.

Exhibit 12.5   Finding housing is a challenge for many newly released inmates. This transitional home for women in Missouri is run by nuns who try to help the residents adjust to life outside prison.

Source: Getty

When transitional housing beds are available, they are often tied to drug treatment because federal and state money can be accessed by providers. In 2015, the *New York Times* investigated halfway houses (or what were called "three-quarter" houses) for the homeless, many of whom were referred by the criminal justice system, and found that conditions were abysmal and treatment questionable.[19]

Some argue that the problems of parolees are more serious today than they have been in the past, partly because of a lack of in-prison programming, and partly because prisoners have more barriers to overcome. Recall the high numbers of prisoners with drug dependency/addiction and/or mental disorders. These individuals face greater challenges upon re-entry, especially when there is a lack of transitional treatment.

In a study of releasees in one state, utilizing a sample of 414 men and 262 women, it was found that 37 percent had no high school diploma or GED; and only half of the sample had held a job for two years or more prior to their prison term. In this sample, 87 percent indicated they would need some or a lot of help in finding a job. Only 15 percent had a job waiting for them upon release. About 60 percent of this sample had not received any drug treatment, even though close to 60 percent reported cocaine use and one-quarter reported heavy daily use. A significant percentage of this sample (almost 20 percent) reported mental health problems and about 30 percent reported a diagnosis of depression.[20]

Unfortunately, inmates do not receive much programming in prison to help them with these re-entry problems. In one state, for instance, the number of prisoners who participated in vocational programs dropped from 31 percent in 1991 to 27 percent in 1997; the number who had participated in education programs dropped from 43 percent to 35 percent, and the number who received any formal substance abuse treatment dropped from 25 percent to 10 percent.[21] Prison treatment programs only comprise 1 percent to 5 percent of prison budgets each year, and most of these are not specifically pre-release programs.[22]

One study points out that the pre-release programs that were more popular in past decades may have been instrumental in reducing recidivism. Researchers found that, of 3,244 Massachusetts inmates released between 1973 and 1976, those who participated in both a pre-release and furlough program had a 9 percent recidivism rate; those who only participated in furloughs had a 17 percent recidivism rate; those who participated only in the pre-release program had a 26 percent rate; and those who participated in neither had a 29 percent recidivism rate (holding prisoner age and prior record constant).[23] Even assuming that those who were allowed to participate in furloughs might have been better risks overall, this does indicate that pre-release programs should be considered essential tools in reducing recidivism.

In many cases, families are unlikely to be of much assistance to the parolee. In a Texas study, two-thirds of the sample reported that at least one family member had been convicted of a crime. More than one-third reported that a family member was currently in prison. Two-thirds reported having a family member with a serious drug or alcohol problem. Most (54 percent) had children under eighteen years old, and 59 percent of these people had lived with one or more children prior to imprisonment.[24]

It may be that prisoners who leave prison underestimate the difficulties they will encounter upon release. In the Texas study, almost 80 percent believed it would be easy to renew relationships with family, and 82 percent thought their family would be supportive. About 63 percent expected to live with family after prison, and about half (54 percent) expected financial support from their families. Further, 65 percent who did not have housing lined up thought that it would be easy or very easy to find housing, and 72 percent thought that it would be easy to stay out of trouble. Fully 84 percent thought it would be easy to stay out of prison after release, and 81 percent thought it would be easy to avoid any parole violations. Most also thought it was unlikely that they would commit a crime (87 percent) or use drugs (81 percent). Despite their optimism, parolees indicated they needed education (73 percent), job training (72 percent), and financial assistance (73 percent).[25]

Several research efforts have documented the difficulties of women after release. Women are more likely than men to have histories of drug and alcohol use, long-term unemployment, few or no skills, and a history of sexual abuse.[26] In one study of Texas releases, it was found that women were more likely than male offenders to have serious histories of drug use, but less likely to have received any treatment. About 42 percent reported daily cocaine use before prison, compared to only 17 percent of the men. More men expected to live with families than women. In this same study, female parolees reported less family support and more negative family influences than did men.[27]

The legal, financial, and emotional difficulties of reuniting with children comprise the most important distinguishing factor between male and female offenders. Women often mention the difficulty of regaining custody of children and/or re-establishing parental bonds. Interestingly, women seem to be more likely than men to view their parole officers as a positive force, and look to them for assistance and resource referrals.[28] One of the differences between male and female offenders is that it seems as though women's relationships with men are more central to their offending; thus, upon parole, they are less likely to stay out of trouble if they are in a relationship with a criminal partner. It is also true that women are less likely to have relationships to return to and they are wary of old partners who may be instrumental in their falling back into drug use.[29]

WHAT ARE COLLATERAL CONSEQUENCES OF A CRIMINAL CONVICTION?

Collateral consequences refer to things that happen along with a prison sentence. Most often, they refer to **civil disabilities** that are civil rights lost or compromised after a criminal conviction. Many disabilities exist, including rights regarding voting, certain types of employment, licensing, jury service, eligibility to hold public office, and the right to own a firearm. Collateral consequences also refers to the requirement that some offenders register where they live and the list may be public information (such as sex offenders or offenders who committed crimes involving children). As mentioned earlier, those convicted of drugs may be barred from public housing and public assistance. Here is a quote from a recent report that describes these collateral punishments:

> One recent study estimated that 65 million people—one in four adults in the United States—have a criminal record. At the same time, the collateral consequences of conviction—specific legal restrictions, generalized discrimination and social stigma—have become more severe, more public and more permanent. These consequences affect virtually every aspect of human endeavor, including employment and licensing, housing, education, public benefits, credit and loans, immigration status, parental rights, interstate travel, and even volunteer opportunities. Collateral consequences can be a criminal defendant's most serious punishment, permanently relegating a person to second-class status. The obsession with background checking in recent years has made it all but impossible for a person with a criminal record to leave the past behind. An arrest alone can lead to permanent loss of opportunity. The primary legal mechanisms historically relied on to restore rights and status—executive pardon and judicial expungement—have atrophied or become less effective.[30]

In most states, ex-offenders do not have the right to vote. Only Maine and Vermont have no restrictions on voting by ex-felons. Three states (Florida, Kentucky, and Virginia) have a lifetime ban on voting rights, and in eleven other states, the offender can petition to have their voting rights restored upon successful completion of their sentence. Ex-offenders cannot serve on juries (31 states permanently take away this right) or possess firearms (28 states permanently take away this right).[31] In about half of all states, ex-offenders cannot hold public office, and close to half of all states allow imprisonment to be used as a reason for permanent deprivation of parental rights.[32] The states that have the most exclusionary policies generally are in the South, but also include Arizona, Kansas, and Nebraska. The most inclusive states (with the fewest civil disabilities for returning felons) are generally in the Northeast, but also include Indiana, Ohio, Oregon, and Utah.[33]

Collateral consequences also refers to what happens to the offenders' families and communities. In some communities, primarily minority communities, up to one-quarter of all adult men are in prison on any given day.[34] The effect of imprisonment on these neighborhoods is that there is a shortage

Go to an interactive website that offers a state-by-state inventory of collateral consequences at http://www. abacollateral consequences.org/

of men, leading to single head-of-households struggling to juggle work and parenthood. Another result is that the lifetime earnings of individuals are diminished because a prison sentence will affect one's employability forever. Another effect is that children will have to deal with the experience of having a parent in prison.

It is estimated that about 1.5 million children have a parent (or parents) in prison.

Children of incarcerated women are especially affected because their living situation is often disrupted and, in fact, some estimates indicate that these children are moved an average of six times during the course of their mother's imprisonment. Children of men in prison are less likely to change their custody arrangements, because about 90 percent of them remain with their mother;

Exhibit 12.6 It is estimated that 1.5 million children have a parent in prison. These children were able to make a Christmas-time visit to their mother in a prison in Texas, but they were not permitted to touch her.

Source: AP

however, statistics indicate that children who have family members in prison are six times more likely to be delinquent.[35] Of course, it may be the case that the removal of a violent family member is a positive factor in a child's life, but when a prisoner comes home, re-entry poses its own problems.

Researchers have found that imprisonment seemed to have some positive effects on a community, but it appears that when it reaches a certain level, there are some negative effects as well and the destabilization in families and communities may lead to more crime, not less. Some policy recommendations that have come from this research include the following:

1. Provide services to families of incarcerated offenders that include short-term financial assistance, crisis counseling, parenting classes, medical care, child care, and adult mentors for children.
2. Facilitate continued communication between the offender and his or her family that includes assistance with costs of telephoning and transportation to the prison.
3. Provide services to the children of incarcerated individuals that include counseling and assistance in maintaining contact with the incarcerated parent.
4. Provide assistance with comprehensive transition plans for release that includes job assistance, counseling, housing, and other services.
5. Reduce financial burdens of offenders that include supervision fees and court costs, at least in the short term, as well as financial restrictions that place barriers to successful re-entry (such as prohibitions against felons in public housing projects).
6. Increase access to low-cost drug treatment programs.
7. Provide services at neighborhood centers that include mentoring, awareness programs, and ex-offender counseling.[36]

WHAT IS THE SECOND CHANCE ACT?

Re-entry assistance has increased in recent years with support from the federal government. In his 2004 State of the Union address, President Bush made special mention of the need for re-entry services and advocated a $300 million federal initiative to provide financial support for state programs to give parolees and releasees a "second chance" through job training, transitional housing, and other forms of support. States were given grants to create such programs. The Second Chance Act of 2007[37] (passed in 2008) was a reauthorization of this earlier Act with new funding. Federal funding is authorized for states and local jurisdictions to try innovative programs to assist re-entry efforts.

The Second Chance Act monies have continued to be awarded by Congress and are administered through the Bureau of Justice Assistance of the Office of Justice Programs. The Council of State Governments Justice Center has a webpage that tracks programs across the country that target re-entry and recidivism. Since 2009, more than 700 awards have been made to grantees across 49 states. Funded programs include those that coordinate mental health services in the community for releasees, job training and readiness programs, and family-based drug treatment programs.

To read about the funded research projects on re-entry, go to http://www.nij.gov/topics/corrections/reentry/pages/evaluation-second-chance.aspx

For more information about programs to assist re-entry funded by the Second Chance Act, go to the Council of State Governments Justice Center webpage at http://www.nationalreentryresourcecenter.org/

WHAT IS THE PROCESS FOR PAROLE REVOCATION?

Similar to caseload supervision in probation, parolees are supervised by parole officers. According to a recent survey by the Association of Paroling Authorities, the average caseload size is thirty-eight, but it is unclear whether this figure utilizes all employees or only those employees who supervise caseloads.[38] Only about 14 percent of parolees are under some form of intensive parole. A very small number (about 3 percent) are under some form of specialized supervision (such as sex offenders). Intensive parole and specialized caseloads cost more than twice what regular parole costs per year.[39] Intensive parole is similar to intensive probation programs in that smaller caseloads allow officers to more intensely supervise offenders. For instance, in one state's intensive parole program, offenders who are high risk because they have committed an act of violence are supervised in caseloads of fourteen. Officers see the offender at least fifteen times per month with at least six "face-to-face" contacts, six drive-bys, and one home visitation. Offenders are on twenty-four-hour electronic monitoring and must submit and have approved a twenty-four-hour schedule of where they will be every hour of the day.[40]

Parole officers not only monitor parolees to make sure they are not arrested for new crimes; they also enforce conditions (rules). Similar to probationers, all parolees are required to abide by conditions established at the time of the parole release. Generally, standard conditions are like those of probation; the offender must report monthly, notify the officer of any moves, hold a job, not commit a crime, and so on. Parolees are expected to pay supervision fees and/or victim compensation fees. Other conditions may be treatment oriented, such as participating in a treatment program or obtaining a GED; or custody oriented, such as following a curfew, or not going anywhere near children. A list of typical conditions is offered in Exhibit 12.7.

Exhibit 12.7 Parole Conditions

- Pay supervision fees and restitution.
- Do not use controlled substances except by prescription.
- Submit to drug testing.
- Remain in the state.
- Find gainful employment or participate in education.
- Obtain permission to change residence.
- Submit to searches of home and visits to workplace.
- Consent to search of person.
- Obey all laws.
- Cooperate in all ways with parole officer.
- Do not possess any weapons.

As with probation, parole officers could write a violation report if any of the conditions are violated which might result in a revocation hearing in front of the parole board or a hearing examiner (some state's parole boards delegate the task to hearing examiners who often have a legal background). **Technical violations** are those that involve only violating conditions of parole. Parolees are also revoked for committing new crimes, with or without formal prosecution.

The Supreme Court decided in *Morrissey v. Brewer*[41] that the deprivation of parole was not as serious a deprivation as probation and, therefore, less due process applied. The Supreme Court held that the following elements must be granted before parole revocation:

- bifurcated hearing (preliminary and full hearing)[42]
- written notice of parole violation
- disclosure to parolee of evidence against him
- opportunity to be heard in person and to present witnesses and documentary evidence
- conditional right to confront and cross-examine (denied if there is reason to keep identity of witnesses, such as police informers, secret)
- neutral and detached hearing body
- written statement of fact finders as to evidence against and reasons for decision.

Many offenders waive the preliminary hearing, and the full revocation hearing is often located in the prison after the offender is sent back. In another case, the Supreme Court held that Oklahoma's "pre-parole" status was equivalent to parole and, therefore, *Morrissey v. Brewer*'s due process analysis applied when the state sought to deprive the pre-parole participants of their liberty.[43] A violation hearing doesn't always result in revocation, but if parole is revoked, the individual is returned to prison. The term for re-arrest or return to prison is recidivism.

HOW MANY OFFENDERS RECIDIVATE AND WHO IS MOST LIKELY TO RECIDIVATE?

The success rate for parolees is lower than that of probationers. Exhibit 12.8 shows the percentages of parolees exiting parole in 2014 who successfully completed parole compared to those who were returned to prison on new convictions or for technical violations.

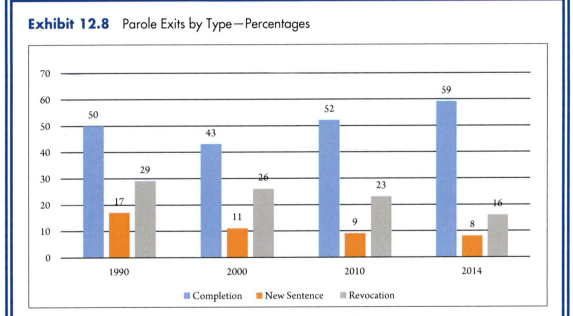

Exhibit 12.8   Parole Exits by Type—Percentages

Other types of exits and unknowns deleted. The unknown number increased in 2014.

Source: D. Kaeble, L. Maruschak and T. Bonczar, *Probation and Parole in the United States, 2014*, p. 20; L. Maruschak and T. Bonczar, *Probation and Parole in the United States, 2012*, p. 9; L. Glaze, *Probation and Parole in the United States, 2006*, p. 7; L. Glaze, *Probation and Parole in the United States, 2001*, p. 6. Washington, DC: Bureau of Justice Statistics.

The number of parolees successfully completing their parole is about 60 percent. States seem to vary tremendously in their patterns of success. Whether this is due to stricter decisions in response to violation reports or more violations is impossible to say. Exhibit 12.8 shows that at least twice as many parolees are revoked for technical violations as those who are returned to prison for new crimes with new sentences. The large number of returns based on technical violations seems to indicate that the revocation process may be too harsh and intermediate community sanctions should be used because the violations are not necessarily new crimes; however, it may be the case that prosecutors are urging parole authorities to use revocations in lieu of new charges and prosecutions. If an offender is going back to prison anyway, new charges and a new sentence may be redundant. There is no way to know whether technical violations are overused, or used in lieu of new charges, without further research.

Exhibit 12.8 is a "snapshot" of completions in a given year. Recidivism studies are different in that they track a cohort of ex-offenders who are released in a given year for a period of time to determine if and when they fail, either due to a new crime or a violation and revocation. According to an older Bureau of Justice Statistics study, about 66 percent of parolees are re-arrested within three years of release. In this study, one in three were arrested in the first six months, and 44 percent in the first year. This study showed that property offenders were most likely to recidivate (about 75 percent) compared to 66 percent of drug offenders and 62 percent of public order and violent criminals. Unfortunately, this study is quite old and used data from 1984 and 1994, tracking a cohort of ex-prisoners from each year. About 63 percent of the offenders released in 1984 and 68 percent of the ex-prisoners released in 1994 were re-arrested.[44]

In 2004, the Bureau of Justice Statistics analyzed nonviolent offenders who were released from prison on parole.[45] Nonviolent offenders included property, drug, and public order offenses. Seven in ten were re-arrested within three years, half were reconvicted, and one-quarter returned to prison. One in five was re-arrested for a violent crime.

The most recent Bureau of Justice Statistics study tracked a cohort who were released in 2005 and found recidivism figures of 68 percent within three years and 75 percent within five years. Researchers at Abt Associates argue, however, that by utilizing a sample cohort released in any given year, the study over-samples recidivistic criminals (who are likely to be in prison and released and returned). In their own study, they used a data set of prison terms for a larger population and over a longer period of time (fifteen years). They found that two out of three people who serve time in prison never come back, and only 11 percent come back multiple times.[46] Neither methodology is wrong, but the two show quite different pictures of the recidivism of ex-prisoners.

It also appears that recidivism figures are improving. The Council of State Governments Justice Center has been issuing fact sheets on recidivism of states that have taken concerted efforts to reduce recidivism, with results illustrated in Exhibits 12.9 and 12.10.

Exhibit 12.9 Three-Year Recidivism Percentage for Releases, 2005 and 2007

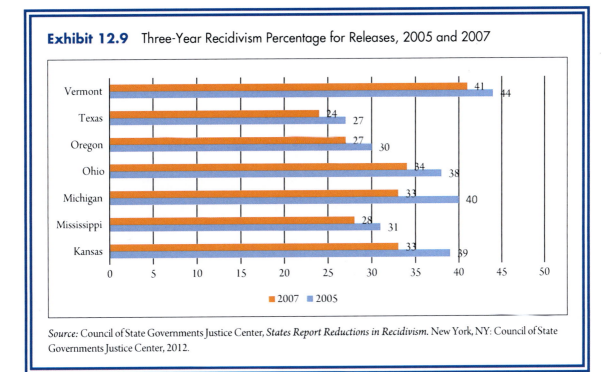

Source: Council of State Governments Justice Center, *States Report Reductions in Recidivism.* New York, NY: Council of State Governments Justice Center, 2012.

Exhibit 12.10 Three-Year Recidivism Percentage for Releases, 2007 and 2010

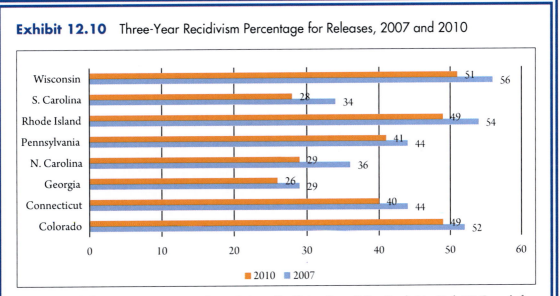

Source: Council of State Governments Justice Center. *Reducing Recidivism: States Deliver Results.* New York, NY: Council of State Governments Justice Center, 2014.

A number of studies have looked at what factors seem to be associated with recidivism while on parole or supervised release. In one study of 167 participants in a "day reporting" program, it was found that the factors associated with success were age (older offenders were more likely to be successful), family responsibilities, and no drug use history. In fact, those with a drug history were three times more likely to fail. Further, offenders with three or more criminal counts and those who received institutional detention were more likely to fail, as were repeat offenders and those with longer sentences.[47] Many studies find that failure is most likely to occur in the first three months of release; therefore, it is recommended that all services be concentrated at the front end of release, in the first three months. Jobs and housing continue to be identified as factors in recidivism.[48]

Some research indicates women are less likely to fail on parole than men. According to the Bureau of Justice Statistics, about 45 percent of female parolees were returned to prison or had absconded. National statistics indicate that probably the most significant factor in recidivism is having a prior arrest history. While only 21 percent of the women with only one prior arrest recidivated, nearly eight in ten of those with eleven or more priors were re-arrested. Those who had employment and stable living arrangements were more likely to succeed on parole.[49] One study reported on the types of needs identified at intake from a sample of 546 female parolees. Researchers found that if a female parolee was employed, had stable living arrangements, and was assessed as needing and receiving some type of drug and/or alcohol program intervention, she was less likely to fail on parole. The study found that many female parolees had drug and alcohol treatment needs, as well as employment, housing, and other needs that were not assessed or addressed. The authors speculate that parole is more custodial than treatment oriented, and point out that these needs are associated with failure on parole; therefore, they should be addressed.[50]

There is good evidence that some programs can reduce recidivism by as much as 30 percent. Programs that use cognitive-behavioral content, address drug addiction, and provide extended support in the community have particularly positive results.[51] An evaluation of California's Preventing Parolee Crime Program (PPCP) found modest success in reducing recidivism. Those who completed program services had a recidivism rate that was eight percentage points lower than non-participants (52 percent of nonparticipants versus 4 percent participants). Recidivism went down even further for those who completed treatment goals (13 percent).[52] A Rand study of California inmates found that inmates who participated in correctional education programs were 43 percent less likely to return to prison within three years of release in comparison to those who did not participate. They were also 13 percent more

Exhibit 12.11   Some post-prison programs have been shown to reduce recidivism by up to 30 percent. Here former inmates graduate from a re-entry program in Texas.

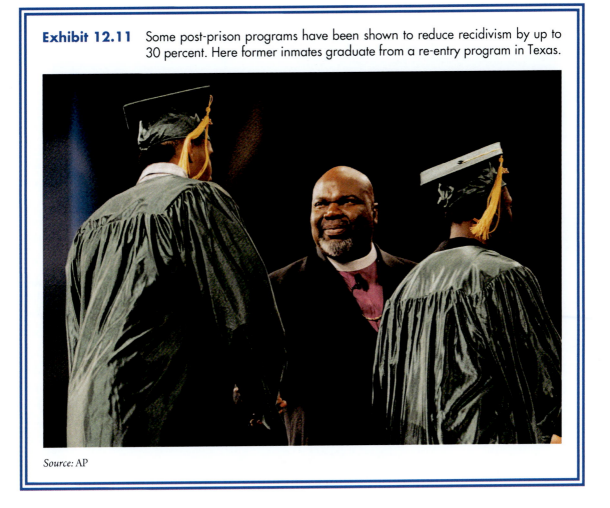

Source: AP

likely to find jobs after being released. Prisoners who participated in vocational training programs were 28 percent more likely to be employed after release.[53]

In a recent study of a prison drug treatment program with an aftercare component, it was found that improving services in the community led to better outcomes for ex-offenders. The researchers showed that creating a network of services for ex-offenders was associated with more successful completion of the aftercare component. They urge that the parole model be adapted to include the utilization of an aftercare plan and clinical case managers who work with parole agents to ensure that releasees complete their program. In the last cohort studies, 70 percent of the participants successfully completed the aftercare component of the program.[54]

FOCUS ON DATA: WHAT IS THE "JUSTICE REINVESTMENT INITIATIVE" AND "JUSTICE REALIGNMENT"? HAVE THESE APPROACHES INCREASED CRIME?

Some estimates are that corrections consume $1 in every $15 of state funds; however, it is difficult to determine the true costs of corrections.[55] Estimating total costs is difficult because some estimates include capital construction costs for prisons, while other estimates do not. Prison costs vary tremendously from state to state, and even within a state, maximum-security institutions cost more than minimum-security, and special-needs offenders cost more to house and care for than regular inmates. Intensive probation or parole costs much more than regular supervision, and probation and parole supervision that includes electronic monitoring and/or GPS tracking is also more expensive. All that means is that cost estimates are probably more accurate within states rather than national estimates and range widely in accuracy.

It seems safe to say, however, that all costs associated with the criminal justice system have risen dramatically in the last twenty years. The Bureau of Justice Statistics reported that the total costs for justice expenditures (not just corrections) between 1986 and 2006 increased by 301 percent from $54 billion to $214 billion. These increases are after the costs were adjusted for inflation.[56] According to one source over the past twenty years, state spending on corrections has skyrocketed—from $12 billion in 1988 to more than $52 billion in 2011.[57] A study involving 40 states revealed that the total taxpayer cost in 2010 ranged from a low of $76 million in Maine to a high of well over $3 billion in New York and Texas.[58]

Partly as a result of a growing recognition that correctional costs are absorbing too much of federal and state budges, disparate groups (e.g., liberal and conservative foundations) have come together to urge a re-evaluation of this country's incarceration patterns.[59] Activity has taken place in two major areas. The first area of activity is to reduce recidivism—the Second Chance Act and re-entry programs across the county discussed above have seemed to be successful in helping states begin to reduce the numbers of individuals re-arrested and sent back to prison. The second target area is to reduce the numbers of individuals sent to prison.

The Justice Reinvestment Initiative and Justice Realignment are sometimes confused because they have overlapping goals. The terms seem to be used interchangeably by some, but the Justice Reinvestment Initiative refers to technical assistance funded by the Bureau of Justice Assistance and the Pew Charitable Trusts that address ways for states to reduce correctional costs by shifting more punishment to the community level. The funds saved by reducing the number of prisoners is supposed to be then re-invested in crime prevention programs that are evidence-based and data-driven. Justice Realignment refers to what has happened in California after a state law passed in response to *Brown v. Plata* (2011), the Supreme Court case discussed in Chapter 11 that resulted in California being required to drastically reduce its prison population. In this discussion we will discuss the two separately.

The Justice Reinvestment Initiative (JRI) refers to a strategy spearheaded by the Council of State Governments (CSG) and funded by the Pew Charitable Trusts and Bureau of Justice Assistance (BJA). About twenty-seven states have been the recipients of JRI technical assistance from either the Council of State Governments Justice Center, the Pew Research Center, or the Vera Institute. Of those, eighteen have enacted JRI-recommended legislation for the purpose of stabilizing corrections populations. The concept is that each state is unique in its offender population, laws, and criminal justice system, and so specific plans and objectives must be developed within each state after data about the criminal justice population in that state is collected and analyzed. According to a summary report, Justice Reinvestment has helped in four states to adopt policies that are projected to generate more than $1 billion in savings over five years, and in Texas alone Justice Reinvestment efforts resulted in $1.5 billion in construction savings and $340 million in annual averted operations costs.[60] The various types of legislative initiatives and programs under the umbrella of Justice Reinvestment is large, ranging from intensive supervision to victim advocacy. Justice Reinvestment strategies include helping jurisdictions adopt classification tools utilizing the R/N/R approach described in Chapter 10. Millions of dollars have been spent on model programs, evaluations, and technical assistance.[61]

To read about the Justice Reinvestment Initiative, go to https://www.bja.gov/programs/justicereinvestment/index.html

There are some who argue that the Justice Reinvestment Initiative has had only modest success in reducing prison populations and goals have become so diffuse that the initiative has moved away from its original mission of reducing prison populations, to one of simply controlling the rate of increase. One critical report notes that in the initial phases of the JRI between 2002 and 2008, several states (Connecticut, Kansas, Texas, Rhode Island, and Arizona) passed legislation that was successful in reducing prison populations by reducing revocations for technical violations of parole and probation, increasing the number of parole hearings, or re-establishing earned "good time" credits, but since 2008, the mission and language used by JRI partners has become generalized and open-ended and that it has abandoned the original mission of reducing the number of prisoners.[62] Further, critics allege that money saved is not going to services for high incarceration communities as originally promised, but instead has gone in some states to law enforcement or the development of risk assessment models.[63] These critics argue that the prison population reductions JRI partners take credit for are too high because they used projected populations of states without taking into account almost all states were seeing a plateauing and reduction of prison populations even without JRI intervention. In fact, some states reduced their prison populations dramatically without any JRI involvement. The states with the most dramatic declines in their prison populations between 2006 and 2014 include: California (27 percent), Hawaii (25 percent), New Jersey (24 percent), Colorado (19 percent), Alaska (19 percent), New York (18 percent) and South Carolina (18 percent).[64] California's decrease came about largely because of Justice Realignment, which we will discuss below. Of the remaining states, JRI lists only Hawaii and South Carolina as having received JRI technical assistance.[65] The other states reduced their prison populations through a variety of ways. New York experienced reductions in the number of felony arrests coupled with increases in non-prison sentences (which only occurred in New York City). New Jersey increased the parole-grant rates because of litigation, reformed drug crimes, and reduced parole revocations.[66]

We posed the question whether the Justice Investment Initiative led to increased crime rates, but the assumption of that question was that it was responsible for reducing the number of people in prison. Since we cannot conclude that it has, we will not move to the question of whether it has reduced crime rates. JRI partners note that the process of influencing state criminal justice systems is extremely complicated. It is also an extremely complicated question as to whether the effects of one intervention like JRI can be isolated given the myriad of influences on imprisonment and crime rates. Concentrating on one state may be more helpful, but California is a good example of why even one state's experience is still a difficult research question.

As noted before, the United States Supreme Court in *Brown v. Plata* (2011) ordered California to reduce prison overcrowding to 137.5 percent of design capacity by June 2013. Since California was not financially able to build several new prisons, this eventually meant reducing the prison population by about 30,000. To reduce the state prison population California passed the Public Safety Realignment Act ("Realignment") under Assembly Bill (AB) 109 in October 2011. This policy redirected people convicted of nonserious, nonviolent, and nonsexual offenses (non-non-non offenses) from state to county jurisdictions to serve their sentences in jails or county probation. Realignment also shortened mandatory parole supervision from one year to six months and required that people who were revoked spend only six months in a county jail (rather than return to prison).[67]

Realignment created the following three populations of offenders: (1) offenders released from state prison to county supervision (instead of state parole) with current convictions that are nonviolent and nonserious (Post-Release Community Supervision or PRCS); (2) felony offenders with no current or prior serious, violent, or sexual offenses who were previously eligible for state prison sentences and state parole supervision, but who now must be incarcerated and supervised at the county level (California Penal Code Section 1170(h)); and (3) serious or violent offenders, mentally disordered offenders, and high-risk sex offenders—all of whom remain under state parole supervision upon release from prison and only become part of the realigned population if they violate the terms of their supervision and are revoked to jail custody.[68]

California was one of the states that had abolished parole but all prison releasees had a mandatory supervision period after prison. The rate of revocation and return to prison was extremely high. Before Realignment three-year re-arrest rates had held at about 75 percent of those paroled. Re-convictions rates were also high—about 49 percent by three years after release. In comparison, less than half of released offenders were returned to prison in a national sample.[69] After Realignment, one-year return-to-prison rates dropped from 32 percent to 7 percent, an incredible decrease. The one-year re-arrest rate dropped from 59 percent to 56 percent after Realignment, although the felony re-arrest rate rose from 37 percent to 43 percent.[70] In order to better determine Realignment recidivism, one study adjusted for differences in offender characteristics before and after Realignment, and found that the percentage of prison releases returned to custody within one year dropped 25 percentage points for offenders released in the post-Realignment period.[71] Other findings show that in the early post-Realignment period, counties experienced worse recidivism outcomes for the same population that had been supervised by state parole officers pre-Realignment. There was great disparity between counties, however, and many counties experienced decreases. The change in reconviction rates under Realignment also varied across counties in California. Some counties adoped a greater enforcement emphasis than treatment emphasis, and spent upwards of four times as much of Realignment funds on law enforcement and jails rather than programs for offenders. These counties showed higher recidivism figures.[72]

Studies that examined whether Realignment increased crime rates either use a methodology that forecasts what might have happened if offenders had continued to be imprisoned by modeling from past years, or they compare counties within California between those that had sent many offenders to state prisons (and now can't) and those that never did. One study, for instance, found that in the time period affected by Realignment, California's crime rates declined by 9 percent and violent crime declined by 10 percent. Simply looking at crime declines doesn't say much because California might have had even greater declines if offenders had remained in prison, so researchers undertake extremely sophisticated modeling analyses to try to determine what would have happened.[73]

Several available analyses have found no strong relationships between Realignment and crime, except some studies find a small increase in motor vehicle theft. One study compared California with other jurisdictions controlling for pre-Realignment crime rates. These researchers found a small, non-statistical increase in violent crime during the first study period (2010) but a decrease in 2013 and 2014. Similarly, there was a small, non-significant increase in property crime which disappeared in later years. Even motor vehicle theft, which earlier studies found had increased under Realignment, did not show any increase from what projections indicated might have happened without Realignment in later years.[74]

In 2014, California passed Proposition 47 with the support of 58 percent of California voters. The law "de-felonized" a range of crimes to misdemeanors—including possession of small amounts of cocaine, heroin, and methamphetamine. The law also reduced theft and other property crimes under $950 from being charged as a felony. There was also a provision that made the law retroactive—thereby making over 5,000 California jail and prison inmates immediately eligible for release. By 2015, after the law went into effect, the prison population was reduced by 3 percent and the jail population by 11 percent. Recent news articles argue that the law has led to an increase in violent and property crime in most California cities and law enforcement has reduced narcotics arrests because nothing happens to those they arrest. Drug offenders opting for drug treatment had been reduced by half since they find short jail sentences are easier.[75]

Now it will be difficult to measure the effects of Realignment from the effects of Proposition 47. One thing is certain—attributing an increase in crime in some counties or locations to the effects of any legislation or progam is probably not accurate. Crime may increase for a variety of reasons, and simply looking at crime increases after Proposition 47 went into effect does not prove that the increase is due to the change in punishment structure. Crime has increased in other jurisdictions and decreased in some. Even in California, different jurisdictions show different patterns. Unfortunately, there are no easy answers to causal questions such as we have posed here. The importance of a critical thinking approach is to ask careful questions and seek multiple sources of data.

To read why a group of national law enforcement leaders endorse reducing incarceration, go to the Law Enforcement Leaders website at http://lawenforcementleaders.org/our-mission/ and click the hyperlink for "Statement of Principles."

SUMMARY

What Is the History of Parole?

The history of parole can be traced back to transportation in Australia, Maconochie's mark system on Norfolk Island, and the "ticket of leave" system in Ireland. In this country, an early form of parole was begun at Elmira Reformatory.

Who Is on Parole?

The decision to release on parole is made by a paroling authority (typically a parole board); however, only about fifteen states still retain full discretionary release. There were 856,900 people on parole in 2014. About 88 percent of parolees are men. In 2014, the crimes of convictions for parolees was fairly evenly split between drugs (31 percent) and violent crimes (31 percent), with a bit fewer convicted of property crimes (22 percent). About 39 percent of parolees are Black, 43 percent White, and 16 percent Hispanic.

What Are the Problems of Re-Entry?

The major issues for parolees are jobs (up to 70 percent are unemployed a year after release), housing (with many not eligible for public housing), and remaining drug free (especially when they were not able to access drug treatment in prison).

What Are Collateral Consequences of a Criminal Conviction?

Collateral consequences of a conviction include civil disabilities (losing the right to vote, run for public office, serve on a jury), losing rights to obtain licenses for certain employment or being barred from some employment fields, not being able to possess a firearm, and a range of other consequences that are often for a lifetime.

What Is the Second Chance Act?

The Second Chance Act was a federal law that funded a range of programs designed to address these issues of re-entry and the collateral consequences of imprisonment.

What Is the Process for Parole Revocation?

A parole officer files a violation report when there is a new crime and/or when there is a technical violation (violating one of the conditions). In some states the parole board holds the revocation hearing, but in other states a hearing examiner does so, evaluates the evidence and determines what to do. Parolees get some due process notice—right to a neutral hearing body, present evidence, cross-examine when it is appropriate, and appeal.

How Many Offenders Recidivate, and Who Is Most Likely to Recidivate?

About half of all parolees are successfully discharged. BJS recidivism studies have followed cohorts to find about 66 percent recidivate, but newer recidivism studies place the number of successful offenders much higher because of a different methodology.

Critical Thinking Exercises

1. Create a "Focus on Data" report covering whether the Justice Reinvestment states have lowered recidivism, but also whether those states have seen an increase of crime using UCR data.
2. Research a re-entry program and determine the best way to evaluate its effects. If there is an evaluation provided, does it "control for" all other variables that might have affected success or failure?

NOTES

1 J. Petersilia, *Reforming Probation and Parole.* Lanham, MD: American Correctional Association, 2002, p. 129.

2 R. Hughes, *The Fatal Shore.* New York: Vintage Books, 1986.

3 H. Barnes and N. Teeters, *New Horizons on Criminology*, 3rd edn. Englewood Cliffs, NJ: Prentice Hall, 1959; J. Petersilia, *Reforming Probation and Parole.* Lanham, MD: American Correctional Association, 2002, p. 130.

4 D. Rothman, *Conscience and Convenience.* Boston, MA: Little, Brown & Co, 1980.

5 J. Petersilia, note 1.

6 J. Petersilia, note 1, p. 131.

7 T. Bonczar, *Characteristics of State Parole Supervising Agencies, 2006.* Washington, DC: Bureau of Justice Statistics, 2008.

8 *Greenholtz, Chairman, Board of Parole of Nebraska et al. v. Inmates of the Nebraska Penal and Correctional Complex,* 442 U.S. 1, 1979.

9 Note that states may "create" a right by statutory language, that is, in *Board of Pardons et al. v. Allen et al.,* 482 U.S. 369 (1987), the use of the word "shall" in the enabling statute created a parole right that was then deemed to be a protected liberty interest.

10 R. Burns, P. Kinkade, M. Leone and S. Phillips, "Perspectives on parole: The board members' viewpoint." *Federal Probation* 63 (1) (1999): 16–22.

11 K. Morgan and B. Smith, "Victims, punishment and parole: The effect of victim participation on parole hearings." *Criminology and Public Policy* 4 (2) (2005): 333–360.

12 D. Kaeble, L. Maruschak and T. Bonczar, *Probation and Parole in the United States, 2014.* Washington, DC: Bureau of Justice Statistics, 2015, p. 20; L. Maruschak and T. Bonczar, *Probation and Parole in the United States, 2014.* Washington, DC: Bureau of Justice Statistics, 2015, p. 2.

13 L. Glaze and T. Bonczar, *Probation and Parole in the United States, 2008.* Washington, DC: Bureau of Justice Statistics, 2009.

14 L. Glaze, T. Bonczar and F. Zhang, *Probation and Parole in the United States, 2009.* Washington, DC: Bureau of Justice Statistics, 2010, p. 36; D. Kaeble, L. Maruschak and T. Bonczar, *Probation and Parole in the United States, 2014.* Washington, DC: Bureau of Justice Statistics, 2015, p. 20.

15 Reentry Council, *Report of the Re-entry Policy Council.* New York, NY: Council of State Governments, 2003, p. 384. Available at www.reentrypolicy.org.

16 D. Pager, "The mark of a criminal record." *American Journal of Sociology* 108 (2003): 937–960.

17 J. Petersilia, *When Prisoners Come Home: Parole and Prisoner Reentry.* Chicago, IL: University of Chicago Press, 2003; J. Travis, *But They All Come Back: Facing the Challenges of Prisoner Reentry.* Washington, DC: Urban Institute Press, 2005

18 Reentry Council, *Report of the Re-entry Policy Council.* New York, NY: Council of State Governments, 2003, p. 362. Available at www.reentrypolicy.org.

19 K. Barkeraug. "Tenants move out of unregulated homes, but remain in limbo." *New York Times*, August 3, 2015. Related articles: "Profiting from addiction: A choice for recovering addicts: relapse or homelessness," May 30, 2015. "New York City task force to investigate 'three-quarter' homes." June 1, 2015. "New York City allocates $5 million to move tenants out of 'three-quarter' homes.'" June 24, 2015.

20 N. LaVigne and V. Kachnowski, *Texas Prisoners' Reflections on Returning Home*. Washington, DC: Urban Institute, 2005.

21 Unfortunately, more recent statistics are not available. J. Watson, A. Solomon, N. LaVigne and J. Travis, *A Portrait of Prisoner Reentry in Texas*. Washington, DC: Urban Institute, 2004, p. 21.

22 J. Petersilia, "Meeting the challenges of prisoner reentry." In American Correctional Association, *What Works and Why: Effective Approaches to Reentry*. Lanham, MD: American Correctional Association, 2005, p. 178.

23 D. LeClair and S. Guarino-Ghezzi, "Does incapacitation guarantee public safety? Lessons from the Massachusetts furlough and prerelease programs." *Justice Quarterly* 8 (1) (1991): 9–36.

24 N. LaVigne and V. Kachnowski, note 20.

25 N. LaVigne and V. Kachnowski, note 20, p. 6–7.

26 L. Greenfield and T. Snell, *Women Offenders*. Washington, DC: Bureau of Justice Statistics, 2000.

27 N. LaVigne and V. Kachnowski, note 20.

28 P. O'Brien, *Making It in the "Free World": Women in Transition from Prison*. Albany, NY: SUNY Albany Press, 2001; M. Dodge and M. Pogrebin, "Collateral costs of imprisonment for women: Complications of reintegration." *Prison Journal* 81 (1) (2001): 42–54.

29 E. Ritchie, "Challenges incarcerated women face as they return to their communities: Findings from life history interviews." *Crime and Delinquency* 47 (3) (2001): 368–389.

30 National Association of Criminal Defense Lawyers, *Collateral Damage: America's Failure to Forgive or Forget in the War on Crime: A Roadmap to Restore Rights and Status After Arrest or Conviction*. Washington, DC: National Association of Criminal Defense Lawyers, 2014, p. 12.

31 Re-Entry Policy Council, *Voting Restrictions for People with Felony Convictions, 2004*. Retrieved 12/30/2005 from http://www.reentrypolicy.org/documents/votingrestrictions.pdf; M. Love, *Relief from the Collateral Consequences of a Criminal Conviction: A State by State Resource Guide*. New York, NY: Open Society Institute, 2005.

32 C. Hemmens, "The collateral consequences of conviction." *Perspectives* 25 (1) (2001): 12–13.

33 J. Petersilia, note 22, p. 182; J. Travis and M. Waul, *Prisoners Once Removed: The Impact of Incarceration and Reentry on Children, Families and Communities*. Washington, DC: Urban Institute Press, 2004.

34 M. Mauer, *Race to Incarcerate*. Washington, DC: The Prison Project, 2000.

35 J. Pollock, *Women, Prison, and Crime*. Belmont, CA: Wadsworth Publishing, 2005.

36 T. Clear, D. Rose and J. Ryder, "Incarceration and the community: The problem of removing and returning offenders." *Crime and Delinquency* 47 (3) (2001): 335–351.

37 Public Law 110–199.

38 S. Kinney and J. Caplan, *Findings from the APAI International Survey of Releasing Authorities*. Philadelphia, PA: Center for Research on Youth and Social Policy, 2008, p. 2. Available through the National Parole Resource Center at www.apaintl.org/documents/surveys/2008.pdf

39 J. Petersilia, note 1, p. 158.

40 Reentry Council, *Report of the Re-entry Policy Council*, Council of State Governments, New York, 2003, p. 362. Available at www.reentrypolicy.org.

41 *Morrissey v. Brewer*, 408 U.S. 471, 1972.

42 While earlier analyses of this case concluded the court meant that two hearings were required, later writers and some lower court holdings have determined that there can be one hearing as long as all elements are present. See R. del Carmen, S. Ritter and B. Witt, *Briefs of Leading Cases in Corrections*. Newark, NJ: LexisNexis/Matthew Bender, 2005, p. 176.

43 *Young v. Harper*, 520 U.S. 143, 1997.

44 P. Langan and D. Levine, *Recidivism of Prisoners Released in 1994*. Washington, DC: Bureau of Justice Statistics, 2002. See also A. Solomon, V. Kachnowski and A. Bhati, *Does Parole Work? Analyzing the Impact of Post-Prison Supervision and Rearrest Outcomes, Research Report*. Washington, DC: Urban Institute, 2005.

45 M. Ducrose and C. Mumola, *BJS Fact Sheet: Profile of Nonviolent Offenders Exiting State Prisons*. Washington, DC: Bureau of Justice Statistics, 2004.

46 W. Rhodes, G. Gaes, J. Luallen, R. Kling, T. Rich and M. Shively. "Following incarceration, most released offenders never return to prison." *Crime and Delinquency*, September 29, 2014, doi: 10.1177/0011128714549655.

47 S. Roy, "Factors related to success and recidivism in a day reporting center." *Criminal Justice Studies* 17 (1) (2004): 3–17.

48 J. Austin, "Prisoner reentry: Current trends, practices and issues." *Crime and Delinquency* 47 (3) (2001): 314.

49 L. Greenfield and T. Snell, *Women Offenders*. Washington, DC: Bureau of Justice Statistics, 2000.

50 P. Schram, B. Koons-Witt and F. Williams, "Supervision strategies and approaches for female parolees: Examining the link between unmet needs and parolee outcome." *Crime and Delinquency* 52 (3) (2006): 450–471.

51 P. Burke and M. Tonry, *Successful Transition and Reentry for Safer Communities: A Call to Action for Parole*. Silver Spring, MD: Center for Effective Public Policy, 2006, p. 15.

52 S. Zhang, R. Roberts and V. Callanan, "Preventing parolees from returning to prison through community-based reintegration." *Crime and Delinquency* 52 (4) (2006): 551–571.

53 L. Davis, *Evaluating the Effectiveness of Correctional Education: A Meta-Analysis of Programs That Provide Education to Incarcerated Adults*. Los Angeles, CA: Rand Corporation, September 16, 2013.

54 D. Olson, J. Rozhon and M. Powers, "Enhancing prisoner reentry through access to prison-based and post-incarceration aftercare treatment: Experiences from the Illinois Sheridan correctional center therapeutic community." *Journal of Experimental Criminology* 5 (2009): 299–321.

55 S. Listwan, C. Jonson, F. Cullen and E. Latessa, "Cracks in the penal harm movement: Evidence from the field." *Criminology and Public Policy* 7 (5) (2008): 423–465.

56 Bureau of Justice Statistics, *Expenditures and Employment Extracts, 2010*. Retrieved 10/27/2010 from http://bjs.ojp.usdoj.gov/index.cfm?ty=tp&tid=5

57 Council of State Governments Justice Center, *Lessons from the States: Reducing Recidivism and Curbing Corrections Costs Through Justice Reinvestment*. Washington, DC: Council of State Governments Justice Center, 2013, p. 1.

58 Ohio Community Corrections Association, *Ohio Dept. of Rehabilitation and Correction Funded Community Corrections Fact Sheet* (February 6, 2013). Available at http://www.occaonline.org/pdf/fact_sheet/Fiscal%20Year%202012%20Fact%20Sheet%20Combined%20.pdf; C. Henrichson and R. Delaney, *The Price of Prisons: What Incarceration Costs Taxpayers*. New York, NY: Center on Sentencing and Corrections, July 20, 2012. Available at http://www.vera.org/sites/default/files/resources/downloads/Price_of_Prisons_updated_version_072512.pdf

59 Eckhom, E. "A.C.L.U. in $50 million push to reduce jail sentences." *New York Times*, November 7, 2014, A14.

60 Council of State Governments Justice Center, *Lessons from the States: Reducing Recidivism and Curbing Corrections Costs Through Justice Reinvestment*. Washington, DC: Council of State Governments Justice Center, 2013, p. 2.

61 Council of State Governments Justice Center, note 60.

62 J. Austin, E. Cadora, T. Clear, K. Dansky, J. Greene, V. Gupta, M. Mauer, N. Porter, S. Tucker and M. Young, *Ending Mass Incarceration: Charting a New Justice Reinvestment*. Washington, DC: Sentencing Project, 2013. Available via NCJRS at https://www.ncjrs.gov/App/Publications/abstract.aspx?ID=264175, p. 10.

63 Ibid, p. 14.

64 L. Eisen and J. Cullen. *Update: Changes in State Imprisonment*. New York, NY: Brennan Center, 2015, p. 2.

65 Council of State Governments Justice Center, note 60, p. 5.

66 J. Austin, E. Cadora, T. Clear, K. Dansky, J. Greene, V. Gupta, M. Mauer, N. Porter, S. Tucker and M. Young, note 62.

67 M. Males. *Realignment and Crime in 2014: California's Violent Crime in Decline.* Center on Juvenile and Criminal Justice, August 2015; J. Sundt, E. Salisbury and M. Harmon, "Is downsizing prisons dangerous? The effect of California's Realignment Act on public safety." *Criminology and Public Policy* 15 (2) (2016).

68 M. Bird and R. Gratten, "Realignment and recidivism." *Annals of the American Association of Policy Sciences* 664 (2016): 176–195, p. 183.

69 Ibid., p. 184.

70 Ibid., p. 185.

71 Ibid., p. 187.

72 Ibid., p. 189.

73 M. Males, note 67, p. 4.

74 J. Sundt, E. Salisbury and M. Harmon, note 67

75 J. Domanick. "The message of California's Prop 47." *Los Angeles Times*, November 7, 2014; C. Chang, M. Gerber and B. Poston, "Unintended consequences of Prop. 47 pose challenge for criminal justice system." *LA Times*, November 6, 2015.

JUVENILE JUSTICE AND CORRECTIONS

13

Throughout a good portion of this country's history, we have excused juveniles from their crimes because of a belief that their immaturity prevented them from engaging in the rational deliberation that is required for criminal (and moral) culpability. It is the same reasoning that supports laws which prevent juveniles from drinking alcohol or buying cigarettes, voting, or serving in the military until they reach the legal age of maturity, which can be 16, 18, or 21 depending on the issue and jurisdiction. Others argue that we should not excuse criminal culpability, since even young children know it is wrong to murder, rob, or steal. Before we can discuss the issue, the history and present-day elements of the juvenile justice system should be understood.

Chapter Preview

- How Is the Juvenile Justice System Different from the Adult System?
- What Have Been the Trends in Juvenile Crime?
- What Is the Profile of the Juvenile Offender?
- Focus on Data: Are Girls Becoming More Violent?
- What Rights Do Juvenile Offenders Have?
- Can Juveniles End Up in Adult Courts? How?
- What Are People Referring to by the Terms "Zero Tolerance" and "School-To-Prison Pipeline"?
- How Many Juveniles Are on Probation?
- How Many Youths Are Sent to Secure Detention Facilities?
- Are Juveniles as Recidivistic as Adults?
- Summary
- Critical Thinking Exercises

HOW IS THE JUVENILE JUSTICE SYSTEM DIFFERENT FROM THE ADULT SYSTEM?

The juvenile justice system is a separate and parallel justice system to the adult criminal system. Many police departments have specialized juvenile divisions; states have specialized juvenile courts; and the juvenile corrections system is separate from the adult corrections system. The terminology in the juvenile justice system is different, as is its origin, history, and mission. A fundamental difference between the two systems is the underlying philosophy that children are less responsible for their actions than adults.

The juvenile justice system and family court operate under the legal concept of **parens patriae** (literally "parent of the country"), which refers to the state's power to take the place of the parent. The spirit of the juvenile justice system is based on the notion that (a) the culpability of very young offenders is less than that of adults because they don't have the maturity to determine right and wrong and/or control their actions, (b) young people are more malleable than adults and can be reformed, and (c) the youths who commit delinquent acts are also often the ones who engage in youthful misbehavior (truancy) and are not being properly parented and/or are neglected or abused. These assumptions support the approach to treat all juveniles, no matter what they have done, as different from adults.

One major difference between the juvenile and adult justice systems is that the juvenile system handles both **delinquents** (those who commit an act that is defined as a crime by the penal code) and **status offenders** (whose behavior is prohibited only because they are juveniles, e.g., running away, truancy, breaking curfew, or being "incorrigible"). In some cases, juveniles who are taken into state custody have done nothing wrong. They have been declared either neglected or abused and the state takes the child away from the parent for their own protection. There is an idea that youth who lack supervision and/or who are difficult to control will graduate to more serious forms of delinquency; thus, most states have created the authority to intervene upon a finding that the juvenile fits the description of CHINS, PINS, or MINS (children in need of supervision, persons in need of supervision, minors in need of supervision).

Before the 1800s, children received very little protection or special treatment from society or the legal system. Only children under the age of seven were presumed to be incapable of criminal culpability; all others were punished similar to adults. In the early jails of this country, children and adults were housed together. Gradually, there came recognition that children should receive greater protections and that the state should step in when parents either could not or would not provide a safe and nurturing environment. The **child saver movement**[1] involved upper-middle-class women who took on, as a reform project, the terrible living conditions of immigrant children in Northeastern cities. These orphaned and/or poverty-stricken children roamed the streets as beggars and engaged in petty crimes to survive. In the late 1800s and early 1900s, the child saver movement resulted in states creating solutions such as foster care, orphanages, houses of refuge, and, eventually, the juvenile justice system.

The first juvenile court was established in Chicago in 1899, and, by 1919, almost all states had created a separate judicial system for youth.[2] Very soon afterward, juvenile probation was established. The concept of a separate system for juveniles was based on the idea that children were different from adults—in their culpability and in their vulnerability. Originally, the differences between children who committed crimes and children who were neglected or abused by

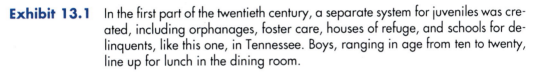

Exhibit 13.1   In the first part of the twentieth century, a separate system for juveniles was created, including orphanages, foster care, houses of refuge, and schools for delinquents, like this one, in Tennessee. Boys, ranging in age from ten to twenty, line up for lunch in the dining room.

Source: AP

their parents were de-emphasized because of the idea that all were in need of care. Status offenders, who might not have done anything other than run away from an intolerable home life, were housed with juvenile delinquents, who could have been serious offenders. In the 1970s, many recognized the injustice of this situation. The 1974 Juvenile Justice and Delinquency Prevention Act mandated, among other things, that neglected and abused children and status offenders needed to be removed from secure detention facilities. Further, if there was a determination that a status offender be sent to a residential placement, then there had to be a sight-and-sound separation between status offenders and juvenile delinquents if housed in the same facility. This led to a substantial decrease in the number of status offenders housed in secure detention, and the incentive to find community placements for those who posed no threat to the community. Other cases led to more due process rights for juveniles.

An increase in juvenile crime in the 1980s and early 1990s led to a "toughening" of the juvenile justice system, with more institutional placements and more judicial **waiver**s to adult court (sending youth to adult criminal courts to be tried and punished). Depending on the state, the juvenile who is adjudicated in adult court may serve their sentence in an adult facility; thus, we have come almost full circle back to where we were before the child saver movement more than a century ago.

Several key differences exist between the juvenile and adult justice systems in the United States. Unlike the criminal justice system, the juvenile justice system can consider extralegal factors in deciding how to handle cases. The juvenile court system can bypass all formal sanctions and judicial action, opting instead to handle matters informally.[3] The language of juvenile corrections is different from adult corrections, as shown in Exhibit 13.2. For instance, juveniles are not sentenced to jail, nor are they incarcerated. Instead, juveniles are adjudicated with dispositions ranging from informal or formal community supervision to secure confinement in training schools. Training schools are juvenile incarceration facilities that serve as a residential placement for the most serious juvenile offenders. The juveniles often live in dorms instead of prison cells, and are considered students, not inmates. These subtle differences in language may be mere euphemisms, but they reflect the historical mission of juvenile justice.

The process from offense through adjudication (conviction) for juveniles has several similarities to the adult system. First, juveniles suspected of wrongdoing come into contact with the police. During this initial contact, law enforcement officers investigate a delinquent act and decide whether to proceed with informal or formal sanctions. Just as with adult criminals, an

Exhibit 13.2 Terminology Differences for Juvenile and Criminal Justice Systems

Juvenile Justice Terminology	Criminal Justice Terminology
Respondent	Defendant
Detain	Arrest
Petition	Indictment
Intake	Prosecution
Hearing	Arraignment
Adjudication hearing	Trial
Finding	Verdict
Secure detention	Pre-trial detention
Disposition	Sentencing
Commitment	Imprisonment
Aftercare	Parole
Secure confinement	Imprisoned
Training school, state school, or residential placement	Jail/prison

Source: Author

officer's reactions are based primarily on the seriousness of the offense committed. Informal sanctions include ignoring the behavior, admonishing the juvenile and consulting his or her parents, referring the family to a social service agency, or detaining the juvenile with a "station adjustment."[4] If the officer decides to officially respond to juvenile delinquency, the officer will detain the juvenile.

Although some states require that juveniles have counsel or parents present when being interrogated by police, other states have no such requirement, or the juvenile is allowed to waive that right. Advocates for juveniles argue that children or youthful suspects are simply unable to protect their own interests and are vulnerable to manipulation and intimidation by interrogators.

Significant differences exist between the intake process in the juvenile system as compared to the prosecution process in the criminal justice system. Some communities do not have facilities for juveniles and, instead, they are housed in the jail (although sight and sound separation from adults is supposed to occur). In most communities, however, there is a juvenile detention facility and the juvenile meets with an intake officer. These officers are typically juvenile probation officers. An intake/probation officer can request that the case be placed on **deferred adjudication** or informal probation, during which time the juvenile must stay out of trouble so that all the charges will be discharged. If the case moves forward toward prosecution, the intake officer files a petition for an adjudication hearing with the juvenile court.[5]

The adjudication hearing is the juvenile version of a trial in a criminal court. During this hearing, a judge may review a motion to waive the juvenile over to adult court to be tried as an adult. If the juvenile remains in juvenile court, the judge reviews the charges and evidence, and renders a decision about the juvenile. These hearings are less formal than criminal trials and are conducted in closed courtrooms to protect the anonymity of the youthful suspect. Rarely are adjudication hearings heard by juries, because states are not required to provide jury trials for juvenile processing. Drug courts exist in the juvenile system as well as the adult system. In these special courts, juveniles who are identified as drug abusers are provided with specialized services. Cases are assigned to a specialized caseload and juveniles may be provided with mental health counseling, as well as family counseling and other services, in addition to drug treatment.[6]

When the court finds that a juvenile committed the offense charged, the youth will appear at a disposition hearing. This disposition hearing is equivalent to a sentencing hearing in a criminal court. The key difference is that there are more options available for youthful offenders than for adults, including everything from informal sanctions to incarceration in an adult prison.[7]

There has been quite a bit of research lately on juvenile brain development and how youth are indeed different from adults in their thinking patterns. The National Academies of Science has summarized research that shows adolescents are less able than adults to regulate their behavior when they are emotional, they are more sensitive to peer pressure and immediate rewards, and they have less ability to make judgments that require forward-thinking. These differences are traced back to the biological immaturity of the brain; more specifically, the brain system that influences pleasure-seeking and emotional reactivity develops more rapidly than the brain system that supports self-control.[8] Thus, today, we have scientific evidence for the different mission and emphases that originated in the 1800s.

WHAT HAVE BEEN THE TRENDS IN JUVENILE CRIME?

Consistent with the dramatic decline of crime among adults, the crime rates of juveniles have also dramatically decreased. Juvenile arrest rates reached their peak in the mid-1990s and have decreased since then. Exhibit 13.3 illustrates the decline in juvenile arrest rates (per 100,000) for all crimes. Exhibit 13.4 illustrates the decline in juvenile arrest rates for violent crime rates. Exhibit 13.5 illustrates property crime arrest rates. Exhibit 13.6 shows drug crime arrest rates for juveniles.

The peak in violent crime came in about 1995 and the decline occurred very rapidly. For property crime, there was greater stability in the arrest rates through the 1980s and first half of the 1990s, at which time the rates began to decline although there was a slight uptick around 2008. Exhibit 13.5 shows that there was a dramatic rise in arrest rates for drug crimes in the mid-1990s and it has declined since then, especially after 2010. The exhibits show the number of juveniles arrested per 100,000 in the population; however, Exhibit 13.7 shows juvenile arrests *as a percentage of total* arrests. Thus, not only have the number of juvenile arrests declined per capita, their *share* of total arrests as compared to adults has also declined, with the most dramatic decline in their share of arrests for property crimes, going from over one-third to less than 20 percent of all arrests.

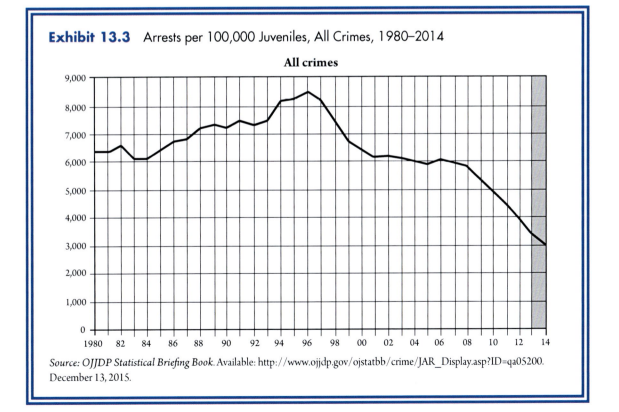

Exhibit 13.3   Arrests per 100,000 Juveniles, All Crimes, 1980–2014

All crimes

Source: OJJDP Statistical Briefing Book. Available: http://www.ojjdp.gov/ojstatbb/crime/JAR_Display.asp?ID=qa05200. December 13, 2015.

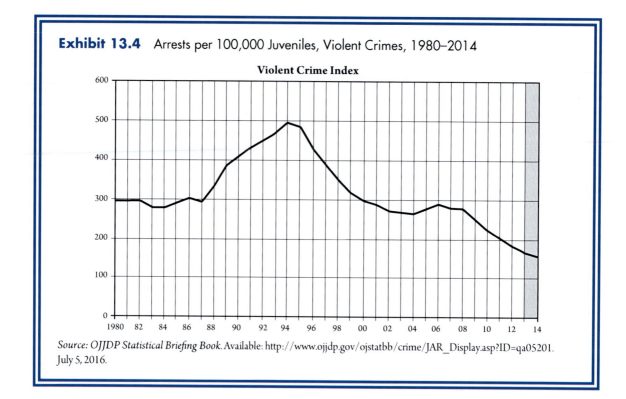

Exhibit 13.4   Arrests per 100,000 Juveniles, Violent Crimes, 1980–2014

Source: OJJDP Statistical Briefing Book. Available: http://www.ojjdp.gov/ojstatbb/crime/JAR_Display.asp?ID=qa05201. July 5, 2016.

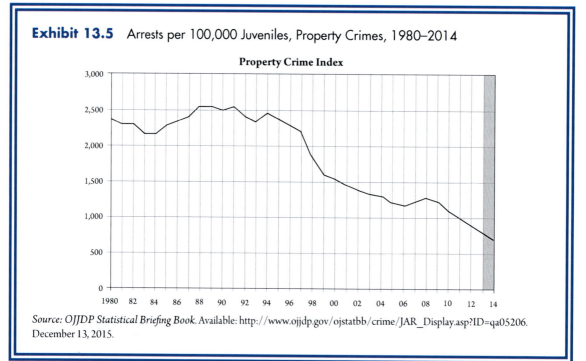

Exhibit 13.5   Arrests per 100,000 Juveniles, Property Crimes, 1980–2014

Source: OJJDP Statistical Briefing Book. Available: http://www.ojjdp.gov/ojstatbb/crime/JAR_Display.asp?ID=qa05206. December 13, 2015.

Exhibit 13.6 Arrests per 100,000 Juveniles, Drug Abuse Violations, 1980–2014

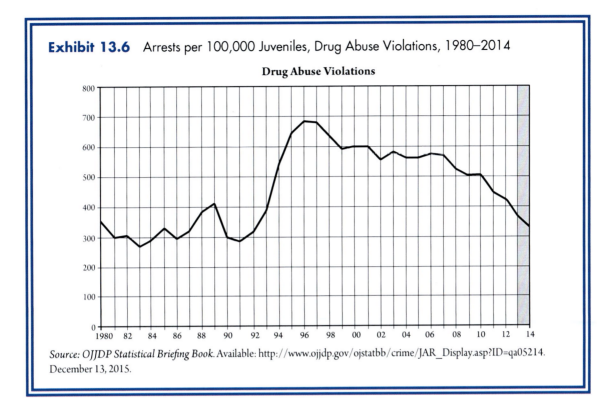

Source: OJJDP Statistical Briefing Book. Available: http://www.ojjdp.gov/ojstatbb/crime/JAR_Display.asp?ID=qa05214. December 13, 2015.

Exhibit 13.7 Percentage of Total Arrests — Juveniles

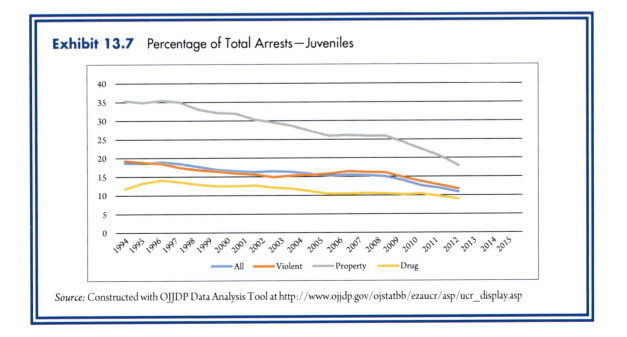

Source: Constructed with OJJDP Data Analysis Tool at http://www.ojjdp.gov/ojstatbb/ezaucr/asp/ucr_display.asp

WHAT IS THE PROFILE OF THE JUVENILE OFFENDER?

Most juveniles who are arrested are not gang members, but a very important component of juvenile delinquency is membership in juvenile gangs. Membership in a juvenile gang does not automatically mean the juvenile is also committing delinquent or criminal acts. A good portion of gang activity

Exhibit 13.8 Gang membership is an important component of juvenile delinquency. These alleged gang members were arrested in the Bronx, New York, in 2016.

Source: Getty

is noncriminal, especially for female gang members. However, estimates indicate that gang members commit three times as much crime as nongang members.

Juvenile gangs have been associated with a range of criminal activity, up to and including murder. Gangs are identified as the primary distributor of drugs in the United States, although this statement includes adult gangs as well as delinquent. Recently, they have been identified as the major cause of the spike in homicides in cities such as Chicago and Baltimore. Gang members are more likely to be both offenders and victims according to researchers.[9] It was reported in 2008 that there were 27,900 gangs with 774,000 members in the United States based on law enforcement estimates, an increase of 28 percent from 2002.[10] A more recent study estimates that over a million youth are in gangs, about 2 percent of the total juvenile population.[11]

Similar to the adult population, Black and other minority youth are disproportionately likely to be arrested or referred, formally processed, and end up in juvenile or adult facilities compared to Whites. Exhibit 13.9 shows that

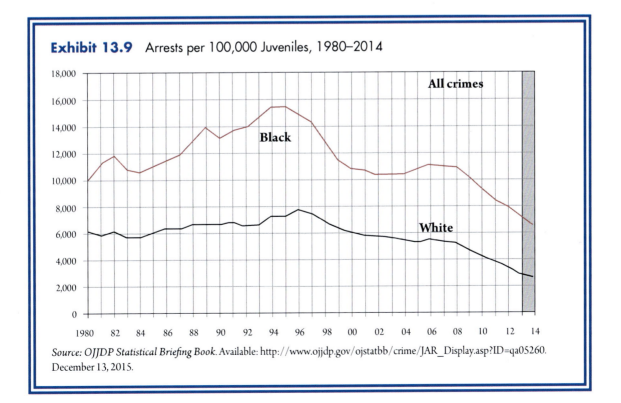

Exhibit 13.9 Arrests per 100,000 Juveniles, 1980–2014

Source: OJJDP Statistical Briefing Book. Available: http://www.ojjdp.gov/ojstatbb/crime/JAR_Display.asp?ID=qa05260. December 13, 2015.

arrest rates of both Black and White youths declined, but Whites have always had lower arrest rates.

Looking specifically at violent crime in Exhibit 13.10, we see that there was a dramatic increase in the rate for Black youths during the mid-1990s that declined just as dramatically, reducing the ratio of arrests between Whites and Blacks. The rate of arrests for White youth showed more modest changes during these years.

These official statistics under-represent the divergence between minorities and Whites because they do not identify ethnicity; most Hispanics are combined with Whites, which masks the differences between the groups. In almost every indicator, Hispanics fall somewhere between Blacks and Whites on such things as arrests, detentions, and victimization.

Drug arrests, displayed in Exhibit 13.11, show an interesting pattern in that arrest/referrals for Black youth increased dramatically in the mid-1990s, but there also emerged a very large divergence in arrest/referral rates between Black and White youth. Arrest rates between the two groups were about the same in 1980 but then Blacks' arrest/referrals rose dramatically, creating a very

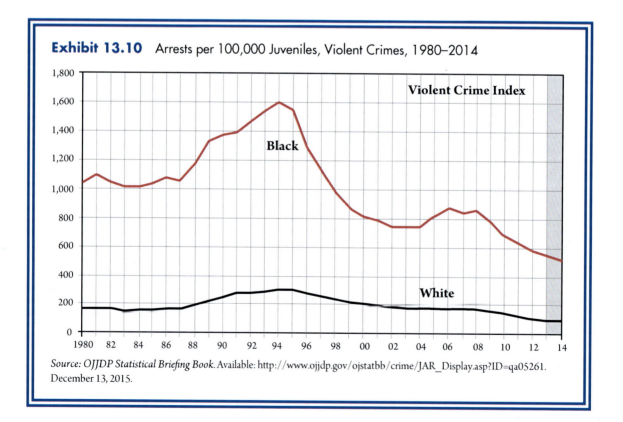

Exhibit 13.10 Arrests per 100,000 Juveniles, Violent Crimes, 1980–2014

Source: OJJDP Statistical Briefing Book. Available: http://www.ojjdp.gov/ojstatbb/crime/JAR_Display.asp?ID=qa05261. December 13, 2015.

large ratio difference between the two groups that has gradually declined again in recent years. It is not clear why this arrest/referral pattern has occurred, although it may have been due to the police focus on crack markets in the inner cities.

Contrary to the popular belief that drugs are a greater problem in minority communities, a recent study found that minority youths were much less likely to have cocaine addiction than Whites in a longitudinal study of a sample of juveniles detained in Cook County (Chicago) during 1995–1998. In the twelve years after detention, non-Hispanic White youths had thirty times the odds of cocaine use disorder compared with African Americans. Hispanic youths had more than twenty times the odds compared with African Americans. Black youth were also less likely than Whites to use hallucinogens, PCP, opiates, amphetamines, and sedatives in this study of youth involved in the juvenile justice system.[12]

The next step in the system is detainment before adjudication (similar to pre-trial detainment in jails for adults). The proportion of cases detained of the total number of arrests was slightly larger in 2013 (21 percent) than in 1985 (19 percent).[13] Minorities are over-represented in the youth detained. While

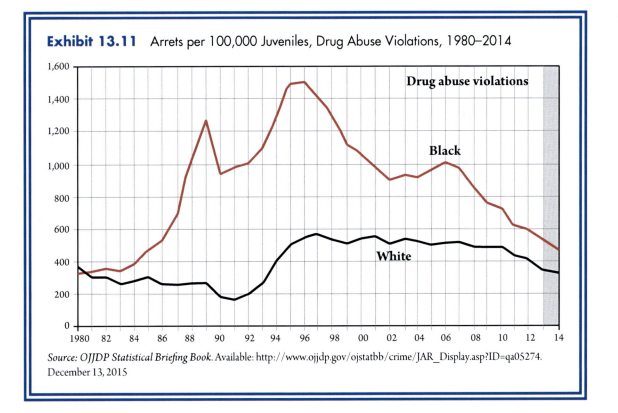

Exhibit 13.11   Arrets per 100,000 Juveniles, Drug Abuse Violations, 1980–2014

Source: OJJDP Statistical Briefing Book. Available: http://www.ojjdp.gov/ojstatbb/crime/JAR_Display.asp?ID=qa05274. December 13, 2015

Black youth represented 35 percent of the overall delinquency caseload in 2013, but they made up 42 percent of the detention caseload.[14] Exhibit 13.12 shows that Black juveniles are more likely than Whites to end up detained for each crime category. This exhibit shows the percentage of arrest/referrals who are identified as Black compared to the percentage of detainments identified as Black. One would expect those to be similar but they are not. Detainments include a higher percentage of Blacks, especially in some arrest categories. Of course, factors other than race may go into the decision to place in secure facilities (e.g., home environment, prior record, level of injury).

Between 1985 and 2013, the likelihood of juveniles being formally processed increased: from 48 percent to 58 percent for public order cases, from 43 percent to 53 percent for property offense cases, from 53 percent to 57 percent for person offense cases. Drug cases are slightly different, there was an increase from 43 percent in 1985 to 49 percent in 2013, but that is down from the peak year (1991) when 65 percent of cases were petitioned.[15] The proportion of delinquency cases petitioned increased for all racial groups between 1985 and 2013: from 43 percent to 52 percent for White youth, from 55 percent to 61 percent for Black youth, from 42 percent to 55 percent for American Indian youth, and from 42 percent to 58 percent for Asian youth.[16]

Exhibit 13.13 shows that Whites contribute the majority of cases in most crime categories. Exhibits 13.3 to 13.6 present the *rate of arrests* for Black

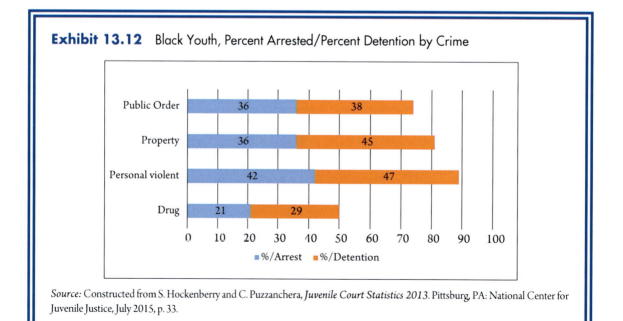

Exhibit 13.12 Black Youth, Percent Arrested/Percent Detention by Crime

Source: Constructed from S. Hockenberry and C. Puzzanchera, *Juvenile Court Statistics 2013*. Pittsburg, PA: National Center for Juvenile Justice, July 2015, p. 33.

Exhibit 13.13   Total Juvenile Court Cases—Percentage White

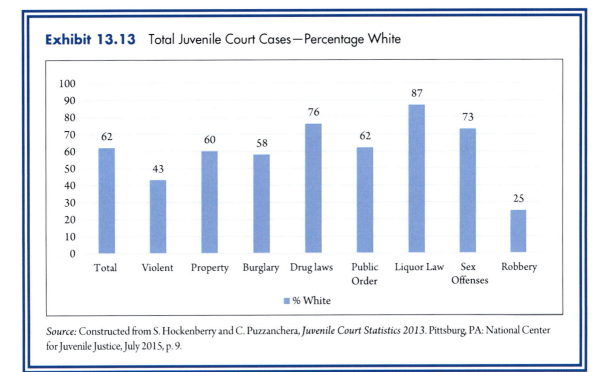

Source: Constructed from S. Hockenberry and C. Puzzanchera, *Juvenile Court Statistics 2013.* Pittsburg, PA: National Center for Juvenile Justice, July 2015, p. 9.

and White juveniles per 100,000 of the population and clearly Blacks' rates of arrests (per 100,000) are higher. However, even though White juveniles may have lower rates of arrests, there are many more Whites than Blacks in the population so White juveniles contribute most of the cases in the juvenile system for many crime categories. Some crimes do stand out, however. Note that for liquor law violations, Whites account for 87 percent of all arrest/ referrals, but for robbery, Whites comprise only 25 percent of all arrest/ referrals.

Minority youth are increasingly over-represented at each successive phase of the system. Researchers note that minority youth are over-represented in juvenile incarceration facilities, when compared to their percentage of arrest/ referrals. Further, they are more likely to be found in public facilities, while White youth are more likely to be found in private "treatment" facilities.[17] Studies indicate that race does play a factor in judicial decisions to send to secure confinement, even after controlling for legal factors of the case, such as seriousness.[18]

Girls' arrest/referral rates also declined since the mid-1990s, but their decline has not been as dramatic. In Exhibit 13.14, both male and female juvenile arrest rates are displayed.

Exhibit 13.14   Arrest Rates of Juveniles for All Offenses

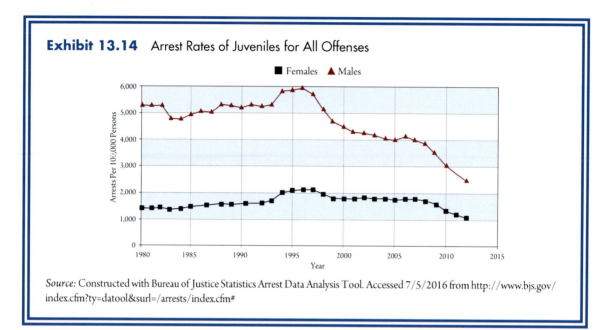

Source: Constructed with Bureau of Justice Statistics Arrest Data Analysis Tool. Accessed 7/5/2016 from http://www.bjs.gov/index.cfm?ty=datool&surl=/arrests/index.cfm#

Exhibit 13.15   Girls, like this suspected gang member detained by a U.S. Marshal in California, make up about 30 percent of all juvenile arrests/referrals.

Source: AP

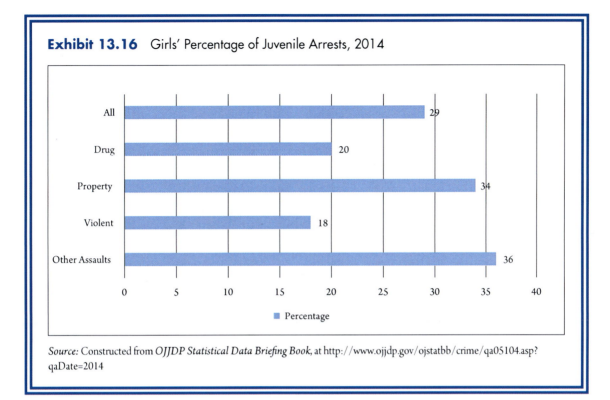

Exhibit 13.16 Girls' Percentage of Juvenile Arrests, 2014

Source: Constructed from *OJJDP Statistical Data Briefing Book,* at http://www.ojjdp.gov/ojstatbb/crime/qa05104.asp? qaDate=2014

Girls comprise about 30 percent of all juvenile arrest/referrals. This is a higher proportion than in past decades. In 1985, the delinquency case rate for males was four times greater than the rate for females; by 2013, the male rate was only about 2.5 times the rate of female juveniles.[19]

Exhibit 13.16 shows girls' percentage of juvenile arrests by type of crime.

"Other assaults" is a category that is not included in the FBI's violent crime index. While aggravated assault is a felony and is typically determined by extent of injury or use of a weapon, "other assaults" in the FBI arrest statistics can cover a wide range of assaultive behavior, including simple pushing and mutual fighting. Girls' rate of arrest/referrals and percentage of total figures for this crime category have increased dramatically and this increase has spurred many to presume that girls are becoming more violent today. Whether they have or not will be covered in our Focus on Data section.

FOCUS ON DATA: ARE GIRLS BECOMING MORE VIOLENT?

As seen in Exhibit 13.14, both male and female juveniles' arrest rates declined, but male juveniles' arrest rates declined much more dramatically than girls, reducing the so-called **gender disparity** between them. This led to many headlines that girls were becoming more criminal. More specifically, there has been a persistent and prevalent message that girls are becoming more violent, spurred, again, by the decreased ratio between male and female arrest/referrals rates for violent crimes and for "other assaults." These questions are difficult to answer with the data sources we have because formal statistics represent only partially the actions of the offender(s); they also are a reflection of the actions of the criminal justice system actors. If girls are more likely to be arrested in recent years than in the past, then it will appear they are more criminal even when their behavior patterns have not changed. We have to attempt to find a way to measure without depending solely on official statistics. We also have to guard against assumptions that girls are becoming more violent based on a few news stories of girls engaging in violent behavior since there has always been a small portion of women who engaged in violent crimes. Exhibit 13.17 shows arrest rates for the violent crime index.

If data is presented that shows male and female arrest rates as ratios or girls' arrest as percentage of total juvenile arrests, then it would certainly appear that girls are becoming more violent because they would appear to have increased their proportion of violent crime dramatically. What Exhibit 13.17 shows,

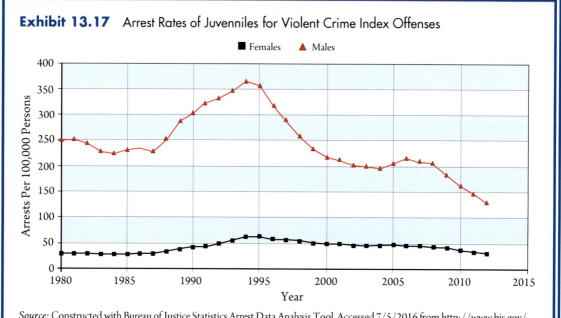

Exhibit 13.17   Arrest Rates of Juveniles for Violent Crime Index Offenses

Source: Constructed with Bureau of Justice Statistics Arrest Data Analysis Tool. Accessed 7/5/2016 from http://www.bjs.gov/index.cfm?ty=datool&surl=/arrests/index.cfm#

however, is that the girls' arrest rate for violent crime increased a bit in 1995 and then rates gradually declined; however, male juveniles' rates spiked dramatically and then declined dramatically as well. In other words, it is not so much that girls have increased their violent crimes as that boys have decreased theirs that has led to the reduced gender disparity.

Recall that in Exhibit 13.16, girls represented 36 percent of "other assaults." This is quite high in relation to other crimes and contributes to the perception that girls are becoming more violent. Exhibit 13.18 shows the arrest trends for "other assaults," indicating that there has been a significant increase in girls' arrest/referrals for this crime since 1980. Exhibit 13.19 illustrates "aggravated assaults," which shows only a very slight increase since 1980.

It seems somewhat suspicious that both types of assaults would not increase with the same pattern; instead only "other assaults" shows a significant increase. Girls "other assaults" arrests are five times as high as the aggravated assault arrests, but boys' arrests/referrals for simple assault are only 3.5 times higher. Some argue this finding indicates that girls' non-serious assaultive behavior is being treated more formally than boys' (increasing girls' arrest/referral numbers in this crime category only). Another suspicious finding is that other assault arrests of girls increased, but there was no increase in homicide or robbery. If

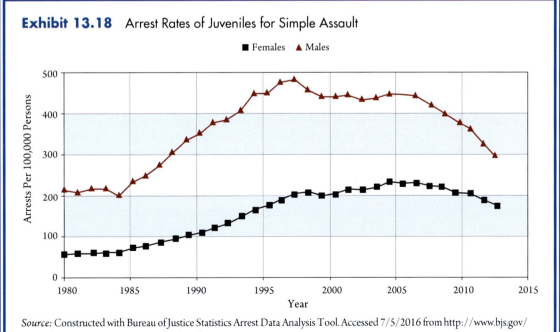

Exhibit 13.18   Arrest Rates of Juveniles for Simple Assault

■ Females   ▲ Males

Source: Constructed with Bureau of Justice Statistics Arrest Data Analysis Tool. Accessed 7/5/2016 from http://www.bjs.gov/index.cfm?ty=datool&surl=/arrests/index.cfm#

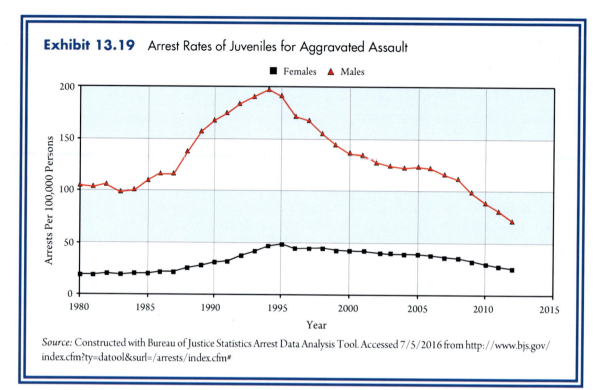

Exhibit 13.19 Arrest Rates of Juveniles for Aggravated Assault

■ Females ▲ Males

Source: Constructed with Bureau of Justice Statistics Arrest Data Analysis Tool. Accessed 7/5/2016 from http://www.bjs.gov/index.cfm?ty=datool&surl=/arrests/index.cfm#

girls were actually becoming more violent, arrests in these other violent crime categories should also increase. Another bit of evidence that girls' arrests for "other assaults" is not simply due to a change in girls' behaviors is that self-reports and the NCVS have not shown the same rate of increase as official arrest/referral numbers.[20]

Steffensmeier and his colleagues[21] compared victim reports and self-reports to arrest statistics. Findings indicated that arrest numbers increased while the other two sources of crime did not show similar increases. These authors speculated that arrest/referrals are more likely to be made for minor incidents today, there is more formal policing of domestic violence which comprises a large portion of girls' violence, and there is a less tolerant or understanding attitude toward girls today. Case studies indicated that girls were arrested for family altercations in incidents of mutual violence or self-defense, or in schools which had zero tolerance policies utilizing police officers to arrest/referral in discipline cases that had been dealt with by school officials in past decades.[22] Other sources show that 50 percent of juvenile assault arrests are for acts against parents and 50 percent of arrests were made of children under thirteen years of age.[23] Buzawa and Hotaling[24] found that 91 percent of girls in domestic violence calls (assaults on parents) were arrested compared to 75 percent of boys.

They also reported from other sources that self-reported assaultive behavior of girls did not increase but arrest/referrals and convictions did, indicating a system change rather than a behavioral change.

Another study utilized data on assault arrests from the National Incident-Based Reporting System. Results indicated that in the assault cases analyzed, holding victim, offender, and offense characteristics constant, arrests for girls were 11 percent higher than that for boys, a statistically significant effect. These results suggested that mandatory arrest policies for domestic violence may disproportionately affect girls, as a greater proportion of girls' offenses than boys' offenses take place at home, requiring the application of domestic violence policies with less discretion by police officers to respond with any response other than arrest/referral.[25] While not definitive, the research above lends support to a formal system response theory; that is, girls are more likely to be arrested today for "other assaults" than in the past. This, combined with the dramatic decline of boys' assaults, has reduced the **gender differential** (the ratio of boys' arrests to girls' arrests).

WHAT RIGHTS DO JUVENILE OFFENDERS HAVE?

A major development that occurred in the 1970s was a shift in perception that, even though the mission of the juvenile system was to help the young offenders, they still deserved the same due process rights as adults. The Supreme Court decided a sequence of cases in the late 1960s and 1970s that established due process rights for juveniles and led to a greater formalization of the court process. These cases are described in Exhibit 13.20. Other due process rights have not been accorded to juveniles, however, including the right to a trial by jury.

Exhibit 13.20 Supreme Court Cases on Juvenile Rights

Kent v. United States 383 U.S. 541 (1966)

Required a hearing before waiver to adult court

In re Gault 387 U.S. 1 (1967)

Required some due process in juvenile proceedings

In re Winship 397 U.S. 358 (1970)

Required juvenile courts be held to the "beyond a reasonable doubt" standard in finding of guilt, instead of the preponderance standard

McKeiver v. Pennsylvania 403 U.S. 528 (1971)

Decision that juveniles did not require a jury trial under the 6th or 14th Amendments

In 2005, the United States joined the majority of nations in banning the execution of juveniles. In *Roper v. Simmons* (2005),[26] the Supreme Court, in a 5–4 decision, held that the 8th and the 14th Amendments barred the execution of anyone who committed their crime before the age of eighteen. At the time, twenty states allowed the execution of offenders who committed their crimes when they were sixteen or seventeen. In 2010, the Supreme Court decided *Graham v. Florida,*[27] holding that juveniles could not be held under a sentence of life without parole for non-homicide crimes. In Graham's case, he had been convicted of robbery at sixteen and was found guilty of committing another at seventeen and violating his probation. The majority of the court held that his sentence was a violation of the 8th Amendment's prohibition against cruel and unusual punishment. In *Miller v. Alabama* (2012),[28] the Supreme Court also extended that ruling to those juveniles who committed homicide before the age of eighteen, and in *Montgomery v. Louisiana* (2016),[29] the Supreme Court held that states must conduct resentencing hearings for all those who were sentenced prior to *Miller* to determine the juveniles' release date. The reasoning behind these cases is that capital punishment should be reserved for the "worst of the worst" criminal offenders, otherwise it is disproportional punishment. Because juveniles are young, malleable, and have less ability for rational thought, they cannot be the "worst of the worst" offenders. The dissent argued vigorously that juveniles who commit murder certainly know right from wrong, but the majority referenced scientific studies that showed that juveniles' brains are actually different than adults with less pre-frontal lobe development (the part of the brain responsible for forward-thinking and rationality). While earlier cases pushed for the right of juveniles to have the same due process rights as adults, the more recent cases are establishing the right of juveniles to be treated differently from adults because of their immaturity.

CAN JUVENILES END UP IN ADULT COURTS? HOW?

Waiver refers to when a juvenile court transfers a case over to adult court. Only four states do not have enabling statutes for waivers. The type of crime and the age of the youth eligible for waiver are set by state statute. Before waiver to adult court, juveniles must be determined to be **competent**. This legal concept means that juveniles are mature enough to know what is happening, be able to judge the consequences of the decisions they make, and be able to assist in their defense. This determination requires that juveniles understand right from wrong, but it does not require that juveniles understand why they did what they did, or that they be able to control their actions. Other factors that influence a waiver decision include: the seriousness of the offense, lengthy juvenile offense history, unsuccessful past rehabilitation interventions, and the age of the minor.

Judicial waivers increased 73 percent between 1988 and 1994, but decreased 28 percent between 1994 and 1997. They comprise only about 1 percent of all juvenile cases.[30] The Office of Juvenile Justice and Delinquency Prevention indicates that 1994 was the peak of juvenile waivers (with 12,100) and since 1994 the percentage of juvenile cases waived to adult court has declined. In 2007, there were about 8,500 cases waived.[31] In 2009, there were 7,600 and in 2013 only about 4,000.[32]

The decline in the use of waiver may not mean there are fewer juveniles in the adult system because states are increasingly using other methods such as "**direct file**" and "**statutory exclusion**." Statutory exclusion is when a certain crime is statutorily excluded from juvenile jurisdiction, regardless of who commits the crime, so that the juvenile is automatically tried as an adult. There are 29 states that have these statutory exclusion laws. In some states, and for certain crimes, both adult and juvenile jurisdictions exist concurrently. In this situation, a prosecutor may choose to file charges on the juvenile in the adult system (direct file) without needing to go through a judicial waiver hearing. There are fourteen states that have enabling legislation for direct file by the prosecutor. It appears that the majority of cases where juveniles end up in the adult system now are not through waiver, but rather through either direct filing by the prosecutor or statutory exclusion.[33]

In the last several years, there has been a growing belief that punitive policies have gone too far, and states are ratcheting back harsh legislation that forced juveniles into adult criminal justice systems. Although two states (North Carolina and New York) set juvenile court jurisdiction as low as fifteen (meaning sixteen- and seventeen-year-olds are automatically tried in the adult system), most states (38) set the juvenile court jurisdiction at seventeen years of age.

Since 2001, 21 states have increased the upper age of jurisdiction of the juvenile court (meaning older youth can be dealt with in the juvenile system rather than the adult system). Most recently, a 2012 Colorado law bars district attorneys from charging juveniles as adults for many low- and mid-level felonies. The Act also disallows fourteen- and fifteen-year-olds from being charged as adults.[34]

Research on youth who have been waived to adult court indicates that they are more likely to recidivate than those who were retained in juvenile court. In one study, 49 percent of the transferred offenders recidivated compared to 35 percent of those retained in the juvenile system. Reasons for the higher

To read a report about New York's effort to divert sixteen- and seventeen-year-olds, go to a study published by the Center for Court Innovation at: http://www.courtinnovation.org/research/criminal-justice-response-16-and-17-year-old-defendants-new-york

The National Center for Juvenile Justice is an organization dedicated to research on the juvenile justice system. On its website (under "National Projects") there is an interactive map where you can find out about your own state's waiver policy and juvenile justice system at http://www.jjgps.org/jurisdictional-boundaries

recidivism may include the negative effects of the greater stigma of adult punishments, a sense of injustice, learning of criminal mores and behavior from adults, or the decreased focus on rehabilitation in the adult system. Unless careful controls are used, however, such findings can occur because arguably more serious offenders are those who are waived.[35] Some researchers indicate that juvenile court judges are more likely to transfer minority delinquents to adult court than White delinquents, even after controlling for seriousness of crime,[36] but more research is needed to determine whether all other factors are controlled for in these findings showing differential treatment. It is important to note that many youths transferred to adult court have been accused of property and drug crimes; they are not all violent offenders.

For an interesting article on juvenile waivers to adult court, go to http://www.ojjdp.gov/pubs/232932.pdf

WHAT ARE PEOPLE REFERRING TO BY THE TERMS "ZERO TOLERANCE" AND "SCHOOL-TO-PRISON PIPELINE"?

In the 1980s and 1990s, there was a real and perceived increase in juvenile crime. In the mid-1990s, some researchers were quoted in the media as predicting an explosion of juvenile crime led by "super predators." Their predictions supported the punitive trend in legislation. The evidence for a predicted explosion of juvenile crime was that there had been spikes in violent crime fueled by easy access to handguns and the crack markets in urban areas. The predicted "bloodbath" did not occur and, in fact, the decline in juvenile crime had already begun and continued in the latter half of the 1990s.

For an interesting documentary about the super-predator prediction and how social science researchers impacted policies with faulty predictions, go to http://www.eji.org/node/893 for a link.

Even though the criminal violence in the late 1980s and early 1990s was largely confined to inner cities, the perception that youth were out of control spurred many states to enact new laws or change existing laws to increase the controls and sanctions over juveniles. These laws included the following:

- curfew laws
- parental responsibility laws
- antigang laws
- juvenile boot camps
- gun laws
- removing laws that seal juvenile records
- waiver laws (allowing waiver to adult courts)
- concurrent jurisdiction laws (extending criminal court jurisdiction to more crimes).

Even though the violent crime spike in the mid-1990s had already started to decline, the 1999 Columbine High School shooting and others (Springfield,

Oregon, 1998; Santee, California, 2001) solidified the pervasive view that juvenile crime was growing and the juvenile justice system was too lenient. At about the same time (late 1990s), the **zero tolerance approach** was being touted as a way to reduce crime. This policing strategy found its way into the schools as well, so that full prosecution of minor crimes on the street became translated to full prosecution and suspension for minor misconduct in the school, in the hope that this would prevent more serious violent crimes on school grounds.

In some cases the zero tolerance approach toward violence reached extreme levels: a ten-year-old girl who whispered "I could kill her" after she wet her pants because her teacher refused to let her go to the bathroom, a ten-year-old who said "I oughtta murder his face" when a classmate messed up his desk, a classmate who uttered a threat after he was pushed, a nine-year-old boy who shot a wad of toilet paper, and a kid in the school cafeteria line who warned his classmates if they ate all the potatoes he would "get them" were all suspended for these "threats of violence." Increasingly, students were arrested for acts that would have received school-based discipline in past decades. As early as 2001, the American Bar Association passed a resolution condemning zero tolerance policies that allow no discretion in defining children's acts as criminal.[37]

Ironically, the zero tolerance approach gained momentum during a period when juvenile crime was actually declining. As Exhibits 13.3 to 13.6 showed, the decade of 1995–2005 was a time when the majority of the public believed that juvenile crime was increasing and becoming more violent, and legislation and public responses to juvenile crime were becoming increasingly harsher, while, in reality, the rate of juvenile crime was declining at dramatic levels.

Zero tolerance policies in schools have resulted in many more suspensions. According to one source, the percentage of students suspended at least once in grades K through 12 has nearly doubled over the last four decades (from 3.7 percent to 6.7 percent). The percentage of Black children suspended is 15 percent. In 2006, almost one-third of Black boys (28 percent) were suspended, compared to 10 percent of White boys. Study authors caution that the numbers probably under-represent what is happening because school districts do not report all suspensions.[38] In many cases, a suspension leads to the student dropping out of school, forever handicapping his or her future. Some have argued that the increased suspension rates have occurred partially in response to national pressure to increase scores on standardized tests. If the lower-performing students are suspended, they do not have to be counted in the school's averages.[39]

To read one group's description of the zero tolerance approach, go to http://cfyj.org/images/pdf/Zero_Tolerance_Report.pdf

Another major change that took place on school grounds was the increasing number of "school safety officers" or "school resource officers" who may be assigned by the local police department or be peace officers employed by an independent school district police department.

Exhibit 13.21   Beginning in the 1980s, many schools began adding resource or safety officers like this one, at West Springfield High School in Springfield, Virginia.

Source: Getty

These officers began to be placed in schools as DARE officers in the 1980s (to teach about drugs) and, after school mass shootings like Columbine, the idea was that they would be the first responder to a mass shooting incident. What has occurred is a "formalization" of discipline so that a fistfight between two boys in junior high that might have been dealt with by the school principal is now handled by the school safety officer, with citations for disorderly conduct or public disturbance, and the involvement of the municipal court. This formal court intervention may occur with or without a school suspension. One study showed that schools with a school safety officer were five times more likely to have disorderly conduct arrests than schools without an officer.[40] Critics observe that their training influences school safety officers to see everything as a criminal justice issue and they may be inclined to use force when it is unnecessary.[41]

Read an article about a North Carolina officer who used what some called excessive force to remove a girl from a classroom at http://www.csmonitor.com/USA/Justice/2015/1027/S.C.-video-spotlights-police-in-schools-Do-they-help-or-hurt

The so-called "school-to-prison pipeline" refers to the idea that once students are suspended or sent to the juvenile justice system, they are much more likely to drop out, become engaged in crime, and end up in the adult criminal justice system. Numerous studies have showed a correlation between those who are punished and subsequent drop-out rates and involvement in the juvenile justice system although because this is correlational research, it is difficult to attribute causation. What this means is that one interpretation of a high correlation between suspension and eventual involvement in the criminal justice system (e.g., future criminality and a prison term) is that the school suspensions led to the latter; however, another explanation could be that the same kids who get suspended are those who would have ended up in the criminal justice system anyway, even without the formal discipline.

> To read more about the school-to-prison pipeline, go to The Justice Institute's webpage about it at http://www.justicepolicy.org/news/8775

By the early 2000s, some jurisdictions chose to retreat from the aggressive discipline policies that utilized formal arrest or suspension. Other jurisdictions were forced to change by courts. For instance, in 2010, the North Carolina Supreme Court held that a school district could not suspend students and deny them alternative school placement or home tutoring without "substantial reasons."[42] Up to this point, school districts did not have to give any reason for denying alternative schooling options. Advocates for youth herald this as a breakthrough and a persuasive authority in other states that have been challenged with similar cases. Interestingly, the public has never supported purely punitive approaches toward juveniles. In studies of public opinion, there has continued to be a great deal of support for rehabilitative responses to juvenile crime. One study found, for instance, that 72 percent of respondents were willing to pay for rehabilitation for serious juvenile offenders, 65 percent supported early childhood prevention efforts, and 59 percent were willing to pay for longer sentences for youthful offenders.[43]

> For information about the juvenile justice system and juvenile crime, go to the website for the Office of Juvenile Justice and Delinquency Prevention at http://ww.ojjdp.gov

HOW MANY JUVENILES ARE ON PROBATION?

Many juvenile offenders are never formally adjudicated and, therefore, are never formally disposed. Frequently, these alternative sanctions are discussed as dispositions despite the fact that there are no formal sanctions by a juvenile court. The most serious disposition is secure confinement, the juvenile version of jail or prison. Exhibit 13.22 illustrates the types of dispositions available for juvenile offenders.

The likelihood of a delinquency adjudication decreased between 1985 and 2013 for both White juveniles (8 percentage points) and Black juveniles (7 percentage points). For both racial groups, the likelihood of adjudication decreased more for drug offense cases than for other general offense

Exhibit 13.22   Types of Dispositions for Juvenile Offender

Disposition	Definition
Dismissal of case	The case is dismissed and the juvenile is released.
Restitution/fines	Restitution and/or damages are ordered by the court. This includes formal or informal supervision by probation officer.
Therapy	The juvenile must attend group and/or individual counseling sessions to address specific mental health concerns; formal or informal supervision by probation officer.
Mental hospitalization	The juvenile is committed to a mental health facility to treat a specific mental illness.
Group home placements	The juvenile is sent to a group home or residential treatment facility, sometimes targeted to address specific problems. Outward bound or wilderness programs or camps also are possible placements.
House arrest/electronic monitoring	The juvenile is required to be confined to home, except for school and court appearances, with or without electronic monitoring.
Probation	The juvenile is supervised in the community and required to meet set rules such as curfew, school attendance, and clean drug tests to stay out of a training school/state school facility.
Day treatment/day reporting centers	The juvenile is supervised in the community and required to attend special classes or check-ins at set times at day centers. These centers usually have mental health services, vocational training, and other services to meet the needs of the juveniles.
Secure confinement	The juvenile is sent to a placement in a state school or training school where he or she is expected to attend classes and rehabilitate. This sanction is the most serious for juvenile offenders who are not certified as adults.
Adult prison	The juvenile is certified as an adult and a trial is conducted in a criminal (not juvenile) court. The juvenile is then sentenced to serve time in a prison. The juvenile may serve part of the sentence in a juvenile facility until he or she is old enough to be placed in an adult prison.

Source: J. Austin, K.D. Johnson and R. Weitzer, *Alternatives to the Secure Detention and Confinement of Juvenile Offenders.* Washington, DC: Office of Juvenile Justice and Delinquency Prevention, 2005; R.V. del Carmen, C.R. Trulson, *Juvenile Justice: The System, Process, and Law.* Belmont, CA: Thompson-Wadsworth, 2006.

categories between 1985 and 2013: from 70 percent to 56 percent for White juveniles and from 65 percent to 47 percent for Black juveniles.[44] Exhibit 13.23 shows a breakdown of what happened to the 1,058 delinquency cases in 2013.

Note from Exhibit 13.23 that probation is the most common resolution for youth who are in the system, either as an informal or formal disposition. Of the million or so juveniles in the system, about one-third (383,600) ended up on probation. Of those who were formally adjudicated, 64 percent ended up on probation, that is a greater percentage than in either 2002 (62 percent) or 2007 (56 percent).[45]

Probation is the oldest and most widely used model of community-based corrections. All states have had juvenile probation since the 1930s, and probation is used for all types of juvenile offenders including first-time, low-risk, and serious offenders.[46] This community-based supervision allows the juvenile to remain in a community while following a set of rules that are specifically tailored to the individual's circumstances. As with adult offenders, probation can be revoked if the juvenile violates the prescribed conditions, which may result in secure confinement for the juvenile offender.

Failure on probation is distressingly common. The factors that have been associated with failure include adjudication for a delinquent act before age thirteen and several prior police contacts.[47] Intensive probation programs have

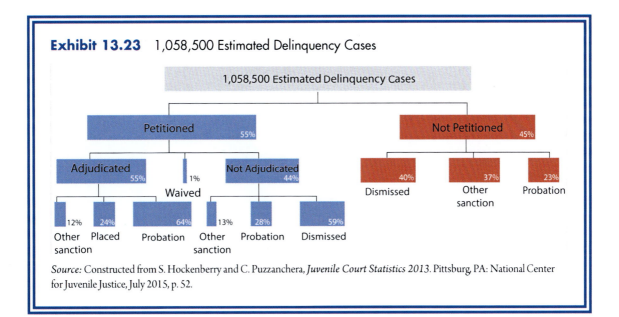

Exhibit 13.23   1,058,500 Estimated Delinquency Cases

Source: Constructed from S. Hockenberry and C. Puzzanchera, *Juvenile Court Statistics 2013.* Pittsburg, PA: National Center for Juvenile Justice, July 2015, p. 52.

been offered as a solution to the failure of regular probation to prevent juveniles from violating probation. Such programs have been evaluated and findings indicate that, similar to adult intensive probation, no significant difference exists between recidivism rates for intensive supervision caseloads and regular probation supervision.[48]

Other innovations have included enriched programming, offering adjudicated youths a range of counseling and educational services. In one such integrated program in Los Angeles, program youth were exposed to self-esteem building, educational tutoring, individual and group counseling, mental health services, substance abuse education and treatment, gang prevention alternatives, crisis intervention, family preservation services, education in parenting skills, housing and financial aid information, career development planning, and employment services. In one study, youth were assigned randomly to a treatment group or a control group who experienced regular probation. Although the treatment group performed better in school and received fewer violations, after the initial six-month reporting period there were no statistically significant differences found between the two groups.[49] Arguably, the program did not result in significant differences in outcome because both groups had fairly high success rates (about 80 percent in both groups did not violate their probation). Critics argue that the evaluation did not take into account the high **attrition** (dropout) rate, especially in the treatment group, where twice as many youths were removed to secure facilities for more intensive counseling or treatment. Those who were left, perhaps, might have performed successfully with or without such enriched services.[50] This illustrates the difficulty of developing, implementing, and evaluating treatment programs for youthful offenders.

HOW MANY YOUTHS ARE SENT TO SECURE DETENTION FACILITIES?

The number of cases adjudicated delinquent that resulted in out-of-home placements (secure facilities, group homes, or other dispositions) decreased to its lowest overall level in 2013. While 105,055 youth were held in out-of-home placement in 1997, that number had declined to 54,148 in 2013.[51] Overall, about one-quarter of youth found delinquent receive residential placement. The number of youth who are placed has been steadily declining since 2000.[52] Exhibit 13.24 shows that the percentage of youth who received out-of-home placements in 1985 and 2013 declined for both Black and White youth in the selected crime categories.

Juveniles can also end up in prisons for adults. In 2005, there were 2,266 inmates under age eighteen in adult prisons. In 2008, the number of juveniles

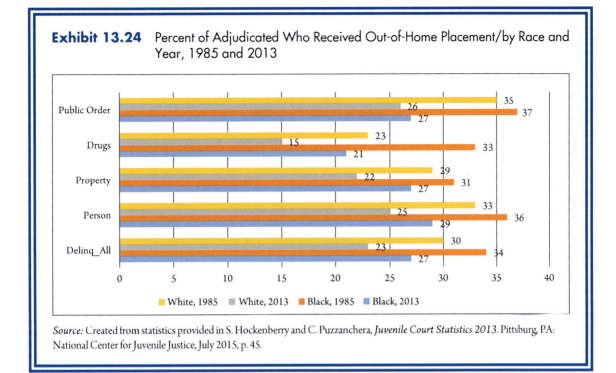

Exhibit 13.24 Percent of Adjudicated Who Received Out-of-Home Placement/by Race and Year, 1985 and 2013

Source: Created from statistics provided in S. Hockenberry and C. Puzzanchera, *Juvenile Court Statistics 2013*. Pittsburg, PA: National Center for Juvenile Justice, July 2015, p. 45.

incarcerated in adult prisons had increased to 3,670, but by 2014, the number of juveniles under eighteen in prison declined to just over 1,000. In 2005 there were 6,759 juveniles in jails and, in 2008, that number had increased to 7,703 juveniles in jails. However, the number of juveniles in jails also declined to about 4,200 juveniles age seventeen or younger in local jails at midyear 2014.[53]

Secure facilities for juveniles sometimes resemble their adult counterparts with high walls and razor wire. Most, however, have cottage-style architecture instead of cell blocks, and they have enriched educational programming. Many youth facilities operate under a token or a phase system that requires juveniles to work toward release. Even in states with determinate sentencing for adults, youth offenders typically have indeterminate sentences, so that facility staff may have a great deal of input into when the juveniles are released. Youth earn points or move through phases by following rules and participating in programming.

Experts in juvenile justice agree that secure confinement in "training schools," correctional schools, or detention centers should be used only as a last resort and reserved for serious, violent offenders.[54] While these facilities for juveniles generally offer more educational and vocational programming than adult institutions, there seem to be as many scandals and problems associated with their management as with the adult prisons.[55] In Pennsylvania, in the so-called "kids for cash" scheme, former judges Michael Conahan and Mark Ciavarella were convicted of a range of charges after it was discovered that they were taking payments from the owners of a private juvenile detention facility in return for sending juveniles who appeared in their courtrooms to the detention facility.[56] This evidently went on for years even though defense attorneys and juvenile probation officers knew that the sentences handed out in that county were disproportionately harsh compared to other counties.

Unfortunately, in some cases, correctional facilities may cause juveniles to become more delinquent or exacerbate psychological problems.[57] Studies consistently show that, at the very least, recidivism is often no better than it would be in a less restrictive community-based environment for the juvenile.[58] Small residential facilities in which juveniles' specific issues are targeted in a therapeutic environment offer an alternative to secure confinement. These facilities have several different names, including group homes and residential treatment facilities, but they are usually in the juvenile's own community rather than in a rural location. Typically, each facility targets a particular issue such as substance abuse or sex offending. Mandatory completion of programs provided in these residential facilities is usually required to avoid secure confinement. The effectiveness of these programs varies according to each facility's mission. Boot camps, for example, are not particularly effective in reducing recidivism, but some sex-offender treatment facilities show success in reducing recidivism.[59]

A troubling finding is that secure confinement seems to be the alternative chosen disproportionately for minorities, even after controlling for crime. Among males born in 2001, one in three African Americans and one in six Hispanics will be incarcerated at some point during their lifetimes—compared with one in seventeen Caucasians.[60] Minority youth accounted for 68 percent of youth in residential placement in 2013, with Black males forming the largest share. The national detention rate for Black youth was nearly six times the rate for White youth, and their commitment rate was more than four times the rate for White youth.[61]

Females accounted for 14 percent of the placement population in 2013. Males tended to stay in facilities longer than females.[62] Throughout the 1960s and 1970s, girls were more likely to be incarcerated in secure facilities for status offenses (misconduct but not crimes), while boys in the same facilities were likely to have committed delinquent acts. About 11 percent of females in residential placement were status offenders in 2013—compared to 4 percent of boys.[63] Note that this doesn't mean by itself that girls are more likely than boys to be sent to a residential placement for similar status offenses, it probably has more to do with the fact that boys are more likely to commit delinquency so their share of status offenses is smaller when looking at a residential population.

Today research finds that girls in detention facilities are still more likely to be less serious offenders than boys. Even though earlier case holdings restricted residential placement decisions purely on status offenses, girls are sent to placement because of contempt charges. What happens is that judges place female status offenders or less serious delinquents on probation with **conditions** (rules). Then, the girl who violates a court order to not run away or skip school is found in contempt of court, which is a delinquent act and, with that finding, the girl is detained in a secure facility.[64] Girls now represent about 15 percent of those held in juvenile facilities and as much as 34 percent in some states.[65]

In 2013, 37 percent of detained girls were locked up for status offenses or technical violations, compared with 25 percent of boys, and 21 percent of girls were detained for simple assault and public order offenses (excluding weapons), compared with 12 percent of boys. In 2013, Black girls were 20 percent more likely to be sent to secure facilities than White girls and American Indian/Alaska Native girls were 50 percent more likely to be detained.[66] In many cases, these girls have babies and are mothers before their age of majority. More research is needed to understand the type of youth who receives secure detention, and what programs might be beneficial in breaking the cycle of state intervention.

Theoretical research indicates that girls and boys may come to delinquency from different paths. Girls involved in the juvenile justice system are very likely to have experienced physical abuse (about 61 percent) and sexual abuse (about 54 percent). More than half have attempted suicide. A substantial number have been diagnosed with one or more psychiatric disorders.[67] Even more so than boys, delinquent girls come from dysfunctional backgrounds. In one study, it was found that girls involved as wards of the state in the child protective services system were four times more likely to be subsequently delinquent, while boys who had been in care were only twice as likely to be adjudicated as delinquent.[68]

To read a research report about the issues of incarcerated female juveniles, go to http://www.nationalcrittenton.org/wp-content/uploads/2015/09/Gender_Injustice_Report.pdf

ARE JUVENILES AS RECIDIVISTIC AS ADULTS?

Approximately 100,000 juvenile offenders are released each year from secure correctional placements, including state schools, residential treatment facilities, and adult jails and prisons.[69] However, once released, most juvenile offenders will recidivate. Data show that recidivism rates for juvenile offenders released from correctional facilities are 55 percent or higher.[70] Juvenile offenders who are released from adult facilities have equal or higher rates of recidivism as youth released from juvenile facilities.

Juvenile offenders who are confined to a secure facility are likely to function well below their age-appropriate grade level in school, and a significant proportion of these offenders are functionally illiterate. Schools are reluctant to welcome back the re-entering juveniles, and often juveniles are forced to start midyear, which puts them even further behind. As a result, many of these youths never go back to high school and have excessive free time when they return to the community. In addition, many mental and physical health conditions go untreated or undertreated while juveniles are confined. Research estimates that at least one out of every five youth in the juvenile justice system has serious mental health problems.[71] Deteriorating mental health can affect a juvenile's ability to stay out of trouble. Substance abuse problems are often also left untreated while confined. Approximately half of all juvenile offenders who are confined have substance abuse problems. Yet, many of these juveniles never receive any treatment for abuse and addiction problems. Once these offenders are released, their substance abuse problems frequently lead to other acts of delinquency.[72]

Successful juvenile aftercare programs include positive social skills, drug and alcohol abuse, education, and employment opportunities. A study of one such program found that after 90 days, the control group was twice as likely as the aftercare group to recidivate and use drugs or alcohol, and three times as likely to have returned to old peer networks. After one year, the recidivism rate of the control group was 53 percent compared to 32 percent of the treatment group.[73] In an analysis of 40 promising programs, it was found that the elements associated with successful reduction of recidivism included systematic assessment, appropriate styles of service, and treatment "fidelity," which is the extent to which the program sticks to the original program elements.[74]

Many researchers and practitioners argue that prevention is more effective than correctional rehabilitation and prevention would include early prevention programs that target very young children. The following preventions are suggested by researchers who argue that scientific evidence supports their effectiveness:

- early prevention (developmental and social programs that intervene during infancy and before school)
- individual prevention (preschool enrichment, social skills training, social competence programs for high-risk children)
- family prevention (parenting programs to teach effective discipline)
- school prevention (discipline management programs, instructional management, reorganization of grades or classes and cognitive programs to increase self control; also, after-school programs and mentor programs).[75]

SUMMARY

How Is the Juvenile Justice System Different from the Adult System?

The juvenile system has a different history, mission, and emphasis than the adult system; it focuses on helping the juvenile to reform. The juvenile system, unlike the adult system, also targets juveniles who have committed only misconduct, not crimes (status offenses) and even children who have done nothing wrong but are neglected or not given proper supervision. There is a completely different terminology used in the juvenile system and the legal process is more informal.

What Have Been the Trends in Juvenile Crime?

Juvenile crime peaked in the mid-1990s and has declined dramatically since then. Black juveniles, especially males, showed a much more pronounced increase and decrease, especially for violent crime.

What Is the Profile of the Juvenile Offender?

As with the adult system, minorities are over-represented and become increasingly more so at each stage of the system. Girls comprise a larger percentage of the juvenile system than they do in the adult system.

What Rights Do Juvenile Offenders Have?

Due process rights include a hearing before waiver to adult court, many of the due process elements found in adult courts (such as the right to a hearing, presentation of evidence, counsel), and the right to be found guilty only after the prosecution has proven the charges "beyond a reasonable doubt." Juveniles do not have the right to a jury trial. Juveniles also have the right not to be subjected to capital punishment or life without parole.

Can Juveniles End Up in Adult Courts? How?

Yes. "Waiver" to adult court is made when juveniles are presumed to be mature enough to know right from wrong. Waiver can be discretionary but, increasingly, it can be from a statutory exclusion (states decide some crimes at some age levels will automatically go to adult court), or from direct filing (where the prosecutor has the discretion to file in adult court) without a waiver hearing.

What Are People Referring to by the Terms "Zero Tolerance" and "School-To-Prison Pipeline"?

Zero tolerance refers to the increasing use of suspension and formal juvenile justice responses to misbehavior in schools (such as fighting) that used to be dealt with informally by school officials. The "school-to-prison pipeline" refers to the research that shows students who are subjected to suspension and/or formal processing are much more likely to end up in the criminal justice system later.

How Many Juveniles Are on Probation?

Of all delinquency cases, about 383,600 juveniles ended up on probation (either formally or informally). Of those formally adjudicated, about 64 percent were given probation (about 205,000).

How Many Youths Are Sent to Secure Detention Facilities?

About 54,000 juveniles are in secure detention facilities. Of those 14 percent are female and 68 percent are minority. The numbers in secure detention have been declining from their high in 1997.

Are Juveniles as Recidivistic as Adults?

Juveniles are more recidivistic than adults; over half recidivate. Youth who are incarcerated in adult prisons are more likely to recidivate.

Critical Thinking Exercises

1. Determine what your state's juvenile justice system looks like—what is the waiver policy? What percentage of adjudicated youth end up in secure facilities? Evaluate any advocacy groups' claims in your state as to the need for change.
2. Read the sequence of Supreme Court cases on capital punishment for juveniles. Construct the legal argument as to why they should not be criminally culpable using the definition of cruel and unusual and the evidence presented in the court holdings. Are you persuaded? Why or why not?

NOTES

1 A. Platt, *The Child Savers: The Invention of Delinquency*. Chicago: University of Chicago Press, 1977.

2 A. Platt, note 1.

3 H. Snyder and M. Sickmund, *Juvenile Offenders and Victims: 2006 National Report*. Washington, DC: Office of Juvenile Justice and Delinquency Prevention, 2006.

4 R. del Carmen and C. Trulson, *Juvenile Justice: The System, Process, and Law*. Belmont, CA: Thomson-Wadsworth, 2006, p. 21.

5 R. del Carmen and C. Trulson, note 4; C. Bartollas and S. Miller, *Juvenile Justice in America*, 4th edn. Upper Saddle River, NJ: Pearson/Prentice Hall, 2005.

6 Office of Juvenile Justice and Delinquency Prevention, Juvenile Drug Court Programs, Washington, DC: Office of Juvenile Justice and Delinquency Prevention, 2001. Retrieved from http://www.ncjrs.org/pdfiles1/ojjdp/184744.pdf

7 R. del Carmen and C. Trulson, note 4; C. Bartollas and S.J. Miller, note 5.

8 National Academies of Science, *Reforming Juvenile Justice: A Developmental Approach. Report Brief.* Washington, DC: National Academies of Justice, 2012.

9 D.C. Pyrooz, R.K. Moule and S.H. Decker, "The contribution of gang membership to the victim-offender overlap." *Journal of Research in Crime and Delinquency* 51 (2013): 315. DOI: 10.1177/0022427813516128.

10 J. Whitehead and S. Lab, *Juvenile Justice: An Introduction.* New Providence, NJ: LexisNexis/Matthew Bender, 2009; A. Egley, J. Howell and J. Moore, *Highlights of the 2008 National Youth Gang Survey.* Washington, DC: Office of Juvenile Justice and Delinquency Prevention, U.S. Department of Justice, 2010; E. Harrell, *Violence by Gang Members, 1993–2003.* Washington, DC: Bureau of Justice Statistics, 2005; A. Liberman, *The Long View of Crime: A Synthesis of Longitudinal Research.* Washington, DC: Springer, 2008.

11 D. Pyrooz and G. Sweeten, "Gang membership between ages 5 and 17 years in the United States." *Journal of Adolescent Health* (2015); DOI: 10.1016/j.jadohealth.2014.11.018.

12 K. Samuelson, "Among delinquent teens, whites more likely than blacks to abuse hard drugs." Northwestern University News Center, March 17, 2016. Retrieved 6/8/2016 from http://www.northwestern.edu/newscenter/stories/2016/03/race-delinquent-youth-substance-use-disorder.html

13 S. Hockenberry and C. Puzzanchera, *Juvenile Court Statistics 2013.* Pittsburg, PA: National Center for Juvenile Justice, July 2015, p. 16.

14 S. Hockenberry and C. Puzzanchera, note 13, p. 13.

15 S. Hockenberry and C. Puzzanchera, note 13, p. 36.

16 S. Hockenberry and C. Puzzanchera, note 13, p. 37.

17 B. Feld, "The politics of race and juvenile justice: The 'due process revolution' and the conservative reaction." *Justice Quarterly* 20 (4) (2003): 7.

18 M. Leiber and K. Fox, "Race and the impact of detention on juvenile justice decision making." *Crime and Delinquency* 51 (4) (2005): 470–497.

19 S. Hockenberry and C. Puzzanchera, note 13, p. 14.

20 M. Zahn, *Girls Study Group: Understanding and Responding to Girls' Delinquency.* Washington, DC: Office of Juvenile Justice and Delinquency Prevention, Department of Justice, 2010.

21 D. Steffensmeier, J. Schwartz, H. Zhong and J. Ackerman, "An assessment of recent trends of girls' violence using diverse longitudinal sources: Is the gender gap closing?" *Criminology* 43 (2005): 355–405.

22 Steffensmeier et al., 2005, note 21, p. 366; also see T. Stevens, M. Morash and M. Chesney-Lind, "Are girls getting tougher, or are we tougher on girls? Probability of arrest and juvenile court oversight in 1980 and 2000." *Justice Quarterly* 28 (2010): 710–744.

23 M. Ducrose, C. Harlow, P. Langan, M. Motivans, R. Rantala and E. Smith, *Family Violence Statistics: Including Statistics on Strangers and Acquaintances.* Washington, DC: Bureau of Justice Statistics, U.S. Department of Justice, 2005.

24 E. Buzawa and G. Hotaling, "The impact of relationship status, gender, and minor status in the police response to domestic assaults." *Victims and Offenders* 1 (2006): 373–393.

25 T. Vaughan, J. Pollock and D. Vandiver, "Sex differences in arrest for juvenile assaults." *Violence and Gender,* March 2 (2015): 24–34.

26 *Roper v. Simmons,* 543 U.S. 551, 2005.

27 *Graham v. Florida,* 560 U.S. 48, 2010.

28 *Miller v. Alabama,* 132 S. Ct. 2455, 2012.

29 *Montgomery v. Louisiana,* 136 S. Ct. 718, 2016.

30 J. Petersilia, *Reforming Probation and Parole.* Lanham, MD: American Correctional Association, 2002, p. 47.

31 C. Puzzanchera, *Delinquency Cases Waived to Criminal Court, 1989–1998*. Washington, DC: Office of Juvenile Justice and Delinquency Prevention, 2003. Available at www.ncjrs.gov/pdf-files1/ojjdp/fs200135.pdf; D. Bishop, "Race, delinquency, and discrimination: Minorities in the juvenile justice system." In P. Benekos and A. Merlo (Eds.), *Controversies in Juvenile Justice and Delinquency*, 2nd edn. New Providence, NJ: LexisNexis/Matthew Bender, 2009, pp. 223–253.

32 B. Adams and S. Addie, *Delinquency Cases Waived to Criminal Court, 2009*. Washington, DC: Office of Juvenile Justice and Delinquency Prevention, Office of Justice Programs, 2010; S. Hockenberry and C. Puzzanchera, note 13.

33 G. Rainville and S. Smith, *Juvenile Felony Defendants in Criminal Courts: Survey of 40 Counties, 1998*. Washington, DC: Bureau of Justice Statistics, 2003.

34 S. Brown, *Trends in Juvenile Justice State Legislation: 2001–2011*. Denver, CO: National Conference of State Legislatures, 2012, pp. 4–5.

35 R. Redding, *Juvenile Transfer Laws: An Effective Deterrent to Delinquency?* Washington, DC: Office of Juvenile Justice and Delinquency Prevention, 2010.

36 B. Feld, "The politics of race and juvenile justice: The 'due process revolution' and the conservative reaction." *Justice Quarterly* 20 (4) (2003): 765–800.

37 K. Zernike, "Crackdown on threats in schools fails a test." *New York Times*, May 17, 2001. Retrieved 5/17/2001 from www.nytimes.com/2001/05/17/nyregion/17THRE.html

38 "One strike and they're out." *New York Times*, September 19, 2010. Retrieved 10/8/2010 from http://www.nytimes.com/2010/09/19/opinion/19sun3.html

39 A. Payne, "Crime and education: Moving school discipline from exclusion and criminal justice to restoration and social justice." *Criminologist* 35 (5) (2010): 1–5.

40 M. Thereiot, "School resource officers and the criminalization of student behavior." *Journal of Criminal Justice* 37 (2009): 280–287.

41 E. Eckholm, "With police in schools, more children in court." *New York Times*, April 12, 2013; J. McKenna and J. Pollock, "Law enforcement officers in schools: an analysis of ethical issues." *Criminal Justice Ethics*, 2014, http://dx.doi.org/10.1080/0731129X.2014.982974. J. McKenna, Examining the Use of Full-Time Police in Schools: How Roles and Training May Impact Responses to Misconduct. Doctoral Dissertation, Texas State University, 2016.

42 E. Eckholm, "Ruling limits state's power in school suspensions." *New York Times*, October 9, 2010. Retrieved 10/9/2010 from http://www.nytimes.com/2010/10/09/us/09suspend.html

43 D. Nagin, A. Piquero, E. Scott and L. Steinberg, "Public preferences for rehabilitation versus incarceration of juvenile offenders: Evidence from a contingent valuation survey." *Criminology and Public Policy* 5(4) (2006): 627–652.

44 S. Hockenberry and C. Puzzanchera, note 13, p. 45.

45 H. Snyder and M. Sickmund, *Juvenile Offenders and Victims: 2006 National Report*. Washington, DC: Office of Juvenile Justice and Delinquency Prevention, 2006, p. 172; C. Knoll and M. Sickmund, *Delinquency Cases in Juvenile Court, 2007*. Washington, DC: Office of Juvenile Justice and Delinquency Prevention, Department of Justice, 2010, p. 3.

46 H. Snyder and M. Sickmund, *Juvenile Offenders and Victims: 2006 National Report*. Washington, DC: Office of Juvenile Justice and Delinquency Prevention, 2006.

47 R. Sharp, "The early offender project: A community-based program for high risk youth." *Juvenile Family Court Journal* 39 (1) (1988): 13–20.

48 W. Barton and J. Butts, "Viable options: Intensive supervision programs for juvenile delinquents." *Crime and Delinquency* 36 (2) (1990): 238–256.

49 S. Zhang and L. Zhang, "An experimental study of the Los Angeles county repeat offender prevention program: Its implementation and evaluation." *Criminology and Public Policy* 4 (2) (2005): 205–236.

50 D. Mackenzie, "The importance of using scientific evidence to make decisions about correctional programming." *Criminology and Public Policy* 4 (2) (2005): 249–258.

51 S. Hockenberry, *Juveniles in Residential Placement, 2013*. Washington, DC: Office of Juvenile Justice and Delinquency Prevention, May 2016.

52 S. Hockenberry and C. Puzzanchera, note 13, p. 45.

53 Bureau of Justice Statistics, *Prison and Jail Inmates at Mid-Year, 2005*. Washington, DC: Bureau of Justice Statistics, 2006; H. West and W. Sabol, *Prison Inmates at Mid-Year 2008*. Washington, DC: Bureau of Justice Statistics, 2009; T. Minton and W. Sabol, *Jail Inmates at Mid-Year 2008*. Washington, DC: Bureau of Justice Statistics, 2009; T. Minton and Z Zeng, *Jail Inmates at Mid-Year, 2014*. Washington, DC: Bureau of Justice Statistics, 2015; *OJJDP Statistical Briefing Book*. Available: http://www.ojjdp.gov/ojstatbb/corrections/qa08701.asp?qaDate=2014. Released on December 13, 2015.

54 L. Arthur, "Ten ways to reduce detention populations." *Juvenile Family Court Journal* 52 (1) (2001): 29–36.

55 S. McGonigle and D. Swanson, "Feds knew about TYC abuse cases." *Dallas News*, August 5, 2007. Retrieved 8/8/2007 from http://www.dallasnews.com/sharedcontent/dws/news/texassouth-west/stories/080507dnmettycabuse.389a816.html; see also N. Blakeslee, "Hidden in plain sight: How did alleged abuse at a youth facility in West Texas evade detection for so long?" *Texas Observer*, August 8, 2007. Retrieved 8/8/2007 from http://www.texasobserver.org/article.php?aid=2428

56 H. Grezlak and L. Strupczewski, "Pa. judicial corruption probe said to be eyeing criminal cases." Law.com, June 1, 2009. Retrieved on 4/6/2010 from http://www.law.com/jsp/law/LawArticleFriendly.jsp?id=1202431103066, 2009; T. Wilson, "Ex-judge pleads guilty in Luzerne "kids-for-cash" scandal." *Philadelphia Inquirer*, April 30, 2010. Retrieved 10/13/2010 from http://www.philly.com/inquirer/local/pa/20100430_Ex-judge_pleads_guilty_in_Luzerne_kids-for-cash_html, 2010.

57 J. Austin, K. Johnson and R. Weitzer, *Alternatives to the Secure Detention and Confinement of Juvenile Offenders*. Washington, DC: Office of Juvenile Justice and Delinquency Prevention, 2005; W. Barton, "Incorporating the strengths perspective into intensive juvenile aftercare." *Western Criminology Review* 7 (2) (2006): 48–53; H. Snyder and M. Sickmund, *Juvenile Offenders and Victims: 1999 National Report*. Washington, DC: Office of Juvenile Justice and Delinquency Prevention, 1999, p. 98.

58 M. Lipsey, "Juvenile delinquency treatment: A meta-analytic inquiry into the variability of effects." In T. Cook, D. Cordray, H. Hartman, L. Hedges, R. Light, T. Louis and F. Mosteller (Eds.), *Meta-Analysis for Explanation: A Casebook*. New York, NY: Russell Sage Foundation, 1992, pp. 83–127.

59 J. Austin, K. Johnson and R. Weitzer, note 57; H. Snyder and M. Sickmund, *Juvenile Offenders and Victims: 1999 National Report*. Washington, DC: Office of Juvenile Justice and Delinquency Prevention, 1999.

60 K. Samuelson, "Among delinquent teens, whites more likely than blacks to abuse hard drugs." Northwestern University News Center, March 17, 2016. Retrieved 6/8/2016 from http://www.northwestern.edu/newscenter/stories/2016/03/race-delinquent-youth-substance-use-disorder.html

61 S. Hockenberry, note 51.

62 S. Hockenberry, note 51.

63 S. Hockenberry, note 51.

64 M. Chesney-Lind, "Judicial paternalism and the female status offender." *Crime and Delinquency* 23 (1977): 121–130; M. Chesney-Lind, *The Female Offender: Girls, Women, and Crime*. Thousand Oaks, CA: Sage, 2006.

65 S. Brown, *Trends in Juvenile Justice State Legislation: 2001–2011*. Denver, CO: National Conference of State Legislatures, 2012, p. 12.

66 F. Sherman and A. Balck, *Gender Injustice: System-level Juvenile Justice Reforms for Girls*. Crittenton Foundation, National Women's Law Center. Available at: http://www.nationalcrittenton.org/wp-content/uploads/2015/09/Gender_Injustice_Report.pdf

67 J. Pollock, *Women's Crimes, Criminology, and Corrections*. Prospect Heights, IL: Waveland, 2014; B. Dohrn, "All ellas: Girls locked up." *Feminist Studies* 30 (2) (2004): 307.

68 B. Dohrn, note 67.

69 S. Brown, *Trends in Juvenile Justice State Legislation: 2001–2011*. Denver, CO: National Conference of State Legislatures, 2012, p. 12.

70 W. Barton, "Incorporating the strengths perspective into intensive juvenile aftercare." *Western Criminology Review* 7 (2) (2006): 48–53.

71 J. Cocozza and J. Shufelt, *Juvenile Mental Health Courts: An Emerging Strategy*, National Center for Mental Health and Juvenile Justice. Delmar, NY: Policy Research Institute, 2006. Retrieved 11/25/2006 from http://www.ncmhjj.com/pdfs/publications/JuvenileMentalHealthCourts.pdf?tr=y&auid=1879566

72 W. Barton, "Incorporating the strengths perspective into intensive juvenile aftercare." *Western Criminology Review* 7 (2) (2006): 48–53.

73 D. Josi and D. Seachrest, "A pragmatic approach to parole aftercare: Evaluation of a community reintegration program for high-risk youthful offenders." *Justice Quarterly* 16 (1999): 51–80. See also L. Goodstein and H. Sontheimer, "The implementation of an intensive aftercare program for serious juvenile offenders." *Criminal Justice Behavior* 24 (1997): 332–359.

74 A. Leschied, A. Cummings and L. Baker, "Models of supervision relevant to the delivery of effective correctional service." In American Correctional Association, *What Works and Why: Effective Approaches to Reentry*. Lanham, MD: American Correctional Association, 2005, pp. 35–60.

75 B. Welsh and D. Farrington, "Save children from a life of crime." *Criminology and Public Policy* 6 (4) (2007): 871–880.

Section 5

CONCLUDING OUR CRITICAL THINKING APPROACH TO CRIMINAL JUSTICE

A CRITICAL THINKING APPROACH TO CRIMINAL JUSTICE

Throughout this book, we have modeled a critical thinking approach to the issues relevant to the various components of the criminal justice system. In this last chapter we will reiterate the approach and take a last look at a few current issues. We also will discuss the steps taken in preventing terrorist actions in this country, and discuss how that challenge overlaps with domestic criminal justice issues.

Recall that critical thinking has many definitions and no set formula, but, in general, it is an approach to problem solving that utilizes the following steps:

(a) Identify and clearly formulate relevant questions or issues.

(b) Gather and assess relevant information, noting the source of the information to identify any bias or vested interest.

(c) Utilize data to develop well-reasoned conclusions and solutions and test them.

Chapter Preview

- What Are the Major Issues in Studying Crime Today?
- What Are the Major Issues in Policing Today?
- What Are the Major Issues in Courts Today?
- What Are the Major Issues in Corrections Today?
- What Is the Role of Criminal Justice Actors in the War on Terror?
- Focus on Data: Last Thoughts
- Critical Thinking Exercises

(d) At all times be aware of assumptions that may bias your perception of data and lead to selective perception, tunnel vision, or cognitive distortion.

(e) Be aware of the implications and practical consequences of findings.[1]

WHAT ARE THE MAJOR ISSUES IN STUDYING CRIME TODAY?

In earlier chapters, we have noted that all three measures of crime, the Uniform Crime Reports, arrest statistics, and victim self-reports in the National Crime Victimization Survey have tracked an historic decline of crime over the last two decades. The triangulation of data makes it more likely that this decline is real. Recently, there has been an increase in homicides in some large cities. Researchers are currently trying to determine whether this trend will continue, and many complain that there are no good sources for current data. It takes six months to a year before the Uniform Crime Reports and arrest statistics are available and the NCVS findings take even longer. There is currently a partnership between the Bureau of Justice Statistics and the FBI to make these data available sooner, but until we have more current data, analysis is difficult. Cities vary, but some have extremely sophisticated data collection and analysis, and these cities have much more current data than we have available nationally. It is important, however, not to equate crime patterns of a few major cities to crime as a whole across the country since suburban and rural crime patterns are very different from the crime patterns of major cities. It is also important to wait to see if this signals a trend or is an aberration since despite the general downward trend of crime rates over the last two decades, there have been some yearly increases in some locations.

One issue with the UCR is that it does not give us much information about the crimes that many people are concerned with today—specifically, identity theft (including credit card theft), cybercrime, and other forms of white-collar crime. These crimes are not part of the **index crimes**, and they are submerged in arrest statistics under general crime categories such as forgery, fraud, embezzlement, or larceny-theft. The National Incident Based Reporting System (NIBRS) provides more information about such crimes because fraud is broken down into identity/credit card/ATM fraud, among other types of frauds, but still many forms of white-collar crime are reported as "all other offenses." NIBRS also includes a data entry for whether the offender used a computer in the crime; therefore, computer crime statistics will be more accessible as law enforcement agencies begin to report under NIBRS. The Bureau of Justice Statistics has begun to publish a report on identity theft that provides more information than we have had in the past.

For the 2014 BJS report on identity theft, go to http://www.bjs.gov/index.cfm?ty=pbdetail&iid=5408

Identity theft is obtaining and using, or attempting to use, another person's identity (name, Social Security number, address) without the owner's permission and/or the unauthorized use of a credit card or a bank account.

Exhibit 14.1   Identity theft affects millions of Americans every year. The NYPD Identity Theft Task Force collected this evidence, including fraudulent credit cards and drivers' licenses, during an investigation.

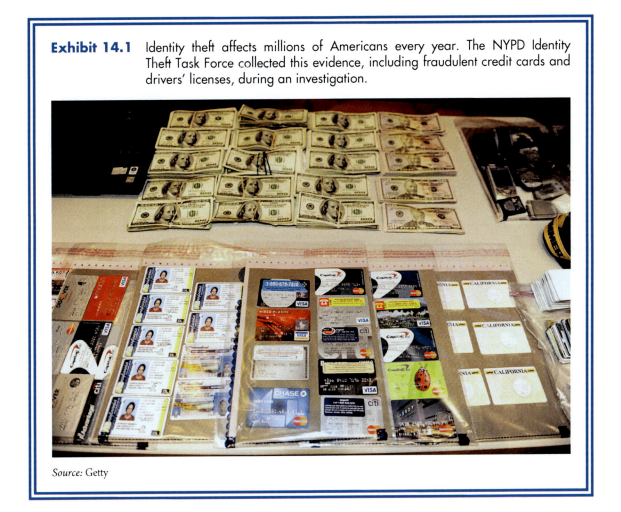

Source: Getty

Identity theft is both a state and a federal crime. In addition, crimes utilizing identity theft may violate federal wire-fraud and credit card fraud laws. The Bureau of Justice Statistics reports an estimated 17.6 million persons, or about 7 percent of U.S. residents age sixteen or older, were victims of at least one incident of identity theft in 2014. In 2014, the most common type of identity theft was the unauthorized misuse or attempted misuse of an existing account— experienced by 16.4 million persons. About 8.6 million victims experienced the fraudulent use of a credit card, 8.1 million experienced the unauthorized or attempted use of existing bank accounts (checking, savings, or other) and

1.5 million victims experienced other types of existing account theft, such as misuse or attempted misuse of an existing telephone, online or insurance account; some victims reported multiple types of victimization.[2]

The majority of identity theft victims did not know how the offender obtained their information, and nine in ten identity theft victims did not know anything about the offender. Two-thirds of identity theft victims reported a direct financial loss. The majority of identity theft victims (52 percent) were able to resolve any problems associated with the incident in a day or less, while about 9 percent spent more than a month. It is important to note that fewer than one in ten identity theft victims reported the incident to police. The majority (87 percent) of identity theft victims contacted a credit card company or bank to report misuse or attempted misuse of an account or personal information, while 8 percent contacted a credit bureau. More females (9.2 million) were victims of identity theft than males (8.3 million) in 2014. People in households with an annual income of $75,000 or more had the highest prevalence of identity theft (11 percent), compared to those in all other income brackets.[3]

In 2007, about 8 million households had at least one member report being a victim of this type of crime and, in 2014, 17.6 million reported being victimized. Thus, if the counting is comparable between 2007 and 2014, there was an over 100 percent increase in the prevalence of identity theft (note that these are just raw counts, not rates so we do not know how many more people there were in the population, how many more people had credit cards, or whether there were different counting methods of identity theft).

In Exhibit 14.2 we see the 17.6 million people who reported identity theft in 2014 can be compared to the 2.9 million who experienced burglary and the 664,210 who reported robbery in 2014.[4] Identity theft has more than doubled since 2004. In 2014, 7 percent of American households experienced some form of identity theft compared to 4 percent in 2004.[5]

Clearly, modern criminals are much less likely to use a gun or burglary tools today when they can use a computer or stolen credit card. Cases of identity theft have increased dramatically with the increasing use of computers. "**Phishing**" refers to false emails that appear to be from banks or other accounts that request the user to enter passwords and other private information. Generally, once an identity has been obtained, the offender can access and steal from bank accounts, use credit card numbers to make purchases, and/or set up credit in the victim's name and incur huge amounts of debt. Identity theft is difficult to investigate and many cases go unreported. Merchants and banks continue to improve their security devices to guard against identity theft and computer crimes, including enhanced encryption and authentication techniques, but there is no doubt that it is one of the most pervasive crime problems in America today and should be considered when discussing the crime decline.

Exhibit 14.2   Crime Comparison

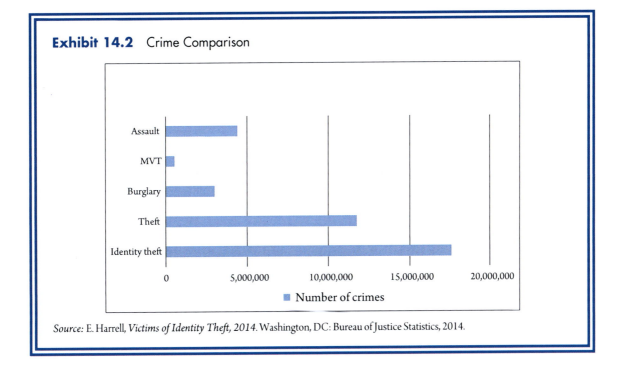

Source: E. Harrell, *Victims of Identity Theft, 2014.* Washington, DC: Bureau of Justice Statistics, 2014.

It is a paradox that the American public is so unaware of the historic low crime rates, especially of violent crime. The perception that crime is increasing, and especially violent crime, is no doubt due to pervasive media coverage. Whether homicide and other violent crime will continue to increase in major cities is a question that can be answered by accessing the available data sources. A critical thinking approach to understanding crime patterns includes using multiple data sources, e.g., FBI's Uniform Crime Reports and arrest statistics, along with NCVS data from the Bureau of Justice Statistics. Crime trends can be better understood when looking at longer periods of comparison. It is unlikely that crime rates can fall much farther since they are at historic lows. It will become important to note the factors associated with increased crime rates.

WHAT ARE THE MAJOR ISSUES IN POLICING TODAY?

We are in a new era where crime occurs on a worldwide platform, which means law enforcement agencies in this country must deal with narcoterrorism, drug cartels, cybercrimes, worldwide money laundering and other financial crimes, corporate criminality on a worldwide scale, and human trafficking. A recent scandal involving a Panamanian bank uncovered income tax evasion by American citizens. Often, identity theft rings steal information in the United States to be used by criminals in Africa or Eastern Europe. Other crimes include arms smuggling, counterfeiting, cyberhacking, and corporate espionage. The Russian mafia, Japanese yakuza, as well as the drug cartels, have joined older organized crime organizations in this country, and American law enforcement agencies, especially those in large cities, must respond. Each of these areas requires cooperation and involvement with Interpol and foreign law enforcement agencies. It is also important for the law enforcement and investigative agencies in the United States to work together. It is indeed a small world and the problems of Mexico or Somalia quickly become our problems as well.

One example of the international nature of crime today is human trafficking.

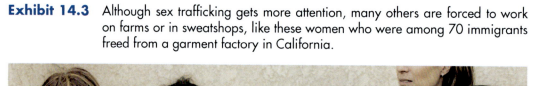

Exhibit 14.3   Although sex trafficking gets more attention, many others are forced to work on farms or in sweatshops, like these women who were among 70 immigrants freed from a garment factory in California.

Source: AP

It is estimated that 600,000 to 2 million people are trafficked internationally each year. In many cases, there is a "willing" person who agreed to illegally enter this country for some type of work, but once they arrive they are held in jail-like conditions and work (typically in agriculture or food service) in various forms of debt bondage. In other trafficking cases, women are brought into the country to work as virtual sex slaves in brothels. Estimates are that 50 percent of trafficked persons are minors. While the victims of domestic, restaurant, and farm labor trafficking probably exceed the numbers of those trafficked in the sex industry, the most attention has been focused on sex trafficking. The Department of State indicates that approximately 14,500 to 17,500 victims are trafficked into the United States every year, although other sources estimate that 50,000 victims are trafficked into the country each year. The majority of victims seem to come from Southeast Asia, Central America, and Eastern Europe. If these women and girls are returned to their own countries, they are subject to shame and ridicule for returning home after their parents have obtained money for their services, and/or when they have been given away as a wife in return for a bride price. They face extreme challenges and hurdles in adjusting and adapting to the demands they face, even if they are rescued from a trafficking situation. The victims have no identity papers, do not speak English, and are constantly threatened with beatings, rapes, and exposure to immigration authorities who, traffickers warn, will put them in prison. Law enforcement officers sometimes have difficulty identifying victims of trafficking and treat them as criminals or immigration violators, especially because the victims are afraid to give evidence against the trafficker. If they are deported, they may fall back into the hands of the traffickers. Local law enforcement agencies may not have officers with the language skills necessary to communicate, much less gain the trust of these victims. Any investigations require the involvement of multiple state and federal agencies.

In 2000, Congress passed the Victims of Trafficking and Violence Protection Act of 2000 (VTVPA), which created or revised federal crimes targeting traffickers, including "human trafficking," "sex trafficking of children," "document servitude," and "forced labor." The Act also increased the penalties associated with these crimes. This legislation was amended four times in 2003, 2005, 2008, and 2013; it continues to be amended and ratified at different levels of government to best combat trafficking and provide services for victims. The VTVPA created agencies designed to combat trafficking both internationally, by identifying problematic countries, and domestically, by supporting task forces between federal and state agencies so that investigation and prosecution can occur more smoothly. The T-visa was created, along with other avenues, to keep the victim in this country in order to assist law enforcement and prosecution and, in some cases, the victim is granted a permanent visa in return.

Trafficking is not easy to investigate or prosecute, however, and there are relatively few successful cases when compared to the scope of the problem.[6]

This is a troubling time for law enforcement. They are facing scrutiny and, in recent years, fatal attacks, spurred perhaps by the widespread perception that there have been abuses of the great power that we entrust to them. In the summer of 2016, after the killings of law enforcement officers in Dallas and Baton Rouge, many leaders spoke about the idea that when there is an attack on police, there is an attack on society itelf because they represent law and order. Critics and supporters of law enforcement have often succumbed to generalizations and bias when discussing the issues. Calm and reasoned thinking is vitally necessary to address the problems of police–community relations.

The President's Task Force on 21st Century Policing utilized a critical thinking approach in that experts (academics, community organizers, and police practitioners) came together and listened to hundreds of people from all sides in many locations across the country. They then outlined some priorities and objectives that emerged from this information. The next step in a critical thinking approach would be to implement some of the changes recommended and carefully track the results to determine effectiveness in crime prevention, community relations, and/or police officer satisfaction and health. This is currently being done.

To read about the Task Force report, go to http://www.cops.usdoj.gov/policingtaskforce

WHAT ARE THE MAJOR ISSUES IN COURTS TODAY?

The Innocence Project refers to groups of attorneys and other volunteers in many states who take cases of inmates claiming innocence. It seems that every day in the news is a new case of someone being released after spending years in prison for a crime they did not commit.

Some estimates indicate that between 1 percent and 3 percent of those in prison are actually innocent or innocent of the specific charges they were convicted of; more may be factually guilty but due process was violated in the steps leading up to their conviction. To date, the Innocence Project lawyers have been instrumental in exonerating 342 inmates, usually through the use of DNA testing, and 147 true perpetrators have been identified. Some of these individuals had been incarcerated for decades, and some were days away from being executed before found to be innocent.

To read more about the Innocence Project, go to http://www.innocenceproject.org/?gclid=CK_-vdyKy6QCFQ5O2godgy9KEg

The reasons for false convictions and imprisonment are usually a combination of eyewitness error, prosecutorial misconduct, defense attorney ineffectiveness, and false confessions (sometimes through coercion). Efforts are underway by researchers to determine the weak points in the system in order to prevent wrongful convictions in the future. What these cases do show is that even with the protections mandated by our Bill of Rights and state constitutions, individuals

EXHIBIT 14.4 The Innocence Project works to free wrongly convicted people, like John Nolley, who served nineteen years before he was released.

Source: Getty

may be falsely accused and punished when individuals subvert or ignore their duties to uphold due process. More importantly, if there are systemic problems that cause such miscarriages of justice, they need to be identified and improved.

There has been increasing concern about the lack of adequate defense for indigents. This issue is related to wrongful convictions and, perhaps, to the numbers of people in prison since someone without adequate legal assistance is more likely to be incarcerated. Another related topic is the issue of the "poverty penalty"; the fact that poor defendants get caught up in the system while those with financial means can "purchase" freedom by paying off fines, fees, and court costs. There are currently attempts underway to determine if pre-trial release programs can identify those who can be released before trial without bail, but also with no risk to public safety. The prediction instruments that have been developed continue to be refined but there has to be the public will to implement them.

To read about sentinel event research in this area, go to http://www.nij.gov/topics/justice-system/Pages/sentinel-events.aspx

To read the report of a group tracking progress in providing pre-trial justice, go to http://www.pretrial.org/download/infostop/Implementing%20the%20Recommendations%20of%20the%20National%20Symposium%20on%20Pretrial%20Justice-%20The%202013%20Progress%20Report.pdf

WHAT ARE THE MAJOR ISSUES IN CORRECTIONS TODAY?

As reported in earlier chapters of this book, crime is at a thirty-year low in some categories, yet the expenditures related to criminal justice keep increasing. The current rate of increase cannot be sustained, especially as some states face billion-dollar deficits and all states are struggling with reduced budgets. The question is how to utilize correctional dollars in the most efficient way without undue risk to the public.

One of the clear issues of the day is what to do about the 700,000 individuals released from prison each year, many of whom have been in prison since the early and mid-1980s. These individuals have served long periods of time, decades even, without any meaningful programs to help them conquer addictions and adapt to their freedom on the street. Although the historic unemployment high of almost 10 percent has dropped by half it is still very difficult for ex-offenders to get jobs.

Those on probation and released from prison often go back to criminogenic communities that have pervasive social problems. These "million-dollar blocks" refer to areas of the city where more than a million dollars is spent incarcerating, returning, and revoking offenders. Typically, the communities that offenders come from and go home to are characterized by longstanding poverty from lack of jobs and business development. Schools underperform and drop-out rates are high. The residents are heavy users of government services. There is a substantial overlap between neighborhoods that are recipients of TANF (Temporary Assistance to Needy Families) and those who receive a disproportionate share of offenders (released on parole or probation).[7]

Research is beginning to show that the huge increase in incarceration that occurred since the 1980s has not necessarily been helpful to the communities hardest hit by crime. Research has found a "**tipping effect**" occurs at high rates of imprisonment where imprisonment seemed to result in more crime in certain communities.[8] Positive effects of incarceration included removal of problem family members and reducing the number of dangerous individuals in the community, but negative effects for communities included the stigma attached to returning offenders for the offender and his or her family, the financial impact of imprisonment for both the offender and his or her family, and the difficulty of maintaining interpersonal relationships through a prison sentence. High levels of incarceration reduce the number of potentially positive role models for children, result in transient populations, and affect the ability of the community to control its members through informal and affective ties.[9] Incarceration can reduce crime by the removal of criminal offenders; on the other hand, if a community experiences high levels of incarceration, it increases social mobility and social disorganization, and weakens the ability of the community to utilize parochial methods of control.[10]

Re-entry efforts have included job training/placement, drug treatment, and housing assistance, as these are identified as the major problems of those released from prison. The Second Chance Act and other state and local programs that assist ex-offenders in obtaining employment should continue to be evaluated for effectiveness. Further, programs that receive Justice Reinvestment monies should be rigorously evaluated to determine if they are meeting their mandate. This requires objective evaluators who have no stake in the outcome or can put aside their biases in implementing and conducting evaluations. Skeptical outside reviews should be welcome since they serve as a check to bias. Although it is frustrating to have contradictory evaluations, having multiple researchers or methodologies carefully evaluating how taxpayers' money is spent is an important element to a critical thinking approach to crime prevention.

Currently, there are massive changes underway in some states' sentencing structures, such as Realignment in California, that shift the correctional population to the community. Proponents of decarceration applaud such efforts while others warn that any reduction in the use of incarceration will lead to more crime. It is important, first, to note the positions of interest groups. For instance, the correctional officer union in California opposed legislative changes to the three-strikes bill that reduced the number of inmates serving long sentences and, indeed, correctional officer unions tend to oppose any legislation that would reduce prison populations. This position may be arrived at through a careful and reasoned review of the evidence or it could be colored by self-interest. Indeed, news items occur periodically describing prison workers' opposition to closing prisons. On the other side, research by advocacy groups who have a mission to reduce the number of incarcerated should also be evaluated for objectivity. These non-profits have been successful at raising awareness of the problem of mass imprisonment, and their work has made data much more accessible, but a critical thinking approach requires us to not reject information outright, but also, not to accept it without scrutiny. Rather, we want to consider the data, note any potential bias, and, if possible, check multiple sources to be more sure of the facts.

To peruse the websites of some of these groups, go to http://www.sentencing project.org/; http://famm.org/; http://www.justicepolicy.org/index.html

WHAT IS THE ROLE OF CRIMINAL JUSTICE ACTORS IN THE WAR ON TERROR?

We have, throughout this book, concentrated primarily on domestic crime and state and local responses to it. However, since 9/11, the response to terrorism has been a shared effort among all levels of law enforcement. Just as the first responders to the World Trade Towers tragedy were New York City police officers and firefighters, in any terrorist plot police play an integral role in both response and prevention.

More recently, international terrorist attacks in Brussels (March 2016), Paris (November 2015), and Nice (July 2016), and domestic attacks in San Bernadino (December 2015) and Orlando (June 2016) illustrate that local police are responsible for responding to and preventing these tragic events. In September 2016, Ahmad Khan Rahami was captured only two days after he allegedly was responsible for planting several bombs in various locations in New York City. Although at this point he is presumed innocent until proven guilty, it is a testament to the efficiency of law enforcement agencies that he was identified as the prime suspect and apprehended so quickly.

EXHIBIT 14.5   Local police are increasingly responsible for responding to terrorist attacks, like the one at Pulse nightclub in Orlando in 2016 that left 49 people dead.

Source: Getty

What limits should be placed on their surveillance powers? Should the 1033 program where military surplus can be given to local law enforcement, including armored vehicles and grenade launchers, be continued? What is the appropriate and legal use of robots (such as the one that was used to kill the shooter in the Dallas killings of five police officers)?

The governmental response to the threat of terrorism within the boundaries of the country has dramatically reshaped the organization and the mission of federal law enforcement. It has also created new questions for the courts to resolve and pitted federal courts against the executive branch in arguments regarding torture, renditions, executive privilege, wiretapping, civil liberties, and the security classification of government documents. Fear of crime has now been eclipsed by fear of terrorism, and new legal and ethical questions regarding the appropriate response to this threat have taken center stage in national debates.

Terrorism, whether domestic or with international elements, has been present from the beginning of this country's history, and so, too, have been government efforts to combat it. In earlier decades, communism was the enemy and the target of government investigation and suppression efforts. The first Alien and Sedition Acts were passed a mere twenty-two years after the birth of the United States, in 1798. The Alien Act gave the government the right to deport those thought to be a danger to the country, and the **Sedition Act** gave the government the right to punish those who spoke against the government's actions. These Acts were criticized by many prominent individuals as being contrary to the 1st Amendment and eventually disappeared; however, the Bolshevik bombings and advocacy of communism led to the Espionage Act of 1917 and the 1918 Sedition Act. The United States government, fearful that Russian immigrants would import their revolution as well, had thousands arrested. Under the Sedition Act, anyone who expressed support for communism could be arrested. Attorney General Palmer arrested 16,000 Soviet resident aliens in 1918 and 1919, and detained them without charges and without trial. The government targeted emerging labor unions, especially the Industrial Workers of the World movement, as threats to the nation, and widespread violence occurred on both sides.[11]

The next chapter in the government's campaign against communism was carried out by J. Edgar Hoover, who was appointed in 1924, and rose to prominence as director of the FBI. His continued investigation of communists eventually led to the McCarthy hearings (House Un-American Activities Committee) in the 1950s. Throughout the 1960s and 1970s, the FBI continued to infiltrate and investigate groups and individuals that were considered threats to the nation. At one point, Hoover had a card index of 450,000 people who were identified or suspected of having left-wing political views.[12]

This was during a time period when violent groups advocated and used violence, such as the Symbionese Liberation Army, which utilized kidnapping and robberies, and the Black Panthers, who used armed robbery and hijacking to advance their cause. Terrorism worldwide was on an upswing, including the horrific hostage-taking and slaying of Israeli athletes that occurred by Palestinian terrorists at the 1972 Munich Olympics, a series of IRA bombings in England, and the Baader-Meinhof (Red Army Faction) terrorist group in Germany that was responsible for a number of assassinations. However, the focus of investigations carried out by the government also included those who, objectively, did not pose a danger to the government, such as Martin Luther King Jr., Hollywood actors who espoused liberal views, and student and community groups that advocated nonviolent means of protest.

It was the abuses of the powers granted by antiterrorist legislation as well as the misuse of government intelligence by those in the Nixon administration that led to Congress dramatically curtailing the powers of federal law enforcement. The Senate created the Select Committee on Intelligence in 1976 and strengthened the Freedom of Information Act. In 1978, the Foreign Intelligence Surveillance Act (FISA) was created and it mandated procedures for requesting authorization for surveillance. A secret court was created (the Foreign Intelligence Surveillance Court—FISC), which consisted of seven federal district court judges appointed by the Supreme Court's Chief Justice. Federal law enforcement officers were required to obtain permission from the court to conduct surveillance. They had to show that their target was an agent of a foreign power and information was in furtherance of counterintelligence. FISA originally approved only electronic eavesdropping and wiretapping, but was amended in 1994 to include covert physical entries, and later in 1998 to permit "pen/trap" orders and business records.[13]

Typical search warrants are obtained only on a showing of probable cause that the target of the search will be found in the location specified, and that it is evidence or an instrumentality of a crime. However, FISA court approval may be obtained merely upon a showing that the target is a foreign power or agent and the search is relevant to a counterintelligence investigation. If the target is a U.S. citizen, there must be probable cause that their activities may involve espionage.[14]

Throughout the 1980s and 1990s, the activities and the rhetoric of the PLO, and, later, Hamas and Hezbollah, became more and more anti-American and many analysts argued that the United States, in addition to Israel, was or would become a central target of terrorist actions. The government did not sit idle, of course. President Reagan utilized national security decision directives rather than Congress to craft and employ a government response to the growing international threats. These directives established a hierarchy of authority regarding response to threats via aviation and kidnapping. Public laws were also passed, including:

- Act to Combat International Terrorism (1984), which sought international cooperation.
- Public Law 99–83 (1985), which allowed funding to be cut off to countries that supported terrorism.
- Omnibus Diplomatic Security and Antiterrorism Act (1986), which expanded the jurisdiction of the FBI to overseas when investigating acts of terrorism against U.S. citizens abroad or at home.[15]

Two of the most important pre-9/11 antiterrorist laws were passed during the Clinton administration. The Omnibus Counterterrorism Act of 1995 greatly expanded the role of the federal government over local and state law enforcement in investigating and prosecuting acts of terrorism, such as bombings, within the boundaries of the United States, and also expanded U.S. jurisdiction overseas when committed against U.S. embassies. It also criminalized fundraising for groups defined as terrorist. It expanded federal law enforcement authority to use "pen registers" and "trap-and-trace" devices, which track telephone calls. It also gave federal law enforcement the power to seek a wide range of personal and business documents with "national security letters," rather than warrants, when investigating terrorism which allowed government agents to begin surveillance while waiting for FISA approval.

This Act was replaced by the Anti-Terrorism and Effective Death Penalty Act of 1996, which incorporated most of the provisions discussed earlier, and added others, such as expanding the authority of INS to deport accused terrorists and other resident aliens, and increasing the penalties for such crimes. The other part of the Act applied to all offenders, and changed habeas corpus protections, eliminating multiple appeals and removing legal barriers to executions.[16]

Prior to 9/11, events foretold the possibility of a major attack: the 1993 bombing of the World Trade Center, the attacks on the USS *Cole* and on U.S. embassies in Africa, and the stated aim of Osama Bin Laden to "cut off the head of the snake," meaning the United States and, more specifically, U.S. economic dominance in the world. Generally, however, the FBI was largely concerned with domestic terrorism. This focus was not misplaced given the tragedy of the Oklahoma City bombing carried out by Timothy McVeigh and Terry Nichols, and the presence of other radical groups that still exist and have expressed and indicated a willingness to use violence to advance their goals. In the aftermath of the terrorist attacks on September 11, 2001, Congress enacted Public Law 107–56, which is titled Uniting and Strengthening America by Providing Appropriate Tools Required to Intercept and Obstruct Terrorism Act. This Act is known as the **USA Patriot Act** of 2001.

The Patriot Act slightly revised the definition of terrorism in the United States Code. The Act's definition included: use of weapons of mass destruction, acts of terrorism transcending national boundaries, financial transactions, providing material to terrorists, and providing material support or resources to designated foreign terrorist organizations and defined international terrorism as activities that "involve violent acts or acts dangerous to human life that are a violation of the criminal laws of the United States or of any State, or that would be a criminal violation if committed within the jurisdiction of the United States or of any State" and that appear to be intended to do one or more of the following:

(a) to intimidate or coerce a civilian population
(b) to influence the policy of a government by intimidation or coercion, or
(c) to affect the conduct of a government by assassination or kidnapping.[17]

The Patriot Act amended that definition to include assassination or kidnapping as one of the acts that constitutes terrorism. In addition, "domestic terrorism" was included.

The Patriot Act also expanded the concept of terrorism to include the actions of individuals who attack Americans outside of the boundaries of the United States. This expansion allowed for the prosecution of John Phillip Walker Lindh, who was charged under this Act with conspiracy to murder nationals of the United States, including American military personnel and other government employees serving in Afghanistan. He was not convicted of violating the statute, but was found guilty of other offenses.[18]

The Patriot Act expanded the section that made it a crime to provide material support to terrorist groups to include anyone outside of the United States; previously it had been directed only to those who provided support within the United States. This allows legal action against anyone in the world if they provide material support to terrorists. The Patriot Act also made the President the decision maker as to which groups were determined to be terroristic.

Other elements of the Patriot Act expand federal powers of investigation. Title II, Enhanced Surveillance Procedures, substantially changed the provisions of the FISA described earlier. Specifically, the Act lowered the standard required to obtain permission to use surveillance against suspects; roving wiretaps were authorized that allowed agents to tap any phone the suspect might use; further, pen registers were allowed that followed any phone number called by the suspect. The Patriot Act also authorizes law enforcement agencies charged with investigating terrorism to share investigative information with domestic law enforcement investigators and vice versa. In summary, some of the provisions that are most controversial include:

- expanding the range of crimes trackable by electronic surveillance
- allowing the use of roving wiretaps to track any phone a suspect might use
- allowing the "sneak and peek" search (not notifying suspects of searches)
- allowing federal warrants to search records with less than probable cause
- lowering barriers of information sharing between domestic and international investigations
- creating new tools for investigating money laundering (by requiring banks to file reports on suspicious behaviors).

On March 7, 2006, Congress approved the renewal of the USA Patriot Act. Most provisions of the Act were made permanent. The bill also created a national security division in the Department of Justice. Three provisions of the Act were set to expire in 2010, but Congress voted to extend them and President Obama signed the bill in February 2010. The provisions were as follows:

- "Lone wolf" provision: allows federal agents to track and investigate a suspect with no discernible affiliation with known terrorist groups or foreign powers.
- "Business records": allows investigators access to suspect's records (i.e., telephone, financial) without his or her knowledge.
- "Roving wiretaps": allows agents to monitor phone lines or Internet accounts used by a suspect even if owned or also used by others (must receive FISA authorization).

Congress passed the Protect America Act of 2007, which was an amendment to the FISA. It basically removed any culpability for secret wiretapping that had occurred before its passage, but mandated that any future wiretapping of citizens would require authorization from the FISC. It removed the warrant requirement for non-citizens and those outside of the United States. It also protected the telecommunications companies that assisted the government in accessing private accounts from any civil liability.

President Bush created the Department of Homeland Security in March 2003. The Department of Homeland Security consolidated 22 federal agencies and more than 180,000 federal employees under one umbrella agency. It had a budget of $30 billion in 2005 and $65 billion in 2016.[19] While the CIA is not one of the agencies that has been merged into the Department of Homeland

To read more about the Department of Homeland Security, go to https://www.dhs.gov/

Security, the idea of a national intelligence center is at the heart of the effort, and the CIA director is no longer the titular head of the U.S. intelligence function, as that role has shifted to the Department of Homeland Security. The Immigration and Naturalization Service was dismantled and the functions distributed to two agencies, U.S. Immigration and Customs Enforcement (ICE), and the U.S. Customs and Border Protection Agency, which also subsumed and redistributed the functions of the Border Patrol and U.S. Customs. The Customs and Border Protection Agency has about 40,000 employees; together, the two agencies employ 55,000 people.

Between 2001 and 2005, nearly 200 suspected terrorists or associates have been charged with crimes and, according to authorities, 100 terrorist plots disrupted.[20] Since then, a steady string of terrorist acts have occurred. The 2009 mass shooting at Ft. Hood by Nidal Hasan ended in thirteen deaths; a May 2010 potential bombing effort in Times Square was thwarted; the 2013 Boston Marathon bombing by the Tsarnaev brothers killed three and injured 264; the San Bernandino shooting in 2015 killed fourteen; and an attack at a Florida nightclub resulted in 49 deaths. Many other plots have been discovered and thwarted by government agents. "Self-radicalization" refers to the process by which any individual can become a terrorist, typically by interacting with terrorist groups such as ISIS via the Internet. These "lone-wolf" terrorists are much harder to track, identify, and catch before they commit acts. The major defense against them is to monitor Internet chatrooms which are becoming increasingly protected with encryption. Another source of information is tips from concerned friends and family. Indeed, one of the arguments against intemperate generalizations about Muslims and Muslim communities that seem to have spurred a rise in hate crimes directed against them is that Muslim community members are and will continue to be important sources of information for law enforcement about self-radicalized individuals in these communities.

Since 9/11, several major drug raids have uncovered ties between drug dealers and terrorist groups, such as Hezbollah, leading to the term "narcoterrorism." Opium from Afghanistan, although condemned by the Taliban, is now believed to be one of the largest sources of funding for Al Qaeda and, more recently, ISIS. Reports indicate that Mexican drug cartels may be engaged in business arrangements with Islamic terrorists, sending their "soldiers" to be trained and, in return, allowing terrorists to utilize their drug smuggling routes to secretly enter the United States.

Since 9/11, more resources have been directed to first responder training. This type of training gives law enforcement officers the skills to approach, engage, and coordinate responses to major threats, such as terrorist actions. Local police, especially those in major metropolitan areas, must assume that they will be first responders when targets of terrorist attacks are located in their city. Bridges, buildings, schools, transportation, sports complexes, other venues where there are large crowds, and nuclear reactors and power plants are the likely targets of terrorists. Actually, there are a wide range of targets that might be vulnerable to terrorist attacks. In addition to those already mentioned, the water supplies of major cities can be contaminated with toxic agents, the banking industry can be immobilized by computers, the nation's ports can be blocked with explosions, or the nation's oil and gas supplies can be sabotaged—bringing to a standstill industry, commerce, and basic services. Police are the first line of defense, both in terms of preventive observation and surveillance, as well as response and intervention.

Fusion centers employ civilian analysts to track and analyze information that might lead to uncovering terrorist plots. Joint task forces between local and federal agents have also been funded. State antiterrorism agencies have also been created to coordinate local law enforcement agencies in the state. Some cities, such as New York City, have antiterrorism units that engage in worldwide investigations.

Exhibit 14.6   Some larger cities, like New York, have dedicated counterterrorism units that conduct investigations and patrol the streets, like this officer on guard in front of the French Embassy after the terror attacks in Paris in 2015.

Source: Getty

To read about fusion centers, go to https://www.dhs.gov/state-and-major-urban-area-fusion-centers

Other smaller cities, however, may be woefully under-resourced. Their arsenal of weapons may not even match that of a well-armed militia group, the surveillance equipment may be inadequate to monitor suspected terrorists, and their communication networks may be deficient. Further, local officers may not be trained to investigate even domestic cybercrime, much less terrorists who use cybertactics. Further, local agencies may not have the expertise to investigate, or training to recognize, biological threats, or even forensic accountants to track international money laundering.

There is tension between national security and individual liberties played out with both federal counterterrorism agents and local law enforcement. One area of conflict is immigration control. Some cities and their police departments have refused to notify federal authorities or check the immigration status of victims or witnesses of crimes while other cities participate in the Secure Communities program whereby they partner with INS to check all people booked into jail for immigration status. Police departments that refuse to be the enforcers of federal laws argue that their role is domestic and involves only local security and crime fighting. These so-called **sanctuary cities** basically respond to crime victims or criminals, for that matter, without regard to any suspicion that the individual is an illegal alien. This issue has created a firestorm of controversy with some states (e.g., Arizona) passing laws requiring police officers to notify INS if they suspect a detainee does not have authorization to be in the country, some cities passing sanctuary city ordinances that prohibit police from doing so, and Congress threatening to withhold all federal monies from sanctuary cities. These arguments swirl around states' rights, civil liberties, and the goals and mission of law enforcement.

Local law enforcement has also been faced with difficult decisions in balancing their investigative activities against individual liberties. Federal law enforcement has sometimes taken aggressive actions in response to the threat of terrorism, especially in regard to Muslim residents and individuals of Middle Eastern descent. Immediately after 9/11, more than 5,000 resident aliens were detained without charges. Many were subsequently deported for minor immigration violations. Those who were released alleged that they were subject to illegal detention and abuse during their imprisonment. The FBI also asked local law enforcement agencies to conduct surveillance and/or question Muslims and foreign residents without any reason other than their nationality or religion. The Portland, Oregon, Police Department gained notoriety when it refused the FBI's request that it conduct interviews with all foreign students in the area. Portland police supervisors thought that they had no authority to do so because the FBI did not articulate any reasonable suspicion, the questions were in areas that were constitutionally protected, such as their religion, and did not relate to criminal matters.[21] Police and federal agents are called upon to balance civil liberties against serious threats to security in the interpretation of their powers.

We have all felt the effects of the nation's efforts to prevent terrorism. Travelers endure searches and, more recently, body scans, and a constant revision of rules concerning what can be carried onto airplanes. We learned through Edward Snowden that the National Security Agency (NSA) has been collecting "metadata"—mindboggling amounts of data on all of our electronic transmissions that it stores in semi-secret facilities in Utah and elsewhere. Whether they peek into electronic communications without warrants is a question that we cannot know the answer to since all court cases that have pushed for discovery have been dismissed on the grounds of national security.

Generally, the public has been supportive of the USA Patriot Act. In 2003, only 28 percent of those polled believed that it gave the government too much power over individual liberties, and 51 percent believed that people had to give up some individual freedom to fight terrorism.[22] However, a 2013 Gallup poll showed only 37 percent of Americans approved of the NSA's collection and storage of electronic data with 53 percent registering disapproval. Note also, though, that ideology affects our opinion about this and with all topics. Conservatives' and liberals' views have reversed from when President Bush was in office (when a majority of liberals disagreed with wiretapping) to President Obama's administration (when a majority of conservatives disagree with wiretapping).[23] Not surprisingly, even in the area of civil liberties our opinions are influenced by predispositions, in this case, political; all the more reason to practice critical thinking.

FOCUS ON DATA: LAST THOUGHTS

Throughout this text we have modeled a critical thinking approach which means to be aware of one's biases, ask well-constructed questions, and be a critical consumer of facts. This last chapter has identified a few more current issues, but another 100 pages could be written to address more. The fact is that no textbook can comprehensively cover all current issues and, in fact, is probably already out of date in some areas by the time you read it. However, the tools to continue the exercise of critical thinking are at your disposal. The Internet is an incredible resource that instantaneously allows you to access information. Follow the path of critical thinking and you will be able to create your own Focus on Data segments or do further study on any of the issues that have been raised in this text or others that you wish had been covered.

First, identify what you want to know; phrase it as a question that can be answered. Clearly define your terms and limit your inquiry to what can be addressed with facts. Don't include presuppositions in the phrasing of your question.

Second, gather facts. The Bureau of Justice Statistics (http://www.bjs.gov/) and the FBI's Uniform Crime Reporting (https://ucr.fbi.gov/ucr) are the two most helpful sources that provide information on crime, law enforcement, courts, and corrections. The Office of Juvenile Justice and Delinquency Prevention (http://www.ojjdp.gov/) is an excellent resource for inquiries related to juvenile justice. The National Institute of Justice (http://www.nij.gov/Pages/welcome.aspx) has funded literally hundreds of studies on a wide range of topics through the years which you can access through its website. Go to these websites and just browse the wide array of available information. You can even use the data analysis tool on the BJS website to construct your own graphs and tables of crime and victimization.

There is a myriad of other Internet sources as well. Just because a source of data may be from an advocacy group doesn't mean the information is false, but it does mean that you will want to look for alternative sources to confirm. Be careful of your own biases as well—do not ignore sources that contradict what you believe. Many of the questions that you will want answers to require sophisticated data analysis and you may not understand the methodology. Actually, many criminologists don't understand some of the data analysis done by others either. Fortunately, articles in academic peer-reviewed journals have been evaluated by those who do understand it, so you can be more confident in the findings. That is why an academic journal is a better data source than an opinion piece in a newspaper (although there still may be conflict between academic researchers that is typically presented in the article itself). The Crime and Justice Research Alliance (http://crimeandjusticeresearchalliance.org/) is a shared project between the two major academic organizations in the field, the American Criminology Society and the Academy of Criminal Justice Sciences. This webpage provides information from researchers who are experts on a range of relevant topics.

The National Academies of Science and other panels and task forces that put together numbers of researchers from different fields are also good sources of information. In effect, these panels practice a critical thinking approach because they frame a question and then bring experts in to gather and evaluate evidence. You will find that there is often still disagreement over some topical areas, which usually arises because of different methodologies resulting in conflicting findings.

If your question is a legal one, law review articles are the necessary source, along with caselaw itself. Once again, the Internet has made legal research much easier than it used to be. For Supreme Court cases, you can simply type in the case name and you will get numerous websites that provide the case holding. Several websites even provide audio or transcripts of the oral arguments before the court (e.g. https://www.oyez.org/).

The third step is to test your findings. While that may not be feasible, there are usually policy implications of the answer or answers you have arrived at. Have such policies been implemented with success? Look at your findings in a different way and determine if you can approach the issue from other data sources. Another test is to present your findings to someone who may disagree with them. Let them probe for weaknesses in your data sources or conclusion.

Critical thinking avoids generalizations, suppositions, oversimplifications, prejudicial thinking, narrow-mindedness, tunnel vision, and cognitive distortions. Done correctly, it helps us step back from any topic area (no matter how emotional) and gain a deeper understanding of the facts relevant to the issue. An accurate understanding of facts is necessary to develop and implement successful solutions. We need no less in the field of criminal justice. Hopefully, your exploration has only just begun.

Critical Thinking Exercises

1. Take any of the "Focus on Data" sections throughout the book and update it with new information gleaned either from academic journals or other sources. Rewrite it if the conclusion seems to be inconsistent with the new information.
2. Write your own section called "Current Issues in Criminal Justice." Of the topics you identify as most important, choose one and rephrase as a question, then construct a methodology that would be adequate to provide an answer to the question.

NOTES

1 Adapted from The Critical Thinking Community, 6/9/2016 from http://www.criticalthinking.org/pages/our-concept-of-critical-thinking/411

2 E. Harrell, *Victims of Identity Theft, 2014* (NCJ 248991). Washington, DC: Bureau of Justice Statistics. Retrieved 12/10/2015 from http://www.bjs.gov/

3 E. Harrell, note 2.

4 J. Truman and L. Langton, *Criminal Victimization, 2014.* Washington, DC: Bureau of Justice Statistics. Retrieved from http://www.bjs.gov/content/pub/pdf/cv14.pdf

5 K. Baum, *Identity Theft, 2014.* Washington, DC: Bureau of Justice Statistics, April 2006.

6 J. Pollock and V. Hollier, "T visas: Prosecution tool or humanitarian response?" *Women and Criminal Justice* 20 (1) (2010): 127–146; S.T. Green, "Protection for victims of child sex trafficking in the United States: Forging the gap between U.S. immigration laws and human trafficking laws." *U.C. Davis Journal of Juvenile Law and Policy* 12 (2008): 309–379; K. Hyland, "Protecting human victims of trafficking: An American framework." *Berkeley Women's Law Journal* 16 (2001): 29–70; T. Kyckelhahn, A. Beck and T. Cohen, *Characteristics of Suspected Human Trafficking Incidents, 2007–2008.* Washington, DC: Bureau of Justice Statistics, 2009.

7 Re-entry Policy Council, *An Explanation of Justice Mapping: Three Examples, 2005.* Retrieved 12/30/2005 from www.reentrypolicy.org/report/justice-mapping.php.

8 T. Clear, D. Rose and J. Ryder, "Incarceration and the community: The problem of removing and returning offenders." *Crime and Delinquency* 47 (3) (2001): 335–351; T. Clear, D. Rose, E. Waring and K. Scully, "Coercive mobility and crime: A preliminary examination of concentrated incarceration and social disorganization." *Justice Quarterly* 20 (1) (2003): 33–64.

9 T. Clear, note 8.

10 J. Lynch and W. Sabol, "Assessing the effects of mass incarceration on informal social control in communities." *Criminology and Public Policy* 3 (2) (2004): 267–294.

11 J.A. Fagin, *When Terrorism Strikes Home: Defending the United States.* Boston, MA: Allyn and Bacon, 2006, p. 39.

12 J.A. Fagin, note 11, p. 51.

13 D. Cole and J. Dempsey, *Terrorism and the Constitution.* New York, NY: Free Press, 2002.

14 R. Ward, K. Kiernan and D. Mabrey, *Homeland Security: An Introduction.* Newark, NJ: LexisNexis/Matthew Bender, 2006, p. 254.

15 J.A. Fagin, note 11, p. 57.

16 J.A. Fagin, note 11, p. 62.

17 Title 18 U.S.C. § 2331

18 *United States v. Lindh,* 227 F. Supp. 2d 565 (E.D. Va. 2002).

19 DHS Budget in Brief, retrieved 7/8/2016 from https://www.dhs.gov/sites/default/files/publications/FY_2016_DHS_Budget_in_Brief.pdf

20 Cited in Fagin, note 11, p. 127.

21 Cited in J. Fagin, note 11, p. 71.

22 Cited in J. Fagin, note 11, p. 77.

23 http://www.gallup.com/poll/163043/americans-disapprove-government-surveillance-programs.aspx

Glossary/Index

Note: Page numbers followed by 'p' refer to Photos
      Page numbers in bold type refer to Exhibits
      Text in bold type refers to Glossary terms

abortion   70–71, 237, 252
abscond   281
actuarial approach   360
actus reus   238, **239, 241**
adjudication hearing   454
affirmative defense   288
age (crime prone)   77–78, **77**, 86
Agnew, R.   95
Aid to Families with Dependent Children (AFDC)   352
airport searches   **199**, 511
Al Qaeda   508
alcohol–blood level   201–202
alcohol dependency   353
alcoholism   244
Alien Act (1798)   503
ambush-style killings   116–117
American Civil Liberties Union (ACLU)   18
American Revolution   124
American Sniper (Kyle)   244
American Society for Industrial Security (now ASIS International)   129
amygdala   89
ancient laws   11–12
Andrews, D.   91, 361
anti-gang laws   231
Anti-Terrorism and Effective Death Penalty Act (1996)   505
antisocial personality disorder   90
antiterrorist legislation   504
appellate: courts   262, 263; judges   274
Apple iPhone hack   152
appointed counsel system   269–270

Argersinger v. Hamlin (1972)   269

argot   391, 393

argot roles   393

arraignment   6, 285

arrest   6, 192–193; of black people 78, **79**, 80–81; common arrests 44, **44**; crime category **73**; drug offenses 44, **44**; due process 280; **gender differential** 72–73, **73**, 74–75, 75–76, **76**; of girls 463, **464**, **465**; immigrants 27; juvenile rates 454–455, **455**, **456**, **457**, **459**, 462–463, **462**, **464**; **Mendenhall test** 193; rates 27, 35–36, 39, 102; urine samples 353; use of force 169, *see also* stops and arrests (seizures)

Arrestee Drug Monitoring Program (ADAM II)   353

assault; aggravated   467, **468**; sexual 235; simple 31–32, 467, **467**, *see also* rape; sexual assault

Assault Weapons Ban (AWB)   213

Atkins, D.   **319**, 319p

attendant circumstance   **239**, 241

attention deficit disorder (ADD)   89

attenuation   208–209

Attica prison riot   **387**

Attorney General   268

attrition   478

Auburn system   384–385

Augustus, J.   343–344

Australia   418

automobile searches   197–198

Baader-Meinhof   504

bail   281–284

Bandura, A.   91

banishment   336

"banning the box" movement   424

Batson v. Kentucky (1986)   289

battered woman syndrome   244, 246

Beccaria, C.   84–85

bench trial   6, 273

benefit of clergy   343

Bentham, J.   85

Berkeley Police Department   132

beyond a reasonable doubt   287–288

BFOQ (bona fide occupational qualifications)   145

Bill of Rights 185–186, 194, 230–231, **230**; **due process** 186–187; 4th Amendment 186, 187, 194, 199; 5th Amendment 186, 187, 201, 204; 6th Amendment 279; 8th Amendment 281; 10th Amendment 14, **14**, 226; 14th Amendment 186–187, 194

biological theories of crime 85–90, 97, **341**; **epigenetics** 90; **eugenics** 86; genetic influences 86, 87–88, 90; monoamine oxidase (MAO) 88; personality traits 88; **phenotypes** 85; police implications **341**; serotonin levels 88; sex differences 89; testosterone 88

birth control 237

Black awareness movement (1960/1970s) 386

"Black Lives Matter" movement 17, 113

Black Panthers 504

Blacks: arrest data 78, **79**, 80, 163; cocaine use 163, **163**; detainment 462, **462**; homicide rates 47, 49, **49**; **incarceration rates** 378–379, 390, 392; juvenile arrest rates 459–461, **460**, **461**, **462**, **464**; killed by police 174–175; police confidence 61, 114–115, 160, **161**, 162; police officers 120–121; sentencing 298, 322, 324–325; stop-and-frisk policies 164–165; victimization levels 80, 81; violent crime 80–81, 83, 84, **84**

Blackstone, W. 13, 225

Blakely v. Washington (2004) 306

blood–alcohol level 201–202

blood samples 201–202

Bloom, B. 352

blue curtain of secrecy 154

"bobbies" 129

body cameras 152

Bolshevik bombings 503

bona fide occupational qualifications (BFOQ) 145

bond agents 282, **282**

Bonta, J. 91, 361

booking 6, 280

border searches **199**, 511

Boston Marathon bombing (2013) 508

Bow Street Runners 129

Bowery Boys 130, **130**

Brady motion 287

Brady v. Maryland (1963) 287

brain chemicals 88, 89

brain tumour 86

branks **337**

Bratton, W.   135, 150

breathalyzer test   202

Brennan Center for Justice   17

Brockway, Z.   418

"broken windows" theory   134

Brown, M.   **53**, 54, 116, 159–160

Brown v. Plata (2011)   381–382, 439, 440

Brussels   502

burden of guilt   287–288

Bureau of Justice Statistics   15

burglary   288; city rates 36, **36**, 37; **clearance rates** 40; country comparison 52, **52**; race rates **79**; trends by sex **74**

burnout   153

Bush, President G.W.   507

business records   507

"buy bust" incidents   149

California   382

"Canadian school" of correctional intervention   361

Carter, J.   235–236

casework model   356

Castile, P.   113, 171

categories of crime   71

Cato Institute   18

causes of crime *see* correlate (of crime); theories of crime

cellphone: hacking   152; police officers' use 151–152; tracing technology 151, 200–201; use while driving 33, **33**

Centers for Disease Control   211

Central Intelligence Agency (CIA)   8, 507–508

Challenge of Crime in a Free Society, The (1967)   8

challenges for cause   290

challenges to criminal justice system   16–21

change of venue   286

charging documents   284

Chicago Police Department   160

Chicago School   93, 94

chief of police   127, 132

child saver movement   450–451, 452

children: custody of   427; lead levels 86–87, **87**; learning issues 89; of prisoners 429–430, **429**; role models 500; sex trafficking 497, *see also* juvenile justice system

chivalry theory   72

Ciavarella, M.   480

CIT (Crisis Intervention Training)   148, 174

citizen satisfaction   147–148

City of Chicago v. Morales (1999)   231

city code violations   7, 14

city comparisons   36–37; homicide 55–56, **56**, **57**

city ordinances   7, 14, 227

civil disabilities   427

civil law   228

civil rights   186; protests 9, 15, 134

civilian review/complaint boards   158

classical school   84–85

classification and risk assessment: **actuarial approach**   360; **clinical approach** 360; **false negatives** 359–360; **false positives** 359; female offenders 364–365; LSI-R classification 361, 362–364; mental health issues 399; R/N/R classification 361–362, 399

clearance rates   39–40; burglary 40

clemency   307–309, **309**, 340

Clemency Project   308

clinical approach   360

Clinton, W. (Bill): administration   505

closing arguments   291

co-occurring disorder   397–398, **398**

cocaine   **163**, 306–307

Code of Hammurabi   11–12, 225, 336

code of silence   154

cohort study   43, 86, 96

collateral consequences   427–430; on minority communities 428–429; voting rights 428

Colson Commission   20

Columbine High School shooting (1999)   472–473, 474

Columbus, Ohio   83–84, **84**

Commentaries on the Laws of England (Blackstone)   225

Commission on 21st Century Policing (2015)   17, **18**, 113, 139, 175–176; Six Pillars 176

Commission on Crime and Administration of Justice (1965)   8, **9**, 10, 15, 16

common crimes   44–46

common law   13, 225

communism   503–504

communities: incarceration effect on   500–501; Muslim 508, 510; and **reintegration era** 338–339

community corrections   342

community courts   263–264

community as crime causation   94

community mental health centers   396

community policing   134–139, **136**, 140; critics of 137–138; demise of 139; strategies used **137**

community reparative boards   315

community service   **347–348**

commutation *see* **clemency; shortening a sentence**

competent   470

Compstat   150–151, **150**

Conahan, M.   480

conceal carry permits   213

concordance   88

conditions   481

conducted energy devices (CEDs)   170

congregate system   384

consent searches   195, **198**

consent stops   187, 188–189

constitutional challenges, law creation   226, 228, 230–231; equal protection violations 233–235; ex post facto laws 232–233; First Amendment Rights 235–236; privacy violations 237; vagueness 231–232

constructed reality   32, **32**

contraception   237

contract attorney model   269

contractual duties   239–240

control theory   94–95

"controlled for"   82

controversies: current legal   252–253

conviction integrity units   19

"cooking" the numbers (of crime)   39

corporal punishment   381

correctional institution   7, 335–336, 386; classification and risk assessment 359–361; cost of 15, 438, 500; drug offenders 353–354; **gender-specific programming** 351–353, 364–365; goals of 335, 336, 338–340; incarceration rates 20–21; LSI-R classification 362–363, 364–365; major issues 500–501; offender profiles 348–351, **349**, **350**; organization of 7; R/N/R classification 361–362; **reintegration era** 338–339; and theories of crime 340–341, *see also* probation correctional officer unions   501

Corrections Corporation of America   400

correlate (of crime)   71, 212; age 77, **77**, 78; gender 72–73, **73**, **74–75**, 75–76, **76**; race and/or ethnicity 78, **79**, 80–84, **82**, **83**, **84**, *see also* theories of crime

correlation   16, 25, **87**, 88, 212–214, 475; negative 86

corruption 155–156, 157–159, **158**; **early warning or audit system** 158; **ends-orientated thinking** 156; **graft** 156; **gratuities** 156; "honest services" law 232; **noble cause corruption** 156; reducing police 158, **158**

cortical arousal   88–89

costs: of criminal justice system   15

counterfeiting   226, **227**

country comparisons   51–52, **52**

county law enforcement agencies   126–127

court of last resort   263

court surety programs   282–283, 342

court systems: **appellate**   262, 263; **court of last resort** 263; domestic violence 266; jurisdictions 260; levels of 7, 259–260; major issues 498–499; specialized 263–266; trial 260–261, 263; wrongful convictions 19–20, 498–499, **499**

courts of limited jurisdiction   260, 273

Craig v. Boren (1976)   235

crime: comparison statistics   494, **495**; definition 31, 70–71; elements of 238–242; yearly fluctuations 57, 59, 61

crime control ideology   21–22

crime fighter role   138, 139

crime labs: investigators   156; scandals 202–203

crime mapping   150–151

crime patterns   16–17, 35–43, 69–70, 495; decline 49–50, **50**; homicide 46–49, 55–57, **56**, **57**, *see also* theories of crime

crime rate   20, 500; comparison other countries 51–52, **52**; female 91; illegal immigrants 27; public perception **51**; sex differential 94

crime spikes   54, 86, 472–473

criminal law   222–223, 228; recent issues 252–253

criminal threat: definition   236

criminogenic knowledge structure (CKS)   100

criminogenic needs   362

criminology   8–9, 17, 70, 100; biological research 86; positivism 85; white-collar crime 99, **99**, *see also* theories of crime

Crisis Intervention Training (CIT)   148, 174

critical criminology   98–99

critical thinking   491–492, 513

Crofton, W.   418

cultural deviance theory   93

custody of children   427

Customs and Border Protection Agency   508

cybercrimes   151, 492

DARE officers   474

dark figure of crime   32

data sources   17, 492, 511–513; cohort studies 43; **National Crime Victim-ization Survey** (NCVS) 9, 41–42, 45, 492; self-report studies 27, 42–43, 492; **Uniform Crime Reports** (UCR) 9, 35–41, **38**, 492; victimization studies 9, 41–42, 45, 81

day fines   347

day reporting centers   **346**

D.C. v. Heller (2008)   230

de-escalation policies   148–149

de-policing   52, 53, 58–60, 62

Dead Rabbits gang   130, **130**

death penalty   317–322; juveniles 243, 318, 470; mentally handicapped 318–319, **319**, 320; method 321; numbers **321**, **322**; public support **320**, 321

deaths in custody   113

Deaths in Custody Reporting Act (2000)   173

debt: offenders   303–305

debtors' prisons   303–304

decarceration *see* Justice Realignment

decline in crime   49–50, **50**; explanations for 67–69, **69**; lead-based paint 86

defense attorney: appointed counsel system   269; contract model 269; public defender system 269; right to 206, 269, 357; role 268

defenses   242; burden of proof 288; diminished capacity 244; duress 246, 247; entrapment 250–251; ignorance or mistake 251; infancy 242; insanity 243–244, 246; mental capacity 243–246, **245**; necessity 247; post-traumatic stress syndrome (PTSD) 244–245, **245**; self-defense 247–249; statute of limitations 252

deferred adjudication   342–343, 454

deferred sentencing   357

delinquents   89, 94, 450; adjudication 475, 477; early onset 97; girls 481; integrated theory of 97–98; late onset 97

Denno, D. 89, 97

Department of Homeland Security (DHS) 8, 124, 507

Department of Justice (DOJ) 15

Department of Public Safety (DPS) 164

deportation 25, 26–27

deprivation theory 391

detainment 461

determinate sentence 300

deterrence 299, 303, 336, 340

deterrence theory(ies) 96, 103

deviance 70

differential association theory 94

differential enforcement 80

diminished capacity defenses 244

direct examination 290

direct file 471

disadvantaged distributions 83–84, **83, 84**

discretion 297

disparity 297, 306

displacement effect 148

disposition hearing 454

disrespectful treatment 165–166

DNA samples 201, 202

docket 261

domestic violence: courts 266; mandatory arrest 149, 193; police units 149;
    reporting of 34, **34**

Dotson, S. 54

double jeopardy 285

drones 151

drug courts 264–266, **264**; juvenile justice system 454

drugs: addiction 293, 366, 436; arrests 44, **44**; federal assistance ban 352;
    housing bans 428; offenders in system 353–354; race/ethnicity 163, **163**,
    461; sentencing 306–310; smuggling 226, 251; and terrorist groups 508

drunken driving 201–202

DSM-V (*Diagnostic and Statistical Manual*) 90, 246

ducking stool **337**

Dudley and Stephens case (1884) 247

due deference era (1980–today) 380

due process 186, 232, 278–280; **arraignment** 285; **arrest** 280; **bail**
    281–284; **booking** 280; **indictment** 284; **information** 284; initial

appearance 280–281; juvenile rights 469–470, **470**; **parole** 432; **plea bargain** 285; **pre-trial motions** 285–287; **preliminary hearing** 284–285; **probation** 354, 357; protections 279
due process ideology   22–23
DUI   201–202
duress   246
Durkheim, E.   92

early warning or audit system   158
economic success   93–94
electronic monitoring (EM)   200–201, **346**
electronic surveillance   199–201, 507, 511
Elmira Reformatory   385–386, 418
eminent domain   279
employment   94; after re-entry 424; **transitional jobs** 424
en banc   274
encounter characteristics   174–175
endogeneity   406
ends-orientated thinking   156
enriched programming   478
Enron   232
entrapment   149, 250–251
environmental conditions   89
environmental criminology   96
environmental toxins   86
epigenetics   90
equal protection violations   233–235, 252–253
Escobedo v. Illinois (1964)   204
ethnicity *see* race/ethnicity
eugenics   86
evidence: presentation of   290–291
ex post facto laws   230, 232–233
exclusionary rule   207–209; "good faith" exception 208
"exigent circumstances"   195, **196–197**

Fair Sentencing Act (2010)   307
fair trial   **286**
"faith-based" statutes   252
false negatives   359–360

false positives 359, 360

family group conferencing 315–317

Farrington, D.: Ohlin, L. and Wilson, J. 96–97

Federal Bail Reform Act (1984) 283–284

Federal Bureau of Investigation (FBI) 8, 510–511; Apple hack 152; arrest data 39, 78; crime data 17, 35; crime lab 20; homicide reports 47, **47**, 55, 173; National Incident-Based Reporting System (NIBRS) 41, 492; terrorism 503, 505, 510–511; **Uniform Crime Reports** (UCR) 9, 35–41, **38**, 492; violent crime index 465; website 62

federal court system 8; appointed attorneys 269–270; jurisdiction of 276–277; military law 275; organization of 274–276, **275**; overcriminalization 16

federal government: powers 13–14, 224, 226

federal law enforcement agencies 8, 124–126, **125**, 504; Central Intelligence Agency (CIA) 8, 507–508; counterterrorism agents 510–511; Customs and Border Protection Agency 508; **Department of Homeland Security** (DHS) 8, 124, 507; employment statistics **125**; Federal Bureau of Investigation (FBI) 8, 510–511; U.S. Customs Service 124

Federal Law Enforcement Training Center (FLETC) 147

federal laws 8, 126, 226

fee system 402

felonies 238, 300–302, 403; de-felonized crimes 442

felony murder 318

Ferguson Effect 19, 52, 53, **53**, 54

fiduciary duty 232

field training officer (FTO) programs 146–147

Fielding, H. 129

filial responsibility laws 239

fines and fees 303–305, **305**; **probation** 304, 345, **347**, 348

fingerprints 203, 204

First Amendment Rights 235–236

first responder training 508–509

Five Points neighborhood 130, **130**

FiveThirtyEight.com 56–57

flag burning 236

Flint, Michigan 86–87

Floyd v. City of New York (2013) 191

force: excessive 170; region variations 169; tasers 170; use of 168–170

Foreign Intelligence Surveillance Court (FISA) 504

forensic science 19–20, 201–203

fraud 492

Freedom of Information Act (1967) 504

Ft. Hood mass shooting (2009) 508

FTOs 146–147

Furman v. Georgia (1972) 317

fusion centers 509

Gall v. United States (2007) 306

gambling 71, 225

gangs 93; anti-gang laws 231; juvenile membership 458–459, **458**; prison 392–393

Gangs of New York (2002) 130

gaol 129, 402

Garner, E. 114, 116

gender differential 72–73, **73–74**, 75–76, **76**, 92; juvenile 465–469, **466**, **467**, **468**, 480–481

gender disparity *see* **gender differential**

gender-specific programming 351–353

Gendreau, P. 361

general deterrence 336

general jurisdiction courts 260, 263, 273

general responsivity 362

general strain theory 95

general theory of crime 95

genetic traits 86, 87–88, 90

geographic jurisdiction 260

Gideon v. Wainwright (1963) 269

girls: arrest/referrals 463, **465**; delinquents 480–481; violence 465–469

Glass, J.M. 132

Goldstein, H. 134–135

"good faith" exception 208

Good Samaritan laws 240

Gottfredson, M. 95

GPS-tracking devices 200–201, **346**

graft 156

Graham v. Connor (1989) 168, 172

Graham v. Florida (2010) 243, 470

grand jury hearing 6, 284

gratuities 156

Greece: ancient   12

Griswold v. Connecticut (1965)   237

"guardian" model   139

guilty but mentally ill   244

gun: control laws   209–214, 230–231; ownership and homicide 212; registration 210–211

gun-related deaths   209, **210**

gun-related violence   54, 60–61, 209, 210–212, 213–214

habeas corpus   262

hacking   152

halfway houses   425

Hammurabi (Babylon 1975–1750 BCE)   11–12

hands-off era   380

harmless error   262

Hawaii's Opportunity Probation with Enforcement (H.O.P.E.)   359

hearsay   290, 298

"hedonistic calculus"   85

heroin   61

Hezbollah   508

Hiibel v. Sixth Judicial District Court of Nevada (2004)   190

Hirschi, T.   94, 95

Hispanics: arrest data   78; **incarceration rates** 378, 390; mental health 396; and police force 121, 159–160, 167; sentencing 322, 324, **326**; victimization levels 80

Hobbes, T.   11, 13, 223

Holder, E. (Attorney General)   20, 270

Holtzclaw, D.   156, **157**, 157p

home intruder   249

homeless   425

homicide   46–49; African American rates 47, 49, **49**; causes of increase 60–62; city comparisons 55–56, **56**, **57**; FBI reports 47, **47**, 55, 173; and gun ownership 212; justifiable 173, 248; rates 16, 46, **46**, 51, 55–58, **56**, victim/offender relationship 47, **47**, **48**

homosexuality: in prison   394

"honest services" law   232

Hoover, J. Edgar   503

"hot pursuit exception"   197

hot spots   148

housing beds   424–425, **425**

Howard, J.   402

human trafficking   496–498, **496**

hyperactivity   89

identification procedures   203–204

identity theft   492, 493–494, **493**, 495–496, **495**

ideology   21–23, 28; **crime control** 21–22; **due process** 22–23

ignorance of a law   251

immigrants: crime correlation   23–24, **24**, 25, 27; deportation 25, 26–27, 510; illegal 23–27, 510; **incarceration rate** 25, 26; Latino 26; loss of status 25; **recidivism** 26; **sanctuary city rules** 25; Secure Communities program 26–27

Immigration and Customs Enforcement (ICE)   25, 508

Immigration and Naturalization Service (INS)   124

implicit bias   159

importation theory   391

imprisonment rate   373–375, **375**; decline 379–380; race/ethnicity/sex 377–379, **378**, **379**; **tipping effect** 500

incapacitation   336, 338

incarceration rate   20–21, 25, 373–375, **375**, **376**, 377–378; Blacks 378–379, 390, 392; and crime rate 405–409, **405**; decline in 68, 379–380; effects on community 500–501; Hispanics 378, 390; international comparison 375, **377**; re-evaluation of 438

incompetent   243

incorporation   187

indeterminate sentence   299–300

index crimes   37, 492

Indian reservations   127, **128**

indictment   284

indigency   20, 269, 270–272, 280–281, 499

"inevitable discovery" exception   208

infancy   242–243

information   284

initial appearance   280–281

inmate code   391–392

Innocence Projects   19, 498, **499**

insanity   243–244, 246

integrated theories   97–98

integrity testing   **158**

intensive supervision programs   359

inter-race marriage   234, **234**

intermediate sanctions   344–345

International Association of Chiefs of Police   155

international crime   496–497

internet chatrooms   508

interrogation; of juveniles   453; rights during 204, **205**, 206–207

intra-racial crime   83

inventory searches   **198**

investigatory detentions   165, 166, 187, 189–191; "pat-downs" **196**

involuntary acts   239

Inwald Personality Inventory (IPI)   144

ISIS   508

jail   7, **7**, 401–404; **fee system** 402; **incarceration rate** 20–21, 25, 373–375, **375**, **376**, 377–378; inmates' legal rights 383; mentally ill 396–399, **397**, **398**; in the past 402–403; race/ethnicity 403, **403**; size 404; standards of 404; suicide rate 402

jailhouse lawyers   381

John Jay College of Criminal Justice   58

Johnson, President L.   8, **9**, 10, 14, 15

judges   272; appellate 274; **docket** 261; of limited jurisdiction 273; **recusal** 287; selection of 272–273; trial 273–274

judicial immunity   354–355

judicial waivers   471

juries: deliberation   291; ex-offenders 428; exemption from 289; instructions to 291; and judges' influence 273, 274; selection of 288–290

Justice Realignment   438–442, 501; and crime rate 441–442; **recidivism** 441

Justice Reinvestment Initiative (JRI)   438–442, 501

justices of the peace   260

justifiable homicides   173, 248

juvenile   242–243; brain development 454, 470; criminal violence 472–473; gang membership 458–459, **458**; mental health 482; **recidivism** 481–482

Juvenile Justice and Delinquency Prevention Act (1974)   452

juvenile justice system   7, 242, 449–454; adjudication 454, 475, 477; arrest rates 454–455, **455**, **456**, **457**, **459**, 462–463, **462**, **464**; **child saver movement** 450–451, 452; death penalty 243, 318, 470; **deferred adjudication** 454; detainment 461–462; detention facilities 453–454; **direct file** 471; disposition alternatives **476**; disposition hearing 454; **drug courts** 454; 1800–early 1900s 450–451; enriched programming 478; **gender differential** 465–469, **466**, **467**, **468**, 480–481; interrogation 453;

jurisdiction 471; offenders' rights 469–470, **469**; offense through adjudication 452–454; overcriminalization 16; **parens patriae** 450; prior to 1800s 450; **probation** 451, 454, 475, 477–478; race and adjudication rates 475, 477; residential placement 452; **school-to-prison pipeline** 16, 475; secure confinement **476**, 478–481; sentencing 470; **status offenders** 450, 452; **statutory exclusion** 471; terminology **453**; training schools 452, 479–480; waiver to adult court 452, 470–472, 478–479

Kagan, E.   277, 278
Kansas City Preventive Patrol Study   147
Katz v. United States (1967)   199
Keeler v. Superior Court (1970)   225
Kelling, G.   134
"kids for cash" scheme   480
King, R.   113, 134
Krivo, L.   83
Kyle, C.   244–245, **245**
Kyllo v. United States (2001)   200

labeling theory   94
Laub, J.   98
law: purpose of   222–224, *see also* legal system
Law Commentaries (Blackstone)   13
law creation   13–14, 33, 227; constitutional challenges to 228, 230–237
law enforcement agencies 5, 7, 140; county 126–127; federal 124–126, **125**; ideologies 21–23; municipal 7, 127; private 127–129; scrutiny 17–19, 54, 58, 498; special jurisdiction 119, 127; state 126, *see also* policing
Lawrence v. Texas (2003)   223, 237
lead toxins   86–87, **87**
learning theory   91
lease-labor system   386
legal aid   269–271, **271**
legal duties   239–240
legal moralism   224
legal system   3–10, 226; changes to 10, 14–15; flowchart of 4, **5**; historical foundation 13–14; origins 13–14, 225–227; state differences 10; subsystems 4–5
legislation   33
legitimacy   95–96
lethal force   248; police powers 171–175

Level of Service Inventory-Revised (LSI-R)   362–363; criticism of 362–364; and women 364

lex talionis   336

line-ups   203

Littlefield, C.   245, **245**

Liu, W.   116

local law enforcement agencies   8, 14; immigration control 510

Locke, J.   11, 223

lockstep march   384, **385**

lockups   280

Lombroso, C.   85

London Metropolitan Police Force   129

"lone-wolf" terrorists   507, 508

longitudinal research   43, 86, 96, 96–97

Los Angeles: City Guards   131; county jail 26; police department 131–132; Rangers 131

Los Angeles Times   56

Louisiana   13, 17

Loving, M. and R.   **234, 234p**

loyalty   155

McCleskey v. Kemp (1987)   318

MacDonald, H.   54, 58

McDonald, L.   160

McDonald v. Chicago (2010)   230

Maconochie, A.   418

macro-level crime theories   69–70, 92

McVeigh, T.   **286**, 286p

Madoff, B.   99, 99p

magistrate   194

Major Cities Chiefs Association (MCCA)   54

"Make My Day" statutes   249

mala prohibita   222

mala in se   222

mandatory arrest statues; domestic violence   149, 193

mandatory minimum sentences   300, 303, 309, 327

Manhattan Bail Project   283

Mapp v. Ohio (1961)   194

marijuana: legalization   60, 253–254; patterns of use 80; possession of 101, 247

mark system   418

marriage: inter-race   234, **234**; same-sex 223, **224**, 237, 252

Martin, T.   248

Martinez, R.   25–26

Maryland v. King (2013)   202

mass imprisonment   20, 501

mass shootings   211, 213

matched pairs   212–213

maxed out   421

Mendenhall test   193

mens rea   **239**, 240–242, **241**

mental capacity defense   243–246, **245**; time of offense 243

mental illness: call outs to   148; **co-occurring disorders** 397–398, **398**; death penalty 318–319, **319**, 320; definition 246, 396; Hispanics 396; in jail/prison 396–399, **397**, **398**; **juvenile** 482; **parole** 426

meta-analyses   323

metadata   511

Metropolitan Police Act (England, 1929)   129

Mexican drug cartels   508

micro-level theories   70, 92

military law   275

Mill, J.S.   223

Miller v. Alabama (2012)   243, 470

"million-dollar blocks"   500

Minnesota   17

Minnesota Multiphasic Personality Inventory (MMPI)   144

minority communities: disrespectful treatment   165–166; men in prison 428–429; police discrimination against 159–168; and police legitimacy 61, 62, 113–115, **115**, 121–122, **122**; **racial profiling** 164–165; sentencing disparity 322–327, **325**; within policing 120–122, **121**, **122**, 134

Miranda, E.   **205**, 205p

Miranda v. Arizona (1966)   204

Miranda warning   204, **205**, 206–207, 280

miscegenation laws   234, **234**

misdemeanors   238

Missouri Plan   272

Missouri v. McNeely (2013)   202

mistake of fact defense   251–252

"mistaken weapon"   174

mixed zones   93

M'Naghten test   243
Model Penal Code   240
modeling   91
monoamine oxidase (MAO)   88
morals   223–225
Morrisey v. Brewer (1972)   432–433
motion   285–286
motion in limine   286
motivation for crime   69–71, *see also* theories of crime
Munich Olympics (1972)   504
municipal courts   260
municipal law enforcement agencies   7, 127
murder *see* homicide
Muslim communities   508, 510

"narcoterrorism"   508
National Academies of Science   20, 202–203, 409, 454
National Crime Victimization Survey (NCVS)   9, 41–42, 45
National Incident-Based Reporting System (NIBRS)   41, 492
National Institute of Justice (NIJ)   55, 61
National Law Enforcement Officers Memorial Fund   116
National Night Out   135–136
National Registry of Exonerations   19
National Security Agency (NSA)   511
national statistics   9, 15
National Survey on Drug Use and Health (NSDUH)   353
Native American tribes   127, **128**
natural law   222
nature versus nurture   88, 89
necessity defense   247
neighborhoods: "**broken windows theory**"   134–135; **mixed zones** 93; TANF 500; and urban crime 83–84, **83**, **84**, *see also* communities
Neri-Jorge, N.   **24**
net-widening   316
New York City: burglary rates   36–37; counterterrorism units 509, **509**; criminal court system 260, **261**; Five Points neighborhood 130, **130**; police department 130–131, 191; stop-and-frisks 58, **59**; **zero tolerance approach** 135
New York City Transit Police   135
New Zealand   315–316

NIBRS (National Incident Based Reporting System)   41, 469, 492

Nice   502

Nixon, President R.: administration   504

no bill   284

"noble cause" corruption   156

Obama, President B.   17, **18**, 20, 113, 139, 175, 254, **308**, 308p, 507

Obergefell, J.   **224, 224p,** 252

Obergefell v. Hodges (2015)   223, 252

offenders: debts from court costs   303–305; drugs 44, **44**, 306–310, 352, 353–354, 428; profile statistics 348–351, **349**, **350**; **recidivism** 433–434, **433**, 436–437; violent 389, **390**

Office of Community Oriented Policing Services (COPS)   139

Office of Law Enforcement Assistance (LEAA)   8, 15

Ohlin, L.: Wilson, J. and Farrington, D.   96–97

Oklahoma City bombing (1995)   505

Omnibus Counterterrorism Act (1995)   505

"open fields" doctrine   **198**

opening statements   290

opiate deaths   61

order maintenance   112

organizational justice   152–153, 156–157

organized crime organizations   496

Orlando nightclub massacre (2016)   209, 230, 502, **502**

Osama Bin Laden   505

out-of-home placements   478–481; by race and year 478–479, **479**; **status offenders** 452

overcriminalization   16, 310, **310**

Owen, B.   352

Packer, H.   21–23

Palmer, A.M. (Attorney General)   503

pardon   419

parens patriae   450

Paris attacks   502, **509**

parol (*parole d'honneur*)   417

parole   7, 342; board members 419, **420**, 421; conditions attached **432**; due process 432; eligible for 419; employment 424, 426; families 426–427; hearings 420–421; history of 417–419; housing 424–425, **425**, 427; numbers on 422, **422**; parolees' crimes 422, **423**; race/ethnicity 423;

recidivism 433–434, **435**, 436–437; **rehabilitative era** 419; revocation process 431–433, **433**; **technical violations** 303, 432–433, 434; violation hearing 432; women on 427, 436, *see also* re-entry problems/services

parole guidelines 420

paternalistic laws 223

patrol and investigation 147–149; domestic violence units 149; Kansas City Preventive Patrol Study 147; mentally ill calls 148–149; patrol cars 151; saturated patrols 148; social media 151; technology 150–152

Peel, R. 129

penal codes 13–14

penitentiary 383–384, **383**; **Auburn system** 384–385; **congregate system** 384; **lockstep march** 384, **385**; **Pennsylvania system** 384; **reformative era** 338, 385–386; **rehabilitative era** 386; **separate system** 384; transition to **correctional institutions** 386; **warehouse prison** 387

Pennsylvania system 384

perceptions of crime 50, **51**

peremptory challenges 289

Personal Responsibility and Work Opportunity Reconciliation Act (PRWORA) (1996) 352

personality traits 88, 90–91; of police officers 144, 145

Petersilia, J. 358

Peterson, R. 83

petit jury 284

phenotype 85

phishing 494

photo array 203–204

physical fitness test 145

"plain view" doctrine 194–195, **198**

plea bargain 6, 273, 285; racial disparity 323

PLRA (Prison Litigation Reform Act) (1996) 380

Police Executive Research Forum (PERF) 147

police misconduct 115, 155–159; abuse of authority 156; **blue curtain of secrecy** 154; individual explanations 156; organizational explanations 156–157; scrutiny 17–19, 54, 58; societal explanations 157, *see also* corruption

police officers: discrimination against minorities 159–168; fatal attacks on 113, 116–118, **117**, **118**; female 122–123, **123**; minority percentages 120–122, **121**, **122**, 134; social lives 154; statistics about 118–123, **122**, **123**, 140; stress levels 152–153; **subculture** 153–155 police operations: patrol and investigation   147–149; screening out process 144; selection criteria 143–145; training 145–147, **146**

police personality   145

police power   14, 226; abuses of 115, 156; lethal force 171–175; use of force 168–170

police shootings   19, 53, 171–175

police subculture   153–155; **blue curtain of secrecy** 154; **socialization** 154

policing: decentralization   124, 137; function of 112–113, 139; height and weight requirements 144–145; juvenile delinquency 452–453; legitimacy crisis 61, 62, 113–115, **115**; major issues 113–115, 495–498; modern background 12, 129–132, 140; pro-active policing 54, 60–62, 147–149; problem-orientated 138; professionalization of 132–134; reactive policing 147–149; scrutiny 17–19, 54, 58, 498; and technology 150–152; in 20th Century 132–134, *see also* de-policing; police misconduct

politics in policing   132

population base   37, 374

Portland Police Department   510–511

positivism   85, 222–223

positivist law   222

post-traumatic stress syndrome (PTSD)   244–245, **245**

"poverty penalty"   303, 499

pre-release programs   426, 499

pre-sentence report (PSR)   354–355

pre-trial diversion programs   342, 343; community service **347–348**; **day fines** 347; day reporting centers **346**; electronic monitoring (EM) 346; **restitution** 346–347; **Scarlett Letter** conditions **348**

pre-trial motions   285–286, 288

pre-trial release programs   342

PREA (Prison Rape Elimination Act) (2003)   394–395

prefrontal cortex   89

preliminary hearing   6, 284–285

premenstrual syndrome (PMS)   244

"preponderance of the evidence"   288

presidential nomination process   23

pretext stop   164, 190

pretrial diversion   6

pretrial hearing   6

prevalence of crime   44–46, 50

Preventing Parolee Crime Program (PPCP)   436

prevention programs for children   482

preventive detention   283–284

primary deviance   94

prison: admission versus population   390, **390**; **civil disabilities** 427–428; **collateral consequences** 427–430; conditions 381–382, 388; **corporal punishment** 381; costs 15, 438; crimes of conviction **389**; education programs 426; **hands-off era** 380; immigrant groups 26; **imprisonment rates** 373–380, **375**, **378**, **379**; **incarceration rates** 373–377, **375**, **376**, **377**; inmate to inmate correspondence 382; **jailhouse lawyers** 381; juveniles in adult 452, 470–472, 478–479; legal rights 380–382; mail censorship 382; **maxed out** 421–422; mental illness 396–399, **397**, **398**; offenders' families 430; **PLRA** 380; police recommendations 430; pre-release programs 426, 499; Prison Rape Elimination Act (PREA) (2003) 394–395; privately run 399–401; privileges 386; race issue 392; race-based violence 388; race/ethnicity 377–379, **378**, **379**, 389–390, **391**; **rational relationship test** 382–383; release 421–422, **421**; religious freedom 382–383; rights era (1960–1980) 380; rights lawsuits 380–381; riots 386–387, **387**; sexual assault in 394–395; sexual victimization in 395; substance abuse 396–397, 425, 426; treatment programs 382, 436–437; vocational programs 426; women's 386, 387, 392, 394, *see also* Justice Reinvestment Initiative (JRI); **penitentiary**; prison subculture; re-entry problems/services

Prison Rape Elimination Act (PREA) (2003)   394–395

prison subculture: **argot**   391, 393; **argot roles** 393–394; **deprivation theory** 391; gangs 392–393; **importation theory** 391; **inmate code** 391–392; **prisonization** 391; **pseudofamilies** 393; violent offenders 392; women 392, 394; younger prisoners 392

prisoner samples   43

prisonization   391

privacy: after arrest   202; reasonable expectation of 199–200, 202, 203; right to 237, 252

private law enforcement   127–129

private prisons   399–401

proactive policing   54, 60–62, 147–149; undercover operations 149

probable cause   188, **188**, 192, **192**, 280

probation   7, 302, 342; caseload 360, 361; **casework model** 355–356; classification levels 360–361; community service 347–348; completion figures 345, 357; conditions attached to 344–345, **345**; current issues 354–356; electronic monitoring (EM) **346**; fines 304, 345, **347**, 348; gender-specific programming 351–353; history of 339, 343–344; juvenile

451, 454, 475, 477–478, **477**; monthly visits **355**, 355p, 356; officers 4, 344, 354–355; pre-sentence report (PSR) 354–355; profile statistics 350–351; progress reports 274; R/N/R classification 360; recidivism rates 359; **restitution** 346–347; revocation of 345, 356–357; **Scarlet Letter** conditions **348**; technical violations 345, 356, 357, **358**; "warning" hearings 359; warrantless searches 356, *see also* **recidivism**

problem-orientated policing   138; **SARA model** 138

problem-solving courts   263–264; effectiveness 264–266

procedural justice   96, 153

Progressive Movement   338

proof   287–288

property crimes   37, **38**

"prophylactic" right   206

Proposition 47 (2014)   442

prosecutors: decision-making ability   268, 323; misconduct 287; **noble cause corruption** 156; office 267; racial disparity 323–324; role of 268; special 267

Protect America Act (2007)   507

pseudofamilies   393

psychological theories of crime   90–92, **341**; **antisocial personality disorder** 90; **DSM-IV** 90; personality traits 90–91; policy implications **341**; psychopathy 90; **sociopathy** 90

psychopathy   90

public: laws   12; peace officers 128; punishment **337**

public defender system   269–271; resources 270, 271, **271**

"public safety" exception   208

Public Safety Realignment Act (2011)   440

punishment   335–336; early eras 336, **337**; public **337**

purchase permits   213

Quetelet, A.   92

race riots   134

race/ethnicity: arrest numbers   27; cocaine use 163, **163**; and crime 78, **79**, 80–84, **81**, **82**, **83**; disadvantaged neighborhoods 83–84, **83**, **84**; drug use 163, **163**, 461; jails 403, **403**; juvenile arrest rates 459–461, **460**, **461**; **parole** 423; perceptions of police 160, **161**, 162, **162**; prison population figures 377–379, **378**, **379**; **racial invariance hypothesis** 83; sentencing hearing disparity 322–327, **325**, **326**, *see also* Blacks; Hispanics; minority communities

racial invariance hypothesis   83

racial profiling 164–165, 190

racism 159–160

Rahami, A.K. 502

Ramos, R. 116

random sampling 42

rape: equal protection law 235; officers on duty 156, **157**; in prison 394–395; statutory 235; victims 34

rates 35–37

rational choice theory 96

rational relationship test 382–383

re-entry problems/services 500, 501; employment 424; families 426–427; housing 424–425, **425**, 427; *Second Chance Act* (2007) 430–431; women 427

reactive policing 147–149

Reagan, President R. 504–505

reasonable suspicion 189, 190, **199**

recidivism 17, 358–359; definition 345; drug sentence clemency 309; failure factors 358–359, 436; immigrants 26; juvenile 481–482; LSI-R classification 361, 362–363; measuring of 345; **parole** 433–434, **435**, 436–437; predictors of 360, 361–363; privately run prisons 400; program intervention 436–437, **437**; R/N/R classification 361–362; Realignment initiative 441; reducing rates 359; specialized courts 265–266; state by state **435**; of women 352, 364–365

recuse/recusal 287

reformatory era 338, 385–386

Regina v. Dudley and Stephens (1884) 247

rehabilitation 336, 338

rehabilitative era 338, 339, 386; **parole** 419

reinforcement 91

reintegration era 338–339

release on recognizance (ROR) program 281–283, 342

religious delusions 244

religious objections 252

reporting crime rates 34–35, **34**, 45, **45**; unreported crime **34**, 39

residential placements 452, 480, *see also* secure detention facilities

residual effect 148

restitution **346**–347; **victim-centered** 347

restorative justice (movement) 313–314, **314**, **315**, 341; community reparative boards 315; criticisms of 316; family group conferencing 315–317; research 316–317; victim–offender mediation 314–315

retribution 336

rights: during interrogation   204, **205**, 206–207; juvenile offenders' 469–470, **469**; to counsel 206, 269, 357, *see also* **due process**

Riley v. California (2014)   201

risk prediction instruments *see* classification and risk assessment

Risk/Needs/Responsivity (R/N/R) classification   361–362

Riverside v. McLaughlin (1991)   280

Roe v. Wade (1973)   237, 252

Roosevelt, T.   131

Roper v. Simmons (2015)   243, 318, 470

Rostker v. Goldberg (1981)   235

Rousseau, J.J.   11

Routh, E.R.   244–245, **245**, **245p**

routine activities theory   96

roving wiretaps   199, 507

Ruffin v. Commonwealth (1878)   380

Russia   503

St Bridig's Well   402

Salient Factor Score   360

same-sex marriage   223, **224**, 237, 252

Sampson, R.   98

San Bernadino shooting (2015)   502, 508

sanctuary cities   25, 510

Sandy Hook Elementary School   209

Santee, California   473

SARA model   138

saturated patrols   148

Saunders, R.   128: 128p

Scarlet Letter conditions   **348**

schizophrenic delusions   244

school: DARE officers   474; formalization of discipline 474; re-entering juveniles 482; safety officers 473–474, **474**; suspension 473, 475; zero tolerance 16, 473

school-to-prison pipeline   16, 475

Schrag, C.   393

Scott, W.   171–172, **171**

searches: airport   **199**, 511; automobile **197–198**; border **199**; **consent searches** 195, **198**; exigent circumstances **196–197**; **hot pursuit exception** 197; inventory **198**; weapons **196**, *see also* warrantless searches; warrants seat belts 223

Seattle 59–60

Second Chance Act (2007) 430–431, 501

Secure Communities programs 26–27

secure detention facilities **476**, 478–481; gender statistics 480–481; "kids for cash" scheme 480; minorities within 480–481; **recidivism** 480

Sedition Act (1918) 503

seizures *see* stop and arrest (seizures)

Select Committee on Intelligence 504

self-control 95

self-defense 247–249; basic elements of 247; "Make my Day" statutes 249; "stand your ground" laws 248–249

self-incrimination 186

self-radicalization 508

self-report studies 27, 42–43, 492

Sensenbrenner-Scott Over-Criminalization Task Force Safe, Accountable, Fair, Effective (SAFE) Justice Reinvestment Act (2015) 16, **310–313**

sentencing **6–7**, 297–298; common sentence 302–303, **302**; **discretion** 297; **disparity** 297–298, 306; fines and fees 303–305; gender disparity 324; goals 299; guidelines 306–310, 324; **hearsay** 298; Hispanics 322, 324, **326**; juveniles 470; lengths given 72, **72**, 302–303, 306, 324, 326, **326**; mental state impact on 245–246; process 298; racial disparity 322–327, **325**, **326**; reform 310–313; **three-strikes** 300–302, **301**, 501; trial courts 292–293; types of sentences 299–300

separate system 384

September 11 terrorist attack (2001) 139, 501–502

serotonin levels 88

"set-ups" 149

sex differentials 89, 94, 95

sex offenders' registration 233, 427–428

sex toys 237

sex trafficking 496–497, **496**

"sexting" 253

sexual assault: laws 235; in prison 394–395, *see also* rape

sexual victimization 395

sheriffs 126–127; early 129

shire reeve 129

shootings: by police 19, 53, 171–175; fleeing subject 171–172, **171**, 193; mass 211, 213

show-up 203–204

"silver platter doctrine"   207

Simpson, O.J.   228, **292**

Skilling, J.   232

Skilling v. United States (2010)   232

Slager, M.T.   171

Snowden, E.   511

sobriety checkpoint   187, 189

social contract   11, 28, 223

social control   11–13, 28

social disorganization theory   94

social media   151

social process theories   94

social schematic theory   100

social support theory   94

socialization   11, 154

societal morals   223–224

sociological theories of crime   92–96, 97, **341**; **control theory** 94–95; **cultural deviance theory** 93; **differential association theory** 94; **general strain theory** 95; general theory of crime 95; **labeling theory** 94; **mixed zones** 93; policy implications **341**; **social disorganization theory** 94; **social process theories** 94; **social support theory** 94; **strain/opportunity theory** 93; **subcultural theory** 93; **subcultures** 93

sociopathy   90

sodomy laws   223

Special Constables Act (1831)   129

special jurisdiction law enforcement agencies   119, 127

specialized courts   263–264; effectiveness 264–266

specific deterrence   336

specific responsivity   362

split sentencing and shock incarceration   7, 299

Springfield, Oregon   472–473

spurious associations   212

"stand your ground" laws   248–249

stare decisis   13

state differences   10

state jails   7

state law enforcement agencies   5, 126

state supreme court   7, 263

status offenders   450, 452

Statute of Limitations   252

statutory crimes   226

statutory duties   239

statutory exclusion   471

statutory rape   235

Steinle, K.   25

Sterling, A.   113, 171

stocks   **337**

stop-and-frisk policies   54, 58, **59**, 164–165, 190–191, **191**

stops and arrests (seizures)   188, 192–193; consent stop 187, 188–189; investigatory detentions 165, 166, 187, 189–191; sobriety checkpoints 187, 189; traffic offense stops 164–165, 166, 167, *see also* **arrest**

strain/opportunity theory   93, 95

stress   152–153

sub-systems: of criminal justice system   4, 5, **5**

subcultural theories   93

subculture   93, 153–155, *see also* police subculture; prison subculture

subject matter jurisdiction   260

substance abuse   **363**; and **drug courts** 482; in jail 396; **juveniles** 482; in prison **398**, 426; **recidivism** 352, 365; residential facilities for 480

Supreme Court   276–277; members of 277; nominee appointments **278**

"surveillance" society   152, 503

suspended sentence   357

Sutherland, E.   94

Sykes, G.   386

Symbionese Liberation Army   504

systems approach   10

tasers   170

Task Force on Policing   17, **18**, 113, 139, 175–176, 498; Six Pillars 176

tax evasion   495

technical violations   345, 356, 357, **358**; **parole** 303, 432–433, 434

technology in policing   150–152

television coverage   15

Temporary Assistance to Needy Families (TANF)   500

Tennessee v. Garner (1985)   172, 174, 193

terminology differences   **453**

terrorism   501–511; antiterrorist legislation 504, 505; first responder training 508–509; **fusion centers** 509; Hezbollah 508; ISIS 508; "lone-wolf" 507, 508; "narcoterrorism" 508; Oklahoma City bombing 505; post 9/11 508–509; prior to 9/11 503–505; *Protect America Act* (2007) 507;

Sedition Act (1918) 503; self-radicalization 508; **USA PATRIOT Act (of 2001)** 8, 506, 511

terroristic threat   236

"Terry stops"   189–191, **196**

Terry v. Ohio (1968)   189

testilying   156

testosterone   88

Texas   382

Texas v. Johnson (1989)   236

theories of crime   84–85, 96–100, **101**, 169–171; biological 85–90, 97; **classical school** 84–85; and corrections system 340–341; **critical criminology** 98–99; **deterrence theories** 96; **environmental criminology** 96; **integrated theories** 96–98; **longitudinal research** 43, 86, 96–97; macro-level 69–70, 92; micro-level 70, 92; neighborhood influences 84; psychological 90–92; **routing activities theory** 96; sociological 92–96, 97

thermal-imaging   151, 200

third generation classification   361; and women 364

"three strikes"   sentences 300–302, **301**, 501

ticket of leave system   418

tipping effect (of imprisonment)   500

Tison v. Arizona (1987)   318

torts   228, **229**

totality of circumstances   381

traffic courts   260

traffic offense stops   164–165, 166, 167; **pretext stops** 190

traffic ticket   193

training schools   452, 479–480

transferred intent   240–241

transitional housing beds   424–425, **425**

transitional jobs   424

transportation   402, 418

treason   238

treatment programs: juvenile   478; in prison 382, 436–437; **recidivism** 480

trial court   6, 260–262, 263, 287–288; closing arguments 291, **292**; evidence presentation 290–291; judges 273–274; jury deliberation 291; jury instructions 291, **292**; jury selection 288–290; opening statements 290; sentencing 292

tribal court system   127

tribal police forces   127, **128**

"turning points"   98

twin studies   88
two-strikes legislation   301
Tyler, T.   95–96

undercover operations   149
Uniform Code of Military Justice   275
Uniform Crime Reports (UCR)   9, 35–41, **38**, 492; criticism of 39
United Nations (UN): Office of Drugs and Crime   51
United States Code   8
United States (US): attorney   276; Customs Service 124; Marshals Service 124
United States v. Wade (1967)   203
University of California   132
unsecured bonds   283
urbanity   82
urine samples arrestees   353
USA PATRIOT Act (of 2001)   8, 506–507, 511; Title II 506

vagueness   231
Vera Institute of Justice   283
victim impact statements   421
victim-centered restitution   **347**
victim-harming crimes   71, 98–99
victim–offender mediation   314–315
victimization: Blacks   80, 81; Hispanics 80; levels by race 80–82, **81**, **82**;
      sexual 395; urban areas 82; of women 351, *see also* **restorative justice
      (movement)**
victimization surveys   9, 41–42, 45, 81, 492
victimless crimes   71
Victims of Trafficking and Violence Protection Act (VTVPA) (2000)   497
Vietnam War   9, 15
vigilante justice   131
violation report   345, 356
Violence Against Women Act (1994)   266
Violent Crime Control and Law Enforcement Act (1994)   168–169
violent crimes   37, **38**, 58, 465; girls 465–469; increase in 60, 495; and race
      84, 460, **460**
violent offenders   389, **390**
voir dire   6, 289
Vollmer, A.   132
voting rights   428

Wackenhut Corporation   400

waiver   452, 470–472, 478–479; **direct file** 471; **statutory exclusion** 471

Wall Street Journal   54

Walnut Street Jail   383–384, **383**

"war of all against all" (Hobbes)   11, 13

warehouse prisons   387

warnings   204, **205**, 206–207

warrantless searches   **196–197**; automobile searches 197–198; exigent circumstances 196–197; non-intrusive collection 203–204; probation 356; weapons 196

warrants   194–195, **196**; for arrest 192, **192**; example **196**; exclusionary rule 207–209; forensic evidence 201–203; GPS-tracking devices 200; terrorism 504; thermal-imaging 200; wiretapping 199

Warren court era   380

weapons: searches for   196

West Springfield High School   **474**

white-collar crimes   99, 492

who commits crime *see* correlate (of crime); theories of crime

Wilson, D.   159

Wilson, J.   134; Farrington, D. and Ohlin, L. 96–97

wiretapping   199, 507

women: classification instruments   364–365; and crime 94, 351; **imprisonment rates** 377–379, **378**, **379**; **parole** 427, 436; police officers 122–123, **123**; prisoner subculture 392; prisons 386, 387, **388**, 392; **recidivism** 352; reformatories for 386, *see also* gender differential; sex differentials

writ of certiorari   263

wrongful convictions   19–20, 498–499, **499**; and forensic science 19–20

Wyatt v. Stickney (1971)   396

zero tolerance approach   135, 473

zero tolerance policing   135